D0887110

Texts and Monographs in Computer Science

Editor

David Gries

Advisory Board
F.L. Bauer
S.D. Brookes
C.E. Leiserson
F.B. Schneider
M. Sipser

Texts and Monographs in Computer Science

(continued after index)

What Computing Is All About

Jan L.A. van de Snepscheut

With 78 Illustrations

Springer-Verlag

New York Berlin Heidelberg London Paris
Tokyo Hong Kong Barcelona Budapest

Jan L.A. van de Snepscheut
California Institute of Technology
Computer Science 256-80
Pasadena, CA 91125
USA

Series Editor:
David Gries
Department of Computer Science
Cornell University
Upson Hall
Ithaca, NY 14853-7501
USA

Library of Congress Cataloging-in-Publication Data
Snepscheut, Jan L. A. van de, 1953–
    What computing is all about / Jan L. van de Snepscheut.
        p.   cm. — (Texts and monographs in computer science)
    Includes bibliographical references and index.
    ISBN 0-387-94021-9 (New York : acid-free paper). — ISBN
3-540-94021-9 (Berlin : acid-free paper)
    1. Programming (Electronic computers)   I. Title.   II. Series.
QA76.6.S6163   1993
005.1—dc20   93-12238

Printed on acid-free paper.

Production managed by Bill Imbornoni; manufacturing supervised by Vincent Scelta.
Photocomposed from the author's LaTeX files.
Printed and bound by Hamilton Printing Co., Castleton, NY.
Printed in the United States of America.

9 8 7 6 5 4 3 2 1

ISBN 0-387-94021-9 Springer-Verlag New York Berlin Heidelberg
ISBN 3-540-94021-9 Springer-Verlag Berlin Heidelberg New York

Preface

I have always been fascinated with engineering. From Roman bridges and jumbo jets to steam engines and CD players, it is the privilege of the engineer to combine scientific insights and technical possibilities into useful and elegant products. Engineers get a great deal of satisfaction from the usefulness and beauty of their designs. Some of these designs have a major impact on our daily lives, others enable further scientific insights or shift limits of technology. The successful engineer is familiar with the scientific basis of the field and the technology of the components, and has an eye for the envisioned applications. For example, to build an airplane, one had better understand the physics of motion, the structural properties of aluminum, and the size of passengers. And the physics of motion requires a mastery of mathematics, in particular calculus.

Computers are a marvel of modern engineering. They come in a wide variety and their range of applications seems endless. One of the characteristics that makes computers different from other engineering products is their programmability. Dishwashers have some limited programming capability, but it is not the key part of the device. Their essential part is some enclosed space where the dishes are stored and flushed with hot water. Computers are embedded in many different environments, but in their case the programming capability is the essential part.

All computers are programmed in more or less the same way. A program, together with the quantities on which it operates, is a long string of zeros and ones, called bits. The computer's operation consists in repeatedly fetching some of those bits, and possibly changing them. Some bits are connected to other devices and they reflect what is going on inside the computer, by opening or closing valves, switching lights on and off, or moving arms. The hardware engineer studies methods for representing bits by physical devices and for implementing the various operations. The absence of structure in the string of bits allows the operations to be performed by a reasonably simple machine. It also makes it possible to use the machine for a wide range of applications because there are hardly any built-in limitations. The software engineer studies methods of building structure from the unstructured bit strings to represent the objects that play a role in the application at hand, and designs algorithms for carrying out the relevant operations.

Organization of the text

This text offers an introduction to the fundamental issues in computing. Because computing is as wide a field as any, there is no way to cover every aspect of it in great detail. This leads to a choice: either the whole field is covered at an informal, descriptive level, or a selection of topics is made and these topics are treated in more detail. I have chosen the latter option, because it seems to be easier to learn a new topic once you have mastered some related topics than to learn several topics when you have only a sketchy impression of each of them. The choice of topics is necessarily a personal one. Some topics are absolutely essential for every computer scientist, whereas others are more remote. More important than the topics themselves is the way they are discussed. In each case, I have tried to give an idea of what the important notions are, what the relevant problems are, and what kind of mathematics one uses to describe and solve the problems.

Grammars have been chosen as the first topic, since almost everyone who has had some programming experience has seen the grammar of a programming language. Grammars allow the introduction of some fundamental notions and form a gentle introduction to some of the mathematical notions and notations that we will be using. Grammars are a stepping stone to parsing, which in turn serves as a stepping stone for discussing the halting problem which is an example of a problem that cannot be solved by computer. Regular expressions and finite automata are described as an alternate to a certain class of grammars. Here the purpose is to show that different formalisms may be equivalent in some sense, and at the same time have very different strengths and weaknesses. Integrated circuits are discussed as a medium for implementing finite automata. Two different kinds of programming languages are discussed: those that do have a notion of state (imperative programs) and those that don't (functional programs). The former category is discussed more extensively, including the mathematics for reasoning about them as well as heuristics that play a role in their design. Implementations of both kinds of programming languages are described. These implementations serve a dual role. On the one hand, they give some insight into how computers execute programs. On the other hand, they serve as examples of larger programs. Program inversion falls both under the heading of heuristics for program design and implementation considerations. (Although the real reason for its inclusion is that it is fun.)

Because computing is largely a branch of engineering, there is a strong emphasis on getting things right. The designer of an airplane does extensive calculations and other checks to make sure that the design is free from errors. When the design, consisting of a large collection of drawings, assembly procedures, tolerances for the parts, and so on, is executed then this is done by a skilled crew of people. It is possible that they find some errors or inaccuracies during the fabrication process, which may lead to improvements in the design. Their attention increases the trustworthiness of the final product. Computer programs are executed by computers, without any intelligent attention to errors or inaccuracies. If a mistake is made, the computation continues with incorrect results, and the quality of the final product suffers. This is one of the reasons why computer programmers have to pay even more attention to the correctness of their designs than do other engineers. Because a program often consists of millions of bits and takes billions of operations to execute, there is no way to understand the program by trying to envision the execution. An understanding at the level of the program text rather than its execution is required, and this tends to be a more formal activity.

Also, the airplane designer knows the properties of the materials from which the plane is being constructed and this provides a lot of design heuristics. A program is built from zeros and ones, and they do not offer an overwhelming amount of heuristic value. Instead, the heuristics are mainly due to the problem that is being solved, and the mathematical theory that is being used to describe and solve it. Again, the software engineer relies more on the formalism than most other designers do.

This text evolved from handouts for a course I teach at Caltech. The course was set up to bridge the gap between the introductory programming course and the advanced courses offered by the department. Some programming experience is an essential prerequisite. Most of the mathematics we use is discrete mathematics, especially predicate calculus. More important than a thorough training in this area is that one understands the role of the formalism. It serves both a descriptive and a calculational purpose. The descriptive role of the formalism is to make clear and unambiguous what we are talking about: it is often much shorter than saying the same thing in plain English. The calculational role of the formalism is to derive results from formulae that have already been established. Calculation is a good way to obtain results (including program texts) that are hard to get right without the formalism. The only difference with ordinary calculus is that we calculate mainly with predicates, and it takes some time to get used to them, just as it takes time to get used to integrals.

When teaching this course, I always find it a pleasure to see that students do not shy away from fundamental issues, that they are thrilled by the beauty and elegance of many topics and the relations between them. As a result, we always seem to have a lot of fun. I hope that some of that excitement is preserved in this text.

Some of the programs in this book can be obtained by anonymous ftp from `cs.caltech.edu` in directory `jan`. Log in with username `ftp` or `anonymous` and enter your email address as password.

Acknowledgments

I am most grateful to the Caltech computer science community. The students of course CS20 have been subjected to my teaching for the past three years. Their enthusiasm is a never-failing source of inspiration. The faculty have allowed me to teach a course that is more compressed and less compartmentalized than most computer science courses. I would never have ventured to teaching such a course without the encouragement of Chuck Seitz, who suggested that I teach a sophomore class. The TA's, Ulla Binau, John Cortese, Robert Harley, Rustan Leino, Johan Lukkien, and more than anyone else Peter Hofstee, have been instrumental in making this course as enjoyably to teach as it is. Without their efforts, this text would not have been the same.

During the course, many programs are developed and run. The lab assignments have not been included here but are an important part of the course. Access to various computer systems was found to be very stimulating. Especially, access to Mosaic multicomputers developed by Chuck Seitz's research group under funding from DARPA is greatly appreciated.

Those familiar with the work of Edsger W. Dijkstra and of Tony Hoare will recognize their influence throughout this text. The influence of lectures by Wim Feijen and Frans Kruseman Aretz, especially their strife for elegance, should be obvious to those who have shared the pleasure of listening to them.

I am grateful to David Gries for encouraging me to rework my class handouts into a publishable text. David read the first drafts and provided linguistic and technical suggestions on almost every paragraph.

I am grateful to the following people who have commented substantially on drafts of the book: Richard Bird, Dian de Sha, Peter Hilbers, Jayadev Misra, Juris Reinfelds, and Berry Schoenmakers. I am especially indebted to Ralph Back, Rich Hehner, and Doug McIlroy for their constructive criticisms. Thanks to Karen Kosztolnyik of Springer-Verlag editorial for suggesting the title.

Calvin Jackson provided much-needed help in coding this book with the LATEX system. Harjanto Sumali executed the drawings.

Finally, I thank my wife, Trees, and children, Suzanne, Marieke, and Jasper, for their love and patience during the past years.

Contents

1

What Is Computing All About?

We begin our explorations of what computing is all about by studying a game. It's a one-person domino game, so it is a little boring, for there is no opponent to beat. This version of the domino game is played with three differently configured pieces, each of which is available in unlimited quantity. The three pieces are as in Figure 1.1.

The game is played on a sufficiently large rectangular board that has exactly one flat bottom labeled P at the upper edge, and a finite sequence of (zero or more) flat tops, each labeled a or b, at the lower edge. The object of the game is to eliminate all flat sides through proper placement of the dominos. Two flat sides are eliminated if the two labels match, hence the name *domino*. Dominos can not be played upside-down and connections cannot be crossed, but they can be stretched. For example, if the initial configuration is as in Figure 1.2, then the game can be completed by playing one each of the three different pieces. A possible first move is shown in Figure 1.3, and the final configuration is shown in Figure 1.4. If the initial configuration is as in Figure 1.5, then there is no way of successfully completing the game. It is not too difficult to see that the game can be completed successfully if the initial sequence of a's and b's at the lower edge is a palindrome — well, a palindrome of even length, including the empty string. The game cannot be completed if the sequence is not a palindrome. (A palindrome is a sequence of letters that reads the same backward or forward.) We avoid the ugly phrase "if and only if" and say that the game can be completed just when the sequence of a's and b's is

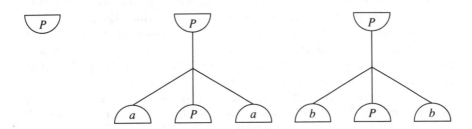

FIGURE 1.1. The three pieces.

FIGURE 1.2. Initial configuration.

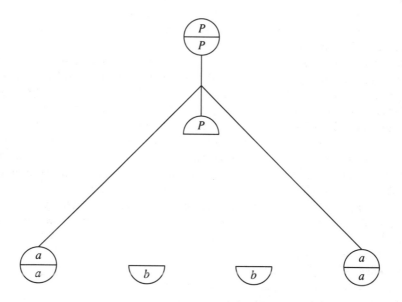

FIGURE 1.3. Intermediate configuration.

a palindrome. There is no bound on the length of a palindrome and the set of palindromes is infinite. The set of sequences for which the game terminates depends, of course, on the different domino pieces that are available and is often called the *language* generated by the dominos, or the language generated by the grammar. The game was created in the study of natural languages; hence this funny terminology.

Can you see which set of sequences, which language, results if we add the dominos of Figure 1.6? What if we add the domino from Figure 1.7 instead? And what if we perform both extensions?

The game as discussed so far is called *parsing*. Parsing can be seen as a computation that takes a symbol sequence as input (the sequence at

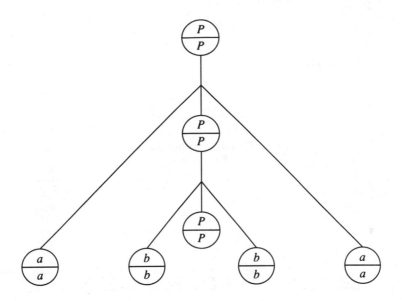

FIGURE 1.4. Final configuration.

FIGURE 1.5. Unsuccessful configuration.

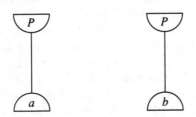

FIGURE 1.6. Additional dominos.

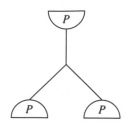

FIGURE 1.7. Another domino.

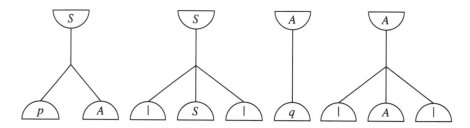

FIGURE 1.8. p - q dominos.

the bottom) and outputs one bit of information: either yes, the sequence is in the language, or no, it is not in the language. Sometimes the entire configuration of dominos on the board is used as the output; this is called the *parse tree* for that particular input string. We will return to parsing in a later chapter, including a discussion of efficient strategies for playing the parsing game. In this introduction we want to see what computing is in general, so we will now change the rules of the game and look at another example, the dominos of which are given in Figure 1.8.

If we insist that symbols p, q, and | be at the lower edge and S be at the upper edge, the language is the set of sequences

$$|^m \ p \ |^n \ q \ |^{m+n}$$

for all natural numbers m and n . (Yes, 0 is a natural number.) $|^m$ denotes the sequence of m occurrences of symbol | . If $m = 0$, this is the empty sequence. We now change the rules of the game. Instead of submitting a complete sequence at the lower edge, we set up a sequence of the form $|^m \ p \ |^n \ q$, for some m and n , and see how far we can get in eliminating all the flat tops and the flat bottom labeled S that are initially on the board. It turns out that there is only one way of doing this, leading to a configuration as in Figure 1.9, in which there is an unmatched sequence $|^{m+n}$.

Or does another solution exist? Well, other solutions exist, namely those in which unmatched flat bottoms labeled | exist to the left of the path

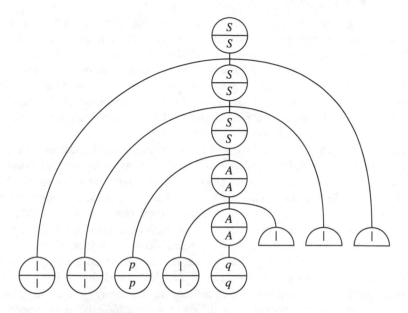

FIGURE 1.9. A complete configuration.

leading from the top S to the bottom q. If we stick to the rule that all unmatched flat sides are to the right of this path, then we have completely defined our second game — and our solution is the only one. This second game is called addition: given as input two natural numbers m and n, encoded through the sequence $|^m\ p\ |^n\ q$, the output is their sum, $m + n$, encoded as the sequence $|^{m+n}$. I am not claiming that this is the only, or best, way of encoding numbers (it is pretty good, though, if you're keeping track of the number of beers you've had) or that addition is a very exciting computation. It does show the essentials of computation, however: all that is done during a computation is to follow the uninterpreted rules of some game. The domino game is not about numbers or addition — these are the result of interpreting $|^m$ as the number m, and p and q as + and =, respectively. Other interpretations are possible; not all are equally useful. Examples are given in the table.

$|^m$	p	q
2 to the power m	multiplication	=
m	=	taken from
true if $m = 0$ and false if $m > 0$	conjunction	=
m	maximum	$\leq$
$|^m$	catenation	=

What does this game tell us about computing? What are the fundamental notions in computer science? What subjects do we address in this text?

One thing that we learn from this game is that computing is a sort of formal symbol manipulation. The computation is carried out in accordance with some set of rules, independent of their interpretation. As a result, computer scientists have, and have to have, a strong interest in notational issues. Can you come up with a grammar for addition for the case in which numbers are not encoded as a sequence of strokes but in decimal notation? Or as Roman numerals? How hard the problem is, or whether it can be done at all, often depends on notations.

Another aspect that we address is the question: can all possible computations be performed by a set of rules as simple as those for the domino game? It turns out that this is not the case. In the versions of the game that we have described so far, each domino piece has one flat side on the top and zero or more flat sides on the bottom. If we allow one or more flat sides on the top (and still disallow crossing of interconnections), more computations can be cast in the framework of our domino game — in fact, all computations can. This is something that we cannot prove, since a mathematical definition of a computation does not exist. (We could define it to be the domino game ...) There is a strong indication, however, that we may take the statement for granted: utterly different games have been proposed in the past — by Church, Kleene, McCulloch, Post, Turing — and they have all been shown to be equivalent, for each induces the same set of possible computations. This is a very important thesis, usually referred to as the Church-Turing thesis. It tells us that anything that can be computed at all, by any existing or future computer, can be computed by one of these simple games. We shall also see, however, that a number of important problems have no solution at all in this set of computations, so they cannot be solved by any computer.

Yet another branch of computer science is concerned with the construction of computers. We may be able to invent wonderful and exciting games, but these games may be of little use if it is impossible to build a device for playing the game. (One-person games may be fun to analyze, but they tend to be rather boring to play.) Suppose the game is played from left to right, and from top to bottom. At any moment, a tree-like structure branches out from the piece that is at the top of the board, and a (possibly empty) part at the left bottom of the tree is matched with a prefix of the input sequence. All that one needs to know to continue playing the game is the unmatched *fringe* of the tree-like structure plus the unmatched suffix of the input sequence. The unmatched part of the fringe is called the *state*. A mode of operation that has been studied a lot is one in which only the state is stored in the machine, and in which the input sequence is presented to the machine one symbol at a time. The machine is activated in the initial state. At every step, the next symbol is input and the machine transits to its next state. The final state corresponds to the output. The machine's set of states is independent of the input sequence; it depends on the grammar only. One may distinguish between finite and infinite machines, that is, machines that have a finite or infinite set of states. It seems unreasonable to think that infinite machines can be physically realized, since all things that we can build consist of a finite number of simple parts. Of course, practically useful approximations of infinite machines can be constructed. We will see what can and what cannot be computed by finite machines. And we will have a look at how fast, in how many steps, a computation can be performed. This is often expressed in terms of the number of input symbols n. Computations may require a number of steps that is linear in n, quadratic in n, exponential in n, or even worse.

On the more physical side, one may ask how a machine's state and state transition mechanism are represented by physical quantities. Most current machines are built from VLSI chips in which states are represented by a large number of digital electrical signals and state transitions are effectuated through transistor networks. It is instructive to understand the operation of these circuits, and we will have a short look at them in due time. Many other ways of representing a machine's state and effectuating its state transitions are possible. Analog circuits inspired by neural networks as found in the brain are beginning to be explored as a means for carrying out computations. Experiments in the area of visual processing are beginning to reveal the possibilities and limitations of what is called computational neuroscience. One may also go down to the microphysical level and ask questions like: How many elementary particles are needed to perform a particular computation? How much energy does it take? Physical phenomena at this level are reversible, for they play their game at the edge of the second law of thermodynamics. One may wonder what reversibility means in terms of computations.

On the more practical side, we will address a number of implementation issues of computers. The design of a well-balanced, effective computer requires a great deal of insight into the nature of computations and physics. Computers have been constructed over a wide range of performance and cost levels, and we will look at some of the issues that determine performance and cost. One of these is concurrency. It can be argued that a conglomerate of harmoniously cooperating small computers that concurrently carry out a computation is in principle more efficient than a single, large computer. Making the principle work, however, is far from trivial, and this has a big impact on everything from program design to computer design.

And then there is an area called *programming*. We have discussed a game with a fixed set of rules. The parameter of the game, so to speak, is the set of domino pieces with which the game is played. This may be viewed as the program that, in conjunction with the rules of the game, relates the input and the output. If the specification — the relationship between input and output — is given, one may try to find or design a set of dominos, a program, that will satisfy this relation. This activity is called *program design*, or programming for short. It is an extremely challenging activity for all but the most trivial specifications.

Of course, dominos form a primitive program notation, not one that lends itself well to being reasoned about in an effective, succinct way. Many other notations are used, and we will have a look at some of them. We will discuss issues in programming methodology: the heuristics of proceeding in a more or less orderly fashion from specification to program. Programming is a rather nonconventional discipline. On the one hand, it is a mathematical activity because, as we have seen, computing is formal symbol manipulation. On the other hand, it is an engineering activity, because a product is designed that is supposed to satisfy a given specification. We will return to programming issues a number of times.

It is sometimes remarked that all important things in mathematics and the sciences have been pioneered by the Greeks. It seems that the old Greek philosophers did not build any computers as we know them nowadays, but they certainly have constructed a number of interesting algorithms that are used to this very day. One famous algorithm is Euclid's algorithm for computing the greatest common divisor of two natural numbers. Other algorithms that the Greeks proposed are of a geometric nature, using compass and straightedge, for bisecting an angle; for constructing perpendicular lines; for constructing a regular pentagon, and so on. Many of these algorithms were short: the angle-bisection algorithm takes only four instructions. Its proof of correctness can be found as Proposition 9 in Euclid's Elements. (The proof is longer than the algorithm.) Only a few algorithms were substantially longer than a handful of instructions, and in even fewer cases did the number of steps depend on the "input". A nice aspect of these geometric algorithms is that anyone who knows how to handle a straightedge and compass can "execute" the algorithm, hence, can bisect any angle, even without understanding why it works. This is the same fortunate situation when executing computer programs: no interpretation is required — just do what the program says, one instruction after another. The fact that no understanding of the algorithm is required becomes more important when the algorithm is more involved, such as for constructing a pentagon. If, however, you are interested in designing new algorithms, it is more important to understand them than to execute them!

What are the differences between our present computer algorithms and these geometric algorithms? A major difference is the choice of elementary instructions. One reason for a different choice is that operations with compass and straightedge are not easy to automate or perform by machine. Another reason is that a number of useful operations cannot (simply) be described by compass-and-straightedge operations. The set of instructions on which our current computers are based is of a rather different nature; and if we may believe the Church-Turing thesis, this set is good in the sense that anything that can be done at all can be done with these instructions. Another difference with the old geometric algorithms is that our present algorithms typically require many more steps, the number of which depends on the input. This implies that we are more than ever interested in proofs that do not imitate execution of the algorithm. We may, therefore, expect a lot of proofs by mathematical induction (and our proofs are typically longer than the algorithms!). Yet another difference is that the tasks assigned to computers are often more complicated than most geometric constructions. It is far from trivial to specify those tasks. And even if the specification is unambiguous and crystal clear, it may require a lot of work and ingenuity to come up with an algorithm that satisfies the specification. More about that later.

2

Grammars

In our introductory chapter, we have defined a grammar to be a set of domino pieces, and we have not been too precise about dominos. In the present chapter, we are more rigorous and define a grammar and a language in a less graphical way — exit dominos. The definitions and notations that we will be using are more conventional and convenient than domino drawings are.

2.1 Strings and Languages

An *alphabet* is a set of symbols. For all practical purposes, alphabets will be finite. An example of an alphabet is the set of 26 Roman letters. Another example is the set of 10 digits: $\{0, 1, \ldots, 9\}$.

A *string* is a sequence of symbols. The *symbols* are elements of an alphabet. For example, 19800816 is a string over the alphabet of digits. All our strings are of finite length, including the empty string denoted by ϵ.

An important operation on strings is catenation. If x and y are strings, then string xy is called the catenation of x and y. It is string x followed by string y. For example, if $x = 19800$ and $y = 816$, then $xy = 19800816$. Repeated catenation is denoted by exponentiation: a^n is the string consisting of n instances of a. For example, $7^0 = \epsilon$, $7^3 = 777$, and $y^2 = 816816$.

For strings x, y, and z, we say that x is a prefix of xyz, y is a substring of xyz, and z is a suffix of xyz. Any prefix or suffix is also a substring (since any of x, y, and z can be ϵ).

A *language* is a set whose elements are strings. Catenation is extended to languages. For languages V and W, catenation VW is the set of all strings that are obtained by catenating a string from V and one from W.

$$VW = \{xy \mid x \in V \ \wedge \ y \in W\}$$

We have

$$V\emptyset = \emptyset V = \emptyset$$
$$V\{\epsilon\} = \{\epsilon\}V = V$$

for all sets V. Again, we write exponentiation for repeated catenation. A language over an alphabet is a set of strings whose symbols are elements of the alphabet. The empty set $\emptyset$ and the singleton set $\{\epsilon\}$ are two distinct languages over any alphabet, even the empty one. For any alphabet A, the set containing all strings over A is denoted by A^*. It is the largest language over A, so to speak, since any language over A is a subset of A^*. A^* satisfies the following property.

$$A^* = \{\epsilon\} \cup A^* A$$

For example, if $A = \{\circ, |\}$ then $A^* = \{\epsilon, \circ, |, \circ\circ, \circ|, |\circ, ||, \circ\circ\circ, \ldots\}$. Although alphabet A is finite and all strings in A^* are finite, set A^* itself is an infinite set. The dots are not a very precise way of denoting an infinite set. If the structure of the language is slightly less obvious, another convention is called for. This is where grammars enter the picture.

2.2 Grammars

A grammar is a means for defining a language (although grammars are often more interesting than the languages they define). A grammar uses two finite, disjoint sets of symbols. These are the set T of *terminal* symbols and the set N of *nonterminal* symbols. The union of N and T is called V. In the palindrome example, we have $T = \{a, b\}$ and $N = \{P\}$. The terminal symbols occur in the strings forming the language. The nonterminal symbols are used in the definition only.

The main part of the grammar consists of a finite set of *production rules* that describe how strings in the language can be generated. A production is a pair of strings. Such a pair is denoted as $x \longrightarrow y$. Both x and y are strings of symbols from N and T. There is a restriction that x contain at least one element of N, that is, $x \in V^* N V^*$ and $y \in V^*$. In Chapter 1, we saw a number of examples of production rules, such as $P \longrightarrow \epsilon$, $P \longrightarrow a P a$, and $P \longrightarrow b P b$. Production rules are used to derive one string from another. If string s contains left-hand side x of a production $x \longrightarrow y$ as a substring, then we can *derive* from s the string t obtained by replacing an occurrence of x in s by y. This will be denoted by $s \Longrightarrow t$. For example, from $a\,a\,P\,a\,a$ we can derive $a\,a\,a\,P\,a\,a\,a$, $a\,a\,b\,P\,b\,a\,a$, and $a\,a\,a\,a$. Through repeated application of these rules we get a possibly infinite set of derivable strings. We write $x \Longrightarrow y \Longrightarrow z$ for $x \Longrightarrow y \ \wedge \ y \Longrightarrow z$. If we want to indicate why $x \Longrightarrow y$ and why $y \Longrightarrow z$, we prefer the following format for presenting a derivation.

$$x$$
$$\Longrightarrow \qquad \{ \text{ hint that explains why } x \Longrightarrow y \ \}$$
$$y$$
$$\Longrightarrow \qquad \{ \text{ hint that explains why } y \Longrightarrow z \ \}$$
$$z$$

The format is especially useful if y is a long string. The hints have no special meaning: they are suggestions to the reader why the next line can be derived from the previous one. An example is

$$P$$
$$\Longrightarrow \quad \{ \ P \longrightarrow a \, P \, a \ \}$$
$$a \, P \, a$$
$$\Longrightarrow \quad \{ \ P \longrightarrow a \, P \, a \ \}$$
$$a \, a \, P \, a \, a$$
$$\Longrightarrow \quad \{ \ P \longrightarrow \epsilon \ \}$$
$$a \, a \, a \, a \qquad .$$

In addition to the production rules an *initial string* is still needed as a starting point: it is given as the fourth component of the grammar. It can be any string, but usually it is just a nonterminal symbol. The language defined by the grammar is the set of strings that consist of terminal symbols only and that can be derived in a number of steps from the initial string.

We use the notation $\Longrightarrow^*$ to denote repeated application (zero or more times) of derivation. Operator $\Longrightarrow^*$ is the reflexive, transitive closure of $\Longrightarrow$. Formally, $\Longrightarrow^*$ is defined by

$x \Longrightarrow^* x$, for all x;

if $x \Longrightarrow^* y$ and $y \Longrightarrow z$ then $x \Longrightarrow^* z$, for all x, y, and z;

$x \Longrightarrow^* y$ holds only if it does so on account of the two rules above.

We use the word "derived" informally for the transitive closure also.

What is the language that corresponds to grammar (T, N, R, S), where T is the set of terminal symbols, N is the set of nonterminal symbols, R is the set of production rules, and S is the initial string? It is the set

$$\{ x \mid x \in T^* \ \wedge \ S \Longrightarrow^* x \} \qquad .$$

As a notational shorthand for representing a set of productions with the same left-hand side,

$$x \longrightarrow u \mid v \mid w$$

is an abbreviation for

$$x \longrightarrow u$$
$$x \longrightarrow v$$
$$x \longrightarrow w \qquad .$$

In the even-length palindrome example, the set of production rules is then written as

$$P \longrightarrow \epsilon \mid a \, P \, a \mid b \, P \, b \qquad .$$

The complete grammar, including the two sets of symbols and the initial string, is compactly written as the quadruple

$$(\{a, b\}, \ \{P\}, \ \{P \longrightarrow \epsilon \mid a \, P \, a \mid b \, P \, b\}, \ P) \qquad .$$

Here is another example of a grammar. The language it defines resembles the set of arithmetic expressions, in a restricted way. The grammar is

$$(\{i, +, \times, (,), \}, \; \{E, T, F\}, \; R, \; E) \qquad ,$$

where R consists of the production rules

$$E \longrightarrow E + T \mid T$$
$$T \longrightarrow T \times F \mid F$$
$$F \longrightarrow (E) \mid i \quad .$$

An example of a derivation is

$$
\begin{aligned}
&E\\
\Longrightarrow \quad &\{ \; E \longrightarrow E + T \; \}\\
&E + T\\
\Longrightarrow \quad &\{ \; E \longrightarrow T \; \}\\
&T + T\\
\Longrightarrow \quad &\{ \; T \longrightarrow F \; \}\\
&F + T\\
\Longrightarrow \quad &\{ \; F \longrightarrow i \; \}\\
&i + T\\
\Longrightarrow \quad &\{ \; T \longrightarrow T \times F \; \}\\
&i + T \times F\\
\Longrightarrow \quad &\{ \; T \longrightarrow F \; \}\\
&i + F \times F\\
\Longrightarrow \quad &\{ \; F \longrightarrow i \; \}\\
&i + i \times F\\
\Longrightarrow \quad &\{ \; F \longrightarrow i \; \}\\
&i + i \times i \quad .
\end{aligned}
$$

Halfway along in the derivation, we have the string $i + T$; then $i \times i$ is derived from T, but there is no way of obtaining $E \times i$ and letting the E go to $i + i$. This we interpret as expressing the convention that $\times$ binds stronger, or has higher priority, than $+$. The parse tree in Figure 2.1 contains this same information: the two occurrences of i surrounding $\times$ are combined, and the result is combined with the first i in the addition.

The grammar also expresses that $+$ and $\times$ are left-associative, that is, $i + i + i$ is understood as $(i + i) + i$, because it is possible to derive $i + i + i$ from E via $E + i$ but not via $i + E$. The parse tree for $i + i + i$ is given in Figure 2.2. It shows that the first two terms are combined, and the result thereof is combined with the last term. Only one parse tree for this string exists.

In every step of the derivation in the example, we have applied the leftmost substitution possible. Other derivations of the string $i + i \times i$ exist that differ in the order in which substitutions are made. The parse trees that would result in the case of the corresponding domino game would be

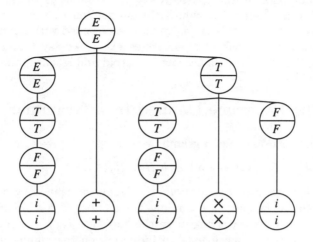

FIGURE 2.1. Parse tree for $i + i \times i$.

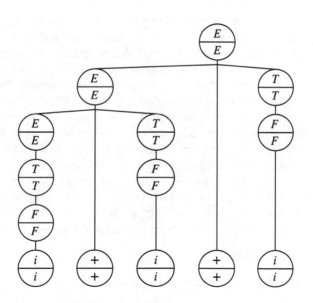

FIGURE 2.2. Parse tree for $i + i + i$.

the same, however. In other cases, that is, in the case of other grammars, a string may have distinct parse trees. An example is the grammar we encountered in Chapter 1 in which the production rule $P \longrightarrow P\,P$ was added. Every string in this language can be obtained with infinitely many parse trees. If more than one parse tree exists, we say that there is an *ambiguity*. When we discuss parsing, we avoid ambiguous grammars.

2.3   The Language Defined by a Grammar

Here is another example of a grammar.

$$(\{a, b\}, \{H\}, \{H \longrightarrow a \mid H\,b\,H\}, H)$$

We show how we can reason about the language defined by a grammar. Let $f(x)$ be the number of a's minus the number of b's in string x. We can prove that for every string x in the language $f(x) = 1$. Such a proof is best conducted by mathematical induction on the number of steps in a derivation of x from H. However, $f(x) = 1$ is not a strong property. Many strings x have $f(x) = 1$ and are not derivable from the grammar, such as string $aaabb$. We also have the property $f(x) = 1$ if we were to change the production rules to

$$H \longrightarrow a \mid b\,H\,H \quad ,$$

which defines quite a different language. What exactly is the language in the first grammar? Let $alt(x)$ be the property that string x begins and ends with an a and in which a's and b's alternate. We prove that the language defined by the first grammar is set $\{x \mid alt(x)\}$. The proof is in two steps. First, we prove that every string x in the language has property $alt(x)$. This part is by induction on the number of steps in the derivation. A derivation of only one step uses rule $H \longrightarrow a$, and string a has property $alt(a)$. A derivation of more than one step leading to string z begins with rule $H \longrightarrow H\,b\,H$. The first occurrence of H leads to a string x and the second occurrence of H leads to a string y. It follows that $z = xby$. From the induction hypothesis we infer $alt(x)$ and $alt(y)$, and, hence, $alt(z)$. We conclude: $(H \Longrightarrow^* x) \Rightarrow alt(x)$, in which $\Rightarrow$ denotes implication.

Second, we show that every string x for which $alt(x)$ holds can be derived. The proof is by mathematical induction on the length of the string.

- induction hypothesis:

  if $alt(x) \ \wedge \ |x| = k$ then $H \Longrightarrow^* x$

- base case: show that the induction hypothesis holds for $|x| = k = 1$.

  The only string x with $alt(x) \wedge |x| = 1$ is string a, and since $H \longrightarrow a$, the induction hypothesis follows.

- step: let $|x| = n > 1$ and assume that the induction hypothesis holds for all k in the range $1 \leq k < n$. Show that it holds for $k = n$ as well.

> Since $alt(x)$ $\wedge$ $|x| = n > 1$, strings y and z exist with the property $x = ybz$ $\wedge$ $alt(y)$ $\wedge$ $alt(z)$. Because $|y| < n$ and $|z| < n$, the induction hypothesis applies and we have $H \Longrightarrow^* y$ and $H \Longrightarrow^* z$. Using rule $H \longrightarrow H\, b\, H$, we conclude $H \Longrightarrow^* x$.

This completes the proof of $alt(x) \Rightarrow (H \Longrightarrow^* x)$.

Things become more complicated when more than one symbol appears in the left side of a production, as in the following grammar.

$(\{a, b, c\},$
$\quad \{R, L\},$
$\quad \{Rb \rightarrow bR,\ Rc \rightarrow Lbcc,\ R \rightarrow \epsilon, bL \rightarrow Lb,\ aL \rightarrow aaR\},$
$\quad aRbc)$

We prove that the language is the set $\{a^n b^n c^n \mid n \geq 1\}$. The proof is in two steps. First, we prove that each string of the form $a^n b^n c^n$ is in the language. Second, we prove that the language contains no other strings.

To prove that each string of the form $a^n b^n c^n$ is in the language, we prove, by mathematical induction on n, that $a^n Rb^n c^n$ can be derived from $aRbc$, that is, $aRbc \Longrightarrow^* a^n Rb^n c^n$. Basis $n = 1$ follows from the reflexivity of $\Longrightarrow^*$. For all $n \geq 1$ we have

$\qquad aRbc$
$\Longrightarrow^* \qquad \{\ \text{induction hypothesis}\ \}$
$\qquad a^n Rb^n c^n$
$\Longrightarrow^* \qquad \{\ n\ \text{applications of}\ Rb \longrightarrow bR\ \}$
$\qquad a^n b^n Rc^n$
$\Longrightarrow \qquad \{\ Rc \longrightarrow Lbcc\ \}$
$\qquad a^n b^n Lbc^{n+1}$
$\Longrightarrow^* \qquad \{\ n\ \text{applications of}\ bL \longrightarrow Lb\ \}$
$\qquad a^n Lb^{n+1} c^{n+1}$
$\Longrightarrow \qquad \{\ aL \longrightarrow aaR\ \}$
$\qquad a^{n+1} Rb^{n+1} c^{n+1}$

Thus, the induction hypothesis holds for $n + 1$ also. We conclude that $aRbc \Longrightarrow^* a^n Rb^n c^n$ for all $n \geq 1$. On account of $R \longrightarrow \epsilon$, we then have $aRbc \Longrightarrow^* a^n b^n c^n$ for all $n \geq 1$, which completes the first part of the proof.

For the second part of the proof, we consider all possible forms of strings that can be derived from $aRbc$. We claim that each derivable string has one of three forms:

$\qquad a^n b^n c^n,\ a^n b^i Rb^j c^n,\ a^n b^i Lb^{j+1} c^{n+1}$

where $n \geq 1$, $i \geq 0$, $j \geq 0$, $i + j = n$. The proof is by mathematical induction on the length of the derivation. For length 0 the claim is true because initial string $aRbc$ is of the second form (with $n = j = 1, i = 0$). Now, assume the hypothesis holds for some derived string. We must show that applying any of the five production rules to any of the three forms to which it is applicable yields a string of one of the three forms, thus showing that the claim holds for the longer derivation.

$R \longrightarrow \epsilon$ applies only to the second form, yielding a string of the first form;

$Rb \longrightarrow bR$ applies only to the second form if $j > 0$, yielding a string of the same form with $i, j := i + 1, j - 1$;

$Rc \longrightarrow Lbcc$ applies only to the second form if $j = 0$, yielding a string of the third form;

$bL \longrightarrow Lb$ applies only to the third form if $i > 0$, yielding a string of the same form with $i, j := i - 1, j + 1$;

$aL \longrightarrow aaR$ applies only to the third form if $i = 0$, yielding a string of the second form with $n, j := n + 1, j + 1$.

We have now established that each derivable string has one of the three forms. The last two forms contain nonterminal symbols. Hence, each string in the language is of the first form. This completes the second part of the proof.

The grammar that we have discussed came out of the blue, and so did the induction hypothesis. How did I come up with these? I had some program in mind that builds up any string of the form $a^n b^n c^n$ by starting with string abc, and then extending it in every step by inserting an a, a b, and a c at appropriate positions. The insertions are performed by a "token" that moves over the string, making a full sweep from that position that separates a's and b's to that position that separates b's and c's, and then back again. The position of the token and the direction in which it travels is indicated by nonterminal L or R in the string. At each reversal of direction it inserts one or two characters, namely bc when changing direction from right to left, and a when changing direction from left to right. At the end of each sweep, the string has the form $a^n b^n c^n$, and the process may be stopped by removing the token.

No general method exists for "designing" a grammar that generates a given language. The discovery of solutions depends a great deal on one's experience and talents and a great deal on the way in which the problem is formulated. Grammars are far from an ideal vehicle for carrying out a systematic design. In later chapters, we address the problem of systematic design in the context of notations that are especially tailored to programming. In Chapter 3, we look at a program notation, or programming language, that is in the mainstream of Pascal- and C-like notations.

We discuss how to prove properties of these programs; only later do we reverse the roles and try to design a program that satisfies a given set of properties. However, we will return to issues related to grammars every now and then because grammars lend themselves well for formulating some of the problems that we are interested in.

If you write a computer program for solving some given problem, you are unlikely to succeed unless you know what the "meaning" of the variables in your program is. Similarly, if you try to construct a grammar for defining some given set of strings, you are unlikely to succeed unless you know what the "meaning" of the nonterminals in your grammar is. When we listed all possible forms that derivable strings can have, we were essentially listing the "meaning" of the symbols. The relationships among symbols in a derivation are limited by the list of possible forms. When reasoning about programs, especially programs with a loop, we will do the same thing, and call this relation the invariant of the loop. It is the crux to understanding the design.

2.4 Bibliographic Notes

Grammars were first used by Chomsky in the study of natural languages. He proposed a classification of grammars into different types [Cho59] that we will encounter in later chapters. The use of grammars in the definition of programming languages was pioneered in the ALGOL 60 report (cf. [Nau63]). The form of grammar used is known as *Backus Naur Form*. An excellent survey of the role of grammars in the definition of programming languages is [Bac79]. A good account of the theory of grammars and languages can be found in [AU72]. It includes a lot of aspects that we will get to in later chapters. The domino game is from [DeR74].

The format in which we present our proofs and derivations was first suggested by W.H.J. Feijen. See also [DS90], [vG90], and [vdS85b].

2.5 Exercises

1. Consider the grammar for expressions, given in Section 2.2. How many derivations of string $i + i \times i$ exist?

2. Describe the language generated by the H-grammar which contains rule $H \longrightarrow a \mid b\,H\,H$.

3. Given is a string over characters a and b. Write an efficient iterative program to determine whether the string is an element of the language in the previous exercise. Prove the correctness of your program.

4. The similarity between the proofs for

$$(H \Longrightarrow^* x) \;\Rightarrow\; alt(x)$$

and for

$$alt(x) \;\Rightarrow\; (H \Longrightarrow^* x)$$

suggests that they can be combined into one proof. Prove equality

$$(H \Longrightarrow^* x) \;=\; alt(x)$$

by induction.

5. Consider grammar

$$(\{a, b\},\; \{A, B, C, E\},\; R,\; E)$$

where R is the set

$$E \longrightarrow \epsilon \mid aA \mid bB$$
$$A \longrightarrow aE \mid bC$$
$$B \longrightarrow bE \mid aC$$
$$C \longrightarrow aB \mid bA \qquad .$$

Show that the language defined by this grammar is the set of all strings over $\{a, b\}$ with the property that the number of a's and the number of b's are both even. In the dot-dot-dot notation, it is the set

$$\{\epsilon,\, aa,\, bb,\, aabb,\, abab,\, abba,\, baab,\, baba,\, bbaa,\, aaaabb, \ldots\} \qquad .$$

(The number of a's and b's need not be the same, but both are even.)

6. Show that the following grammar defines the same language.

$$(\; \{a, b\},$$
$$\{S, D, E\},$$
$$\{S \longrightarrow aa \mid bb,\; D \longrightarrow ab \mid ba,\; E \longrightarrow \epsilon \mid SE \mid DEDE\},$$
$$E)$$

7. Given is a string over characters a and b. Write an iterative program to determine whether the string is an element of the language in the previous exercise. Prove the correctness of your program. Can you do it without using integer variables for counting a's and b's but using booleans instead? Can you do it with only one boolean variable? How about with none?

8. Suppose we extend the simplified grammar for arithmetic expressions with a division operator that has the same priority that multiplication has, but, for some obscure reason, we want it to associate to the right. To that end, we extend the production rule for T to

$$T \longrightarrow T \times F \mid F/T \mid F \quad .$$

Does this lead to any problems?

9. Consider the simplified grammar for arithmetic expressions. Change the grammar to include exponentiation, which should have a higher priority than addition and multiplication. Make your grammar such that exponentiation associates to the right.

10. Give a grammar that generates the language over $\{a, b\}$ of all strings that have twice as many a's as b's.

11. Give a grammar that generates the language over $\{a, b, c\}$ of all strings that consist of equal numbers of a's, b's, and c's.

12. Give a grammar that generates the language $\{a^{n^2} \mid n \geq 1\}$; show that your grammar generates exactly the required language.

13. Give a grammar that generates the language $\{a^{f(n)} \mid n \geq 1\}$; show that your grammar generates exactly the required language. Function f yields Fibonacci numbers: $f(0) = 0$, $f(1) = 1$, and $f(n+2) = f(n) + f(n+1)$ for all $n \geq 0$.

14. Give a grammar that generates the carré language over $\{a, b\}$, in which every string is the catenation of two equal strings, that is, the language $\{xx \mid x \in \{a, b\}^*\}$. (Carré is the French word for square; can you guess why the language is called that way?)

15. Given is a string of even length over the characters a and b. Write an efficient program to determine for each prefix of even length whether the prefix is an element of the carré language.

16. Show that grammar

$$(\{a, b, c\}, \{A, B\}, R, A)$$

where R is the set of rules

$$
\begin{aligned}
A &\longrightarrow aABc \mid \epsilon \\
cB &\longrightarrow Bc \\
aB &\longrightarrow ab \\
bB &\longrightarrow bb
\end{aligned}
$$

generates $\{a^n b^n c^n \mid n \geq 0\}$.

3

A Program Notation

3.1 Introduction

In this chapter, we introduce a notation for writing programs. It is sufficiently similar to Pascal and C to warrant only a short introduction, so we concentrate on describing the effects brought about by a program written in such a language. Let us start with an example of a Pascal program.

```
program example;
   var q, r, a : integer;
begin  read(a);  q := 0;  r := a + 1;
          while r ≥ 4 do begin
              q := q + r div 4;  r := r div 4 + r mod 4
          end;
          write(q, r − 1)
end.
```

What does the program compute for some given input a? Let it be given that input a is a natural number, that is, $a \geq 0$. If $a < 3$, the computation is quite easy, because the condition guarding the loop is *false*. How about some larger numbers? Tracing execution of the program for some larger input values leads to the following table.

$a = 29$	$a = 86$	$a = 87$
$q, r := 0, 30$	$q, r := 0, 87$	$q, r := 0, 88$
$7, 9$	$21, 24$	$22, 22$
$9, 3$	$27, 6$	$27, 7$
	$28, 3$	$28, 4$
		$29, 1$
$output = 9, 2$	$output = 28, 2$	$output = 29, 0$

In each of the three examples, the output consists of two numbers that are the quotient and the remainder of dividing the input number by 3. Is there a way to convince ourselves that this holds for each possible input other than by checking each and every one (and there are lots of natural numbers)? The only effective way that I know of is to find a "good" characterization of all the intermediate values. It must be good in the sense that it admits a correctness argument that is independent of the number of intermediate values assumed, that is, independent of the number of lines in the table. The characterization is a relation between the values of the variables, q and r, and the input value, a. In this example, such a relation is

$$a + 1 = 3 \cdot q + r \ \wedge \ r \geq 1 \quad .$$

How do we go about proving that this relation holds for all values assumed by the variables? That it is an invariant relation? The proof is similar to a proof by mathematical induction: we prove that the relation holds initially (that is, it is established through execution of $q := 0; \ r := a + 1$) and that every subsequent execution of the loop maintains the relation. In proving the latter, we may take advantage of the fact that the body of the loop is performed only if the condition guarding the loop is *true*, that is, if $r \geq 4$.

Here is the proof of the first part. The statements $q := 0; \ r := a + 1$ indeed establish relation $a + 1 = 3 \cdot q + r \ \wedge \ r \geq 1$, provided $a \geq 0$, which is exactly the condition that we had already imposed on the input.

The second part of the proof consists of showing that, if

$$a + 1 = 3 \cdot q + r \ \wedge \ r \geq 1 \ \wedge \ r \geq 4$$

before execution of

$$q := q + r \ \textbf{div} \ 4; \ r := r \ \textbf{div} \ 4 + r \ \textbf{mod} \ 4$$

then

$$a + 1 = 3 \cdot q + r \ \wedge \ r \geq 1$$

afterwards. The two conditions are called the precondition and the postcondition of the statement, respectively. The standard argument is that this is trivial. A slightly more convincing argument would be welcome, however. As we will argue in a minute, the argument should be that the precondition implies the postcondition in which the substitutions prescribed by the assignment statements are performed in right-to-left order. (This order may seem a bit surprising — in fact, it is, but I ask you to just accept it for now.) So, we take the postcondition, replace in it every occurrence of r by $r \ \textbf{div} \ 4 + r \ \textbf{mod} \ 4$, then replace in the result thereof any occurrence of q by $q + r \ \textbf{div} \ 4$, and show that the result is implied by the precondition. (Remember that **div** and **mod** bind as strong as multiplication, hence stronger than addition.) Substitution of F for x in E is written as E_F^x. Symbol $\Leftarrow$ denotes "follows from" and is the dual of $\Rightarrow$ which denotes "implies". Here we go.

$$((a + 1 = 3 \cdot q + r \ \wedge \ r \geq 1)_{r \, \textbf{div} \, 4 + r \, \textbf{mod} \, 4}^{r})_{q + r \, \textbf{div} \, 4}^{q}$$
$$= \quad \{ \text{ rule of substitution } \}$$
$$(a + 1 = 3 \cdot q + r \ \textbf{div} \ 4 + r \ \textbf{mod} \ 4 \ \wedge$$
$$r \ \textbf{div} \ 4 + r \ \textbf{mod} \ 4 \geq 1)_{q + r \, \textbf{div} \, 4}^{q}$$
$$= \quad \{ \text{ rule of substitution } \}$$

$$a + 1 = 3 \cdot (q + r \ \textbf{div} \ 4) + r \ \textbf{div} \ 4 + r \ \textbf{mod} \ 4 \ \wedge$$
$$r \ \textbf{div} \ 4 + r \ \textbf{mod} \ 4 \geq 1$$

$=$ { arithmetic }

$$a + 1 = 3 \cdot q + 4 \cdot (r \ \textbf{div} \ 4) + r \ \textbf{mod} \ 4 \ \wedge$$
$$r \ \textbf{div} \ 4 + r \ \textbf{mod} \ 4 \geq 1$$

$=$ { arithmetic, in particular $4 \cdot (r \ \textbf{div} \ 4) + r \ \textbf{mod} \ 4 = r$ }

$$a + 1 = 3 \cdot q + r \ \wedge \ r \ \textbf{div} \ 4 + r \ \textbf{mod} \ 4 \geq 1$$

$\Leftarrow$ { arithmetic, in particular $r \geq 4 \Rightarrow r \ \textbf{div} \ 4 \geq 1$ }

$$a + 1 = 3 \cdot q + r \ \wedge \ r \geq 4$$

$\Leftarrow$ { predicate calculus, in particular $P \wedge Q \Rightarrow P$ }

$$a + 1 = 3 \cdot q + r \ \wedge \ r \geq 1 \ \wedge \ r \geq 4$$

For proving that the last line implies the first, we used the same format that we have used for displaying a sequence of derivations in the case of grammars. In the present case, we have connected the lines with equality signs and implication signs. The implications were "the wrong way": the last line implies the preceding line rather than the other way around. Of course, we could have started with the last line and worked our way to the first line. The first step would then have been a conventional implication rather than the unconventional "follows from". The advantage of using "follows from" in the example is that the steps do not come as a big surprise when reading from top to bottom. It is better to have implications in both directions available than to resort to surprises.

We have shown that the values of a, q, and r are related as

$$a + 1 = 3 \cdot q + r \ \wedge \ r \geq 1 \quad .$$

How do we conclude that the program computes both the quotient and the remainder of dividing a by 3? We know that the loop terminates when the condition that guards the loop is *false*, that is, when $r < 4$. Combined with the invariant, we have

$$a + 1 = 3 \cdot q + r \ \wedge \ r \geq 1 \ \wedge \ r < 4 \quad ,$$

or, equivalently,

$$a = 3 \cdot q + r - 1 \ \wedge \ 0 \leq r - 1 < 3 \quad .$$

The output consists of q and $r - 1$, and the previous formula expresses that they are the required quotient and remainder. (The last inequality is essential.)

This completes the proof of our program. Or does it? We have shown that the quotient and remainder are printed if the loop terminates. We have not shown, however, that the loop terminates — it might loop forever. In order to show termination, we use a device called a *bound function*, which is an integer function on the program variables that is an upper bound on the number of iterations still to be performed. (It is often too difficult, or plainly impossible, to postulate the exact number of iterations — an upper bound will do.) For this interpretation to make sense, it should be clear that each iteration of the loop should decrease the bound function (by at least one, since it is an integer number), and that the bound function is positive as long as the loop has not terminated. In our example, we take the bound function to be r. We have to show that r is positive as long as execution of the loop continues and that r decreases in each iteration. We use our knowledge about q and r, as embodied in the invariant relation, as well as the condition guarding the loop, to good advantage in these proofs. First, we prove that r is positive:

$$\begin{aligned} & r > 0 \\ = \quad & \{ \text{ use the guard } r \geq 4 \ \} \\ & true \end{aligned}$$

and, next, we prove that r decreases.

$$\begin{aligned} & r^r_{r\,\textbf{div}\,4+r\,\textbf{mod}\,4} < r \\ = \quad & \{ \text{ rule of substitution } \} \\ & r \ \textbf{div} \ 4 + r \ \textbf{mod} \ 4 < r \\ = \quad & \{ \text{ arithmetic, in particular } r = 4 \cdot (r \ \textbf{div} \ 4) + r \ \textbf{mod} \ 4 \ \} \\ & 0 < 3 \cdot (r \ \textbf{div} \ 4) \\ = \quad & \{ \text{ arithmetic } \} \\ & r \geq 4 \\ = \quad & \{ \text{ use the guard } r \geq 4 \ \} \\ & true \end{aligned}$$

We have now really fulfilled our proof obligations.

By the way, in a sense I have been a bit sloppy by using the terminology "the loop terminates". Of course, the loop terminates. It is a loop of only three lines, and terminates with the symbol **end** that occurs two lines below the symbol **while**. What I meant was that execution of the loop terminates. I will stick to the sloppy terminology.

3.2   The Simple Statements

For describing the meaning, or the semantics, of the statements in our program notation we use the following notation: $\{ \, P \, \} \, S \, \{ \, Q \, \}$. Both P and Q are conditions, and S is a statement; P is called the *precondition* and Q is called the *postcondition*. We will also use the term *predicate* for condition. By $\{ \, P \, \} \, S \, \{ \, Q \, \}$ we mean that if statement S is executed, starting in an initial state that satisfies P, then execution is guaranteed to terminate, and the final state will satisfy Q. Construct $\{ \, P \, \} \, S \, \{ \, Q \, \}$ is called a *Hoare triple*. It is a boolean property: a property that is either *true* or *false*. From the operational definition, it should be clear that if $\{ \, P \, \} \, S \, \{ \, Q \, \}$ is *true*, then $\{ \, P' \, \} \, S \, \{ \, Q' \, \}$ is also *true*, where P' is stronger than P (that is, $P' \Rightarrow P$) and where Q' is weaker than Q (that is, $Q \Rightarrow Q'$). We usually refer to this by saying that we may strengthen the precondition and weaken the postcondition. Given a postcondition, we are particularly interested in the *weakest precondition*. Similarly, given a precondition, we are particularly interested in the *strongest postcondition*. (Strictly speaking, we should not have said that P' is stronger than P, but that P' is at least as strong as P — but this is *very* strictly speaking.)

We mentioned that the rule for a sequence of assignments consists of a sequence of substitutions performed from right to left. Since this may be unexpected, we have a look at this now. For a single assignment statement, $x := e$, with precondition P and postcondition Q, we have to figure out what the relation between these three components should be. If the state satisfies P initially, and x is replaced by e, we obtain a new state that has to satisfy Q. Looking at the operation of the machine, one might tend to think that the proper relation is $P_e^x \Rightarrow Q$. We claim, however, that it should be the other way round: $P \Rightarrow Q_e^x$. Here is an explanation. Since the value of e has been stored in x after completion of the assignment, Q will be *true* after execution of the assignment just when Q with the value of x replaced by e is *true* before execution. The following examples should make you more familiar with this idea. We write the examples in the notation $\{\ P\ \}\ x := e\ \{\ Q\ \}$ to express that $P \Rightarrow Q_e^x$ is *true*.

- $\{\ 29 = 29\ \}\ x := 29\ \{\ x = 29\ \}$. Hence, execution of $x := 29$ establishes the postcondition $x = 29$ for any initial state. (Any state satisfies condition $29 = 29$, that is, *true*, which is the weakest or least restrictive of all conditions.)

- $\{\ x + 1 = 11\ \}\ x := x + 1\ \{\ x = 11\ \}$. Hence, increasing x by 1 leads to final state $x = 11$ if the initial state is $x = 10$.

- $\{\ x^2 = 100\ \}\ x := x^2\ \{\ x = 100\ \}$. Squaring x leads to $x = 100$ if initially $x^2 = 100$, for example, if $x = -10$.

- $\{\ 2x + 1 > 11\ \}\ x := 2x + 1\ \{\ x > 11\ \}$.

We have ignored the problem of undefined expressions. For example, assignment $x := 1/y$ is undefined if $y = 0$. The complete definition of the assignment statement is therefore that $\{\ P\ \}\ x := e\ \{\ Q\ \}$ is the same as $P \Rightarrow (well\ defined(e)\ \wedge\ Q_e^x)$ in which Q_e^x is not computed if *well defined(e)* is *false*. We will leave out definedness of expressions wherever possible.

We generalize the Pascal assignment statement a bit. The traditional assignment statement allows the update of one variable. We have seen that it corresponds to substitution of an expression for a variable in the postcondition. Substitution is traditionally applied to a list of expressions and a list of variables. This suggests that we extend the definition of an assignment to lists in the obvious way. For example, we define $\{\ P\ \}\ x, y := e, f\ \{\ Q\ \}$

to be equivalent to $P \Rightarrow Q_{e,f}^{x,y}$. The substitutions of e for x and f for y are performed simultaneously, so that e and f are "unaffected" in case x or y occur in them. For example, if $Q \equiv (y = x^2)$ then $Q_{y+2x+1,x+1}^{y,x} \equiv (y + 2x + 1 = (x+1)^2)$.

Check that statement $x, y := y, x$ swaps x and y. In order to describe the pre- and postconditions of the swap, we have to introduce so-called logical variables. They are not part of the program but are part of the reasoning about the program only, as in

$$\{x = X \wedge y = Y\} \ x, y := y, x \ \{x = Y \wedge y = X\} \quad .$$

One may wonder what the definition is of some "crazy" constructs like substituting two different values for the same variable, such as $x, x := 1, 2$. The mathematical notion of substitution does not apply to this case, and we dismiss "double substitution" as a nonsensical operation. There is nothing wrong with $x, x := 1, 1$ even though it may not appear to be the most useful thing to do. However, $a[i], a[j] := a[j], a[i]$ is an instance hereof in the case where $i = j$, and this is definitely useful.

The simplest method for composing a bigger statement out of smaller ones is sequential composition: a number of statements in a given sequence are executed one after the other. In Pascal it is indicated by the semicolon:

$$S0; \ S1$$

means $S0$ followed by $S1$. In terms of Hoare triples, we define the semicolon as: if both $\{ \ P0 \ \} \ S0 \ \{ \ P1 \ \}$ and $\{ \ P1 \ \} \ S1 \ \{ \ P2 \ \}$, then $\{ \ P0 \ \} \ S0; \ S1 \ \{ \ P2 \ \}$. Sometimes we retain the "intermediate" $P1$ in the program text for reference purposes, sometimes we don't. For example, we have

$$\begin{aligned} \{ \ x = X \wedge y = Y \ \} \ & x := x + y; \\ & y := x - y; \\ & x := x - y \ \{ \ x = Y \wedge y = X \ \} \quad . \end{aligned}$$

In this case, we can figure out what the two intermediate states are by performing substitution from right to left, to obtain the state $x - y = Y \wedge y = X$ at the last semicolon and $y = Y \wedge x - y = X$ at the first. Sometimes, when we have more complicated statements than assignments, it may not be that easy. If $\{ \ P0 \ \} \ S0 \ \{ \ P1 \ \}$, $\{ \ P1 \ \} \ S1 \ \{ \ P2 \ \}$, and $\{ \ P2 \ \} \ S2 \ \{ \ P3 \ \}$ then $\{ \ P0 \ \} \ S0; \ S1 \ \{ \ P2 \ \}$ and hence $\{ \ P0 \ \} \ (S0; \ S1); \ S2 \ \{ \ P3 \ \}$. But also $\{ \ P1 \ \} \ S1; \ S2 \ \{ \ P3 \ \}$ and hence $\{ \ P0 \ \} \ S0; \ (S1; \ S2) \ \{ \ P3 \ \}$, from which we conclude that sequential composition is associative. This allows us to omit the parentheses.

We introduce two more basic statements, mainly for reasons of elegance. These are the zero- and unit-elements of semicolon, so to speak. The zero-element is *abort*, and the unit-element is *skip*. The *abort*-statement is only mildly useful from a computational point of view. In fact, one had better make sure that it is never executed, for if execution ever reaches *abort*, then no final state will be reached at all. In practice, an implementation on an actual computer is likely to abort execution of the program and print a message indicating that something is in error. In terms of pre- and postconditions, we can define *abort* as satisfying $\{$ *false* $\}$ *abort* $\{$ *P* $\}$ for every predicate P. No predicate weaker than *false* can be found as a precondition for *abort*. Since no state satisfies condition *false*, the statement cannot be executed; therefore, it reaches no final state. (*false* is the strongest or most restrictive of all conditions.)

Assignment is the basic statement that brings about a change of state. The *skip*-statement causes no change of state; it is an empty statement that has no effect whatsoever. In Pascal, the empty statement is written by writing nothing: it is invisible; we prefer to make it visible and write *skip*. Its semantics are given by triple $\{$ *P* $\}$ *skip* $\{$ *P* $\}$ for every predicate P.

3.3 The Conditional Statement

Virtually every programming language has some sort of conditional statement that allows execution of substatements to be dependent on the state of the program's variables. In Pascal, it is the if-statement. For example,

> **if** $x \geq 0$ **then** $z := x$ **else** $z := -x$

stores the absolute value of x in z. Execution of the if-statement starting from an initial state satisfying P amounts to execution of $z := x$ if $x \geq 0$, and to execution of $z := -x$, otherwise. Hence, the preconditions of those two assignments are $P \wedge x \geq 0$ and $P \wedge x < 0$, respectively. There is a slight asymmetry in the way in which the two alternatives are dealt with, and this tends to get worse when more alternatives are added.

> **if** $a[i] < b[j]$ **then** $i := i + 1$
> $\quad\quad$ **else if** $a[i] > b[j]$ **then** $j := j + 1$
> $\quad\quad\quad\quad$ **else** $i, j := i + 1, j + 1$

It is not a spectacular improvement, but definitively more pleasing, to write the condition under which an alternative is selected explicitly.

> $[\ x \geq 0 \rightarrow z := x \ \|\ x \leq 0 \rightarrow z := -x\ ]$

(It is not unusual to find **if** and **fi** instead of the square brackets in the literature — I just happen to like the brackets better.) Let us, for once, start with the rule about pre- and postconditions and discuss execution later. We stipulate that the triple

> $\{\ P\ \}\ [\ B0 \rightarrow S0 \ \|\ B1 \rightarrow S1\ ]\ \{\ Q\ \}$

is equivalent to the conjunction of

$$\{\,P \wedge B0\,\}\ S0\ \{\,Q\,\}$$
$$\{\,P \wedge B1\,\}\ S1\ \{\,Q\,\}$$
$$P \ \Rightarrow\ (B0 \vee B1) \qquad .$$

In the case of our example, we find that

$$\{\ true\ \}\ [\ x \geq 0 \rightarrow z := x\ \|\ x \leq 0 \rightarrow z := -x\ ]\ \{\ z = |x|\ \}$$

is equivalent to the conjunction of

$$\{\ x \geq 0\ \}\ z := x\ \{\ z = |x|\ \}$$
$$\{\ x \leq 0\ \}\ z := -x\ \{\ z = |x|\ \}$$
$$true \ \Rightarrow\ (x \geq 0\ \vee\ x \leq 0) \qquad ,$$

and that all three of them are *true*, as expected. This gives us some confidence that the rule is not completely without sense. How can we think about it in an operational way, that is, how might this funny if-statement be executed? The interpretation of

$$\{\ P\ \}\ [\ B0 \rightarrow S0\ \|\ B1 \rightarrow S1\ ]\ \{\ Q\ \}$$

is that if execution of the statement is begun in a state satisfying P, then execution will terminate, and it will do so in a state satisfying Q. If $P \wedge B0$ happens to be *true* initially, then Q can be established by execution of $S0$. (This is exactly what $\{\ P \wedge B0\ \}\ S0\ \{\ Q\ \}$ is telling us.) Similarly, if $P \wedge B1$ happens to be *true* initially, then Q can be established by execution of $S1$. Finally, conjunct $P \ \Rightarrow\ (B0 \vee B1)$ assures that $B0$ or $B1$ is *true* if P is. Hence, in any state satisfying P it is possible to select one of the two alternatives and establish Q.

The definition is symmetric in the two alternatives; their order doesn't matter. Hence, it is easy to generalize the definition to any number of alternatives (see Exercise 12).

For the sake of curiosity: which alternative is chosen if both $B0$ and $B1$ are *true*? The description above does not provide an answer to this question. If you manage to prove the three relevant conjuncts, the choice is irrelevant with respect to the relation between pre- and postcondition. The choice may, therefore, be made on other grounds, such as: select the shorter alternative, select one randomly, select the first, select the one that hasn't been chosen for the longest time, etc. This choice is of no concern to us; we don't mind which alternative is chosen by the implementation. (If we had reasons to prefer one over the other, say $S0$ over $S1$, we should have written $B1 \wedge \neg B0$ as the condition guarding $S1$.) Since the choice is open, the if-statement is said to be *nondeterministic*.

The bad news about nondeterministic programs is that if you run them twice, you may get different answers, even if the inputs are exactly the same. An example is

$$[\ true \rightarrow x := 1\ \|\ true \rightarrow x := -1\ ] \qquad ,$$

in which we can conclude that the postcondition is $|x| = 1$. Neither $x = 1$ nor $x = -1$ can be asserted, however. The good news about nondeterministic programs is that if you run them twice, you may get different answers, even if the inputs are exactly the same. This discourages you from trying to get your programs right by running them to see if they work. The answer may be perfect when you try it for yourself, yet wrong when the TA is looking over your shoulder. Thinking more carefully about what you are trying to do improves the quality of your work. Another advantage of nondeterminism is that the programmer need not always make irrelevant choices. In the absolute value example, it doesn't matter whether $z := x$ or $z := -x$ is selected when $x = 0$. In Pascal, you have to make a choice; in the notation that we use, you need not. (Of course, the choice, in this example, is not one that requires a lot of thought — it is more elegant, however, not to specify a choice if such is irrelevant.)

At the other end of the scale: which alternative is chosen if both $B0$ and $B1$ are *false*? In this case, you have made a mistake in your last proof obligation, namely in the proof of $P \Rightarrow (B0 \ \lor \ B1)$. So, whatever happens, you have no reason to complain. Again, what happens exactly is not prescribed by the rules above. Anything may happen and it is likely that the same thing will happen as happens upon execution of an *abort*-statement. In fact, one can prove that $\{ P \} \, [\, false \rightarrow S] \, \{ Q \}$ is equivalent to $\{ P \} \, abort \, \{ Q \}$ for all P, Q, and S.

3.4   The Iterative Statement

The while-loop as we know it in Pascal has the form **while** B **do** S, where B is a boolean expression, and S is a statement. S is sometimes called the body of the loop, and B is the condition guarding the loop (or the guard, for short). We write this same loop as $*[B \rightarrow S]$. In the literature, you may encounter **do** $B \rightarrow S$ **od**, which explains why the loop is also called the do-statement. The present form suggests generalization to the loop

$$*[B0 \rightarrow S0 \ | \ B1 \rightarrow S1 \ldots \ | \ Bn \rightarrow Sn] \qquad .$$

Note the similarity between the if-statement and the do-statement. Each is a set of pairs, guard plus statement, enclosed in a bracket pair. Such a pair is called a *guarded command*.

Here is how a loop can be executed. Iterate the following as long as at least one guard Bi is *true*: choose an i for which Bi is *true* and execute the corresponding statement Si. It follows that upon termination of the loop all guards are *false*.

The order in which the alternatives are listed in the loop is irrelevant, just as in the case of the if-statement. The same kind of nondeterminism is in action: if two or more guards are *true*, any one of them may be chosen but no more than one per iteration.

We write BB for the disjunction of the guards; that is, BB is *true* just when at least one Bi is. The operational description suggests that

$$*[B0 \rightarrow S0 \parallel B1 \rightarrow S1 \ldots \parallel Bn \rightarrow Sn]$$

is equivalent to

$$*[BB \rightarrow [B0 \rightarrow S0 \parallel B1 \rightarrow S1 \ldots \parallel Bn \rightarrow Sn]] \quad .$$

This explains why we can get by with only the simple while-loop. Nevertheless, we stick to the general form because it is useful in the development of programs. And some programs just look a lot nicer, such as good ol' Euclid's algorithm for computing the greatest common divisor of two positive integers:

$$*[a > b \rightarrow a := a - b \parallel b > a \rightarrow b := b - a] \quad .$$

We now turn to the formal definition of a loop. This is more complicated than any of the previous statements, partly due to the possibility of non-termination. Let us first give a definition in which we ignore termination for a moment. (As in the case of the if-statement, we define the loop for the case of two alternatives, leaving the generalization to the exercises.) The triple

$$\{\ P\ \}\ *[B0 \rightarrow S0 \parallel B1 \rightarrow S1]\ \{\ Q\ \}$$

follows from the conjunction of

$$\{\ P \wedge B0\ \}\ S0\ \{\ P\ \}$$
$$\{\ P \wedge B1\ \}\ S1\ \{\ P\ \}$$
$$(P \wedge \neg B0 \wedge \neg B1) \Rightarrow Q \quad .$$

Let's check whether this conforms to the operational description and to our interpretation of a Hoare triple. Given the three conjuncts, we have to convince ourselves that starting execution of the loop in a state satisfying P will, upon termination of the loop, lead to a state satisfying Q. Here we go. If initially P is *true* and all guards are *false*, then the last conjunct implies that Q is *true*. The operational meaning of the loop is that no further iterations are performed when all guards are found to be *false*, that is, the loop terminates in a state satisfying Q. Great! If, however, at least one guard is *true*, then one of them is selected and the corresponding statement is executed. For example, if $B0$ is *true*, then $S0$ may be executed. According to the first conjunct, execution of $S0$ from a state in which $P \wedge B0$ is *true* leads to a state in which P is *true* again; that is, we have returned to a situation similar to the initial state. This state may differ wildly from the initial state, but it does satisfy P, and that is the only thing we have been using here. Hence, no matter how many times the body of the loop is iterated, predicate P is *true* for any state reached. (Of course, we are not considering intermediate states that may be reached "in the middle" of $S0$ or $S1$.) Predicate P is referred to as an *invariant*. The notion of an invariant is one of the most fundamental notions, showing up in mathematics (as invariants in group theory, or as "induction hypotheses" in proofs by mathematical induction), in physics (under the name of "conservation laws"), and in most other branches of science and engineering. It is the key to being able to handle a possibly unlimited number of steps in an execution by following a limited number of steps in an argument about the execution.

Here is an example of applying the rules to a simple loop. The property that

$$\{ N \geq 0 \}$$
$$s, n := 0, 0;$$
$$\{ 0 \leq n \leq N \ \wedge \ s = \sum_{i=1}^{n} i^3 \}$$
$$*[n \neq N \rightarrow n := n + 1; \ s := s + n^3]$$
$$\{ s = \sum_{i=1}^{N} i^3 \}$$

holds follows from three parts: from

$$\{ N \geq 0 \} \ s, n := 0, 0 \ \{ 0 \leq n \leq N \ \wedge \ s = \sum_{i=1}^{n} i^3 \}$$

to show the correctness of the initialization; from

$$\{ 0 \leq n \leq N \ \wedge \ s = \sum_{i=1}^{n} i^3 \ \wedge \ n \neq N \}$$
$$n := n + 1; \ s := s + n^3$$
$$\{ 0 \leq n \leq N \ \wedge \ s = \sum_{i=1}^{n} i^3 \}$$

to show the invariance; and from

$$(0 \leq n \leq N \ \wedge \ s = \sum_{i=1}^{n} i^3 \ \wedge \ n = N) \ \Rightarrow \ s = \sum_{i=1}^{N} i^3$$

to justify the postcondition. None of these presents any particular difficulties.

In this example, it is also clear that the loop terminates; it takes exactly N iterations to complete. In a nondeterministic program, the number of iterations is not necessarily fixed by the initial state. An example is

$$x := 20; \ *[x \geq 1 \rightarrow x := x - 1 \ \| \ x \geq 2 \rightarrow x := x - 2] \qquad ,$$

which terminates after anything from 10 through 20 steps. In any case, the final state satisfies $x = 0$.

In general, we look for an integer-valued function on the variables that can be interpreted as an upper bound on the number of iterations. In the last example, x is such a function; in the summation example, $N - n$ will do. In the formal definition below, we call it bf, for bound function. It may be compared to a convergence criterion in mathematics. The full definition of the Hoare triple for loops is that

$$\{ P \} \ *[B0 \rightarrow S0 \ \| \ B1 \rightarrow S1] \ \{ Q \}$$

follows from the conjunction of

bf is an integer function
$$\{ \, P \wedge B0 \wedge bf = BF \, \} \ S0 \ \{ \, P \wedge bf < BF \, \}$$
$$\{ \, P \wedge B1 \wedge bf = BF \, \} \ S1 \ \{ \, P \wedge bf < BF \, \}$$
$$P \wedge (B0 \vee B1) \ \Rightarrow \ bf > 0$$
$$(P \wedge \neg B0 \wedge \neg B1) \ \Rightarrow \ Q \quad .$$

BF is one of those auxiliary variables that we have mentioned earlier. It is a logical variable that does not occur in the program, and the boolean value of the two Hoare triples in which it occurs should not depend on it. Stated differently, the Hoare triples must be *true* for each value of BF. In the last conjunct but one, we might just as well have written $bf \geq 0$, or $bf > 29$, or any other number — any lower bound that is independent of the variables will do, although we can interpret bf as a bound on the number of iterations only if the lower bound that we specify is positive.

In the case of the if-statement, I mentioned that the Hoare triple is equivalent to the conjunction of three predicates. In the case of the do-statement, I have chosen to say that it follows from the conjunction of a number of predicates. The latter wording ("follows from" instead of "is equivalent to") is clearly weaker. Is there a reason for the weaker formulation? Well, we know that

$$\{ \, P \, \} \ * [B0 \rightarrow S0 \ \| \ B1 \rightarrow S1] \ \{ \, Q \, \}$$

implies

$$\{ \, P' \, \} \ * [B0 \rightarrow S0 \ \| \ B1 \rightarrow S1] \ \{ \, Q \, \}$$

if P' is stronger than P. However, it may not be the case that the stronger P' satisfies all four conditions that P satisfies. The problem is in the invariance conditions $\{ \, P \wedge Bi \, \} \ Si \ \{ \, P \, \}$, since the invariant occurs in both the pre- and postcondition. Here is an example:

$$\{x = 8\}$$
$$* [\ \ 0 < x \leq 10 \ \rightarrow x := x - 1$$
$$\| \ 10 < x \leq 20 \ \rightarrow x := x + 1$$
$$\| \ 20 < x \leq 30 \ \rightarrow x := 0$$
$$]$$
$$\{x = 0\}$$

Predicate $0 \leq x \leq 8$ is an invariant that satisfies all conditions on invariants; in fact, it is the strongest one to do so. The weaker predicate $0 \leq x \leq 10$ is also an invariant. But, then, the even weaker $0 \leq x \leq 20$ fails to be an invariant even though it is always *true*. However, if we weaken this even further to $0 \leq x \leq 30$, we have another invariant. In fact, it is the weakest invariant. If any invariant exists at all, then there is a strongest invariant (the conjunction of all invariants) and a weakest invariant (their disjunction). But not every predicate that is in between the two is necessarily an invariant.

In some older texts on programming, you may not find a discussion of invariants, whereas they are central to our discussion of loops. Instead, it is often claimed that all you need to do is to state the meaning of the variables that are used in the program. For a program that adds array elements, one might write

> n is the number of array elements scanned so far, and
> s is the sum as computed so far.

One of the problems with "so far" is that it is not clear where the scan started, for example, at the low end or the high end of the array, or are the even indices done first and then the odd indices? Expressing in a formula which elements have been scanned so far, we get

$$s = \sum_{i=1}^{n} a[i]$$

and we add

$$0 \le n \le N$$

to clarify that n is in the proper range. And now we have got our invariant. The formula expresses exactly what the "meaning" of the variables is, and does so concisely. Invariants are not an extra burden to the programmer, they just contain the essential information that was needed to understand the program anyway.

We make a short excursion into a notational issue here. We wrote

$$s = \sum_{i=1}^{n} a[i]$$

to express that s is the sum of $a[1]$ through $a[n]$. Proving the program's correctness involves only manipulations with the range of i, and no manipulation of the term $a[i]$ is called for. It is therefore preferable to express the range as one expression rather than to split it into an upperbound and a lowerbound. In the sequel we write

$$s = \langle \sum i : 1 \le i \le n : a[i] \rangle$$

for the summation. Quantifier $\sum$ is followed by the bound variable, next comes the range of the variable, and finally we have the term. For a continued disjunction (existential quantification) we use exactly the same notation with $\exists$ instead of $\sum$, and for a continued conjunction (universal quantification) we write $\forall$ instead of $\sum$.

We conclude this section with a slightly exotic program. (The program contains a choice if both x and y are positive, but don't be distracted by this nondeterminism. If it bothers you, change the first guard to $x > 0 \;\wedge\; y = 0$, or the second guard to $x = 0 \;\wedge\; y > 0$.)

$$\{ x \geq 0 \ \wedge \ y \geq 0 \}$$
$$*[\ x > 0 \rightarrow x := x - 1; \ y := any \ natural \ number$$
$$\| \ y > 0 \rightarrow y := y - 1$$
$$]$$

We would like to conclude that the loop terminates. The precondition serves as invariant, but what is the bound function? Unfortunately, no integer function will do the job. If only we knew that statement

$y :=$ *any natural number*

assigns to y a number from a bounded range, say $0 \leq y < N$ for some given constant N, then we could choose $x \cdot N + y$. It is the *unbounded nondeterminism* that tricks us. By the way, we can interpret $x \cdot N + y$ as a two–digit number written in a number system with base N instead of our usual base ten. The order of natural numbers coincides with their alphabetic order as strings (when of equal length). How do the pairs (x, y) encountered during execution of the program compare when using alphabetic order and without assuming a bounded range for y? Sure enough, every step decreases the pair, and every sequence of decreases is finite (but there is no bound on the length of such a sequence of decreasing pairs). Mathematics uses the term *well-founded order* for exactly such an order. We will return to it in a later chapter. For now, it suffices to state that a well-founded order is exactly what is needed to show that a program terminates eventually. This may not be what you need in practice, though, because a program that terminates eventually cannot be distinguished by experiment from a program that doesn't terminate at all. If the program hasn't terminated after five seconds, you just have to wait a little longer. If you are still waiting after five weeks, you just have to wait a little longer. And even after five years, you have (formally) no reasons to suspect that the programmer goofed. If you want to avoid this situation, you have to insist on termination within a bounded number of steps, not just a finite number of steps. This corresponds to our bound function. The function that guarantees the weaker property that a program terminates eventually is called a *variant function.*

3.5   Procedures

One important program construct remains: the procedure. The procedure, also known as the routine or subroutine, is a mechanism for labeling a piece of program text. It is mainly used for the purpose of abstraction: singling out the relevant properties of the piece of text and forgetting those that are irrelevant. The main property that we are interested in is: what is the effect achieved by the program? The property that we want to omit from consideration is how the effect is achieved. For example, the effect of

$$\{\ x = X \land x \geq 0\ \}$$
$$y, z := 1, x; \quad * [z \neq 0 \rightarrow y, z := 2y, z - 1]$$
$$\{\ x = X \land y = 2^x\ \}$$

is to set y to 2^x without affecting x. The postcondition listed here is not the strongest possible. It does not specify what the value of z is; apparently this is considered an irrelevant detail in this case.

If we use this piece of program, we want to know the pre- and post-conditions only, and we are not interested in the code itself. This is the essential idea of abstraction, of a black box: we don't care what is inside. Therefore, the specification of a procedure consists of a precondition and a postcondition, possibly containing logical variables, like X in the example. We write a procedure declaration as follows.

> **procedure** pr;
> $\{\ x = X \land x \geq 0\ \}$
> $|[$ **var** $z : integer$;
> $\qquad y, z := 1, x; \quad * [z \neq 0 \rightarrow y, z := 2y, z - 1]$
> $]|$
> $\{\ x = X \land y = 2^x\ \}$

The pre- and postcondition are written before and after the so-called procedure body, and the whole thing is prefixed with the procedure heading that indicates the name, pr, of the procedure. (If you care about documentation, then it is probably wise to write both pre- and postcondition near the heading, because that is where they are easiest to find.) Brackets $|[$ and $]|$ delineate the scope of local variable z. Having defined pr in this way, we may write

> pr

as a statement. Its effect will be to transform a state that satisfies the precondition into a state that satisfies the postcondition. We find, for example, that

$$\{\ x = X \land x \geq 0\ \}\ pr\ \{\ x = X \land y = 2^x\ \};\ \ y := y + 1\ \{\ y = 17\ \}$$

requires $x = X = 4$ in the intermediate state, hence $x = 4$ in the initial state. So far, so good.

What is a possible implementation of the procedure statement? In a state where the precondition of the procedure body holds, execution of the statement should lead to a state in which the postcondition of the body holds. This can be realized by executing the procedure body for the procedure statement, and this is exactly how procedures are implemented.

Procedure pr operates on global variables x and y and cannot be used for anything else. If we need the same operation for a different pair of variables, we have to write the same procedure again, with the other variables substituted for x and y. Parameters of procedures serve the purpose of taking care of this kind of systematic substitution. For example,

$$\textbf{procedure } p(x : integer; \ \ \textbf{var } y : integer);$$
$$\{ \ x = X \wedge x \geq 0 \ \}$$
$$|[\ \textbf{var } z : integer;$$
$$\quad y, z := 1, x; \ \ * [z \neq 0 \rightarrow y, z := 2y, z - 1]$$
$$]|$$
$$\{ \ x = X \wedge y = 2^x \ \}$$

allows us to write

$$p(x, y)$$

to do the same thing that we used pr for, but also

$$p(a, b)$$

to store 2^a in b. Parameters make procedures a lot more useful. Various technical difficulties arise because of parameters. Let us, therefore, try to give a precise definition of the procedure call. We assume that procedure p has value parameter x and reference parameter y, just as in the example. Let S be the body of p. We assume that execution of statement

$$p(a, b)$$

is identical to execution of

$$|[\ \textbf{var } x, y; \ \ x, y := a, b; \ \ S; \ \ b := y \ ]| \qquad .$$

Note the difference between x and y : the final value of y is stored in b, but the final value of x is not stored in a. This is the one and only difference between value parameters and reference parameters. A consequence is that b is restricted to be a variable, whereas a can be any expression. From the equivalence of procedure statement and its body with substitution, we conclude

$$\{ \ B \ \} \ S \ \{ \ C_y^b \ \} \ \Rightarrow \ \{ \ B_{a,b}^{x,y} \ \} \ p(a, b) \ \{ \ C \ \} \qquad .$$

This can be seen by mere substitution:

$$\{ \ B_{a,b}^{x,y} \ \} \ |[\ \textbf{var } x, y; \ \ x, y := a, b; \ \ \{ \ B \ \} \ S \ \{ \ C_y^b \ \}; \ \ b := y \ ]| \ \{ \ C \ \}$$

which also shows that predicate C should be independent of x and y. This is a nice way to characterize the semantics of a procedure, but it misses the point: we would like to relate the pre- and postcondition of $p(a, b)$ without referring to body S. Instead, we want to formulate this in terms of the pre- and postcondition of S. Let us call them U and V, respectively: $\{ \ U \ \} \ S \ \{ \ V \ \}$. U and V are fixed for the procedure definition, but B and C differ from one call to another. We would like to know under which circumstances V implies C_y^b. In general, V does not imply C_y^b, since the latter may include variables and properties that are specific to some procedure call. Therefore, we look for an additional condition A strong enough to conclude

$$A \wedge V \;\Rightarrow\; C_y^b \qquad .$$

Predicate A is known as the *adaptation*. In view of the fact that A is going to capture the state at the procedure statement, we assume $\{\,A\,\}\,S\,\{\,A\,\}$. We then have

$$\begin{array}{rl}
& \{\,A\,\}\,S\,\{\,A\,\}\ \wedge\ \{\,U\,\}\,S\,\{\,V\,\} \\
\Rightarrow & \quad\{\ \text{conjunction of pre- and postconditions (Exercise 5) }\} \\
& \{\,A\wedge U\,\}\,S\,\{\,A\wedge V\,\} \\
\Rightarrow & \quad\{\ \ A\wedge V\;\Rightarrow\;C_y^b\ \} \\
& \{\,A\wedge U\,\}\,S\,\{\,C_y^b\,\} \\
\Rightarrow & \quad\{\ \text{rules of assignment and ; }\} \\
& \{\,(A\wedge U)_{a,b}^{x,y}\,\}\,\|[\ \textbf{var}\ x,y;\ \ x,y := a,b;\ \ S\ ;\ \ b := y\,]\|\,\{\,C\,\} \\
= & \quad\{\ \text{definition of procedure statement }\} \\
& \{\,(A\wedge U)_{a,b}^{x,y}\,\}\,p(a,b)\,\{\,C\,\} \qquad .
\end{array}$$

It remains to find a condition under which we can guarantee $\{\,A\,\}\,S\,\{\,A\,\}$ without checking A versus procedure body S. This condition is called: A is *transparent*. One such condition is that A is independent of x and y and of all global variables modified by S. One of the easiest ways to achieve this independence is to insist that S does not modify x or any global variables and that y does not occur in A. A slightly more general rule is: S does not modify x if x occurs in A, S does not modify any global variable that occurs in A, and y does not occur in A. This rule requires that we include the list of global variables and value parameters modified by S in the specification of the procedure; this allows us to have a concise proof rule, and is considered to be good practice anyway. Here is a summary of the rule.

> Let A be a predicate that is transparent with respect to the procedure body and that satisfies $A \wedge V \;\Rightarrow\; C_y^b$;
>
> then, $\{\,(A\wedge U)_{a,b}^{x,y}\,\}\,p(a,b)\,\{\,C\,\}$.

If the procedure has more than one reference parameter, then the corresponding actual parameters should be distinct for the expression C_y^b to make sense. Compare this with the similar case of the concurrent assignment statement.

Let us now try to show that $\{\,w = 29\,\}\,p(a,b)\,\{\,w = 29\,\}$, which should be easy enough since w is not even referenced in our procedure $p(a,b)$. Without the adaptation A, this is impossible, but with A we can do it: just choose A to be $w = 29$. Since A does not contain any value parameter or global variable modified by the body of p, A is transparent and we can apply the rule for procedures. We have to check the postcondition:

$$A \wedge V \;\Rightarrow\; (w = 29)_y^b$$

(which is *true*) and the precondition:

$$w = 29 \;\Rightarrow\; (A \wedge U)^{x,y}_{a,b}$$

(which is *true* just when $a \geq 0$). It turns out that we need the additional constraint $a \geq 0$ in the precondition to show that $w = 29$ is an invariant of $p(a, b)$, that is, we have $\{ w = 29 \wedge a \geq 0 \} \; p(a, b) \; \{ w = 29 \}$ instead of $\{ w = 29 \} \; p(a, b) \; \{ w = 29 \}$. This is no surprise, because inspection shows that the procedure will not terminate if $a < 0$.

The implementation of our y parameter requires that b be copied to y at procedure entry, and that y (which may have been modified by then) be copied back to b at procedure exit. We have called this a reference parameter, although it is sometimes called a value result parameter. A true reference parameter is implemented as follows. At procedure entry, the address of b is stored in y. During execution of the body, every reference to y is treated as an indirect reference to b. For example, an assignment to y in S has the immediate effect of assigning to b. Nothing happens at procedure exit. The advantage of reference parameters is that no copies need to be made, which is especially important if y is a large data structure, such as a big matrix. The disadvantage is that every reference requires more time. Our proof rule applies to either implementation if the actual parameter b is not one of the global variables inspected or modified by the procedure body. And if there is more than one reference parameter, they should be pairwise distinct and all of them should be distinct from the global variables inspected or modified by the procedure body.

3.6   Recursion

The rule for procedures discussed in the previous section applies to their common use, but there is another way in which procedures are sometimes used, namely recursively. It is true that all recursive programs can be written without recursion, but often the recursive solution is elegant and efficient. What do we have to add to our proof rule for procedures to accommodate recursion? Well, the only problem that recursion gives us is that for all conditions U and V

> **procedure** $p(x : integer;$ **var** $y : integer)$;
> $\{ \, U \, \} \; p(x, y) \; \{ \, V \, \}$

meets all our formal requirements, and yet we know that it does not do what it is supposed to do: execution of the procedure goes into a nonterminating recursion and therefore does not terminate in a state satisfying V. This is similar to the loop

$$*[\; true \;\rightarrow\; skip \;] \qquad ,$$

which maintains every invariant P, and also $P \wedge \neg B \Rightarrow R$ for every postcondition R. The problem is that the loop doesn't terminate, and that is why we introduced a bound function that bounds the number of iterations. Similarly, the repeated substitution of body for procedure call does not terminate in the example, and we have to introduce a bound function that bounds the number of recursive procedure calls. Since the situation is so similar to the loop, but only notationally more involved, we refrain from formalization. We conclude with an example of recursive procedure.

US mail sells N different stamps. The face value of stamp i is $v[i]$, where $v[1..N]$ is a given array of distinct positive integers. Given a certain amount that needs to be put on a letter, how many different ways exist of producing this value from the stamps? Many copies of the same stamp may be needed, but the order in which they are glued on the envelope is considered irrelevant. For example, if we have stamps whose face values are 1, 4, and 25, then the amount 29 can be composed in ten different ways. Write a program for computing the number of combinations.

We tackle the problem as follows. Let $c(x, n)$ be the number of combinations in which x can be produced from stamps 1 through n, where $x \geq 0$, $0 \leq n \leq N$. Function c satisfies

$$c(0, n) = 1 \qquad \text{for all } n;$$
$$c(x, 0) = 0 \qquad \text{for } x > 0;$$
$$c(x, n) = \langle \sum i : 0 \leq i \cdot v[n] \leq x : c(x - i \cdot v[n], n - 1) \rangle$$
$$\text{for } n > 0 \ \wedge \ x > 0.$$

The reasoning for the three alternatives is as follows. An amount of 0 can be composed in one way only: by using no stamps at all. A positive amount cannot be composed if no stamps can be used. If amount x is composed using i copies of stamp n then the number of ways of doing so is the number of ways of composing the remaining amount with the other stamps. The range for i is $0 \leq i \cdot v[n] \leq x$, while the remaining amount is $x - i \cdot v[n]$, which can be composed in $c(x - i \cdot v[n], n - 1)$ ways from the remaining stamps. We write a procedure that is equivalent to $y := y + c(x, n)$.

```
procedure p(x, n : integer; var y : integer);
  { x = x' ≥ 0  ∧  0 ≤ n = n' ≤ N  ∧  y = y' }
  |[ var k : integer;
    [ x = 0              → y := y + 1
    ‖ x > 0 ∧ n = 0      → skip
    ‖ x > 0 ∧ n > 0      →
```

$$k := 0;$$
$$\{ \ inv: \ y = y' + \langle \sum i : 0 \le i < k : c(x - i \cdot v[n], n - 1) \rangle$$
$$\wedge \ k \ge 0 \ \wedge \ (k-1) \cdot v[n] \le x \ \}$$
$$\{ \ bf: \ x \ \textbf{div} \ v[n] - k \ \}$$
$$*[k \cdot v[n] \le x \to p(x - k \cdot v[n], n - 1, y); \ k := k + 1]$$
$$]$$
$$]|$$
$$\{ \ y = y' + c(x', n') \ \}$$

The recursion is well defined, since parameter n is bounded from below on account of the precondition (which includes $n \ge 0$), and it is less in the recursive call (where it is $n - 1$). The problem to compute $c(x, N)$ is now solved by the following statements.

$$y := 0; \ p(x, N, y) \ \{ \ y = c(x, N) \ \}$$

3.7   Bibliographic Notes

Hoare triples were introduced in [Hoa69]. We have written $\{ P \} S \{ Q \}$ to mean that if statement S is executed, starting in an initial state that satisfies P, then execution is guaranteed to terminate, and the final state satisfies Q. Hoare's original paper instead used $P \{S\} Q$ with the meaning that if statement S is executed, starting in an initial state that satisfies P, then execution may or may not terminate; if it terminates, the final state satisfies Q. This version is sometimes referred to as *partial correctness* whereas we have focussed on *total correctness*.

We are usually interested in the weakest precondition P for which $\{ P \} S \{ Q \}$ holds. Following [Dij75], this is written as $wp(S, Q)$. This is also the paper that introduced guarded commands. The weakest precondition P for which $P \{S\} Q$ holds is referred to as the weakest liberal precondition $wlp(S, Q)$. Both wp and wlp are studied in [Dij76]. See also [DS90] and [dB82].

The idea of using assertions is usually attributed to [Flo67]. The essential idea can also be found in [Tur49]. Consult [Apt81] for an overview of defining program semantics by Hoare triples and for related work, and refer to [Jon92] for an historical overview.

The problem of the Dutch National Flag (Exercise 37) is due to [Dij76]. Program *Find* is due to [Hoa71]. Program *Quicksort* (Exercises 44 and 45) is due to [Hoa62].

The semantics of procedures is adapted from [Mar83]. See also [Gri81].

3.8   Exercises

1. Give the weakest expression that can be substituted for the dots

in each of the following cases. (We want the weakest because any
stronger condition, such as *false*, will do also.)

$$\{ \dots \} \, x := x + 1 \, \{ \, x = 24 \, \}$$
$$\{ \dots \} \, x := x + 1 \, \{ \, x^2 > 45 \, \}$$
$$\{ \dots \} \, x := x + 1 \, \{ \, x^2 - x > 87 \, \}$$
$$\{ \dots \} \, x := x^2 - x + 1 \, \{ \, x \geq 23 \, \}$$
$$\{ \dots \} \, x := x^4 - x^2 - 6 \, \{ \, x \geq 23 \, \}$$
$$\{ \dots \} \, x := (x - 1) \cdot (x + 1) \, \{ \, x \geq 0 \}$$
$$\{ \dots \} \, x := 1 \, \{ \, x = 10 \, \}$$
$$\{ \dots \} \, x := y \, \{ \, x < 0 \, \}$$
$$\{ \dots \} \, x := x + y \, \{ \, x > 0 \; \wedge \; y > 0 \, \}$$
$$\{ \dots \} \, b := b \wedge c \, \{ \, b \, \}$$
$$\{ \dots \} \, b := b \wedge c \, \{ \, b \Rightarrow c \, \}$$
$$\{ \dots \} \, b := b \wedge c \, \{ \, c \Rightarrow b \, \}$$
$$\{ \dots \} \, b := b \wedge c \, \{ \, b = c \, \}$$
$$\{ \dots \} \, x, y, z := y, z, x \, \{ \, x = X \; \wedge \; y = Y \; \wedge \; z = Z \, \}$$
$$\{ \dots \} \, z, y := z \cdot x, y - 1 \, \{ \, y \geq 0 \; \wedge \; z \cdot x^y = a^b \, \}$$

2. Give the strongest expression that can be substituted for the dots
   in each of the following cases. (We want the strongest because any
   weaker condition, such as *true*, will do also.)

$$\{ \, x = 10 \, \} \, x := x + 1 \, \{ \dots \}$$
$$\{ \, x^2 > 45 \, \} \, x := x + 1 \, \{ \dots \}$$
$$\{ \, x \geq 10 \, \} \, x := x - 10 \, \{ \dots \}$$
$$\{ \, 0 \leq x < 10 \, \} \, x := x^2 \, \{ \dots \}$$
$$\{ \, x^3 = y \, \} \, x := |x| \, \{ \dots \}$$

3. Derive the weakest precondition.

$$\{ \dots \} \, y := y + 2x + 1; \; x := x + 1 \, \{ \, y = x^2 \, \}$$
$$\{ \dots \} \, y := y + 3z + 3x + 1; \; z := z + 2x + 1; \; x := x + 1$$
$$\{ \, y = x^3 \; \wedge \; z = x^2 \, \}$$
$$\{ \dots \} \, y := y^2; \; x := x \, \mathbf{div} \, 2 \, \{ \, y^x = z \, \}$$
$$\{ \dots \} \, b := b \equiv c; \; c := b \equiv c; \; b := b \equiv c \, \{ \, b \equiv B \; \wedge \; c \equiv C \, \}$$
$$\{ \dots \} \, b := b \not\equiv c; \; c := b \not\equiv c; \; b := b \not\equiv c \, \{ \, b \equiv B \; \wedge \; c \equiv C \, \}$$

4. Find appropriate assignments to substitute for the dots.

$$\{ \, z = x^y \; \wedge \; y \geq 0 \, \} \, \dots; \; y := y + 1 \, \{ \, z = x^y \; \wedge \; y > 0 \, \}$$
$$\{ \, 0 \leq n < 100 \; \wedge \; s = \sum_{i=1}^{n} i^3 \, \} \, \dots; \; n := n + 1$$
$$\{ \, 0 < n \leq 100 \; \wedge \; s = \sum_{i=1}^{n} i^3 \, \}$$
$$\{ \, P \, \} \, x := 2x + 1; \; \dots \, \{ \, P \, \} \; \text{for all} \; P$$

5. Consider the case where we have $\{ \, P \, \} \, S \, \{ \, Q \, \}$ and $\{ \, P' \, \} \, S \, \{ \, Q' \, \}$.
   From the interpretation of a Hoare triple, prove $\{ \, P \wedge P' \, \} \, S \, \{ \, Q \wedge Q' \, \}$
   and $\{ \, P \vee P' \, \} \, S \, \{ \, Q \vee Q' \, \}$.

6. We have defined the *abort*-statement to satisfy for all P the triple $\{\,false\,\}\ abort\ \{\,P\,\}$. Discuss the "inverse" hereof, that is, a statement characterized by $\{\,P\,\}\ troba\ \{\,false\,\}$ for all P. Would this be a useful statement to have in a programming language? Can you think of a possible implementation?

7. Find the weakest P that satisfies

$$\{\,P\,\}$$
$$[w \le r \to q, r := q + 1, r - w \parallel w > r \to skip]$$
$$\{\,q \cdot w + r = x\ \wedge\ r \ge 0\,\}\quad.$$

8. Prove

$$\{\,z \cdot x^y = X^Y\ \wedge\ y > 0\,\}$$
$$[odd(y) \to z := z \cdot x \parallel even(y) \to skip];$$
$$x, y := x^2, y\ \textbf{div}\ 2$$
$$\{\,z \cdot x^y = X^Y\ \wedge\ y \ge 0\,\}\quad.$$

9. What is the Hoare triple for the if- and do-statement if well-definedness of the guards is taken into account?

10. Calculate boolean expressions $b0$ and $b1$ that satisfy

$$\{P \wedge x \ne y\}\ [b0 \to x := x - y \parallel b1 \to y := y - x]\ \{P\}\quad,$$

where P is given by $x > 0\ \wedge\ y > 0$.

11. Explain which mistake has been made in the following example.

$$\{\,true\,\}\ *[true \to x := x - 1]\ \{\,true\,\}$$
$$inv:\quad true$$
$$bf:\quad 2^x$$

Check all proof obligations and list those that are in error.

12. Consider the general definition of the if-statement with n guarded commands. Simplify the formula for $n = 0$, and give (for this case only) an equivalent statement that contains no boolean expression. Similarly for the do-statement.

13. Give a grammar for the programming language introduced in this chapter.

14. Write expression $\langle \sum i : 2 \le i \le N\ \wedge\ prime(i) : i \rangle$ in the traditional notation with a lowerbound and an upperbound for a summation.

15. Prove

$$\{\, k > 0 \,\} \;*\, [x < 0 \rightarrow x := x + k] \; \{\, x \geq 0 \,\} \,.$$

16. Prove

$$\{\, true \,\} \;*\, [x < y \rightarrow x, y := y, x] \; \{\, x \geq y \,\} \,.$$

17. Prove

$$\{\, true \,\}$$
$$*[i < j \rightarrow i := i + 1 \;\|\; j < k \rightarrow j := j + 1 \;\|\; k < i \rightarrow k := k + 1]$$
$$\{\, i = j = k \,\} \quad .$$

18. We have observed that for given P, Q, B, and S, several invariants may exist to infer $\{\, P \,\} \, * [B \rightarrow S] \, \{\, Q \,\}$. (By invariant, we mean a predicate that satisfies all criteria listed for invariants.) Prove that the conjunction and disjunction of two invariants are also invariants.

19. Let f be the Fibonacci function as defined in Exercise 2.13. Prove

$$\{\, N \geq 0 \,\}$$
$$n, x, y := 0, 0, 1;$$
$$\{\, inv : \; 0 \leq n \leq N \;\wedge\; x = f(n) \;\wedge\; y = f(n-1)\}$$
$$\{\, bf : \; N - n \,\}$$
$$*[n \neq N \rightarrow x, y := x + y, x; \; n := n + 1]$$
$$\{\, x = f(N) \,\} \quad .$$

You will find that you need to define $f(-1)$ in such a way that the recurrence equation that we have given for f applies to the case $n = -1$.

20. Prove

$$\{\, N \geq 0 \,\}$$
$$s := 0; \; n := N;$$
$$*[n \neq 0 \rightarrow n := n - 1; \; s := s \cdot x + a[n]]$$
$$\{\, s = \langle \textstyle\sum i : 0 \leq i < N : a[i] \cdot x^i \rangle \,\} \quad .$$

This algorithm is known as *Horner's rule* for evaluating a polynomial.

21. Prove

$$\{\, N \geq 0 \,\}$$
$$a, b := 0, N + 1;$$
$$*[\; b - a \neq 1 \rightarrow c := (a + b) \textbf{ div } 2;$$
$$\qquad\qquad [\; c^2 \leq N \rightarrow a := c$$
$$\qquad\qquad \| \; c^2 > N \rightarrow b := c$$
$$\qquad\;\;] \qquad\qquad]$$
$$\{\, a^2 \leq N < (a + 1)^2, \text{ that is, } a \text{ is the integer part of } \sqrt{N} \,\} \quad .$$

22. Prove

$$\{ N \geq 0 \}$$
$$a := N;$$
$$*[a^2 > N \rightarrow a := (a + N \textbf{ div } a) \textbf{ div } 2]$$
$$\{ a^2 \leq N < (a+1)^2, \text{ that is, } a \text{ is the integer part of } \sqrt{N} \} \qquad .$$

23. f is a natural function on natural arguments, satisfying

$$f(0, y) = y;$$
$$f(x, 0) = x;$$
$$f(x, y) = f(x, y + k \cdot x) = f(x + k \cdot y, y) \text{ for all } x, y, k \geq 0.$$

Prove

$$\{ X \geq 0 \ \wedge \ Y \geq 0 \}$$
$$x, y := X, Y;$$
$$*[\ x > y > 0 \rightarrow x := x \textbf{ mod } y$$
$$\| \ y > x > 0 \rightarrow y := y \textbf{ mod } x$$
$$]$$
$$\{ \max(x, y) = f(X, Y) \} \qquad .$$

Use $\lfloor \log(xy+1) \rfloor$ as a bound function, which shows that the program is a fast one, running in logarithmic time. (All logarithms that we use are to the base 2.) Can you describe function f in words, possibly assuming that not both arguments are zero?

24. You know how to compute the quotient and remainder of dividing two "large" numbers through a process called long division. Describe this algorithm, and prove its correctness.

25. Prove

$$\{ x \geq 0 \ \wedge \ y > 0 \}$$
$$q, r, w := 0, x, y; \quad * [r \geq w \rightarrow w := w \cdot 2];$$
$$*[\ w \neq y \rightarrow w := w/2; \ q := q \cdot 2;$$
$$[r \geq w \rightarrow q, r := q + 1, r - w \ \| \ r < w \rightarrow skip]$$
$$]$$
$$\{ q = x \textbf{ div } y \ \wedge \ r = x \textbf{ mod } y \} \qquad .$$

26. Prove

$$\{ x \geq y \ \wedge \ y \geq 0 \}$$
$$*[x \neq y \rightarrow y := y + 1; \ x := x - x \textbf{ mod } y]$$
$$\{ x = y \} \qquad .$$

27. Prove

$$\{\, N \geq 0 \,\}$$
$$x, y, k := 0, 0, 0;$$
$$*[k \neq N \rightarrow x := x + f(k); \quad y := y + x; \quad k := k + 1]$$
$$\{\, y = \langle \sum i : 0 \leq i < N : (N - i) \cdot f(i) \rangle \,\} \quad .$$

28. Prove termination of the following algorithm.

$$\{\, x \bmod 3 \neq 0 \,\}$$
$$*[x \text{ is not a power of } 2 \rightarrow x := x + 3]$$
$$\{\, true \,\}$$

29. Can you prove or disprove termination of the following algorithm?

$$\{\, n \geq 1 \,\}$$
$$*[n \neq 1 \rightarrow [odd(n) \rightarrow n := 3 \cdot n + 1 \ \| \ even(n) \rightarrow n := n/2]]$$
$$\{\, true \,\}$$

If you have trouble finding a bound function, you might want to trace execution of this algorithm for $n = 15$ or $n = 27$. This will not help you much in finding a bound function, but it may give you a feeling of why this is nontrivial.

30. We have discussed the semantics of value result parameters and we have discussed when they may be implemented as reference parameters. Can you think of a proof rule for reference parameters that is consistent with a reasonable implementation?

31. Given positive integer N, prove

    var $a :$ **array** $[0..N - 1]$ **of** $integer$;
    procedure $search(x : integer;$ **var** $b : boolean)$;
      $\{\, true \,\}$
      $a[0] := x; \quad b := true$
      $\{\, b = \langle \exists i : 0 \leq i < N : a[i] = x \rangle \,\} \quad .$

32. Given positive integer N, prove

    var $a :$ **array** $[0..N - 1]$ **of** $integer$;
    procedure $search(x : integer;$ **var** $b : boolean)$;
      $\{\, a = a' \,\}$
      $x := a[0]; \quad b := true$
      $\{\, a = a' \ \wedge \ b = \langle \exists i : 0 \leq i < N : a[i] = x \rangle \,\} \quad .$

33. Given positive integer N, prove

    var $a :$ **array** $[0..N - 1]$ **of** $integer$;
    procedure $search(x : integer;$ **var** $b : boolean)$;
      $\{\, a = a' \ \wedge \ x = x' \,\}$

$$\begin{aligned}
&\|[\ \textbf{var}\ k : integer; \\
&\quad b := false;\ \ k := 0; \\
&\quad *[k \neq N \wedge \neg b \rightarrow b := a[k] = x;\ \ k := k+1] \\
&]\|
\end{aligned}$$
$$\{\ a = a'\ \wedge\ b\ =\ \langle \exists i : 0 \leq i < N : a[i] = x' \rangle\ \}\quad .$$

Also, show that the procedures in the previous two exercises do not meet the present specification.

34. Given integer $N > 2$, prove

$$\begin{aligned}
&\textbf{var}\ t : \textbf{array}\ [2..N]\ \textbf{of}\ boolean; \\
&\quad n : integer; \\
&\textbf{procedure}\ prime(x : integer;\ \textbf{var}\ p : boolean); \\
&\quad \{\ 1 \leq n \leq N\ \wedge\ \langle \forall i : 2 \leq i \leq n : t[i]\ =\ i\ \text{is prime}\rangle\ \wedge \\
&\quad\quad 2 \leq x = x' \leq N\ \} \\
&\quad \|[\ \textbf{var}\ k : integer; \\
&\quad\quad *[\ n < x \rightarrow n := n+1;\ \ k := 2;\ t[n] := true; \\
&\quad\quad\quad\quad\quad\quad *[k^2 \leq n\ \wedge\ t[n] \rightarrow t[n] := n\ \textbf{mod}\ k \neq 0; \\
&\quad\quad\quad\quad\quad\quad\quad\quad\quad\quad\quad\quad\quad\quad\quad k := k+1 \\
&\quad\quad\ ]\quad\quad\quad\quad]; \\
&\quad\quad p := t[x] \\
&\quad]\| \\
&\quad \{\ 1 \leq n \leq N\ \wedge\ \langle \forall i : 2 \leq i \leq n : t[i]\ =\ i\ \text{is prime}\rangle\ \wedge \\
&\quad\quad p\ =\ x'\ \text{is prime} \\
&\quad \}\quad .
\end{aligned}$$

35. Given integer $N > 0$, prove

$$\begin{aligned}
&\textbf{var}\ a : \textbf{array}\ [0..N-1]\ \textbf{of}\ integer; \\
&\textbf{procedure}\ choose(m, n : integer;\ \textbf{var}\ x : integer); \\
&\quad \{\ 0 \leq m < n \leq N\ \wedge\ m = m'\ \wedge\ n = n'\ \wedge\ a = a'\ \} \\
&\quad x := a[(m+n)\ \textbf{div}\ 2] \\
&\quad \{\ \langle \exists i : m' \leq i < n' : a[i] = x\rangle\ \wedge\ a = a'\ \}\quad .
\end{aligned}$$

36. Given integer $N > 0$, prove

$$\begin{aligned}
&\textbf{var}\ a : \textbf{array}\ [0..N-1]\ \textbf{of}\ integer; \\
&\textbf{procedure}\ choose(m, n : integer;\ \textbf{var}\ x : integer); \\
&\quad \{\ 0 \leq m < n \leq N\ \wedge\ m = m'\ \wedge\ n = n'\ \wedge\ a = a'\ \} \\
&\quad \|[\ \textbf{var}\ u, v, w : integer; \\
&\quad\quad u := a[m];\ \ v := a[(m+n)\ \textbf{div}\ 2];\ \ w := a[n-1]; \\
&\quad\quad [\ u \leq v \leq w \rightarrow x := v \\
&\quad\quad \|\ v \leq w \leq u \rightarrow x := w \\
&\quad\quad \|\ w \leq u \leq v \rightarrow x := u \\
&\quad\quad] \\
&\quad]\| \\
&\quad \{\ \langle \exists i : m' \leq i < n' : a[i] = x\rangle\ \wedge\ a = a'\ \}\quad .
\end{aligned}$$

37. Given integer $N > 0$, prove

> **var** $a : $ **array** $[0..N-1]$ **of** *integer*;
> **procedure** $DNF(m, n, x : integer;$ **var** $l, r : integer);$
> $\{\, 0 \le m < n \le N \;\;\wedge\;\; m = m' \;\;\wedge\;\; n = n' \;\;\wedge\;\; a = a' \,\}$
> $\|[$ **var** $j : integer;$
> $l, j, r := m, m, n;$
> $*[\, j \ne r \;\rightarrow\;\; [\; a[j] < x \;\rightarrow\; a[j], a[l] := a[l], a[j];$
> $j, l := j + 1, l + 1$
> $[\!]\; a[j] = x \;\rightarrow\; j := j + 1$
> $[\!]\; a[j] > x \;\rightarrow\; a[j], a[r-1] := a[r-1], a[j];$
> $r := r - 1$
> $]$ $]$
> $]\|$
> $\{\, perm(a, a') \;\wedge$
> $\langle \forall i : 0 \le i < N : a[i] = a'[i] \;\;\vee\;\; m' \le i < n' \rangle \;\;\wedge$
> $m' \le l \le r \le n' \;\;\wedge\;\; \langle \forall i : m' \le i < l : a[i] < x \rangle \;\;\wedge$
> $\langle \forall i : l \le i < r : a[i] = x \rangle \;\;\wedge\;\; \langle \forall i : r \le i < n' : a[i] > x \rangle$
> $\}$,

where $perm(a, a')$ is *true* just when a and a' are possibly different permutations of the same bag of numbers. This problem is known as the Dutch National Flag, which has three stripes, red, white, and blue. It relates to the program when numbers less than x are red, numbers equal to x are white, and numbers greater than x are blue.

38. Given integer $N > 0$, prove

> **var** $a : $ **array** $[0..N-1]$ **of** *integer*;
> **procedure** $Find(k : integer);$
> $\{\, 0 \le k < N \;\;\wedge\;\; k = k' \;\;\wedge\;\; a = a' \,\}$
> $\|[$ **var** $x, m, l, r, n : integer;$
> $m, n := 0, N;$
> $*[\, n - m \ne 1 \;\rightarrow\;\; choose(m, n, x); \;\; DNF(m, n, x, l, r);$
> $[\; k < l \;\;\;\;\;\;\; \rightarrow\; n := l$
> $[\!]\; l \le k < r \;\rightarrow\; m, n := k, k + 1$
> $[\!]\; r \le k \;\;\;\;\;\;\; \rightarrow\; m := r$
> $]$ $]$
> $]\|$
> $\{\, perm(a, a') \;\wedge$
> $\langle \forall i : 0 \le i < k' : a[i] \le a[k'] \rangle \;\;\wedge$
> $\langle \forall i : k' < i < N : a[k'] \le a[i] \rangle$
> $\}$,

where $perm(a, a')$ is *true* just when a and a' are possibly different permutations of the same bag of numbers. This procedure finds the least-but-k element in array a. It does so by rearranging the array elements in such a way that the least-but-k element is $a[k]$.

39. What is the adaptation needed to show the correctness of the recursive call in the body of the procedure that solves the stamps problem?

40. Solve the stamps problem under the additional restriction that the envelope has space for at most M stamps, where M is a given natural number.

41. Given is a collection of N rocks, numbered from 0 on. Rock i has mass $m[i]$, where $m[0..N-1]$ is a given array of positive integers. Write a program for determining the number of ways in which the collection can be partitioned into two sets with equal total mass.

42. Given are positive integers N and V, and positive integer arrays $v, w[0..N-1]$. We consider a set of N articles, numbered from 0 on. Article i has volume $v[i]$ and weight $w[i]$. A set of articles "fit" if their total volume is at most V. Show that the following program assigns to m the maximum weight of any set of articles that fit.

```
var m, x, y : integer;
procedure p(j : integer);
    [ j = N → m := y
    ‖ j < N → y := y − w[j];
                [ y > m → p(j + 1) ‖ y ≤ m → skip ];
                y, x := y + w[j], x + v[j];
                [ x ≤ V → p(j + 1) ‖ x > V → skip ];
                x := x − v[j]
    ];
m, x, y := 0, 0, ⟨∑ i : 0 ≤ i < N : w[i]⟩;
p(0)
```

43. Let f be the Fibonacci function, as defined earlier. Show

```
procedure fib(n : integer; var a, b : integer);
    { n′ = n ≥ 0 }
    ‖[ var x, y : integer;
        [ n < 2 → a, b := n, 1
        ‖ n ≥ 2 → fib(n div 2, x, y);
                    [ odd(n) → a, b := x² + y², y² + 2xy
                    ‖ even(n) → a, b := 2xy − x², x² + y²
        ]                ]
    ]‖
    { a = f(n′)  ∧  b = f(n′ + 1) }          .
```

Hint: first show

$$f(i+j-1) = f(i)f(j) + f(i-1)f(j-1)$$

for all positive i, j.

44. Assume that we have procedures *choose* and *DNF* as specified in previous exercises. Given integer $N > 0$, prove

> **var** a : **array** $[0..N-1]$ **of** *integer*;
> **procedure** *Quicksort*$(m, n : integer)$;
> $\quad \{\, 0 \le m < n \le N \;\; \wedge \;\; m = m' \;\; \wedge \;\; n = n' \;\; \wedge \;\; a = a' \,\}$
> $\quad |[\;$ **var** $l, r, x :$ *integer*;
> $\qquad choose(m, n, x);\;\; DNF(m, n, x, l, r);$
> $\qquad [\; l - m > 1 \rightarrow Quicksort(m, l)\; |\; l - m \le 1 \rightarrow skip\;];$
> $\qquad [\; n - r > 1 \rightarrow Quicksort(r, n)\; |\; n - r \le 1 \rightarrow skip\;]$
> $\quad]|$
> $\quad \{\; perm(a, a')\; \wedge$
> $\qquad \langle \forall i : 0 \le i < N : a[i] = a'[i] \;\; \vee \;\; m' \le i < n' \rangle \;\; \wedge$
> $\qquad \langle \forall i : m' < i < n' : a[i-1] \le a[i] \rangle$
> $\quad \}$.

Procedure call $Quicksort(0, N)$ is, on the average, an extremely efficient method for sorting array $a[0..N-1]$. Its execution time is proportional to N^2 in the worst case, but is proportional to $N \log(N)$ in the average case.

45. Same problem for

> **var** a : **array** $[0..N-1]$ **of** *integer*;
> **procedure** *Quicksort*$(m, n : integer)$;
> $\quad \{\, 0 \le m < n \le N \;\; \wedge \;\; m = m' \;\; \wedge \;\; n = n' \;\; \wedge \;\; a = a' \,\}$
> $\quad |[\;$ **var** $l, r, x :$ *integer*;
> $\qquad *[\; n - m > 1 \rightarrow$
> $\qquad\quad choose(m, n, x);\;\; DNF(m, n, x, l, r);$
> $\qquad\quad [\; l - m \ge n - r \rightarrow Quicksort(r, n);\;\; n := l$
> $\qquad\quad |\; n - r \ge l - m \rightarrow Quicksort(m, l);\;\; m := r$
> $\qquad\quad]\;\;]$
> $\quad]|$
> $\quad \{\; perm(a, a')\; \wedge$
> $\qquad \langle \forall i : 0 \le i < N : a[i] = a'[i] \;\; \vee \;\; m' \le i < n' \rangle \;\; \wedge$
> $\qquad \langle \forall i : m' < i < n' : a[i-1] \le a[i] \rangle$
> $\quad \}$.

4

Regular Expressions

In Chapter 2, we discussed grammars as a means of defining languages. In Chapter 1, we mentioned that it seems unreasonable to think that machines with an infinite set of states can be physically realized. In this chapter, we explore the class of languages that can be accepted with finite-state machines, the class of *regular languages*. We study several ways of defining regular languages (right-linear grammars, transition graphs, regular expressions, and finite-state machines) and show their equivalence. For reasons that are beyond me, the terminology that has developed around these notions is slightly different. For example, one says that a language is "generated" by a grammar, "accepted" by a machine, and "denoted" by a regular expression. I will use all terms (as well as the term "defined") to mean the same thing.

4.1 Right-Linear Grammars

The first device with which we define a regular language is a right-linear grammar. A right-linear grammar is a grammar (T, N, R, S) that satisfies the following restrictions:

- initial string S is a nonterminal symbol;

- every production rule is of the form $A \to xB$ or of the form $A \to x$ where x is a string of terminal symbols ($x \in T^*$) and A and B are nonterminal symbols ($A, B \in N$).

(It should come as no surprise that one can define left-linear grammars in the obvious way by switching from xB to Bx. It may come as a surprise that to every right-linear grammar corresponds a left-linear grammar that defines the same language, and vice versa. It is important that left-linear and right-linear production rules not be mixed, because the result of a mixture need not be regular.)

Why does the class of languages defined by right-linear grammars correspond to the class of languages that can be accepted with finite-state machines? We give only a hint now and provide a proof later. Consider the domino game once more. Assume that a left-to-right, top-to-bottom parsing strategy is used to check whether an input string can be generated by the grammar. At any moment, a tree-like structure branches out from the piece that is at the top of the board, and a possibly empty part at the left bottom of the tree is matched with a prefix of the input string. The unmatched fringe of the tree-like structure is still to be matched against the unmatched suffix of the input string. The fringe has, at any moment, the following structure: it is the suffix of the right-hand side of one of the production rules. (Check that this is an invariant by checking that it holds initially and that every step maintains the invariant. Convince yourself that you need the restrictions on right-linear grammars.) Hence, given the right-linear grammar, only a limited number of distinct fringes or states exists, namely, the number of those suffixes.

4.2   Transition Graphs

Sometimes a diagram conveys information more clearly and compactly than does text. (Not always, however, and this certainly varies from person to person; try to imagine a picture that illustrates the expression "a picture is worth a thousand words" as clearly as these seven words do.) We discuss how right-linear grammars may be represented by diagrams called *transition graphs*.

A transition graph is a finite set of nodes plus a finite set of directed edges. One node is called the start node, and one node is called the final node. (It is okay for one node to be both the start and the final node.) Each edge is labeled with a string of terminal symbols and leads from a source node to a destination node. (It is okay for the source and destination to be the same node.) The diagrammatic representation of the transition graph is the usual representation of a graph consisting of a circle per node and an arrow per edge, plus a pointer to the start node labeled "start" and a double circle for the final node.

So much for the transition graph itself. Next, we define the language that corresponds to the graph. A path is a finite sequence of edges in which the destination of any edge is the source of the next edge in the path. (It is okay for a path to contain cycles.) A successful path through a transition graph is a path beginning at the start node and ending at the final node. (It is okay for a path to continue beyond the final node as long as the final node is also the last node on the path; in this case the path contains a cycle.) To each successful path corresponds one string: it is obtained by catenating in order the strings that label each edge in the path. The language defined by the transition graph is the set of all strings corresponding to successful paths.

Consider the right-linear grammar (we have seen this one in Exercise 2.5)

$$(\{a, b\}, \{A, B, C, E\}, R, E) \qquad ,$$

where R is the set

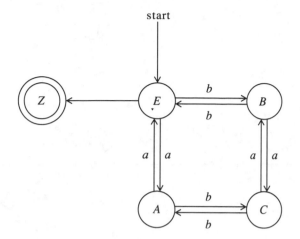

FIGURE 4.1. Graph for even numbers of a's and b's.

$$E \longrightarrow \epsilon \mid aA \mid bB$$
$$A \longrightarrow aE \mid bC$$
$$B \longrightarrow bE \mid aC$$
$$C \longrightarrow aB \mid bA \quad .$$

The diagrammatic representation by a transition graph is shown in Figure 4.1. We will describe the process to construct the graph from the grammar in Section 4.4. There may be other graphs that define the same set of strings. For example, the graph obtained by deleting node Z from Figure 4.1 and by double-circling node E defines the same language.

We may also play the game in reverse and construct a right-linear grammar from a transition graph. For example, the grammar corresponding to the graph in Figure 4.2 is

$$(\{a, b, c\}, \ \{A, B, C, S\}, \ R, \ S) \qquad ,$$

where R is the set

$$S \longrightarrow aS \mid bS \mid cS \mid aA \mid bB \mid cC$$
$$A \longrightarrow a \mid aA \mid bA \mid cA$$
$$B \longrightarrow b \mid aB \mid bB \mid cB$$
$$C \longrightarrow c \mid aC \mid bC \mid cC \quad .$$

The corresponding language is the set of all nonempty strings over $\{a, b, c\}$ whose last symbol also appears previously in the string; for example, aba is included, but aab is not.

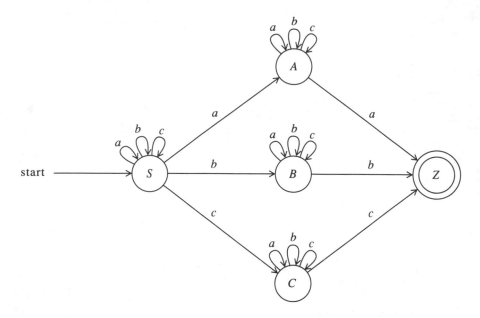

FIGURE 4.2. Graph for replicated symbol.

4.3   Regular Expressions

Transition graphs look like flow charts (or flaw charts). It is common to prefer the use of repetition and selection statements like *[...] and [...] to express the structure of an algorithm. Similarly, one can use *regular expressions* instead of transition graphs or grammars to define a regular language.

Regular expressions make extensive use of the * operator (defined in Chapter 2). It is used whenever something is repeated an indefinite number of times, and this usage is closely related to the *[...] in programming. In Chapter 2, the * operator was applied to alphabets only, that is, to sets of symbols. We extend its definition so that it can be applied to arbitrary sets of strings. If S is a set of finite strings, then S^* is the set of all finite strings formed by catenating strings from S, where any string may be used as often as we like (including zero times). The most trivial example is $\emptyset^* = \{\epsilon\}$. The second simplest example is $\{\epsilon\}^* = \{\epsilon\}$. (In fact, these are the only two instances for S that turn S^* into a finite set; all other S's make S^* an infinite set.) Slightly less trivial, $\{aa, b\}^*$ is the set of strings over $\{a, b\}$ in which consecutive a's come in groups of even length. Strings *bbb* and *baabaaaa* are in $\{aa, b\}^*$, but *aabaaaba* is not. As another example, $\{a, ab\}^*$ is the set of all strings over $\{a, b\}$ except those that start with b and those that contain the substring *bb*.

Operator * is called the "closure operator" or "Kleene closure", because set S^* is closed under catenation: if we take any two strings in S^* and catenate them, we get another string in S^*. In general, S is not closed under catenation, but S^* is.

The next and last operation on sets of strings that we use in the context of regular expressions is set union. It is usually denoted by $\cup$ but with regular expressions one mostly sees $+$ or $|$; we will stick to $+$. As an example, $(\{a\} + \{b\})(\{a\} + \{b\})$ denotes the set of all strings of length two over $\{a, b\}$. Since all these curly brackets for singleton sets look so silly, we decide to drop them and let a stand for the symbol a or for the singleton set $\{a\}$, whichever is appropriate in the context. The example is then written as $(a + b)(a + b)$.

So, what are regular expressions? A regular expression is an expression for denoting a set of strings that uses no operators other than union, catenation, and closure. The class of regular expressions can be defined recursively as follows.

- $\emptyset$ is a regular expression;

- ϵ is a regular expression;

- a is a regular expression, for each symbol a;

- If E and F are regular expressions then

    - $E + F$ is a regular expression,

    - EF is a regular expression,

    - E^* is a regular expression, and

    - (E) is a regular expression;

- Nothing else is a regular expression.

Expression $a + bc$ can be parsed in different ways, and we have to use a binding convention to understand whether we mean $a + (bc)$ or $(a + b)c$. The convention we use is this: operator * binds more strongly (that is, has a higher priority) than any other operator, and catenation binds more strongly than $+$ does. Since catenation is associative, and since $+$ is associative ($+$ also happens to be symmetric), no further rules are needed. Hence, $a + bc = a + (bc)$; both represent the set $\{a, bc\}$.

For each regular expression, we can figure out which language is denoted by the expression. For each such language, there is an infinity of regular expressions that denote the same language. We say that two regular expressions are equal ($=$) if they denote the same set.

Regular expressions look much like the expressions used in ordinary algebra. Make sure, however, not to apply all rules you are familiar with in a different context — they may not be valid. For instance, if $S + T = S + U$, one may not conclude $T = U$. An example hereof is

$$(a + b)^* + (a + b)^* = (a + b)^* + a^*$$

but not

$$(a + b)^* = a^* \quad .$$

Similarly, if $ST = SU$, one is not to conclude $T = U$. An example is

$$(a + b)^*(a + \epsilon) = (a + b)^*(a + b)^*$$

but not

$$(a + \epsilon) = (a + b)^* \quad .$$

Some algebraic properties of regular expressions are stated in the following table. (I have not included associativity and symmetry. These are so basic that I use them without explicit reference. For the same reason, we had already decided not to include the superfluous parentheses. Letters e, f, and g stand for any regular expression.)

$$e(f + g) = ef + eg \qquad\qquad (e + f)g = eg + fg$$
$$\epsilon e = e\epsilon = e \qquad\qquad \emptyset e = e\emptyset = \emptyset$$
$$(e + f)^* = (e^* + f^*)^* \qquad\qquad e^{**} = e^*$$
$$(ef)^* = \epsilon + e(fe)^*f \qquad\qquad e + \emptyset = e$$

We give a few examples of equalities that can be derived from this table. The first one is $e^* = \epsilon + ee^*$.

$$\epsilon + ee^*$$
$$= \qquad \{ \; e = \epsilon e \; \}$$
$$\epsilon + e(\epsilon e)^*$$
$$= \qquad \{ \; f = f\epsilon \text{ with } f := e(\epsilon e)^* \; \}$$
$$\epsilon + e(\epsilon e)^*\epsilon$$
$$= \qquad \{ \; (ef)^* = \epsilon + e(fe)^*f \text{ with } f := \epsilon \; \}$$
$$(e\epsilon)^*$$
$$= \qquad \{ \; e\epsilon = e \; \}$$
$$e^*$$

The next one is $\emptyset^* = \epsilon$.

$$\emptyset^*$$
$$= \qquad \{ \text{ previous result, with } e := \emptyset \; \}$$
$$\epsilon + \emptyset\emptyset^*$$
$$= \qquad \{ \; \emptyset e = \emptyset \text{ with } e := \emptyset^* \; \}$$
$$\epsilon + \emptyset$$
$$= \qquad \{ \; e + \emptyset = e \text{ with } e := \epsilon \; \}$$
$$\epsilon$$

Finally, we show $\epsilon^* = \epsilon$.

$$\epsilon^* = \epsilon$$
$$= \quad \{ \text{ previous result twice } \}$$
$$\emptyset^{**} = \emptyset^*$$
$$= \quad \{ \ e^{**} = e^* \text{ with } e := \emptyset \ \}$$
$$true$$

We have written the latter proof slightly differently in the sense that every line is a boolean expression, rather than a regular expression. Sometimes one format is more convenient, sometimes the other. These proofs do not refer to the "meaning" of the expressions involved, they refer to the given properties only. This tends to reduce the errors in proofs, and makes them a lot easier to check because the underlying assumptions have been made explicit. These proofs were given in great detail. With more experience, one would probably combine a few small steps into one bigger step.

4.4 The Relation Between the Three Formalisms

We are about to prove the main theorem of this chapter, which expresses that right-linear grammars, transition graphs, and regular expressions are in a sense equivalent.

Property

For each language L, the following three statements are equivalent:

    (0)   Set L can be defined by a regular expression;
    (1)   Set L can be defined by a transition graph;
    (2)   Set L can be defined by a right-linear grammar.

Proof

The proof is in three parts. First, we assume that L is given by a regular expression and construct a transition graph that also defines L. Second, we assume that L is given by a transition graph and construct a right-linear grammar that also defines L. Third, we assume that L is given by a right-linear grammar and construct a regular expression that also defines L. We do not conduct our three proof-parts in great detail. (You may not even think of them as proofs.)

First part of the proof: $(0) \Rightarrow (1)$.

Language L is defined by a regular expression, E, say. We construct a transition graph with the same language by following the structure of E. Since the structure of E is given by cases, the construction of the transition graph is given by cases also. In the drawings, we identify the initial and final states of the transition graphs that correspond to E by i_E and f_E. Figure 4.3 contains the graphs for the three basic cases: $E = \emptyset$, $E = \epsilon$, and $E = a$. Figure 4.4 contains the graphs for the three compound cases:

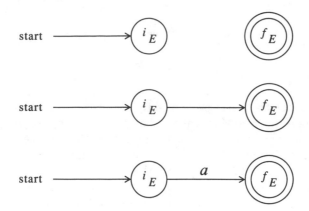

FIGURE 4.3. The three basic graphs.

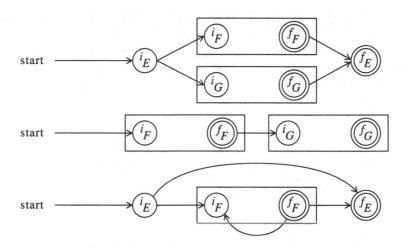

FIGURE 4.4. The three compound graphs.

$E = F + G$, $E = FG$, and $E = F^*$. In the case $E = FG$ we have $i_E = i_F$ and $f_E = f_G$. Of the subgraphs for F and G, only the initial and final nodes have been indicated and all edges have been omitted from the figure.

The correctness of the construction follows from the definitions of regular expression and of transition graph. Here is an example of applying the construction to $ab + c^*$. The resulting graph contains lots of ϵ-edges, as shown in Figure 4.5. When doing the construction by hand, one can often spot shortcuts in the construction process that will reduce the number of ϵ-edges. A smaller graph for the same example is given in Figure 4.6, but incorporation of shortcuts in an algorithm may not be too easy. How

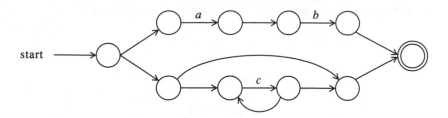

FIGURE 4.5. Graph obtained through systematic application of rules.

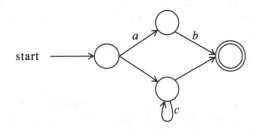

FIGURE 4.6. A smaller graph.

bad can the graph actually be? If we count the number of operators plus symbols in the regular expression then we have a measure for the size. The number of nodes produced by the construction method is at most twice the number of symbols in the expression, and the number of edges is at most four times the number of symbols. Thus, it isn't too bad after all: it is a linear function of the size.

Second part of the proof: (1) ⇒ (2).

Language L is defined by a transition graph. We construct a right-linear grammar that defines the same language. The set of terminal symbols is going to be the set of all symbols that appear in the labeling of the edges. The set of nonterminal symbols is exactly the set of nodes. The initial string is the starting node. For each edge, labeled with string x from node A to node B, we have a production rule $A \longrightarrow xB$ in the grammar. Finally, we add production $Z \longrightarrow \epsilon$ for final node Z. Again, we give only the construction, and not the proof. The correctness relies on the fact that each string that contains a nonterminal symbol and that can be derived from the initial string is of the form xA. A path from the initial node to node A exists whose labeling is exactly x. Application of rule $Z \longrightarrow \epsilon$ is the only way to "eliminate" nonterminal symbols. Since Z is the final node, this makes the path a successful path.

Third part of the proof: (2) ⇒ (0).

Language L is defined by a right-linear grammar. We construct a regular expression denoting L. This is done by regarding the grammar as defining a set of simultaneous equations. For example, the productions

$$A \longrightarrow \epsilon \mid aA \mid bB$$
$$B \longrightarrow aA$$

can be regarded as two simultaneous equations

$$A = \{\epsilon\} \cup \{a\}A \cup \{b\}B$$
$$B = \{a\}A$$

where A is a set of strings (obviously corresponding to nonterminal symbol A in the grammar), and similar for B. In the notation of regular expressions, we dispense with $\{$ and $\}$ and write $+$ instead of $\cup$ so that we have the shorter

$$A = \epsilon + aA + bB$$
$$B = aA$$

instead. The first step in solving this set of equations is to substitute the value of B into the equation for A. Actually we do not know the value of B, but we do know that it satisfies the last equation, so we can substitute the right-hand side, yielding

$$A = \epsilon + aA + baA$$
$$B = aA \qquad .$$

Since we are interested in solving for A, we may omit the last equation. In order to solve

$$A = \epsilon + aA + baA$$

we apply the "magic" *conversion rule* which states that

$$\text{equation } V = xV + y \text{ has solution } V = x^*y \qquad .$$

(To verify the rule, substitute x^*y for V and observe that the two sides are equal, that is, that they define the same set.) Returning to our equation, we find that we can rewrite it into

$$A = (a + ba)A + \epsilon$$

and then apply the conversion rule with $x := a + ba$, $y := \epsilon$ to obtain

$$A = (a + ba)^*\epsilon = (a + ba)^* \qquad .$$

Alternatively, we may obtain

$$
\begin{aligned}
& A \\
= \quad & \{ \text{ equation for } A \ \} \\
& aA + baA + \epsilon \\
= \quad & \{ \text{ symmetry } \} \\
& baA + aA + \epsilon
\end{aligned}
$$

$=$ { apply conversion rule with $x, y := ba, aA + \epsilon$ }
$(ba)^*(aA + \epsilon)$
$=$ { distribution and ϵ-catenation }
$(ba)^* aA + (ba)^*$
$=$ { apply conversion rule with $x, y := (ba)^* a, (ba)^*$ }
$((ba)^* a)^* (ba)^*$

or

A
$=$ { equation for A }
$aA + baA + \epsilon$
$=$ { apply conversion rule with $x, y := a, baA + \epsilon$ }
$a^*(baA + \epsilon)$
$=$ { distribution and ϵ-catenation }
$a^* baA + a^*$
$=$ { apply conversion rule with $x, y := a^* ba, a^*$ }
$(a^* ba)^* a^*$.

If we have more than one equation to solve, then we solve them one after the other. For example, in

$$A = aB + cA + \epsilon$$
$$B = aC + bB$$
$$C = aA + bC$$

we apply the conversion rule to the last equation, yielding $C = b^* aA$, and substitute in the equation for B. Thus we obtain $B = b^* ab^* aA$ and, finally, $A = (ab^* ab^* a + c)^*$. We do not dwell on this proof any further but would like to point out an analogy. Operations $+$ and catenation on regular expressions are similar to addition and multiplication on (real) arithmetic expressions. The axioms given in the table point out the similarities (and differences: $e + e = e$ is not true of most numbers, and catenation is not symmetric — you win, you loose). The conversion rule also has an analog in real arithmetic, in which equation $V = xV + y$ has the solution $V = \frac{y}{1-x}$. Moreover, since $\frac{1}{1-x} = 1 + x + x^2 + x^3 + \ldots$ (for $|x| < 1$), we have $V = y + xy + x^2 y + x^3 y + \ldots$, which looks much like $V = x^* y$. Thus, you should not be surprised if the process of finding a regular expression reminds you of Gaussian elimination.

We conclude this third part of the proof with the remark that the solution of a system of equations need not be unique. The conversion rule tells us to go from $V = xV + y$ to $V = x^* y$, and it is easily checked that this is a solution indeed. However, if x denotes a set that contains ϵ, then $V = x^*(y+z)$ is also a solution, for all z. Thus, the equation has infinitely many solutions. In situations like this, we shall use the smallest solution, which we call the *least fixpoint* of the equation. The least fixpoint is $x^* y$. It is the appropriate solution since the equations originated from a grammar, that is, $V = xV + y$ comes from $V \longrightarrow xV \mid y$. The language defined by this grammar (if x and y are terminal strings) is the set $\{y, xy, xxy, xxxy, \ldots\}$, which is the set denoted by x^*y and not $x^*(y + z)$. This concludes [our discussion of] the proof that the three formalisms are equivalent.   □

4.5 Equivalence Relations and Finite-State Automata

In this section, we discuss two more formalisms that are closely related to the three formalisms discussed before. They are equivalence relations and finite-state automata.

Let $\sim$ be a binary relation over set V. Relation $\sim$ is called

reflexive   if $a \sim a$ for all $a \in V$,
symmetric   if $a \sim b = b \sim a$ for all $a, b \in V$, and
transitive   if $a \sim b \ \wedge \ b \sim c \Rightarrow a \sim c$ for all $a, b, c \in V$.

A binary relation that is reflexive, symmetric, and transitive is called an *equivalence relation*. . We use $[a]$ to denote the subset of V that contains the elements that are equivalent to a:

$$[a] \ = \ \{b \in V \mid b \sim a\} \quad .$$

Such a set is called an *equivalence class*. The number of equivalence classes is called the *index* of the equivalence relation. We have

$$b \in [a] \ = \ b \sim a \qquad \text{and}$$
$$([a] = [b]) \ = \ a \sim b \quad .$$

The set of equivalence classes is referred to as the quotient $V / \sim$.

$$V / \sim = \ \{[a] \mid a \in V\}$$

The equivalence classes form a partitioning of V.

In this section we are interested in equivalence relations that are defined over sets of the form A^*. Equivalence relation $\sim$ is called *right invariant* if

$$x \sim y \ \Rightarrow \ xz \sim yz$$

for all $x, y, z \in A^*$.

Next, we define what a finite-state automaton is. In Chapter 1, we gave an informal definition, namely, something that is activated in an initial state and that makes a number of steps, one after the other. In every step, it receives an input symbol and transits to a new state. The state determines whether the sequence of input symbols received thus far forms a string in the language accepted by the finite-state automaton. We will now be a bit more explicit about the state transition mechanism.

The important thing about the state transition mechanism of a finite-state automaton is that it is deterministic. By this we mean that the new state is completely determined by the present state and the input. Nothing else is involved; no random or other choice is involved; no knowledge of how the automaton got into its present state is involved; the state of the automaton twenty-some steps ago is irrelevant. In short, the state transition mechanism is a function that maps a state and a symbol to a state. This leads to the following definition.

A finite-state automaton is a five-tuple $(Q,\ A,\ \delta,\ q_0,\ F)$, where

Q is a finite set of states;

A is a (finite) alphabet;

δ is a function from $Q \times A$ to Q;

q_0 is an element of Q, and it is called the initial state; and

F is a subset of Q, and is called the set of final states.

The state transition mechanism is δ: if the automaton is in state q and receives input a it transits to state $\delta(q, a)$. The initial state is q_0. If the current state is in F, then the sequence of input symbols received so far is a string in the language accepted by the automaton; otherwise, it isn't.

Function δ is from $Q \times A$ to Q. We extend δ from mapping a symbol to mapping a string, that is, from $Q \times A^*$ to Q:

$\delta(q, \epsilon) = q$ for all $q \in Q$.

$\delta(q, xa) = \delta(\delta(q, x), a)$ for all $q \in Q, x \in A^*, a \in A$.

We have used the same name, δ, for the original function and for the extended function. This is normal practice (and good practice) because the restricted version can be replaced by the extended one in all occurrences without making any difference. (Yes, the type, or signature, of the functions is different, but their use is not, and that is what counts.)

Using the (extended) function δ, we define the language accepted by the finite-state automaton to be the set of all strings that lead from the initial state to a final state, that is, the language is

$\{x \mid \delta(q_0, x) \in F\}$.

Here is the finite-state automaton that corresponds to the even a and even b language that we have encountered in the forms of a transition graph, a right-linear grammar, and a regular expression. Compare the finite-state automaton and the state-transition graph — the two are closely related. The automaton is the five-tuple

$(\{q_0,\ q_1,\ q_2,\ q_3\},\ \{a,\ b\},\ \delta,\ q_0, \{q_0\})$,

where the nonextended δ is

$\delta(q_0, a) = q_2, \quad \delta(q_1, a) = q_3 \quad \delta(q_2, a) = q_0 \quad \delta(q_3, a) = q_1$

$\delta(q_0, b) = q_1, \quad \delta(q_1, b) = q_0 \quad \delta(q_2, b) = q_3 \quad \delta(q_3, b) = q_2$.

It is easily seen that any string x leads the finite-state automaton to state q_i, where $i = 2 \cdot (x\#a \bmod 2) + (x\#b \bmod 2)$. The proof is best given by induction on the length of x. ($x\#a$ is the number of a's in x.) As a result, the language is the set of strings over $\{a, b\}$ having an even number of a's and an even number of b's.

4.6 Bridling Nondeterminism

In previous sections, we discussed transition graphs. These graphs look a lot like finite-state machines, but there is one important difference: the graphs are nondeterministic and the machines are deterministic. A string is in the language defined by a transition graph if a successful path exists from the initial node to the final node that has the appropriate labeling. Given the string, many paths starting from the initial node may exist that have the proper labeling, some leading to the final node, some leading elsewhere. In the case of a machine, the string uniquely determines the path from the initial state. If the state to which it leads is a final state, then the string is contained in the language; otherwise it is not. The element of choice that is present in transition graphs is absent in state machines. The question that we look at in this section is: does this freedom buy us anything? The answer will be neither yes nor no, but both. Every language that can be defined by a transition graph can also be defined by a state machine, which is the 'no' part. However, the number of states needed in the state machine can be much larger than the number of nodes needed in the transition graph — even exponential growth is possible — and this is the 'yes' part.

Let us first go for the equivalence in expressive power. It should be fairly obvious that any state machine can be converted into a transition graph that defines the same language. Here is a possible construction. The set of nodes is the set of states, extended with one extra node that is going to be the final node. The initial node is the initial state. For state q and every symbol a, the graph contains an edge labeled with a from node q to node $\delta(q, a)$. In addition, for every state q in the set of final states, there is an edge labeled ϵ from node q to the specially designated final node that does not correspond to any state.

Next, consider the construction the other way around, which is known as the *subset construction*. Given a transition graph, we define a finite-state automaton that accepts the same set of strings. The set of states is the powerset of the set of nodes, that is, each state is a subset of the set of nodes. The initial state is the singleton set that consists of the starting node only. The final state is the singleton set that consists of the final node only. The state transition function is: $\delta(q, a)$ is the set of all nodes that can be reached from any node in set q via a path of one or more edges, of which one is labeled a and all others are labeled ϵ.

The proofs that the two formalisms are equivalent is omitted. We have given the constructions to go from one to the other, but we have not shown that they accept the same set of strings. The proofs can be given by induction on the length of the string. The (surprising) conclusion is that nondeterminism does not increase the expressive power of finite machines. In the literature, the terms 'transition graph' and 'finite-state automata' are often used interchangeably, sometimes prefixed with either 'deterministic' or 'nondeterministic' for emphasis.

To construct a (deterministic) finite automaton from a (nondeterministic) transition graph, however, we had to resort to the set of all possible nodes that might be reached from the initial node with the present input string. If the number of nodes is k then the number of states is 2^k, which, while it is still finite, is definitely a large number. The exponential growth is where nondeterminism buys us something. The (nondeterministic) transition graph may be a lot smaller than the (deterministic) automaton, and, therefore, a lot easier to understand and to work with.

Next we prove an important theorem that establishes the relation between finite-state automata and right-invariant equivalence relations. In the previous section, we established the equivalence of right-linear grammars, regular expressions, and state transition graphs. We have also indicated the equivalence of transition graphs and finite state automata. The next property therefore implies that just about everything in this chapter has the same expressive power.

Property

For each language L over alphabet A, the following three statements are equivalent:

(0) language L is accepted by some finite-state automaton;

(1) language L is the union of some of the equivalence classes of a right-invariant equivalence relation of finite index;

(2) equivalence relation $\sim$ defined by

$$x \sim y \;=\; \langle \forall z : z \in A^* : xz \in L \;=\; yz \in L \rangle$$

is of finite index.

Proof

The proof is in three parts.
(0) $\Rightarrow$ (1)

Let L be accepted by automaton (Q, A, δ, q_0, F) and let $\approx$ be the equivalence relation

$$x \approx y \;\equiv\; \delta(q_0, x) = \delta(q_0, y) \quad .$$

Since

$$x \approx y$$
$=$ { definition of $\approx$ }
$$\delta(q_0, x) = \delta(q_0, y)$$
$\Rightarrow$ { calculus }
$$\langle \forall z : z \in A^* : \delta(\delta(q_0, x), z) = \delta(\delta(q_0, y), z) \rangle$$
$=$ { definition of δ }
$$\langle \forall z : z \in A^* : \delta(q_0, xz) = \delta(q_0, yz) \rangle$$
$=$ { definition of $\approx$ }
$$\langle \forall z : z \in A^* : xz \approx yz \rangle \quad ,$$

$\approx$ is right invariant. The index of $\approx$ is finite since the index is at most the number of states in Q. Furthermore, L is the union of those equivalence classes whose elements x satisfy $\delta(q_0, x) \in F$. This is well defined since

$$x \approx y \Rightarrow (\delta(q_0, x) \in F = \delta(q_0, y) \in F) \quad .$$

$(1) \Rightarrow (2)$

We show that any equivalence relation $\approx$ satisfying (1) is a refinement of $\sim$ as defined in (2), that is, every equivalence class of $\approx$ is a subset of some equivalence class of $\sim$. As a consequence, the index of $\sim$ is at most the index of $\approx$ and, hence, finite. For all $x, y \in A^*$, we have

$$x \approx y$$
$\Rightarrow$ { $\approx$ is right invariant }
$$\langle \forall z : z \in A^* : xz \approx yz \rangle$$
$=$ { L is the union of some of the equivalence classes }
$$\langle \forall z : z \in A^* : xz \in L = yz \in L \rangle$$
$=$ { definition of $\sim$ }
$$x \sim y \quad .$$

$(2) \Rightarrow (0)$

Let Q' be the finite set of equivalence classes of $\sim$, that is, $Q' = A^*/\sim$. Since

$$[x] = [y]$$
$=$ { definition of $[\,]$ }
$$x \sim y$$
$=$ { definition of $\sim$ }
$$\langle \forall z : z \in A^* : xz \in L = yz \in L \rangle$$
$\Rightarrow$ { calculus }
$$\langle \forall a, z : a \in A \wedge z \in A^* : xaz \in L = yaz \in L \rangle$$
$=$ { definition of $\sim$ }
$$\langle \forall a : a \in A : xa \sim ya \rangle$$
$=$ { definition of $[\,]$ }
$$[xa] = [ya] \quad ,$$

we can define δ' as $\delta'([x], a) = [xa]$. Let q_0' and F' be defined as $q_0' = [\epsilon]$ and $F' = \{x : x \in L : [x]\}$. Finite-state automaton M', defined as $(Q', A, \delta', q_0', F')$, accepts L, since

x is in the language accepted by M'
$$=$$
$$\delta'(q_0', x) \in F'$$
$$= \quad \{ \text{ definition of } \delta' \text{ and } q_0' \ \}$$
$$[x] \in F'$$
$$= \quad \{ \text{ definition of } F' \ \}$$
$$x \in L \quad .$$

This completes the proof.   ☐

Finally, we prove our last theorem of this chapter. Many automata exist that accept the same set of strings. The automata may differ in the number of states and in the state transitions. The theorem shows that the automaton with the minimum number of states is, essentially, uniquely determined by the language.

Property

The minimum state automaton accepting L is unique up to an isomorphism (renaming of the states) and is given by M' as constructed in the third part of the proof above.

Proof

As shown above, any finite automaton $M = (Q, A, \delta, q_0, F)$ that accepts L induces an equivalence relation that is a refinement of $\sim$. Hence, the number of states of M is at least the number of states of M'. If equality holds, then each state of M can be identified with a state of M', as follows. Since for all $x, y \in A^*$

$$\delta(q_0, x) = \delta(q_0, y)$$
$$\Rightarrow \quad \{ \text{ definition of } \sim \text{ as in previous property } \}$$
$$x \sim y$$
$$= \quad \{ \text{ construction of } M' \text{ above } \}$$
$$\delta'(q_0', x) = \delta'(q_0', y) \quad ,$$

we may identify any state $q \in Q$ with $\delta'(q_0', x)$, where x is any string that satisfies $\delta(q_0, x) = q$. Since M has the minimum number of states, each state is reachable and such an x exists.   ☐

Various algorithms exist for computing the minimum finite-state automaton. In a later chapter, we discuss one of those algorithms.

We have encountered nondeterminism in two different places: in the selection of a guarded command in our program notation and in the selection of the next state in transition graphs. The two forms of nondeterminism are very different. In our program notation, the rules are such that a program is considered to be correct only if every possible choice of a guarded command (with a guard that is *true*) leads to the correct postcondition. If we have given a proof of the program, no strategy of making the choices will cause the program to fail. Not even a demon controlling the choice can crash the program. This form of nondeterminism is called *demonic nondeterminism.* This gives the implementation a lot of freedom, since any choice will do the job. One may be faster than another, but each one is correct.

The other form of nondeterminism that we have seen is in transition graphs. A string is in the language defined by a transition graph if a successful path exists from the initial node to the final node that has the appropriate labeling. When a string is read, and a path is followed through the graph, some outgoing edges of a node may have the same label, and a choice has to be made. Foresight may be required to make the correct choice in order to end up in the final node. This form of nondeterminism is called *angelic nondeterminism.* The implementation is, in general, nontrivial. If we want to avoid backtracking, then a transformation to a deterministic version may be necessary. We have shown how this can increase the number of states in the system, even for the finite case.

We have now established a handful of formalisms that each have their strengths and weaknesses, and that share the character of finiteness. The set of strings in a language defined by any of these formalisms need not be finite, but if it is infinite there is some regular structure in it that can be described in a simple way, namely by the pumping lemma, mentioned in Exercise 19.

4.7   Bibliographic Notes

Regular expressions and their equivalence with finite-state machines were first discussed in [Kle56]. A good source of information on finite-state machines is [Koh70]. More information on the relation between certain classes of grammars and machines can be found in [HU69]. See also [AU72].

The term flaw chart is from [Gri81].

4.8   Exercises

1. Construct a right-linear grammar for identifiers as in Pascal, and one for real numbers.

2. Construct a right-linear grammar for the set of all strings over $\{a, b\}$ in which the number of a's minus the number of b's in every prefix of every string is at least 0 and at most 2.

3. How many strings of length two are in the language denoted by $(a + b)^*$? Of length 3? Of length n? How many of length n or less?

4. How many strings of length two are in the language denoted by $(aa + b)^*$? Of lengths 3 through 6? How many of length n?

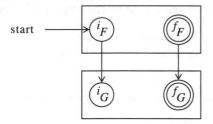

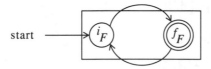

FIGURE 4.7. Alternative graphs.

5. Show that for every regular expression e, we have $e + e = e$. Hint: first prove the property for the case $e = \epsilon$. Use only the given properties and the results that have been derived from them in the text.

6. Same question for $e^* e^* = e^*$. Hint: first prove $\epsilon + e^* = e^*$. You may use the result of the previous exercise.

7. Can you prove

$$(a + b)^* a(a + b)^* b(a + b)^* + bb^* aa^* + a^* + b^* \ = \ (a + b)^*$$
$$a(a + b)^* + b(a + b)^* + \epsilon \ = \ (a + b)^*$$
$$(a + b)^* \ = \ a^*(ba^*)^*$$

from the given properties? If you can't, do you think that equality holds nevertheless?

8. Describe the language defined by

$$(aa + bb + (ab + ba)(aa + bb)^*(ab + ba))^* \quad .$$

9. Can we change the graph for $F + G$ into the alternative graph given in Figure 4.7, in which $i_E = i_F$ and $f_E = f_G$? Can we change the graph for F^* into the alternative graph in which $i_E = i_F$ and $f_E = f_F$? How about both changes?

10. Extend the construction of a transition graph from a regular expression for the case in which we extend regular expressions with operators for "zero-or-one" and "at-least-once".

11. Think of a construction that introduces no ϵ-edges.

12. Give a method for converting a left-linear grammar into a transition graph. (This is trickier than the conversion from a right-linear grammar.)

13. Give a method for converting a transition graph into a left-linear grammar.

14. Find a regular expression that describes the same language as

$$(\{a, b, c\},\ \{A, B, C, S\},\ R,\ S)\quad,$$

where R is the set

$$
\begin{aligned}
S &\longrightarrow aS \mid bS \mid cS \mid aA \mid bB \mid cC \\
A &\longrightarrow a \mid aA \mid bA \mid cA \\
B &\longrightarrow b \mid aB \mid bB \mid cB \\
C &\longrightarrow c \mid aC \mid bC \mid cC \quad.
\end{aligned}
$$

15. Find a regular expression that describes the same language as

$$(\{a, b\},\ \{A, B, C, E\},\ R,\ E)\quad,$$

where R is the set

$$
\begin{aligned}
E &\longrightarrow \epsilon \mid aA \mid bB \\
A &\longrightarrow aE \mid bC \\
B &\longrightarrow bE \mid aC \\
C &\longrightarrow aB \mid bA \quad.
\end{aligned}
$$

16. Set up a grammar for all strings over $\{a, b\}$ whose number of a's is a multiple of three. Construct a regular expression for the same language. Construct the regular expression according to the method discussed in the third part of the proof. Compare the outcome to the expression you had before.

17. Give a regular expression, right-linear grammar, or transition graph that defines the set of Roman numerals less than ten. Same question for the Roman numerals less than a thousand. Write a program for printing a number less than a thousand in Roman numerals.

18. In Section 4.5, we defined an equivalence relation as a relation that satisfies three specific conditions. Show that the conjunction of those three conditions is equivalent to the conjunction of the following two conditions.

$a \sim a$ for all $a \in V$,

$a \sim b \ \wedge \ c \sim b \Rightarrow c \sim a$ for all $a, b, c \in V$.

19. ("Pumping Lemma") Prove the following lemma. Let L be a regular language. A constant, k, exists with the following property. Every string in L with length at least k can be written as the catenation of three parts, where the middle part is nonempty and with the property that every string with the same prefix and suffix and with the middle part repeated any number of times, is also in L. (Note. It is not stated that a string of length at least k exists in L; but if it exists, then it can be decomposed and its interior part can be repeated. The value of k depends on L but is independent of the string.) If you really like quantifiers, you may write the problem as follows.

$$\langle \forall L : L \text{ is a regular language} : \langle \exists k :: \langle \forall w : w \in L \wedge |w| > k :$$
$$\langle \exists x, y, z : w = xyz \wedge 0 < |y| \le k : \langle \forall n : n \ge 0 : xy^n z \in L \rangle \rangle \rangle \rangle \rangle$$

20. Use the Pumping Lemma (previous exercise) to show that language $\{a^i b^i \mid i \ge 0\}$ is not regular.

21. Compute the (deterministic) finite-state automaton corresponding to the transition graph in Figure 4.2.

5

Integrated Circuits

Interest in computations and computing theory got a big boost when digital computers were first being built, for they demonstrated the feasibility of having machines carry out computations with complete accuracy.

Of course, some sort of calculators had already been known for some time. The idea of linking a series of gear wheels such that each time one wheel makes a complete rotation the next wheel turns so as to record the carry of one unit is very old, appearing in the writings of Heron of Alexandria. It was the 17th century before the idea was converted into the construction of an adding machine. The German astronomer Wilhelm Shickard built one around 1624; a little bit later (1642–1645), the French scientist and philosopher Blaise Pascal built another one. Somewhat later, the great mathematician, Gottfried Leibnitz, constructed a machine (designed in 1671; built in 1694) that allowed a multi-digit number to be set up beforehand and then be added to the number already in the accumulator with the turn of a handle. This allowed multiplication to be performed by repeated turns of the handle, and by shifting the position of the carriage relative to the accumulator, rather than by repeatedly setting up, digit by digit, the number that was to be multiplied. The next big step was made by Charles Babbage, who devised the difference engine, a device capable of automatically generating successive values of algebraic functions by means of the method of finite differences. The difference engine was capable of handling two orders of difference. In fact, it was the only machine he ever completed — his full-fledged difference engine never saw the light of day; the part of it that was finished by 1833 is now in the London Science Museum. Lots and lots of mechanical calculating machines were built during the next hundred years. It is not obvious exactly what the influence of these early machines has been on present-day computers. A major importance was that they led to the general acceptance of the idea of mechanized digital calculation, thereby, helping to pave the way for the development of automatic computers.

The idea of using a sequence control mechanism to enable the machine to carry out a complex action as a sequence of simple actions is also a golden oldie. The oldest implementation that we know of was described by Heron of Alexandria (again) and was the forerunner of the revolving pegged cylinder found in music boxes. In the early versions, ropes were wound on the cylinder, from peg to peg, in patterns that caused a short sequence of small actions by other devices when the ropes were unwound. Directly using the pegs themselves is a technique used to control decorative figures on large church clocks as early as the fourteenth century. Later, they were used to control pipe organs. The idea of controlling a machine by sequencing information held on a separate medium, that is, separating the general-purpose device and the specific series of actions, is due to Basile Bouchon (1725). He used a perforated tape to assist in weaving patterns into the silk. His machine was improved by Joseph Marie Jacquard, who turned it into an automatic loom (1801).

In the 1930s and 1940s, many interesting automatic computers were constructed: mechanical, relay, and electronic — but we will skip the discussion thereof. Many advances in the material sciences have enabled the development of the modern electronic computer. One of those was the development of the field-effect transistor, invented by Julius Edgar Lilienfeld (1926), which appeared to work to some extent although no one quite knew why. In the sequel, we look at how such devices can now be constructed and how we may understand their operation. The level of understanding we aim for is superficial; we are talking classical physics, whereas a less than superficial explanation requires a dive into quantum physics, which is way beyond the scope of these discussions.

5.1   Semiconductor Physics

We may think of atoms as consisting of a massive, positively-charged nucleus surrounded by a bunch of less massive, negatively-charged electrons that make the whole thing electrically neutral, for the negative charges balance the positive charge. Each atom has preferred groupings of electrons, which we may think of as concentric shells, each capable of holding a limited number of electrons. In balancing the positive charge of the nucleus, electrons fill the innermost shell first, then the second-innermost shell, and so on, until balance is achieved. The outermost nonempty shell is extremely important. It may or may not be filled up to capacity. The electrons in this shell are called the valence electrons. We can distinguish solid matter on the basis of how strongly the atoms bind their valence electrons. There are three categories: insulators, conductors, and semiconductors.

In insulators, electrons are so strongly bound to atoms that they can be torn free from the atom only by large forces. Even when such a "loss" occurs, electrons within the solid cannot move about to try to compensate for it. Consequently, if an electric imbalance is evoked, then it remains the way it is until new electrons are added from the outside.

In conductors, we have the opposite situation. Valence electrons are quite easily separated from the atoms and are free to travel throughout the conductor in all directions, wiggling around at high speed. The number of free electrons contributed to the "electron sea" by each atom is small: most

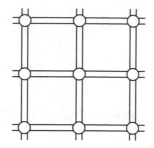

FIGURE 5.1. Two-dimensional representation of the crystal.

metals have a valence of one or two. The other electrons remain bound to the nucleus. Because the free electrons are all negatively charged, they repel each other; thus, they distribute themselves quickly throughout the solid in the manner of a diffusing gas. Injecting a load of electrons in one place in the solid charges up the whole thing. A conductor is electrically neutral, but only the negative charge carriers contribute to electrical conduction.

Semiconductors are a completely different story. A semiconductor atom has four valence electrons; these are not free to move through the solid, but, instead, participate in the covalent bonds that hold the semiconductor atoms together in a periodic crystalline arrangement. Each silicon atom in the crystal has four direct neighbors, and it shares its valence electrons with them. We usually represent the three-dimensional structure in the two-dimensional format shown in Figure 5.1. This representation retains the important features of the actual situation: four direct neighbors and an equal sharing of the valence electrons with these neighbors. Each covalent bond contains two electrons — each line represents one electron. The covalent bonds are a "trick" to fool the atom. The silicon atom has a capacity of 8 electrons in its outermost shell, but with only 4 valence electrons, there is room for another 4. But, because of the imbalance in charge that would result, there is no way to add those 4 electrons to the atom. The covalent bonds make it appear as if 8 electrons are orbiting the silicon nucleus. When the valence electrons are constrained in covalent bonds, no electrical conduction is possible. Consequently, a material in this arrangement behaves as an insulator. Diamond, the crystalline form of carbon, is an example of such a material.

In semiconductors, the covalent bond is not very strong. As a result, a number of covalent bonds are incomplete — the higher the temperature, the more incomplete bonds exist. The few broken bonds (roughly 1 in 10^{10}) that occur at normal temperatures result from the thermal vibration of the valence electrons. A few electrons acquire enough energy to escape from the bonds and become free. These free electrons, scarce as they are, have an enormous effect on the properties of the semiconductor; they make

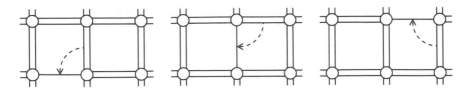

FIGURE 5.2. Mobile holes.

conduction possible by providing charge carriers in a configuration where otherwise none would exist.

Two distinct, and largely independent, groups of charge carriers exist that support electric currents in semiconductors. The mobile electrons that escape from a covalent bond are negative-charge carriers that move around just like the free electrons in a conductor. The other charge carrier is the hole that remains where a valence electron escapes from a covalent bond. Because of the escaped electron, the broken bond is a region with positive charge. The hole can move around because a valence electron in a nearby bond can fill the vacancy, thereby causing the hole to travel in the opposite direction. It takes less energy for a valence electron to move this way from one complete bond to a broken bond than to escape a bond. Therefore, the hole can move throughout the material. In practice, the mobility of holes is about one third the mobility of free electrons. One may also think about holes as repelling each other just like electrons do. The process of moving holes is illustrated in Figure 5.2. So far, the number of holes equals the number of conduction electrons, since each of these is the result of a broken covalent bond. Semiconductor crystals can, however, be enriched either in holes or in electrons by adding minute amounts of impurities, or dopants, to the semiconductor.

An atom of phosphorus or arsenic has 5 valence electrons; an atom of boron or aluminum has 3. When atoms of either kind are integrated with the silicon lattice, their contribution to the electrical properties of the material becomes dominant. For example, one of the five valence electrons of each phosphorus atom is promptly freed. (It is not needed for any covalent bond.) The electron then moves about through the semiconductor as a conduction electron. The impurity atom is left behind as an immobile, positive charge. This atom has donated one to the set of conducting electrons without contributing one to the set of mobile holes. This form of impurity is called a donor.

Similarly, each boron atom's covalence deficit is promptly covered by a silicon neighbor, which accepts a hole in exchange. The impurity atom produces a single mobile hole, and a single, immobile negative charge. This form of impurity is called an acceptor.

In summary, semiconductors conduct electricity as a consequence of the independent motion of two oppositely charged groups of charge carriers: holes and electrons. They can be created in three ways:

- a very small fraction of the covalent bonds is broken as the result of thermal movements of the valence electrons; this contributes an equal number of electrons and holes;

- donor impurity atoms contribute only electrons (and immobile holes that we may ignore);

- acceptor impurity atoms contribute only holes (and immobile electrons that we may ignore).

The process of replacing silicon atoms in the lattice with impurity atoms is called doping. Semiconductors doped with donors are said to be of n-type, for they have an excess of negatively charged carriers, while semiconductors doped with acceptors are said to be of p-type, for they have an excess of positively charged carriers. Doping can be done by adding the impurity element to molten silicon and letting the result cool and crystallize, or by diffusing the dopant as vapor through the surface of the crystalline solid at high temperatures when the whole crystal is vibrating so much that the impurity atoms can shake into some position without distorting the crystal too much. The heavier the doping, the better the conductivity. In the jargon, heavily doped material is typed as n^+- or p^+.

5.2 Semiconductor Junctions

We will now discuss two different kinds of junctions: the np-junction and the field-induced junction. We discuss them separately and then combine them into a transistor.

The semiconductor devices in which we are interested have lots of np-junctions: regions of semiconductor material in which there is an abrupt change from n-type material to p-type material within the same crystal structure. Particles that are free to move in one half of the crystal are also free to move into and within the other half: there is no fault in the crystal structure at the boundary between the two. Let us pretend that we have adjoined a block of n-type and a block of p-type silicon, as in Figure 5.3. See what happens. Acceptor impurities cause the hole concentration to exceed the electron concentration in the p-type region; donor impurities cause the electron concentration to exceed the hole concentration in the n-type region. The difference in concentration levels is such that electrons diffuse from the n-type to the p-type region, whereas the holes diffuse in the opposite way. Where they meet, they may annihilate one another. However, the electrons that diffuse away from the n-type region leave behind them a growing number of positively-charged, immobile phosphorus ions; their

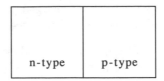

FIGURE 5.3. The semiconductor np-junction.

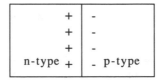

FIGURE 5.4. The charge-carrier depletion zone.

charge is no longer balanced by the electrons that are traveling around in the n-type material. Similarly, the holes that diffuse away from the p-type region leave behind them a growing number of negatively-charged ions, whose charge is no longer balanced by the free holes. As a result, an electrostatic potential builds up; in the case of silicon, this potential is roughly 0.7 volts. The electric field associated with it is directed from the n-type to the p-type. (Remember that the n-type gets a positive charge, the p-type a negative charge.) Thus, it opposes the diffusive flow of both the holes and the electrons. In equilibrium there is, therefore, no flow of charge carriers across the np-junction; the diffusive spread of majority carriers turned out to be a self-limiting process. At the interface between the two regions, we find a carrier-depletion zone, illustrated in Figure 5.4.

Next, consider the effects of connecting a battery to this device. We can apply a voltage across the junction by connecting the two terminals of the battery to the two regions. Two experiments can be done, depending on how the connections are made. See Figure 5.5. In the first case, we connect the battery's + to the n-type region and the battery's − to the p-type region of np-junction. As a result, the battery increases the height of the potential barrier. Therefore, the charge carriers cannot cross the junction and there is hardly any current. We say that the junction insulates when the voltage is applied in reverse polarity. The depletion zone grows thicker.

If the battery is connected in the opposite way, then the battery voltage reduces the height of the potential barrier. If the battery voltage exceeds the threshold of 0.7 volts (in silicon), then the reduction in the potential barrier admits a flow of charge carriers from the region in which they are in the majority to the other region. Both the electron and the hole flow are sustained by the generation of carriers at the battery connections. The

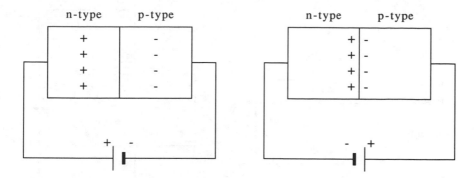

FIGURE 5.5. Conduction through an np-junction.

+ side of the battery pulls out free electrons, leaving free holes in the p-type region, and the − side of the battery injects free electrons in the n-type region. The junction conducts well when the voltage is applied in forward polarity, and the depletion zone narrows. Actually, we should be careful with a two-valued discrimination of states: the value of the forward voltage applied across the junction determines directly how large the flow through the device is. It is incorrect to say that there is no flow below threshold and perfect flow above. The specific properties of how the current depends on the voltage can be used to good advantage in what are called analog circuits. In this chapter, we confine ourselves to digital circuits; in these, a voltage is either way below or way above threshold, and then the binary distinction makes sense. We will exploit the asymmetry in electrical behavior by isolating one region from another, thus confining the charge to flow within only one of them. By laying out paths of one type material within a block of opposite-type material, and by arranging for the proper voltages, we can effectively construct conducting paths, or wires.

Next, consider the other kind of junction, the field-induced junction, which is the basic control mechanism in all MOS circuits. It is shown in Figure 5.6. A semiconductor substrate (in the example a block of p-type silicon), is covered with an insulating layer. By the way, a very good insulator is silicon dioxide, usually called glass, although it has to be in such a pure form that we should call it quartz rather than ordinary glass. (Ordinary glass contains too much table salt to act as a proper insulator.) On top of the insulator is a metal (or any other conductive) plate. It is the structure of this junction that gave rise to the name MOS: it is a metal-oxide-silicon (from top to bottom) sandwich. Again, a battery is connected: + to plate, − to substrate, thereby creating an electric field. The battery conducts away some of the electrons in the plate, leaving it with some positive charge, and injects some electrons in the substrate, providing it with some negative charge. The negative charge does not diffuse evenly

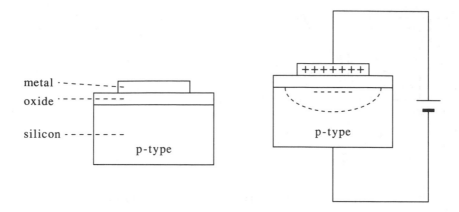

FIGURE 5.6. Field-induced junction.

throughout the substrate, for it is attracted by the electric force field and comes to rest below the insulating layer; well, perhaps not at rest, for they are still wiggling around, but most are close to the insulator. There is another effect: the free holes that are wiggling under the insulator are pushed away by the electric field, thus leaving negatively-charged, immobile regions under the insulator. Both effects contribute to the creation of a negatively-charged layer that sits under the insulator beneath the positively-charged conducting plate. This layer is referred to as an n-type inversion layer in the p-type substrate. It is filled partly with immobile negative phosphorus ions and partly with free electrons. The result is a layer in which a flow of electrons is possible, but only if we can make connections to the ends of the layer, which is what is being done in an MOS transistor. There is one other important effect, which is that if the battery is disconnected, the situation persists. Because of the good insulating layer, the charge that is trapped in the conducting plate will remain intact, and so will the inversion layer. It is possible to use this effect to store something, which is the basis on which computer memories are built. By the way, why do we use silicon for making semiconductor devices, rather than germanium or gallium-arsenide? (Gallium-arsenide seems to be especially attractive, since the mobility of its charge carriers is higher than in silicon, promising faster circuits.) One reason is that it is quite easy to make silicon dioxide, which is a good insulator, and not nearly so easy to make a good insulator on top of the other materials.

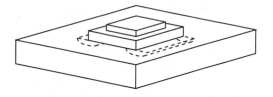 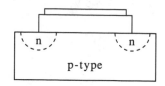

FIGURE 5.7. The n-channel MOS transistor.

5.3 MOS Transistors

The structure of a typical MOS field-effect transistor (abbreviated to MOS-FET) is illustrated in Figure 5.7, together with a drawing of the cross section. The device is made of a p-type silicon substrate in which two n-type regions have been embedded. In this context, the two regions are called *source* and *drain*. Which is which depends on how the transistor is going to be used, and their roles may change during operation of the circuit. The portion of the substrate between the two is called the channel. The channel region is covered by an insulating layer of silicon dioxide. A thin layer of conducting material is deposited on top of the insulator; this is called the gate. The gate is sometimes made of metal, although nowadays it is more usual to find gates made of polycrystalline silicon, or poly for short. How does the device operate? We stick to the rule that the substrate is always at the lowest potential, that is, it is connected to ground, and that all other signals are nonnegative. As a result, we know from the discussion of np-junctions that the n-type regions are electrically separate from one another. If, in addition to that, the gate is at a zero voltage level, then there are no extra effects, and little or no current results at either source or drain in response to any externally imposed drain-to-source voltage. If, however, the gate is at a high voltage, higher than the threshold, then a conducting inversion layer forms in the channel, and this layer admits a flow of electrons between the two n-type regions. If a positive drain-to-source voltage is imposed, then electrons will flow from the source to the drain; hence, this terminology. Hardly any holes flow in the channel. It is therefore called an n-channel MOSFET. The channel itself has few electrons. The source supplies electrons in large quantities and the channel transports them across to the drain. These electrons in the channel enhance the conductivity of that path. The degree of enhancement depends on the voltage difference between gate and channel (or between the gate and the average of source and drain). Again, as mentioned before, we concentrate on digital circuits, circuits in which the voltages are way above or way below threshold. As a result, we may think of transistors as being switches: either there is or there is not a conducting path between source and drain. In order to emphasize this binary view of voltages and conductances, we discuss the circuits that

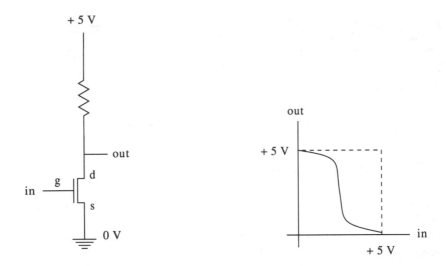

FIGURE 5.8. Circuit drawing of MOS inverter.

are to come in the terminology of boolean expressions. We let a high voltage represent the boolean value *true* and a low voltage the boolean value *false*, and we try to figure out which boolean function is implemented by a circuit.

The first circuit is given in Figure 5.8. It illustrates the symbol that we use for an MOS transistor. Notice that although the substrate (and its connection to ground) is not depicted, it is understood to be connected to ground to ensure proper operation. (And an even lower voltage for the substrate wouldn't hurt.) Next to the circuit, we have drawn the graph of the input versus the output voltages, that is, V_{gs} versus V_{ds}. The actual values depend on such properties as the ratio between the resistance of the "pull-up" resistor and the resistance of the transistor's channel. The latter decreases when V_{ds} increases, and also depends on the geometry of the channel. If the distance between source and drain is increased, then the resistance of the channel increases. If the width of the path between source and drain is increased, then the resistance of the channel decreases. When laying out a transistor, or a circuit, these parameters have to be taken into account, but we ignore them for now.

Interpreting the graph in a binary way, we see that a *true* input (high input voltage) produces a *false* output (low output voltage), and vice versa; that is, the circuit is an inverter: it computes the boolean negation of its input.

For our next circuit, let us interchange the position of transistor and resistor. (There is not much else we can do with only these two elements.) Figure 5.9 contains the circuit and its input output graph. Again we may

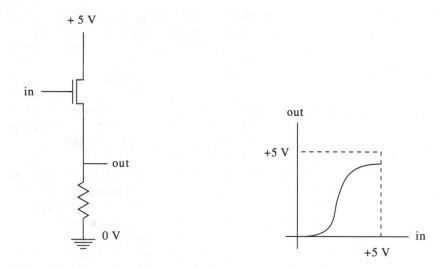

FIGURE 5.9. A poor circuit.

interpret this circuit as computing a boolean function. It is the identity function, not the most interesting of functions. Note, however, that the high output voltage is not as high as the voltage provided by the power supply. We have mentioned before that if the voltage between gate and channel decreases below the threshold, then the channel has a high resistance, and turns off. Hence, the voltage level of the output, which is connected to the source, is limited by the power supply's voltage minus the threshold. Informally speaking, we often say that the n-channel transistor is good for conducting lows and not so good for conducting highs. How can we make a transistor that is better suited for conducting high voltages? On account of symmetry, one may expect that a p-channel transistor made with p-type source and drain regions in an n-type substrate makes a good conductor for highs; in fact, it does. In CMOS technology, where the C stands for complementary, both types of transistor are being used to good advantage. Hence, this a more appealing technique. It has other attractive properties as well, including a lower power consumption, but we will ignore CMOS in our present discussion.

We conclude this section with another technical detour: how do we make a good resistor in this silicon technology? It is important that the resistance of the pull-up resistor in the inverter be large compared to the resistance of the conducting channel of the pull-down transistor to ensure that the output voltage of the inverter goes down well below the threshold voltage. (This is vital in order for the output to be usable as input for a next circuit.) The resistance of the conducting channel is quite high, mainly because the channel conducts only a very shallow flow of charge and, hence, has a small cross section. The resistance of even minimum-width lines of various available conducting elements is far less and would, therefore, require impractically long lines to produce resistors. One solution is to use a transistor with its gate permanently connected to the positive side of the power supply. When we make it a transistor whose channel length-to-width ratio is much higher, say by a factor of 10 or 20, than that of the pull-down transistor, then we have a reasonably large resistor. Remember, however, the problems that we observed with a transistor: it doesn't allow the output to increase above a threshold below the power supply's high voltage.

A better solution is offered by a technological trick. This pull-up transistor need never be off. In fact, a problem developed when the transistor was turned off as the source voltage began to increase. It would be nice if we could change the channel's structure to always be in the conducting state. One method is to add some donor impurity atoms to the channel, thereby causing the channel to contain many more free electrons. The channel is thus p^+-type, and the substrate is p-type. The result is that there is always a conducting path between source and drain. Actually, what happens is that the threshold is drastically decreased and, thus, has become negative. If the gate voltage is decreased to an even lower negative level, then the channel would no longer be conductive at all. In our applications, however, the gate is always positive. By connecting the gate to either source or drain, the fiddled-with transistor has a conducting path between source and drain. Such a transistor is called a depletion-mode transistor (as opposed to the enhancement-mode transistor discussed before). With the proper length-to-width ratio, the depletion-mode transistor serves as a good pull-up resistor. (The proper ratio is roughly four or five times larger than the pull-down transistor: it is not for free!) In the sequel, we will just draw resistors for the pull-ups.

5.4   Combinational Circuits

We have seen how the combination of a transistor and a resistor produces an inverter. How about using two transistors in combination with one resistor? (Resistors consume more area than transistors, so we do not dare to think about using more resistors than transistors.) We can put the two transistors either in series or in parallel, leading to the two circuits in Figure 5.10. For the sake of completeness we also give the layout of the two circuits in Figure 5.11. The left circuit, in which the transistors are in series, has a conducting path between output and ground just when both transistors are conducting, that is, when both inputs are high. In boolean terms: the output is *false* just when both inputs are *true*. The circuit computes the negation of the conjunction of its inputs — it is invariably called the NAND gate. (I understand why it is called a NAND; I do not see why it is called a gate.) Using our notation for boolean expressions, we have $c = \neg(a \wedge b)$.

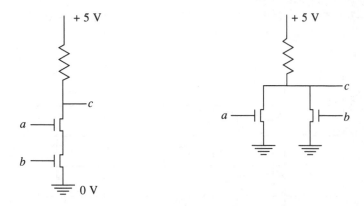

FIGURE 5.10. NAND and NOR circuits.

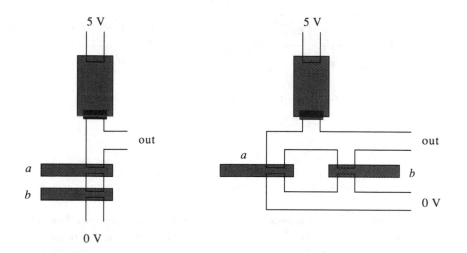

FIGURE 5.11. Layout of NAND and NOR circuits.

You will not be surprised to hear that the other circuit is a NOR gate. It establishes $c = \neg(a \vee b)$.

Now that we have the hang of it, we can probably see how to implement any boolean function as a circuit. We construct a series/parallel composition of transistors that is conducting just when the boolean function is to be *false*; this network is extended with one pull-up transistor, and we are done! Well, there are some problems with the transistor ratios: if there is a long sequence of transistors in series in the pull-down network, then there may be a large resistance in that conducting path; this implies that the pull-up has to be an even larger resistor. It will not only make the circuit large, but will also make the circuit slow: it won't pull up very fast because

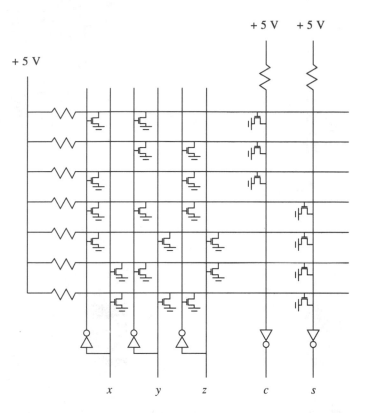

FIGURE 5.12. An example of a larger circuit.

the pull-up has a big resistance and, hence, only a small current. The other problem is that it may be difficult to lay the circuit out in the plane. The irregularities of the boolean function at hand are reflected by irregularities in the layout if the latter is closely imitating the former.

Next, we discuss a circuit whose suggested layout is virtually independent of the function it computes. Here is an example. The triangles with a little circle in Figure 5.12 are inverters; the dot indicates the output wire. (We have seen how to make inverters.) Consider the topmost horizontal line first. It is the output of one of our previous circuits: a NOR with inputs $\neg x$ and $\neg y$, that is, the value of this horizontal line is $x \wedge y$. In this way, each of the horizontal functions can be written as the conjunction of a number of optionally negated inputs. This is the first stage of the circuit.

The second stage is dominated by vertical lines. Consider one of those vertical lines, say the rightmost one. It, too, is the output of a NOR circuit, and because of the inverter at the bottom, the output of the circuit is the OR of some of the horizontal lines. That is, the output is a disjunction of a number of terms; each term is the conjunction of a number of literals, where a literal is either an input or the negation of an input. An expression written in this form is said to be in *disjunctive normal form*. With some generalization from the example, we see how to implement any expression in disjunctive normal form with a two-stage circuit. A surprising result in the theory of boolean expressions is that every boolean expression can be written in disjunctive normal form. (Or, for every boolean function, a defining expression in disjunctive normal form exists; an expression in disjunctive normal form is a disjunction of one or more terms, where a term is a conjunction of one or more literals, and where a literal is a variable or a negated variable.) Consequently, every expression can be computed with a two-stage circuit. How can that be? How can the number of stages be independent of the complexity of the expression? The trick, if that is what you want to call it, is that the number of intermediate results, which correspond to the horizontal lines, is not limited to 2, or to the number of inputs, but may, in the worst case, grow exponentially with the number of inputs. In practice, functions requiring an awful lot of intermediate results seem to be of little interest; hence, these two-stage circuits are most useful. (We have mentioned earlier that the transistor size ratios play a role in the proper functioning of NOR and NAND circuits. Also, in the case of these two-stage circuits, the ratio is not fixed by the number of vertical input and output lines. Thus, they must be given a worst-case value or be calculated dependent on the function to be implemented.)

A two-stage circuit like this is called a PLA, which stands for Programmable Logic Array. (A two-dimensional rectangular structure is often called an array; boolean expressions are often equated, or confused, with logic; and all that needs to be done to tailor, or program, the circuit to the boolean expression at hand is to indicate at which intersections there is to be a transistor.)

The PLA in the example computes the following functions:

$$c = (x \land y) \lor (x \land z) \lor (y \land z) \qquad \text{and}$$
$$s = (x \land y \land z) \lor (x \land \neg y \land \neg z) \lor (\neg x \land y \land \neg z) \lor$$
$$(\neg x \land \neg y \land z) \quad .$$

Now suppose that we switch from booleans to integers and write 1 for *true* and 0 for *false*. In that case we may write

$$c = (x + y + z) \text{ div } 2$$

and

$$s = (x + y + z) \text{ mod } 2 \quad .$$

Combining the two, we have

$$c \cdot 2 + s = (x + y + z) \text{ div } 2 \cdot 2 + (x + y + z) \text{ mod } 2 = x + y + z$$

which expresses that c and s are the more- and less-significant bits of the sum of three one-bit numbers, x, y, and z.

Now, imagine how addition can be performed in the binary number system. It consists of repeatedly adding two binary digits and a carry in from the previous step, that is, it consists of adding three binary digits — we need not distinguish between the carry and the other two digits. The sum is written as one binary digit plus a carry out to the next step. The PLA in the example computes just that: given three digits, x, y, and z, sum s and carry c are produced. This circuit is called a full adder. Cascading n full adders, and possibly simplifying the first one in the sequence, produces a circuit that adds two n-bit numbers.

5.5   State-Holding Devices

Every interesting computation consists of a large number of smaller computations. This can be arranged for by having a large array of small circuits and feeding the output of each circuit to the inputs of other circuits further down the line of the array. The combined circuit then computes the combined function. The size of the circuit is in direct correspondence with the complexity of the function to be evaluated. Every little circuit is used only once in the evaluation of the whole thing. It is more efficient, when measuring the size of the circuit, to break down the computation in a number of steps and try to reuse the circuitry. This requires that intermediate results be stored somewhere, as part of the circuit. In this section we discuss how information can be stored and how operations can be sequenced.

We start with a couple of circuits known as *flip-flops*. A flip-flop is a circuit that has two stable states — when set to one of the stable states it will remain in that state as long as the battery lasts. Bistability is provided by a cross-connection between negating combinational circuits. Figure 5.13 shows a version of an *RS* flip-flop based on a pair of NORs. Check that there are two stable states when both R and S are *false*, that is, at a low voltage. One is where Q and Q' are high and low, the other where they are low and high, respectively. Also, check the other combinations as listed in the table.

R	S	Q	Q'
lo	lo	lo	hi
lo	lo	hi	lo
lo	hi	hi	lo
hi	lo	lo	hi
hi	hi	lo	lo

As you can see, R and S can be used to impose the stable state: they force the circuit into a particular stable state, and when they go low again, the flip-flop remains in that state. Problems arise when R and S are made high at the same time. We will make a detour on that problem in a moment. When the problem is avoided, the Q and Q' outputs are each

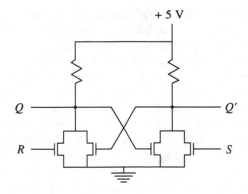

FIGURE 5.13. An *RS* flip-flop.

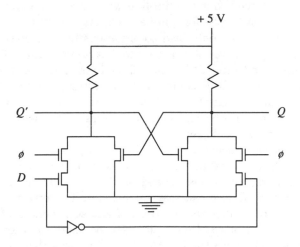

FIGURE 5.14. A *D* flipflop.

other's negation, and we may consider Q' as representing $\neg Q$.

The *RS* flip-flop is not the only possible flip-flop. One that is often useful is the *D* flip-flop shown in Figure 5.14. This flip-flop can change state only during specific time intervals dictated by an external "clock" signal. When clock signal ϕ is high, input *D* is copied to output *Q*; when clock signal ϕ is low, input *D* is ignored. The output of the *D* flip-flop is, consequently, stable only during intervals at which ϕ is low. In the next stage of the circuit, one may expect another clock signal to be used whose intervals are different: the output of the *D* flip-flop is useful only when stable and is, therefore, used in the next step when ϕ is low. As a result, we usually see a two-phase nonoverlapping clock: a clock providing intervals at which $\phi 1$ is high for use in every other stage of the circuit, and intervals at which $\phi2$ is high for use in the in-between stages. The two intervals do not overlap, which ensures that changes in the state of one stage do not interfere with the actions in the next stages.

Here we make the detour. As remarked, the RS flip-flop should not be used with its R and S inputs high at the same time. What happens if they are both high and are released at roughly the same time? The Q and Q' both begin to rise because there is no longer a conducting path between them and ground. As they rise, however, they turn on the two transistors in parallel to the R and S transistors, thus providing two conducting paths to ground. So the voltages at Q and Q' begin to fall again. If the circuitry is very fast, the voltages may swing up and down a number of times until some unpredictable event causes the difference between the two to become so large that the situation resolves into one of the two stable states. If the circuitry is very slow, then maybe the up and down swings are not so pronounced, but the flip-flop will remain in a state with both Q and Q' at about 2 volts for quite a while. Asymmetries in the circuitry do not really help: they only lead to situations like 1.5 volts for Q and 2.5 volts for Q' in the problematic state, but do not resolve the problem. Similarly, input D to the D flip-flop should not change at the end of the interval during which D is copied into Q. When ϕ is about to go low, D should be stable, or else the D flip-flop enters this weird state in which Q and Q' are not at the high and low voltages that correspond to the boolean values they should represent.

It can be shown that every device that has two stable states also has a *metastable state*. (That is, metastable states exist in every device in which signal changes are continuous instead of discrete.) This is a state that is not stable, but the device can stay in this state for some period of time. It is impossible to predict the duration of any such period. One can only state that these periods are more likely to be short than long, the odds falling exponentially with the length of time in a way that varies in detail from circuit to circuit. Figure 5.15 shows a system with two stable states: the pebble is in the left trough, or the pebble is in the right trough. The metastable state is the state in which the pebble is on top of the hill separating the two troughs. One might be tempted to think that noise will resolve the metastability — send the pebble one way or the other. But then, the noise may also send the pebble back to the top if it starts rolling down one way.

These metastable states, or "glitches" as they are sometimes confusingly called, are unavoidable. Well, they are unavoidable in a circuit built from continuous components. It is usual to assume that all physical signals change continuously, although this may sometimes be hard to reconcile with quantum physics. For example, an electron has an up or down spin, and it may change from one to the other state instantaneously. It may be hard to tell exactly when it changes state, but it is never in a "halfway" state. I do not know whether metastability occurs in quantum physics; maybe nobody

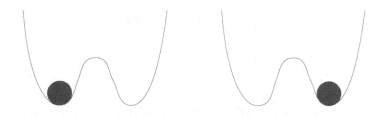

FIGURE 5.15. Two stable states.

knows.

Lots and lots of "solutions" have been proposed, and some of them have been published. Sometimes it isn't easy to see where the mistake is, but you can be assured there always is one: there is no way around the problem. Given that metastability is unavoidable, how can we live with it? Can we always ensure that D is stable by the end of the clocking interval? If the D signal is coming from a circuit that is orchestrated by the same clock signal as the D flip-flop is, then it is well possible to meet the requirements. If D is coming from an external circuit, say from a key that is being pushed by a person sitting at a keyboard, then it is impossible to guarantee that the signal is stable at the right time. It is possible to reduce the probability of failure, usually at the expense of adding a delay between the input and the synchronized output. Reduction is possible by cascading a number of flip-flops, all clocked by the same signal, and then the probability of metastability is reduced to (roughly) the products of the probabilities of each individual, metastable flip-flop. When the probability is on the order of once in the lifetime of the universe, it is deemed acceptable. (Or, probably, a bit sooner than that.) A more radical solution is to abolish clocks altogether. This can be done by employing so-called self-timed circuits. They totally avoid the problem of invalid signals, but they sacrifice predictability of response time. The latter seems to be no problem, and, in some cases, the circuits work faster than their clocked counterparts. They can work properly only through a more explicit scheme of signaling when the operation has completed and new inputs may be supplied. It is a fascinating subject, but we will leave it at that for now. So much for the detour.

5.6   Sequential Circuits

We have seen state-holding devices whose operation is controlled by clock signals for proper sequencing, and we have seen PLAs used as a method for

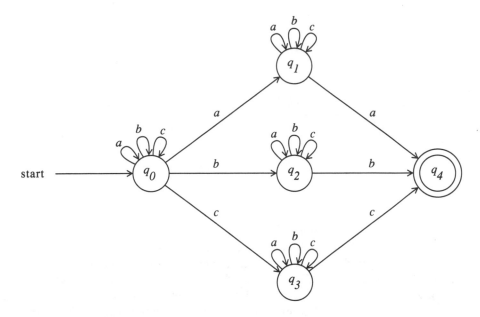

FIGURE 5.16. A transition graph.

implementing a number of boolean expressions. In this section, we let the two combine forces to form a *sequential circuit*, a circuit in which certain operations are performed in sequence. An interesting source of sequential stuff that we have discussed in the past comes from grammars. Grammars define languages that consist of strings, which are sequences of symbols. We set ourselves the following task. Given a regular language (regular for the sake of implementability), can we devise a circuit such that, as its input, the device receives one symbol per clock tick, and as its output, the device produces one boolean value per clock tick. The boolean value is *true* just when the input sequence received so far is an element of the language. We know how to convert between transition graphs, regular expressions, and right-linear grammars, so we can pick any of those. We select a transition graph; we assume that every edge is labeled with exactly one symbol, that is, it has no ϵ-edges and no edges with labels of two or more symbols. It may, however, be as nondeterministic as you like. Figure 5.16 has an example.

How do we go from the graph to a circuit? Remember that a string is in the language if a path exists from the initial node to the final node whose labeling corresponds to the string. In general, many nodes can be reached from the initial node, given one string. Furthermore, given the reachable nodes, it is easy to figure out what the reachable nodes will be if the string is extended by some symbols: for each node in the old set, compute the set of nodes that can be reached from it via a path whose labeling corresponds to the suffix added to the original string. The union of those new sets is the set of nodes reachable from the initial node using the whole string.

We introduce a boolean per node to record the set of reachable nodes. In the case of the example, we have boolean q_i to record that state q_i is reachable from the initial node along a path whose labeling is the sequence of symbols received so far. Because of the nondeterminism, more than one of these booleans may be *true* at any point in time. Initially, q_0 is *true*, and the other ones are *false*. The output that we are interested in is q_4, since that is the final state; others are used only for computing it. Here is the statement that sets the q's to their new values. Boolean a is supposed to be *true* just when the input is the symbol a; similarly, for inputs and symbols b and c. (This may not be the most efficient encoding of the input when counting the number of wires, but it will do for this example.) In the statement that assigns a value to q_i, we have a disjunct per incoming edge to node q_i. Each disjunct is the conjunction of the edge's source node and the edge's label (well, of the booleans that correspond to them). This sets the boolan variables to their proper values only if every edge is labeled with exactly one symbol (see also Exercise 7).

$$
\begin{aligned}
q_0, q_1, q_2, q_3, q_4 := \ & (q_0 \wedge a) \vee (q_0 \wedge b) \vee (q_0 \wedge c), \\
& (q_0 \wedge a) \vee (q_1 \wedge a) \vee (q_1 \wedge b) \vee (q_1 \wedge c), \\
& (q_0 \wedge b) \vee (q_2 \wedge a) \vee (q_2 \wedge b) \vee (q_2 \wedge c), \\
& (q_0 \wedge c) \vee (q_3 \wedge a) \vee (q_3 \wedge b) \vee (q_3 \wedge c), \\
& (q_1 \wedge a) \vee (q_2 \wedge b) \vee (q_3 \wedge c)
\end{aligned}
$$

The boolean expressions in this statement are all in disjunctive normal form, which means that they are in a form suitable for evaluation by a PLA. Note that q_0 is invariantly *true* : it is *true* initially and it is never changed since in every step one of a, b, and c is *true*. We may, therefore, remove it from our considerations and simplify the other expressions.

$$
q_1, q_2, q_3, q_4 := q_1 \vee a, \ q_2 \vee b, \ q_3 \vee c, \ (q_1 \wedge a) \vee (q_2 \wedge b) \vee (q_3 \wedge c)
$$

Without further ado, this translates into the circuit in Figure 5.17. The flip-flops are somewhat divided up between the $\phi 1$ and $\phi 2$ parts. The left half of the circuit copies the input (q_1, q_2, q_3, a, b, c) during $\phi 1$ to the corresponding inverters. The charge trapped on the gate of the inverters remains there when $\phi 1$ goes low; especially, the PLA is stable during $\phi 2$ when it is supposed to produce a stable value that is copied to the inverters at its output. These inverters, in turn, are stable during $\phi 1$ when the left half's input is indeed required to be stable. Very nice, indeed.

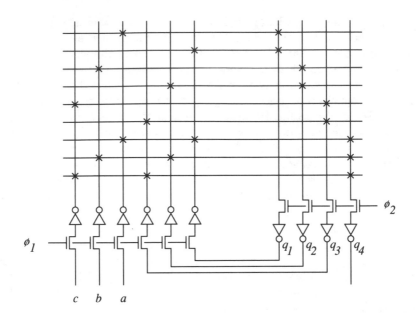

FIGURE 5.17. A circuit implementation of a transition graph.

5.7   Variations

We may also write regular expressions in the notation that we have been using for our programs. For example, the expression that corresponds to the transition graph of Figure 4.1 can be written as follows.

$$
\begin{aligned}
&st := 0; \\
&*[\ true \rightarrow read(in); \\
&\qquad\qquad [\ st = 0 \ \wedge \ in = a \rightarrow st := 1 \\
&\qquad\qquad \|\ st = 0 \ \wedge \ in = b \rightarrow st := 2 \\
&\qquad\qquad \|\ st = 1 \ \wedge \ in = a \rightarrow st := 0 \\
&\qquad\qquad \|\ st = 1 \ \wedge \ in = b \rightarrow st := 3 \\
&\qquad\qquad \|\ st = 2 \ \wedge \ in = a \rightarrow st := 3 \\
&\qquad\qquad \|\ st = 2 \ \wedge \ in = b \rightarrow st := 0 \\
&\qquad\qquad \|\ st = 3 \ \wedge \ in = a \rightarrow st := 2 \\
&\qquad\qquad \|\ st = 3 \ \wedge \ in = b \rightarrow st := 1 \\
&\ \ ] \qquad\quad]
\end{aligned}
$$

The output, that indicates that the input string read so far has both an even number of a's and an even number of b's, is $st = 0$. If we want to add a second output that indicates that both numbers are odd, we may add $st = 3$. The same results are produced by the following program, although the corresponding circuit is different.

$x := false, y := false;$
$*[\ true \rightarrow read(in);$
$\qquad\qquad [\ \neg\ x\ \ \wedge\ \ in = a \rightarrow x := true, bothodd := y$
$\qquad\qquad \|\quad x\ \ \wedge\ \ in = a \rightarrow x := false, botheven := \neg y$
$\qquad\qquad \|\ \neg\ y\ \ \wedge\ \ in = b \rightarrow y := true, bothodd := y$
$\qquad\qquad \|\quad y\ \ \wedge\ \ in = b \rightarrow y := false, botheven := \neg y$
$\quad]\qquad\quad]$

An even shorter version is

$x, y := false, false;$
$*[\ true \rightarrow read(in);$
$\qquad\qquad [\ in = a \rightarrow x, bothodd, botheven := \neg x, \neg x \wedge y, x \wedge \neg y$
$\qquad\qquad \| in = b \rightarrow y, bothodd, botheven := \neg y, x \wedge \neg y, \neg x \wedge y$
$\quad]\qquad\quad]\quad .$

By the way, the second program is shorter than the first, due to the encoding of the state. Finding a good encoding is called the *state-assignment problem*; it is a notoriously tough problem.

Another example is a clock circuit that produces an output signal called *slow* on every sixth clock tick, an output signal called *medium* on every third clock tick, and an output signal called *fast* on every second clock tick. We use one further abbreviation: if the right-hand side of an assignment is *true*, it is omitted; if it is *false*, both left-hand side and right-hand side are omitted. As a result, statement

$t := 4, medium$

is short for

$t := 4, fast := false, medium := true, slow := false$.

$*[\ t = 0 \rightarrow t := 1, fast, medium, slow$
$\| t = 1 \rightarrow t := 2$
$\| t = 2 \rightarrow t := 3, fast$
$\| t = 3 \rightarrow t := 4, medium$
$\| t = 4 \rightarrow t := 5, fast$
$\| t = 5 \rightarrow t := 0$
$\quad]$

We will use this notation again in a later chapter. In the form of a regular expression, with a proper understanding of what is input and what is output, one might be tempted to write

$(\sqrt{}, fast, medium, slow; \sqrt{}; \sqrt{}, fast; \sqrt{}, medium; \sqrt{}, fast; \sqrt{})^*$

where $\sqrt{}$ stands for a clock tick, but we do not pursue this avenue.

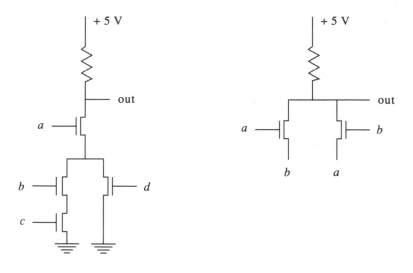

FIGURE 5.18. Two more circuits.

5.8   Bibliographic Notes

The reference work for studying integrated circuits is [MC80]. It contains a wealth of information on operation, design, and fabrication of integrated circuits. In Chapter 7 of this book, C.L. Seitz discusses various aspects of timing, including a discussion of the metastable state and of circuits that do not require a clock at all ([Sei80]). Metastability in arbiters and synchronizers was independently discovered by many researchers and engineers in the late 1950's and early 1960's. Two standard references are [CM73] and [Sci73].

5.9   Exercises

1. Figure out which boolean functions are computed by the two circuits given in Figure 5.18.

2. Prove that every boolean expression can be written in disjunctive normal form. (Hint: first prove that every expression can be written with conjunctions, disjunctions, and negations, and no other operators. Then, prove the existence of a normal form.) Contrary to what the name suggests, the normal form need not be unique. For example, $a \wedge b$ and $(a \wedge b) \vee (a \wedge b \wedge c)$ are equivalent, and both are in normal form. It should be noted, however, that the terminology is not "completely consistent" throughout the literature.

3. Find a disjunctive normal form for each of the following expressions.

$$((a \wedge b) \vee c) \quad \wedge \quad (d \vee (b \wedge \neg d))$$
$$a \equiv b$$
$$a \equiv b \equiv c$$
$$(a \equiv b) \quad \wedge \quad (b \equiv c)$$
$$(\neg(a \wedge c) \vee \neg d) \quad \wedge \quad \neg(b \vee (c \wedge e))$$

4. It goes almost without saying that a conjunctive normal form exists. Can you think of a variation of the PLA that employs this form?

5. A circuit is given two 2-bit binary numbers, x and y, as its input. Design a PLA that produces three outputs, corresponding to the boolean expressions $x < y$, $x = y$, and $x > y$, respectively.

6. Suppose we change the definition of a transition graph a bit. We allow a set of final nodes instead of insisting on a single final node, and we declare a string to be in the language if a path with proper labeling exists from the initial node to at least one of the final nodes. This obviously does not extend the class of languages that can be defined by transition graphs, because we can always go back to one with a single final node by adding an extra node, adding ϵ-transitions from all final nodes to the new node, and making the new node the one and only final node. The difference is in the following statement, which is true for the graphs with a set of final nodes and which is not true for the graphs with a single final node: every transition graph can be converted into a transition graph that defines the same language and in which every edge is labeled with a single symbol; that is, it has no ϵ-edges and no labels of two or more symbols. Prove this statement. Show that it is not true for graphs that have exactly one final node. How do we cope with the situation of more (or less) than one final node in our circuits?

7. We have shown how to construct a sequential circuit when given a transition graph in which every edge is labeled with exactly one symbol. Explain the problem that arises when there is an ϵ-edge in the graph. How would you make a circuit for such a graph?

8. Construct a transition graph for the language over $\{a, b\}$ in which the number of a's minus the number of b's in every prefix of every string is at least 0 and at most 2. Convert the graph into a circuit.

9. Construct a transition graph for all strings over $\{a, b\}$ whose number of a's is a multiple of 3. Convert the graph into a circuit.

6

Recursive Descent Parsing

We have encountered grammars a number of times. We started our discussions of what a computation is by looking at grammars. We defined languages by devising grammars for defining them. We translated right-linear grammars into transition graphs and then into VLSI circuits. In this chapter, we study programs for parsing input strings, that is, programs that determine whether a given input string can be derived from a given grammar. In the case of right-linear grammars, we had a severe restriction on the grammar: every rule has a left-hand side of exactly one nonterminal and a right-hand side of a sequence of zero or more terminals followed by at most one nonterminal. This restriction corresponds to finite machines. In this chapter, the restriction is less severe. The left-hand side is still restricted to be one nonterminal but the right-hand side is unrestricted. This class of grammars is called the class of *context-free grammars*. Later on, we have to impose further restrictions to admit efficient parsing algorithms; in fact, we discuss only one parsing strategy. This strategy is called *top-down parsing*. We give an implementation in the form of a set of recursive procedures, and then the parsing method is sometimes referred to as parsing by *recursive descent*. This method is limited to grammars that satisfy the $LL(1)$ condition, which is discussed later. We begin by discussing the parsing method in the context of the domino game, and we have a look at its implementation in the form of a set of recursive procedures. We explore the theoretical limitations, and we discuss ways of improving the practical feasibility of this method.

6.1 Top-Down Parsing

In order to illustrate the method of top-down parsing and its implementation in the form of a set of recursive procedures, we use the following grammar for arithmetic expressions.

$$(\{0, 1, \ldots 9, (,), +, -, \backslash, /, *, \uparrow\}, \{E, T, F, P, N, D\}, R, E)$$

where R is the following set of production rules.

$$E \longrightarrow T \mid -T \mid E + T \mid E - T$$
$$T \longrightarrow F \mid T * F \mid T/F \mid T\backslash F$$
$$F \longrightarrow P \mid P \uparrow F$$

$$P \longrightarrow N \mid (E)$$
$$N \longrightarrow D \mid N \ D$$
$$D \longrightarrow 0 \mid 1 \mid 2 \mid 3 \mid 4 \mid 5 \mid 6 \mid 7 \mid 8 \mid 9$$

(As far as parsing is concerned, it doesn't matter which arithmetic operations are denoted by / and \ — nor any other of the operators, for that matter. When we discuss evaluation of the expression, we take it that they stand for integer division and remainder, respectively.)

Parsing is complicated by the presence of ambiguities. A famous ambiguity in Pascal is the "dangling else". Consider the rules

$ST \longrightarrow$ **if** b **then** ST **else** ST | **if** b **then** ST | st .

The grammar is ambiguous since string

if b **then if** b **then** st **else** st

can be derived in two essentially different ways:

$$
\begin{aligned}
& ST \\
\Longrightarrow \quad & \textbf{if } b \textbf{ then } ST \textbf{ else } ST \\
\Longrightarrow \quad & \textbf{if } b \textbf{ then if } b \textbf{ then } ST \textbf{ else } ST \\
\Longrightarrow^2 \quad & \textbf{if } b \textbf{ then if } b \textbf{ then } st \textbf{ else } st
\end{aligned}
$$

and

$$
\begin{aligned}
& ST \\
\Longrightarrow \quad & \textbf{if } b \textbf{ then } ST \\
\Longrightarrow \quad & \textbf{if } b \textbf{ then if } b \textbf{ then } ST \textbf{ else } ST \\
\Longrightarrow^2 \quad & \textbf{if } b \textbf{ then if } b \textbf{ then } st \textbf{ else } st \qquad .
\end{aligned}
$$

They are "essentially different" since in the first case the symbol **else** corresponds to the first **if** whereas in the second case it corresponds to the second **if**. That is, the string can be interpreted either as

if b **then** (**if** b **then** st) **else** st

or as

if b **then** (**if** b **then** st **else** st)   .

These two interpretations are illustrated by the two parse trees shown in Figure 6.1. In the ALGOL 60 "Revised Report", this ambiguity was carefully ruled out by the grammar, and the example is not a syntactically correct statement. In Pascal it is a correct statement, and in the Pascal report it is stated in English (but not in the formalism) that the second interpretation is the intended one. In this chapter, we avoid grammars that are ambiguous. The reason is the following. Grammars are used to define a set of strings, and in a second stage, some sort of a meaning is attached to the strings. For example, the meaning could be the effect when executed by

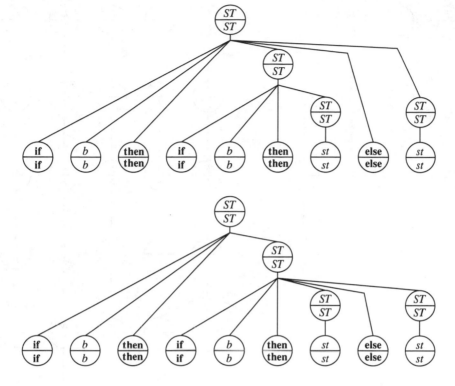

FIGURE 6.1. The two parse trees.

a computer. Often the meaning is defined via the grammar. In the example, one would say: the effect of

if b **then** st_0 **else** st_1

is the effect of st_0 if b is *true*, and it is the effect of st_1 if b is *false*. The effect of

if b **then** st

is the effect of st if b is *true*, and it has no effect if b is *false*. The ambiguous statement

if *true* **then if** *false* **then** st_0 **else** st_1

has no effect in the first interpretation, and has the effect of st_1 in the second interpretation. In general, it is therefore a good idea to avoid ambiguous grammars, and we restrict ourselves to nonambiguous grammars in this chapter. It would be nice to have a program that takes a grammar as its input and decides whether the grammar is ambiguous. In the next

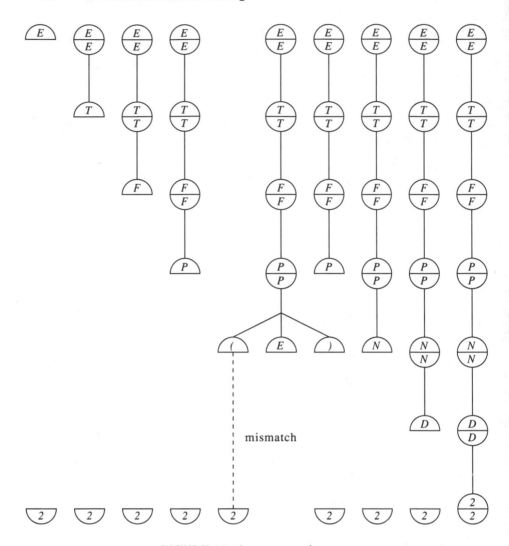

FIGURE 6.2. A sequence of moves.

chapter, we show that not all problems can be solved by computers, and, unfortunately, the test for ambiguity is one of them.

We begin our explorations of top-down parsing, or predictive parsing, with a simple-minded and extremely inefficient algorithm. It is a kind of a top-down, left-to-right strategy. We do so in the terminology of the domino game. The process is illustrated in Figure 6.2. The sequence of configurations is shown from left to right. The initial configuration is that the string corresponding to the grammar's initial string is set up with flat-bottom pieces at the top of the board, and the input string is set up with flat-top pieces at the bottom of the board. The rule for which domino to play next is the following. Select the leftmost unmatched flat bottom. If it contains a terminal symbol that equals the terminal symbol on the leftmost unmatched flat top, which is part of the input string, then we have a match, and the two flat sides are positioned against each other; if the two terminal symbols differ, there is no match and the present derivation fails. If, however, the leftmost unmatched flat bottom contains a nonterminal symbol, then we try all the corresponding dominos. Trying all dominoes is often implemented by trying one first and, if the derivation fails, trying another one while starting from the same configuration in which the first one was tried. The latter action is called *backtracking*. The game is said to terminate successfully when all flat sides have been eliminated.

This simple strategy is not necessarily efficient; in fact, it is extremely inefficient in all but a few uninteresting cases. In the grammar that we use, one should be very careful about recursive productions like $E \longrightarrow E + T$, since they might lead the player of the game into a never-ending loop in which this domino is played over and over again without succeeding in eliminating any flat sides.

The source of the inefficiency is the choice between the various production rules for a nonterminal symbol. If the "wrong" choice is made, then some backtracking will result later in the game. What we need is a mechanism for selecting "the right" production rule. Here is the mechanism that one opts for in the case of $LL(k)$ parsing (k is a positive integer): the choice is based on the leftmost k unmatched symbols from the input string (these are called the *lookahead symbols*) and on the dominos played so far. This means that the only restriction is that the remainder of the input beyond the lookahead is not taken into consideration. It should be obvious that if we happen to have a grammar to which this strategy applies, then parsing can be done much more efficiently: no backtracking is called for. We may go even a bit further and base the choice only on the k lookahead symbols, and on the leftmost unmatched flat-bottom symbol. This is called strong $LL(k)$ parsing. It is even more efficient than $LL(k)$ parsing because much fewer symbols are taken into account when making a choice. Below, we discuss how this choice is made.

The first L in $LL(k)$ stands for reading the input left to right. The second L stands for playing the dominos top to bottom, which is the same as left to right in a production rule. Parameter k stands for the number of lookahead symbols. We restrict ourselves to the case $k = 1$. One can also imagine parsing strategies in which the right-hand side of a production rule is reduced to a left-hand side. This is called $LR(k)$ parsing.

First, we discuss exactly how the decision is made in an $LL(1)$ parser; then we show that it doesn't help to look around in the remainder of the configuration on the board — this may safely be ignored.

To every production rule $A \longrightarrow u$ corresponds a so-called *lookahead set* $L(A \longrightarrow u)$. The lookahead set is a set of terminal symbols; it depends on the grammar but not on the input string. (We give its definition in the next paragraph.) When a decision is to be made, for example, between $A \longrightarrow u$ and $A \longrightarrow u'$ while the lookahead symbol is a, then $A \longrightarrow u$ is chosen if $a \in L(A \longrightarrow u)$, whereas $A \longrightarrow u'$ is chosen if $a \in L(A \longrightarrow u')$. The strategy of $LL(1)$ parsing is applicable just when the lookahead sets for all rules with the same left-hand side are disjoint.

The definition of a lookahead set presents a technical problem. The problem is that although all input symbols may already be matched to flat bottoms, some other flat bottoms are still unmatched; that is, no more lookahead symbols exist, but the game is not yet over. This case may occur if we have ϵ productions for those flat bottoms. The way out is to extend the input with one symbol that represents the end of the input sequence explicitly. We use the symbol $\perp$ for that purpose. We augment the grammar by replacing initial string S with initial string $S \perp$. We make sure that $\perp$ occurs nowhere else in the grammar and nowhere else in the input. Then the adjoining of the two $\perp$'s is the last act of the $LL(1)$ parser, and our problem with running out of lookahead symbols is gone.

Here is our first attempt at defining the lookahead sets. For each rule $A \longrightarrow u$, the lookahead set $L(A \longrightarrow u)$ is defined to be $\{a\}$ if u begins with terminal symbol a; if u begins with a nonterminal, say B, then the lookahead set is the set of all terminals that may show up as the first symbol of any string that can be derived from B. There is a complication: suppose that the empty string can be derived from B. Well, in that case the second symbol from u should be included in the lookahead set $L(A \longrightarrow u)$, and so on. Unfortunately, there is a problem with the "and so on". If the whole of u can be reduced to the empty string, then which terminal symbols are to be included? It is the set of all symbols that can follow A in some derivation. All this is captured in the following definition.

$$L(A \longrightarrow u)$$
$$=$$
$$\{a \mid \langle \exists v, x, y, z :: S \perp \Longrightarrow^* xAv \Longrightarrow xuv \Longrightarrow^* xyv \Longrightarrow^* xaz \rangle\}$$

(Throughout this section, we have initial string $S \perp$, nonterminal A, production rule $A \longrightarrow u$, $a \in T \cup \{\perp\}$, $u, v \in (T \cup \{\perp\} \cup N)^*$, and $x, y, z \in (T \cup \{\perp\})^*$; and the same naming convention applies to primed variables. We have omitted the range of the bound variables in the existential quantification.) The complexity in the discussion is captured by the possibility of various strings being ϵ. For example, if $u \Longrightarrow^* \epsilon$, then $y = \epsilon$, and if A can be followed by a, then a is the first symbol of the terminal symbol sequence to which v reduces.

We are now going to prove that using these lookahead sets is the right thing to do; that is, we prove that if the lookahead sets are not disjoint, then the grammar is not $LL(1)$. In other words, if the lookahead sets are not disjoint, then there is no other way of telling from the lookahead symbol and from the remaining configuration on the board which rule must be applied. (It should be rather obvious that if all lookahead sets with the same left-hand side are disjoint, then the grammar can be parsed with the $LL(1)$ strategy.) Here we go.

The proof is by contradiction. Suppose we have two lookahead sets that are not disjoint. We show that either the grammar is ambiguous, a case that we have already excluded, or that a choice cannot be based on other information that is available. Let the intersecting lookahead sets be $L(A \longrightarrow u)$ and $L(A \longrightarrow u')$. We then have the existence of sequences v, x, y, z, v', x', y', and z' for which

$$\begin{aligned} &S \perp \Longrightarrow^* xAv \Longrightarrow xuv \Longrightarrow^* xyv \Longrightarrow^* xyz \\ \wedge\ &S \perp \Longrightarrow^* x'Av' \Longrightarrow x'u'v' \Longrightarrow^* x'y'v' \Longrightarrow^* x'y'z' \\ \wedge\ &first(yz) = first(y'z') \quad . \end{aligned}$$

(All these symbol sequences exist since $L(A \longrightarrow u) \cap L(A \longrightarrow u') \neq \emptyset$.) We distinguish between two cases.

- If $y = y' = \epsilon$ then

$$\begin{aligned} S \perp \Longrightarrow^* xAv \Longrightarrow xuv \Longrightarrow^* xv \Longrightarrow^* xz \qquad &\text{and} \\ S \perp \Longrightarrow^* xAv \Longrightarrow xu'v \Longrightarrow^* xv \Longrightarrow^* xz \quad &, \end{aligned}$$

  which implies that we have two derivations of the same string, thus the grammar is ambiguous.

- If at least one of y and y' is nonempty, say $y \neq \epsilon$, then

$$\begin{aligned} &S \perp \Longrightarrow^* x'Av' \Longrightarrow x'uv' \Longrightarrow^* x'yv' \Longrightarrow^* x'yz' \ \wedge \\ &S \perp \Longrightarrow^* x'Av' \Longrightarrow x'u'v' \Longrightarrow^* x'y'v' \Longrightarrow^* x'y'z' \ \wedge \\ &first(yz') = first(y) = first(yz) = first(y'z') \quad . \end{aligned}$$

  (We have $first(yz') = first(y) = first(yz)$, since $y \neq \epsilon$, and we have $first(yz) = first(y'z')$ from our assumptions.) When the choice between reducing A to u or to u' is to be made, the dominos played so far in the two situations are equal (they correspond to the derivation $S \perp \Longrightarrow^* x'Av'$); hence, they don't provide any information. The lookahead symbol is also the same in the two cases: it is $first(yz')$ or $first(y'z')$; therefore, the grammar is not $LL(1)$.

This completes the proof.

6.2 Recursive Descent Parsing

In this section, we discuss how the $LL(1)$ parsing algorithm can be implemented as a set of recursive procedures. We do not build the derivation tree explicitly, since we are interested only in the binary decision of whether the input is in the language. We discuss the example of the grammar for arithmetic expressions, and we also show how the expression can be evaluated on the fly.

We have one procedure per nonterminal. All procedures operate on global variable *sym* whose value is the lookahead, that is, the leftmost unmatched input symbol. The input file contains the remaining unmatched input symbols. The input can be advanced over one position by calling procedure *getsym*. The input is a sequence of characters, *sym* is of type *char*, and *getsym* is equivalent to

if *eof*(*input*) **then** *sym* :=$'\perp'$ **else** *read*(*input*, *sym*)   .

For every nonterminal, say A, a call of procedure A amounts to playing all dominos on the board that form the subtree below a flat-bottom labeled A. As we have seen before, this can be done by looking at the input, by advancing the input when symbols match, and by ignoring the rest of the domino board. The operation of the procedure is, therefore, independent of the context in which it is called. This implies that no further information in the form of global variables or parameters is involved. Here is the first procedure. It corresponds to nonterminal D in the grammar, which generates any digit. This procedure presents no problems whatsoever, because the lookahead sets are easy to calculate: no empty productions or other nonterminals are involved. For example $L(D \longrightarrow 3) = \{'3'\}$. We have made one minor optimization: the ten alternatives come out exactly the same, so instead of writing

$[$ *sym* $= '0' \rightarrow$ *getsym*
$\|$ *sym* $= '1' \rightarrow$ *getsym*
$\ldots$

we have taken the disjunction of the guards and written the command only once.

procedure D;
$\|[$ $[$ *sym* $\in \{'0'..'9'\} \rightarrow$ *getsym*
$\|$ *sym* $\notin \{'0'..'9'\} \rightarrow$ *error*
$]$
$]|$

Procedure *error* reports errors, that is, it reports that the input string is not an element of the language defined by the grammar. If procedure *error* is not called during execution of the program then the input string is an element of the language. One may wonder what has to be done when an error is detected: print informative messages, try to get the parser back on the rails, suggest minor modifications to the input string to make it syntactically correct, or whatever. Back-on-the-rails strategies were important in the days of batch processing. In the interactive mode of working with

computers that prevails nowadays, it is more attractive to report one error
and quit, especially if the syntax check can be done quickly.

Ah, we promised to calculate the value of the arithmetic expression on
the fly! What is the value of the arithmetic expression that consists of
only one digit? It is the number represented by that single digit. Using
Pascal function *ord*, the value is calculated as $ord(sym) - ord('0')$. We
extend every procedure that corresponds to a nonterminal with an integer
parameter that is assigned the value of the (part of the) expression that
it parses. In case of an error, the parameter is undefined. Thus, we obtain
our final D.

> **procedure** $D(\mathbf{var}\ x : integer)$;
> $\|[\ [\ sym \in \{'0'..'9'\} \rightarrow x := ord(sym) - ord('0');\ getsym$
> $\ \|\ sym \notin \{'0'..'9'\} \rightarrow error$
> $\ ]$
> $]\|$

On to the second-simplest procedure. This corresponds to nonterminal P,
for which we have two production rules. One begins with terminal symbol
$'('$, which implies that this is the only symbol in the lookahead set for that
rule. The other rule consists of nonterminal N from which numbers are
derived. Every number begins with a digit, so the lookahead set for that
rule is the set of digits.

> **procedure** $P(\mathbf{var}\ x : integer)$;
> $\|[\ [\ sym = '(' \qquad\qquad \rightarrow getsym;\ E(x);$
> $\qquad\qquad\qquad\qquad\qquad [sym = ')' \rightarrow getsym \ \| \ sym \neq ')' \rightarrow error]$
> $\ \|\ sym \in \{'0'..'9'\} \qquad \rightarrow N(x)$
> $\ \|\ sym \notin \{'(',' 0'..'9'\} \rightarrow error$
> $\ ]$
> $]\|$

Next, we consider the procedure for F. We have two production rules
for F, $F \longrightarrow P \uparrow F$ and $F \longrightarrow P$, and they begin with the same
nonterminal. Hence, the lookahead sets for the two rules are not disjoint.
Of course, we may factor out the P from the two right-hand sides and
write

> $F \ \longrightarrow P\ F'$
> $F' \longrightarrow \uparrow\ F$
> $F' \longrightarrow \epsilon \qquad .$

The lookahead set for the alternative $F' \longrightarrow \uparrow F$ is simply $\{\uparrow\}$, the
lookahead set for $F' \longrightarrow \epsilon$ is the set of all symbols that may follow an F
in any derivation, that is, $\{\perp, +, -, *, /, \backslash,)\}$. Hence, we get the following
procedure F. We do not write a separate procedure F' since it would be
called only once. We replaced the call of F' by its body instead.

procedure $F(\textbf{var } x : integer)$;
$\lVert\ \textbf{var } y : integer$;
$\quad P(x)$;
$\quad [\ sym = '\!\uparrow' \rightarrow getsym;\ F(y);\ x := x \uparrow y$
$\quad \Vert\ sym \in \{'\perp','+','-','*','/','\backslash',')'\} \rightarrow skip$
$\quad \Vert\ sym \notin \{'\perp','+','-','*','/','\backslash',')','\!\uparrow'\} \rightarrow error$
$\quad]$
$\rbrack\rbrack$

Of course, if the program notation used for writing the parser does not
have exponentiation, then $x := x \uparrow y$ is to be replaced with a slightly
more elaborate, equivalent program. If so desired, we may guard the exponentiation with tests, ensuring that x and y are in the range in which x^y
is well-defined, that is, something like

$$[\ (x \neq 0 \wedge y \geq 0) \vee (x = 0 \wedge y > 0) \rightarrow x := x \uparrow y$$
$$\Vert\ (x = 0 \vee y < 0) \wedge (x \neq 0 \vee y \leq 0) \rightarrow error$$
$$]\qquad.$$

We ignore errors like this one, including the possibility of overflow, in the
present chapter.

Just to make sure that the proper result is computed, we verify that
$4 \uparrow 3 \uparrow 2$ is indeed evaluated as $4 \uparrow (3 \uparrow 2)$. The procedure F calls $P(x)$
to parse and evaluate the 4, it advances the input over the first $\uparrow$ and
calls $F(y)$ to parse and evaluate $3 \uparrow 2$, thereby storing 9 in y, and finally
stores the value 262144 in variable x, as it should. It appears that $\uparrow$ is
right associative indeed.

Strictly speaking, the body of F should have been

$$[\ sym \in L(F \longrightarrow P\ F') \rightarrow P(x);$$
$$[\ \dots\ ]$$
$$\Vert\ sym \notin L(F \longrightarrow P\ F') \rightarrow error$$
$$]$$

However, since $P\ F'$ is the only replacement for F, no errors will go
undetected in our simpler version. If an error occurs, it will still be reported
at the same input position, that is, no further calls to *getsym* will have
been made, but the reporting is delegated from F to P. It simplifies
the program text and is therefore to be preferred. A similar simplification
exists for the if-statement in F. It checks whether *sym* is in lookahead
set $L(F' \longrightarrow \uparrow F)$ or in $L(F' \longrightarrow \epsilon)$. If *sym* is in neither set, an error is
reported. One may also check whether *sym* equals $\uparrow$, in which case the
first alternative is selected, or not, in which case the second alternative is
selected. If *sym* is not in $L(F' \longrightarrow \epsilon)$ then the error is reported at some
later stage, but not much later: the output will not yet be advanced, but
a larger part of the derivation will have been performed. In our example,
the error reporting will be delegated from F to the procedure that calls
F. The shorter, and more attractive, version of F is given below.

```
procedure F(var x : integer);
|[ var y : integer;
   P(x);
   [ sym = ' ↑ ' → getsym;  F(y);  x := x ↑ y
   | sym ≠ ' ↑ ' → skip
   ]
]|
```

There is another hard nut to crack: the procedure for nonterminal N.
We have just dealt with F, which was right recursive, and we are now faced
with a left-recursive rule: $N \longrightarrow D \mid N\ D$. Again, there is no way that the
two lookahead sets are going to be disjoint. Factoring out the common D
doesn't help in this case, because the choice between ϵ and N cannot be
based on lookahead sets: every N starts with a digit, and every ϵ is, in this
context, followed by a D; that is, its lookahead set is the set of digits also.
Fortunately there is a way out. In Chapter 4, we discussed the conversion
rule used in going from right-linear grammars to regular expressions. The
conversion rule is: from $V = xV + y$ go to $V = x^*y$. Phrased for left-
recursion, and changing the notation to grammar notation, we have: from
$V \longrightarrow Vx \mid y$ go to $V \longrightarrow yV'$ and add nonterminal V' with rules
$V' \longrightarrow xV'$ and $V' \longrightarrow \epsilon$. Applying this conversion rule we transform
the two rules for N into rule $N \longrightarrow D\ N'$ together with $N' \longrightarrow D\ N'$
and $N \longrightarrow \epsilon$.

```
procedure N;
|[ D;  N' ]|
procedure N';
|[ [ sym ∈ {'0'..'9'} → D;  N'
   | sym ∉ {'0'..'9'} → skip
   ]
]|
```

The tail recursion in N' can be replaced by iteration. The only remaining
call of N' is then in N and we replace it by the body of N'. The result
follows, together with the computation of the result value.

```
procedure N(var x : integer);
|[ var y : integer;
   D(x);  *[ sym ∈ {'0'..'9'} → D(y);  x := x · 10 + y ]
]|
```

Let's check again to see whether we have fooled ourselves; that is, let's check
whether the left recursion is translated correctly into left associativity of
the silent multiply-by-ten-and-add operator. We check how 432 is dealt
with. It should give rise to $(4 \cdot 10 + 3) \cdot 10 + 2$ and not to $4 \cdot 10 + (3 \cdot 10 + 2)$.
Procedure N calls $D(x)$, which stores 4 in x and enters the loop. It calls
$D(y)$, which parses the 3 and stores 3 in y. The loop then stores 43 in x

and in the next iteration stores 2 in y and sets x to its final value 432 —
okay, it works.

Note that left recursion is to be translated into a loop (cf. N), whereas
right recursion is to be translated into a right-recursive procedure call
(cf. F). Never, ever, should we confuse the two. Well, never... if the operator involved is associative, then it doesn't matter whether we translate it
into left or right associativity. Hence, in such a case we have a choice.

The remaining two procedures present no further difficulties. They are
listed below. Both implement left-recursive production rules and are, therefore, coded with a loop.

$$
\begin{aligned}
&\textbf{procedure } E(\textbf{var } x : integer); \\
&|[\textbf{ var } y : integer; \\
&\quad [\; sym \neq \,'-' \to T(x) \\
&\quad | \; sym = \,'-' \to getsym; \; T(x); \; x := -x \\
&\quad]; \\
&\quad *[\; sym = \,'+' \to getsym; \; T(y); \; x := x + y \\
&\quad | \; sym = \,'-' \to getsym; \; T(y); \; x := x - y \\
&\quad] \\
&]| \\
&\textbf{procedure } T(\textbf{var } x : integer); \\
&|[\textbf{ var } y : integer; \\
&\quad F(x); \\
&\quad *[\; sym = \,'*' \to getsym; \; F(y); \; x := x * y \\
&\quad | \; sym = \,'/' \to getsym; \; F(y); \; x := x \textbf{ div } y \\
&\quad | \; sym = \,'\backslash' \to getsym; \; F(y); \; x := x \textbf{ mod } y \\
&\quad] \\
&]|
\end{aligned}
$$

(By the way, observe the elegance of having loops with more than one
guard.) We have applied the same simplification of delaying error reporting:
the if-statement in E chooses $E \longrightarrow T$ unless lookahead synbol sym is
in $L(E \longrightarrow -T)$.

Now that we have all our procedures lined up, all that remains to be
done is to get the machinery going. This corresponds to the initial string.
In our case, the initial string is $E \perp$, which leads to the program fragment

$$
\begin{aligned}
&|[\textbf{ var } x : integer; \\
&\quad initsym; \quad \{ \text{ initialize lookahead } \} \\
&\quad E(x); \\
&\quad [sym =\,'\perp' \to print(x) \; | \; sym \neq\,'\perp' \to error] \\
&]|
\end{aligned}
$$

which concludes our discussion of recursive descent parsing.

6.3 Limitations

In this section, we discuss some limitations of $LL(k)$ parsing. We have already seen that the grammar should not be ambiguous. Rules with the same left-hand side should have disjoint lookahead sets, although we may be able to transform the rules into another grammar that defines the same language and that has disjoint lookahead sets.

We have seen that if $k = 1$, all parsing decisions can be based on the leftmost unmatched symbol from the input string and on the leftmost unmatched flat bottom on the board; it doesn't help to consider the other dominoes on the board. For $k > 1$, however, it does make a difference. Taking all the other dominoes into account is called $LL(k)$ parsing, and if they are ignored it is called strong $LL(k)$ parsing. Here is an example of a grammar that is $LL(2)$ but not strong $LL(2)$. It is going to be a very simple grammar because we have to show that it is possible to do an $LL(2)$ derivation for every string. The grammar (due to [Bac79]) is

$$(\{a, b\}, \{S, A\}, \{S \longrightarrow aAaa, S \longrightarrow bAba, A \longrightarrow b, A \longrightarrow \epsilon\}, S)$$

which defines the language $\{aaa, abaa, bbba, bba\}$. The lookahead sets for the two A-rules are

$$L(A \longrightarrow b) = \{ba, bb\}$$

and

$$L(A \longrightarrow \epsilon) = \{ba, aa\}$$

which are obviously not disjoint. (In the case of $LL(k)$ parsing the lookahead sets consist of strings of length k.) Hence, the grammar is not strong $LL(2)$. How do we show that it is $LL(2)$ nevertheless? We have to show all configurations on the domino board when A is about to be parsed and show that a choice between the two rules can be made. Fortunately, the number of configurations is small, so we can draw all of them, as in Figure 6.3. In every configuration, we have underlined the lookahead. In the first and last configuration, no problems exist. In the second and third configurations, the lookahead is the same, ba in both cases; but we can make a choice on the basis of the preceding terminal symbol, which is a in the second and b in the third configuration.

A not-so-elegant way out exists. We can encode the choice between $S \longrightarrow aAaa$ and $S \longrightarrow bAba$ by introducing two different version of A. They have exactly the same production rules. Grammar

$$(\{a, b\},$$
$$\{S, A, A'\},$$
$$\{S \longrightarrow aAaa, S \longrightarrow bA'ba, A \longrightarrow b, A \longrightarrow \epsilon, A' \longrightarrow b, A' \longrightarrow \epsilon\},$$
$$S)$$

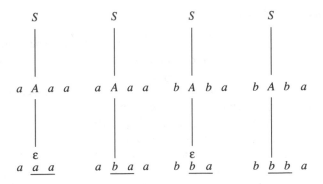

FIGURE 6.3. $LL(2)$ but not strong $LL(2)$.

defines the same language as the previous grammar, and is strong $LL(2)$. This coding technique does not really work satisfactorily, because one can come up with examples in which the number of new nonterminals grows beyond any bound — in fact, one would need an infinite amount of them. This cannot be done in a grammar, because we have required the set of nonterminals and the set of production rules to be finite.

Here is another example of the kind of problems that one may run into when using recursive-descent parsing. We have seen definitions of arithmetic expressions, and one may come up with similar definitions for boolean expressions. Suppose that we give a definition for an expression, which can be either an arithmetic or a boolean expression. Including a rule like

$$E \longrightarrow A \mid B$$

is temptingly simple. Unfortunately, it is not $LL(k)$ for any k. The problem is caused by parentheses: if an expression starts with k or more left parentheses, there is no way to tell whether it is going to be an arithmetic or a boolean expression. We have both

$$E \Longrightarrow A \Longrightarrow^* (^k 0)^k$$

and

$$E \Longrightarrow B \Longrightarrow^* (^k true)^k \quad .$$

Thus, the $LL(k)$ condition is violated. The route that is taken in the Pascal report is to include expressions like $2 \vee 3$, $true + (x = 1)$, and $0 \vee true$ in the syntax. The restriction of type-compatibility is expressed in informal English prose, not in the formalism. (This doesn't mean that it is less clear!) The parser "computes" the type of an expression on the fly, just as we have computed the value of an arithmetic expression in the previous section, and checks for type compatibility wherever required. (Incorporating things like type compatibility into the grammar requires using non-context-free grammars or decorating the nonterminals with attributes that are much like the parameters of our parsing procedures; we refrain from doing so.)

Another instance where Pascal is not an $LL(1)$ language is the problem of the dangling **else**. (Why are we picking on Pascal so often? Well, I guess the definition of Pascal is so clear that you can find out where the problems are. For example, the definition of C is not nearly so clear; in addition to that, it is well known that C has many, many pitfalls — it is just too easy to point out problems; everyone can do it. On the other side, we have ALGOL 60, where the number of problems is much less. Probably, people have become less precise over the years.) Consider the rules for the ambiguous if-statement given before. The procedure that corresponds to ST is the following.

> **procedure** ST;
> |[[$sym = $ **if** $\rightarrow$ $getsym$; b;
>   [$sym = $ **then** $\rightarrow$ $getsym$ ‖ $sym \neq $ **then** $\rightarrow$ $error$];
> ST;
>   [$sym = $ **else** $\rightarrow$ $getsym$; ST
>   ‖ $sym \in \{$';', **end**, **until**, **else**, $\cdots\} \rightarrow skip$
>   ‖ $sym \notin \{$';', **end**, **until**, **else**, $\cdots\} \rightarrow error$
>   ]
> ‖ $sym \in \{...\} \rightarrow st$
> ‖ $sym \notin \{$**if**, $...\} \rightarrow error$
>]
>]|

The ambiguity results in two lookahead sets that both contain **else**. In Pascal, the ambiguity is resolved by stating that **else** binds to the closest possible if-clause. In the parser this is reflected by giving priority to the rule with the else part over the rule without an else part. After applying the technique of delaying the error reporting, we get the following parser. It is quite possible that some compiler writers have done so automatically, without realizing that there was a problem.

> **procedure** ST;
> |[[$sym = $ **if** $\rightarrow$ $getsym$; b;
>   [$sym = $ **then** $\rightarrow$ $getsym$ ‖ $sym \neq $ **then** $\rightarrow$ $error$];
> ST;
>   [$sym = $ **else** $\rightarrow$ $getsym$; ST
>   ‖ $sym \neq $ **else** $\rightarrow skip$
>   ]
> ‖ $sym \in \{...\} \rightarrow st$
> ‖ $sym \notin \{$**if**, $...\} \rightarrow error$
>]
>]|

6.4 Lexical Analysis

We have discussed the construction of a parser in the context of strings of symbols. When discussing the parser, we assumed that every symbol is represented by a single character. More often than not this is not the case. It is not unusual to find phrases like "any number of blanks can be inserted between consecutive symbols". Therefore, we rewrite the procedure *getsym* to skip blanks. This solution is much to be preferred over the alternative, in which one tries to incorporate the irrelevant blanks in every production rule into the grammar. The situation is further aggravated by switching to new lines, inserting comments, and so forth. A final complication is the fact that many symbols are made of a sequence of characters, rather than a single character. For example, **begin** is made up of five characters, and $\leq$ is often represented by the two-character sequence $<=$. Converting the sequence of input characters to a more manageable sequence of terminal symbols is the task of the extended procedure *getsym*. This procedure is usually called the *lexical analyzer*, or the scanner. It allows us to ignore the representation of symbols in the rest of the parser.

It has become a tradition to study lexical analysis in the context of regular languages. It is true that the sequence of symbols recognized by a scanner can be described by a right-linear grammar, but it is also true that one does not use that particular theory in order to program an efficient scanner. So, we break with the theory-tradition here and subscribe to the ad-hoc way.

As far as lexical analysis is concerned, all identifiers are equal. They must, however, be distinguished from the so-called reserved words, such as *begin*, which look like identifiers but represent other symbols, such as **begin**. The distinction can be made by first scanning the characters as if they represent an identifier, and then comparing that sequence of characters with the representation of each reserved word. Various methods exist to reduce the number of comparisons, such as binary search and hashing, but we will not discuss them. In our scanner, we have incorporated a simple but effective test that avoids many comparisons. For every letter c, $lens[c]$ is a set of integers. Each integer in the set is the length of a keyword starting with letter c. Choosing a method that will work efficiently is very important. One should not be surprised to find that a compiler spends a significant fraction of its time in the scanner. Horror stories exist about compilers that spend up to half of their time skipping blanks! Here is what part of a scanner might look like.

```
type symbol = ( andsym, arraysym, ..., whilesym, withsym,
                identifier, integerconst, ..., plus, minus, ...,
                endoftext);
     string = array [0..?] of char;
```

```
var   ch : char;
      sym : symbol;
      idl : integer;
      id : string;
      repr : array [andsym..withsym] of string;
      reprl : array [andsym..withsym] of integer;
      lens : array [char] of set of integer;
procedure getch;
|[...]|   { handles new lines and end of file }
procedure getsym;
|[ *[ch ∈ {' ', eol} → getch];
   [ ch ∈ {'a'..'z',' A'..'Z'} →
         id[0] := ch;  idl := 1;  getch;
         *[ ch ∈ {'a'..'z',' A'..'Z','0'..'9'} →
               id[idl] := ch;  idl := idl + 1;  getch
            ];
         [ idl ∈ lens[id[0]] → sym := andsym
         ‖ idl ∉ lens[id[0]] → sym := identifier
         ];
         *[ sym ≠ identifier cand
               (reprl[sym] ≠ idl cor repr[sym] ≠ id) →
                  sym := succ(sym)
            ]
   ‖ ch ∈ {'0'..'9'} → ···
   ‖ ch = ';' → getch;  sym := semicolon
   ‖ ch = '>' → getch;
         [ch = '=' → getch;  sym := geq ‖ ch ≠ '=' → sym := gtr]
   ···
   ‖ ch = '⊥' → sym := endoftext
   ‖ ch ∉ {'A'..'Z',' a'..'z','0'..'9',';',' >',···,'⊥'} →
         error
   ]
]|
procedure initsym;
|[ var c : char;  s : symbol;
   reprl[andsym] := 3;  repr[andsym] := 'and';
   ···
   reprl[withsym] := 4;  repr[withsym] := 'with';
   for c ∈ {'a'..'z',' A'..'Z'} do lens[c] := ∅;
   for s ∈ {andsym..withsym} do
       lens[repr[s][0]] := lens[repr[s][0]] ∪ {reprl[s]};
   reset(input);  getch;  getsym
]|
```

We have given a systematic method of deriving the parser for an $LL(1)$

grammar. One might wonder whether it is practical to automate this process, and write a parser generator, a program that takes a grammar as its input and produces a parser as its output. In fact, this can be done quite easily. The main task is to compute the lookahead sets for every rule. Computing the lookahead sets in an efficient manner is a substantial program that we will not discuss here. It involves three computations for every nonterminal: whether the empty string can be derived from it, what the set of leading terminal symbols is of all strings that can be derived from it, and what the set of nonterminal symbols is that can follow it in any derivation. In each case, it is rather easy to find some relations from the grammar rules, but what is needed then is always the transitive closure of that relation. In a later chapter, we will discuss an algorithm for computing the transitive closure.

6.5 $LR(k)$ Parsing

In the literature, one finds a lot of information about $LR(k)$ parsing. What is the difference between $LL(k)$ and $LR(k)$? Let me summarize what $LL(k)$ is in terms of the domino game. Dominos are played from top to bottom, and from left to right. At every moment, the leftmost k unmatched input symbols are used, together with the leftmost unmatched nonterminal, to select which domino to play next. After the parsing game has been completed, this domino will, possibly via a big tree of more dominos, cover part of the input sequence. This is the part of the input that is derived from the particular nonterminal "on top of" the domino. In the case of $LL(k)$ parsing, the first k symbols thereof have been used in the choice of the domino (and if the sequence is shorter than k symbols, then the symbols following it up to a total length of k have been used).

In the case of $LR(k)$ parsing, dominos are played from left to right and from bottom to top. Which domino to play next is based not on the first k symbols of the input part that it derives, but on the input part that it derives plus the first k symbols following it. This shows that much more information is available than in the case of $LL(k)$ parsing. The difference is illustrated in Figure 6.4. Assume that substring y is derived from nonterminal A via rule $A \longrightarrow uvw$. In the case of $LL(k)$, the choice $A \rightarrow uvw$ is based on A and on the first k symbols of input string yz. In the case of $LR(k)$, the choice $A \rightarrow uvw$ is based on uvw and on the first k symbols of input string z. Part y of the input has already been read, and the fact that y is derived from uvw is already known when the choice $A \rightarrow uvw$ is made in the case of $LR(k)$ parsing; y has not been read and it has not been established that it is derived from uvw in the case of $LL(k)$ parsing. It should therefore be no surprise that $LR(k)$ is "more powerful" than $LL(k)$, in the sense that every grammar that is $LL(k)$ is also $LR(k)$, and that some $LR(k)$ grammars are not $LL(k)$. It should

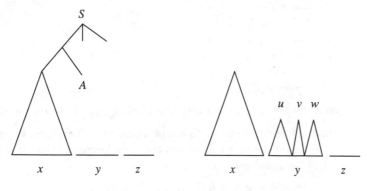

FIGURE 6.4. *LL(k)* versus *LR(k)* parsing.

also come as no surprise that *LR(k)* is harder to implement than is *LL(k)*. We have seen a simple implementation of *LL*(1). No simple implementation of *LR(k)* exists, except for the case $k = 0$. (The case $k = 0$ does not make much sense for *LL* parsing; for *LR* parsing, it does make sense, but very few grammars are *LR*(0).) Many simplifications or approximations of *LR*(1) exist, known as *SLR*(1) and *LALR*(1). Grammars exist that are *SLR*(1) or *LALR*(1), and that are not *LL*(1). However, the opposite is also the case: some *LL*(1) grammars are neither *SLR*(1) nor *LALR*(1). The *LL*(1) parsing method seems easier to understand and the parser seems easier to extend with extra statements to generate code or to perform additional checks.

6.6 Bibliographic Notes

The method of parsing by recursive descent (cf. [Luc61]) is so simple that nobody bothers to write much about it. The theory of LL parsing was developed by [LS68]. See also [Knu71]. An excellent reference work on syntax analysis is [Bac79]. Consult [DeR71] for a discussion of a practical *LR(k)* parsing method. An early and still relevant text on compilation, including parsing, is [Gri71]. See also [AU72].

6.7 Exercises

1. Transform the following grammar into *LL*(1) form, while preserving the language that it defines. The starting string is *S*.

$$S \longrightarrow A \mid P$$
$$A \longrightarrow V := E$$
$$P \longrightarrow i \mid i\,(\,L\,)$$
$$L \longrightarrow E \mid E, L$$
$$E \longrightarrow V$$
$$V \longrightarrow i \mid a[i]$$

2. Do the same thing with the last line changed to $V \longrightarrow i \mid a(i)$.

3. Following is the Algol 60 definition of a number. Transform the grammar into $LL(1)$ form, while preserving the language that it defines. The set of terminal symbols is

$$\{0, 1, 2, 3, 4, 5, 6, 7, 8, 9, +, -, {}_{10}, .\}$$

and the capital letters are the nonterminal symbols (they were much longer identifiers in the official report). The nonterminal that defines numbers is N.

$$D \longrightarrow 0 \mid 1 \mid 2 \mid 3 \mid 4 \mid 5 \mid 6 \mid 7 \mid 8 \mid 9$$
$$J \longrightarrow D \mid J\,D$$
$$I \longrightarrow J \mid +J \mid -J$$
$$E \longrightarrow {}_{10}\,I$$
$$F \longrightarrow .\,J$$
$$G \longrightarrow J \mid F \mid J\,F$$
$$U \longrightarrow G \mid E \mid G\,E$$
$$N \longrightarrow U \mid +U \mid -U$$

List the lookahead sets for all production rules.

4. Let a and b be terminal symbols, just like **if, then, else, while,** and **do.** Consider grammar rules

$$S \longrightarrow \textbf{if } b \textbf{ then } S \textbf{ else } S \mid \textbf{if } b \textbf{ then } S \mid \textbf{while } b \textbf{ do } S \mid a$$

in which S is both the initial string and the only nonterminal symbol. This grammar is ambiguous. Construct a nonambiguous context-free grammar that defines the same set of strings. Your grammar should formalize the rule that **else** binds to the closest possible if-clause. Your grammar need not be $LL(1)$.

5. Give the precondition and postcondition of procedure A for parsing nonterminal A using the $LL(1)$ method.

6. Write a program whose input is a grammar. The program is supposed to check that the grammar is in $LL(1)$ form.

7. Write a program whose input is a grammar in $LL(1)$ form. The program is supposed to generate a recursive-descent $LL(1)$ parser.

8. Construct a lexical analyzer for Pascal or for C, whichever you prefer.

7

The Halting Problem and Formal Proofs

In this chapter, we make a detour into an area that is remotely related to the subject of the previous chapter. We have seen how to write a procedure that parses an expression and, on the fly, evaluates the expression. In this chapter, we consider extensions of the grammar for expressions, essentially extending it to a "real" programming language, and conclude that it is then no longer possible to write a function for evaluating all interesting attributes of strings in the language. In particular, it is impossible to determine whether an arbitrary program evokes a finite or an infinite computation. By doing so, we explore some fundamental limitations of programming languages and computers, while ignoring some of the practical limitations, such as cost. Some programmers have attempted to solve problems that are probably unsolvable, and some have attempted to solve problems that are provably unsolvable. The practicing programmer is well advised to learn about the existence of such problems. The inability to check mechanically whether execution of a program terminates, let alone to check its correctness, is all the more reason to write only correct programs. Hard as it may be, we try to do so by developing programs in a well-organized way in which we design the program hand in hand with an outline of its correctness proof. We rarely give the proof in full detail, but by being so careful at every step, we are convinced that we could give the full proof should the need arise.

7.1 The Halting Problem

A program for parsing and evaluating an expression is called an *interpreter*. All sorts of conversions take place in executing that program: a sequence of characters is converted to a number, operator / is converted to an application of **div**, and so on. We have written the program as a procedure that returns an integer and operates on a global input file. We might also write it as a function that takes a character string as an argument and returns the integer value represented by the string.

> **function** $E(e : string) : integer$;
> { $E(e)$ = the value of e }

For example, we have $E('3+4') = 7$. We can extend the definition of expressions to incorporate constructs like

    '**const** $x = 3$; $x + 4$'

and have them evaluated by E. The interpreter can maintain a table of pairs, containing identifiers and their "meanings"; it adds the pair that couples identifier x with the integer 3 when the construct

    '**const** $x = 3$; '

is analyzed. Even constructs like

    '**var** x; $x := 3$; $x := x + 1$; $x + 4$'

present no particular difficulties. The value-part of the pair in the table is updated when an assignment statement is analyzed. Conditional statements do not present any problems. How about loops or, equivalently, recursive definitions? Can we handle

    '**var** x;
      function r; $[x \neq 0 \rightarrow x := x - 1;\ r \parallel x = 0 \rightarrow 29]$;
      $x := 41;\ r$'   ,

which contains a function declaration? We can do a similar thing as we did to handle x, namely make a table in which the correspondence between identifier r and string

    '$[x \neq 0 \rightarrow x := x - 1;\ r \parallel x = 0 \rightarrow 29]$'

is stored. Whenever r is invoked in the string to be interpreted, the definition is looked up and inserted. Now, however, we are running the risk of nontermination: it is not obvious that our interpreter terminates on all inputs. In the example, there will be 42 calls of r leading to $x = 0$ and to the result 29. However, if the initial value of x is changed to -1, the interpreter loops forever. It would be useful to have a boolean function, say h, that returns *true* just when its parameter is a string on which our interpreter terminates. We could then write something like

$$[h(s) \rightarrow write(E(s)) \parallel \neg h(s) \rightarrow write('program\ loops\ forever')]$$

and guarantee termination of interpreter E on input string s. If the language from which s is selected is sufficiently restricted, then it is not very difficult to write h. If the language contains recursion, it becomes more difficult. In fact, we show that it is impossible to write function h by assuming that h exists and then deriving a contradiction. Consider string

    '**function** f; $[h(f) \rightarrow *[true \rightarrow skip];\ 7 \parallel \neg h(f) \rightarrow 3]$;
     f'   ,

which contains a definition of function f, and a call of f. The body of f contains an invocation of our hypothetical function h. If $h(f)$ is found to be *true*, then f goes into an infinite loop and never returns 7, otherwise, f returns the value 3. Function h is called with f as its parameter; in the way we have described the correspondence table, which stores the definitions of identifiers, f is indeed linked to a string, namely to

$$\text{`} [h(f) \to *[true \to skip]; \ 7 \parallel \neg h(f) \to 3] \text{'} \qquad .$$

Now, look at the definition of h and see what $h(f)$ is, and look at the definition of f to see when it terminates properly instead of going into an infinite recursion.

$$
\begin{aligned}
& h(f) \\
=\ & \qquad \{ \text{ definition of } h \ \} \\
& f \text{ terminates} \\
=\ & \qquad \{ \text{ definition of } f \ \} \\
& \neg h(f)
\end{aligned}
$$

Here we have our contradiction: $h(f) = \neg h(f)$. We cannot escape the conclusion that it is impossible to write function h. We have cheated on one point: we should have included the definition of h in the string that we used to obtain the contradiction because f invokes h. That is, it should look like

> `function` $h(s)$; $\cdots$;
> `function` f; $[h(f) \to *[true \to skip]; \ 7 \parallel \neg h(f) \to 3];$
> f '

and the conclusion is then read as: it is not possible to program a function that determines whether any function written in the same language terminates. If you don't like the idea of writing interpreters and prefer to spell out the whole proof in more traditional mathematical terminology then this can be done. It is a lot of hard work. It was done by Alan M. Turing, who first proved the unsolvability of the halting problem (cf. [Tur36]).

The idea on which the proof is based is to apply h to itself and sneak in a negation. Self-reference is what is needed to make the contradiction apparent. The same idea is found in Russell's paradox. Consider sets of sets. One might think of set U, which contains all sets that contain themselves, that is, $U = \{x \mid x \in x\}$. U is a big set, but it is not sheer nonsense. Another set is $I = \{x \mid x \text{ is an infinite set }\}$. We have $I \in I$. Next, define R to be the set that contains all sets that do not contain themselves, that is, $R = \{x \mid x \notin x\}$. Is R well defined? Consider the question of whether R is an element of R. For every x, predicate $x \in R$ is, according to the definition of R, equivalent to $x \notin x$. Substituting R for x, we obtain a contradiction.

$$R \in R$$
$$= \quad \{ \text{ definition of } R \ \}$$
$$R \notin R$$

The halting problem is also closely related to Cantor's diagonal argument and Gödel's incompleteness result. We examine both of them in some detail.

7.2   Logic and Boolean Expressions

In previous chapters, we found ourselves writing many boolean expressions, especially in correctness proofs of programs and to establish the relation between grammars and languages. We have discussed VLSI circuits and have seen how these circuits can be used for evaluating boolean expressions. In this section, we take a closer look at boolean expressions and how to manipulate them. If we are relying on proofs made out of boolean expressions for convincing ourselves of the correctness of programs (or, for that matter, of anything else), we had better make sure that we are proficient at working with boolean expressions or else the proof will not be very convincing, that is, it will not be a proof.

What kind of objects are these boolean expressions that we are talking about? They look like propositions and predicates that you have probably encountered in mathematical logic. The similarity is misleading, however, and in fact our boolean expressions are a lot closer to algebraic expressions or to arithmetic expressions as you know them from analysis. Let us have a look at logic first.

Propositions and predicates are strings that satisfy certain syntactic restrictions. These strings are called the well-formed formulae. For example, $p \wedge (q \vee r)$ and $x < y + 3$ are well formed, and $x < (y = 7)$ and $x(>$ are not. Next, the wff's (as they are referred to) are partitioned into two sets: those that are called derivable and those that are not. The definition of derivable strings is a recursive one:

- some strings are given to be derivable (the axioms),

- some rules are given as to how new derivable strings can be constructed from other, already derivable strings (inference rules),

- no other strings are derivable.

An example of an inference rule is *Modus Ponens* : if p is a derivable string and $p \supset q$ is a derivable string, then q is a derivable string. This rule is often written as

$$\frac{p, \ p \supset q}{q} \qquad .$$

Another rule, called *Hypothetical syllogism*, is

$$\frac{p \supset q, \; q \supset r}{p \supset r} \quad .$$

Note the similarity between strings derivable in a logic and the language generated by a grammar. One of the questions that logicians are interested in is: what is a minimal set of axioms and inference rules that produces an "interesting" set of derivable wff's.

A device that is used a lot in logic is called a *model* or a *meaning*, and is a function from the set of wff's to the set $\{true, false\}$ of boolean values. Defining such a function may involve concepts other than strings or booleans, such as numbers. The meaning function maps some substrings to those concepts instead of to boolean values, so the function actually has a wider domain and a wider range. Remember the grammar over $\{|, p, q\}$ that we used in the introduction. It is readily translated into a logic in which $||p|q|||$ is derivable, and $||||p|q||$ isn't. One can think of a model mapping these strings to *true* and *false*, respectively. For example, for mapping $\mathcal{M}$, we might want to write something like:

$$\mathcal{M}(x\mathsf{p}y\mathsf{q}z) = true \text{ if } \mathcal{M}(x) + \mathcal{M}(y) = \mathcal{M}(z)$$
$$\mathcal{M}(x\mathsf{p}y\mathsf{q}z) = false \text{ if } \mathcal{M}(x) + \mathcal{M}(y) \neq \mathcal{M}(z)$$
$$\mathcal{M}(\epsilon) = 0$$
$$\mathcal{M}(x|) = \mathcal{M}(x) + 1 \qquad \text{for all } x \in \{|\}^*$$

without much problem. (That is, until you begin to ask questions like: what does 0 mean? What is $+$? What is $=$? etc.) Since the natural numbers are included in the range of $\mathcal{M}$, for example $\mathcal{M}(||||) = 3$, we say that a string like $||p|||q|||||$ which is mapped to *true* expresses a fact about natural numbers. If, in a more complex case, some notion of booleans was incorporated, we would like to write

$$\mathcal{M}(b \wedge c) = \mathcal{M}(b) \wedge \mathcal{M}(c)$$

where the first $\wedge$ is a string character and the last $\wedge$ denotes conjunction. (It would be less confusing but also less legible if we would use two different symbols, as we did for p and $+$.) In the sequel, we shall carefully distinguish between string characters and other symbols by using string quotes where necessary. It looks like we're defining the meaning of a string containing addition in terms of addition, and conjunction in terms of conjunction. Well, that's the way it is. We cannot start from scratch; some understanding has to be present before we can begin. However, we can define complex notions in terms of simpler notions — just as we would have done without models. The idea is that the model gives some sort of trustworthiness to what we are doing. In fact, the following two concepts play a central role in logic: consistency and completeness. A logic (plus model) is consistent when every derivable wff maps to *true*. The logic is complete when every wff that maps to *true* is derivable. Consistency is a minimal requirement —

an inconsistent system allows us to conclude just about everything, even false statements. Completeness is at the other end of the scale: it is the maximum one may hope for.

Every logic can be made consistent by selecting a trivial model: map every wff to *true*. This is not an interesting model, however. It becomes more interesting when ||p|q||| is mapped to *true* and ||||p|q|| is mapped to *false*. It is far from trivial to extend the logic to express all statements from number theory, and to construct a model that maps all true statements to *true* and all false statements to *false*. For example, we need to include strings that express quantifications like: $x + y = y + x$ for all x and y. However, if the system is this powerful, if it can express all statements from number theory, we meet Gödel's theorem. This famous theorem says that every powerful (in the sense given) logic plus model is either inconsistent or incomplete. Gödel's theorem has had profound consequences and we will show its relation to the halting problem.

7.3   Gödel's Incompleteness Result

At the turn of the century, a small group of mathematicians were very excited about the idea of formalizing all of mathematics. David Hilbert put forward a program to work on this subject. The hope was to come up with a formal logical system, with axioms and inference rules as we have discussed them, and to show that all mathematical results can be formulated in this framework. But in 1931, Kurt Gödel proved that this was too much to hope for. Here, we give an outline of Gödel's proof. As before, the essence of the proof is the construction of a self-reference. Gödel carried out the encoding of a theorem that refers to itself in terms of natural numbers; we shall use strings instead. We will be careful in writing all string quotes in this section since the proof that follows becomes very confusing if we don't.

The "meaning" function $\mathcal{M}$, the interpreter that maps a string to its intended meaning, is identical to function E that we discussed in the first section of this chapter. We stick to $\mathcal{M}$ to emphasize its role as a meaning function. For example, we have

$$\mathcal{M}(\text{ 'true' }) = true, \text{ and}$$
$$\mathcal{M}(\text{ ' } \neg \text{ ' } x) = \neg\mathcal{M}(x), \text{ and}$$
$$\mathcal{M}(\text{ '||p|q|||' }) = true \qquad .$$

We have written ' $\neg$ ' x for the string whose first character is $\neg$ and whose remaining characters form string x; we have once again omitted the operator for string catenation. $\mathcal{M}$ acts as the inverse of quotation marks: it unquotes its operand. We need a second function, say Q, called the "norming" function by Gödel, although it is called Quining (after the logician W.V.O. Quine) when doing the same for strings. When given a string s as its parameter, Q returns s with all occurrences of character q in it replaced by string s (excluding the outer string quotes since they are not elements of s). For example, in $Q(\,$'Iraq'$\,) = $ 'IraIraq' the argument is a string of four characters and the result is a string of seven characters. Again, with some confidence in our programming capabilities, we know how to write a program for Q, that is, we can be assured that Q can be defined properly. In order for $\mathcal{M}$ to be a complete meaning function, it must apply to all strings representing wff's, including those that start with Q. The rule for these strings is

$$\mathcal{M}(\,\text{'Q('}\ x\ \text{')'}\,) = \mathcal{M}(Q(x))\qquad ,$$

and it is in the same vein as the above-mentioned rule for negation, so it should not present any particular difficulties. 'Q('$\ x\ $')' stand for a string whose first character is Q, whose second character is (, whose last character is), and whose interior part is called x. Given $\mathcal{M}$ and Q, we derive a contradiction.

$$\mathcal{M}(\,\text{'Q(}\neg\text{Q(q))'}\,)$$
$$=\qquad \{\ \text{definition of } \mathcal{M}(\,\text{'Q('}\ x\ \text{')'}\,)\ \}$$
$$\mathcal{M}(Q(\,\text{'}\neg\text{Q(q)'}\,))$$
$$=\qquad \{\ \text{definition of } Q\ \}$$
$$\mathcal{M}(\,\text{'}\neg\text{Q(}\neg\text{Q(q))'}\,)$$
$$=\qquad \{\ \text{definition of } \mathcal{M}(\,\text{'}\neg\text{'}\ x)\ \}$$
$$\neg\mathcal{M}(\,\text{'Q(}\neg\text{Q(q))'}\,)$$

The last line is the negation of the first line, yet we have proven them equal, so we have an inconsistency. To save the logic from inconsistency, we must withdraw something that we used in the proof of the contradiction. We can withdraw the ability to define functions like Q, but then we have a very weak formalism. We can withdraw one of the rules for $\mathcal{M}$, leaving it as an incompletely defined interpreter, that is, making the logic incomplete. We cannot just change the rules for $\mathcal{M}$, because then it would not be an interpreter at all.

From our programmer's point of view, however, we know that applying interpreter $\mathcal{M}$ to string 'Q($\neg$Q(q))' will cause the interpreter to go into an infinite execution and yield neither *true* nor *false*. In these terms, Gödel's incompleteness result is again the halting problem.

From another point of view, there is no problem at all. There is no inconsistency, the only thing is that $\mathcal{M}$ is not a total function; $\mathcal{M}$ is a partial function, and string 'Q($\neg$Q(q))' is an example of a string of 8 characters for which it is not defined, a string that is outside the domain of the function. The only discomforting aspect is that there is no way to turn $\mathcal{M}$ into a total function that can be viewed as an interpreter.

Actually, Gödel was a little more clever. Here is his proof.

$$\neg\mathcal{M}(Q(\,\text{'}\neg\text{M(Q(q))'}\,))$$
$$=\qquad \{\ \text{definition of } Q\ \}$$
$$\neg\mathcal{M}(\,\text{'}\neg\text{M(Q('}\neg\text{M(Q(q))'}))\text{')'}\,)$$

Gödel's definition of Q replaces q with the entire string including quotes (actually, replaces a free variable —q— with a number that encodes the entire formula; encoding is quoting). The inner quotes are just characters in the string enclosed in the outer quotes. We have

$$G = \neg\mathcal{M}(\text{'G'})$$

where G stands for $\neg\mathcal{M}(Q(\text{'}\neg\texttt{M(Q(q))'}))$. Gödel argues that if $\mathcal{M}$ is a complete interpreter then

$$G = \mathcal{M}(\text{'G'})$$

and obtains an inconsistency. If we have been so careful in the development of our definitions that we can believe that the logic is consistent, then the assumption that $\mathcal{M}$ is complete must be dropped; in particular, it does not apply to 'G'.

Gödel's proof is more clever than the one we gave because he does not need the rule we gave for $\mathcal{M}$ when applied to strings starting with Q. His definitions of $\mathcal{M}$ and Q do not invoke themselves, so in principle the names are not needed. He avoids the recursion by using quantifiers. We could also write unnamed functions instead of $\mathcal{M}$ and Q — we will see how to write anonymous functions later — but this makes G rather complicated. So for clarity of explanation, we have deviated from Gödel by using a string encoding rather than a numeric encoding, by defining $\mathcal{M}$ recursively rather than with quantifiers, and by defining Q as a function rather than as a relation as Gödel did.

7.4   Cantor's Diagonal Argument

Cantor's diagonal argument shows that there are more real numbers than integers. It is usually presented as follows, in which the reals are restricted to the range 0 through 1, and the integers to the natural ones. Write an infinite sequence of reals, one per line. The lines are numbered with natural numbers. On each line we have an infinite sequence of digits. (Don't worry about .3999999... and .4000000... representing the same real number; just avoid one of the two sequences.)

```
0:      .8352094562383...
1:      .7376237612872...
2:      .1237238724322...
3:      .5428290637366...
4:      .2045292629929...
   ⋮
```

We form an infinite sequence that is not in the table by taking its n th digit different from the n th digit in the n th row. Hence, although there is one line for every natural number, a real number exists that occurs nowhere in the table: the number of reals exceeds the number of integers.

How is this related to the halting problem? It is through the formalist's point of view. The formalist does not insist that every proof be given formally (at least, I hope not) but that it can be formalized when one insists. For the sake of argument, we insist. How do we make Cantor's argument a formal proof? On the first row, we do not have an infinite sequence of digits, although this was promised. We have 13 digits followed by 3 dots. If we want to formalize it, then we cannot expect to have an infinite sequence written down somewhere, but we have to provide a mechanism that defines an infinite sequence of digits. That's easy: instead of 13 digits and 3 dots, we write a program for printing the digits. Since the sequence is to be infinite, the program is a nonterminating program. This takes care of the horizontal dots. How do we get rid of the vertical dots? We need an infinite sequence of nonterminating programs. We can certainly write a program that generates all programs one after the other. For example, one generates all strings in order of increasing length, and per length in lexicographic order. Leave out all those strings that are not syntactically correct — this we know how to do. Leave out all those programs that are terminating programs — and here we have our friend, the halting problem. We are unable to say which programs to leave out, so we are formally unable to to define a sequence consisting of infinite sequences of digits. When Cantor's diagonal argument is formalized in this manner, it again becomes an instance of the halting problem.

The formalist wonders how one can conclude that there are more reals than integers. One might just as well conclude that it is impossible to write an infinite sequence of reals. Who would conclude from the inability to list all nonterminating programs that there are more of those programs than there are natural numbers?

7.5   Calculating with Boolean Expressions

One of the consequences of Gödel's theorem is that logicians are mainly concerned with the validity and limitations of formal processes, and much less with actually finding out whether a formula is *true* or *false* or how it is related to another formula. The latter is the kind of thing we find interesting in algebra or calculus. For example, we might write a distribution property as

$$x \cdot (y + z) = x \cdot y + x \cdot z$$

or (replace $x\cdot$ by $\frac{\delta}{\delta x}$)

$$\frac{\delta}{\delta x}(y + z) = \frac{\delta}{\delta x}y + \frac{\delta}{\delta x}z \qquad .$$

The first rule applies to numbers x, y, z, and also to functions. The second rule makes sense only if y and z are functions of x. It might be argued that it is better to write the dependence on x explicitly, which leads to $\frac{\delta}{\delta x}(y(x) + z(x)) = \frac{\delta}{\delta x}y(x) + \frac{\delta}{\delta x}z(x)$ but this looks definitely more confusing. Once we understand that both y and z depend on x, the formula looks much better without the four occurrences of (x). It becomes a pain in the neck to drag it along all the time. What we are really doing then is using a name for an expression instead of using a name for the function. For example, we write

$$f = x^2 + 1$$

instead of the more conventional

$$f(x) = x^2 + 1$$

or, equivalently,

$$f = \lambda x.x^2 + 1 \quad .$$

We can apply this "abbreviation trick" only if we know exactly what the domain of the functions is. For example, if it is understood that we are working in the two-dimensional Euclidean space with orthogonal coordinates x and y, then expression $x^2 + 1$ denotes the function that maps every point (x, y) to the number $x^2 + 1$. Similarly, expression $x^2 + y$ maps every point (x, y) to $x^2 + y$, but $x^2 + z$ makes sense only if z is a given number. Just as arithmetic expressions denote functions from the well-understood but anonymous domain to the numbers, boolean expressions denote functions that map to the booleans. If it is understood that we are working in the same domain as before, expression $x > 0$ denotes a boolean function that maps every point (x, y) in the two-dimensional Euclidean space to a boolean value; it maps to *true* if x is positive and to *false* otherwise. Expression $(x + y)^2 = x^2 + 2xy + y^2$ maps every point to *true*, and expression $(x + y)^2 = x^2 + 2xy$ is equivalent to expression $y = 0$.

The last two examples might be confusing. You "know" that $(x + y)^2 = x^2 + 2xy + y^2$ is right and $(x + y)^2 = x^2 + 2xy$ is wrong. The difference with what we did in the previous paragraph, is that there we were talking in the context of a given state space with coordinates x and y. In such a context, $(x + y)^2 = x^2 + 2xy$ is equivalent to $y = 0$. Traditionally, formulae like $(x + y)^2 = x^2 + 2xy + y^2$ are universally quantified over all free variables. If we make this quantification explicit, we get

$$\langle \forall x, y :: (x + y)^2 = x^2 + 2xy + y^2 \rangle \quad ,$$

and this is *true*, whereas

$$\langle \forall x, y :: (x + y)^2 = x^2 + 2xy \rangle$$

is *false*. We stick to the tradition of leaving out those universal quantifications, but it does require one to know which variables are free. And if x and y are given to be coordinates of the state space, then they are not free variables.

The situation is a bit more complicated in the presence of quantifications and bound variables. For example, $\int_1^x \frac{y}{t} dt$ denotes the function that maps every point (x, y) to $y \cdot \ln(x)$. Variable t is not a coordinate of the space in which we are working and $\int_1^x \frac{y}{t} dt$ is not a function on points (x, y, t). Subexpression $\frac{y}{t}$ is a function on points (y, t). The collection of variables grows and shrinks, so to speak, with the scope of the variables involved. Variable t has a scope that is restricted to the subexpression $\frac{y}{t}$; we say that t is bound to this part of the expression. We find the same thing in programming languages where local variables are declared in a block: they have a scope that is limited to that block only. Not all programming languages require that all variables be declared, and not all expressions used in everyday mathematics declare the bound variables explicitly. For example, in $\{x \mid x \geq 0\}$, it isn't hard to guess; in $\{x + 1 \mid x \geq 1\}$, it is also "guessable"; and in $\{x + y \mid x \geq y\}$, we can do it only because of the previous two examples. If the previous examples had been $\{y \mid 0 \geq y\}$ and $\{1 + y \mid 1 \geq y\}$, we might have guessed differently.

When reasoning about programs, we know exactly what the domain of the functions is: it is given by the variables in the program. If the program's variables are i and k, we understand that $i = 2^k$ is a boolean function that maps all points (i, k) to *true* if i is the kth power of 2 and to *false* otherwise. We borrow some terminology from the discussion above: we will talk about the space spanned by i and k. Program variables are like names of coordinates in mathematics, and not like mathematical variables. We return to this issue in Chapter 10.

So much for the formal status of our boolean expressions. Given that we know what they are, and given that we have some fixed state space in which we understand the functions, we are interested in figuring out some relationships between various boolean expressions. This is what algebra or calculus is about. In order to be able to do some sort of algebra, we have to have some operators. The operators we use are

$\lor$	disjunction (or)
$\land$	conjunction (and)
$=$	equivalence (equivales)
$\neq$	discrepancy (exclusive or)
$\Rightarrow$	implication (implies)
$\Leftarrow$	explication (explies, follows from)
$\neg$	negation (not)

The last operator is a unary prefix operator, whereas all the others are binary infix operators. (Discrepancy is not used a lot; explication, however, is.) We define all the operators.

- conjunction $p \wedge q$ is *true* in every point of the state space where both p and q are *true*, and *false* elsewhere.

- disjunction $p \vee q$ is *false* in every point of the state space where both p and q are *false*, and *true* elsewhere.

- equivalence $p = q$ is *true* in every point of the state space where p and q have the same value, and *false* elsewhere.

- discrepancy $p \neq q$ is *false* in every point of the state space where p and q have the same value, and *true* elsewhere.

- implication $p \Rightarrow q$ and explication $q \Leftarrow p$ are *false* in every point of the state space where p is *true* and q is *false*, and *true* elsewhere.

- negation $\neg p$ is *false* in every point of the state space where p is *true*, and *true* elsewhere.

It follows that $\vee$, $\wedge$, $=$, and $\neq$ are both symmetric (commutative) and associative; $\Rightarrow$ and $\Leftarrow$ are neither symmetric nor associative. From the fact that $\vee$ is associative, it follows that we need not write any parentheses in $p \vee q \vee r$.

Similarly, from the fact that $=$ is associative, it follows that we need not write any parentheses in $p = q = r$, even though this may surprise you a bit. The associativity of $\neq$ is probably least surprising to electrical engineers who have worked with exclusive or.

The associativity of $=$ is cause for concern, because we are used to thinking of $p = q = r$ as an abbreviation of $p = q \ \wedge \ q = r$. This is similar to $a \leq b \leq c$. We never have a need for reading the latter as $(a \leq b) \leq c$ for numbers a and b and for boolean c because $\leq$ is not defined for booleans. But $=$ is, and it is useful. And $p = q \ \wedge \ q = r$ is completely different from $(p = q) = r$. Just look at $p = false$, $q = false$, and $r = true$. In order to resolve this, we introduce another operator, written $\equiv$. For all p and q, expressions $p \equiv q$ and $p = q$ are equivalent — they have the same boolean value in each point of the state space. We will use $p \equiv q \equiv r$ to stand for the boolean expression that you might also read as $(p \equiv q) \equiv r$ or $p \equiv (q \equiv r)$, whereas $p = q = r$ stands for $p = q \ \wedge \ q = r$. It is the only difference between $\equiv$ and $=$. We will never use associativity of $=$ and $\neq$ but we do use associativity of $\equiv$ and $\not\equiv$. Note that $\equiv$ and $\not\equiv$ are even mutually associative, so that $p \equiv q \not\equiv r$ can be read as either $(p \equiv q) \not\equiv r$ or $p \equiv (q \not\equiv r)$, with the same meaning.

It also follows that $\vee$, $\wedge$, $=$, and $\neq$ have a unit element.

$$(p \vee false) \ = \ p$$
$$(p \wedge true) \ = \ p$$
$$(p = true) \ = \ p$$
$$(p \neq false) \ = \ p$$

We also have the following properties.

$$(p \lor true) = true$$
$$(p \land false) = false$$
$$(p = false) = \neg p$$
$$(p \neq true) = \neg p$$
$$(false \Rightarrow p) = true$$
$$(p \Rightarrow true) = true$$
$$(p \lor p) = p \qquad \text{idempotence of } \lor$$
$$(p \land p) = p \qquad \text{idempotence of } \land$$

To avoid writing lots of parentheses, we introduce a number of precedence rules. We use the conventional priority rules for the arithmetic operators: $*$ binds tighter than $+$, so we may write $x * y + z$ for $(x * y) + z$. The arithmetic infix operators have a higher binding power, or a higher priority, than the boolean infix operators. For example, $+$ binds tighter than $\lor$. Of the boolean operators, $\neg$ binds tightest; next come $\lor$ and $\land$, with the same binding power, and finally $\equiv$, $\not\equiv$, $\Rightarrow$, and $\Leftarrow$, all with the same binding power. Some operators have been given the same binding power in order to preserve a certain symmetry in useful formulae. As a result, we may not write $p \land q \lor r$, because it is not clear whether $(p \land q) \lor r$ or $p \land (q \lor r)$ is meant. The table lists operators in order of decreasing binding power. Operators on the same line have the same binding power. The first line contains the prefix operators, all others are infix operators.

$$\neg \quad + \quad -$$
$$=$$
$$\cdot \quad / \quad \text{div} \quad \text{mod}$$
$$+ \quad -$$
$$\lor \quad \land$$
$$\equiv \quad \not\equiv \quad \Rightarrow \quad \Leftarrow$$

From the definitions, we can derive many algebraic laws. We list some of them. Some of them may be "obvious" while others may be "surprising".

$$(p \Rightarrow q) \equiv \neg p \lor q \qquad \text{definition of } \Rightarrow$$
$$(p \Rightarrow q) \equiv p \lor q \equiv q \qquad \text{definition of } \Rightarrow$$
$$(p \Rightarrow q) \equiv p \land q \equiv p \qquad \text{definition of } \Rightarrow$$
$$p \Rightarrow p \lor q \qquad \text{weakening}$$
$$p \land q \Rightarrow p \qquad \text{weakening}$$
$$p \equiv q \equiv (p \Rightarrow q) \land (q \Rightarrow p) \qquad \text{mutual implication}$$
$$p \land q \equiv p \equiv q \equiv p \lor q \qquad \text{golden rule}$$
$$\neg(p \land q) \equiv \neg p \lor \neg q \qquad \text{De Morgan's rule}$$
$$\neg(p \lor q) \equiv \neg p \land \neg q \qquad \text{De Morgan's rule}$$
$$p \land (q \lor r) \equiv (p \land q) \lor (p \land r) \qquad \text{distribution}$$
$$p \lor (q \land r) \equiv (p \lor q) \land (p \lor r) \qquad \text{distribution}$$
$$p \land (q \not\equiv r) \equiv (p \land q) \not\equiv (p \land r) \qquad \text{distribution}$$

$$p \vee (q \equiv r) \;\equiv\; (p \vee q) \equiv (p \vee r) \qquad \text{distribution}$$
$$p \vee (p \wedge q) \;\equiv\; p \qquad \text{absorption rule}$$
$$p \wedge (p \vee q) \;\equiv\; p \qquad \text{absorption rule}$$
$$p \vee (p \not\equiv q) \;\equiv\; p \vee q \qquad \text{absorption rule}$$
$$p \wedge (p \equiv q) \;\equiv\; p \wedge q \qquad \text{absorption rule}$$
$$p \vee (\neg p \wedge q) \;\equiv\; p \vee q \qquad \text{complement rule}$$
$$p \wedge (\neg p \vee q) \;\equiv\; p \wedge q \qquad \text{complement rule}$$
$$(p \Rightarrow q) \wedge (q \Rightarrow r) \;\Rightarrow\; (p \Rightarrow r) \qquad \text{transitivity}$$

We give the proof of the first absorption rule.

$$p \vee (p \wedge q)$$
$$= \qquad \{ \ true \ \text{is unit element of conjunction} \ \}$$
$$(p \wedge true) \vee (p \wedge q)$$
$$= \qquad \{ \ \text{distribution} \ \}$$
$$p \wedge (true \vee q)$$
$$=$$
$$p \wedge true$$
$$=$$
$$p$$

Because of implication's transitivity, we write proofs in the form

$$p$$
$$\Rightarrow \qquad \{ \ \text{hint why} \ p \Rightarrow q \ \}$$
$$q$$
$$\Rightarrow \qquad \{ \ \text{hint why} \ q \Rightarrow r \ \}$$
$$r$$

to establish $p \Rightarrow r$. We can mix implications and equivalences. Here is an example. The law $(p \Rightarrow q) \;\Rightarrow\; (p \vee r \;\Rightarrow\; q \vee r)$ follows from

$$p \Rightarrow q$$
$$= \qquad \{ \ \text{definition of implication} \ \}$$
$$\neg p \vee q$$
$$\Rightarrow \qquad \{ \ \text{weakening} \ \}$$
$$\neg p \vee q \vee r$$
$$= \qquad \{ \ \text{complement rule} \ \}$$
$$(\neg p \wedge \neg r) \vee q \vee r$$
$$= \qquad \{ \ \text{De Morgan's rule} \ \}$$
$$\neg(p \vee r) \vee q \vee r$$
$$= \qquad \{ \ \text{definition of implication} \ \}$$
$$p \vee r \;\Rightarrow\; q \vee r \qquad .$$

7.6   Formal and Informal Mathematics

The subject of this chapter is (too) often linked to philosophy. So, let me shortly describe two of the philosophies to which people subscribe. I will describe them in terms as close to mathematics as I can get; in the case of physical sciences, the debate seems to be less heated.

The prevailing philosophy is that of platonism. According to the platonist, mathematical objects exist "out there", and all that the mathematician does is discover mathematical truths about them. The way we express those truths may be a result of human involvement, but the truths are independent of us, have always existed, and will always exist.

This point of view has been formulated in an extreme way in a speech by E. Everett delivered at Gettysburg (November 19, 1863), which lasted for hours.

> In the pure mathematics we contemplate absolute truths, which existed in the Divine Mind before the morning stars sang together, and which will continue to exist there, when the last of their radiant host shall have fallen from heaven.

This formulation is not one that I find myself very much attracted to, but that is beside the point. The point is that in this view, mathematical objects exist independent of our knowledge of them — we can discover some of them, but we cannot create any new of our own.

The opposing view is called formalism. The formalist has it that mathematics is created. The definitions and the rules for going from one formula to another are the subject matter. The word "truth" does not play a role in the game, but "provable" does. It means that a definite procedure exists for obtaining some formula from the initially given formulae and a fixed set of inference rules. This is what we usually call a proof. One may study different theories, theories with different sets of rules related to different expressions; or, even, different rules and the same expressions. What can be proved with one set of rules may not be provable, derivable, in the other set. These rules are human creations, each set of rules existing only because someone proposed them and probably found them interesting. This point of view was put forward by D. Hilbert, who wrote

> Mathematics is nothing more than a game played according to certain simple rules with meaningless marks on paper.

I usually have a hard time in making up my mind about these two extreme points of view. (Is it reasonable to expect that the gray stuff in our skull can be characterized by one boolean parameter?) Many arguments in favor of either position can be put forward, but I refrain from doing so.

Not all mathematicians feel at ease with a formal, abstract view of mathematics; neither do all computing scientists feel at ease with a formal view of computing. For example, when we discuss the construction of VLSI circuits, we are looking at concrete silicon structures — not very abstract, right? Partly right. I think that one of the fascinating aspects of computing is that anything can be computed at all without requiring that the executing agent understand what is being computed. The executing agent must be able to apply the rules of the game but need not understand the justification of those rules and need not understand what the objects stand for. In the case of VLSI circuits, the rules have been carefully chosen to coincide with the rules of semiconductor physics. It is a great achievement whenever such a set of rules is created. For example, when we constructed the full adder, we had three boolean inputs and two boolean outputs. We could come up with an interpretation of the booleans as representing one-bit integers and then the boolean expressions would correspond to addition. For the operation of the circuit, however, it is not essential that they stand for numbers.

The correct execution of a computer program, whether it is in hardware or software, does not depend on the interpretation of the quantities that are involved. In order to be able to say objectively that a program is correct, independent of interpretation, we proceed as follows. We first write a specification that we hope captures our intent; this part depends on interpretation. After that, we are finished with interpretation. We can prove that a program is correct with respect to a specification by using inference rules. And this is where we enter the realm of formal mathematics.

It is sometimes said that formalism stifles creativity. The practicing mathematician, the practicing engineer, the practicing programmer should not be constrained by the limitations of the formal methods that they have at their disposal. Of course they shouldn't, but besides complaining about the limitations of formal methods one should also appreciate them for the simplicity of well-chosen abstractions and for the aid offered by their calculational support. And if something can be obtained by calculation instead of by intuition, then the result is usually more reliable. (A well-known joke: compute 2345×9876 by intuition alone.) The use of formal methods often allows one to concentrate one's creativity on those parts where it is required; formalism doesn't stifle creativity, it just makes creativity superfluous in those cases where the formalism can already do the job for you. Focus your creativity on choosing the proper abstractions, on selecting the next step in a proof; don't waste it on routine problems. Experience shows that doing routine problems by calculation is easier than doing them by logical inference rules. I think the main reason is that "replacing equals by equals" is a simple and effective rule, and, therefore, equality is an important thing to have. It also appears to scale better to somewhat larger problems. This is why we prefer to conduct our proofs in a calculational style.

7.7   Bibliographic Notes

The halting problem was first settled by Turing (cf. [Tur36]). Our description of Gödel's Theorem and its relation to the halting problem was inspired by [Heh90] and substantially refined by [Heh92]. Exercise 2 is from this paper also. The "Golden Rule" is from [DS90]. Exercise 7 is due to J. Misra who dubbed it the "Californian Game".

7.8 Exercises

1. Study the following Pascal program. What does the program print when executed? Can you come up with a shorter one that does a similar job? (In order to get a decent listing here, the program was spread out over a number of lines. Read it as a one-line program without inserting any spaces at line boundaries.)

   ```
   program self(output);type xstring=array[1..186]of char;
   ystring=array[1..5]of char;procedure p(q,c:char;x:
   xstring;y:ystring);begin writeln(x,q,q,q,q,c,q,c,q,c,q,x
   ,q,c,q,y,q,y)end;begin p('''',',',','program self(output);
   type xstring=array[1..186]of char;ystring=array[1..5]
   of char;procedure p(q,c:char;x:xstring;y:ystring);
   begin writeln(x,q,q,q,q,c,q,c,q,c,q,x,q,c,q,y,q,y)end;
   begin p(',')end.')end.
   ```

2. Consider function $\mathcal{M}$ defined in this chapter. We introduce a new symbol, say H, for Hehner, and define it to be a string of five characters.

   $$H = \text{'}\neg\text{M(H)'}$$

   We define the effect of $\mathcal{M}$ on string 'H'.

   $$\mathcal{M}(\text{'H'}) = \mathcal{M}(H) = \mathcal{M}(\text{'}\neg\text{M(H)'}) \quad .$$

   Show $\mathcal{M}(H) = \neg\mathcal{M}(H)$.

3. Actually, for Cantor's diagonal argument it is not required that every line consists of an infinite sequence of digits. What is required is that the n th line has at least n digits. Show that checking whether a program prints at least n digits is as hard as checking whether the program halts.

4. Logicians talk about *modus ponens*, mathematicians about *Joe Moe's Theorem*, and physicists about *conservation of momentum*. What does this tell you about their philosophies?

5. Prove

   $$(p \wedge q) \vee r \equiv p \wedge (q \vee r) \equiv (r \Rightarrow p)$$

6. Prove

$$(p \wedge q) \vee (q \wedge r) \vee (r \wedge p) \equiv (p \vee q) \wedge (q \vee r) \wedge (r \vee p)$$
$$(p \Rightarrow q) \equiv (\neg p \Leftarrow \neg q)$$
$$p \wedge (p \Rightarrow q) \equiv p \wedge q$$
$$q \vee (p \Rightarrow q) \equiv p \Rightarrow q$$
$$p \equiv q \equiv (p \wedge q) \vee (\neg p \wedge \neg q)$$

7. In a finite set of married couples (traditional couples consisting of one husband and one wife):

- the oldest man and the oldest woman have the same age;
- for any two married couples, if partners are swapped, then the younger partner in one of the new couples has the same age as the younger partner in the other new couple.

Show that in every married couple, husband and wife have the same age.

8. n light bulbs are arranged in a circle. Each light bulb is either on or off. In the middle of the circle is a push button. Pushing the button has the following effect on the light bulbs:

a light bulb is on after the button is released just when this light bulb and its right-hand neighbor were both on or both off before the button was pressed.

Show that, if n is a power of 2, all light bulbs are on after the button is pushed n times, independent of the initial configuration.

8

Some Programming Heuristics

A good conjurer will not disclose how the tricks are done. In the exposition of the programs that we have encountered before, we have been pretty good conjurers: we did argue the correctness of our programs but we never explained where they came from — like rabbits, they were pulled out of the magician's hat. But a professional programmer is not a conjurer. A programmer should be able to explain how the program was derived, because program design is at the heart of computer science. In this chapter, we discuss a number of heuristics that often, but not always, lead to nice, efficient programs for solving programming problems. The heuristics are illustrated by example, but my real interest is in how heuristics help in designing algorithms. The emphasis is, therefore, on trying to avoid interpreting the formulae but to look at their structure and see what this tells us. Our goal is not to prove the correctness of given programs, the goal is to determine how to construct a program that will do the job, and will do it efficiently. It turns out that thinking about the correctness argument gives clues about what the program might look like. As a result, we discuss the proofs and the programs at the same time. We concentrate on simple programs first, that is, programs that consist of only one loop. The leitmotiv throughout this chapter is: given the specification of what the program is supposed to do, that is, given its pre- and postcondition, develop the invariant relation governing the loop; this is usually the hard part. Next, think of a bound function and a statement inside the loop that will decrease it. Finally, think of statements that maintain the invariant in spite of that change. The programs that we discuss here are of the form

$$\{ \text{ precondition } G \}$$
$$S0;$$
$$*[B \to S]$$
$$\{ \text{ postcondition } R \} \qquad .$$

We are given G and R, and have to come up with the rest, including invariant P of the loop. One of our proof obligations is $\{G\}\ S0\ \{P\}$. Sometimes this gives a clue to what P might look like, but more often than not it doesn't. Another proof obligation is $P \wedge \neg B \Rightarrow R$. This part often does give some insight as to which P to choose, and also which guard B to use in conjunction with P. How R may suggest P is what we discuss next. Here we go.

8.1   Omit a Conjunct

The postcondition is often a conjunction of terms. One possible suggestion is: take some of the conjuncts as invariant and the negation of the others as the guard. Here is an example.

Given natural number N, write a program that assigns to variable a a value that satisfies

$$R: \quad a \geq 0 \ \wedge \ a^2 \leq N \ \wedge \ N < (a+1)^2 \quad .$$

Taking the square root of the last two terms in R, we find that a is to be assigned the largest integer not exceeding $\sqrt{N}$.

Deleting the last conjunct of R leads to a possible invariant

$$P: \quad a \geq 0 \ \wedge \ a^2 \leq N$$

and its companion program skeleton

```
{ N ≥ 0 }
S0; {inv : P }
*[ (a + 1)² ≤ N → S ]
{ R }      .
```

The only variable that we have is a, which does not leave much room for the bound function. Since the only "obvious" initial value for a is 0, it is unavoidable that a is going to be increased somehow. We, therefore, select $N - a^2$ as our bound function. (We might also take $N - a$.) The easiest way to make progress is to increase a by the least amount possible, namely, to increase a by 1. This leads to

```
{ N ≥ 0 }
a := 0; {inv : P }
*[ (a + 1)² ≤ N → a := a + 1 ]
{ R }      .
```

No other statements are needed. We show that P is indeed an invariant of the loop. According to the rule for the loop, the invariance of P follows from

$$\{ P \ \wedge \ B \} \ a := a + 1 \ \{ P \} \quad ,$$

which, according to the rule of assignment, is equivalent to

$$P \ \wedge \ B \ \Rightarrow \ P^a_{a+1} \quad .$$

The proof hereof is

$$
\begin{aligned}
& P^a_{a+1} \\
= \quad & \{ \text{ substitution } \} \\
& a + 1 \geq 0 \ \wedge \ (a+1)^2 \leq N \\
\Leftarrow \quad & \{ \text{ choice of } B \} \\
& P \ \wedge \ B \quad .
\end{aligned}
$$

We omit the proofs that the bound function decreases, that it is bounded from below, and that the initialization establishes P, all of which are quite easy.

Other choices for P and B are possible with this same R. For example, we may select $a \geq 0 \ \wedge \ (a+1)^2 > N$ as invariant and the negation of the remaining term as guard $a^2 > N$. This might lead to the program

$$\{ N \geq 0 \}$$
$$a := N; \ \{inv : (a+1)^2 > N \}$$
$$*[\ a^2 > N \rightarrow a := a - 1 \ ]$$
$$\{ R \}$$

or to the more efficient program in Exercise 3.22.

Another example to which this technique applies is the one we discussed in Chapter 3, computing $q = a$ **div** 3 and $r - 1 = a$ **mod** 3. This postcondition was rewritten to read

$$a = 3 \cdot q + r - 1 \ \wedge \ 0 \leq r - 1 \ \wedge \ r - 1 < 3 \qquad ,$$

the guard was taken to be the negation of the last term, and the invariant was taken to be the conjunction of the first two terms.

Our final example of this technique is called linear search. Given is a boolean array $b[0..N-1]$, $N > 0$, that contains at least one element that is *true*. Find the first occurrence of *true*; that is, write a program to store in variable j the least natural number for which $b[j]$ is *true*. In a formula, the minimization is expressed by writing that $b[j]$ is *true* and that $b[i]$ is *false* for all i less than j.

$$R : \quad 0 \leq j \ \wedge \ \langle \forall i : 0 \leq i < j : \neg b[i] \rangle \ \wedge \ b[j]$$

We may obtain invariant P by omitting the last conjunct of R.

$$P : \quad 0 \leq j \ \wedge \ \langle \forall i : 0 \leq i < j : \neg b[i] \rangle$$

The program reads as follows.

$$j := 0;$$
$$*[\ \neg b[j] \rightarrow j := j + 1 \ ]$$

It is fairly easy to see that execution of $j := j + 1$ under the condition $P \ \wedge \ \neg b[j]$ leads to a state satisfying P, that is, P is an invariant of the loop. The proof of $P \wedge \neg b[j] \ \Rightarrow \ P_{j+1}^{j}$ is:

$$P_{j+1}^{j}$$
$$= \qquad \{ \text{ substitution } \}$$
$$0 \leq j + 1 \ \wedge \ \langle \forall i : 0 \leq i < j + 1 : \neg b[i] \rangle$$
$$\Leftarrow \qquad \{ \text{ strengthen first term } \}$$
$$0 \leq j \ \wedge \ \langle \forall i : 0 \leq i < j + 1 : \neg b[i] \rangle$$
$$= \qquad \{ \ 0 \leq i < j + 1 \ \equiv \ (0 \leq i < j \vee i = j) \ \}$$
$$0 \leq j \ \wedge \ \langle \forall i : 0 \leq i < j \vee i = j : \neg b[i] \rangle$$

$=$ { distribute $\lor$ of range over universal quantification }
$$0 \leq j \;\land\; \langle \forall i : 0 \leq i < j : \neg b[i] \rangle \;\land\; \langle \forall i : i = j : \neg b[i] \rangle$$
$=$ { apply one-point rule to last quantification }
$$0 \leq j \;\land\; \langle \forall i : 0 \leq i < j : \neg b[i] \rangle \;\land\; \neg b[j]$$
$=$ { definition }
$$P \;\land\; \neg b[j] \quad .$$

The steps we made in this proof are minuscule. We rarely bother with so much detail and usually proceed from the second line to the last-line-but-one in a single step. It occurs so frequently, it is so standard, that we take it for granted that the details can be filled in when we are not absolutely sure about a step. The bigger step is still fairly easy to do right.

It is also fairly easy to see that $j := 0$ establishes P, since universal quantification over an empty range is *true*. Quantification over an empty range is something that you should feel most comfortable with because it occurs so often in initializing statements. Make sure that you are familiar with universal quantification over an empty range (*true*), existential quantification over an empty range (*false*), summation over an empty range (0), and product over an empty range (1).

Don't be surprised by this attention to extreme cases: we have to work with the initialization, with the finalization, and with the "general case". The extreme cases are two out of three; they are bound to be important to us (and, fortunately, they will often turn out to be easy).

The example was a solution to the problem of finding the least index where the array element is *true*. Of course, the array can be replaced with an arbitrary boolean function and we can still solve the problem in the same manner, which is known as *linear search*. Here is the principle embodied by linear search.

> To find a minimum value with a given property, check values
> starting from the lower bound in increasing order. When looking
> for a maximum value, check values from the upper bound in
> decreasing order.

A different solution to this problem is to search from the highest index and record the least value j thus far for which $b[j]$ is *true*. The linear search principle tells us not to do so, but to start at the lowest index. One reason is that linear search gives us a slightly simpler program. Another reason is that, in general, it may not be so easy to start at the highest index, since it may not always be a given value. (N was not used in our solution.) And the best reason is that execution of the program would always have to reference all array elements and cannot stop once a *true* element has been found. Linear search provides a program that is both simpler and more efficient.

Where did we use the fact that b contains an element with value *true* ? So far we didn't, and indeed we have not shown that our program terminates. There are two ways for doing this. The hard way is to strengthen the invariant so as to include the given fact. Either

$$0 \leq j \ \wedge \ \langle \forall i : 0 \leq i < j : \neg b[i] \rangle \ \wedge \ \langle \exists i : 0 \leq i < N : b[i] \rangle$$

or

$$0 \leq j \ \wedge \ \langle \forall i : 0 \leq i < j : \neg b[i] \rangle \ \wedge \ \langle \exists i : j \leq i < N : b[i] \rangle$$

will do. The invariance of either of these two can be verified using the rule for the assignment statement. From either of these stronger invariants, we can conclude $j < N$; that is, $N - j$ is bounded from below and makes a perfect bound function. Since $j := j + 1$ decreases the bound function, the loop terminates.

The easier way is to use the fact $\langle \exists i : 0 \leq i < N : b[i] \rangle$ in the proof that $N - j$ is bounded from below. Using a fact that depends only on fixed quantities is good practice. The quantities don't change anyway, so why bother to prove the invariance of such a fact? We will often use our common sense to omit the obvious — but this should never be used as an excuse to omit the nonobvious. For example, we rarely show that the bound function decreases. Progress is often too obvious to waste time and space on. We promise to pay attention when it is nonobvious.

8.2   Replace a Constant by a Variable

Suppose we want a program for storing N^2 in variable x, for given natural number N, using addition as the only arithmetic operation.

$$R: \quad x = N^2$$

A technique for constructing an invariant that is used very often is to replace a constant by a variable. In this case, R contains two constants: N and 2. We opt for replacing N by a variable, n say. Postcondition R has been established when the constant and the variable that took its place are equal: $P \ \wedge \ n = N \Rightarrow R$.

$$P: \quad x = n^2$$

In order to enable initialization , n is set to a small constant, and it is increased in the loop, maintaining $x = n^2$ in every step. Since N might be as small as 0, we let 0 be the smallest value of n also. We strengthen the invariant to include the range of n.

$$P: \quad x = n^2 \ \wedge \ 0 \leq n \leq N$$

The program reads

```
x := 0;  n := 0;
*[ n ≠ N → ...;  n := n + 1 ]        ,
```

where the dots stand for a statement that updates variable x. We prefer to have the increment of n at the end, because that allows us to figure out the pre- and postcondition of the dots: the precondition is $P \land n \neq N$ and the postcondition is P_{n+1}^n. Rewriting this postcondition a bit yields $x = n^2 + 2n + 1$. Comparing this with precondition $x = n^2$ suggests that we substitute statement $x := x + 2n + 1$ for the dots or, without multiplications,

$$x := 0; \quad n := 0;$$
$$*[\, n \neq N \rightarrow x := x + n + n + 1; \quad n := n + 1\,]$$

We have included the term $0 \leq n \leq N$ in the invariant for two reasons. First, the part $n \leq N$ is needed for termination (in combination with bound function $N - n$). Second, in rewriting P_{n+1}^n, one often needs a restriction on the range of n in order to rewrite one of the terms. This was not the case in the present example. Had we considered a summation of n terms, however, say $s = \sum_{i=0}^{n-1} f(i)$, then we would need the fact $n \geq 0$ to rewrite $s = \sum_{i=0}^{n} f(i)$ into $s = \sum_{i=0}^{n-1} f(i) + f(n)$. This "splitting off a term" from a quantification occurs so frequently that we almost automatically insert range restrictions on new variables in the invariant.

Mildly more complicated is the program for computing N^3. Following the line laid out above, we find invariant

$$x = n^3 \land 0 \leq n \leq N \quad ,$$

and we need to come up with a statement whose precondition is $x = n^3$ and postcondition is $x = (n + 1)^3$. The latter can be rewritten as $x = n^3 + 3n^2 + 3n + 1$, which tells us that x is to be increased by $3n^2 + 3n + 1$. In our previous example, the increase of x was $2n + 1$ and this is easily computed from the variable n. The value $3n^2 + 3n + 1$, however, is not so easily derived from n. This is where another heuristic comes in: if a value is needed that is not easily computed from the variables that already occur in the invariant, introduce a fresh variable. The value that is needed is equated to this fresh variable and this equation is added as a new term to the invariant. Let y be the fresh variable. Our next invariant becomes

$$x = n^3 \land y = 3n^2 + 3n + 1 \land 0 \leq n \leq N \quad ,$$

and we find that we need to update y also, setting it to $3(n+1)^2 + 3(n+1) + 1$. This being equal to $3n^2 + 3n + 1 + 6n + 6$, we add one more variable,

$$x = n^3 \land y = 3n^2 + 3n + 1 \land z = 6n + 6 \land 0 \leq n \leq N$$

and obtain the program

$$x, y, z := 0, 1, 6; \quad n := 0;$$
$$*[\, n \neq N \rightarrow x, y, z := x + y, y + z, z + 6; \quad n := n + 1\,] \quad .$$

The term $3n^2 + 3n + 1$ is sometimes referred to as the first (discrete) derivative of the term n^3, because it represents the difference between $(n+1)^3$ and n^3.

Here is another example to which the heuristic of adding new variables to the invariant applies. Given array $a[0..N-1]$, $N \geq 0$, all of whose elements are either 0 or 1, write a program for computing the number of pairs i, j in the range $0 \leq i < j < N$ for which $a[i] = 0 \ \wedge \ a[j] = 1$. We use quantifier $\mathbf{N}$ for denoting such a number. For example,

$$\langle \mathbf{N} i : 0 \leq i < 10 : odd(i) \rangle$$

denotes the number of odd values for bound variable i, taken from the range $0 \leq i < 10$. (It is 5.) The postcondition can thus be written as

$$R: \quad x = \langle \mathbf{N} i, j : 0 \leq i < j < N : a[i] = 0 \wedge a[j] = 1 \rangle \quad .$$

Replacing constant N by variable n, we obtain our first invariant.

$$P: \quad x = \langle \mathbf{N} i, j : 0 \leq i < j < n : a[i] = 0 \wedge a[j] = 1 \rangle \ \wedge$$
$$0 \leq n \leq N$$

Increasing n by 1 leads to a state satisfying P, provided that P^n_{n+1} in the state prior to the increase. (We ignore the range of n for a moment.)

$$P^n_{n+1}$$
$$= \qquad \{ \text{ substitution } \}$$
$$x = \langle \mathbf{N} i, j : 0 \leq i < j < n+1 : a[i] = 0 \wedge a[j] = 1 \rangle$$
$$= \qquad \{ \text{ split range of } j \text{ in two disjoint parts } \}$$
$$x = \langle \mathbf{N} i, j : 0 \leq i < j < n : a[i] = 0 \wedge a[j] = 1 \rangle$$
$$\quad + \langle \mathbf{N} i, j : 0 \leq i < j = n : a[i] = 0 \wedge a[j] = 1 \rangle$$
$$= \qquad \{ \text{ eliminate } j \text{ from last line } (j = n) \ \}$$
$$x = \langle \mathbf{N} i, j : 0 \leq i < j < n : a[i] = 0 \wedge a[j] = 1 \rangle$$
$$\quad + \langle \mathbf{N} i : 0 \leq i < n : a[i] = 0 \wedge a[n] = 1 \rangle$$

We might be tempted to introduce a variable whose value equals the last term. However, there is a problem since this term depends on $a[n]$. After the last step, we have $n = N$ and $a[n]$ is undefined. This means that the last step sets this fresh variable to an undefined value, and we may expect trouble. Observe, however, that term $\langle \mathbf{N} i : 0 \leq i < n : a[i] = 0 \wedge a[n] = 1 \rangle$ equals 0 if $a[n] \neq 1$ and equals $\langle \mathbf{N} i : 0 \leq i < n : a[i] = 0 \rangle$ if $a[n] = 1$. Since $\langle \mathbf{N} i : 0 \leq i < n : a[i] = 0 \rangle$ does not depend on $a[n]$ it is a more promising candidate for inclusion in the invariant. We therefore decide to strengthen the invariant with condition

$$Q: \quad y = \langle \mathbf{N} i : 0 \leq i < n : a[i] = 0 \rangle$$

to make the update of x doable. We have to look at the update of y also.

$$Q_{n+1}^n$$
$$= \quad \{ \text{ substitution } \}$$
$$y = \langle \mathbf{N} i : 0 \le i < n+1 : a[i] = 0 \rangle$$
$$= \quad \{ \text{ split range of } i \text{ into two disjoint parts } \}$$
$$y = \langle \mathbf{N} i : 0 \le i < n : a[i] = 0 \rangle + \langle \mathbf{N} i : i = n : a[i] = 0 \rangle$$

The last term is 1 if $a[n] = 0$, and 0 otherwise. This yields our final program.

$$x, y := 0, 0; \ n := 0;$$
$$*[\ n \ne N \to [a[n] = 0 \to y := y+1 \ | \ a[n] = 1 \to x := x + y];$$
$$n := n+1$$
$$]$$

Our next example is more complicated. It is sort of a convolution of Fibonacci numbers, hence its name: Fibolucci. Given integers x and y, not necessarily positive, we define f by

$$f(0) \ = \ 0;$$
$$f(1) \ = \ 1;$$
$$f(i+2) \ = \ x \cdot f(i) + y \cdot f(i+1) \ \text{ for all } \ i \ge 0.$$

The problem is to compute

$$\langle \sum i : 0 \le i < N : f(i) \cdot f(N-i) \rangle$$

for given $N \ge 0$. Replacing constant N in the postcondition by variable n produces an invariant.

$$P0: \quad a = \langle \sum i : 0 \le i < n : f(i) \cdot f(n-i) \rangle \ \wedge \ 0 \le n \le N$$

We have replaced both occurrences of N by n. Sometimes replacing one of them will do; in this case, we would get stuck soon, and replacing both turns out to be the better choice. Let's do our calculations.

$$P0_{n+1}^n$$
$$= \quad \{ \text{ substitution } \}$$
$$a = \langle \sum i : 0 \le i < n+1 : f(i) \cdot f(n+1-i) \rangle$$
$$= \quad \{ \text{ we cannot apply the recurrence to } f \text{ because of }$$
$$\text{the range of } i, \text{ but we can split off a term } \}$$
$$a = \langle \sum i : 0 \le i < n : f(i) \cdot f(n+1-i) \rangle$$
$$+ f(n)$$
$$= \quad \{ \text{ we cannot split off a term because of the range of } i,$$
$$\text{but we can apply the recurrence } \}$$
$$a = \langle \sum i : 0 \le i < n : f(i) \cdot (x \cdot f(n-1-i) + y \cdot f(n-i)) \rangle$$
$$+ f(n)$$
$$= \quad \{ \text{ split summation into two terms;}$$
$$\text{move constant factors outside summation } \}$$
$$a = x \cdot \langle \sum i : 0 \le i < n : f(i) \cdot f(n-1-i) \rangle$$
$$+ y \cdot \langle \sum i : 0 \le i < n : f(i) \cdot f(n-i) \rangle \rangle + f(n)$$

The new term in this formula is the first summation (the second one is already in $P0$), so we allocate a fresh variable to it,

$$P1: \quad b = \langle \sum i : 0 \le i < n : f(i) \cdot f(n-1-i) \rangle \quad ,$$

and we calculate $P1_{n+1}^n$.

$$
\begin{aligned}
& P1_{n+1}^n \\
=\; & \{ \text{ substitution } \} \\
& b = \langle \sum i : 0 \le i < n+1 : f(i) \cdot f(n-i) \rangle \\
=\; & \{ \; f(n-n) = 0 \; \} \\
& b = \langle \sum i : 0 \le i < n : f(i) \cdot f(n-i) \rangle
\end{aligned}
$$

The latter summation is one we've seen before: it equals a in $P0$. There was another new term in $P0_{n+1}^n$, namely $f(n)$; it is taken care of by adding variable c and extend the invariant with $c = f(n)$, which in turn requires a term for $f(n+1)$. The last conjunct of the invariant, therefore, reads

$$P2: \quad c = f(n) \; \land \; d = f(n+1) \quad .$$

The program is

```
a, b, c, d := 0, 0, 0, 1;  n := 0;
*[ n ≠ N → a, b, c, d := x · b + y · a + c, a, d, x · c + y · d;
           n := n + 1
 ]   .
```

We consider another example of the technique of replacing a constant with a variable. It is known as the *maximum segment sum* problem. Given is integer array $a[0..N-1]$, $N \ge 0$. A *segment* is a contiguous subsequence of the array. A segment may even be the empty subsequence or the whole array. Every segment has a sum: the sum of all integers in it. Write a program for computing the maximum of all those segment sums. For example, if the array is the sequence $4, 3, -12, 2, 3, -2, 5$, then the maximum segment sum is 8 (for the segment $2, 3, -2, 5$). The program need not figure out which segment assumes the maximum sum, since only the value of that maximum is called for. The maximum segment sum is uniquely determined by the array, while there may be many segments that assume this same maximal sum.

We define $f(i,j)$ to be the sum of all the numbers in the segment from i up to and excluding j; that is, $f(i,j) = \langle \sum h : i \le h < j : a[h] \rangle$ for all $0 \le i \le j \le N$. Postcondition R is written as follows.

$$R: \quad s = \langle \mathbf{MAX} i,j : 0 \le i \le j \le N : f(i,j) \rangle$$

Replacing constant N by variable n suggests

$$P: \quad s = \langle \mathbf{MAX} i,j : 0 \le i \le j \le n : f(i,j) \rangle \; \land \; 0 \le n \le N$$

as a first shot at the invariant. The corresponding bound function is

$$bf: \quad N - n \quad ,$$

and the program is going to be

$$s, n := 0, 0; \quad \{ P \}$$
$$*[\, n \neq N \rightarrow s := \ldots; \ n := n + 1 \,]$$

We compute P_{n+1}^n to find the proper assignment to s.

$$P_{n+1}^n$$
$$=\qquad \{ \text{ substitution } \}$$
$$s = \langle \textbf{MAX} i, j : 0 \leq i \leq j \leq n + 1 : f(i,j) \rangle \ \wedge \ 0 \leq n + 1 \leq N$$
$$\Leftarrow\qquad \{ \text{ domain split; strengthen } 0 \leq n + 1 \ \}$$
$$s = \max \, (\langle \textbf{MAX} i, j : 0 \leq i \leq j \leq n : f(i,j) \rangle$$
$$, \langle \textbf{MAX} i, j : 0 \leq i \leq j = n + 1 : f(i,j) \rangle) \ \wedge$$
$$0 \leq n < N$$
$$=\qquad \{ \text{ eliminate } j \text{ from last quantification } \}$$
$$s = \max \, (\langle \textbf{MAX} i, j : 0 \leq i \leq j \leq n : f(i,j) \rangle$$
$$, \langle \textbf{MAX} i : 0 \leq i \leq n + 1 : f(i, n + 1) \rangle) \ \wedge$$
$$0 \leq n < N$$

At this point it is tempting to introduce a variable whose value equals the last quantification. However, if we add

$$r = \langle \textbf{MAX} i : 0 \leq i \leq n + 1 : f(i, n + 1) \rangle$$

to the invariant, we have a problem. The problem is that the invariant admits $n = N$ as a value for n and expression $f(i, n + 1)$ is undefined if $n = N$ (since $a[N]$ is undefined). Therefore, we cannot add this term to the invariant; the last iteration of the loop is bound to refer to a nonexisting array element. Instead, we continue our simplification of P_{n+1}^n from the point where we stopped. We focus on the last quantification. The problem with $n = N$ does not occur in this simplification, because we have $n < N$ here.

$$\langle \textbf{MAX} i : 0 \leq i \leq n + 1 : f(i, n + 1) \rangle$$
$$=\qquad \{ \text{ split range of } i \ \}$$
$$\max(\langle \textbf{MAX} i : 0 \leq i \leq n : f(i, n + 1) \rangle, f(n + 1, n + 1))$$
$$=\qquad \{ \ f(n + 1, n + 1) = 0 \ \}$$
$$\max(\langle \textbf{MAX} i : 0 \leq i \leq n : f(i, n + 1) \rangle, 0)$$
$$=\qquad \{ \ f(i, n + 1) = f(i, n) + a[n] \text{ for } i \leq n \ \}$$
$$\max(\langle \textbf{MAX} i : 0 \leq i \leq n : f(i, n) + a[n] \rangle, 0)$$
$$=\qquad \{ \ + \text{ distributes over } \textbf{MAX} \ \}$$
$$\max(\langle \textbf{MAX} i : 0 \leq i \leq n : f(i, n) \rangle + a[n], 0)$$

Can we introduce a variable whose value equals the quantification in this last line? Term $\langle \mathbf{MAX}i : 0 \leq i \leq n : f(i,n) \rangle$ includes well-defined values only, even if $n = N$ and therefore we can strengthen the invariant with

$$Q: \quad r = \langle \mathbf{MAX}i : 0 \leq i \leq n : f(i,n) \rangle$$

and we have the following program.

$$r, s, n := 0, 0; \quad \{ \ P \ \}$$
$$*[\ n \neq N \rightarrow r, s := \ldots, \max(s, r + a[n], 0); \ n := n+1 \ ]$$

We still have to calculate the update of r

$$\begin{aligned} &Q^n_{n+1} \\ = \quad &\{ \text{ substitution } \} \\ &r = \langle \mathbf{MAX}i : 0 \leq i \leq n+1 : f(i, n+1) \rangle \end{aligned}$$

and find exactly the same formula as we had before. The program is, therefore

$$r, s, n := 0, 0, 0; \quad \{ \ P \ \wedge \ Q \ \}$$
$$*[n \neq N \rightarrow r, s := \max(r + a[n], 0), \max(s, r + a[n], 0); \ n := n+1]$$

which may be rewritten to

$$r, s, n := 0, 0, 0; \quad \{ \ P \ \wedge \ Q \ \}$$
$$*[n \neq N \rightarrow r := \max(r + a[n], 0); \ s := \max(s, r); \ n := n+1]$$

Bound function $N - n$ is bounded from below because the invariant contains the term $n \leq N$. It decreases by one in every step of the iteration.

Here is the verification of the same solution in English rather than in formulae. We check all items that need to be proved, but present an a posteriori proof rather than a simultaneous derivation of program and proof. It has been included only to give you the opportunity for comparing formalism and text. The main reason for not giving all proofs in this style is the lack of rules for English proofs, and the danger of ambiguity.

We define the maximum sum of any segment terminating in $n - 1$ to be the maximum sum of any segment whose rightmost element has index $n - 1$. We include in this category the empty segment with sum 0 that is located between $n - 1$ and n. We define the maximum segment sum to the left of n to be the maximum sum over all segments terminating in an index that is less than n. Postcondition R, invariant P, and bound function bf are as follows.

$R:$ $s = $ the maximum segment sum to the left of N
$P:$ $s = $ the maximum segment sum to the left of n,
    $r = $ the maximum sum of any segment terminating in $n - 1$,
    n is in the range from 0 through N
$bf:$ $N - n$

The program is

$$r, s, n := 0, 0, 0; \quad \{ P \}$$
$$*[\, n \neq N \rightarrow r := \max(r + a[n], 0); \quad s := \max(s, r); \quad n := n + 1 \,]$$

and the verification proceeds as follows:

- initialization

$$P^{r,s,n}_{0,0,0}$$

$=$ { substitution }
0 = the maximum segment sum to the left of 0,
0 = the maximum sum of any segment terminating in -1,
0 is in the range from 0 through N

$=$ { both maxima involve the empty segment between -1 and 0 only }

$N \geq 0$

- finalization

$$P \;\wedge\; n = N \;\Rightarrow\; R \text{ is immediate}$$

- invariance of P

$$((P^n_{n+1})^s_{max(s,r)})^r_{max(r+a[n],0)}$$

$=$ { substitution }
$\max(s, \max(r + a[n], 0)) =$
     the maximum segment sum to the left of $n + 1$,
$\max(r + a[n], 0) =$
     the maximum sum of any segment terminating in n,
$n + 1$ is in the range from 0 through N

$\Leftarrow$ { domain split; strengthen range restriction of n }
$\max(s, r + a[n], 0) =$ the maximum of two things:
     the maximum segment sum to the left of n and
     the maximum sum of any segment terminating in n,
$\max(r + a[n], 0) =$
     the maximum sum of any segment terminating in n,
n is in the range from 0 through $N - 1$

$=$ { domain split }
$\max(s, r + a[n], 0) =$ the maximum of three things:
     the maximum segment sum to the left of n and
     $a[n] +$ the maximum sum of any segment terminating
         in $n - 1$ and
     the sum of the empty segment between $n - 1$ and n,
$\max(r + a[n], 0) =$ the maximum of two things:
     $a[n] +$ the maximum sum of any segment terminating
         in $n - 1$ and
     the sum of the empty segment between $n - 1$ and n,
n is in the range from 0 through $N - 1$

$$\Leftarrow \quad \{ \text{ definition of } P; \text{ calculus } \}$$
$$P \ \wedge \ n \neq N$$

- *bf* bounded

$$P \ \Rightarrow \ bf \geq 0$$

- termination

    bf is decreased by 1 in every step of the iteration.

We conclude this section with a description of *binary search*. It is an algorithm that every programmer should know, because it is both simple and efficient. Linear search takes N steps in the worst case and $N/2$ steps in the average case, but binary search takes $\log_2(N)$ steps. However, it is also an algorithm that one easily gets wrong, as testified by many published incorrect solutions.

We are given integer array $a[M..N]$, $M < N$, and integer x. It is given that $a[M] \leq x < a[N]$. Eventually we will need the property that a is sorted (monotonically nondecreasing), but we postpone this as long as possible. The program should store in variable i a value for which

$$R: \quad M \leq i < N \ \wedge \ a[i] \leq x < a[i+1]$$

holds. We obtain our invariant by replacing constant 1 with a variable, and this variable is also the bound function. In fact, the formulae come out a bit nicer if we replace $i+1$ with a variable.

$$P: \quad M \leq i < j \leq N \ \wedge \ a[i] \leq x < a[j]$$
$$bf: \quad j - i$$

The idea of binary search is to reduce the size of the interval i through j because we are done if the size thereof equals 1. This suggests the following program. Condition $i < m < j$ is inserted to make sure that the bound function decreases; we will not check this part.

$$i, j := M, N;$$
$$*[\ j \neq i+1 \rightarrow m := \cdots; \ \{ \ i < m < j \ \}$$
$$[\ \cdots \rightarrow i := m$$
$$[\!] \ \cdots \rightarrow j := m$$
$$]\qquad\qquad]$$

It remains to fill out the dots. First, let us compute the guards of the if-statement. The first alternative selects $i := m$ and therefore we compute

$$P^i_m$$
$$= \qquad \{ \text{ substitution } \}$$
$$M \leq m < j \leq N \ \wedge \ a[m] \leq x < a[j]$$
$$\Leftarrow \qquad \{ \text{ definition of } P \ \}$$
$$P \ \wedge \ i < m < j \ \wedge \ a[m] \leq x \qquad .$$

The second alternative selects $j := m$ and we have

$$P^j_m$$

$$= \quad \{ \text{ substitution } \}$$
$$M \leq i < m \leq N \ \wedge \ a[i] \leq x < a[m]$$
$$\Leftarrow \quad \{ \text{ definition of } P \}$$
$$P \ \wedge \ i < m < j \ \wedge \ x < a[m] \quad .$$

(We did not need the monotonicity of array a here.) All that remains to be done is to select the value to be assigned to m. The value should be between i and j, given $j - i > 1$. One expression that will do is $i + 1$, and $j - 1$ is another. For reasons of efficiency, we choose yet another expression. The quintessence of binary search is to reduce the size of the interval i through j by dropping the part that is to the left of m or to the right of m. In the worst case, the smaller of the two parts is dropped, and therefore the smaller of the two should be as big as possible. This can be realized by choosing both parts the same size. Assignment $m := (i + j)$ **div** 2 will do just that, which yields the following program.

$$i, j := M, N;$$
$$*[\ j \neq i + 1 \rightarrow m := (i + j) \textbf{ div } 2; \ \{ \ i < m < j \ \}$$
$$\qquad [\ a[m] \leq x \ \rightarrow i := m$$
$$\qquad \| \ x < a[m] \ \rightarrow j := m$$
$$\ ] \qquad\qquad\quad]$$

Many variations of binary search exist, some of them right, most of them wrong. One of the errors that is often made is to terminate the loop when i and j are equal. Termination of the algorithm is ensured not by postulating $i < m < j$ (which is impossible if $j = i + 1$) but the weaker $i \leq m < j$. The assignment to j is then replaced with $j := m - 1$. However, $(i + j)$ **div** $2 < j$ then depends on the fact that **div** rounds down instead of up. In many cases, **div** is defined to round toward 0, which is down if $i + j > 0$ and up if $i + j < 0$. (Remember that M might have been negative.) If division by two is implemented by shifting, and if the machine uses two's complement notation, it rounds down for both positive and negative arguments. Therefore, some of the algorithms fail to terminate under certain conditions. The algorithm we gave is insensitive to the direction of rounding.

Binary search is often used to check for the presence or absence of a given integer in a given array. How can our algorithm be used to do just that? Obviously, if the algorithm terminates with $a[i] = x$ then x occurs in the array. What if $a[i] \neq x$? In order to conclude that x does not occur in the array if it does not occur at index i, we need monotonicity. If a is monotonically nondecreasing, and given that $a[i] \leq x < a[i + 1]$, we conclude that $a[i] \neq x$ implies that x does not occur in the array. This is the only place where we need the monotonicity.

8.3 Enlarge the Range of a Variable

We start this section with an alternative correctness proof of linear search.
It is a different proof of correctness of the same program. The attraction of
this proof is that the complicated part of the invariant disappears. The key
is to introduce a name for an object that plays an essential role, in this case
the least index for which $b[i]$ is *true*. All the complexity is concentrated
in this name. Let us use the name k for this index. We then have that k
satisfies

$$0 \leq k \ \land \ \langle \forall i : 0 \leq i < k : \neg b[i] \rangle \ \land \ b[k] \quad .$$

The program is supposed to store k in variable j, of course without using
k in the program. We may, however, use k in the proof. The invariant
that we come up with is, in this case, obtained by weakening postcondition
$j = k$ to invariant

$$Q: \quad 0 \leq j \leq k \quad ,$$

which enlarges the range of j. Bound function bf is $k - j$. Here is the
proof. It is given in full detail to show that nothing has been left out from
the invariant, even though it looks, and is, so simple. The program is

$$j := 0; \ * [\ \neg b[j] \rightarrow j := j + 1 \ ] \quad .$$

The loop invariant is established initially.

$$
\begin{aligned}
& Q_0^j \\
= \quad & \{ \text{ substitution } \} \\
& 0 \leq 0 \leq k \\
= \quad & \{ \ k \text{ is given to be at least } 0 \ \} \\
& true
\end{aligned}
$$

The loop maintains the invariant and decreases the bound function.

$$
\begin{aligned}
& Q_{j+1}^j \ \land \ bf_{j+1}^j < BF \\
= \quad & \{ \text{ substitution } \} \\
& 0 \leq j + 1 \leq k \ \land \ k - j - 1 < BF \\
\Leftarrow \quad & \{ \text{ arithmetic } \} \\
& 0 \leq j \leq k \ \land \ j \neq k \ \land \ k - j - 1 < BF \\
\Leftarrow \quad & \{ \text{ from the definition of } k, \text{ we have } \neg b[j] \Rightarrow j \neq k \ \} \\
& Q \ \land \ \neg b[j] \ \land \ bf = BF
\end{aligned}
$$

The bound function is bounded from below.

$$
\begin{aligned}
& k - j \geq 0 \\
= \quad & \{ \text{ definition of } Q \ \} \\
& true
\end{aligned}
$$

The loop establishes the postcondition.

$$
\begin{aligned}
&\quad Q \;\wedge\; b[j] \\
&= \quad \{ \text{ definition of } Q \ \} \\
&\quad 0 \le j \le k \;\wedge\; b[j] \\
&= \quad \{ \text{ definition of } k \ \} \\
&\quad j = k
\end{aligned}
$$

Next we do a two-dimensional version of this problem. David Gries dubbed this problem *Saddleback Search*. Given is integer x, that occurs in matrix $a[0..m-1, 0..n-1]$. Furthermore, it is given that each row of a is in ascending order and each column is in descending order; that is, $a[i,j] \le a[i,j+1]$ and $a[i,j] \ge a[i+1,j]$, for appropriate i and j. Construct a program to store values in variables i and j satisfying $a[i,j] = x$. If x occurs more than once in a, it does not matter which occurrence is selected.

We solve this problem by introducing names I and J for the indices of some occurrence of x in a; that is, $a[I, J] = x$. This is not necessarily the index pair that will be stored in the variables i and j, but it is a pair that has the property. The invariant we have is

$$P: \quad 0 \le i \le I \;\wedge\; 0 \le j \le J$$

and the bound function is

$$J - j + I - i \quad .$$

Obviously, assignment $i, j := 0, 0$ can be used to establish P. Next we calculate under which condition i can be increased by 1.

$$
\begin{aligned}
&\quad P_{i+1}^{i} \\
&= \quad \{ \text{ substitution } \} \\
&\quad 0 \le i+1 \le I \;\wedge\; 0 \le j \le J \\
&\Leftarrow \quad \{ \text{ calculus } \} \\
&\quad 0 \le i < I \;\wedge\; 0 \le j \le J \\
&\Leftarrow \quad \{ \text{ columns are descending: } a[i,j] > a[I,j] \Rightarrow i < I \ \} \\
&\quad a[i,j] > a[I,j] \;\wedge\; 0 \le i \;\wedge\; 0 \le j \le J \\
&\Leftarrow \quad \{ \text{ rows are ascending: } a[I,J] \ge a[I,j] \text{ for } 0 \le j \le J \ \} \\
&\quad a[i,j] > a[I,J] \;\wedge\; 0 \le i \;\wedge\; 0 \le j \le J \\
&= \quad \{ \text{ definition of } I \text{ and } J: a[I,J] = x \ \} \\
&\quad a[i,j] > x \;\wedge\; 0 \le i \;\wedge\; 0 \le j \le J \\
&\Leftarrow \quad \{ \text{ definition of } P \ \} \\
&\quad P \;\wedge\; a[i,j] > x
\end{aligned}
$$

Hence, $a[i,j] > x \to i := i+1$ is a guarded command that maintains P. By symmetry, $a[i,j] < x \to j := j+1$ maintains P also. (Check it; why does the inequality come out different?) We have now verified that

$$
\begin{aligned}
&i, j := 0, 0; \\
&*[\, a[i,j] > x \to i := i+1 \ [\!] \ a[i,j] < x \to j := j+1 \,]
\end{aligned}
$$

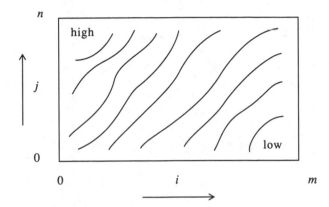

FIGURE 8.1. Lines of constant altitude in a.

establishes and maintains P. What condition do we have upon termination of the loop? From the negation of the two guards, we have $a[i,j] = x$, which is exactly the postcondition that we are after! We do not even need the invariant for this conclusion — it's sole purpose is to show that the bound function is bounded. We cannot assert $i = I \; \wedge \; j = J$ upon termination if x occurs more than once in the array. From P and the definition of I and J, we may conclude that the final value of i,j is the occurrence of x that is closest to $0,0$. (Check that you understand why this is the case.)

A completely different way of tackling the saddleback search is not to name a position at which x occurs, but to maintain invariant

$$x \in a[i..m-1, j..n-1] \; \wedge \; i \geq 0 \; \wedge \; j \geq 0 \quad .$$

It works equally well, leads to the same program, but requires longer formulae. Sometimes this kind of formula is unavoidable; in fact, it is a technique that we explore in the next section.

We have chosen to initialize i,j to $0,0$ and have both i and j increase. Since a matrix has four extremes, four corners, one may wonder whether it is possible to start in any of those and then "work inwards". The answer is no: it is possible to start from two of the four, and it doesn't work from the other two. Why is that? It all depends on the sortedness of the array. In this case, the array was given to be ascending in j and descending in i. We may then draw a picture like that in Figure 8.1. The wiggly lines are isometrics, lines of constant altitude when taking $a[i,j]$ as the altitude in position i,j. (The technical term for isometrics is bath tub rings, but the term is not appropriate here because we have assumed our matrix a to be monotonic: no rings allowed.) Saddleback search can be understood as a walk along a slope near an isometric: whenever the present altitude is too

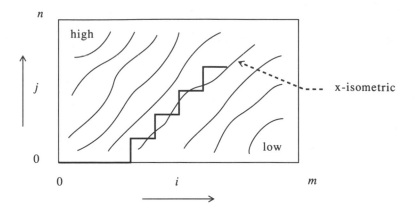

FIGURE 8.2. Path followed by saddleback search.

high, $a[i, j] > x$, the step is down, whenever it is too low, $a[i, j] < x$, the step is up. In the present case, up is either an increase of j or a decrease of i; down is either an increase of i or a decrease of j. The bound function (or, equivalently, the choice of the starting point) tells us in either case which of the two possible actions to choose: one of them decreases the bound function (that's the one we need) and the other one increases it (corresponding to retracing our steps). Figure 8.2 illustrates the process in action. The saddleback-search technique requires a walk near an isometric; that is, in the present case, starting at the left bottom or right top and going towards the opposite corner. It does not work if a walk is attempted that is orthogonal to the isometrics.

8.4   Reduce the Problem Size

In Chapter 3, we gave Euclid's algorithm for computing the greatest common divisor of two given positive integer numbers.

$$*[\ a > b \rightarrow a := a - b \ \|\ b > a \rightarrow b := b - a\ ]$$

How do we prove the correctness of this algorithm? The key idea is that a and b change while the greatest common divisor $\gcd(a, b)$ of a and b remains the same. To express this property, we introduce two auxiliary constants, A and B, that are the initial values of variables a and b. The program is to compute $\gcd(A, B)$. The invariant is

$$P:\quad \gcd(A, B) = \gcd(a, b) \ \wedge\ a > 0 \ \wedge\ b > 0$$

and the bound function is

$$bf : \quad a + b \quad .$$

The verification of the loop is straightforward. We check one alternative, and the other one follows by symmetry.

$$
\begin{aligned}
&\quad P^a_{a-b} \;\wedge\; bf^a_{a-b} < BF \\
=&\qquad \{ \text{ substitution } \} \\
&\quad \gcd(A,B) = \gcd(a-b,b) \;\wedge\; a - b > 0 \wedge b > 0 \;\wedge\; a < BF \\
\Leftarrow&\qquad \{\; \gcd(a,b) = \gcd(a-b,b) \;\} \\
&\quad P \;\wedge\; a > b \;\wedge\; a + b = BF
\end{aligned}
$$

The conclusion $a = \gcd(A,B)$ upon termination of the loop follows from the negation of the guards (together they imply $a = b$) and the invariant, in combination with the property $a = \gcd(a,a)$.

The general technique behind this solution is to reduce the problem size while maintaining a simple relation between the solutions of the big problem and the reduced problem. The reduction is performed repeatedly until the reduced problem has a "trivial" solution. In this case, the solutions to the general and the reduced problems are equal; sometimes we have to add another quantity, which is given by an additional variable. As an example, you may think of adding up the elements of an array. (Yes, replacing a constant by a variable will do just as well in this case.) The invariant is

$$
\begin{aligned}
&\langle \textstyle\sum i : 0 \le i < N : a[i] \rangle = s + \langle \textstyle\sum i : k \le i < N : a[i] \rangle \\
&\wedge\; 0 \le k \le N \quad .
\end{aligned}
$$

It expresses that the required sum is the same as adding s to the summation of the tail part of the array, the part from k on. The bound function is $N - k$ and the program is

```
s := 0;  k := 0;
*[ k ≠ N → s := s + a[k];  k := k + 1 ]
```

The "competing" invariant is

$$s = \langle \textstyle\sum i : 0 \le i < k : a[i] \rangle \;\wedge\; 0 \le k \le N \quad ,$$

and it is easily shown to be equivalent to the one we have used — it just looks a bit different. In other cases, it may make a real difference. Here is an example.

We are given natural number N and we want a program for computing the sum of the digits of N in its decimal representation. We submit that function ds returns the digit-sum of its argument.

$$
\begin{aligned}
&ds(0) = 0 \\
&ds(n) = ds(n \textbf{ div } 10) + n \textbf{ mod } 10 \qquad\qquad \text{for all } n > 0
\end{aligned}
$$

Using ds, we may write the postcondition as $x = ds(N)$. The invariant is

$$P: \quad ds(N) = x + ds(n) \ \wedge \ 0 \le n \le N,$$

that is, the original problem (namely, to compute $ds(N)$) is reduced to a related problem (to compute $ds(n)$) and the difference between the two solutions is stored in a variable (namely, x). The program, which you probably saw in a flash, is

```
x := 0;  n := N;
*[ n ≠ 0 → x := x + n mod 10;  n := n div 10 ]    .
```

An invariant of the form $x = ds(n)$ doesn't fly; we really need the other kind.

The next example that we try is somewhat related to saddleback search. Given integer x and matrix $a[0..M-1, 0..N-1]$, we are going to construct a program for counting how often x occurs as an element of the array. Rows and columns are sorted according to $a[i,j] < a[i,j+1]$ and $a[i,j] > a[i+1,j]$, for appropriate i and j. (This time we are not given that x occurs at least once; instead we are to count the number of occurrences.) We solve this problem by reducing the problem size. In this particular case, we are asked to count the number of x's in a given rectangular region of size $M \times N$. We reduce the problem to counting the number of x's in a smaller rectangular region and add variable k to the outcome thereof to give the number for the $M \times N$ region. We use constant K to stand for the number of x's in the large region.

$$K = \langle \mathbf{N}i, j : 0 \le i < M \wedge 0 \le j < N : a[i,j] = x \rangle$$

The invariant can be written as follows.

$$P: \quad K = k + \langle \mathbf{N}i, j : m \le i < M \wedge n \le j < N : a[i,j] = x \rangle$$
$$\wedge \ 0 \le m \le M \ \wedge \ 0 \le n \le N$$
$$bf: \quad M - m + N - n$$

We always try to make initialization as simple as possible. The left-hand side contains K, the number of x's in the $M \times N$ region, and, therefore, we'd better make sure that the counting in the right-hand side is over the same $M \times N$ region. This suggests setting m, n to $0, 0$ and, hence, k to 0 initially. Upon termination we want to have $K = k$; that is, variable k is the answer. In order to achieve $K = k$, we need the count of x's over the smaller region to be 0, which is best achieved by letting the region be empty. This is implied by $m = M \vee n = N$. The stronger $m = M \wedge n = N$ is not necessary; a rectangular area is empty if either its height or its width is zero. Since $m = n = 0$ initially, the body of the loop contains statements to increase m, or n, or both. We have now established that the program is going to look something like

$$k := 0; \quad m, n := 0, 0;$$
$$*[\ m \neq M \wedge n \neq N \rightarrow [\ \cdots \rightarrow m := m + 1$$
$$\qquad\qquad\qquad\qquad\qquad\| \ \cdots \rightarrow n := n + 1$$
$$\qquad\qquad\qquad\qquad\qquad\| \ \cdots \rightarrow k, m, n := k + 1, m + 1, n + 1$$
$$\ ] \qquad\qquad\qquad\qquad\quad]$$

and we have to think of conditions for the dots such that the statements maintain the invariant. (We have made a bold guess that k is also going to be increased in one of the three alternatives — actually, it is not that bold a guess, since k cannot be constant forever; on the other hand, k cannot be changed if m and n are constant without falsifying the invariant and therefore m or n or both change when k changes; we opt for the most symmetric choice.) We can take advantage of the fact that both m and n are in the index range of a so that $a[m, n]$ is well defined in the body of the loop.

(Note) $a[m, n]$ is not necessarily defined if the program were to terminate under the condition $m = M \wedge n = N$, since that would yield guard $m \neq M \vee n \neq N$, which guarantees that one of the two is in range, but allows that the other one may already be out of range.

What is the proper condition for increasing m, say by 1? As before, this condition is obtained from looking at P^m_{m+1}. Here we go.

$$\begin{aligned}
&P^m_{m+1} \\
=\quad &\{ \text{ substitution } \} \\
&K = k + \langle \mathbf{N}i, j : m + 1 \leq i < M \wedge n \leq j < N : a[i, j] = x \rangle \ \wedge \\
&0 \leq m + 1 \leq M \ \wedge \ 0 \leq n \leq N \\
\Leftarrow\quad & \\
&K = k + \langle \mathbf{N}i, j : m + 1 \leq i < M \wedge n \leq j < N : a[i, j] = x \rangle \ \wedge \\
&0 \leq m < M \ \wedge \ 0 \leq n \leq N \\
=\quad &\{ \ m + 1 \leq i \ = \ (m \leq i \wedge \neg(m = i)) \ \} \\
&K = k + \langle \mathbf{N}i, j : m \leq i < M \wedge n \leq j < N : a[i, j] = x \rangle \\
&\quad - \langle \mathbf{N}i, j : m = i \wedge n \leq j < N : a[i, j] = x \rangle \ \wedge \\
&0 \leq m < M \ \wedge \ 0 \leq n \leq N \\
\Leftarrow\quad &\{ \text{ monotonicity: } a[m, n] > x \Rightarrow a[m, j] > x \text{ for } n \leq j \ \} \\
&K = k + \langle \mathbf{N}i, j : m \leq i < M \wedge n \leq j < N : a[i, j] = x \rangle \ \wedge \\
&0 \leq m < M \ \wedge \ 0 \leq n < N \ \wedge \ a[m, n] > x \\
=\quad & \\
&P \ \wedge \ m \neq M \ \wedge \ a[m, n] > x
\end{aligned}$$

This provides us with one guard of the if-statement. On account of symmetry and the fact that the monotonicities in the rows and columns of a are opposite, we have the second guard also.

$$k := 0; \quad m, n := 0, 0;$$
$$*[\ m \neq M \wedge n \neq N \rightarrow$$
$$\quad [\ a[m, n] > x \rightarrow m := m + 1$$
$$\quad |\ a[m, n] < x \rightarrow n := n + 1$$
$$\quad |\ \cdots \quad\quad\quad \rightarrow k, m, n := k + 1, m + 1, n + 1$$
$$\ ]\quad\quad]$$

One would certainly hope that the third guard turns out to be $a[m, n] = x$. Let us check whether it is.

$$P_{k+1,m+1,n+1}^{k,m,n}$$
$=\quad$ { substitution }

$K = k + 1 +$
$\quad \langle \mathbf{N}i, j : m + 1 \leq i < M \wedge n + 1 \leq j < N : a[i, j] = x \rangle \ \wedge$
$0 \leq m + 1 \leq M \ \wedge \ 0 \leq n + 1 \leq N$

$\Leftarrow$

$K = k + 1 + \langle \mathbf{N}i, j : m + 1 \leq i < M \wedge n < j < N : a[i, j] = x \rangle \ \wedge$
$0 \leq m < M \ \wedge \ 0 \leq n < N$

$=\quad$ { four-way split }

$K = k + 1 + \langle \mathbf{N}i, j : m \leq i < M \wedge n \leq j < N : a[i, j] = x \rangle$
$\quad\quad - \langle \mathbf{N}i, j : m = i \wedge n < j < N : a[i, j] = x \rangle$
$\quad\quad - \langle \mathbf{N}i, j : m < i < M \wedge n = j : a[i, j] = x \rangle$
$\quad\quad - \langle \mathbf{N}i, j : m = i \wedge n = j : a[i, j] = x \rangle \ \wedge$
$0 \leq m < M \ \wedge \ 0 \leq n \leq N$

$\Leftarrow\quad$ { if $a[m, n] = x$ then
$\quad\quad \langle \mathbf{N}i, j : m = i \wedge n = j : a[i, j] = x \rangle = 1$
$\quad\quad$ and the other two counts are 0 (by monotonicity) }

$K = k + \langle \mathbf{N}i, j : m \leq i < M \wedge n \leq j < N : a[i, j] = x \rangle \ \wedge$
$0 \leq m < M \ \wedge \ 0 \leq n < N \ \wedge \ a[m, n] = x$

$=$

$$P \ \wedge \ m \neq M \ \wedge \ n \neq N \ \wedge \ a[m, n] = x$$

Sure enough: the condition is what we expected, or hoped for, which implies that we are done with our program. The invariant implies that the bound function is bounded from below. Each step of the iteration either increases m or n or both, and in each of those cases, decreases the bound function. Hence, the program terminates.

$$k := 0; \quad m, n := 0, 0;$$
$$*[\ m \neq M \wedge n \neq N \rightarrow$$
$$\quad [\ a[m, n] > x \rightarrow m := m + 1$$
$$\quad |\ a[m, n] < x \rightarrow n := n + 1$$
$$\quad |\ a[m, n] = x \rightarrow k, m, n := k + 1, m + 1, n + 1$$
$$\ ]\quad\quad]$$

The kind of invariant used in this example is sometimes referred to as a *tail invariant*. It is illustrated in Figure 8.3. The value of k equals the

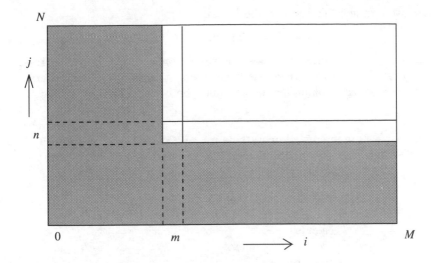

FIGURE 8.3. Illustration of tail invariant.

number of occurrences of x in the shaded, L-shaped area. The invariant expresses this by stating that K, which is the number of occurrences of x in the large rectangle, equals k plus the number of occurrences of x in the smaller, white rectangle. The figure also illustrates the i, j pairs that disappear from the small rectangle when increasing m or n or both. An invariant of the form

$$k = \langle \mathbf{N} i, j : 0 \le i < m \wedge 0 \le j < n : a[i,j] = x \rangle$$

expresses that k is the number of occurrences of x in a rectangle at the left bottom of the figure. In order to enable an increase of m or n, such an invariant must be extended with terms to express that x does not occur in the two legs that make up the remainder of the L-shaped region. This additional complexity is avoided by a tail invariant.

We conclude this section with one more example, known as the *celebrity* problem. Among a group of persons, a celebrity is someone who is known by everyone, but does not know anyone. For a group of N people, numbered from 0 on, the relation

person i knows person j

is represented by boolean $b[i, j]$. Given that a celebrity exists, we are asked to write a program for finding a celebrity. Defining c as

$$c(i) \equiv \langle \forall j : j \ne i : b[j, i] \ \wedge \ \neg b[i, j] \rangle \quad ,$$

the problem is to find an index i in the range 0 through $N-1$ for which $c(i)$ holds, given that it exists . We reduce the problem size by restricting the latter range; this leads to the invariant

$$P: \quad 0 \leq m \leq n < N \ \wedge \ \langle \exists i : m \leq i \leq n : c(i) \rangle \quad .$$

Starting from the maximum possible range, $m = 0 \ \wedge \ n = N - 1$, and stopping when the range comprises one element, $m = n$, which is therefore the index we are looking for, we see that the bound function is

$$n - m$$

and that we are interested in statements $m := m + 1$ and $n := n - 1$. Let us see what their preconditions are. The precondition of $m := m + 1$ is

$$P^m_{m+1}$$
$$= \quad \{ \text{ substitution } \}$$
$$0 \leq m + 1 \leq n < N \ \wedge \ \langle \exists i : m + 1 \leq i \leq n : c(i) \rangle$$
$$\Leftarrow \quad \{ \text{ calculus } \}$$
$$P \ \wedge \ m \neq n \ \wedge \ \neg c(m)$$
$$= \quad \{ \text{ substitution } \}$$
$$P \ \wedge \ m \neq n \ \wedge \ \langle \exists j : j \neq m : \neg b[j, m] \ \vee \ b[m, j] \rangle$$
$$\Leftarrow \quad \{ \text{ choose } n \text{ for } j \text{ since } m \neq n \ \}$$
$$P \ \wedge \ m \neq n \ \wedge \ (\neg b[n, m] \ \vee \ b[m, n])$$

and the precondition of $n := n - 1$ is

$$P^n_{n-1}$$
$$= \quad \{ \text{ substitution } \}$$
$$0 \leq m \leq n - 1 < N \ \wedge \ \langle \exists i : m \leq i \leq n - 1 : c(i) \rangle$$
$$\Leftarrow \quad \{ \text{ calculus } \}$$
$$P \ \wedge \ m \neq n \ \wedge \ \neg c(n)$$
$$= \quad \{ \text{ substitution } \}$$
$$P \ \wedge \ m \neq n \ \wedge \ \langle \exists j : j \neq n : \neg b[j, n] \ \vee \ b[n, j] \rangle$$
$$\Leftarrow \quad \{ \text{ choose } m \text{ for } j \text{ since } m \neq n \ \}$$
$$P \ \wedge \ m \neq n \ \wedge \ (\neg b[m, n] \ \vee \ b[n, m])$$

from which we obtain the following program.

$$m, n := 0, N - 1;$$
$$*[\ m \neq n \rightarrow [\ \neg b[n, m] \ \vee \ b[m, n] \rightarrow m := m + 1$$
$$\| \ \neg b[m, n] \ \vee \ b[n, m] \rightarrow n := n - 1$$
$$] \qquad]$$
$$\{ 0 \leq m = n < N \ \wedge \ c(n) \}$$

We can even strengthen the two guards of the if-statement, although this makes the program a bit less symmetric. (We can always strengthen the guards of an if-statement without affecting the program's correctness, as long as at least one of the guards is *true*.)

$$m, n := 0, N - 1;$$
$$*[\ m \neq n \rightarrow [\quad b[m, n] \rightarrow m := m + 1$$
$$|\ \neg b[m, n] \rightarrow n := n - 1$$
$$]\qquad\qquad]$$
$$\{\ 0 \leq m = n < N \ \wedge\ c(n)\ \}$$

8.5 Random Examples

Here is a variation on binary search. Suppose we are given natural number N. We are to write a program that stores in i the integer part of the square root of N, that is, $i^2 \leq N < (i+1)^2$. The constant to be replaced by a variable is the 1. (Replacing the 2 doesn't seem to be very sensible.) The variable then indicates the size of the interval to which the search for the square root is confined. The idea of binary search is to halve the size of this interval every step, so let us try to let the size be a power of 2.

$$i^2 \leq N < (i + k)^2 \ \wedge\ k \geq 1 \ \wedge\ k \text{ is a power of 2}$$

The program is going to be something like

$$i, k := 0, 1; \quad *[\ k^2 \leq N \rightarrow k := k \cdot 2\ ];$$
$$*[\ k \neq 1 \rightarrow k := k/2;$$
$$[\ (i + k)^2 \leq N \rightarrow i := i + k$$
$$|\ (i + k)^2 > N \rightarrow skip$$
$$]\qquad\qquad\qquad]$$

in which the first loop establishes the invariant. Its own invariant is

$$i = 0 \ \wedge\ k \geq 1 \ \wedge\ k \text{ is a power of 2.}$$

(We omit the verification of the invariance.) Observe that $(i+k)^2$ is computed all the time. Let us try to eliminate this computation. In fact, $(i+k)^2$ is always compared to N. Since $(i + k)^2 = i^2 + 2ik + k^2$, and because of the comparison with N, we decide to introduce the following variables.

$$a = k^2 \ \wedge\ b = i \cdot k \ \wedge\ c = N - i^2$$

Having introduced a, b, and c, variables i and k are redundant, and we remove them from the program. When needed, we can always "recover" their value from a, b, and c. Through this *coordinate transformation*, the program transforms to

$$a, b, c := 1, 0, N; \quad *[\ a \leq N \rightarrow a := a \cdot 4\ ];$$
$$*[\ a \neq 1 \rightarrow a, b := a/4, b/2;$$
$$[\ a + 2 \cdot b \leq c \rightarrow b, c := b + a, c - a - 2 \cdot b$$
$$|\ a + 2 \cdot b > c \rightarrow skip$$
$$]\qquad\qquad\qquad\qquad]\qquad .$$

The answer of the previous program is i. Now, however, i has been "improved" away. Upon termination, however, we had $k = 1$ which implies $b = i$, hence, b is the outcome of the new program. As a final improvement, we avoid the threefold evaluation of $a + 2 \cdot b$.

$$a, b, c := 1, 0, N; \quad *[\ a \leq N \rightarrow a := a \cdot 4\ ];$$
$$*[\ a \neq 1 \rightarrow a := a/4; \quad h := c - a - b; \quad b := b/2;$$
$$[\ h \geq 0 \rightarrow b, c := b + a, h$$
$$|\!|\ h < 0 \rightarrow skip$$
$$]\qquad\qquad]$$

Next comes an example of a program for which you need a good idea in order to get started. The problem is to print the first so-many digits of e, the base of the natural logarithm. The good idea is, in this case, that $e = \sum_{i=0}^{\infty} \frac{1}{i!}$. Infinite sums are hard to work with, so assume that we restrict ourselves to $e \approx \sum_{i=0}^{100} \frac{1}{i!}$. The error that we make is approximately the first term that was left out, that is, $\frac{1}{101!}$, which is less than 10^{-159}. Hence, when we compute the sum accurately, we have e up to the first 159 digits following the decimal point. Since $\sum_{i=0}^{100} \frac{1}{i!} = 2 + \sum_{i=2}^{100} \frac{1}{i!}$, the latter summation is the fractional part of e (since $2 < e < 3$). We are used to writing fractions in decimal notation as a sequence of digits, d_i, standing for $\sum_i \frac{d_i}{10^i}$; hence, the major difference with our previous sum is in the weights of the digits. In our newly-invented factorial notation, digit d_i has weight $\frac{1}{i!}$ instead of the weight $\frac{1}{10^i}$ that it has in decimal notation. Apparently, we can write $e = 2.1111 \cdots$ assuming "factorial" notation, but we really wanted e to be printed in decimal notation. All that remains to be done is to convert from one notation to the other. How do we do that? The leading decimal digit of fraction f is the integer part of $10 \cdot f$. (This observation is independent of the way in which f is represented; the algorithm for computing it does depend on the representation.) The second decimal digit is the integer part of 10 times (the fraction of $10 \cdot f$), and, with poor man's induction, we find that the leading 159 decimal digits of f are printed by performing

print the integer part of $10 \cdot f$; $f := $ fraction of $10 \cdot f$

159 times. Okay, how do we multiply a number by 10? That's easy: multiply each digit d_i by 10. This works fine, because $10 \cdot \sum_i \frac{d_i}{i!} = \sum_i \frac{10 \cdot d_i}{i!}$, just as in the case of decimal notation. However, we are used to the restriction $0 \leq d_i < 10$ in decimal, which is required to make the representation unique. (If we would have a digit that is 10 or more, then it can be normalized by replacing the digit by its remainder modulo 10 and adding the quotient to the next higher digit without changing their weighted sum.) What is the corresponding restriction in factorial notation? It is $0 \leq d_i < i$. Again, if $d_i \geq i$, we can replace d_i by $d_i \bmod i$ and increase d_{i-1} by $d_i \operatorname{div} i$ without affecting the number represented. (Check it!) What happens to the

very first digit when we do this "normalization"? If the number is less than 1, that is, if it is a fraction, then there will be no overflow since $\sum_{i=2}^{100} \frac{d_i}{i!} \le \sum_{i=2}^{100} \frac{i-1}{i!} < \sum_{i=2}^{\infty} \frac{i-1}{i!} = 1$. If the number that is being represented is 1 or more, then there will be "overflow" and the normalization technique will produce a number that is supposedly added to d_1, which doesn't exist in our summation. Had it existed, then its weight would have been $\frac{1}{1!}$; hence, it is the integer part of the number. Thus, we end up with the following algorithm. (We use *write* statements for printing a string or a digit.)

$$i := 100; \quad *[\ i \ne 1 \to d[i] := 1; \ i := i - 1\ ];$$
$$write('e = 2.'); \ j := 0;$$
$$*[\ j \ne 159 \to x := 0; \ i := 100;$$
$$\qquad *[\ i \ne 1 \to p := d[i] \cdot 10 + x;$$
$$\qquad\qquad d[i], x := p \textbf{ mod } i, p \textbf{ div } i; \ i := i - 1$$
$$\qquad\ ];$$
$$\qquad write(x : 1); \ j := j + 1$$
$$]$$

The invariant of the main loop is

the first j digits of the fractional part of e have been printed
$$\wedge \qquad \sum_{i=2}^{100} \frac{d[i]}{i!} = \text{ fractional part of } 10^j \cdot \sum_{i=2}^{100} \frac{1}{i!} \quad .$$

We omit the verification.

The last example is yet another program for computing the greatest common divisor. It is obtained by transforming Euclid's algorithm.

$$a, b := A, B; \quad \{\ \gcd(a, b) = \gcd(A, B) \wedge a > 0 \wedge b > 0\ \}$$
$$*[\ a > b \to a := a - b \ \| \ b > a \to b := b - a\ ]$$
$$\{\ a = b = \gcd(A, B)\ \}$$

In every step the greater of the two variables is decreased by the lesser of the two. It is well known that the program can be postfixed by another such step, which sets one of the variables to zero. (Repeating this step any further does not bring about any further changes since decreasing with zero is the empty operation.) We rewrite the program to implement the additional step as an extra iteration of the loop.

$$c, d := A, B;$$
$$\{\ \gcd(c, d) = \gcd(A, B) \ \wedge \ c \ge 0 \ \wedge \ d \ge 0 \ \wedge \ \max(c, d) > 0\ \}$$
$$*[c \ne 0 \wedge d \ne 0 \to [c \ge d \to c := c - d \ \| \ d \ge c \to d := d - c]]$$
$$\{\ \max(c, d) = \gcd(A, B)\ \}$$

Next, we introduce variables e and f that satisfy

$$e = \min(c, d) \ \wedge \ f = \max(c, d) \quad ,$$

which leads to

$$e, f := \min(A, B), \max(A, B);$$
$$\{ \gcd(e, f) = \gcd(A, B) \;\wedge\; f \geq e \geq 0 \;\wedge\; f > 0 \}$$
$$*[e \neq 0 \rightarrow e, f := \min(e, f - e), \max(e, f - e)]$$
$$\{ f = \gcd(A, B) \;\wedge\; e = 0 \} \qquad .$$

Finally, we introduce variables g and h that satisfy

$$g = f - e \;\wedge\; h = f + e \qquad .$$

Using

$$\max(A, B) - \min(A, B) = |A - B|$$
$$\max(A, B) + \min(A, B) = A + B$$
$$\max(e, f - e) + \min(e, f - e) = f = (g + h)/2$$
$$\max(e, f - e) - \min(e, f - e) = |f - 2e| = |3g - h|/2$$

we obtain

$$g, h := |A - B|, A + B;$$
$$\{ \gcd(\tfrac{g+h}{2}, \tfrac{h-g}{2}) = \gcd(A, B) \wedge h \geq g \geq 0 \wedge h + g > 0 \}$$
$$*[g \neq h \rightarrow g, h := |3g - h|/2, (g + h)/2]$$
$$\{ g = h = \gcd(A, B) \} \qquad .$$

The guards of the loops in the last three programs can be replaced with *true* to obtain a program that sets g and h to $\gcd(A, B)$ after a number of steps and loops forever thereafter without changing the state. The last program has been included as an example of a very short program whose effect is completely obscure when given the program text only. A specification and an invariant make all the difference.

8.6   Conclusion

We have discussed a number of ways to come up with an invariant. All of them derive the invariant from the specification of the problem, especially from the postcondition. Therefore, we have no way of figuring out the invariant if there is no specification. If there is no specification, or if the specification is unclear, work on getting a precise specification before you start to work on solving the problem. Getting a proper specification is not an easy problem, and this is sometimes used as an excuse for starting the program's development in anticipation of its specification. One must be extremely optimistic, naive, or both, to expect that program and specification develop independently into a compatible state. The result is too often that the specification is left undeveloped, and the quality of the product suffers.

It is sometimes said that choosing the right invariant involves a great deal of luck. It may appear that we were often lucky in choosing the proper invariant, but I think it is more experience than luck. I am reminded of an interview with a famous soccer player. It was the goal keeper of the winning team who had led his team to victory with a few spectacular saves. The interviewer remarked that the goalie had been very lucky by jumping to the right corner at the right time. The goalie remarked that he had been practicing a lot over the past years, and he had noticed that over those years he became 'lucky' more and more often.

We have not tried to make the heuristics too precise. In fact, if we could be very precise about them, we might be able to automate the process of program construction. I doubt that we will be able to do this for all problems and hope to get good solutions (where "good" means: "elegant and efficient"). In many cases, a good solution requires the invention of a tiny mathematical theory, a special-purpose theory in the sense that it applies to a small collection of problems only. If we restrict the problem domain to an area in which the operations involved are well understood, then there are reasonable chances that we can go a long way in the right direction. In fact, I have the feeling that we have already come a long way toward that goal by concentrating on uninterpreted formula manipulation, but there is no doubt that we still have a long way to go. It took a long time (for Europeans) to switch from Roman to Arabic numerals, but the switch made it possible to describe simple algorithms for addition and multiplication that require no interpretation of a sequence of digits as a natural number; we can apply the algorithms blindfolded, and we have greater confidence in the answer than with any other method. The major problem is to identify the "Roman numerals" of an interesting class of problems and to come up with a better notation. And this is not going to be easy, for both technical and nontechnical reasons.

8.7   Bibliographic Notes

The use of the term "to pull a rabbit" in the technical meaning of the first paragraph of this chapter has been around for a while. It has been extensively documented and illustrated in [Bro89].

The program for computing decimal digits of e is part of the folklore. As far as I know, it is due to A. van Wijngaarden. The celebrity problem is from [Man89] and [KS90]. The maximum segment sum problem was first published in [Gri82], including a discussion of its history. The problem of counting the number of lattice points that lie in a circle (see Exercise 17) goes back to Gauss. An efficient algorithm for counting them is presented in [KS63]. This paper also contains the essence of the saddle back search. Exercise 21 is due to [BM]. It is an amazingly efficient algorithm. For a generalization, see [MG82].

Most exercises (including examples in the text) are due to W.H.J. Feijen whose unpublished collection of nice problems has been widely circulated for almost two decades and has served an important role in many programming courses. Many of those problems have finally been published in [DF88]. See also [Bac86], [Gri81], [Heh84], [Kal90], and [Mor90].

Martin Rem's column "Small Programming Exercises" in Science of Computer Programming is a good source of interesting programming problems, and their solutions.

I made up the story of the goal keeper. Experience and practice do help.

8.8   Exercises

1. Write a program that finds the largest integer that is a power of 2 and does not exceed a given positive integer N.

2. Given array $a[0..N]$ of $N+1$ integers, write a program for computing the boolean value

$$\langle \exists i : 0 \leq i < N : a[i] = a[N] \rangle \quad .$$

3. Given is sequence $b[0..N-1]$ of $N \geq 0$ boolean values. Write a program for storing in boolean variable c the value of

$$\langle \exists n : 0 \leq n \leq N : \langle \forall i : 0 \leq i < n : \neg b[i] \rangle \ \wedge$$
$$\langle \forall i : n \leq i < N : b[i] \rangle \rangle \quad .$$

4. Given is ascending sequence $a[0..N-1]$ of $N > 0$ integer values. That is, we have $\langle \forall i : 0 < i < N : a[i-1] \leq a[i] \rangle$. Write a program for computing the number of distinct values in a. A *plateau* is a consecutive subsequence of equal values. Write a program to compute the length of a longest plateau in a. (There may be many plateaus of maximum length, but the maximum length is unique.)

5. Prove $j - i > 1 \Rightarrow i < (i+j)$ **div** $2 < j$.

6. Given ascending integer array $a[M..N-1]$, $M \leq N$, and integer x, write a program for assigning to boolean b the value

$$\langle \exists i : M \leq i < N : a[i] = x \rangle \quad .$$

Use binary search to obtain an efficient program, but we are not given $a[M] \leq x < a[N]$, in fact $a[N]$ doesn't exist.

7. We define set H of natural numbers, called the Hamming numbers.

   (0) $1 \in H$;
   (1)   if $k \in H$, then $2k \in H$, $3k \in H$, and $5k \in H$; and
   (2)   no other numbers are in H.

For given positive integer N, write a program to compute the least N elements of set H.

8. Three given sequences $f, g, h(i : i \geq 0)$ have a common element; that is, a number exists that occurs in each of the three sequences (but possibly at different indices). The three sequences are in ascending order. Write a program for computing the least element they have in common.

9. Given are integers A and N and integer array $w[0..N-1]$. We are given

$$A > 0 \ \wedge \ N > 0 \ \wedge \ \langle \forall i : 0 < i < N : w[i-1] < w[i] \rangle \ .$$

In a garage, we have N gearwheels, numbered from 0 on. Wheel i has radius $w[i]$. In the garage are two parallel axles whose distance is A. Two wheels, i and j, fit together on the axles just when $w[i] + w[j] = A$. Write a program for computing the number of pairs of gearwheels that fit together on the axles, that is,

$$\langle \mathbf{N}i, j : 0 \leq i < j < N : w[i] + w[j] = A \rangle \ .$$

10. Prove the correctness of the digit-sum program.

11. Given are two natural numbers. Each has a sequence of digits as its decimal representation; we make it unique by omitting leading zeros. (The representation of 0 is the empty sequence.) These two sequences have a longest common prefix, which might be the empty sequence. This longest common prefix is the decimal representation of another natural number. Write a program for computing the latter number.

    (Hint: here is a reformulation of the gcd problem. We are given two positive, integer numbers. Each has a set of numbers as its divisors, and which is unique. The intersection of the two sets is the set of common divisors, which is nonempty since 1 is in both sets. The greatest number in the intersection is the greatest common divisor.)

12. Given two natural numbers X and Y, where $X > 0 \ \wedge \ Y \geq 0$, write a program for computing X^Y. Develop a program whose number of steps is a logarithmic function of Y. (Hint: Use variables x, y, and z, the latter being the output. Consider $X^Y = z \cdot x^y$ as part of the invariant.) It is required that you do not use y as a bound function, but $\lfloor \log(y) \rfloor$.

13. Given are two strictly increasing integer arrays $f[0..M-1]$ and $g[0..N-1]$. Write a program for computing the number of integers that occur in both f and g.

14. Repeat the problem in the previous exercise for the case in which the two arrays are ascending but not strictly increasing.

15. Given are two ascending integer arrays $f[0..M-1]$ and $g[0..N-1]$. Write a program for computing the minimum "distance" between f and g; that is,

$$\langle \mathbf{MIN} i,j : 0 \le i < M \wedge 0 \le j < N : |f[i] - g[j]| \rangle \quad .$$

16. Given natural number N, write a program for computing the number of ways in which N can be written as the sum of two squares. This can be viewed as the number of grid points on a circle with radius $\sqrt{N}$ whose center is also a grid point. Restrict the count to one octant; that is, write a program for computing

$$\langle \mathbf{N} x,y : 0 \le x \le y : x^2 + y^2 = N \rangle \quad .$$

Use integer arithmetic only.

17. Given natural number r, write a program for computing the number of grid points $A(r)$ on or inside a circle with radius r whose center is also a grid point.

$$A(r) = \langle \mathbf{N} x,y :: x^2 + y^2 \le r^2 \rangle$$

A good approximation of $A(r)$ is πr^2. In fact, it has been shown that for large r, $A(r) - \pi r^2$ is $O(r^\theta)$ for $\theta = 0.65$, and that the same is not the case for $\theta = 0.5$ but the area in between is "still open". It has been conjectured that $A(r) - \pi r^2$ is $O(r^\theta)$ for all $\theta > 0.5$; it is, therefore, interesting to plot $\frac{\ln(|A(r) - \pi r^2|)}{\ln(r)}$ to see how this tends to 0.5.

18. For given positive integer x, write a program for computing the least number n for which

$$\langle \exists k : 0 \le k \le n : \binom{n}{k} = x \rangle \quad .$$

19. For given positive integer x, write a program for computing

$$\langle \mathbf{N} n : n \ge 1 : \langle \exists k : 0 \le k \le n : \binom{n}{k} = x \rangle \rangle \quad .$$

20. We are given integer array $a[0..N-1]$. For $0 \le p \le q \le N$, we define segment $a[p..q-1]$ of length $q-p$ to be a democratic segment if it contains a negative number, a zero, and a positive number. We are given that a as a whole is a democratic segment. Write a program for computing the shortest length of any democratic segment in a.

21. We are given array $b[0..N-1]$, of $N \geq 1$, integer numbers. We are given that a number exists that occurs more than N **div** 2 times in the array. Given the array, this number is fixed. Show that the following program stores that number in variable v.

$$\{ N \geq 1 \ \wedge \ \langle \exists x :: \langle \mathbf{N}j : 0 \leq j < N : b[j] = x \rangle > N \textbf{ div } 2 \rangle \}$$
$$i, c, v := 1, 2, b[0];$$
$$*[\ i \neq N \rightarrow [\ v = b[i] \qquad \rightarrow c, i := c+2, i+1$$
$$\| \ c = i \qquad \rightarrow c, i, v := c+2, i+1, b[i]$$
$$\| \ c \neq i \wedge v \neq b[i] \rightarrow i := i+1$$
$$] \qquad]$$
$$\{ \langle \mathbf{N}j : 0 \leq j < N : b[j] = v \rangle \ > \ N \textbf{ div } 2 \}$$

A suitable choice for the invariant is

$$0 \leq i \leq N \ \wedge \ i \leq c \ \wedge \ c \bmod 2 = 0 \ \wedge$$
$$\langle \mathbf{N}j : 0 \leq j < i : b[j] = v \rangle \ \leq \ c \textbf{ div } 2 \ \wedge$$
$$\langle \forall x : x \neq v : \langle \mathbf{N}j : 0 \leq j < i : b[j] = x \rangle \ \leq \ i - c \textbf{ div } 2 \rangle$$

22. For given integer N, $N \geq 1$, array $a[0..N-1]$ is a permutation of the numbers 0 through N from which one number is missing. Write a program for computing the missing number.

23. Consider the *Fibonacci number system*. We can represent any natural number as a sequence, $b_n b_{n-1} \cdots b_2$, of 0's and 1's. The number that is being represented is $\sum_{i=2}^{n} b_i f(i)$, where $f(i)$ is the ith Fibonacci number. In order to make the representation unique, it is required that there be no two adjacent 1's. Prove that such a representation exists for every natural number. Describe an algorithm that, given an array of bits representing some natural number m in the Fibonacci number system, changes the array to represent $m+1$. (The array has indices from 2 through n, and n is given to be sufficiently large.) Can you describe an algorithm for adding two numbers given in the Fibonacci number system?

24. We have seen an algorithm for computing the nth Fibonacci number $f(n)$ in a time proportional to n. Since

$$\begin{pmatrix} f(n+1) \\ f(n+2) \end{pmatrix} = \begin{pmatrix} 0 & 1 \\ 1 & 1 \end{pmatrix} \cdot \begin{pmatrix} f(n) \\ f(n+1) \end{pmatrix} \quad ,$$

we have

$$\begin{pmatrix} f(n) \\ f(n+1) \end{pmatrix} = \begin{pmatrix} 0 & 1 \\ 1 & 1 \end{pmatrix}^n \cdot \begin{pmatrix} 0 \\ 1 \end{pmatrix} \quad ,$$

which shows that $f(n)$ and $f(n+1)$ can be computed by raising a matrix to the nth power. Since we have seen that exponentiation can be done in $\log(n)$ steps, (cf. Exercise 12) a logarithmic algorithm emerges. Complete this algorithm. This method can be applied to any linear recurrence relation. Apply it to compute Fibolucci numbers in logarithmic time.

25. Given positive integer A, and positive integer function f, satisfying

$$\langle \exists i : i > 0 : \langle \forall j : j > 0 : j > i \; \equiv \; f(j) > A \rangle \rangle \quad ,$$

write a program for computing

$$\langle \mathbf{N} p, q : 1 \leq p < q : \langle \sum i : p \leq i < q : f(i) \rangle = A \rangle \quad .$$

26. Same question for the special case where $f(i) = i$. Go for a solution with a running time that is proportional to $\sqrt{A}$.

9

Efficiency of Programs

A programming problem may admit a variety of solutions that are all in perfect compliance with the specification. Yet, we may have a strong preference for one over the other. By far the most relevant criterion for distinguishing between the programs is the time it takes to execute them. One has to be careful in these matters, though, as illustrated by the following example. Assume that we have two programs PA and PB that each solve our programming problem. We have two machines available, and measuring of execution times of the two programs reveals that they take 3 and 6 seconds on MA, and 6 and 3 seconds on MB, respectively.

	MA	MB
PA	3 secs	6 secs
PB	6 secs	3 secs

Which of the two programs is more efficient? One might say that they are roughly the same, or that it depends on the machine, but it does not make sense to say that PA is 25% faster than PB. Yet, this is what some manufacturers of programs (or, by symmetry, of machines) want you to believe. Here is the reasoning they follow. We cannot compare these absolute timings, they have to be normed first. This means that one program is said to take time 1 (no units) and everything is scaled accordingly. Let PA be the norm; divide the timings in the first column by 3 seconds, and in the second column by 6 seconds.

	MA	MB
PA	1	1
PB	2	0.5

Next, compute the average execution time of each program, averaging over all machines.

	MA	MB	average
PA	1	1	1
PB	2	0.5	1.25

Inspection of the table shows that PB takes 25% longer to execute. I trust that you see that the argument does not hold water, but it is applied over and over again in the literature, mostly in the situation where a number of so-called benchmark programs are run on different computers, and one computer is made to come out best by exactly the argument given here.

One might try to avoid this pitfall by choosing one machine and by sticking to it when comparing programs. However, it is not always the case that the results carry over to another machine. It is, therefore, more attractive to characterize programs in a way that is less dependent on the detailed properties of actual machines. It is then unavoidable that we cannot distinguish between the efficiency of some programs whose relative speeds depend on such properties. On the other hand, such a characterization might give us more insight into a program's efficiency than a table of measured data does. Here is the characterization that is often used. Find one natural number that is the main (or only) parameter that determines the program's execution time. For example, to set to zero all elements of an array of n integers takes time proportional to n. On one machine it might be $29n + 7$ microseconds and on another it might be $16n + 41$ nanoseconds. Ignoring the additive and the multiplicative constants, we say that the program's execution time is of order n, written as $O(n)$. Formally, one defines $O(g(n))$ to be the set of all functions $f(n)$ from naturals to naturals that are bounded by $a \cdot g(n)$, for some constant a and for all sufficiently large n.

$$f(n) \in O(g(n)) \equiv \langle \exists a, k : a, k \geq 0 : \langle \forall n : n \geq k : f(n) \leq a \cdot g(n) \rangle \rangle$$

Because the big-O notion ignores the constants that we had before, we need not worry about actual execution times, but can restrict our attention to the number of steps it takes to execute a program. And even the number of steps can be taken loosely. For example, in the case of

```
i := 0;
*[ i ≠ n → a[i] := 0;  i := i + 1 ]
```

we need not worry whether one step is one reference to a variable, or one assignment, or the evaluation of one expression, or all of those actions combined, because in each case the number of steps comes out to be a function of n that is in $O(n)$. The jargon has it that the program's complexity is $O(n)$. This use of the word complexity has nothing to do with the complexity of the program's structure, or the intricacy of the mathematical theorems upon which its correctness relies. It is just another word for the execution time.

(*Aside*) Sometimes, you will see expressions like $3n+4 = O(n)$ instead of our $3n+4 \in O(n)$ in the literature. This is a terrible mistake, since it destroys the symmetry and associativity of equality, and you can no longer substitute "equals for equals": $3n + 4 = O(n)$ and $4n + 5 = O(n)$ does not imply $3n + 4 = 4n + 5$.

(*Another aside*) Sometimes, you will see $|f(n)| \leq a \cdot g(n)$ in the definition of O in the literature. In general, this is actually better, but we do not have any negative functions in this chapter.

It is the property of hiding the constants that makes the big-O notion easy to use, and independent of details of the actual machine. It turns out that programs with a superior big-O performance are also better in practice, although this is true only if one is interested in running big problems, that is, in executing the program for large values of n. This is often the case.

Here is another example. Given integer array $a[0..n-1]$ and integer x that occurs somewhere in the array, assign to integer i an index at which x occurs in a. The execution time of

$i := 0;$
$*[\ a[i] \neq x \rightarrow i := i + 1\ ]$

heavily depends on the position where x occurs in the array. It could be anything from 1 step to n steps. Is the execution time $O(1)$ or $O(n)$? It depends, but in the worst case it is $O(n)$. The worst-case complexity is usually easier to estimate than, for example, the average-case complexity. It may be completely useless in some problems since the worst case may almost never occur, but it is definitely the one that gives strong guarantees. Worst-case complexity is therefore the one that you will encounter most often.

9.1   A Lower Bound for Searching

We have just seen that the worst-case complexity of linear search is $O(n)$. In Chapter 8, we discussed a more efficient algorithm for the special case in which the array is sorted, the so-called binary search. Its worst-case complexity is $O(\log(n))$. It doesn't make any difference whether the base of the logarithm is 2 or 10 or any other constant, because of the constants in the big-O notion. In this section we show that no algorithm can do better than binary search, that is, no algorithm exists with a worst-case complexity that is lower than $O(\log(n))$. Of course, it may be possible to find algorithms that have a lower constant factor in front of the logarithm, but those are hidden in the big-O. We have to make one assumption, though: the only way that a program may extract any kind of information from the given array and from the number to be located, is by carrying out two-way comparisons. It may compare two elements of the array, or compare an array element with the number sought for, or compare them with anything else. The output of a comparison is *true* or *false*, and not something like: the required position is 17 to the left.

Execution of any proposed program consists of some actions and then reaches the point where it makes its first comparison. Based on the outcome thereof, it continues in one of two possible ways. In each case it again performs some actions, possibly different actions in the two cases, and then reaches another comparison. And so on. We may describe the possible executions of the program by a binary tree. The root is the first comparison; it has two successors that correspond to the next comparison: one for each possible outcome of the first comparison. The edges in the tree correspond to actions that are not comparisons.

For any given program and for each value n, such a tree can be made. The tree is finite since the program terminates on each input that satisfies the precondition. The leaves of the tree correspond to reaching the conclusion about whether and if so, where, the sought-for number occurs in the array. Because there are at least $n + 1$ different outcomes (one for each possible position, and one for absence), the tree has at least $n + 1$ leaves. Of course, there might be more leaves, with several leaves corresponding to the same outcome. We will have shown that the worst-case complexity of the program is at least $O(\log(n))$ if the tree contains at least one path from the root to a leaf whose length is at least $\log_2(n)$. This result follows directly from the following property.

A binary tree of height d has at most 2^d leaves,

where the height of a tree is defined to be the length of a longest path from the root to any leaf. The property can be established by mathematical induction on d.

We write $f(n) \in O(g(n))$ for an upper bound on f, and in the same spirit we write $f(n) \in \Omega(g(n))$ for a lower bound.

$$f(n) \in \Omega(g(n)) \equiv \langle \exists a, k : a, k \geq 0 : \langle \forall n : n \geq k : f(n) \geq a \cdot g(n) \rangle \rangle$$

This notation allows us to express our result as: the complexity of searching is $\Omega(\log(n))$.

9.2   Analysis of Nested Loops

Consider the following problem. We are given integer array $a[0..N-1]$, $N \geq 0$. A 7-segment is defined to be a consecutive subsequence of the array that contains at most 7 occurrences of the integer 0. We postulate that program

$$k, l, m, n := 0, 0, 0, 0;$$
$$*[\ n \neq N \rightarrow [a[n] = 0 \rightarrow k := k + 1 \mid a[n] \neq 0 \rightarrow skip];$$
$$*[\ k > 7 \rightarrow [a[m] = 0 \rightarrow k := k - 1 \mid a[m] \neq 0 \rightarrow skip];$$
$$m := m + 1$$
$$];$$
$$l := \max(l, n + 1 - m);\ \ n := n + 1$$
$$]$$

computes the maximum length of any 7-segment in the given array. An invariant of the outer loop is

$$0 \leq m \leq n \leq N\ \ \wedge\ \ k = c(m, n)\ \ \wedge$$
$$m = \langle \mathbf{MIN} i : 0 \leq i \leq n\ \ \wedge\ \ c(i, n) \leq 7 : i \rangle\ \ \wedge$$
$$l = \langle \mathbf{MAX} i, j : 0 \leq i \leq j \leq n\ \ \wedge\ \ c(i, j) \leq 7 : j - i \rangle$$

where

$$c(m, n)\ =\ \langle \mathbf{N} i : m \leq i < n : a[i] = 0 \rangle\quad .$$

The body of the outer loop is executed N times, and for each iteration of the outer loop, the inner loop is executed at most N times (or $N - 7$ times). It seems that the total number of steps is bounded by N^2. This is true, but a stricter upper bound can be given. Although some of the iterations of the inner loop can be $O(N)$, others take many fewer steps. Integer variable m is increased whenever the inner loop makes another iteration. No statement decreases m. Since $0 \leq m \leq N$, it follows that the total number of times that the body of the inner loop is executed is at most N.

What can we say about the complexity of the inner loop itself? We have seen that it is $O(N)$ in the worst case, but also $O(N)$ for N executions together. Averaged over those N executions, the complexity is $O(1)$. The notion of average complexity is applied to the case where one averages over all possible situations. Here, we average over all executions of a part of the program during the execution of the whole program. This is referred to as the *amortized complexity*. Amortized complexity plays a role when the program part that is being studied maintains a variable that is preserved from one execution to the next (during one execution of the whole program). In the example, the variable is m. In many cases, the variable is a more complicated data structure, and the amortized complexity is not necessarily easy to analyze. A typical example is a data structure for storing a set of items. The operations are to add an item and to test membership of an item. The data structure is reorganized every now and then to facilitate faster execution of the two operations. If reorganization is a time-consuming operation, the worst-case complexity of each individual operation may look bad. But if the reorganization is effective and need not be performed often, then the amortized complexity may be good.

9.3   The Constant Factor

Whenever we use the big-O notation for describing a program's execution time, we ignore the constant hidden in it. In this section we have a short look at that constant. Programs

$$n := 0;$$
$$*[\ n \neq N \rightarrow a[n] := n^3;\ \ n := n + 1\ ]$$

and

$$x, y, z := 0, 1, 6;\ \ n := 0;$$
$$*[\ n \neq N \rightarrow a[n] := x;\ \ x, y, z := x + y, y + z, z + 6;\ \ n := n + 1\ ]$$

each produce a table of third powers (see Chapter 8) in time $O(N)$. If the programs are run on some machine then their execution times may be very different. In most machines, exponentiation and multiplication take a lot longer than addition, and, hence, most machines will execute the second program more rapidly than the first. Even though both programs are linear, the constant factor is smaller in the second program. If, however, one has a machine that multiplies almost as fast as it adds, then the difference between the two vanishes.

As another example, let us look at binary search again. The program we had was the following.

$$i, j := M, N;$$
$$*[\ j \neq i + 1 \rightarrow m := (i + j) \textbf{ div } 2;$$
$$\qquad\qquad [\ a[m] \leq x\ \rightarrow i := m$$
$$\qquad\qquad |\!|\ x < a[m]\ \rightarrow j := m$$
$$\ \ ]\qquad\qquad\ \ ]$$

It is sometimes stated that this program is inefficient, because it might have terminated as soon as $a[m]$ is found to be equal to x;   instead the program just continues until $j = i + 1$. So, a seemingly better algorithm is

$$i, j := M, N;$$
$$*[\ j \neq i + 1 \rightarrow m := (i + j) \textbf{ div } 2;$$
$$\qquad\qquad [\ a[m] < x\ \rightarrow i := m$$
$$\qquad\qquad |\!|\ a[m] = x\ \rightarrow i, j := m, m + 1$$
$$\qquad\qquad |\!|\ a[m] > x\ \rightarrow j := m$$
$$\ \ ]\qquad\qquad\ \ ]\qquad ,$$

and we calculate just how much more efficient it is. Of course, if x does not occur in the array then the improved algorithm will require the same number of steps as the old one. In order to make the improved algorithm look good, we therefore assume that x does indeed occur in the array. In that case, the improved algorithm may terminate many steps earlier than the old algorithm. How many? Well, in order to do the calculations, we assume that $M = 0$ and N is a power of 2, and we also assume that all positions for x are equally likely. If x occurs at an odd index then the old program would inspect it for the first time only at its very last step, and the improved program saves no steps. Since half of the indices are odd, in half the cases the gain is zero steps. If x occurs at an even index, but the index divided by two is odd, then the old program would first inspect it at its last step but one, and the improved program saves one step. In one quarter of the cases, one step is saved. Similarly, in one eighth of the cases, two steps are saved; and so on. The total number of steps saved is therefore given by

$$\sum_i \frac{i}{2^{i+1}} \quad ,$$

in which i ranges from 1 to $\log_2(n)$ (the term with $i = 0$ is 0). Let s be equal to this sum for the case where i ranges from 1 to $+\infty$, and observe

$$s - \frac{s}{2} = \sum_{i \geq 1} \frac{i}{2^{i+1}} - \sum_{i \geq 1} \frac{i}{2^{i+2}} = \sum_{i \geq 1} \frac{i}{2^{i+1}} - \sum_{i \geq 1} \frac{i-1}{2^{i+1}} = \sum_{i \geq 1} \frac{1}{2^{i+1}} = \frac{1}{2}$$

from which $s = 1$ follows. Since the range of i is bounded in the formula for the number of steps saved, the average number of steps saved is less than 1, which is definitely less than we had hoped for. But things may be even worse. The old algorithm executes an if-statement with two alternatives in each step, and the improved algorithm has an if-statement with three alternatives. Suppose that the first if-statement takes time t_2 to execute, and the other one takes time t_3. The total time for the old algorithm is then $\log_2(n) \cdot t_2$, and the improved algorithm takes time in excess of $(\log_2(n)-1) \cdot t_3$. Which one comes out better? We have to assume something about the relation between t_2 and t_3. If the algorithm is coded in Pascal or C, and if the if-statement is written as

> **if** $a[m] < x$ **then** $i := m$ **else**
> **if** $a[m] = x$ **then begin** $i := m$; $j := m+1$ **end**
> $\qquad$ **else** $j := m$

then we may expect $t_3 = \frac{3}{2} t_2$ if we count only comparisons (since two boolean expressions are evaluated if $a[m] \geq x$, which is *true* in half of the cases). We calculate when the improved algorithm is better.

$$(\log_2(n) - 1) \cdot t_3 < \log_2(n) \cdot t_2$$
$$=$$
$$(\log_2(n) - 1) \cdot \tfrac{3}{2} < \log_2(n)$$
$$=$$
$$\log_2(n) < 3$$
$$=$$
$$n < 8$$

It turns out that our improved algorithm is better only for very short arrays. The simpler algorithm is simply better.

9.4   Conclusion

This chapter is a very short one, but from its length one should not infer that efficiency of programs is unimportant. In fact, efficiency is extremely important, and we have developed a great many efficient algorithms in preceding chapters. If it were not for efficiency, most programming problems would be rather easy. Do not make the mistake, however, of focusing on too low a level of detail. It may pay off to tune a program, control the use of specific machine resources, decide which variables are kept in registers, which in main storage, and which on disk. But this tuning is marginal compared to the gains that a better algorithm can provide you with. An order-of-magnitude improvement outweighs any lower-level improvements, if you are interested in large problems. And if you are not interested in large problems, then tuning the low-level details is not worth it either. This kind of tuning should be done only if you are quite sure that you have got the best algorithm. There are numerous examples of assembly-language programs that are outperformed by higher-level programs on the same job, exactly because an assembly language forces one to think about the low-level decisions right away, rather than to invite one to focus on the proper algorithm (and its data structure) first.

We have not touched upon the issue of trading time versus space. In many algorithms, additional variables are introduced to store some intermediate results that are needed later. Introducing those variables saves the effort to recompute the values. It is a technique that we have applied over and over again in preceding chapters, and we do not discuss it in more detail here.

It is sometimes claimed that the importance of efficient algorithms becomes less with the increasing speed of our computer systems. Exactly the opposite is true. Assume that you have a program that takes $3 \cdot 10^9 n$ microseconds, and another program that takes 2^n microseconds for solving the same problem. Both require about a day if $n = 37$. Consider the case where you get a new computer, which runs every program 10 times faster. The linear program will allow you to run a problem with $n \approx 370$ in a day, but the exponential one limits you to $n \approx 40$. The faster the machines become, the bigger the difference between efficient and inefficient programs will grow. There is just no good excuse for writing inefficient programs.

9.5   Bibliographic Notes

The big-O notation was introduced in [Bac94]. The Ω notation is from [Knu76]. We also follow the latter paper in the sense that it describes $O(f(n))$ and $\Omega(f(n))$ as sets of functions.

Since execution aspect is an important property of a program's execution, it should really be part of the specification. Not much work has been done in this area. See [Heh89] for an example of how this might be done.

Amortized complexity has been touched upon only briefly here. See [Tar85] for a thorough discussion.

9.6   Exercises

1. Assume that we have two programs for solving a problem. One program takes time $10^n + 57$ nanoseconds, and the other takes n^{10} microseconds. For which values of n is the running time of these two programs approximately one second? For which values of n is it the time period that has elapsed since the "Big Bang"?

2. Assume that we have an algorithm whose running time is $5 \cdot 2^n$ microseconds. Compute the values of n for which the program can be executed in one minute, one day, and one year respectively. Same questions if the running time is $3n \log_2(n)$ microseconds, and if it is $10n$ microseconds.

3. Prove $3n + 17 \log(n) + 29 \in O(n)$.

4. Prove that any sorting algorithm that extracts information from the given array by comparisons only, requires $\Omega(n \log(n))$ operations.

5. Prove that the worst-case complexity of a sorting algorithm that swaps direct neighbors only, is $\Omega(n^2)$.

6. Given an array of N numbers, and an integer k, $0 \le k < N$. Show that it is possible to find the kth smallest array element in time $O(N)$. Is it possible to find all of the smallest k array elements in time $O(N)$? If so, does this contradict the fact that sorting is $\Omega(N \log(N))$?

7. We are given a bag of nonnegative numbers. The following operation is performed on the bag as long as it has at least two elements. Remove the least two elements from the bag, and add their sum as a new element to the bag. You may assume that the initial bag is given as an array with the elements in ascending order. Design a data structure that allows each step to be executed in $O(1)$.

8. What is the value of $\frac{t_3}{t_2}$ if the if-statement in the "improved" binary search is coded as

if $a[m] = x$ then begin $i := m$; $j := m + 1$ end else
if $a[m] < x$ then $i := m$
                    else $j := m$?

10

Functional Programming

In this chapter, we have a look at a programming style that is quite different from the style that we have seen before. Previously, we wrote programs that operate on variables; one of the basic operations is the assignment statement, which causes the value of an expression to be stored in a variable. It is the only statement that changes the state spanned by the variables. This programming style is called imperative programming.

Variables as used in mathematics are completely different. They do not change because some assignment statement is specified; they are understood to vary over some range, their domain. For example, in $\int_0^1 e^x \, dx$, variable x ranges over the set of all real numbers from the closed interval $[0, 1]$.

In this chapter, we study a style of programming called *functional programming*, in which variables are not changed through assignments but are the bound variables that we are familiar with in mathematics. It is sometimes claimed that this automatically implies an advantage: reasoning about functional programs is more firmly rooted in mathematics than is the machine-oriented, operational reasoning commonly used in reasoning about imperative programs. On the other hand, it often turns out that functional programs are developed with at least as much operational reasoning as are imperative programs. Apparently, the claimed advantage is not automatic.

10.1 LISP

We start our explorations with LISP. LISP (list processing language) is based on λ-calculus. We choose not to present λ-calculus first, but to discuss LISP programs right away. As a result, the firm, but sometimes boring, basis is missing. (As a matter of fact, the relation between LISP and λ-calculus is only sketchy and is often overemphasized.) While λ-calculus may give some insights into the foundations of computing, it hardly contributes to the effective design of reliable programs. We do not attempt to provide a programming-oriented exposition of LISP, but give a bottom-up exposition, starting with some of the features of the language and seeing how they can be used. The main reason for discussing LISP in full length is to allow us to study both the language and its implementation without having to ignore lots of details. (Warning: many, many versions of LISP exist that differ in minor and major details. We discuss only one version, the simplest one of which I am aware.)

One of the differences between functional programs and imperative programs is the nature of the variables. Another difference is that many functional programs operate on values of a different type than we are used to. Quite often, they are lists, or sequences. Lists differ from arrays in the sense that the elements are not equally accessible: the first element can be accessed and the remainder of the list can be accessed. It takes a number of steps to access the fourth element of a list (the first element of the remainder of the remainder of the remainder of the list). The fact that not all elements are accessible in the same number of steps induces a terrific asymmetry, and it has its consequences on the design of programs, especially when efficiency is considered.

In LISP, the list that consists of the elements a, b, and c in that order is written as $(a\ b\ c)$. The elements a, b, and c have no meaning whatsoever, but are arbitrary constants that have no further structure attached to them. Such constants are called atoms. (It's not that computer scientists think that, in physics, atoms have no further substructure: one just needs a name that is good enough for its purpose.) Atoms are denoted by a sequence of letters and digits, just as in C and Pascal, except that the first character may be a digit as well as a letter. Elements of a list are not restricted to being atomic; they may also be lists. An example of a list of lists is $((a\ b)\ (c\ d))$, and an example of a mixed list is $(a\ b\ (c\ d)\ e)$. The empty list is $()$. It is also written as the atom nil, which is, therefore, an atom that does have a "meaning". The two notations for the empty list are interchangeable.

Little can be done with atoms. The major operation on atoms is the test for equality. LISP provides a boolean function on two atoms, whose value is true when the two atoms are equal, and false otherwise. Boolean values need to be represented by atoms; hence two special atoms are needed. We already have one special atom, nil, and we add another one, t. Atom nil serves both as the empty list, and as the boolean value false. Atom t corresponds to true. We thus have

$$(eq\ a\ a)\ =\ t$$

and

$$(eq\ a\ b)\ =\ nil\qquad .$$

The arguments of the function are not separated by commas. The function name is between the parentheses, not in front of them. As a result, the construct $(eq\ a\ b)$ looks like a list. The notation in which LISP programs are written is the same as the notation for the values being manipulated. It is confusing, indeed, but on the other hand, it is one of the properties that allows us to make an extremely concise implementation, to be discussed later.

Boolean function *atom* lets us determine whether its argument is an atom or a list. Since *nil* is both an atom and a list, a choice has to be made here: the function is chosen to be true for *nil*.

$$(atom\ a)\ =\ t$$
$$(atom\ nil)\ =\ t$$
$$(atom\ ())\ =\ t$$
$$(atom\ (a\ b\ c))\ =\ nil$$

How about composing these functions? What is $(atom\ (eq\ a\ b))$? One might expect

$$
\begin{aligned}
&(atom\ (eq\ a\ b)) \\
=\quad &\{\ (eq\ a\ b)\ =\ nil\ \} \\
&(atom\ nil) \\
=\quad &\{\ (atom\ nil)\ =\ t\ \} \\
&t\quad,
\end{aligned}
$$

but, unfortunately, this is not the case. This is because the argument $(eq\ a\ b)$ of *atom* is not evaluated when input $(atom\ (eq\ a\ b))$ is entered. The argument is taken literally, without evaluating it first. In other programming languages, we would write it in quotes. In LISP, the quotes are assumed implicitly on all arguments of the expression that is being input. Hence, this input leads to applying *atom* to a list of three elements: the list $(eq\ a\ b)$. Since this list is not an atom, the result is *nil* instead of t. When defining functions, however, as we will be doing below, while within the expression defining the function, arguments to any further function application will be evaluated before the function is applied. Hence, when we write something like

$$(atom\ (eq\ a\ b))$$

within function definitions, the effect is as expected. (The result is t if both a and b are parameters that have an atomic value, and it is undefined otherwise.)

The next three functions, *car*, *cdr*, and *cons*, decompose or construct values. For a nonempty list x, $(car\ x)$ is the first element of x and $(cdr\ x)$ is the list obtained by dropping the first element of x.

$$(car\ (a\ b\ c))\ =\ a$$
$$(cdr\ (a\ b\ c))\ =\ (b\ c)$$
$$(car\ ((a\ b)\ (c\ d)))\ =\ (a\ b)$$
$$(cdr\ ((a\ b)\ (c\ d)))\ =\ ((c\ d))$$

For any list x and any a, $(cons\ a\ x)$ is the list whose first element is a and whose remainder is x.

$$(cons\ a\ (b\ c))\ =\ (a\ b\ c)$$
$$(cons\ (a\ b)\ (c\ d))\ =\ ((a\ b)\ c\ d)$$
$$(cons\ a\ nil)\ =\ (a)$$

It follows that

$$(car\ (cons\ a\ x))\ =\ a$$
$$(cdr\ (cons\ a\ x))\ =\ x\qquad .$$

Sometimes we will apply *cons* to a second argument that is not necessarily a list. For example, if x is an atom, we still assume the two equalities to hold. The result of such a *cons* is not a list. Instead, it is called a *dotted pair*. It is printed as $(a\ .\ x)$. List $(a\ b\ c)$ is equivalent to $(a\ .\ (b\ .\ (c\ .\ nil)))$.

> *(Aside)* The names *car* and *cdr* are somewhat obscure. These funny names are due to the first implementation of LISP, in which list x would be represented in a register that consists of two parts. The *contents of address field of register* would hold $(car\ x)$ and the *contents of decrement field of register* would hold $(cdr\ x)$.

This completes the set of all functions provided by LISP. When writing programs, we construct more complicated and hopefully more interesting functions from these five base functions. All that remains is some syntax for defining functions. We give examples of function definitions. They look like applications of a function called *define*, but the similarity is deceptive: the syntax is the same, the semantics is completely different. The syntax is inspired by the λ-calculus. For example, in the λ-calculus one would not write

$$sqr(x)\ =\ x^2$$

to define the function that squares its argument, but

$$sqr\ =\ \lambda x.x^2\qquad .$$

The construct $\lambda x.x^2$ is an anonymous function. Such functions are useful in algebraic manipulations. (x^2 is not a function: it is an expression in x; the construct λx "binds" x and turns the expression into a function.) We give two functions that produce the second and third element of their argument respectively, which is supposed to be a sufficiently long list.

$$(define\ (cadr\ (lambda\ (x)\ (car\ (cdr\ x))))$$
$$(caddr\ (lambda\ (x)\ (car\ (cdr\ (cdr\ x))))))$$

The examples illustrate the syntax: *define* has a number of arguments, each of which is a function definition. Each function definition is a list of two elements: the name of the function and the λ-expression defining the function. The λ-expression in turn is a list of three elements: the atom *lambda*, the list of bound variables, and the expression.

The LISP counter part of the if-statement is the conditional expression. A conditional expression is a list whose first element is atom *cond* and whose remaining elements are all of the form $(b_i \ e_i)$:

$$(cond \ (b_0 \ e_0) \ (b_1 \ e_1) \ \cdots \ (b_{n-1} \ e_{n-1}))$$

The b_i are booleans, that is, expressions that evaluate to t or *nil*. The value of the conditional expression is e_j, where j is the least value for which b_j is t. If no such j exists, the expression is undefined. Booleans b_{j+1} through b_{n-1} are not evaluated. It follows that the order of the elements in the conditional expression is relevant. As a result, one often writes t for the last boolean in the list. Here is an example of a function that uses a conditional expression. It is true if the argument is the empty list and false otherwise.

$$(define \ (null \ (lambda \ (x)$$
$$(cond \ ((atom \ x) \ (eq \ x \ nil))$$
$$(t \ nil)))))$$

What is the reason for defining functions at all? After all, we might type something like

$$(null \ (a \ b \ c))$$

and find the LISP system printing *nil*, but we could equally well type

$$((lambda \ (x) \ (cond \ ((atom \ x) \ (eq \ x \ nil)) \ (t \ nil))) \ (a \ b \ c))$$

and obtain the same response. One advantage of defining functions is the fact that the former of the two inputs is definitely shorter, given that *null* has been defined. Also, it allows us to split large programs into smaller pieces that can be used in different places and that are easier to identify when they have a name. Another reason is that the introduction of a name for the function allows the function definition to be recursive. Because of the absence of assignable variables, we do not have iteration in LISP and we find ourselves writing lots of recursive function definitions. Also, the fact that lists are defined recursively invites recursively defined programs.

Here is an example of a recursively defined function. Function *atomlist* applied to a list is supposed to be true if the list consists of atoms only, and false otherwise. The function is undefined if the argument is not a list.

$$(define \ (atomlist \ (lambda \ (x)$$
$$(cond \ ((null \ x) \ t)$$
$$((atom \ (car \ x)) \ (atomlist \ (cdr \ x)))$$
$$(t \ nil)))))$$

Informally, *atomlist* is true either if its argument is the empty list or if both the first element is an atom and the remainder is a list of atoms. Because of the absence of boolean connectives, we have to spell it out in the form of a conditional expression. By doing so, we make sure that functions are never applied to an argument outside their domain. For example,

$(define\ (atomlist\ (lambda\ (x)$
$\qquad\qquad (cond\ \ ((atom\ (car\ x))\ (atomlist\ (cdr\ x)))$
$\qquad\qquad\qquad\ \ ((null\ x)\ t)$
$\qquad\qquad\qquad\ \ (t\ nil)))))$

is an incorrect program because *car* may (and will) be applied to the empty list.

10.2   Well-Founded Definitions

Our definition of *atomlist* is recursive, and in the sequel we will see many more recursive definitions. How do we make sure that recursive definitions are proper definitions? Do they really define the function? When writing the definition for factorial, we write something like

$0! = 1$
$n! = n \cdot (n-1)! \qquad \text{for all } n > 0,$

and we know that this is a proper definition of $n!$ for all natural n because the recursion is well founded: in the definition of $n!$, a recursive invocation of ! occurs, but the argument is $n-1$, which is less than n and thereby implies that eventually the base case 0 is reached. Had we opted for

$0! = 1$
$n! = (n+1)!/(n+1) \qquad \text{for all } n > 0,$

then the situation would have been not nearly so fortunate. The latter line expresses an equality that holds for the factorial function, but it does not define the left-hand side in terms of the right-hand side. In order to stress the asymmetry in this kind of definitional equality, one sometimes writes a triangle over the equality sign. (The resulting symbol still looks symmetric, though.)

In the case of LISP, we need an order on lists instead of on natural numbers to show that the recursion terminates. The order need not be total, but it must be the case that every decreasing sequence of values, that is, a sequence in which every value is smaller in the order than its predecessor in the sequence, is of finite length. Such an order is called *well founded*. A partial order, or for that matter a total order, admits mathematical induction just when it is a well-founded order. A precise formulation of the principle of mathematical induction is as follows. From

$\qquad P(0)$

and

$\qquad \langle \forall n : n \geq 0 : P(n) \Rightarrow P(n+1) \rangle$

follows

$$\langle \forall n : n \geq 0 : P(n) \rangle \quad .$$

Another formulation is sometimes called "strong mathematical induction": from

$$\langle \forall n : n \geq 0 : \langle \forall i : 0 \leq i < n : P(i) \rangle \Rightarrow P(n) \rangle$$

follows

$$\langle \forall n : n \geq 0 : P(n) \rangle \quad .$$

In the latter formulation, the base case is included in the general case (substitute 0 for n) and only one formula suffices. The advantage of the latter formulation is that it generalizes to arbitrary partial orders. Let V be a set with partial order $<$ on its elements. If it is a well-founded order, we have: from

$$\langle \forall y : y \in V : \langle \forall x : x \in V \wedge x < y : P(x) \rangle \Rightarrow P(y) \rangle$$

follows

$$\langle \forall y : y \in V : P(y) \rangle \quad .$$

If the order is not well founded, this conclusion is not warranted. Informally speaking, there need not be a base on which the induction is founded. Or, equivalently, the recursion need not terminate.

What is the well-founded order that we use to show that our recursive function definitions are proper, that is, to admit reasoning by mathematical induction? The order we choose is: one list is less than another if the former is a proper substructure of the latter. For example, for all nonatomic x, both $(car\ x)$ and $(cdr\ x)$ are proper substructures of x, and hence less than x under our order. In most of our recursive definitions, the recursive call is indeed on the car or cdr of one of the parameters.

> In other versions of LISP, lists may sometimes contain loops: a list can be an element of itself. In this case the substructure order is not well founded. In our version of LISP no loops can be constructed.

The induction principle based on this order is sometimes called structural induction. You have been using the substructure order in such cases as defining the derivative of expressions : $\frac{d}{dx}(e + f) = \frac{de}{dx} + \frac{df}{dx}$. Why is this a proper definition, that is, why is it not a circular definition giving the derivative in terms of a derivative? Because e and f are subexpressions of $e + f$: they are both smaller than $e + f$ in the substructure order. (But it is irrelevant whether e is a substructure of f or not: the order need not be total.)

10.3 More Examples of LISP Programs

We continue our exploration of LISP with a list of examples. The first example function computes the last element of its argument, which is required to be a nonempty list.

> (*define*
>   (*last* (*lambda* (*x*)
>   (*cond* ((*null* (*cdr x*)) (*car x*))
>   (*t* (*last* (*cdr x*)))))))

The recursive call in the definition of (*last x*) is one in which the argument is (*cdr x*); that is, it is less than the original argument *x* in the substructure order. In the definition of *equal*, both arguments are smaller in both recursive calls.

The second function is a boolean function that is true just when its two arguments are equal.

> (*define*
>   (*equal* (*lambda* (*x y*)
>   (*cond* ((*atom x*) (*cond* ((*atom y*) (*eq x y*))
>   (*t nil*)))
>   ((*atom y*) *nil*)
>   ((*equal* (*car x*) (*car y*)) (*equal* (*cdr x*) (*cdr y*)))
>   (*t nil*)))))

The asymmetry in the definition of the conditional expression (that is, the relevance of the order of the alternatives) leads to an asymmetry in the way in which *x* and *y* are handled in *equal*.

Having typed in the definitions above, we might have the following "dialogue" with a LISP system. (The output is slightly indented to allow you to see what the input is and what the output is.)

> (*last* (*abcd de f gh*))
>   *gh*
> (*last* ((*a b*) (*c d*) (*xyz f*)))
>   (*xyz f*)
> (*equal a a*)
>   *t*
> (*equal* (*a*) *a*)
>   *nil*
> (*equal* (*a b* (*c d*)) (*a b* (*c d*)))
>   *t*

Our next function takes two lists as its arguments and catenates the two; that is, it returns one list whose elements are the elements of the first argument (in the order given) followed by the elements of the second argument (in the order given).

> *(define (append (lambda (x y)*
>   *(cond   ((null x) y)*
>   *(t (cons (car x) (append (cdr x) y)))))))))*

The recursion is well founded. Let us prove that this definition indeed
defines the function we want to have. (The proof is really very simple,
so we can concentrate on the shape of such a proof rather than on the
actual case.) In order to do so, we need some specification of *append* for
comparison. Here is an informal specification:

> *(append x y)* is the list containing the elements of *x*
> followed by the elements of *y*   .

The proof, by mathematical induction, follows the structure of the definition.

- if $x = nil$ then

>   *(append x y)*
> =   { substitute function body }
>   *y*
> =   { $x = nil$ }
>   the elements of *x* followed by the elements of *y*

  which is as required by the specification.

- if $x \neq nil$ then

>   *(append x y)*
> =   { substitute function body }
>   *(cons (car x) (append (cdr x) y))*
> =   { definition of *cons* }
>   *(car x)* followed by the elements of *(append (cdr x) y)*
> =   { induction hypothesis }
>   *(car x)* followed by the elements of
>   *(cdr x)* followed by the elements of *y*
> =   { $x = (cons (car x) (cdr x))$ }
>   the elements of *x* followed by the elements of *y*

  which is as required by the specification. We rely on the associativity
  of "followed by" in the last step.

Soon we will find ourselves interested in the efficiency of *append*. Here,
what do we mean by efficiency? We cannot talk about the efficiency of a
mathematical function, of course, but we may be asking for the time it
takes to evaluate the application of a function to an argument, given some
mechanism for performing the application. We will discuss a mechanism in
detail later, but for now it suffices to count the number of steps it takes to

arrive at the result by merely substituting a function body for its name. We may count the number of times that this is done for the five elementary functions, for the other functions, or for all functions. In this example, we count the number of *cons* operations only. (This is not a very interesting measure to apply to function *equal*; in most other cases, however, it doesn't really matter what is being counted because all counts come out roughly the same.) Let $f(k)$ be the number of *cons* operations required for *append* -ing a list of length k with another list. (In terms of the parameters, k is the length of x, and $f(k)$ does not depend on y.) According to the function body of *append*, we have

- $f(0) = 0$ because no *cons* operations are required if $x = nil$;

- $f(k) = 1 + f(k-1)$ if $k > 0$ because 1 *cons* operation is required to construct the result and $f(k-1)$ *cons* operations are required to construct the intermediate result.

This pair of equations has one solution for f : the identity function $f(k) = k$. We do not discuss general techniques for finding such solutions. We can make a guess at what the solution is and verify it by substituting in the equations. If the solution is unique, then this suffices. If the LISP function is well defined then the solution to these equations is unique.

The next function is a lot more interesting than the previous ones. It computes the reverse of a list, that is, constructs a list whose elements are the same as those in the argument but they occur in reverse order.

$$(define\ (reverse\ (lambda\ (x)$$
$$(cond\ ((null\ x)\ nil)$$
$$(t\ (append\ (reverse\ (cdr\ x))\ (cons\ (car\ x)\ nil)))))))$$

The recursion is well founded and $(reverse\ x)$ "obviously" constructs the reverse of x. What is the efficiency of this program? Again, let us count the number of *cons* operations required. Let $g(k)$ be the number of *cons* operations required for reversing a list of length k. We have

- $g(0) = 0$

- $g(k) = g(k-1) + f(k-1) + 1$ for $k > 0$, because it takes $g(k-1)$ *cons* operations to reverse $(cdr\ x)$ and it takes $f(k-1)$ *cons* operations to append that result to the list of length 1 that consists of the first element of x only.

Substituting k for $f(k)$ (see above), we obtain

- $g(0) = 0$

- $g(k) = g(k-1) + k$ for $k > 0$,

whose solution is $g(k) = k(k + 1)/2$. We see that the program has a complexity that grows quadratically with the size of its argument. Next, we exhibit a different definition of the same function that has a linear complexity and is, therefore, much to be preferred.

$(define\ (reverse\ (lambda\ (x)$
$\qquad (rev\ x\ nil)))$
$\quad (rev\ (lambda\ (x\ y)$
$\qquad (cond\ ((null\ x)\ y)$
$\qquad\quad (t\ (rev\ (cdr\ x)\ (cons\ (car\ x)\ y)))))))$

First, the recursion is well founded: $(cdr\ x)$ is a proper substructure of x and, hence, smaller. As a result the definition is okay, even though the argument substituted for y, namely $(cons\ (car\ x)\ y)$, is larger. Second, *reverse* is the right function. To that end, we can prove that $(rev\ x\ y)$ is the list of elements of x in reverse order, followed by the elements of y. Substituting *nil* for y reveals that $(rev\ x\ nil)$ is indeed the reverse of x, as required. By induction, we can, but do not, show that *rev* satisfies its specification. Third, we establish the efficiency of *rev*. Let $h(k)$ be the number of *cons* operations required in the application of *rev* to a list of length k with an arbitrary second argument. According to the definition of *rev*, we have

- $h(0) = 0$ because no *cons* operations are required if $x = nil$;

- $h(k) = 1 + h(k-1)$ if $k > 0$, because 1 *cons* operation is required to construct the second argument of *rev* and $h(k-1)$ *cons* operations are required to apply *rev* to $(cdr\ x)$.

Again, this pair of equations has one solution: the identity function. Hence, this is a linear program.

The technique of introducing an auxiliary function with an additional parameter is often used in functional programming. The additional parameter is sometimes called an accumulator. Its introduction corresponds to the introduction of a variable in imperative programming. The example illustrates a programming technique that we have also seen in Chapter 8: reduce the problem size. In an imperative notation, we would write

$x, y := X, nil;$
$\{$ invariant: reverse of X = reverse of x, followed by y $\}$
$\{$ bound: x $\}$
$*[x \neq nil \rightarrow x, y := (cdr\ x), (cons\ (car\ x)\ y)]$

and this relates directly to our LISP program.

We continue this list of examples with two functions that operate on finite sets. A set is conveniently represented by a list of all its elements. The order of the elements in the list is irrelevant. We may or may not decide to avoid duplicate elements in the list — in the examples, we assume that the given lists have no duplicates, and we construct lists that have no duplicates. The first function establishes whether a given value is an element of a given set, that is, for given a and s, it computes the boolean value $a \in s$. The program corresponds to the following two cases:

- either $s = \emptyset$, so $a \in s \equiv$ *false*;

- or $s = \{b\} \cup r$, so $a \in s \equiv a = b \vee a \in r$.

$$(define \ (member \ (lambda \ (a \ s)$$
$$(cond \ ((null \ s) \ nil)$$
$$((equal \ a \ (car \ s)) \ t)$$
$$(t \ (member \ a \ (cdr \ s)))))))$$

The other example of a function on sets is set union: for given sets x and y, compute $x \cup y$. Our solution is, necessarily, asymmetric in x and y. It is based on

- $\emptyset \cup y = y$

- $(\{a\} \cup x) \cup y = x \cup y$ if $a \in y$

- $(\{a\} \cup x) \cup y = \{a\} \cup (x \cup y)$ if $a \notin y$.

$$(define \ (union \ (lambda \ (x \ y)$$
$$(cond \ ((null \ x) \ y)$$
$$((member \ (car \ x) \ y) \ (union \ (cdr \ x) \ y))$$
$$(t \ (cons \ (car \ x) \ (union \ (cdr \ x) \ y)))))))$$

The next two examples illustrate how functions can be used as parameters in exactly the same way that other values can. The first is function *map*, which applies a given function to every element of a given list. For example, $(map \ car \ ((a \ b) \ (f \ gh \ e))) = (a \ f)$. The second function is best explained using infix notation. Suppose x is the list $x_0, x_1, \cdots, x_{n-1}$ and $\oplus$ is some infix operator. We define $(reduce \ \oplus \ x)$ to be the result of inserting $\oplus$ between every two consecutive elements in x, that is, the result of expression $x_0 \oplus x_1 \oplus \cdots \oplus x_{n-1}$. In the case where x is the empty list, the result is the unit element e of the operation $\oplus$, which we, therefore, give as another argument to *reduce*. If operator $\oplus$ is not associative, then we have to clarify how the expression with the $\oplus$'s in it is to be interpreted. We distinguish between the so-called *left-reduce*

$$((e \oplus x_0) \oplus x_1) \oplus \cdots \oplus x_{n-1}$$

and the *right-reduce*

$$x_0 \oplus (x_1 \oplus \cdots \oplus (x_{n-1} \oplus e)).$$

Here are the definitions of *map* and *rreduce*.

```
(define (map (lambda (f x)
          (cond ((null x) nil)
                (t (cons (f (car x)) (map f (cdr x)))))))
       (rreduce (lambda (op e x)
          (cond ((null x) e)
                (t (op (car x) (rreduce op e (cdr x))))))))
```

Suppose function *and* computes the conjunction of two booleans: the result of $(and\ x\ y)$ is t if both x and y equal t, and is *nil* otherwise. Then, expression $(rreduce\ and\ true\ x)$ computes the conjunction of all booleans in list x: it is t if all elements of x are t, and it is *nil* otherwise. For example, we have

$$(rreduce\ and\ t\ (t\ t\ t)) = t\quad,$$
$$(rreduce\ and\ t\ (t\ nil\ t)) = nil\quad.$$

The *map* and *reduce* functions embody common recursion patterns and their use enables the simplification of many programs.

Our next example is a boolean function that checks whether its two arguments have the same *fringe*. The fringe of a value is the list of atoms in their order of occurrence, ignoring the parenthesized structure in the given value. For example,

$$(same\ (a\ (b\ c))\ ((a\ (b))\ (c))) = t$$

and

$$(same\ (a\ (b\ c))\ ((a\ (c))\ (b))) = nil\quad.$$

We give two essentially different solutions to this problem. The first solution constructs the two fringes and compares them.

```
(define
    (same (lambda (a b)
        (samefringe (fringe a) (fringe b))))
    (fringe (lambda (x)
        (cond ((null x) nil)
              ((atom x) (cons x nil))
              (t (append (fringe (car x)) (fringe (cdr x)))))))
    (samefringe (lambda (fra frb)
        (cond ((null fra) (null frb))
              ((null frb) nil)
              ((eq (car fra) (car frb))
                  (samefringe (cdr fra) (cdr frb)))
              (t nil)))))
```

We can make function *fringe* more efficient by adding an accumulating parameter to avoid *append*.

$$(fringe\ (lambda\ (x)$$
$$(fr\ x\ nil)))$$
$$(fr\ (lambda\ (x\ y)$$
$$(cond\ ((null\ x)\ y)$$
$$((atom\ x)\ (cons\ x\ y))$$
$$(t\ (fr\ (car\ x)\ (fr\ (cdr\ x)\ y)))))))$$

In the sequel, we do not refer to this version of *fringe* anymore, but refer
to the first version instead. The next solution is based on the observation
that the first solution constructs two complete fringes and only thereafter
starts comparing them. For the sake of efficiency, it would be much better
if we could combine the two operations and stop both the comparison and
construction processes if the two fringes are found to be different. The
essential idea is to construct function *split* that does not construct the
entire fringe, but rather constructs its first element plus some remainder.
The remainder is any structure whose fringe equals the remainder of the
whole fringe.

if $(fringe\ a)\ =\ nil$ then
$\quad\quad[0]\quad\quad\quad (split\ a)\ =\ nil$
if $(fringe\ a)\ \neq\ nil$ then
$\quad\quad[1]\quad\quad\quad (car\ (fringe\ a))\ =\ (car\ (split\ a))$
$\quad\quad[2]\quad\quad\quad (cdr\ (fringe\ a))\ =\ (fringe\ (cdr\ (split\ a)))$

A consequence of these three rules is

$\quad\quad[3]\quad\quad\quad (null\ (fringe\ a))\ =\ (null\ (split\ a))$.

Instead of function *samefringe* we need a function that compares the leading elements (if any) and, in case of equality, deals with the remainders.
The function definition can be derived from the definition of *samefringe*
by postulating the intended meaning

$\quad\quad (samefringe\ (fringe\ a)\ (fringe\ b))$
$=\quad (samesplit\ (split\ a)\ (split\ b))$

and then calculating from the definition of *samefringe*.

$\quad\quad (samesplit\ (split\ a)\ (split\ b))$
$=\quad\quad\quad \{\ by\ postulate\ \}$
$\quad\quad (samefringe\ (fringe\ a)\ (fringe\ b))$
$=\quad\quad\quad \{\ definition\ of\ samefringe\ \}$
$\quad\quad (cond\ ((null\ (fringe\ a))\ (null\ (fringe\ b)))$
$\quad\quad\quad\quad ((null\ (fringe\ b))\ nil)$
$\quad\quad\quad\quad ((eq\ (car\ (fringe\ a))\ (car\ (fringe\ b)))$
$\quad\quad\quad\quad\quad (samefringe\ (cdr\ (fringe\ a))\ (cdr\ (fringe\ b))))$
$\quad\quad\quad\quad (t\ nil))$
$=\quad\quad\quad \{\ [3]\ \}$

$$
\begin{aligned}
&(cond\ ((null\ (split\ a))\ (null\ (split\ b)))\\
&\qquad ((null\ (split\ b))\ nil)\\
&\qquad ((eq\ (car\ (fringe\ a))\ (car\ (fringe\ b)))\\
&\qquad\qquad (samefringe\ (cdr\ (fringe\ a))\ (cdr\ (fringe\ b))))\\
&\qquad (t\ nil))\\
=\quad &\{\ [1]\ \text{twice}\ \}\\
&(cond\ ((null\ (split\ a))\ (null\ (split\ b)))\\
&\qquad ((null\ (split\ b))\ nil)\\
&\qquad ((eq\ (car\ (split\ a))\ (car\ (split\ b)))\\
&\qquad\qquad (samefringe\ (cdr\ (fringe\ a))\ (cdr\ (fringe\ b))))\\
&\qquad (t\ nil))\\
=\quad &\{\ [2]\ \}\\
&(cond\ ((null\ (split\ a))\ (null\ (split\ b)))\\
&\qquad ((null\ (split\ b))\ nil)\\
&\qquad ((eq\ (car\ (split\ a))\ (car\ (split\ b)))\\
&\qquad\qquad (samefringe\ \ (fringe\ (cdr\ (split\ a)))\\
&\qquad\qquad\qquad\qquad (fringe\ (cdr\ (split\ b))))))\\
&\qquad (t\ nil))\\
=\quad &\{\ \text{postulated meaning of } samesplit\ \}\\
&(cond\ ((null\ (split\ a))\ (null\ (split\ b)))\\
&\qquad ((null\ (split\ b))\ nil)\\
&\qquad ((eq\ (car\ (split\ a))\ (car\ (split\ b)))\\
&\qquad\qquad (samesplit\ \ (split\ (cdr\ (split\ a)))\\
&\qquad\qquad\qquad\qquad (split\ (cdr\ (split\ b)))))\\
&\qquad (t\ nil))
\end{aligned}
$$

Thus, we have obtained the function definition for *samesplit*. This leaves us with the task of defining function *split*. We have a lot of choice here, since all we require of *split* is that it satisfy the relation to *fringe* given by its postulated meaning. One solution is to use *fringe* for *split*, but that defeats the whole purpose: it is correct, but inefficient.

We are now going to define *split*. We might give a calculational derivation similar to that of *samesplit*, but this is left to Exercise 17. Instead, we give an informal argument. On account of [0], we start out with

$$
\begin{aligned}
&(split\ x)\\
=\quad &(cond\ ((null\ x)\ nil)
\end{aligned}
$$

and [1] leads us to extend this to

$$
\begin{aligned}
&(cond\ ((null\ x)\ nil)\\
&\qquad ((atom\ x)\ (cons\ x\ nil)))\qquad .
\end{aligned}
$$

Because $(fringe\ (cons\ (cons\ a\ b)\ c)) = (fringe\ (cons\ a\ (cons\ b\ c)))$, and on account of [1] and [2], we are tempted to add

```
(cond ((null x) nil)
      ((atom x) (cons x nil))
      (t (cons (car (split (car x)))
               (cons (cdr (split (car x))))
                     (cdr x)))))     ,
```

but this is correct only if $(split\ (car\ x))$ is nonempty. Our final version is therefore

```
(cond ((null x) nil)
      ((atom x) (cons x nil))
      ((null (split (car x))) (split (cdr x)))
      (t (cons (car (split (car x)))
               (cons (cdr (split (car x))))
                     (cdr x)))))     .
```

The complete program is as follows. It differs from the one above only in that multiple evaluation of $(split\ (car\ x))$ is avoided.

```
(define
    (same (lambda (a b)
        (samesplit (split a) (split b))))
    (split (lambda (x)
        (cond ((null x) nil)
              ((atom x) (cons x nil))
              (t (f (split (car x)) (cdr x))))))
    (f (lambda (scarx cdrx)
        (cond ((null scarx) (split cdrx))
              (t (cons (car (scarx))
                       (cons (cdr scarx)
                             cdrx))))))
    (samesplit (lambda (spa spb)
        (cond ((null spa) (null spb))
              ((null spb) nil)
              ((eq (car spa) (car spb))
                  (samesplit (split (cdr spa)) (split (cdr spb))))
              (t nil)))))
```

We are about to conclude our list of examples — one more to go. This example is about addition of natural numbers. We have to come up with some representation of the numbers, since in our "pure" version of LISP no built-in numbers exist. One way of representing number n is by a list of n elements, for example, a list of n *nil*'s. It certainly makes addition simple: it is merely the catenation of two lists for which we can use our function *append*. It is, however, not very efficient in time and storage to use a list of length n. The decimal representation that we are familiar with is more compact: a list of $log_{10}(n)$ digits suffices. Of course we may

use any other base than ten (well, the base should be at least two), and
our program is slightly simpler if we use the smallest possible base, that is,
base two. Formally, the value $\mathcal{M}(x)$ represented by a sequence of binary
digits x is

- $\mathcal{M}(nil) = 0$

- $\mathcal{M}(xa) = \mathcal{M}(x) \cdot 2 + a$, where a is one digit, $0 \le a \le 1$.

Adding numbers is a process that proceeds from right to left, that is, from
the least- to the most-significant digit. In every step, the corresponding
digits are added, thereby forming one digit in the sum and a carry to the
next, more significant, position.

Here is how it works in the general case. Let one number be of the form
xa, where x is a sequence of digits followed by the least-significant digit
a, and the other be yb, and let the incoming carry be c; then the sum
of xa, yb, and c is given by the sum of x and y, with incoming carry
$(a + b + c)$ **div** 2 followed by the least-significant digit $(a + b + c)$ **mod** 2.
This definition of *sum* properly forms the sum, since we have

$$\mathcal{M}(sum(xa, yb, c))$$
$$= \quad \{ \text{ definition of } sum \ \}$$
$$\mathcal{M}(sum(x, y, (a + b + c) \ \textbf{div} \ 2)) \cdot 2 + (a + b + c) \ \textbf{mod} \ 2$$
$$= \quad \{ \text{ induction hypothesis } \}$$
$$(\mathcal{M}(x) + \mathcal{M}(y) + (a + b + c) \ \textbf{div} \ 2) \cdot 2 + (a + b + c) \ \textbf{mod} \ 2$$
$$= \quad \{ \text{ arithmetic } \}$$
$$\mathcal{M}(x) \cdot 2 + \mathcal{M}(y) \cdot 2 + (a + b + c) \ \textbf{div} \ 2 \cdot 2 + (a + b + c) \ \textbf{mod} \ 2$$
$$= \quad \{ \text{ arithmetic } \}$$
$$\mathcal{M}(x) \cdot 2 + \mathcal{M}(y) \cdot 2 + a + b + c$$
$$= \quad \{ \text{ arithmetic } \}$$
$$\mathcal{M}(xa) + \mathcal{M}(yb) + c \qquad .$$

Furthermore, we have that the last digit is binary, that is, $0 \le (a + b + c)$ **mod** $2 \le 1$, and the new carry is a binary digit, $0 \le (a + b + c)$ **div** $2 \le 1$, since $0 \le a + b + c \le 3$.

Since we need to work from less to more-significant digits to perform the
addition, and since we can access only the first element of a list efficiently,
it seems wise to store the digits in reverse order in a list. Using base 2, we
get binary numbers, and the representation is something like $(0\ 0\ 1\ 0\ 0\ 1\ 1)$
for a hundred, or also $(0\ 0\ 1\ 0\ 0\ 1\ 1\ 0\ 0)$ if we don't care about leading zeros
(which become trailing zeros in the reverse order), and $()$ or $(0\ 0\ 0)$ for
zero. The list elements are digits 0 and 1, and in our LISP system they are
meaningless identifiers, just as a, x, and *zero* are. We need to interpret
them as constants, however, and to that end the construct $(quote\ x)$ is
introduced. It is an expression, just as x is, but its value is the constant x
rather than the value associated with variable x. Our program for addition
of two numbers, x and y, represented by lists of digits in reverse order

(and possibly different length), is as follows. Note that x and y are lists of digits, whereas c is a single digit.

```
(define
  (add (lambda (x y)
    (sum x y (quote 0))))
  (sum (lambda (x y c)
    (cond ((null x) (cond ((eq c (quote 0)) y)
                          (t (sum (quote (1)) y (quote 0)))))
          ((null y) (cond ((eq c (quote 0)) x)
                          (t (sum x (quote (1)) (quote 0)))))
          (t (cons (mod2 (car x) (car y) c)
                   (sum (cdr x) (cdr y)
                        (div2 (car x) (car y) c)))))))
  (div2 (lambda (a b c)
    (cond ((eq a b) a)
          ((eq b c) b)
          ((eq c a) c))))
  (mod2 (lambda (a b c)
    (cond ((eq a b) c)
          ((eq b c) a)
          ((eq c a) b)))))
```

10.4   A LISP Interpreter Written in LISP

In this section, we present a program for interpreting LISP programs. The input to the interpreter is a LISP program, that is, an expression consisting of constants and functions with their arguments, and the output is the result of evaluating the expression. Hence, the interpreter can be used for running the programs that we have seen so far. An interesting aspect is that the interpreter itself is a LISP program, so the whole thing is a bit circular: in order to run the interpreter you already need to have a LISP implementation, which in turn means that you don't need this interpreter. True, but it serves at least two purposes. First, it is a nice example of a larger LISP program. Second, it serves as a blueprint for an interpreter written in Pascal that we discuss in the next section. It can also be viewed as defining the meaning of LISP programs: if you want to know what the result of executing a LISP program is, just figure out what the interpreter will do with it. This form of definition of the semantics of a programming language is very different from the axiomatic semantics that we have used in previous chapters. Called operational semantics, it defines the semantics in terms of another program. You have to be very careful not to fall in the pit of circular definitions...

How does our LISP interpreter work? A function *apply* exists that applies a function to a list of arguments. For example, if the function is *car* and the list of arguments is $((a\ b\ c))$, then the result is a. The result is not $(a\ b\ c)$, since $((a\ b\ c))$ was said to be the list of arguments, so the first and only argument to *car* is the list $(a\ b\ c)$. What is the result of applying f to $((a\ b\ c))$? This depends on the definition of f, so our program *apply* has to be supplied with the current function definitions. We will also need the values of variables. We use one data structure for recording the value associated with an identifier, the so-called association list, both for variables and functions. It is a long list of pairs, where each pair is an identifier together with its present value. The *car* of the pair is the identifier and the *cdr* is the value. If the identifier is a function, then the value is the λ-expression. For example, if variable a has value t and if function f returns the third element of a list, then the association list could be

$$((a\ .\ t)\ (f\ .\ (lambda\ (x)\ (car\ (cdr\ (cdr\ x)))))))$$

If we have various nested function calls, then it may be the case that one identifier was bound a couple of times, possibly to different values. In our present program, the association list will contain all bindings, and the currently valid one is the one that is closest to the head of the list. For example, the value of variable a is 23 if the association list reads

$$((a\ .\ 23)\ (a\ .\ t)\ (f\ .\ (lambda\ (x)\ (car\ (cdr\ (cdr\ x)))))))$$

Function *assoc* defined below returns the value of an identifier, given the association list. It looks for the first occurrence of x in list a by comparing x to the first identifier, returning its value if they are equal or searching the remainder of the list if they are different.

Function *pairlis* is just the opposite: given a list x of identifiers, a list y of values, and an association list a, it returns association list a extended with the pairs formed by taking matching identifiers and values. Lists x and y are of equal length. If they are empty, then the result is a; otherwise the first identifier in x is paired with the first value in y, and the remainders of x and y are similarly added to a.

These two functions are used in our function *apply*. If the function to be applied is one of the five standard functions, the result is established immediately. If the function is an identifier but not one of the five standard names, then its value (its function body) is looked up in association list a and the result thereof is applied. If function *fn* is not an identifier, then it should be a lambda expression. The result of applying λ-expression *fn* to the list of arguments is obtained by evaluating expression $(caddr\ fn)$ that constitutes the function body in a context where association list a is extended with pairing the list of variables $(cadr\ fn)$ with the list x of arguments. If some of the variables already have a value associated with them, then the new binding should overwrite the old one. This is why function *pairlis* adds the new bindings to the front of the association list.

This leaves us with the problem of evaluating an expression. Well, there are five possibilities. If the expression is a constant (either *t* or *nil*), then the constant is the value of the expression. If the expression is a variable, then its value is the value of the expression. If the expression is of the form (*quote x*), then *x* is the value of the expression without further evaluations. If the expression is of the form (*cond x*), then we have a conditional expression and all the conditions must be checked one after another until one is found that evaluates to true; and the corresponding alternative is the value of the conditional expression. Finally, if the expression is of the form (*f x*), then function *f* is applied to the list of arguments *x*, after evaluating all of those arguments. The interpreter uses auxiliary functions *evcon* and *evlis* for evaluating a conditional expression and for evaluating a list of arguments, respectively.

That's all there is to it. Here is the listing of the LISP interpreter together with all auxiliary functions it needs. *define* has not been implemented in this interpreter. The problem with *define* is that it is not a function that returns some result but instead it changes the global association list. This cannot be done in a purely functional framework.

```
(define
(apply (lambda (fn x a)
    (cond ((atom fn) (cond ((eq fn (quote car)) (caar x))
                           ((eq fn (quote cdr)) (cdar x))
                           ((eq fn (quote cons)) (cons (car x) (cadr x)))
                           ((eq fn (quote atom)) (atom (car x)))
                           ((eq fn (quote eq)) (eq (car x) (cadr x)))
                           (t (apply (assoc fn a) x a))))
          ((eq (car fn) (quote lambda))
              (eval (caddr fn) (pairlis (cadr fn) x a))))))
(eval (lambda (e a)
    (cond ((atom e) (cond ((eq e nil) nil)
                          ((eq e t) t)
                          (t (assoc e a))))
          ((atom (car e)) (cond ((eq (car e) (quote quote)) (cadr e))
                                ((eq (car e) (quote cond)) (evcon (cdr e) a))
                                (t (apply (car e) (evlis (cdr e) a) a))))
          (t (apply (car e) (evlis (cdr e) a) a)))))
(evcon (lambda (c a)
    (cond ((eval (caar c) a) (eval (cadar c) a))
          (t (evcon (cdr c) a)))))
(evlis (lambda (x a)
    (cond ((null x) nil)
          (t (cons (eval (car x) a) (evlis (cdr x) a)))))))
```

$(pairlis\ (lambda\ (x\ y\ a)$
$\qquad (cond\ ((null\ x)\ a)$
$\qquad\qquad (t\ (cons\ (cons\ (car\ x)\ (car\ y))\ (pairlis\ (cdr\ x)\ (cdr\ y)\ a))))))$
$(assoc\ (lambda\ (x\ a)$
$\qquad (cond\ ((eq\ (caar\ a)\ x)\ (cdar\ a))$
$\qquad\qquad (t\ (assoc\ x\ (cdr\ a))))))$
$(null\ (lambda\ (x)$
$\qquad (cond\ ((atom\ x)\ (eq\ x\ nil))$
$\qquad\qquad (t\ nil))))$
$(caar\ (lambda\ (x)\ (car\ (car\ x))))$
$(cadr\ (lambda\ (x)\ (car\ (cdr\ x))))$
$(cdar\ (lambda\ (x)\ (cdr\ (car\ x))))$
$(cadar\ (lambda\ (x)\ (car\ (cdr\ (car\ x)))))$
$(caddr\ (lambda\ (x)\ (car\ (cdr\ (cdr\ x)))))$
$)$

10.5   A LISP Interpreter Written in Pascal

In this section, we convert the LISP interpreter into one that is written in Pascal. The translation requires that one issue be addressed: how are atoms and lists represented in Pascal? Let us start with the lists. Lists are sequences of arbitrary size, and we have to represent them by objects of fixed size. We pursue the possibility of representing a list x by an integer i. In view of the fact that the operations on a list are car and cdr, we introduce two arrays, a and d. They are related to car and cdr by $(car\ x) = a[i]$ and $(cdr\ x) = d[i]$. What is the type of the array elements? Well, it might be that $(cdr\ x)$ is again a list, so d has to be an array of integers. Similarly, a is an integer array. This choice implies that atoms are also represented by integers, and in a second we have to decide how this is done. We also need to decide how lists can be distinguished from atoms (which we have to do for implementing the boolean function $atom$). Let's restrict the index range of a and d to positive integers so that we can use negative integers for atoms. The sign of an integer then tells us whether it represents a list or an atom. For example, the list

$\qquad (x\ y\ z)$

is represented by a positive integer i and we have

$\qquad a[i]$ is the integer that represents x
$\qquad d[i]$ represents the list $(y\ z)$ that is,
$\qquad\qquad a[d[i]]$ is the integer that represents y
$\qquad\qquad d[d[i]]$ represents the list (z) that is,
$\qquad\qquad\qquad a[d[d[i]]]$ is the integer that represents z
$\qquad\qquad\qquad d[d[d[i]]]$ represents the empty list nil

As you see, this representation closely follows the "dotted pair" equivalent of lists where

$$(x \ y \ z) \ = \ (x \ . \ (y \ . \ (z \ . \ nil)))$$.

Now, how are the atoms represented? Atoms are given by a sequence of characters — letters and digits — and two atoms are equal just when the two character sequences are equal. So, we want distinct integer representations for distinct character sequences. We can record the character sequences in an array and use the index in the array as the integer representation. In view of the sign of the integer that represents an atom (it is negative), we choose to use the absolute value of the integer as an index in the array of character strings.

So much for the representation. How about the operations? Well, the boolean functions *eq* and *atom* are easy enough to encode. For example, *atom* checks the sign of its argument and returns the representation of atom t if the sign is negative, and the representation of *nil* otherwise. How about *car* and *cdr*? If i is the representation of some list x, then $a[i]$ is the representation of $(car \ x)$, so it seems to suffice to use this simple implementation for *car*. What if we use this implementation for the assignment $y := (car \ x)$ and subsequently there is a change of variable x? If the value of x changes, does y change also, so that we would have to make a representation for y that copies all elements of the whole list? Fortunately, this problem does not arise in LISP because there are no assignment statements, and we can safely share the representation of equal sublists between variables.

One serious problem remains. Function *cons* is given two arguments x and y, and has to come up with an index i and set $a[i]$ to x and $d[i]$ to y. How is index i selected? Since $a[i]$ and $d[i]$ are being changed, we have to make sure that index i is not presently being used as the representation of any object. One solution to this problem is to use a fresh value for i whenever the function *cons* is invoked. This implies that enormously long arrays a and d are needed in a long computation, even if only a few lists exist simultaneously. It would be better to keep track of the elements that are currently in use, and to recycle the elements that are no longer needed for representing any list. What elements are presently in use? At least all elements that are in the present association list are in use, but there are a few more, namely, all those elements that have already been constructed but have not yet been bound to a variable (and, therefore, have not yet been entered into the association list). For example, the arguments to a function are evaluated in some order. Somewhere halfway through the process some values have already been computed, but they have not yet been bound to the corresponding variables because the binding is done (by *pairlis*) after all arguments have been evaluated. Therefore, we add another list, the so-called object list, which contains all elements that are presently in use and that may or may not yet be part of the association list. Maintaining this list is definitely the most tricky part of the translation of our LISP interpreter from LISP into Pascal.

Recycling elements that are no longer in use is done when a *cons* operation is to be performed and no more cells are available that have been recorded as being free. This causes the so-called *garbage collector* to come into action. It marks all elements that can be reached from the association list or from the object list, and adds all other ones to the so-called free list. (An element can be reached if it is in the association or object list, or if it is the *car* or *cdr* of a reachable element.) The convention that we have followed is that every function makes sure that every element it creates and that must be reachable is reachable, except for the function value that it returns. The calling function is responsible for making it reachable. Many more techniques for collecting garbage exist, but we do not discuss them now.

This completes our description of the essentials of the translation process. As a minor improvement, we have replaced variable *a*, which is a parameter of just about every function in the LISP interpreter, by global variable *alp* (for association list pointer). As a result, we need not drag it along all the time, but this also implies that we explicitly have to reset it to its previous value wherever the LISP version has completed a function call. The object list is also represented by a global variable, namely *olp* (for object list pointer). Furthermore, we have included some rudimentary error checks.

program *lisp*(*input*, *output*);

label 13;

```
const   n       =  10000;
        maxids  =  100;
        nil     =  -1;
        t       =  -2;
        atom    =  -3;
        eq      =  -4;
        kar     =  -5;
        kdr     =  -6;
        kons    =  -7;
        lambda  =  -8;
        cond    =  -9;
        quote   =  -10;
        defyne  =  -11;

type    alfa = packed array[1..8]of char;
        object = -maxids..n;

var  ch : char;
```

```
      nrofids : 0..maxids;
      ids : array[1..maxids]of alfa;
      letters : set of char;
      a, d : array[1..n]of object;
      inuse : array[1..n]of boolean;
      oldalp, alp, olp, Free : object;

procedure erm(n : integer);
begin writeln;
      write( '*** error : ' );
      case n of
        1: writeln( 'illegal application : no function name' );
        2: writeln( 'car of an atom' );
        3: writeln( 'cdr of an atom' );
        4: writeln( 'garbage collector finds no free space' );
        5: writeln( 'symbol ) expected' );
        6: writeln( 'incorrect starting symbol of expression' );
        7: writeln( 'too many identifiers' );
        8: writeln( 'undefined identifier' );
        9: writeln( 'too few actual parameters' );
       10: writeln( 'too many actual parameters' )
      end;
      alp := oldalp; readln; ch := ' ' ; goto 13
end;

function identifier : object;
    var i : 1..maxids; j : 0..8; id : alfa;
begin j := 0; id := '        ' ;
      while ch ∈ letters do begin
          if j ≠ 8 then begin j := j + 1; id[j] := ch end;
          read(ch)
      end;
      if nrofids = maxids then erm(7);
      ids[nrofids + 1] := id; i := 1;
      while ids[i] ≠ id do i := i + 1;
      if i > nrofids then nrofids := i;
      identifier := -i
end;

procedure printatom(x : object);
    var i : 1..8;
begin for i := 1 to 8 do if ids[-x, i] ≠ ' ' then write(ids[-x, i]) end;

procedure skipspaces;
begin while ch ∈ [ ' ' , chr(9)] do read(ch) end;
```

```
function islist(x : object) : boolean;
begin while x > 0 do x := d[x];
      islist := x = nil1
end;

procedure print(x : object);
begin if x < 0 then
         printatom(x)
      else begin
         write( '(' );
         if islist(x) then begin
            print(a[x]);  x := d[x];
            while x > 0 do begin
               write( ' ' );  print(a[x]);  x := d[x]
            end
         end else begin
            print(a[x]);  write( ' . ' );  print(d[x])
         end ;
         write( ')' )
end   end;

procedure mark(ref : object);
begin while (ref > 0) ∧ ¬inuse[ref] do begin
         inuse[ref] := true;  mark(a[ref]);  ref := d[ref]
end   end;

procedure collectgarbage;
      var i : 1..n;
begin for i := 1 to n do inuse[i] := false;
      mark(olp);  mark(alp);
      for i := 1 to n do
        if ¬inuse[i] then begin d[i] := Free;  Free := i end;
      if Free = nil1 then erm(4)
end;

function cons(x, y : object) : object;
      var ref : object;
begin if Free = nil1 then collectgarbage;
      ref := Free;  cons := ref;  Free := d[ref];
      a[ref] := x;  d[ref] := y
end;
```

```
function car(x : object) : object;
begin if x < 0 then erm(2);
      car := a[x]
end;

function cdr(x : object) : object;
begin if x < 0 then erm(3);
      cdr := d[x]
end;

function readitem : object;
    var n : object;
begin skipspaces;
    if ch ∈ letters then
        readitem := identifier
    else begin
        if ch ≠ '(' then erm(6);
        read(ch);  skipspaces;
        if ch = ')' then begin
            read(ch);  readitem := nil
        end else begin
            olp := cons(nil, olp);  n := cons(nil, nil);  a[olp] := n;
            readitem := n;  a[n] := readitem;  skipspaces;
            if ch = '.' then begin
                read(ch);  d[n] := readitem;
                skipspaces;  if ch ≠ ')' then erm(5)
            end else
                while ch ≠ ')' do begin
                    d[n] := cons(nil, nil);  n := d[n];
                    a[n] := readitem;  skipspaces
                end;
            read(ch);  olp := d[olp]
end end end;

function eval(e : object) : object;
    forward;

function evcon(x : object) : object;
begin while eval(car(car(x))) = nil do x := d[x];
      evcon := eval(car(d[a[x]]))
end;

function evlis(x : object) : object;
    var op : object;
```

```
begin if x = ni1 then
          evlis := ni1
      else begin
          op := olp;  olp := cons(ni1, olp);  evlis := olp;
          a[olp] := eval(car(x));  d[olp] := evlis(d[x]);  olp := op
end   end;


function assoc(x : object) : object;
    var al : object;
begin al := alp;
      while (al ≠ ni1) ∧ (a[a[al]] ≠ x) do al := d[al];
      if al = ni1 then erm(8);
      assoc := d[a[al]]
end;


procedure pairlis(x, y : object);
begin if x ≠ ni1 then begin
          if y = ni1 then erm(9);
          pairlis(cdr(x), cdr(y));
          alp := cons(ni1, alp);  a[alp] := cons(a[x], a[y])
      end else if y ≠ ni1 then
          erm(10)
end;


function apply(fn, x : object) : object;
    var ap : object;
begin if fn < 0 then
              if fn = kar   then apply := car(car(x)) else
              if fn = kdr   then apply := cdr(car(x)) else
              if fn = kons then apply := cons(car(x), car(cdr(x))) else
              if fn = atom then if car(x) < 0 then apply := t
                                              else apply := ni1 else
              if fn = eq    then if car(x) = car(cdr(x)) then apply := t
                                                          else apply := ni1
                       else apply := apply(assoc(fn), x)
      else if a[fn] = lambda then begin
          ap := alp;  pairlis(car(d[fn]), x);
          apply := eval(car(d[d[fn]]));  alp := ap
      end else erm(1)
end;


function eval(e : object) : object;
begin if e < 0 then
          if (e = ni1) ∨ (e = t) then eval := e else eval := assoc(e)
      else if a[e] = quote then
```

```
                eval := car(d[e])
        else if a[e] = cond then
                eval := evcon(d[e])
        else begin
                olp := cons(nil, olp);  a[olp] := evlis(d[e]);
                eval := apply(a[e], a[olp]);  olp := d[olp]
end    end;

procedure interpret;
    var e, p : object;
begin  olp := nil;  olp := cons(nil, nil);
        read(ch);  e := readitem;  a[olp] := e;  writeln;
        if car(e) = defyne then begin
                e := d[e];  write( '(' );
                repeat p := car(e);  print(car(p));  alp := cons(nil, alp);
                        a[alp] := cons(a[p], car(d[p]));  e := cdr(e);
                        if e ≠ nil then write( ' ' )
                until e = nil;
                write( ')' )
        end else
                print(apply(a[e], d[e]));
        writeln
end;

begin for Free := 1 to n − 1 do d[Free] := Free + 1;  d[n] := nil;
        Free := 1;
        ids[−nil    ] := 'nil     ';
        ids[−t      ] := 't       ';
        ids[−atom   ] := 'atom    ';
        ids[−eq     ] := 'eq      ';
        ids[−kar    ] := 'car     ';
        ids[−kdr    ] := 'cdr     ';
        ids[−kons   ] := 'cons    ';
        ids[−lambda ] := 'lambda  ';
        ids[−cond   ] := 'cond    ';
        ids[−quote  ] := 'quote   ';
        ids[−defyne ] := 'define  ';
        nrofids := 11;
        letters := [ 'A' .. 'Z' , 'a' .. 'z' , '0' .. '9' ];
        writeln;
        writeln( 'LISP interpreter' );
        writeln;
        alp := nil;  read(ch);
 13 :  repeat oldalp := alp;  interpret until false
end.
```

10.6   Discussion

We conclude this chapter with a short discussion. Let function f be defined
as

$$f(x) = 29$$

and consider $f(1/0)$. In the λ-calculus, one substitutes 29 for the body of
f and finds that $f(1/0) = 29$. In LISP, the argument is evaluated before
the body is substituted and, since $1/0$ is undefined, $f(1/0)$ is undefined.
The semantics used in the λ-calculus gives greater freedom in doing algebraic manipulations since the result is independent of the order in which
the operations are performed. This semantics is known as *lazy evaluation*
and is the semantics chosen by some functional programming languages.
LISP's *eager evaluation* is easier to implement efficiently. The *fringe* example is easy with lazy evaluation: the first solution we gave is just fine. Our
more efficient solution is more efficient only in the case of eager evaluation;
with lazy evaluation, the simple solution is just as efficient as the complex
solution. Our program contains, in a nutshell, the essence of lazy evaluation by postponing the evaluation of expressions until their value is needed.
One of the many consequences of eager evaluation is that LISP requires a
conditional expression, whereas it is superfluous in the λ-calculus.

Another major difference between LISP and the λ-calculus is in the
handling of recursion. We define the function that computes $n!$ as

$$f \ = \ \lambda n.\textbf{if} \ n = 0 \ \textbf{then} \ 1 \ \textbf{else} \ n \cdot f(n-1) \qquad .$$

Next, consider function F, which maps an integer function to an integer
function.

$$F \ = \ \lambda g.\lambda n.\textbf{if} \ n = 0 \ \textbf{then} \ 1 \ \textbf{else} \ n \cdot g(n-1)$$

It follows that our function f satisfies $f = F(f)$. We say that f is a
fixpoint of F. The definition of f is recursive, the definition of F is not. If
we postulate function Y that takes a function as its argument and returns
the fixpoint thereof, then $f = Y(F)$. This is exactly what is done in the
λ-calculus. It avoids recursion and therefore does not require names for
functions. Eliminating the need for names simplifies algebraic calculations.

Our present implementation allows one to write

$$(define \ (f \ (lambda \ (y) \ (equal \ x \ y)))$$
$$(g \ (lambda \ (x) \ (f \ x)))$$
$$(h \ (lambda \ (x) \ (f \ (cons \ x \ x)))))$$

and obtain result t for any call of g and *nil* for any call of h. It looks
strange because x seems not to be defined in f. The implementation with
the association list ignores normal scope rules completely by having one list
of all identifiers. Looking up identifiers x in the association list returns the
value associated with x in g if f is called from g or the value associated

with x in h if f is called from h. If f is called from a function in which x is undefined, an error message will result. As a result, the name of a parameter plays a role outside the function definition, and this can only be considered to be a mistake. It should not be considered as a feature of the language but as a mistake that is not reported by the implementation. It is one of the dangers of defining the semantics of a programming language via an interpreter that restrictions in the language are not made explicit.

10.7   Bibliographic Notes

Lambda notation was first published in [Chu41]. LISP, the first programming language based on the lambda calculus, was published in [McC60]. This paper also contains a version of the LISP interpreter written in LISP. LISP was the first widely used functional language. The connection between lambda calculus and programming languages was more formally explored in [Lan65]. An excellent text on functional programming is [BW88]. It uses a more modern functional programming language than we did. We used LISP because its implementation is a lot simpler, and we wanted to discuss that implementation. The derivation of the *fringe* program is essentially identical to the one in [vdS92]. Exercise 22 is from [Hem80]. Exercise 23 is from [HA72]. Our version of the LISP interpreter written in Pascal was adapted from [Kru75].

10.8   Exercises

1. Prove that the two formulations of mathematical induction (weak and strong) are equivalent for the case of induction over the natural numbers.

2. We define *lexicographic order* on pairs of natural numbers. Pair (a, b) is defined to be less than pair (c, d) just when

$$a < c \ \lor \ (a = c \ \land \ b < d) \quad .$$

   Show that lexicographic order is a well-founded order.

3. Here is a purported definition of the so-called Ackermann function. It is a function that maps two natural numbers to one natural number.

$$
\begin{aligned}
A(m, n) \ = \ & n + 1, & \text{if } m = 0\,; \\
& A(m - 1, 1), & \text{if } m > 0 \land n = 0\,; \\
& A(m - 1, A(m, n - 1)), & \text{otherwise.}
\end{aligned}
$$

   Show that A is a properly defined function. In order to do so, you need to give a well-founded order on the arguments, that is, you need to give a relation R that is well founded and that satisfies $(m-1,1)\ R\ (m,n)$ if $m>0 \wedge n=0$, and both $(m,n-1)\ R\ (m,n)$ and $(m-1,A(m,n-1))\ R\ (m,n)$ if $m>0 \wedge n>0$. Also, compute the value of $A(3,6)$, without using a calculator or computer.

4. Show that the following is also a well-defined function. Its two arguments are natural numbers.

$$
\begin{array}{lll}
g(x,y) & = & 0, & \text{if } x=0 \wedge y=0\,; \\
& & g(x,y-1)+1, & \text{if } x=0 \wedge y>0\,; \\
& & g(x-1,y+1), & \text{otherwise.}
\end{array}
$$

Give a nonrecursive definition for $g(x,y)$.

5. Let function $f(x,y)$ for integers x and y satisfy the following equation.

$$
\begin{array}{lll}
f(x,y) & = & y+1, & \text{if } x=y\,; \\
& & f(x,f(x-1,y+1)), & \text{otherwise.}
\end{array}
$$

Show that $f(x,y)=x+1$ satisfies the equation. Also show that $f(x,y)=\textbf{if } x \geq y \textbf{ then } x+1 \textbf{ else } y-1$ satisfies the equation. What is the function defined by the equation?

6. Write a function of three arguments, x, y, and z, that replaces every occurrence of x in z by y. It may be assumed that x is an atom, and not *nil*.

7. Given two lists of atoms, write a program to determine whether the first list is a consecutive sublist of the second.

8. Write functions that compute the intersection of two sets, their set difference, and the test for equality. Sets are represented as lists without duplicates.

9. Given is a list of distinct atoms. Write a function that returns the list of all permutations of the given list.

10. Relation R is given by a list of pairs. Pair $(x\ y)$ occurs in the list just when xRy holds. Write a function that computes the transitive closure of R. The transitive closure is to be represented by a list of pairs, just like R is.

11. Write a function of one argument that computes the set of all atoms, except *nil*, that occur at least once in the argument. There are no restrictions on the argument: it can be an atom, a list, a list whose elements can be lists, and so on. If, for example, an atom is an element of a list that is an element of the list constituting the argument, the atom occurs in the argument and should be included in the result. As before, the set is to be represented by a list without duplicates.

12. Write function *lreduce* that corresponds to the *left-reduce* as described in the text. Describe function *some* whose definition follows. Is it the same if we replace *lreduce* by *rreduce*?

    (define (some (lambda (x)
        (lreduce (quote (lambda (a b) (cond (a t) (t b))))
        nil
        x))))

13. Write function *reduce* that operates on a nonempty list and an associative operator. It works much like *lreduce* and *rreduce* do, except that we need not specify a unit element; therefore, the implementation differs. What is the effect of

    (reduce (lambda (a b) b) x)

    for an arbitrary nonempty list *x*?

14. Figure out the effect of function *subset*, and explain why it works.

    (define (subset (lambda (x y)
        (all (map (quote (lambda (a) (member a y))) x))))
        (all (lambda (x)
        (lreduce and t x)))
        (and (lambda (a b)
        (cond (a b) (t nil)))))))

    Which of our previously defined functions equals *ama*?

    (define (ama (lambda (x)
        (all (map atom x)))))

15. Write a program for computing the derivative of an expression with respect to some variable. An expression is either a constant, a variable, *(plus e_0 e_1)*, or *(times e_0 e_1)* where e_0 and e_1 are in turn expressions. We restrict constants to 0 and 1, represented by atoms 0 and 1, respectively. Variables are *x* and *y*. For example,

    (deriv (plus x y) x) = *(plus 1 0)*   .

    The result is an expression in the same format.

16. Write a function for simplifying expressions as defined in the previous exercise. For example, *(plus 1 0)* is simplified to 1.

17. We have given a calculational derivation of *samesplit*. Give a similar derivation for *split*.

18. Functions *div2* and *mod2* were given in a symmetrical way. A shorter but asymmetric definition of *div2* is

    (define (div2 (lambda (a b c)
        (cond ((eq a b) a)
            (t c)))))   .

    Can you give a similar definition of *mod2*?

19. Write programs for subtraction and multiplication of binary numbers.

20. Write a program for addition of numbers given in a number system with base $n + 1$, where n is a parameter of the function. You may assume that n is at most 9. (Why do we write base $n + 1$ instead of base n here?)

21. Write a LISP program for solving the "Towers of Hanoi" problem.

22. We are given a list of atoms, each of which is either *a*, *l*, or *r*. When reading *l* and *r* as left and right parentheses, the list is given to be properly parenthesized. Write a program that produces a list that when printed looks like the original list with each *l* replaced by a left parenthesis and each *r* replaced by a right parenthesis. For example, the result of applying the function to *(a l a a r a l r)* is *(a (a a) a ())*. No limit on the nesting depth is given.

23. We have seen how to write a number of function definitions in LISP. Suppose we consider a small subset of the English language, consisting of a fixed set of adjectives only, say the eight words short, long, abstract, understandable, polysyllabic, monosyllabic, autological, and heterological. For each of these adjectives we can write a boolean function that takes one argument and returns *t* if the meaning of the adjective applies to the argument, and *nil* otherwise. The arguments are also restricted to come from a small set of English words, say the same set as above. For example, we have *(short polysyllabic) = nil* and *(monosyllabic short) = t*. The definition of the functions is easy; we can do it by simply comparing the argument with the subset of our eight words to which it applies.

    (define (short (lambda (a)
        (member a (quote (short long abstract)))))))

    We do so for all eight adjectives except for the last two: autological and heterological. An adjective is autological if it applies to itself. For example, polysyllabic has many syllables and is, therefore, autological; similarly for short. An adjective which is not autological is heterological. For example, long is heterological. We may write the definition of these functions as follows.

$$(define \ (not \ (lambda \ (x)$$
$$(cond \ (x \ nil) \ (t \ t))))$$
$$(autological \ (lambda \ (p)$$
$$(p \ p)))$$
$$(heterological \ (lambda \ (p)$$
$$(not \ (p \ p)))))$$

What are the results of evaluating the following expressions?

$$(short \ long)$$
$$(short \ short)$$
$$(short \ heterological)$$
$$(heterological \ short)$$
$$(autological \ short)$$
$$(heterological \ heterological)$$
$$(autological \ autological)$$

What are the proper results of each of these expressions in terms of their true meaning when phrased in English rather than as LISP programs? For example, for the first expression, what is the answer to the question: is the word "long" a short adjective?

24. In Chapter 7 we saw a meaning function $\mathcal{M}$ that served as an interpreter for logic. Gödel showed that it is incomplete, assuming the logic is consistent. Are our LISP interpreters complete? If not, can you give an example for which the interpreter gives no result? Can it be made complete?

25. In the two versions of the interpreter, the association list is a linear list of pairs of names and values. Since it records both the values for local names and globally defined functions, looking up a name for a globally defined function requires scanning through a possibly long list of pairs. (The list gets longer and longer through every (recursive) function call.) Give a modified implementation of the name list that is more efficient in this respect. For example, consider an array of lists of values: one list per identifier.

26. Procedure *mark* contains the boolean expression

$$(ref > 0) \land \neg inuse[ref]$$

which is understood to be *false* if $ref \leq 0$. In this case the second conjunct is undefined. However, the Pascal report states that both conjuncts need to be defined. Rewrite the procedure to meet this requirement.

27. The garbage collector in the Pascal program embodies a recursive marking scheme. Change it into an iterative one, using the Deutsch-Schorr-Waite method described in [SW67].

28. Show that the data structure used in the LISP interpreter contains no cycles. Study the tree-traversal algorithm described by [Mor79]. It requires no extra storage for the traversal of a tree. Adapt it to a graph-marking algorithm for use in the LISP interpreter, even though the data structure in the interpreter is not a tree.

29. Extend the LISP version of the interpreter to include conditional expressions of the form

$$(if \ x \ y \ z) \qquad ,$$

where the value of this expression is defined to be y if $x = t$, and z if $x = nil$.

30. Modify the Pascal version of the interpreter to report errors in a more intelligible way. For example, figure out what is reported when all conditions in a conditional expression are *nil*, and improve this. Also, when an undefined variable is reported, print the name of the variable. What happens if *cons* is called with an incorrect number of arguments?

31. One of the charming aspects of the λ-notation is the possibility of letting a function be anonymous. For example, we wrote

$$((lambda \ (x) \ (cond \ ((atom \ x) \ (eq \ x \ nil)) \ (t \ nil))) \ (a \ b \ c))$$

and the effect is exactly the same as that of

$$(null \ (a \ b \ c)) \qquad .$$

This nice possibility does not apply to recursive functions; therefore, we had to use *define*. Another option, and this is found in many LISP systems, is to write so-called label expressions. A label expression is an expression of the form $(label \ f \ e)$, and it is equivalent to expression e, except that in e every occurrence of identifier f stands for the whole label expression. Invariably, expression e is a λ-expression and, hence, f and the label expression are functions. Here is an example.

$$(label \ last \ (lambda \ (x)$$
$$(cond \ ((null \ (cdr \ x)) \ (car \ x)) \ (t \ (last \ (cdr \ x)))))))$$

is a label expression that is equivalent to

$$(lambda\ (x)\ (cond\ ((null\ (cdr\ x))\ (car\ x))\ (t\ (last\ (cdr\ x)))))$$

except that in the λ-expression every occurrence of *last* stands for the lambda expression, just as with *define*. Hence, the whole thing stands for the function that we know as *last* and

```
((label last (lambda (x)
    (cond ((null (cdr x)) (car x)) (t (last (cdr x)))))))
(a b c))
```

leads to the printing of *c*. Extend both the LISP and the Pascal version of the interpreter to implement label expressions correctly.

32. Procedure *pairlis* in the Pascal program contains the statements

$$alp := cons(ni1, alp);\ a[alp] := cons(a[x], a[y])\qquad.$$

Can we change these two statements to the single statement

$$alp := cons(cons(a[x], a[y]), alp)$$

without affecting the program's correctness? Justify your answer.

11

Program Inversion

Suppose we videotape execution of a program. The tape records all the states in one way or another. When we look at the video, we can more or less tell what the algorithm is. Next, suppose we run the video tape backwards. What do we see? It is the animation of another algorithm, called the *inverse program*. A program may have more than one inverse, while some programs have no inverse at all. We now look at techniques for constructing the inverse of a program, should one exist. No general technique is known, but we can find inverses under various circumstances, depending on how much cheating (or ingenuity) we want to do.

Why in the world would one be interested in figuring out what the inverse of a program is? It so happens that it is sometimes easy to solve the forward problem, whereas the inverse problem seems to be much harder to tackle. In such a case, constructing the forward solution and inverting it can be an attractive way of solving the inverse problem. We will see examples thereof.

11.1 Inversion of Programs

Consider statement S. What is the inverse S^{-1} thereof? The idea is that execution of S; S^{-1} leads from an initial state to some intermediate state and then back to the initial state. Some statements are easy to invert, like *skip*, which is its own inverse. (Doing nothing and doing nothing in reverse is much the same thing.) The inverse of $x := -x$ is no big mystery; it is $x := -x$, that is, this statement is its own inverse. The same holds true for $x, y := y, x$ (read it backwards!) The inverse of $x := x + 1$ is also easy: it is $x := x - 1$. If the expression in the assignment statement is slightly more complicated, we find the inverse statement by swapping variable and expression, and rewriting until the left-hand side is the same variable as in the forward assignment. For example, assignment $x := \sqrt{(x+1)/2}$ can be inverted under precondition $x + 1 \geq 0$.

$$
\begin{aligned}
&(x := \sqrt{(x + 1)/2})^{-1} \\
=\quad &\{ \text{ swap variable and expression } \} \\
&\sqrt{(x + 1)/2} := x \\
=\quad &\{ \text{ square left- and right-hand sides; } x + 1 \geq 0 \} \\
&(x + 1)/2 := x^2
\end{aligned}
$$

$$= \qquad \{ \text{ multiply by 2 } \}$$
$$x + 1 := 2x^2$$
$$= \qquad \{ \text{ subtract 1 } \}$$
$$x := 2x^2 - 1$$

In the case of $x, y := x + y, x - y$, we do some "Gaussian elimination" to find the inverse.

$$x + y := x$$
$$x - y := y$$
$$= \qquad \{ \text{ add second line to the first } \}$$
$$2x \qquad := x + y$$
$$x - y := y$$
$$= \qquad \{ \text{ divide first line by 2 } \}$$
$$x \qquad := (x + y)/2$$
$$x - y := y$$
$$= \qquad \{ \text{ change signs in second line } \}$$
$$x \qquad := (x + y)/2$$
$$y - x := -y$$
$$= \qquad \{ \text{ add first line to the second } \}$$
$$x \qquad := (x + y)/2$$
$$y \qquad := (x - y)/2$$

We thus find the inverse of $x, y := x+y, x-y$ to be $x, y := (x+y)/2, (x-y)/2$. Why don't we need the precondition that $x+y$ and $x-y$ are even?

But some statements are harder to invert. For example, we cannot invert $x := 1$ without knowing the "old" value of x. In other words, we can invert $x := 1$ only if we know the precondition. The inverse of

$$\{ x = 0 \} \ x := 1$$

is

$$\{ x = 1 \} \ x := 0 \qquad .$$

One gets the inverse by reading the original statements backwards and by interchanging the role of statement and assertion. This example shows that we may be able to compute inverses only when the precondition is given. Therefore, we define the inverse with respect to a precondition, that is, we define S^{-1} by $S; \ S^{-1} = skip$, given precondition P. This is the same as requiring $\{ P \wedge Q \} \ S; \ S^{-1} \ \{ Q \}$ for all Q and for given P. (This formulation admits a distinction between a right-inverse, which we have now, and a left-inverse which we would have by writing $S^{-1}; \ S$. I haven't the foggiest idea when the left- and right-inverse are the same.) If inverse S^{-1} of S is independent of the precondition, then we have the inverse with respect to precondition *true*.

Using precondition $x > 0$, we are able to invert $x := x^2$, which we could not do otherwise. However, precondition $x > 0$ provides insufficient information to invert $x := x$ **div** 2. Either $odd(x)$ or $even(x)$ as a pre-condition would do the job, and they lead to different inverses.

It is quite easy to see that *abort* doesn't have an inverse: execution of *abort* doesn't terminate, hence there is no way that execution of *abort* followed by something else (which is then never executed) is equivalent to *skip*.

A sequence of statements connected by semicolons is inverted by inverting all statements in the sequence and reversing their order in the sequence. For example, we have $(x := x + 1; \ y := y \cdot 2)^{-1} = (y := y/2; \ x := x - 1)$. How about the inverse of

$$x := x + y; \ y := x - y; \ x := x - y$$

(which is yet another way to swap x and y)? We have

$$(x := x + y; \ y := x - y; \ x := x - y)^{-1}$$
$$= \qquad \{ \text{ invert in opposite order } \}$$
$$(x := x - y)^{-1}; \ (y := x - y)^{-1}; \ (x := x + y)^{-1}$$
$$= \qquad \{ \text{ split } y := x - y \text{ in two statements temporarily } \}$$
$$x := x + y; \ (y := y - x; \ y := -y)^{-1}; \ x := x - y$$
$$=$$
$$x := x + y; \ (y := -y)^{-1}; \ (y := y - x)^{-1}; \ x := x - y$$
$$=$$
$$x := x + y; \ y := -y; \ y := y + x; \ x := x - y$$
$$= \qquad \{ \text{ combine the middle two statements } \}$$
$$x := x + y; \ y := -y + x; \ x := x - y$$
$$=$$
$$x := x + y; \ y := x - y; \ x := x - y$$

and we find that this program is its own inverse, independent of the pre-condition.

How do we invert an if-statement? Execution of an if-statement must begin with at least one guard *true* or else it is equivalent to the noninvertible *abort*. Hence, the disjunction of the guards has been inserted as the precondition of the statement.

$$\{ B0 \ \lor \ B1 \} \ [\ B0 \rightarrow S0 \ \{ R0 \}$$
$$\| \ B1 \rightarrow S1 \ \{ R1 \}$$
$$] \ \{ R0 \ \lor \ R1 \}$$

Execution terminates with either $R0$ or $R1$, depending on which of the two alternatives is selected, so $R0 \ \lor \ R1$ is the postcondition. In order to execute the if-statement in reverse, either $S0$ or $S1$ has to be executed in reverse, and the choice between the two is made on the the basis of the postcondition of the forward program. If $R0$ holds, then $S0^{-1}$ is to be executed, and if $R1$ holds, then $S1^{-1}$ is to be executed; this means that $R0$ and $R1$ cannot both be true at the same time if the "right" choice has to be made. We therefore require $\neg(R0 \ \land \ R1)$.

(Aside) One might try to develop a different notion of inverse
that does not correspond to the reverse video action, but that
does admit nondeterminism, and merely require that the inverse
program reestablish the initial state of the original program.

Given the restriction $\neg(R0 \land R1)$, the inverse of the if-statement is
straightforward (or straightbackward?). We conjecture that the inverse is
as follows. (We do not give proofs here — they are tedious but not hard.)

$$\{ R1 \lor R0 \} [R1 \to S1^{-1} \{ B1 \}$$
$$\| R0 \to S0^{-1} \{ B0 \}$$
$$] \{ B1 \lor B0 \}$$

The more interesting statement is the loop. We consider the case of a
loop with one guard only, because the general loop can be rewritten as a
loop with one guard and an if-statement as its body. The inverse of such
a loop will also turn out to be a loop with one guard and an if-statement
as its body, which can then be transformed back into a multi-guard loop.
The surprising thing about the inversion of

$$*[B \to S] \{ \neg B \}$$

is that we do not need the loop invariant or the variant function. Through
our previous examples we have come to expect that a precondition is needed
for the inversion and that conditions and guards switch roles. We therefore
introduce precondition $\neg C$ and insert C as the postcondition of S. As
a result, we are looking at

$$\{ \neg C \} *[B \to S \{ C \}] \{ \neg B \}$$

for inversion. It's easy: just read it backwards (and write the asterisk at
the correct position).

$$\{ \neg B \} *[C \to S^{-1} \{ B \}] \{ \neg C \}$$

Why should this be the correct inverse of the loop? Well, all it takes is that
we show that the loop terminates at the right moment, plus confidence in
the fact that S^{-1} is the inverse of S. Why does the loop terminate at
the right moment? Look at the forward program. Either B is false in the
initial state, in which case S is never executed and the loop terminates in a
state satisfying $\neg C$, or B is true initially, in which case S is executed at
least once, thus switching the state from $\neg C$ to C at the first execution of
S and terminating the loop in a state satisfying C. In the reverse game,
either $\neg C$ holds, in which case the inverse program correctly terminates
without executing S^{-1}, or else C holds, in which case the inverse loop
correctly executes S^{-1} until condition C switches from true to false. The
inverse program retraces the steps of the forward program.

(Aside) This is exactly the place where we have most problems
with nondeterministic programs.

(Another aside) If we need to include the precondition in our considerations, then the rules for inverting statements become a bit more complicated. They then read as follows.

- The inverse of $\{\,P\,\}\ x := E_0$ is $x := E_1$, provided $P \Rightarrow (x = E_1\frac{x}{E_0})$ (and the expressions are well-defined).
- The inverse of $\{\,P\,\}\ S0;\ S1$ is $S1^{-1};\ S0^{-1}$, provided $S0^{-1}$ is the inverse of $\{\,P\,\}\ S0$ and $S1^{-1}$ is the inverse of $\{\,Q\,\}\ S1$ for Q where Q satisfies $\{\,P\,\}\ S0\ \{\,Q\,\}$.
- The inverse of

$$\{\,P\,\}$$
$$[\,B0 \to S0\ \{\,R0\,\}\ \|\ B1 \to S1\ \{\,R1\,\}\,]$$
$$\{\,R0\ \lor\ R1\,\}$$

  is

$$[\,R1 \to S1^{-1}\ \|\ R0 \to S0^{-1}\,]\quad,$$

  provided $P \Rightarrow (B0 \lor B1) \land \lnot(B0 \land B1)$, and $\lnot(R0\ \land\ R1)$, and S_i^{-1} is the inverse of $\{\,P\ \land\ B_i\,\}\ S_i$.

- The inverse of

$$\{\,P\ \land\ \lnot C\,\}\ *[\,B \to S\ \{\,P\ \land\ C\,\}]\,\{\,\lnot B\,\}$$

  is

$$*[\,C \to S^{-1}\,]\quad,$$

  provided S^{-1} is the inverse of $\{\,P\ \land\ B\,\}\ S$.

Let us apply the rules to a simple example. Here is a program for storing 2^N in x, assuming proper initialization. Invariant $x \cdot 2^n = 2^N\ \land\ 0 \le n \le N$ has been omitted from the program text.

$$\{\,x = 1 \land n = N\,\}$$
$$*[\,n \ne 0 \to x := 2 \cdot x;\ n := n - 1\,]$$
$$\{\,x = 2^N\,\}$$

In order to compute its inverse, we have to change the annotation a bit. We drop postcondition $x = 2^N$ and replace it with $n = 0$, so that it is the negation of the guard. We weaken the precondition to $x = 1$ and include its negation, $x \ne 1$, as a postcondition of the loop body, which is the only thing that needs to be verified (it follows from the invariant). We then have

$$\{\,x = 1\,\}\ *[\,n \ne 0 \to x := x \cdot 2;\ n := n - 1\ \{\,x \ne 1\,\}\,]\,\{\,n = 0\,\}$$

which fits the rule for inversion of a loop, resulting in

$$*[\,x \ne 1 \to n := n + 1;\ x := x/2\,]\quad,$$

which is exactly what we expected: the familiar program for computing the logarithm base 2 (for the case in which x is an integer power of 2). Our rules do not give an annotated inverse program, so we don't know the invariant of this program. Were it not for the fact that we know the "forward" program, we would have to give a separate proof for the conjecture that this program indeed computes the logarithm.

Here is another example. In this example, we have to cheat a bit because the information is stored in different variables initially and finally. We carefully avoided this problem in the previous example through the reuse of n and x. We are given a sequence of N digits that are the decimal representation of a natural number: $\sum_{i=0}^{N-1} a[i] \cdot 10^i$. We write a few programs that compute the number, given the digits, and then invert them one after the other to obtain programs that compute the digits when given the number. Here are three solutions, together with the invariants that justify their correctness. We are given that $N \geq 0$ and $\langle \forall i : 0 \leq i < N : 0 \leq a[i] < 10 \rangle$.

$S0:$ $s := 0;\ j := N;\ \{\ P0 : s = \sum_{i=j}^{N-1} a[i] \cdot 10^i\ \wedge\ 0 \leq j \leq N\ \}$
      $*[j \neq 0 \rightarrow j := j - 1;\ s := s + a[j] \cdot 10^j]$

$S1:$ $s := 0;\ j := 0;\ \{\ P1 : s = \sum_{i=0}^{j-1} a[i] \cdot 10^i\ \wedge\ 0 \leq j \leq N\ \}$
      $*[j \neq N \rightarrow s := s + a[j] \cdot 10^j;\ j := j + 1]$

$S2:$ $s := 0;\ j := N;\ \{\ P2 : s = \sum_{i=j}^{N-1} a[i] \cdot 10^{i-j}\ \wedge\ 0 \leq j \leq N\ \}$
      $*[j \neq 0 \rightarrow j := j - 1;\ s := s \cdot 10 + a[j]]$

Invariants $P0$ and $P1$ are obtained from the postcondition by replacing a constant with a variable, whereas $P2$ is the invariant of *Horner's rule*. The latter type of invariant is almost always less obvious but leads to more elegant programs.

Let us invert these programs, starting with the last one. Because $j \neq N$ holds as a postcondition of the loop body of $S2$, and because $j = N$ holds as a precondition to the loop, we may use $j \neq N$ as guard in the inverse program. We thus have

$S2^{-1}:$ $\{\ j = 0\ \}$
      $*[\ j \neq N \rightarrow (s := s \cdot 10 + a[j])^{-1};\ j := j + 1\ ]$.

We still need to find the inverse of the assignment to s. The "obvious" answer $s := (s - a[j])/10$ is not correct because the inverse program has to assign a value to $a[j]$ also. Apart from that fact, $s := (s - a[j])/10$ is a perfect inverse. What value E is to be stored in $a[j]$? It has to satisfy the constraint that execution of $s := s \cdot 10 + a[j];\ a[j], s := E, (s - E)/10$ is equivalent to *skip*. We need to guarantee this, however, only for those cases that do occur in the forward program. They can be characterized by giving the condition under which $s := s \cdot 10 + a[j]$ is executed. The precondition $P2'$ of this statement can be obtained from the invariant plus the fact that the given a's are digits. We make a wild guess at E and verify its correctness. The guess is $E = s \bmod 10$; this allows $(s-E)/10$ to be simplified to $s \mathbf{\,div\,} 10$. Formally, for all Q, we have

$$\{P2' \wedge Q\}\ s := s \cdot 10 + a[j];\ a[j], s := s \bmod 10, s \mathbf{\,div\,} 10\ \{Q\}$$

$=$

$$\{P2' \wedge Q\}\ s := s \cdot 10 + a[j]\ \{Q^{a[j],s}_{s \bmod 10, s \mathbf{\,div\,} 10}\}$$

$=$

$$P2' \wedge Q\ \Rightarrow\ Q^{a[j],s}_{(s\cdot 10+a[j])\bmod 10,(s\cdot 10+a[j])\mathbf{\,div\,} 10}$$

$=$

$$P2' \wedge Q\ \Rightarrow\ Q^{a[j],s}_{a[j]\bmod 10, s+(a[j]\mathbf{\,div\,} 10)}$$
$$\{\ 0 \le a[j] < 10\ \}$$
$$P2' \wedge Q\ \Rightarrow\ Q^{a[j],s}_{a[j],s}$$

$=$

true

and the inverse is

$S2^{-1}:$ $\{\ j = 0\ \}$
$\quad *[\ j \ne N \to a[j], s := s \bmod 10, s \mathbf{\,div\,} 10;\ j := j+1\ ]$.

It turns out that the only part of $P2'$ that we needed was $0 \le a[j] < 10$.
  Let us next invert $S1$. It is going to be

$S1^{-1}:$ $\{\ j = N\ \}$
$\quad *[\ j \ne 0 \to j := j - 1;\ (s := s + a[j] \cdot 10^j)^{-1}\ ]$,

in which we still have to invert the assignment to s. Inspired by our previous program and by our understanding of $S1$, we guess $a[j], s := s \mathbf{\,div\,} 10^j, s \bmod 10^j$ and verify it as follows. Precondition $P1'$ of $s := s + a[j] \cdot 10^j$ is the conjunction of invariant $P1$ and the fact that the a's are digits.

$$\{\ P1' \wedge Q\ \}$$
$$s := s + a[j] \cdot 10^j;\ a[j], s := s \mathbf{\,div\,} 10^j, s \bmod 10^j$$
$$\{\ Q\ \}$$

$=$

$$\{\ P1' \wedge Q\ \}\ s := s + a[j] \cdot 10^j\ \{\ Q^{a[j],s}_{s \mathbf{\,div\,} 10^j, s \bmod 10^j}\ \}$$

$=$

$$P1' \wedge Q\ \Rightarrow\ Q^{a[j],s}_{(s+a[j]\cdot 10^j)\mathbf{\,div\,} 10^j,(s+a[j]\cdot 10^j)\bmod 10^j}$$
$$\{\ P1' \Rightarrow 0 \le s < 10^j\ \}$$
$$P1' \wedge Q\ \Rightarrow\ Q^{a[j],s}_{a[j],s}$$

$=$

true

This shows that

$S1^{-1}$: $\{\, j = N \,\}$
    $*[j \neq 0 \rightarrow j := j - 1;\ a[j], s := s\ \textbf{div}\ 10^j, s\ \textbf{mod}\ 10^j]$

is the proper inverse of $S1$. We used the fact that the a's are digits in the inversion of $S2$, whereas we used $0 \le s < 10^j$ in the inversion of $S1$.

Finally, we tackle the inversion of $S0$. We have

$S0^{-1}$: $\{\, j = 0 \,\}$
    $*[j \neq N \rightarrow (s := s + a[j] \cdot 10^j)^{-1};\ j := j + 1]$

and it is tempting to guess

$$(s := s + a[j] \cdot 10^j)^{-1}\ =\ a[j], s := s\ \textbf{div}\ 10^j, s\ \textbf{mod}\ 10^j\quad,$$

just as in the previous case. However, the different precondition does not allow us to infer $0 \le s < 10^j$ and the inversion doesn't work out well. (This is a case where the inverse really depends on the precondition.) So, we make another guess, and after some experiments I came up with

$$a[j], s := s\ \textbf{div}\ 10^j\ \textbf{mod}\ 10, s\ \textbf{div}\ 10^{j+1} \cdot 10^{j+1}\quad.$$

In order to verify the inverse, we look at precondition $P0'$ first. From $P0$, we infer that $P0'$, the precondition of the assignment to s in the loop body of $S0$, implies $s = \sum_{i=j+1}^{N-1} a[i] \cdot 10^i$;   hence, $P0' \Rightarrow s\ \textbf{mod}\ 10^{j+1} = 0$. Next follows the verification.

$\quad\quad \{\, P0' \wedge Q \,\}$
$\quad\quad s := s + a[j] \cdot 10^j;$
$\quad\quad a[j], s := s\ \textbf{div}\ 10^j\ \textbf{mod}\ 10, s\ \textbf{div}\ 10^{j+1} \cdot 10^{j+1}$
$\quad\quad \{Q\}$

$=$

$\quad\quad \{\, P0' \wedge Q \,\}$
$\quad\quad s := s + a[j] \cdot 10^j$
$\quad\quad \{\ Q^{a[j],s}_{s\,\textbf{div}\,10^j\,\textbf{mod}\,10, s\,\textbf{div}\,10^{j+1}\cdot10^{j+1}}\ \}$

$=$

$\quad P0' \wedge Q\ \Rightarrow$
$\quad\quad Q^{a[j],s}_{(s+a[j]\cdot10^j)\,\textbf{div}\,10^j\,\textbf{mod}\,10,(s+a[j]\cdot10^j)\,\textbf{div}\,10^{j+1}\cdot10^{j+1}}$
$\quad\quad \{\ P0' \Rightarrow s\ \textbf{mod}\ 10^{j+1} = 0\ \}$
$\quad P0' \wedge Q\ \Rightarrow\ Q^{a[j],s}_{a[j]\cdot10^j\,\textbf{div}\,10^j\,\textbf{mod}\,10, s+(a[j]\cdot10^j\,\textbf{div}\,10^{j+1}\cdot10^{j+1})}$
$\quad\quad \{\ 0 \le a[j] < 10\ \}$
$\quad P0' \wedge Q\ \Rightarrow\ Q^{a[j],s}_{a[j],s}$

$=$

$\quad\quad$ *true*

This shows that

$$S0^{-1}: \quad \{\, j = 0 \,\}$$
$$*[j \neq N \rightarrow a[j], s := s \text{ div } 10^j \bmod 10, s \text{ div } 10^{j+1} \cdot 10^{j+1};$$
$$j := j + 1$$
$$]$$

is the proper inverse of $S0$.

Next we consider a somewhat larger example. We are given positive number N and array $a[0..N-1]$ that contains a permutation of the numbers 0 through $N-1$. $N!$ such permutations exist, and they can be listed in lexicographic order. To every permutation, we assign a natural number, called its rank, which is the number of permutations by which it is preceded in the lexicographic order. For example, if $N = 3$, we have

$rank(0\ 1\ 2) = 0$
$rank(0\ 2\ 1) = 1$
$rank(1\ 0\ 2) = 2$
$rank(1\ 2\ 0) = 3$
$rank(2\ 0\ 1) = 4$
$rank(2\ 1\ 0) = 5$

We will develop a program that computes the rank of the given permutation and then invert it to obtain a program that computes a permutation given the rank.

We first define the rank of an arbitrary suffix of array a, that is, the rank of $a[i..N-1]$. Note that $a[i..N-1]$ is not necessarily a permutation of the numbers i through $N-1$; it may contain numbers smaller than i, but we do know that all the numbers in $a[i..N-1]$ are distinct. The rank of $a[i..N-1]$ is $(N-1-i)!$ times the number of elements in $a[i+1..N-1]$ that are less than $a[i]$, because all those smaller elements can be the leading element of a lexicographically smaller sequence and there are $(N-1-i)!$ of those sequences per leading element, plus the rank of the remainder of the sequence. This translates to the formula

$$rank(a[i..N-1]) = 0 \text{ for } i = N$$
$$= \langle \mathbf{N}j : i < j < N : a[j] < a[i] \rangle \cdot (N-1-i)!$$
$$+ rank(a[i+1..N-1])$$
$$\text{for all } 0 \leq i < N$$

which can be written as

$$rank(a[0..N-1]) = \sum_{i=0}^{N-1} \langle \mathbf{N}j : i < j < N : a[j] < a[i] \rangle \cdot (N-1-i)!$$

We can now write a program for solving the problem of assigning the value of $rank(a[0..N-1])$ to a variable, say r. The program consists of a loop whose invariant is as follows. (We will need to strengthen it later.)

$$P: \quad r = \sum_{i=0}^{k-1} \langle \mathbf{N}j : i < j < N : a[j] < a[i] \rangle \cdot (N-1-i)!$$
$$\wedge \ 0 \leq k \leq N$$

The program sets r and k to 0 initially, and every step of the loop increases k and updates r. The amount by which r is increased depends on the elements in the sequence $a[k..N-1]$: it is the number of elements that are less than $a[k]$ times some factorial. If we could guarantee that the $N-k$ elements of $a[k..N-1]$ are a permutation of the least $N-k$ natural numbers, that is, a permutation of 0 through $N-k-1$, then $\langle \mathbf{N}j : k < j < N : a[j] < a[k] \rangle$ equals $a[k]$. Since that appears to be attractive, we add this constraint to the invariant. This imposes the requirement, however, that $a[k+1..N-1]$ be modified before increasing k without changing the rank of this sequence. This can be done by changing the numbers as long as their relative order is not changed. Sequence $a[k..N-1]$ is a permutation of 0 through $N-k$ and we must turn $a[k+1..N-1]$ into a permutation of 0 through $N-k-1$. Its rank is not changed if we decrease by 1 the elements that are larger than the "missing" number $a[k]$ and do not change the other elements. In this way, we end up with the following program and invariant. We have also introduced a variable whose value equals $(N-k)!$ to get rid of the factorial in the program. As far as this program is concerned, the order of the inner loop and the assignments to f and r is immaterial: we might just as well update f and r before the loop. The body of the loop depends on $a[k]$, however, and in the inverse program $a[k]$ must have a value before executing the inverse of the inner loop. The value of $a[k]$ is bound to be derived from r (because r is given and a is to be computed); hence, we prefer to update r before the inner loop in the inverse program, that is, after the inner loop in the present program.

$$P: \quad r = \sum_{i=0}^{k-1} \langle \mathbf{N}j : i < j < N : a[j] < a[i] \rangle \cdot (N-1-i)!$$
$$\wedge\ 0 \le k \le N \ \wedge\ f = (N-k)!$$
$$\wedge\ a[k..N-1] \text{ is a permutation of 0 through } N-k-1$$

```
k := 0;  f := 1;  *[ k ≠ N → k := k + 1;  f := f · k];   { f = N! }
k := 0;  r := 0;
*[ k ≠ N → i := k + 1;
      *[ i ≠ N → [ a[i] > a[k] → a[i] := a[i] − 1    { a[i] ≥ a[k] }
      [] a[i] < a[k] → skip                          { a[i] < a[k] }
      ];
      i := i + 1
   ];
   f := f/(N − k);  r := r + a[k] · f;  k := k + 1
]  { k = N  ∧  r = rank(a[0..N − 1])  ∧  f = 1 }
```

The program can be inverted because the loops can be inverted, the if-statement has mutually exclusive postconditions for its two alternatives, and each of the assignments can be inverted. The only assignment that is hard is $r := r + a[k] \cdot f$. How do we invert this one? Similar to the examples with which we started this chapter, we cannot simply write $r := r - a[k] \cdot f$, because $a[k]$ is undefined when this statement is to be executed. Array a was given in the original program, and it has to be assigned a value in the inverse program. We prefix $r := r - a[k] \cdot f$ with an assignment to $a[k]$, and then we have the proper inverse. Inspired by our earlier examples, we observe that we have the following invariant of the original program: r is a multiple of f, and in combination with the properties $f = (N - k)!$ and $0 \leq a[k] < N - k$, we conclude that $(r/f) \bmod (N - k)$ is the right value to store in $a[k]$. We omit the verification hereof and obtain the following inverse program.

$$
\begin{aligned}
&k := N; \ f := 1; \\
&*[\ k \neq 0 \to k := k - 1; \\
&\qquad\qquad a[k] := (r/f) \bmod (N - k); \ r := r - a[k] \cdot f; \\
&\qquad\qquad f := f \cdot (N - k); \ i := N; \\
&\qquad\qquad *[\ i \neq k + 1 \to i := i - 1; \\
&\qquad\qquad\qquad\quad [\ a[i] < a[k] \to skip \\
&\qquad\qquad\qquad\quad |\!|\ a[i] \geq a[k] \to a[i] := a[i] + 1 \\
&\quad\ ]\qquad\qquad]\qquad\qquad\qquad] \\
&\{\ k = 0 \ \land \ r = 0 \ \land \ f = N!\ \}
\end{aligned}
$$

A much nicer program is obtained by choosing a slightly different invariant. Instead of

$$
r = \sum_{i=0}^{k-1} \langle \mathbf{N} j : i < j < N : a[j] < a[i] \rangle \cdot (N - 1 - i)! \qquad ,
$$

we may use

$$
r = \sum_{i=0}^{k-1} \langle \mathbf{N} j : i < j < N : a[j] < a[i] \rangle \cdot \frac{(N - 1 - i)!}{(N - k)!} \qquad ,
$$

which is somewhat similar to Horner's rule; and then we obtain the program

$$
\begin{aligned}
&k := 0; \ r := 0; \\
&*[\ k \neq N \to i := k + 1; \\
&\qquad\quad *[\ i \neq N \to [\ a[i] > a[k] \to a[i] := a[i] - 1 \quad \{\ a[i] \geq a[k]\ \} \\
&\qquad\qquad\qquad\qquad\ |\!|\ a[i] < a[k] \to skip \qquad\qquad\quad \{\ a[i] < a[k]\ \} \\
&\qquad\qquad\qquad\ ]; \\
&\qquad\qquad\qquad\ i := i + 1 \\
&\qquad\quad]; \\
&\qquad\ r := r \cdot (N - k) + a[k]; \ k := k + 1 \\
&\ ]\ \{\ k = N \ \land \ r = rank(a[0..N - 1])\ \} \qquad ,
\end{aligned}
$$

which avoids factorials (and, hence, variable f) altogether. Its inverse is

$$k := N;$$
$$*[\; k \neq 0 \rightarrow k := k - 1;$$
$$\qquad\qquad a[k] := r \bmod (N - k); \;\; r := r \operatorname{div} (N - k); \;\; i := N;$$
$$\qquad\qquad *[\; i \neq k + 1 \rightarrow i := i - 1;$$
$$\qquad\qquad\qquad [\; a[i] < a[k] \rightarrow skip$$
$$\qquad\qquad\qquad \|\; a[i] \geq a[k] \rightarrow a[i] := a[i] + 1$$
$$\qquad]\qquad\qquad]\qquad\qquad\qquad] \;\;.$$

Verifying that this is the proper inverse boils down to checking the assignments to $a[k]$ and r; that is, we have to check

$$\{\, P \wedge Q \,\}$$
$$r := r \cdot (N - k) + a[k]; \;\; a[k] := r \bmod (N - k); \;\; r := r \operatorname{div} (N - k)$$
$$\{\, Q \,\}$$

for all Q, and for the proper precondition P.

$$\left(\left(Q^r_{r \operatorname{div} (N-k)} \right)^{a[k]}_{r \bmod (N-k)} \right)^r_{r \cdot (N-k) + a[k]}$$

$$= $$

$$Q^{r,\; a[k]}_{(r \cdot (N-k) + a[k]) \operatorname{div} (N-k), \;\; r \cdot (N-k) + a[k]) \bmod (N-k)}$$
$$\qquad\quad \{ \text{ invariant, and hence } P, \text{ implies } 0 \leq a[k] < N - k \;\}$$
$$= $$
$$Q^{r,\; a[k]}_{r,\; a[k]}$$

$$= $$

$$Q$$

We conclude this section on program inversion with one more example. From a labeled, binary tree one can derive many sequences of labels. Two of them are the inorder and the preorder traversals, defined below. It is rather easy to construct those sequences from the tree. The inverse problem is to reconstruct the tree from the two traversals. This is the problem that we tackle now.

First, we define the notions that are involved. A labeled binary tree is either

- $\bot$ if it is the empty tree, or

- $\langle t.l, t.d, t.r \rangle$ if it is a nonempty tree t with left and right subtrees $t.l$ and $t.r$ and label $t.d$.

Inorder traversal $in(t)$ of tree t is a sequence of all the labels that occur in t. The order in which they occur in the sequence is defined as follows.

- $in(\bot) = \epsilon$

- $in(t) = in(t.l) \; t.d \; in(t.r)$ for all nonempty t

Sequence $in(t)$ is called the *inorder traversal* because label $t.d$ occurs between $in(t.l)$ and $in(t.r)$. Catenation of sequences and elements is denoted by juxtaposition. The *preorder traversal* is defined similarly.

- $pre(\perp) = \epsilon$

- $pre(t) = t.d\ pre(t.l)\ pre(t.r)$ for all nonempty t

The tree is uniquely defined by its inorder and postfix traversals only if all labels in the tree distinct. We assume they are. Inorder traversal $in(t)$ and preorder traversal $pre(t)$ of tree t are stored in sequence variables x and y through execution of the following algorithm.

$$x, y := \epsilon, \epsilon;\ gen(t)$$

where

> **procedure** $gen(t : tree)$:
> $[\ t = \perp \rightarrow skip$
> $\|\ t \neq \perp \rightarrow y := y\ t.d;\ gen(t.l);\ x := x\ t.d;\ gen(t.r)$
> $]$

The specification of the procedure is

> $\{\ x = X\ \wedge\ y = Y\ \}$
> $gen(t)$
> $\{\ x = X\ in(t)\ \wedge\ y = Y\ pre(t)\ \}$.

We write the pre- and postcondition of a procedure before and after the procedure body. The program produces sequences x and y from left to right. We might also do it the other way round. (Either way is fine; both can be inverted.)

> **procedure** $gen(t : tree)$:
> $\{\ x = X\ \wedge\ y = Y\ \}$
> $[\ t = \perp \rightarrow skip$
> $\|\ t \neq \perp \rightarrow gen(t.r);\ x := t.d\ x;\ gen(t.l);\ y := t.d\ y$
> $]$
> $\{\ x = in(t)\ X\ \wedge\ y = pre(t)\ Y\ \}$

From the specification it follows that $gen(t)$ is equivalent to

$$x, y := in(t)\ x, pre(t)\ y$$

which is somewhat easier to use, since it allows the use of the rule for assignment statements. We verify the correctness of the procedure. Since the program is recursive, the proof is by mathematical induction: in the proof it can be assumed that the recursive calls satisfy their specification because their arguments $t.r$ and $t.l$ are proper subtrees of tree t. Since the procedure body consists of two alternatives, there are two cases to be checked. If $t = \perp$, we have to show

$$x = X\ \wedge\ y = Y\ \wedge\ t = \perp\ \Rightarrow\ x = in(t)\ X\ \wedge\ y = pre(t)\ Y$$

which is immediate from the definition of in and pre. If $t \neq \perp$, we use the assignment statement instead of the recursive calls and obtain

$$x, y := in(t.r) \; x, pre(t.r) \; y; \quad x := t.d \; x;$$
$$x, y := in(t.l) \; x, pre(t.l) \; y; \quad y := t.d \; y \quad .$$

The verification boils down to performing a lot of substitutions, starting from the postcondition, and simplifying until we have the precondition.

$$\begin{aligned}
& ((((x = in(t) \; X \; \wedge \\
& \quad y = pre(t) \; Y)^y_{t.d \; y})^{x,y}_{in(t.l) \; x, pre(t.l) \; y})^x_{t.d \; x})^{x,y}_{in(t.r) \; x, pre(t.r) \; y} \\
= & \quad \{ \text{ substitution } \} \\
& (((x = in(t) \; X \; \wedge \\
& \quad t.d \; y = pre(t) \; Y)^{x,y}_{in(t.l) \; x, pre(t.l) \; y})^x_{t.d \; x})^{x,y}_{in(t.r) \; x, pre(t.r) \; y} \\
= & \quad \{ \text{ substitution } \} \\
& ((in(t.l) \; x = in(t) \; X \; \wedge \\
& \quad t.d \; pre(t.l) \; y = pre(t) \; Y)^x_{t.d \; x})^{x,y}_{in(t.r) \; x, pre(t.r) \; y} \\
= & \quad \{ \text{ substitution } \} \\
& (in(t.l) \; t.d \; x = in(t) \; X \; \wedge \\
& \quad t.d \; pre(t.l) \; y = pre(t) \; Y)^{x,y}_{in(t.r) \; x, pre(t.r) \; y} \\
= & \quad \{ \text{ substitution } \} \\
& in(t.l) \; t.d \; in(t.r) \; x = in(t) \; X \; \wedge \\
& t.d \; pre(t.l) \; pre(t.r) \; y = pre(t) \; Y \\
= & \quad \{ \text{ definition of } in(t) \text{ and } pre(t) \text{ for nonempty } t \; \} \\
& in(t) \; x = in(t) \; X \; \wedge \quad pre(t) \; y = pre(t) \; Y \; \wedge \; t \neq \bot \\
= & \\
& x = X \; \wedge \; y = Y \; \wedge \; t \neq \bot
\end{aligned}$$

So far so good.

Inversion of the program requires that we come up with mutually exclusive postconditions for the two alternatives in the if-statement. No simple conditions seem to exist. Operationally speaking, the problem is that all work is done in the second alternative; no variables change in the first alternative, so it is hard to detect calls that select the first alternative. Therefore, we propose to shift some of the work from the second to the first alternative. Since statement $y := t.d \; y$ is the last state change of the second alternative it is probably indicative of which alternative was chosen, and we don't want to lose that information. Therefore, we move the assignment to x to the first alternative. The problem in doing so, however, is that the label to be prefixed to sequence x is not available in this situation, so we add it as a parameter to the procedure.

procedure $gen(d : label; \; t : tree):$
$\{ \; x = X \; \wedge \; y = Y \; \}$
$\quad [\; t = \bot \rightarrow x := d \; x$
$\quad \| \; t \neq \bot \rightarrow gen(d, t.r); \; gen(t.d, t.l); \; y := t.d \; y$
$\quad]$
$\{ \; x = in(t) \; d \; X \; \wedge \; y = pre(t) \; Y \; \}$

We omit the verification. The program consists of

$$x, y := \epsilon, \epsilon; \quad gen(\emptyset, t)$$

in which $\emptyset$ is a label that does not occur in tree t and that is appended to $in(t)$ in sequence x. With this change, a postcondition of the first alternative is $hd(x) = d$, where $hd(x)$ is the first element of sequence x. We write $tl(x)$ for the remainder of sequence x. A postcondition of the second alternative is $hd(x) = t.d$ if $t.l = \perp$, or $hd(x)$ is a label from $t.l$ if $t.l \neq \perp$. If all labels in the tree are distinct then $t.d \neq d$ and all labels from $t.l$ differ from d also. Hence, the postcondition of the second alternative implies $hd(x) \neq d$. Inversion of procedure gen yields procedure neg, which stores in t the tree whose traversals are given in x and y. It requires that x be extended with label $\emptyset$ that does not occur anywhere else in the two traversals.

procedure $neg(d : label;$ **var** $t : tree)$:
$\{ \ x = in(T) \ d \ X \quad \wedge \quad y = pre(T) \ Y \ \}$
$\quad [\ hd(x) = d \rightarrow t, x := \perp, tl(x)$
$\quad \| \ hd(x) \neq d \rightarrow t.d, y := hd(y), tl(y); \quad neg(t.d, t.l); \quad neg(d, t.r)$
$\quad]$
$\{ \ x = X \ \wedge \ y = Y \ \wedge \ t = T \ \}$

The program is

$\{ \ x = in(T) \ \emptyset \ \wedge \quad y = pre(T) \ \}$
$neg(\emptyset, t)$
$\{ \ x = \epsilon \ \wedge \ y = \epsilon \ \wedge \ t = T \ \}$

which solves our programming problem.

11.2   Reversible Computations

We have seen how we can sometimes invert a program. In this section, we have a look at the physics of computations that can be run backwards.

Computations evoked by our programs can be performed by electronic computers; by biological systems such as our brains; by pencil and paper; and what have you. All implementations share the rather obvious property that they are physical processes and, hence, are subject to the laws of physics. It makes sense, therefore, to ask such questions as: what is the minimum size of any device capable of performing a given computation? What is its maximum size? How much time does it take? What is the minimum amount of energy it takes? We will focus on the latter question. Besides being "just" interesting, it is also a question that is relevant to the construction of many modern computing systems. Energy dissipation is the transformation of "useful" energy into "useless" heat. The rate at which heat can be removed from the machine is roughly proportional to the surface area of the machine, whereas the production of heat is roughly proportional to the number of gates and, hence, the volume of the machine. If we build a larger machine by extending it in all spatial dimensions, then the volume grows faster than the surface and heat becomes a problem. The alternative is to extend the size of the machine in only two of the three dimensions, but then the distance over which signals have to be communicated is increased and the machine is slowed down. As a result, energy dissipation is a serious concern in the construction of computers.

Is there any fundamental lower limit to the energy dissipation? Yes, there is, as the following argument, due to Von Neumann, shows. The argument involves the notion of entropy, so let us see what entropy is. According to information theory, entropy is a measure for the amount of information in a system. Let i range over the possible states of the system, and let p_i be the probability that the system is in state i. Entropy H is defined to be

$$H = -\sum_i p_i \log(p_i)$$

where $\log$ is the logarithm base 2. The unit in which H is expressed is bits. For example, consider a system with two states of equal probability. Then $H = -(0.5 \log(0.5) + 0.5 \log(0.5)) = 1$ bit. If we set the system in one fixed state, then the probability of that state is 1 and of the other state is 0. In this case, the entropy is 0 bits; that is, the action has destroyed 1 bit of information. The notion of entropy also exists in thermodynamics, where it is defined to be

$$S = -k \sum_i p_i \ln(p_i)$$

joules/kelvin. (Actually, entropy is often defined to be $S = k \ln(\Omega)$, where Ω is the number of states in the system — but this is really the same thing when assuming that all states have the same probability, $1/\Omega$.) The thermodynamical notion of entropy is coupled to energy through the temperature T of the system: when the entropy of a system is decreased by some amount, then the system dissipates energy equal to the amount of entropy reduction times the temperature. The observation by Von Neumann is that the two entropies are the same notion, apart from some constant factor, $k \ln(2)$.

Putting things together we find that when the probability distribution of the system is changed so that entropy H is decreased by 1 bit, then entropy S is decreased by $k \ln(2)$ joules/kelvin, and the system dissipates $kT \ln(2)$ joules of energy in the form of heat. Hence, destruction of information implies dissipation of energy.

Here is an example. Suppose a program operates on two boolean variables x and y, and assume that the four possible initial states have the same

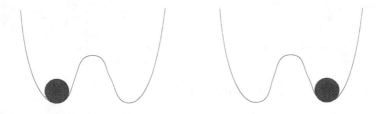

FIGURE 11.1. Two states.

probability. The initial entropy is $-4 \cdot (\frac{1}{4} \log \frac{1}{4}) = 2$ bits. Let the program be the assignment statement

$$x, y := x \lor y, x \land y \quad .$$

As a result, only three final states occur, two of them with probability $\frac{1}{4}$ and one (namely with $x, y = true, false$) with probability $\frac{1}{2}$. The final entropy is therefore $-(2 \cdot \frac{1}{4} \log \frac{1}{4} + \frac{1}{2} \log \frac{1}{2}) = 1.5$ bits, which means that the program decreases the entropy by 0.5 bits. Its execution will, therefore, dissipate at least $\frac{1}{2} kT \ln(2)$ joules of energy.

Figure 11.1 shows another example. A pebble can be in either the left or in the right trough, with equal probability. The action to be performed is to make sure that the pebble ends up in the left trough. If the action is performed when the pebble starts out in the left trough, then nothing needs to be done, and no energy is dissipated. If the action is performed when the pebble starts out in the right trough, then we kick the pebble to the left, supplying it with enough kinetic energy to roll up the hill and then down on the left side. If we slow down the pebble while it is rolling down and collect the energy that is converted from potential to kinetic energy, in such a way that the pebble comes to a halt just when it reaches the bottom of the left trough, then the amount of energy we collect equals the kinetic energy that we applied in kicking it out of the right trough. Again: no energy is dissipated.

What are we saying about energy dissipation? Which mistake have we made? The mistake is that you need to know the position of the pebble before you decide which procedure to apply (do nothing vs. kick). If you know the position of the pebble, then the two states do not have equal probability, and no information is destroyed. If the initial position is not known then the position has to be measured, and if the two states have equal probability this act requires $kT \ln(2)$ joules of energy.

In the sequel, we study methods of performing computations that do not destroy information. This does not yet imply that energy isn't dissipated — other sources of energy dissipation may exist. We give one example of a computation technique that avoids energy dissipation altogether, and we discuss one technique in which the energy dissipation is very low. One

FIGURE 11.2. A switch.

remark seems to be in order to put everything in the proper perspective. We are discussing effects of the order of $kT \ln(2)$ joules. In present day computers, about $10^9 kT$ joules are dissipated per bit operation. We still have a long way to go.

11.3   Circuits Built from Reversible Gates

In this section, we try to perform a computation without destroying information. We have already encountered the destruction of information in a storage element: the pebble that can be in one of two positions. If we add to every flip-flop another flip-flop that contains the previous value, another one to contain the pre-previous value, and so on, then we can assign values to variables without destroying information. Technical problems exist with building and initializing infinitely many flip-flops, but in the name of progress we ignore those for a moment.

What other sources of information destruction do we have? The remaining source is the combinatorial circuitry, circuits that compute some function of their inputs. If the function has no inverse, then information is destroyed. For example, if we know that the output of an adder is 6, we cannot conclude that the input was 2 and 4. From switching theory, we know how all combinational circuits can be built from boolean functions. Of all those functions, only two have an inverse: negation and identity. These two alone do not suffice to construct all functions. (How do we compute a conjunction from negation and identity?) It appears that it does not suffice to consider components that have only one output; we need components with at least two outputs. The simplest one is the switch, shown in Figure 11.2, but it cannot be inverted.

In order to compute the output, we need to know whether the switch is in the left or in the right state. Therefore, we include the signal that determines the state explicitly, both as an input and as an output signal, as in Figure 11.3. The specification of this component can be written as

$$(a \ \wedge \ x0 = y0 \ \wedge \ x1 = y1) \ \vee \ (\neg a \ \wedge \ x0 = y1 \ \wedge \ x1 = y0) \ \ .$$

It is obviously its own inverse. This switch, known to electricians and plumbers for more than a century, is known as the Fredkin-gate. Figure 11.4

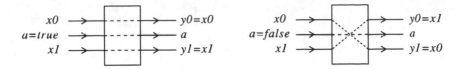

FIGURE 11.3. A switch with control signal.

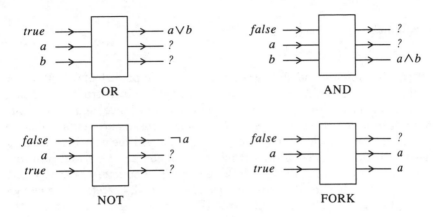

FIGURE 11.4. Four gates built from switches.

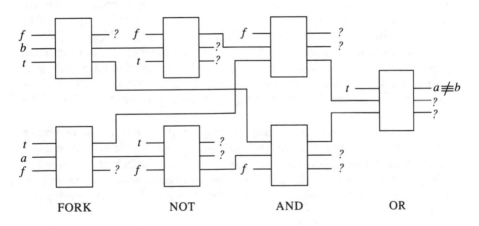

FIGURE 11.5. An exclusive-or circuit.

gives some examples to show how elementary combinational functions can be built from these switches.

These gates can be connected to build arbitrary combinational functions. Figure 11.5 shows how an exclusive-or circuit can be built. It is based on

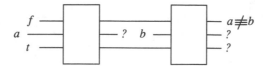

FIGURE 11.6. Another exclusive-or circuit.

the formula

$$a \not\equiv b = (a \wedge \neg b) \vee (b \wedge \neg a) \quad .$$

Often, the simple-minded construction can be improved upon. A better exclusive-or is given in Figure 11.6. In general, the construction method leads to circuits with a number of constant inputs (*true* and *false*), the outputs in which we are interested, and some garbage outputs in which we are not interested. The garbage outputs are a pain in the neck because they need to be thrown away when setting up a new computation, and throwing away a garbage bit requires $kT \ln(2)$ energy. The number of garbage bits is, roughly, proportional to the number of gates and, therefore, the energy dissipation is, roughly, proportional to the number of gates. In general, the number of gates is an exponential function of the number of inputs, which implies that a lot of energy is involved. (It wouldn't be so bad if energy dissipation were proportional to the number of input or output bits, but an exponential function thereof is just too much.) Can we reduce the number of garbage bits in a systematic way? Yes. As illustrated in Figure 11.7, the number of garbage bits can be made equal to the number of input bits (real inputs plus constants) and, furthermore, their values can be made equal to the inputs. Therefore, we know exactly what those values are, and we can remove them without dissipating any energy (see the discussion of the pebble and the two troughs).

It appears that, in order to perform a computation, it is not necessary to change the entropy. The garbage output, x, can be destroyed without dissipation of energy because it is known (x is the input), and the energy dissipation required for the destruction of the "real" output, y, is proportional to the number of output bits and independent of the number of gates required for computing y.

11.4   Reversible Gates Built from Billiard Balls

We have made plausible that an arbitrary computation can be embedded in a reversible one. Next, we have to show that the reversible computation can be performed without dissipation of energy. In this section, we discuss an implementation that requires no energy dissipation at all; it is, however,

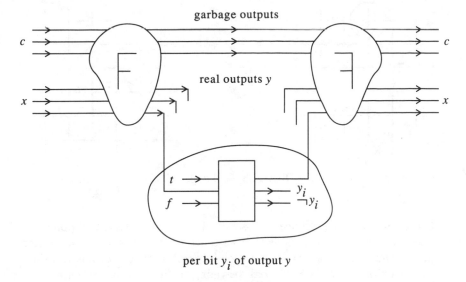

per bit y_i of output y

FIGURE 11.7. Construction for general function F.

somewhat unrealistic in the sense that unachievable precision is required in building the machine. One may use it as a guideline, however, in the design of more realistic implementations, such as the one mentioned in the next section.

The present model, first proposed by Toffoli and Fredkin, is referred to as the *billiard ball* model of computation. The physical effects on which it is based are elastic collisions involving balls and fixed reflectors. The "rules of the game" are the same as those that underly the theory of kinetic gases, where the balls correspond to the gas molecules and the reflectors to the container's walls. (Benioff and Feynman played similar games based on quantum physical principles instead of classical physics; fortunately, the conclusions are the same.) We show that by putting reflectors of the right shape in the right places and by giving the right balls the right initial position and speed, any specified computation can be carries out. We do so by building the switch that we have discussed in the previous section.

Consider a two-dimensional grid, where the spacing between neighboring grid points will be our unit of distance. Assume that we have a number of indistinguishable hard balls of radius $1/\sqrt{2}$ traveling along the grid lines at the velocity of one unit of space per unit of time. At the starting time, the center of each ball is on a grid point, and we will see to it that the centers are on grid points at every integral multiple of the time unit. Because of the choice of the radius, the assumptions are preserved by right-angle elastic collisions between the balls. They are ruined by head-on collisions, so we avoid the latter and only allow the first kind of collision.

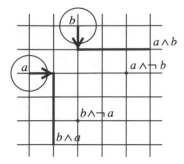 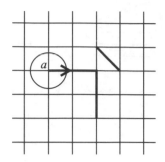

FIGURE 11.8. Colliding balls.

It is clear that the presence or absence of a ball at a given grid point can be viewed as a boolean variable that assumes the value *true* or *false* (for "ball" or "no ball", respectively) at each integral moment in time. Consider the left part of Figure 11.8. If a ball traveling to the East is present at time t at position a and a ball traveling South is present at time t at position b, then balls will be present at time $t + 4$ at the positions labeled $a \wedge b$ and $b \wedge a$. Labels $a \wedge \neg b$ and $b \wedge \neg a$ are found in a similar fashion by assuming that only one ball is present. If no ball is present, then the four boolean expressions are *false*. We stick to the convention that our inputs are on a SW–NE diagonal, that all balls travel to the East or to the South, and that the outputs are also on a SW–NE diagonal. As a result, we can largely ignore the timing, and we do not mention the $t + 4$ any more.

Next, consider the right half of Figure 11.8. It contains one reflector and one ball. The output is a copy of the input, except that the ball is traveling in a different direction. We use this mirror for changing between southern and eastern directions. We can use stationary balls instead of reflecting mirrors, if that is what we like better. (Stationary balls do not move, not even when hit by a moving ball.)

Next, we put these two collision mechanisms together to construct a switch. Using two mirrors, we first obtain a simpler kind of switch, shown in Figure 11.9. Verify the labeling. The ball that exits at the output labeled a may be the ball that entered at either the input labeled a or the input labeled x, depending on whether one or two balls entered this switch. However, since balls are indistinguishable, we need not worry about this. What is the inverse of this circuit? Of course, if we label the two switching inputs $x \wedge a$ and $x \wedge \neg a$, then the output is x. We may, however, also label them $y \wedge a$ and $x \wedge \neg a$, and then the output turns out to be $(y \wedge a) \vee (x \wedge \neg a)$. What else do we need to construct our full-fledged switch? Its specification was

$$(a \ \wedge \ x0 = y0 \ \wedge \ x1 = y1) \ \vee \ (\neg a \ \wedge \ x0 = y1 \ \wedge \ x1 = y0)$$

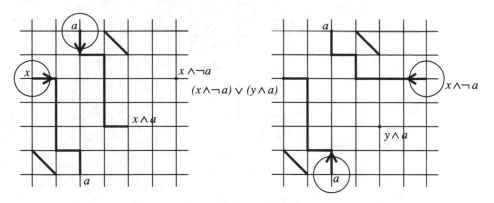

FIGURE 11.9. A simple switch.

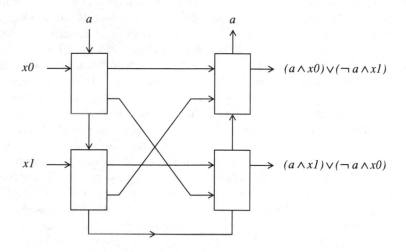

FIGURE 11.10. The complete switch.

and this can be rewritten into

$$(y0 \; = \; (a \wedge x0) \vee (\neg a \wedge x1)) \; \wedge \; (y1 \; = \; (a \wedge x1) \vee (\neg a \wedge x0))$$

in which we recognize two simple switches, and two of its inverses.

In order to put everything together as illustrated in Figure 11.10, we need to make a crossing that is "free from interference"; that is, billiard balls should be able to cross lines even if another ball runs into it at a right angle. Such a crossing can be made as in Figure 11.11. Actually, it is our simple switch, which has been compressed in such a way that two of its outputs coincide.

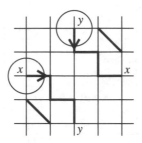

FIGURE 11.11. An interference-free crossing.

11.5   DNA and Turing Machines

The billiard ball computer that can be constructed in this way is somewhat unrealistic. The parts must be built perfectly, they have to be immune to thermal noise, and the machinery has to be started at exactly the right time with the right velocities. Small errors in the initial position or velocity are amplified (by roughly a factor of 2) at each collision between balls. Hence, a small random error in the initial state causes the trajectories to become completely unpredictable after a few dozen collisions. Lots of tricks exist to correct small deviations and they all lead to small amounts of energy dissipation. The resulting design might still be of practical interest, since the amount of energy needed for these corrections might be far less than the kinetic energy that accounts for the speed of the computation. A technique that is completely different does not try to correct the adverse effects of thermal noise, but tries to use the noise to good advantage. The following proposal by Bennett is a machine whose driving force is exactly this Brownian motion (see [Ben82]). It is similar to the transport of electrons in a copper wire to which an electric field (a potential difference) is applied: the electrons jiggle back and forth, due to the Brownian motion, but the movement in one direction slightly exceeds the movement in the opposite direction; the electrons drift, on the average, in one way. There is a net effect dictated by the direction of the field, and this is what we call the electric current. A similar thing happens in the world of chemical reactions, where Brownian motion suffices to bring reactant molecules into contact, orient and bend them into a transition state, and then separate the product molecules after the reaction. The chemical reaction is, in principle, reversible: the same Brownian motion that causes the forward reaction sometimes brings product molecules together, pushes them through the transition state, and lets them emerge as reactant molecules. The chemical reactions involve surmounting potential energy barriers of a few kT in order to reach the transition state. On the other hand, potential barriers on the order of $100kT$, as found in covalent bonds, are typically too big to

be surmounted by Brownian motion. Such barriers prevent DNA from un-
dergoing random rearrangements of its base sequence at room temperature
and thereby facilitate biological life.

How can we construct a Brownian computer? We start from a Turing machine. A Turing machine is essentially a finite-state machine, as discussed
in Chapter 4, but extended with a tape plus a read/write head. The input
to the finite-state machine is supplied as the initial sequence of characters
on the tape, and in every step the machine not only transits to a new state
but also writes an output character on the tape and may move the head
over one position to the left or right. If the tape is infinitely long, then
everything that can be computed at all can be computed by a Turing machine; this is the Church-Turing hypothesis that we mentioned in Chapter
1. (Of course, at every moment in time only a finite part of the tape is
actually in use.) It turns out that every Turing machine computation can
be embedded in a reversible computation, one in which each configuration
has at most one predecessor and at most one successor.

A chemical implementation hereof might consist of a long macromolecule,
similar to DNA or RNA, which for our purposes can be viewed as a string
of symbols (drawn from the alphabet $\{A, T, G, C\}$). A chemical group attached at one site might encode the position of the read/write head and the
state of the machine. Several different kinds of enzymes, one kind for each
of the machine's transition rules, would catalyze reactions of the macromolecule with smaller molecules in the surrounding solution. Such a reaction would transform the macromolecule into its successor as prescribed by
the operation of the Turing machine. The reactions occur in both directions,
corresponding to forward and backward steps in the Turing machine. The
resulting computation speed can be controlled by adjusting the reactant
concentrations. The closer these are to equilibrium, the slower the machinery works, and the less energy is dissipated. If the energy dissipation is E
per step, then the ratio between forward and backward steps is $e^{E/kT}$. For
example, if the four nucleotide pyrophosphates are present in 10 percent
excess over equilibrium concentration, then we would see on the average
11 forward steps per 10 backward steps and the energy dissipation would
be $kT \ln(11/10) \approx 0.1kT$ per effective forward step. This corresponds to
the difference in chemical potential between reactants and products. By
increasing the concentrations, we can increase the effective speed of the
computation and this is accompanied by an increase of the energy dissipation. (It also decreases the errors due to uncatalyzed reactions, but we
ignore this issue here.) In biological life forms, RNA polymerase copies a
DNA strand at a speed of about 30 nucleotides per second, dissipating
about $20kT$ per nucleotide (and making less than one mistake per 10,000
nucleotides).

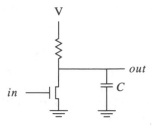

FIGURE 11.12. A driver.

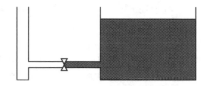

FIGURE 11.13. Connected water containers.

11.6   Hot-Clock nMOS

Although the DNA computer is more realistic than the billiard-ball computer, it is not the kind of machine that we can readily construct yet. But it does give some insights in how to construct energy-efficient nMOS circuits. To understand how we can construct those circuits, we check how energy is dissipated on a chip.

Figure 11.12 shows a driver circuit whose input is copied to the output (and also inverted, but that is not our concern here). The output, a wire, contains some capacitive load. The load is a combination of the input gates from successor circuits and of the parasitic capacitance between the wire and the ground of the chip. Each time that signal out changes from 0 to V volts, the power supply provides a quantity of charge CV at potential V, which makes for an amount of energy CV^2. Half of this energy ends up stored in the capacitance C, and the other half is dissipated in the pull-up transistor. When out changes back from V to 0 volts, the charge stored in C is conducted into the ground connection, via the channel of the pull-down transistor where it is dissipated. Hence, a full up-and-down cycle of the capacitive output dissipates energy CV^2.

How can we get rid of this energy dissipation? Well, consider a huge container filled with water, and a small, empty container as in Figure 11.13. The two containers are connected via a tube with a valve, but the valve is closed. What happens if we open the valve? The water will flow rapidly from the huge container into the small container until the latter is filled to the same level as the huge container. If the small container's cross section is

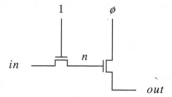

FIGURE 11.14. The elementary hot-clock driver.

C units, and if the water level reaches height V, then the potential energy stored in the container is $\frac{1}{2}CV^2$. Because CV units of water flowed into the container, and because it was supplied from a container whose water level is V higher (if the huge container is huge, its water level doesn't change significantly), the amount of energy supplied is CV^2. Apparently, half of it is lost in the form of heat that has been dissipated. The rapid flow of the water causes a lot of motion of the individual water molecules, the water molecules pick up a lot of kinetic energy, which is dissipated when the molecules finally come to rest. Can we stem the rapid flow of water, and turn it into a gentle flow that causes much less dissipation? Yes, we can by starting from a different configuration. Suppose that we can change the height of the huge container, and that we start with its water level just as high as the bottom of the small, empty container when we open the valve. Nothing happens. If we slowly raise the huge container, then there will be a gentle flow of water into the small container. We want to do this slowly, so that the process is thermodynamically reversible and no energy is dissipated. When the water level finally reaches height V, we have the same final configuration as before, with $\frac{1}{2}CV^2$ energy stored in the small container but without any energy being dissipated. You might say that we needed some energy to raise the huge container. But that is exactly the same amount of energy that was released by lowering the container in the first place, and we might have trapped that energy somewhere, for example, in a big spring holding up the container. We are not cheating!

The analogy to our circuits is that the huge, stationary container is the power supply, and the small container is the capacitive load at the output of our circuit. Can we construct something that is similar to the up-and-down going container? Well, our circuits have a clock, which is exactly a signal that is going up and down all the time. Let us, therefore, make a circuit that is driven from the clock instead of from the power supply.

In Figure 11.14, let 1 be the connection to the power supply, and let ϕ be the clock. We will see that the operation of the circuit depends on the fact that the rightmost of the two transistors is "big" which means that there is a large capacitance between gate and channel when the transistor is in the conducting state. There is only a small capacitance between gate and channel if the transistor is not conducting, or if the transistor is small. Assume that the initial state is S_0.

S_0 : $V_{in} = V_n = V_\phi = V_{out} = 0$
small transistor is on, n is driven
large transistor is off, out is floating

We write V_{in} for the voltage level at node in. We say that a transistor is on if it is in the conducting state (that is, if its gate voltage exceeds the source voltage or the drain voltage by at least the threshold V_{th}), and off otherwise. A node is said to be driven if there is a conducting path between the node and power, ground, or the clock signal; a node is said to be floating otherwise. Check that S_0 is a stable state of the circuit.

Next, assume that V_{in} increases. Since the small transistor is on, V_n increases also. The small transistor turns off when $V_{in} = V_n = V_1 - V_{th}$. Even if V_{in} increases further, V_n remains fixed. So much for the small transistor. Since n is the gate of the large transistor, this transistor turns on when V_n crosses V_{th}. As a consequence, out is driven by the clock. V_{out} does not change, because we already have $V_{out} = 0$. Thus, the circuit reaches its second stable state S_1.

S_1 : $V_{in} \geq V_n = V_1 - V_{th}$; $V_\phi = V_{out} = 0$
small transistor is off, n is floating
large transistor is on, out is driven

In this state there is a noticeable capacitance between the gate and the channel of the big transistor. Therefore, if ϕ switches from 0 to V_1, V_ϕ increases by V_1 and the other terminal of the capacitance also increases by V_1. Consequently, V_n goes to $2V_1 - V_{th}$ which even exceeds the voltage level of the power supply. The circuit reaches its third stable state S_2.

S_2 : $V_{in} \geq V_1 - V_{th}$; $V_n = 2V_1 - V_{th}$; $V_\phi = V_{out} = V_1$
small transistor is off, n is floating
large transistor is on, out is driven

$V_{out} = V_1$ and not $V_{out} = V_1 - V_{th}$, which means that this circuit nicely "restores" high input signals. If clock signal ϕ switches back from 1 to 0, the circuit returns to state S_1. Decreasing V_{in} to 0 leads back to S_0, which completes one cycle of the circuit's operation.

Next, we consider what happens if V_{in} remains fixed at 0. If in state S_0 clock signal ϕ switches from 0 to 1, the circuit enters stable state S_3.

S_3 : $V_{in} = V_n = V_{out} = 0$; $V_\phi = V_1$
small transistor is on, n is driven
large transistor is off, out is floating

If ϕ switches back to 0, the circuit returns to state S_0.

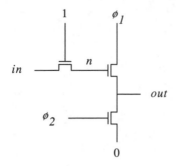

FIGURE 11.15. First variation.

Notice the quintessence of reversibility in this circuit. Whenever a transistor turns on, there is no voltage difference across the channel of the transistor (source and drain are at the same voltage level). Whenever a transistor turns off, there is no current flowing through the channel.

The last circuit is not the last word on circuit design; it has a number of unattractive properties. The most basic one is the fact that *out* may be floating. When ϕ is high, *out* may be floating if $V_{in} = 0$ and, hence, *out* is susceptible to charge sharing. If this situation persists during many cycles, *out* is floating during many cycles, and may accumulate a lot of charge. Also, if V_{in} decreases to 0 while in state S_2, the small transistor turns on again, V_n decreases, and the large transistor turns off. Hence, we still have $V_{out} = V_1$, but *out* is floating. We shortly discuss a number of variations of the basic circuit that avoid *out* floating. All these circuits require a two-phase nonoverlapping clock.

The first variation is shown in Figure 11.15. This is the old circuit, extended with one transistor. It is used to drive *out* by 0 during ϕ_2. During each cycle we now have *out* being driven by 0 part of the time. Although *out* still floats during ϕ_1 if $V_{in} = 0$, the cumulative effect of the charge sharing has been exorcised.

In the second variation, shown in Figure 11.16, the connection to 1 is replaced by ϕ_2. Previously, *in* was required to be stable during ϕ_1 to avoid having *out* floating while $V_{out} = V_1$. Changing 1 to ϕ_2 results in copying V_{in} to V_n during ϕ_2 and isolating node n thereafter, which guarantees that n does not change during the ϕ_1. Hence, it now suffices that *in* has the proper value by the end of ϕ_2.

In the third variation, shown in Figure 11.17, the connection to 0 is replaced by ϕ_1. Node 0 was only connected to *out* during ϕ_2. Since ϕ_1 and ϕ_2 do not overlap, there is no difference at all in the operation of the circuit. There is one nice difference when considering the connections to be made to this driver circuit: we have two clock signals, ϕ_1 and ϕ_2, but the connections to the power supply, 0 and 1, have been eliminated. The

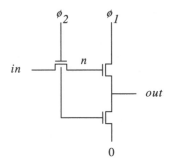

FIGURE 11.16. Second variation.

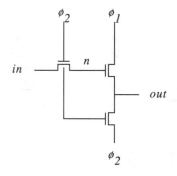

FIGURE 11.17. Third variation.

energy that is required, is supplied by the clock signals, hence the name hot-clock circuits.

11.7   Bibliographic Notes

Program inversion can be traced back to [Dij78]. A good discussion can be found in Chapter 21 of [Gri81]. Constructing a labeled binary tree from its inorder and preorder traversal is a topic that shows up every now and then in places ranging from the writings of Knuth (cf. [Knu73]) to the ACM Programming Competition. Several inefficient solutions have been published in the literature, even though the efficient, recursive solution that we have included here is almost trivial. It has been produced independently by several authors, and has been published in [vdS91]. Several authors have (re)discovered an equally efficient iterative algorithm, such as the one in [CU90]. An earlier algorithm that reconstructs a binary tree from its inorder traversal alone is presented in [GvdS90]. The inorder traversal alone does not uniquely determine the tree; the latter algorithm is nondeterministic. It has the remarkable property that every tree whose inorder traversal equals the given input is a possible outcome of the program. Exercise 5 is from [Dij78] and is discussed in [Gri81].

The billiard ball computer is due to [FT82]. The DNA computer is from [Ben82]. Von Neumann's argument is in [vN66]. Feynman's quantum mechanical, reversible computer can be found in [Fey84]. The paper that pioneered work in this area is [Ben73]. A nice overview paper of this area is [BL85].

A description of hot-clock circuits can be found in [SFM$^+$85].

11.8 Exercises

1. Is $s = 0$ upon termination of the programs $S0^{-1}$, $S1^{-1}$, and $S2^{-1}$?

2. Show that $S0$, $S1$, and $S2$ are the inverses of $S0^{-1}$, $S1^{-1}$, and $S2^{-1}$, respectively.

3. Determine the inverse of $x, y := x + y, x$.

4. Our algorithm for computing the rank takes time proportional to N^2. Write an algorithm whose running time is proportional to $N \log(N)$. Can you invert this program?

5. Let N be a positive integer and let $a[0..N-1]$ be an array that contains a permutation of the numbers 0 through $N-1$. Given N and a, we define a second array, $b[0..N-1]$, as follows: $b[i]$ is the number of values in $a[0..i-1]$ that are less than $a[i]$. Formally:

$$\langle \forall i : 0 \le i < N : b[i] = \langle \mathbf{N}j : 0 \le j < i : a[j] < a[i] \rangle \rangle \quad .$$

Array b is called the *code* of the permutation. Write a program that replaces the contents of array a with array b, that is, a program that replaces the permutation by its code. Invert the program to obtain a program that converts the code back to the permutation. (The existence of these programs proves that for each permutation exactly one code exists, and vice versa.)

6. Consider the following program for multiplying two natural numbers, X and Y.

```
x, y, z := X, Y, 0;
*[ y ≠ 0 → [ odd(y) → x, y, z := 2x, (y − 1)/2, z + x
           ‖ even(y) → x, y := 2x, y/2
           ]
 ]
```

Invert this program under the assumption $X \neq 0$. (Hint: First, figure out an invariant for showing that this program computes the product of X and Y; next, you have to add a term to the invariant that allows you to conclude mutually exclusive postconditions for the two alternatives in the if-statement.) Does the inverse program compute the quotient and the remainder of an integer division?

7. Consider the following program for multiplying two natural numbers X and Y. It is assumed that Y is an N-bit number, that is, $0 \leq Y < 2^N$.

$$x, y, z, k := X, Y, 0, N;$$
$$*[\ k \neq 0 \rightarrow [\ odd(y) \rightarrow x, y, z, k := 2x, (y-1)/2, z+x, k-1$$
$$\quad\quad\quad\quad\ |\ even(y) \rightarrow x, y, k := 2x, y/2, k-1$$
$$\quad]\quad\quad\ ]$$

Invert this program under the assumption $X \neq 0$. (Same hint and question as in the previous exercise.)

8. Prove that for given positive natural numbers X and Y, program

$$x, y, u, v := X, Y, Y, X;$$
$$*[\ x > y \rightarrow x, v := x - y, v + u$$
$$\ |\ y > x \rightarrow y, u := y - x, u + v$$
$$\ ]$$
$$\{\ (x+y)/2 = \gcd(X, Y)\ \wedge\ (u+v)/2 = \mathrm{lcm}(X, Y)\ \}$$

computes the greatest common divisor and the least common multiple of X and Y. Invert the program to reconstruct X and Y.

9. Construct an iterative solution to the problem of reconstructing a labeled binary tree from its inorder and preorder traversals.

10. Consider a system with three boolean variables, a, b, and c. Assume that the eight possible initial states occur with equal probability. How much entropy reduction occurs through execution of the statement $a, b, c := c, c, a \wedge b$?

11. Given are integers i and j, $0 \leq i < 10\ \wedge\ 0 \leq j < 10$. All 100 possible initial states have the same probability. How much does the entropy change through execution of the statement $i, j := i+j, i+j$? Same question for

$$i, j := i + j, i - j$$
$$i, j := i + j, |i - j|$$
$$i, j := j, i$$
$$i, j := i\ \mathbf{div}\ 2, j\ \mathbf{div}\ 2$$
$$i, j := i\ \mathbf{mod}\ 2, j\ \mathbf{mod}\ 2$$

$$i, j := \max(i, j), \min(i, j)$$
$$[\, i \leq j \rightarrow i := 0 \parallel i > j \rightarrow j := 0 \,]$$
$$*[i > j \rightarrow i := i - 1]$$

12. Construct a full adder from billiard balls. A full adder has three binary inputs, say x, y, and z, and produces two binary outputs, $(x + y + z)$ **div** 2 and $(x + y + z)$ **mod** 2. You may have to add constant inputs and you may end up with more outputs.

13. We list a number of gates with two inputs and two outputs each. For each of them, answer the following questions and explain your answers. Can all boolean functions be constructed from the gate? Is the gate reversible? If so, what is the inverse gate? Can the gate be built from billiard balls without using additional input signals and without generating additional output signals? The gates have inputs a and b. The two outputs are

   a and $a \equiv b$

   $a \vee b$ and $a \wedge b$

   $\neg(a \vee b)$ and $\neg(a \wedge b)$

   $\neg(a \vee b)$ and a

   $a \Rightarrow b$ and $b \Rightarrow a$ (where the arrow does not mean that input a goes to output b, but stands for implication).

14. It is sometimes claimed that the formula $E = kT \ln(2)$ is a lower bound on energy dissipation. In this chapter, we have argued that this is not necessarily the case. Discuss two other limits. One is $E = \bar{h}/t$, in which t is the switching time of an elementary action. The other is $E = C \cdot V^2$, in which C is a capacitance and V is the voltage to which it has to be charged.

12

A Collection of Nice Algorithms

12.1 Bresenham's Algorithm

We develop an algorithm for drawing a straight line on a raster. The algorithm is known as Bresenham's algorithm.

Given are four integers, x_0, x_1, y_0, and y_1, satisfying

$$0 \le x_0 < x_1 < 512 \ \wedge \ 0 \le y_0 \le y_1 < 256 \ \wedge \ y_1 - y_0 \le x_1 - x_0 \quad .$$

Write a program for marking all points on the unit grid near the straight line segment between (x_0, y_0) and (x_1, y_1).

For the moment we ignore the details of marking and write $mark(x, y)$ to mark point (x, y). In order to make the specification more precise, especially clarifying what is meant by "near", we propose that the program mark all points $(x, round(f(x)))$ with $x_0 \le x \le x_1$, where

$$f(x) = (x - x_0)\tfrac{dy}{dx} + y_0 \quad ;$$
$$dx = x_1 - x_0 \quad ;$$
$$dy = y_1 - y_0 \quad .$$

We have chosen to mark one point (x, y) for every x instead of for every y since $dx \ge dy$. This guarantees that marked points are not far apart. Marking one point (x, y) for every y leads to fewer marked points, and if $dy = 0$ even only one. If the points are far apart, they do not give a good image of the line segment.

From the postcondition that all points $(x, round(f(x)))$ in the range $x_0 \le x \le x_1$ have been marked, we obtain invariant

all points $(s, round(f(s)))$ with $x_0 \le s < x$ have been marked, and $x_0 \le x \le x_1$.

This leads to program

```
x := x_0;
*[ x ≠ x_1 → mark(x, round(f(x)));  x := x + 1 ];
mark(x, round(f(x)))    .
```

In order to reduce the number of f-evaluations, we introduce variable y and add term $y = round(f(x))$ to the invariant. In view of

$$y = round(f(x))$$
$$= \quad \{ \text{ definition of } round \text{ } \}$$
$$-\tfrac{1}{2} \le y - f(x) < +\tfrac{1}{2}$$
$$= \quad \{ \text{ definition of } f \text{ } \}$$
$$-\tfrac{1}{2} \le y - (x - x_0)\tfrac{dy}{dx} - y_0 < +\tfrac{1}{2}$$
$$= \quad \{ \text{ calculus; } dx > 0 \text{ } \}$$
$$0 \le 2(y - y_0)\,dx - 2(x - x_0)\,dy + dx < 2dx \quad ,$$

we introduce variable t and add term $t = 2(y - y_0)\,dx - 2(x - x_0)\,dy + dx$ to the invariant; we observe that $y = round(f(x))$ is then equivalent to $0 \le t < 2dx$. Statements

$$x, t := x + 1, t - 2dy$$

and

$$y, t := y + 1, t + 2dx$$

maintain $t = 2(y - y_0)\,dx - 2(x - x_0)\,dy + dx$, so

$$x, t := x + 1, t - 2dy;$$
$$*[t < 0 \rightarrow y, t := y + 1, t + 2dx]$$

maintains term $0 \le t < 2dx$ as well. Since $dy \le dx$, the loop will be iterated at most once and can be reduced to an if-statement. This leads to the following refinement of our marking program.

$$dx, dy := x_1 - x_0, y_1 - y_0;$$
$$x, y, t := x_0, y_0, dx;$$
$$*[\; x \ne x_1 \rightarrow mark(x, y);$$
$$\qquad\qquad x, t := x + 1, t - 2dy;$$
$$\qquad\qquad [\; t < 0 \rightarrow y, t := y + 1, t + 2dx$$
$$\qquad\qquad \| \; t \ge 0 \rightarrow skip$$
$$\;] \qquad\qquad\qquad \];$$
$$mark(x, y)$$

This program is known as Bresenham's algorithm. Observe the similarity to saddleback search.

Next, we focus on the marking operation. Marking point (x, y) is performed by operation $d[a] : \oplus b$, where

$$a = y \cdot 64 + x \text{ } \textbf{div } 8$$
$$b = 2^{x \bmod 8}$$

$d[0..16383]$ is an array of integers in the range $0..255$.

The interpretation of $d[a] : \oplus b$ depends on the kind of drawing operation that is to be performed. For example, if a black line is to be drawn on a white background it is often interpreted as $d[a] := b$, but if a line of inverted color is to be drawn on a background that may contain both black and white regions, then $d[a] := d[a] \textbf{ exor } b$ is chosen.

In order to economize on the computation of $y \cdot 64 + x$ **div** 8 and $2^{x \bmod 8}$, we introduce variables a, b, and c and strengthen the invariant with

$$a = y \cdot 64 + x \text{ \textbf{div} } 8 \ \wedge \ b = 2^c \ \wedge \ c = x \bmod 8 \qquad ,$$

which allows us to eliminate y and obtain the following program.

$$
\begin{aligned}
&dx, dy := x_1 - x_0, y_1 - y_0; \\
&x, t := x_0, dx; \\
&a, b, c := y_0 \cdot 64 + x \text{ \textbf{div} } 8, 2^{x \bmod 8}, x \bmod 8; \\
&*[\ x \neq x_1 \rightarrow d[a] : \oplus b; \\
&\qquad\qquad x, t := x + 1, t - 2dy; \\
&\qquad\qquad [\ c = 7 \rightarrow a, b, c := a + 1, 1, 0 \\
&\qquad\qquad \|\ c < 7 \rightarrow b, c := 2b, c + 1 \\
&\qquad\qquad]; \\
&\qquad\qquad [\ t < 0 \rightarrow t, a := t + 2dx, a + 64 \\
&\qquad\qquad \|\ t \geq 0 \rightarrow skip \\
&\qquad\qquad]; \\
&\ ] \\
&d[a] : \oplus b
\end{aligned}
$$

Next, we develop an algorithm for marking points on a circle whose origin is $(0, 0)$ and whose radius is given by positive integer r. We restrict our attention to marking points (x, y) in the octant where $x \leq y$, since the points in the other octants can be obtained by symmetry. Again, the straightforward algorithm is

$$
\begin{aligned}
&x := 0; \ y := round(f(x)); \\
&*[\ x \leq y \rightarrow mark(x, y); \ x := x + 1; \ y := round(f(x))\ ] \qquad ,
\end{aligned}
$$

where f is defined by

$$x^2 + f(x)^2 = r^2 \ \wedge \ 0 \leq f(x) \qquad .$$

The invariant of this algorithm is

$$
\begin{aligned}
&y = round(f(x)), \\
&\text{all points } (s, round(f(s))) \text{ with } 0 \leq s < x \text{ have been marked,} \\
&\text{and } x \geq 0 \qquad .
\end{aligned}
$$

Again, we simplify $y = round(f(x))$:

$$
\begin{aligned}
&\quad y = round(f(x)) \\
&= \qquad \{ \text{ definition of round } \} \\
&\quad -\tfrac{1}{2} \leq y - f(x) < \tfrac{1}{2} \\
&= \\
&\quad y + \tfrac{1}{2} \geq f(x) > y - \tfrac{1}{2} \\
&= \qquad \{ \text{ see note below; } f(x) \geq 0 \ \} \\
&\quad y^2 + y + \tfrac{1}{4} \geq f(x)^2 > y^2 - y + \tfrac{1}{4} \\
&= \qquad \{ \text{ definition of } f(x) \ \}
\end{aligned}
$$

$$y^2 + y + \tfrac{1}{4} \geq r^2 - x^2 > y^2 - y + \tfrac{1}{4}$$
$$= \quad \{ \text{ calculus } \}$$
$$2y + \tfrac{1}{4} \geq r^2 - x^2 - y^2 + y > \tfrac{1}{4}$$
$$= \quad \{\ a > \tfrac{1}{4} \equiv a > 0 \text{ for integer } a\ \}$$
$$2y \geq r^2 - x^2 - y^2 + y > 0 \quad .$$

Thus, we might as well introduce $t = r^2 - x^2 - y^2 + y$, which implies that $y = round(f(x))$ is equivalent to $2y \geq t > 0$. We add this term to the invariant.

One note is in order. The third step in the simplification is valid only if $y - \tfrac{1}{2} \geq 0$, and this is implied by the term $2y \geq t > 0$ that was added to the invariant. The complete invariant is

$$t = r^2 - x^2 - y^2 + y \ \wedge\ 2y \geq t > 0 \ \wedge\ 0 \leq x \quad .$$

The first term is invariant under

$$x, t := x + 1, t - 2x - 1$$

and

$$y, t := y - 1, t + 2y - 2 \quad .$$

Since the statements are executed under the condition $x \leq y$, which is the guard of the loop, the first two terms are invariant under

$$
\begin{aligned}
&x, t := x + 1, t - 2x - 1; \\
&[\ t \leq 0 \rightarrow y, t := y - 1, t + 2y - 2 \\
&\|\ t > 0 \rightarrow skip \\
&]\quad ,
\end{aligned}
$$

which leads to Bresenham's algorithm for marking a circle.

$$
\begin{aligned}
&x, y, t := 0, r, r; \\
&*[\ x \leq y \rightarrow mark(x, y); \\
&\qquad\qquad x, t := x + 1, t - 2x - 1; \\
&\qquad\qquad [\ t \leq 0 \rightarrow y := y - 1; \ \ t := t + 2y \\
&\qquad\qquad \|\ t > 0 \rightarrow skip \\
&]\qquad\qquad]
\end{aligned}
$$

12.2 Computing the Transitive Closure

In this section, we discuss a well-known and often-used algorithm that operates on a relation or a directed graph. A relation is a boolean function on two arguments taken from the same domain, for example, a boolean function on two natural numbers, such as $i \leq j$ or $i \bmod 29 = j$, for natural numbers i and j. A directed graph is a set of nodes together with a set of edges. An edge is a pointer that points from one node to another node. There is a strong correspondence between directed graphs and relations. To each relation corresponds a graph (its set of nodes is the domain of the relation; if the boolean function is true for a pair of arguments, then there is an edge from the first to the second argument), and vice versa.

Given a relation, one can define its *transitive closure*. We have done this, for example, in Chapter 2 for the derivation relation. In terms of the graph, the set of nodes of the transitive closure is the same as in the original graph; the transitive closure has an edge from one node to another just when the original graph has a path of one or more edges. (Replacing "one" by "zero" yields the reflexive transitive closure.) In this section, we discuss an algorithm that, given a directed graph of finite size, computes its transitive closure. This algorithm is known as Warshall's algorithm. The algorithm works in situ, that is, it modifies the variable that records the initial data structure without using a similar variable for holding any intermediate results (except for a few scalar variables). The property of being in situ is an attractive one in the case of a large graph that requires a lot of storage capacity for its representation.

The graph contains N nodes, numbered from 0 on. For nodes i and j and integer k, $0 \leq k \leq N$, predicate $i \xrightarrow{<k} j$ denotes the presence in the initial graph of a path from i to j via zero or more intermediate nodes, all of which have a number less than k. In the sequel, we omit the ranges of i and j. The graph that is being modified is recorded in variable b as an adjacency matrix; boolean b_{ij} is equivalent to the presence of an edge from node i to node j in the graph. The initial value of variable b is given by constant a. We list some properties of predicate $i \xrightarrow{<k} j$.

(0) $\langle \forall i, j :: b_{ij} \equiv i \xrightarrow{<0} j \rangle \equiv (b = a)$

(1) $\langle \forall i, j :: b_{ij} \equiv i \xrightarrow{<N} j \rangle \equiv (b = closure\ of\ a)$

(2) $i \xrightarrow{<k+1} j \equiv i \xrightarrow{<k} j \ \lor \ (i \xrightarrow{<k} k \ \land \ k \xrightarrow{<k} j)$
     for all $0 \leq k < N$

The right-hand sides of properties (0) and (1) are the pre- and postcondition, respectively. An invariant can be obtained by replacing the constant in which their left-hand sides differ by a variable.

$$P: \quad \langle \forall i, j :: b_{ij} \equiv i \xrightarrow{<k} j \rangle \ \land \ 0 \leq k \leq N \quad .$$

Since the initial value of k is going to be 0 (see (0)), and since its final value is going to be N (see (1)), the program will consist of a loop in which k is increased. Therefore, the bound function is

$$bf: \quad N - k \quad ,$$

and we are interested in P_{k+1}^{k}. Here is a rewrite of that formula.

$$P^k_{k+1}$$
$$= \quad \{ \text{ substitution } \}$$
$$\langle \forall i,j :: b_{ij} \equiv i \xrightarrow{<k+1} j \rangle \quad \wedge \quad 0 \le k+1 \le N$$
$$\Leftarrow \quad \{ \text{ restrict range of } k \ ; \ (2) \ \}$$
$$\langle \forall i,j :: b_{ij} \equiv i \xrightarrow{<k} j \quad \vee \quad (i \xrightarrow{<k} k \ \wedge \ k \xrightarrow{<k} j) \rangle$$
$$\wedge \ 0 \le k < N$$

This rewrite suggests the following program.

```
{  b = a  }
k := 0;  { P }
*[ k ≠ N →  forall(i, j :: b_{ij} := b_{ij}  ∨  (b_{ik}  ∧  b_{kj}));  { P^k_{k+1} }
              k := k + 1  { P }
]
{  b = the closure of a  }
```

The correctness proof that we gave of this program applies only to the case where all variables b_{ik} and b_{kj} have the value given in the invariant, that is, they have not yet been updated. Hence, we are done if the **forall** statement performs all the N^2 assignments as one concurrent assignment. What if they are performed sequentially? In that case, some of the b_{ik} and b_{kj} may already have been updated when they are used in an assignment. For example, b_{ik} is assigned the value $b_{ik} \vee (b_{ik} \wedge b_{kk})$, which simplifies to b_{ik}. Hence, b_{ik} does not change. Similarly, b_{kj} does not change. As a result, the program is also correct if the N^2 assignments are performed sequentially, in any order.

12.3   Recording Equivalence Classes

Here is another graph algorithm. This time the graph is undirected. The property of being connected via a path of zero or more undirected edges is an equivalence relation (cf. Chapter 4). Given an equivalence relation, many graphs can be used for representing the relation, and for each graph in turn, many representations exist. The choice of the graph and its representation depend on the application, that is, on the operations performed on it. In this section, we discuss one set of operations and the representation to which it leads. We will mainly use the terminology of the undirected graph.

We consider N nodes, numbered from 0. The graph under discussion varies. The set of nodes is fixed, but the set of edges grows from time to time (see below). Initially, the set of edges is empty. Two operations on the graph need to be programmed.

- $eq(p, q)$ is a boolean function that returns *true* just when nodes p and q are connected in the present graph, that is, when they are equivalent with respect to the equivalence relation;

- $add(p, q)$ is an operation that extends the graph with an edge between nodes p and q; it makes the equivalence relation weaker since more nodes become equivalent.

These two operations are used in lots of applications, including programs that maintain a set of cities in the Los Angeles area that are connected by metro rail (surprisingly, this set is nonempty!), programs that perform the layout and wiring of electrical circuits, and programs for testing whether two finite automata are equivalent.

In order to make the first operation as simple as possible, we might record the graph's equivalence relation by a boolean matrix, as discussed in the section on Warshall's algorithm. Function $eq(p, q)$ then is merely a table-lookup, but adding an edge is an $O(N^3)$ operation.

In order to make the second operation as simple as possible, we might record the list of all edges that have been added so far. This makes the first operation a very time-consuming one.

It seems wiser to strike a balance between the two operations and make both of them do a bit of work. How do we do that? One possibility is to assign unique identifiers (for example, numbers) to each connected component of the graph, that is, to each equivalence class of the equivalence relation. If we store the identity $ec(p)$ of the equivalence class containing node p, then the first operation is simply $ec(p) = ec(q)$ but the second operation needs to update array ec. For example, program

$$
\begin{aligned}
add(p, q): \quad & r := 0; \; ecq := ec(q); \\
& *[\; r \neq N \rightarrow [\; ec(r) = ecq \rightarrow ec(r) := ec(p) \\
& \qquad\qquad\qquad\quad \| \; ec(r) \neq ecq \rightarrow skip \\
& \qquad\qquad\qquad\;]; \\
& \qquad\qquad\quad r := r + 1 \\
& \;]
\end{aligned}
$$

would do the job, but takes time proportional to N, even if both components p and q are small. We may shift some work from add to eq by storing a slightly different table, one from which ec can be derived without great effort. Because the information that is added by $add(p, q)$ is that, from now on, nodes p and q are in the same component, we are led to store function f with the property

nodes k and $f(k)$ are in the same equivalence class

for each k. Since we start out with an initially empty graph, we have no choice but to initialize f to $f(k) = k$, for all k. For a nonempty graph, the obvious choice is now to identify each equivalence class by the identity of one of its nodes; let's call it the characteristic node. By repeatedly applying f to a node number, we hop from one node to another, all the time staying in the same equivalence class. If we can see to it that this eventually leads to the characteristic node (and that we can detect that it is the characteristic node), then we are done. We can do so by postulating for all k

$f(k) = k$ just when k is the characteristic node of its class   ,

and

$\langle \exists j :: f^j(k)$ is the characteristic node of the class containing $k\rangle$.

Given these two postulates, algorithm

$$p_0 := p; \quad * [p_0 \neq f(p_0) \rightarrow p_0 := f(p_0)]$$

terminates with p_0 set to the number of the characteristic node $ec(p)$ of the equivalence class containing p. The correctness of this algorithm follows from invariant

$$ec(p) = ec(p_0)$$

and bound function

$$\langle \mathbf{MIN} j : f^j(p_0) = f^{j+1}(p_0) : j\rangle   ,$$

to which we will refer as the path length of p_0.

The two operations can now be coded as follows. (We have added a variable or two to avoid reevaluation of $f(p_0)$.)

$$eq(p,q): \quad p_0, p_1 := p, f(p); \quad * [p_0 \neq p_1 \rightarrow p_0, p_1 := p_1, f(p_1)]$$
$$q_0, q_1 := q, f(q); \quad * [q_0 \neq q_1 \rightarrow q_0, q_1 := q_1, f(q_1)]$$
$$eq := p_0 = q_0$$
$$add(p,q): \quad p_0, p_1 := p, f(p); \quad * [p_0 \neq p_1 \rightarrow p_0, p_1 := p_1, f(p_1)]$$
$$q_0, q_1 := q, f(q); \quad * [q_0 \neq q_1 \rightarrow q_0, q_1 := q_1, f(q_1)]$$
$$f(p_0) := q_0$$

Of course, it would have been wrong to replace the last line by $f(p_0) := q$ since that might have led to a cycle, breaking the postulate to which the representation was promised to conform. If p and q are not already connected, then $f(p_0) := q$ would have been correct but less efficient, since it increases the path length of nodes p, $f(p)$, $f^2(p)$, ... with the path length of q (plus 1), whereas the version we gave increases those path lengths with only 1. We might, however, have written $f(q_0) := p_0$, and we have no preference for either of the two.

Right now our two programs are correct but one has the feeling that the first one can be improved. Instead of following the sequences

$$p, \; f(p), \; f(f(p)), \; \cdots$$
$$q, \; f(q), \; f(f(q)), \; \cdots$$

all the way down to the characteristic nodes, it would suffice to continue until the first common element of these two chains, if such exists. (If any common element exists, then the first common element is uniquely defined because the only cycles are those of length one at the characteristic nodes.) We know that finding the first common element is easy when the two sequences are monotonic (saddleback search !) and, therefore, we add another postulate:

$f(k) \leq k$ for all k .

By the way, this postulate also makes it easier to see that the only cycles are those around the characteristic nodes, which have $f(k) = k$. Invariant

$$ec(p_0) = ec(p) \ \wedge \ p_1 = f(p_0) \ \wedge$$
$$ec(q_0) = ec(q) \ \wedge \ q_1 = f(q_0) \ \wedge$$
$$(ec(p) = ec(q) \ \Rightarrow \ (fce(p,q) = fce(p_0,q_0))$$

(in which $fce(p,q)$ is the first common element of the sequences starting from p and q) and bound function

path length of p_0 + path length of q_0

suggest that the first algorithm can be rewritten as

$$eq(p,q): \qquad p_0, p_1, q_0, q_1 := p, f(p), q, f(q);$$
$$*[\ p_0 \neq p_1 \wedge p_1 > q_1 \rightarrow p_0, p_1 := p_1, f(p_1)$$
$$\| \ q_0 \neq q_1 \wedge q_1 > p_1 \rightarrow q_0, q_1 := q_1, f(q_1)$$
$$];$$
$$eq := \ p_1 = q_1$$

The program for adding an edge can also be improved with the new representation. It can now be written as follows. The loop is the same as in the previous program, and so are the invariant and the bound function, but the action following the loop is different. It has been changed to comply with the restriction $f(k) \leq k$.

$$add(p,q): \qquad p_0, p_1, q_0, q_1 := p, f(p), q, f(q);$$
$$*[\ p_0 \neq p_1 \wedge p_1 > q_1 \rightarrow p_0, p_1 := p_1, f(p_1)$$
$$\| \ q_0 \neq q_1 \wedge q_1 > p_1 \rightarrow q_0, q_1 := q_1, f(q_1)$$
$$];$$
$$[\ p_1 > q_1 \rightarrow f(p_0) := \ q_1$$
$$\| \ q_1 > p_1 \rightarrow f(q_0) := \ p_1$$
$$\| \ p_1 = q_1 \rightarrow skip$$
$$]$$

The last assignment might be written as $f(q_0) := \ p_0$, but we prefer to assign p_1, since its path length is the same or one less.

The efficiency of our programs looks a lot better now, but it is not yet quite what we would like. Repeatedly adding edges increases path lengths and, consequently, slows down both operations. For any equivalence relation, many possible versions of f exist that satisfy all our postulates. Is it possible to switch to a more efficient version every now and then; that is, can we "clean up" our function f? Many ways are open to us for achieving this, and all of them are known as "path compression". Let us try to find a better value for $f(k)$ whenever $f(k)$ has been accessed. For example, in the case of the eq operation, can we come up with expressions for the dots in program

$$eq(p,q): \qquad p_0, p_1, q_0, q_1 := p, f(p), q, f(q);$$
$$*[\ p_0 \neq p_1 \wedge p_1 > q_1 \rightarrow p_0, p_1, f(p_0) := p_1, f(p_1), \ldots$$
$$\|\ q_0 \neq q_1 \wedge q_1 > p_1 \rightarrow q_0, q_1, f(q_0) := q_1, f(q_1), \ldots$$
$$];$$
$$eq := p_1 = q_1$$

without changing the equivalence relation? The value x to be assigned to $f(p_0)$ should satisfy $ec(x) = ec(p_0)$ and, furthermore, $x \leq f(p_0) = p_1$. The "obvious" choice for x is $f(p_1)$, which effectively halves the length of the paths from p, $f(p)$, $\ldots$ and q, $f(q)$, $\ldots$ until their first common element.

$$eq(p,q): \qquad p_0, p_1, q_0, q_1 := p, f(p), q, f(q);$$
$$*[\ p_0 \neq p_1 \wedge p_1 > q_1 \rightarrow p_0, p_1, f(p_0) := p_1, f(p_1), f(p_1)$$
$$\|\ q_0 \neq q_1 \wedge q_1 > p_1 \rightarrow q_0, q_1, f(q_0) := q_1, f(q_1), f(q_1)$$
$$];$$
$$eq := p_1 = q_1$$

In case of the *add* operation, we can do the same thing, or even be a little smarter. We may not only choose nodes x with $ec(x) = ec(p_0)$, but also those with $ec(x) = ec(q_0)$. Therefore, we may also consider q_0 or, even better, q_1 (better since $q_1 \leq q_0$). Since the guard contains $p_1 > q_1$, the choice q_1 guarantees a real decrease of $f(p_0)$. We then have a bounded integer value that decreases in every step of the iteration, and can be used as a bound function. The terms $p_0 \neq p_1$ and $q_0 \neq q_1$ were present only to guarantee termination, and can now be removed from the program. The loop is then guaranteed to terminate with $p_1 = q_1$, and the if-statement can be eliminated as well.

$$add(p,q): \qquad p_0, p_1, q_0, q_1 := p, f(p), q, f(q);$$
$$*[\ p_1 > q_1 \rightarrow p_0, p_1, f(p_0) := p_1, f(p_1), q_1$$
$$\|\ q_1 > p_1 \rightarrow q_0, q_1, f(q_0) := q_1, f(q_1), p_1$$
$$]$$

12.4 Minimization of Finite Automata

In this section, we discuss an algorithm that, for a given, possibly nondeterministic, finite-state machine computes the minimal finite state machine accepting the same language. From Chapter 4, we know that the minimum automaton, the one that has the smallest possible number of states, is unique up to renaming of states.

The algorithm that we describe centers around the notion of reverse: the reverse of a string and the reverse of an automaton. The reverse $\tilde{x}$ of string x is string x read backwards. For example, if x is string abc, then $\tilde{x}$ is string cba.

The reverse M' of a deterministic automaton $M = (Q, A, \delta, q_0, F)$ is the automaton that is obtained from M by switching states from elements of Q to subsets of Q, by reversing the direction of δ, by interchanging the role of initial and final states, and by restricting attention to reachable states. This second part is the subset construction of Chapter 4. We define

$$M' = (Q', A, \delta', q_0', F')$$

where

> elements of Q' are subsets of Q
> $q \in \delta'(V, a) \equiv \delta(q, a) \in V$ for $q \in Q, a \in A, V \subseteq Q$
> δ' is extended to strings in the usual way
> $V \in F' \equiv q_0 \in V$ for $V \subseteq Q$
> $V \in Q' \equiv \langle \exists x : x \in A^* : \delta'(q_0', x) \in V \rangle$ for $V \subseteq Q$
> $q_0' = F$.

We show that, applying the reversal operation twice to any automaton, by taking the reverse of the reverse of the automaton, produces an automaton that accepts the same set of strings, and does so with the minimum number of states. We do so by showing that the reverse of a deterministic automaton is minimal (but accepts the reversed language). Since the first reversal produces a deterministic automaton, the second reversal produces one that is minimal, and accepts the original language. First, we give a number of related properties.

Property 0

For all $q \in Q, V \in Q', x \in A^*$ we have $q \in \delta'(V, x) \equiv \delta(q, \tilde{x}) \in V$.

Proof

By mathematical induction on the length of x. For the empty string, we have for all q and V

> $q \in \delta'(V, \epsilon)$
> $=$ { definition of δ' }
> $q \in V$
> $=$ { definition of δ }
> $\delta(q, \epsilon) \in V$
> $=$ { definition of reverse of a string }
> $\delta(q, \tilde{\epsilon}) \in V$,

and for a nonempty string, we have for all $q, V, a,$ and x

> $q \in \delta'(V, ax)$
> $=$ { definition of δ' }
> $q \in \delta'(\delta'(V, a), x)$
> $=$ { induction hypothesis }

$$\delta(q, \tilde{x}) \in \delta'(V, a)$$
$$= \qquad \{ \text{ definition of } \delta' \ \}$$
$$\delta(\delta(q, \tilde{x}), a) \in V$$
$$= \qquad \{ \text{ definition of } \delta \ \}$$
$$\delta(q, \tilde{x}a) \in V$$
$$= \qquad \{ \text{ definition of reverse of a string } \}$$
$$\delta(q, \widetilde{ax}) \in V \qquad .$$

$\Box$

Property 1

A string is accepted by an automaton just when the reverse of the string is accepted by the reverse of the automaton.

Proof

For all $x \in A^*$ we have

$$x \text{ is accepted by } M$$
$$=$$
$$\delta(q_0, x) \in F$$
$$= \qquad \{ \text{ property 0 } \}$$
$$q_0 \in \delta'(F, \tilde{x})$$
$$= \qquad \{ \text{ definition of } F' \text{ and } q_0' \ \}$$
$$\delta'(q_0', \tilde{x}) \in F'$$
$$=$$
$$\tilde{x} \text{ is accepted by } M'$$

$\Box$

It follows that reversing twice does not change the set of strings accepted by an automaton. It remains to show minimality. In Chapter 4, it was shown that, for a given set of strings L over alphabet A automaton M'',

$$(A^* / \sim, A, \delta'', [\epsilon], F'')$$

is the minimal automaton for accepting L, where

$$x \sim y \equiv \langle \forall z : z \in A^* : xz \in L \equiv yz \in L \rangle$$
$$x \in [y] \equiv x \sim y$$
$$F'' = \{[x] \mid x \in L\}$$
$$\delta''([x], a) = [xa] \qquad .$$

We can therefore show minimality of our twice-reversed automaton by showing that a once-reversed automaton is equivalent (up to renaming of the states) to M'', provided L is the set of strings accepted by the reverse M' of automaton M.

Property 2

Given the definitions above, we have for all $x, y \in A^*$

$$[x] = [y] \equiv \delta'(q_0', x) = \delta'(q_0', y) \qquad .$$

Proof

$$[x] = [y]$$
$$= \qquad \{ \text{ definitions of } [\,] \text{ and } \sim \ \}$$
$$\langle \forall z :: x\tilde{z} \in L \equiv y\tilde{z} \in L \rangle$$
$$= \qquad \{ \ L \text{ is the set of strings accepted by } M' \ \}$$
$$\langle \forall z :: x\tilde{z} \text{ accepted by } M' \equiv y\tilde{z} \text{ accepted by } M' \rangle$$
$$= \qquad \{ \text{ property 1 } \}$$
$$\langle \forall z :: z\tilde{x} \text{ accepted by } M \equiv z\tilde{y} \text{ accepted by } M \rangle$$
$$= \qquad \{ \text{ definition of set of strings accepted by } M \ \}$$
$$\langle \forall z :: \delta(q_0, z\tilde{x}) \in F \equiv \delta(q_0, z\tilde{y}) \in F \rangle$$
$$= \qquad \{ \text{ definition of } \delta \ \}$$
$$\langle \forall z :: \delta(\delta(q_0, z), \tilde{x}) \in F \equiv \delta(\delta(q_0, z), \tilde{y}) \in F \rangle$$
$$= \qquad \{ \text{ calculus } \}$$
$$\langle \forall q, z : q = \delta(q_0, z) : \delta(q, \tilde{x}) \in F \equiv \delta(q, \tilde{y}) \in F \rangle$$
$$= \qquad \{ \text{ property 0 } \}$$
$$\langle \forall q, z : q = \delta(q_0, z) : q \in \delta'(F, x) \equiv q \in \delta'(F, y) \rangle$$
$$= \qquad \{ \ q_0' = F \ \}$$
$$\langle \forall q, z : q = \delta(q_0, z) : q \in \delta'(q_0', x) \equiv q \in \delta'(q_0', y) \rangle$$
$$= \qquad \{ \ M \text{ has reachable states only } \}$$
$$\langle \forall q :: q \in \delta'(q_0', x) \equiv q \in \delta'(q_0', y) \rangle$$
$$= \qquad \{ \text{ calculus } \}$$
$$\delta'(q_0', x) = \delta'(q_0', y)$$

$\square$

This property allows us to define function f as

$$f([x]) = \delta'(q_0', x) \text{ for all } x \in A^* \qquad .$$

We show that f is an isomorphism that maps M'' into M'. Since f renames the states of M'' into states of M', we have to show that it renames the initial and final states of M'' into the initial and final states of M', respectively, and that it preserves the state transition function.

Property 3

$$f([\epsilon]) = q_0'$$

Proof

$$f([\epsilon])$$
$$= \qquad \{ \text{ definition of } f \ \}$$
$$\delta'(q_0', \epsilon)$$

$$= \\ q_0'$$

☐

Property 4

For all $x \in A^*$ we have $[x] \in F'' \equiv f([x]) \in F'$.

Proof

$$[x] \in F''$$
$$= \quad \{ \text{ definition of } F'' \}$$
$$x \text{ is accepted by } M'$$
$$= \quad \{ \text{ property 1 } \}$$
$$\tilde{x} \text{ is accepted by } M$$
$$=$$
$$\delta(q_0, \tilde{x}) \in F$$
$$= \quad \{ \text{ property 0 } \}$$
$$q_0 \in \delta'(F, x)$$
$$= \quad \{ \text{ definition of } F' \text{ and } q_0' \}$$
$$\delta'(q_0', x) \in F'$$
$$= \quad \{ \text{ definition of } f \}$$
$$f([x]) \in F'$$

☐

Property 5

For all $x \in A^*, a \in A$ we have $f(\delta''([x], a)) = \delta'(f([x]), a)$.

Proof

$$f(\delta''([x], a))$$
$$= \quad \{ \text{ definition of } \delta \}$$
$$f([xa])$$
$$= \quad \{ \text{ definition of } f \}$$
$$\delta'(q_0', xa)$$
$$= \quad \{ \text{ definition of } \delta' \}$$
$$\delta'(\delta'(q_0', x), a)$$
$$= \quad \{ \text{ definition of } f \}$$
$$\delta'(f([x]), a)$$

☐

Property 6

M'' and M' are isomorphic.

Proof

From the definition it follows that f maps the set of states of M'' onto the set of states of M'.
From Property 2 it follows that f is a one-to-one mapping.
From Property 3 it follows that f maps the initial state of M'' to the initial state of M'.
From Property 4 it follows that f maps the final states of M'' to the final states of M'.
From Property 5 it follows that f preserves the state transition function.

$\square$

This concludes our discussion of the minimization algorithm. We leave its implementation to the exercises.

12.5 Oil-Spread Algorithms

In this section, we discuss a few graph-algorithms that are known as oil-spread algorithms. For now, we ignore this name and concentrate on the following problem. Given a finite, directed graph and a node in the graph, compute the set of all nodes that can be reached from the node.

Of course, we could use Warshall's algorithm for computing the transitive closure, but this yields the answer for every possible node, whereas we need it only for one given node. We might therefore be able to do better.

We formalize the problem by introducing function r. For x a set of nodes, $r(x)$ is the set of nodes reachable from x. Function r satisfies

$$r(x) \;=\; x \cup \langle \cup v : v \in x : r(s(v)) \rangle \quad ,$$

where $s(v)$ is the successor set of node v, that is, the set of nodes pointed at by an edge emanating from v. A problem with this equality is that it doesn't serve as a definition of r. For example, for all x, the set of all nodes in the graph satisfies the equality. As usual for recursive definitions, the equality can serve as a definition if we add the requirement that $r(x)$ is the smallest set satisfying the equality, that is, $r(x)$ is the least fixpoint (cf. Exercise 15).

In order to clean up our notation a bit, we extend function s to operate on a set of nodes instead of on a single node. It returns the set of all nodes pointed at by an edge emanating from any element of the argument set. This simplifies r to

$$r(x) \;=\; x \cup r(s(x)) \quad ,$$

which looks a lot better. The problem can now be stated as: given node v, compute $r(\{v\})$. We write the postcondition as

$$R: \quad r(\{v\}) \;=\; x$$

and look for an invariant that will lead to R. We mention two properties of r, the proofs of which are delegated to Exercise 16.

$$s(x) \subseteq x \;\Rightarrow\; r(x) = x$$
$$r(x) \;=\; r(x \cup s(x))$$

The first property suggests a loop of the form

$$*[\; \neg(s(x) \subseteq x) \to \dots \;]$$

together with invariant

$$P0: \quad r(\{v\}) \;=\; r(x) \qquad .$$

This is an invariant of the variety described in Chapter 8 under the heading "reduce the problem size". The second property of r suggests statement $x := x \cup s(x)$ as the loop body. Verification of initialization, invariance, and finalization is mere substitution, and we omit it here. What is the bound function? Set x is extended with $s(x)$ in every iteration of the loop. The guard ensures that $s(x)$ is not a subset of x, so that x is really increased. The number of nodes in the graph minus the number of nodes in x is, therefore, a bound function.

$$x := \{v\};$$
$$*[\; \neg(s(x) \subseteq x) \to x := x \cup s(x) \;]$$

Set x is extended in every iteration of the loop. Function s is, therefore, applied to an ever increasing set. If we want to apply s to the difference between the old and new set only (and obtain a presumably more efficient program), we choose a different invariant. It is obtained by partitioning x in two sets x and y. The new set x contains those elements to which s is not reapplied.

$$P1: \qquad r(\{v\}) \;=\; r(x \cup y) \;\wedge\; s(x) \subseteq x \cup y \;\wedge\; x \cap y = \emptyset$$

The program is

$$x, y := \emptyset, \{v\};$$
$$*[\; y \neq \emptyset \to x := x \cup y; \; y := s(y) \setminus x \;]$$

and the verification is as follows.

- initialization

$$P1_{\emptyset, \{v\}}^{x, y}$$
$$= \qquad \{ \text{ substitution } \}$$
$$\textit{true}$$

- finalization

$$P1 \;\wedge\; y = \emptyset$$
$$\Rightarrow \qquad \{ \text{ substitution } \}$$
$$r(\{v\}) \;=\; r(x) \;\wedge\; s(x) \subseteq x$$
$$\Rightarrow \qquad \{\; s(x) \subseteq x \Rightarrow r(x) = x \;\}$$
$$R$$

- invariance of $P1$

$$(P1^{y}_{s(y)\setminus x})^{x}_{x\cup y}$$
$$= \qquad \{ \text{ substitution } \}$$
$$r(\{v\}) \;=\; r(x \cup y \cup (s(y) \setminus (x \cup y))) \;\wedge$$
$$s(x \cup y) \subseteq x \cup y \cup (s(y) \setminus (x \cup y)) \;\wedge$$
$$(x \cup y) \cap (s(y) \setminus (x \cup y)) = \emptyset$$
$$\Leftarrow \qquad \{\; s(x \cup y) \;=\; s(x) \cup s(y) \text{ twice } \}$$
$$r(\{v\}) \;=\; r(x \cup y \cup s(x \cup y)) \;\wedge\; s(x) \subseteq x \cup y$$
$$= \qquad \{\; r(z) \;=\; r(z \cup s(z)) \text{ with } x \cup y \text{ for } z \;\}$$
$$r(\{v\}) \;=\; r(x \cup y) \;\wedge\; s(x) \subseteq x \cup y$$
$$\Leftarrow$$
$$P1$$

- The number of nodes not in x is a bound function: it is at least zero and it is decreased in every step of the iteration by the number of nodes in y since $x \cap y = \emptyset$. The guard implies that y is nonempty, so that this is a real decrease.

This program is sometimes referred to as a breadth-first search, since all nodes in y have the same distance (number of edges in the shortest path) from v.

If we want to apply successor function s to individual nodes only, we can write statement $y := s(y) \setminus x$ as a loop. We may also code the algorithm as follows.

$$x, y := \emptyset, \{v\};$$
$$*[\; y \neq \emptyset \rightarrow \text{choose } u \text{ such that } u \in y;$$
$$x := x \cup \{u\}; \; y := (y \cup s(u)) \setminus x$$
$$]$$

In this form, it is no longer a breadth-first search.

Let us now turn to the funny name of this algorithm. Why is it called an oil-spread algorithm? Imagine that the algorithm starts out with an initially white graph. Oil is poured on node v and starts spreading out over the graph. Oil propagates via the edges of the graph. After a while, there is a big black blob of oil, completely covering the black nodes in set x, and the oil has just made it to the grey nodes in y. The grey part encloses the black part, so to speak. From y, it continues propagating into the white remainder of the graph, but for nodes in x nothing changes any more.

Although the metaphor may serve as a way to visualize or remember the method, it does not really help us too much. For example, it is obvious from the metaphor that $y \subseteq r(x)$, and that $v \in x \cup y$, but these are properties that we did not need. The metaphor may therefore be both useful and distracting at the same time, which all goes to say that we need to be careful with metaphors.

Let us conclude this section with another application of this method. Consider the case where the edges of the graph have a non-negative length, and we are supposed to write an algorithm for computing for every node the distance to the given node v. The distance between two nodes is the length of a shortest path between them. How do we apply the oil-spread method to this problem? The set of black nodes is the set for which the distance has been established, and a shortest path visits black nodes only. The set of grey nodes is the set for which the length of some path has been established, but it is not necessarily a shortest path. However, of all paths with only black nodes between v and the grey node, it is a shortest one. Nothing has been established about the distance of white nodes, but every path from v to a white node first passes through a grey node. Let $d[u]$ be the recorded distance for any black or grey node u. The question is: how do we select a grey node for blackening? In the previous algorithm, any grey node would do; in the present algorithm, we have to make a careful choice. We are done if there is a grey node whose so-far-established distance from v is the minimal distance in the entire graph. We show that the grey node u whose distance (via black nodes only) from v is the smallest among all grey nodes, will do. Consider any path from v to u, and let its length be l. This path may contain other grey nodes and even white nodes. This path leaves the black region somewhere, since v is black and u is grey; let g be the first grey node on the path. (The first non-black node is grey, not white.) It may or may not be the case that $g = u$. Since u was chosen to minimize $d[u]$, we have $d[u] \leq d[g]$. Since the distance from g to u is nonnegative, we have $d[g] \leq l$. Hence, $d[u] \leq l$, that is, this path is at least as long as the one that led to the recorded distance of u. Therefore, the distance of u from v equals the recorded distance, and u can be colored black. All white successors of u are colored grey and a distance is recorded for each of them, which is the distance from v to u plus the length of the path from u to the successor. All grey successors of u remain grey, but their recorded distance may need to be reduced, namely, if the path via u is shorter. The program is as follows.

$x, y := \emptyset, \{v\}; \ \ d[v] := 0;$
$*[\ y \neq \emptyset \rightarrow \text{choose} \ \ u \ \ \text{such that} \ \ u \in y \land \langle \forall z : z \in y : d[u] \leq d[z] \rangle \ ;$
$\qquad x := x \cup \{u\}; \ \ y := y \setminus \{u\};$
$\qquad \textbf{forall} \ n : n \in s(u) \ \textbf{do}$
$\qquad \quad [\ n \in x \rightarrow skip$
$\qquad \quad \| \ n \in y \rightarrow d[n] := \min(d[n], d[u] + len[u, n])$
$\qquad \quad \| \ n \notin x \cup y \rightarrow y := y \cup \{n\}; \ \ d[n] := d[u] + len[u, n]$
$\ ] \qquad \qquad \quad]$

Many algorithms can be formulated in this black–grey–white terminology. The important differences are: what exactly is the invariant and how is it maintained, that is, what exactly is recorded about black and grey nodes, and which grey node is then colored black?

12.6   Figure 6

We are given a function f that maps integers to integers with the additional property that sequence

$$0, \ f(0), \ f(f(0)), \ \cdots$$

is eventually periodic. Can we write a program for computing the period? Program

$p := 1;$
$*[\ f^p(x) \neq x \rightarrow p := p + 1 \ ]$

does a linear search, returning the correct answer for the period, provided that we start with a number x that occurs somewhere in the cyclic part of the sequence. If x occurs in the part that precedes the cycle, then the program will not terminate. If x does not occur in the sequence at all, then the program may or may not terminate; and if it terminates, then the answer has no relation to the question. So, our problem is now to find a number x that occurs in the cyclic part of the sequence. Given period p, program

$x := 0;$
$*[\ f^p(x) \neq x \rightarrow x := f(x) \ ]$

would do, but we do not have p at our disposal. It seems to be unavoidable that we look for p and x simultaneously. In the first program, the invariant is $f^i(x) \neq x$ for all i in $1 \leq i < p$; and in the second program, the invariant is $f^p(j) \neq j$ for all j that precede x in the sequence we are scanning. In the first one, the bound variable is in the exponent; in the second one, the bound variable is in the argument position. Can we combine the two into one invariant, which then has to be: $f^i(j) \neq j$ for all i and j, where $1 \leq i < p$ and j is the i-th element in the sequence, that is, $j = f^{i-1}(0)$? Substituting the last equality in the first part of the invariant, we get $f^{2i-1}(0) \neq f^{i-1}(0)$ for all $1 \leq i < p$, and all we need to do is convince ourselves that the corresponding linear search terminates. From the existence of a pair i, j with $f^{j+i}(0) = f^j(0)$, it follows that

$$f^{ij-1}(0) = f^{ij+i-1}(0) = \cdots = f^{ij+ij-1}(0) = f^{2ij-1}(0) \quad ,$$

which proves that ij is an upper bound on the number of steps of the linear search. It is a very pessimistic upper bound, though. (See Exercise 22.)

$$i := 1;$$
$$*[\ f^{2i-1}(0) \neq f^{i-1}(0) \rightarrow i := i+1\ ]$$

The complete program is obtained by first computing a number x in the ubiquitous sequence, and then using x to compute the period. This number x is not necessarily the first number in the cyclic part of the sequence. The number of steps of the first loop is a multiple of the period. We strengthen the invariant of the first loop with $x = f^{2i-1}(0)$ and $y = f^{i-1}(0)$, and the invariant of the second loop with $z = f^p(x)$. Variable i is eliminated.

$$x, y := f(0), 0;$$
$$*[\ x \neq y \rightarrow x, y := f(f(x)), f(y)\ ];$$
$$p, z := 1, f(x);$$
$$*[\ x \neq z \rightarrow p, z := p+1, f(z)\ ]$$

12.7   Huffman's Algorithm

We are given a finite set A of symbols, $\#A \geq 1$, and a so-called frequency count f, which is a function that maps each symbol to a positive integer. A code tree of A is a binary tree in which there is a 1-1 correspondence between leaves and symbols of A. Let $d(x, t)$ be the distance (number of edges) between leaf x and the root in tree t. Let weight $w(t)$ be defined as

$$w(t) = \langle \sum a : a \in A : f(a) \cdot d(a, t) \rangle \quad .$$

Huffman's algorithm constructs a code tree of A whose weight is minimal (cf. [Huf52]). We write $d(a, t)$ even though the first argument of d is supposed to be a leaf; we can do so because there is a 1-1 correspondence between leaves and symbols.

The code tree is used for coding and decoding a string over A in the form of a bit string, which makes sense only if $\#A \geq 2$. Each symbol is translated into a bit string, and a string over A is translated by catenating all those individual bit strings. The translation for each symbol is obtained by following the path in the tree from the root to the leaf that corresponds to the symbol. The two subtrees of any non-leaf node are ordered, and each left successor appends a 1 to the path, each right successor appends a 0. If $f(a)$ is the number of occurrences of symbol a in the string that is encoded, then $w(t)$ is the length of the bit string induced by the code tree. It follows that, if we restrict ourselves to coding with trees, minimizing $w(t)$ leads to the shortest possible bit string.

First, we describe the algorithm. To that end, we extend the domain of f from symbols to trees. We need to consider trees that are code trees of some subset of A. $L(t)$ is the set of leaves of code tree t, $L(t) \subseteq A$. For any tree t that is a code tree of some subset of A,

$$f(t) = \langle \sum a : a \in L(t) : f(a) \rangle \quad .$$

We also apply w to trees whose labels are a subset of A :

$$w(t) = \langle \sum a : a \in L(t) : f(a) \cdot d(a,t) \rangle \quad .$$

The algorithm, then, is surprisingly simple, and does not even involve computing any d-value. It operates on one variable, say C, which is a set of trees. Initially, C contains one tree for every symbol in A; each tree consists of one node only. Upon termination, set C consists of one tree, which is an optimal code tree. In every step of the loop, two trees are selected and combined. The two trees are those that have the least f-values. They are combined by making them the two direct subtrees of a newly created root node. We write $\langle y, z \rangle$ for the new tree that is the combination of trees y and z. The two subtrees are unordered. Here is the code of the algorithm.

$$
\begin{aligned}
&C := A; \\
&*[\ \#C \geq 2 \rightarrow \text{choose } y, z \text{ such that } y \in C \land z \in C \land y \neq z \ \land \\
&\qquad\qquad \langle \forall x : x \in C \setminus \{y, z\} : f(x) \geq f(y) \land f(x) \geq f(z) \rangle; \\
&\qquad C := C \setminus \{y, z\} \cup \{\langle y, z \rangle\} \\
&\ ]
\end{aligned}
$$

We rely on the 1-1 correspondence between leaves and symbols to construct the initial value of C. The trees are code trees of subsets of A, and their respective subsets partition A. This part of the invariant is a direct consequence of the updating of C. It follows that tree $\langle y, z \rangle$ that is added to C is not already in it and, hence, every step of the iteration decreases $\#C$ by one. Therefore, termination of the algorithm is obvious. However, optimality is far from obvious. The proof that we give crucially depends on the following invariant:

> an optimal code tree exists that contains each element of C as a subtree.

Initialization establishes this invariant. In order to show that a step of the repetition maintains the invariant, we extend the definition of d. For subtree x of tree t, we define $d(x,t)$ to be the distance in tree t between the root of x and the root of t. For tree z, and for subtree x of tree t, we write $t(x := z)$ for the tree that is obtained from t by replacing subtree x with tree z. When extending this notation to multiple trees, we see to it that the subtrees being replaced are disjoint. We state a property of d and w, that we will prove later. For disjoint subtrees x and z of code tree t,

$$w(t(x, z := z, x)) = w(t) + (f(x) - f(z)) \cdot (d(z, t) - d(x, t)) \quad .$$

Now we return to the invariance property. It states that an optimal code tree exists in which all trees in C are subtrees. Let y and z be two trees in C with lowest f-values, that is,

$$y \in C \ \wedge \ z \in C \ \wedge \ y \neq z \ \wedge$$
$$\langle \forall x : x \in C \setminus \{y, z\} : f(x) \geq f(y) \wedge f(x) \geq f(z) \rangle \quad .$$

We are done when we have shown that an optimal code tree exists in which all trees in $C \setminus \{y, z\} \cup \{\langle y, z \rangle\}$ are subtrees. From the invariant we know that an optimal code tree t exists that contains all elements of C, including y and z. If t also contains $\langle y, z \rangle$, then we are done. If t does not contain $\langle y, z \rangle$, then we construct a code tree t' that contains $\langle y, z \rangle$ in addition to all trees in $C \setminus \{y, z\}$, and whose weight is at most the weight of t. Since tree t contains both y and z but does not contain $\langle y, z \rangle$, a subtree x of t exists that is combined with either y or z, that is, t contains either $\langle x, y \rangle$ or $\langle x, z \rangle$. To guarantee disjointness of the trees involved, we assume that x is combined with y and that the distance between y and the root of t is at least the distance between z and the root of t, that is, t contains $\langle x, y \rangle$ and $d(x, t) = d(y, t) \geq d(z, t)$. We choose

$$t' = t(x, z := z, x)$$

and show $w(t') \leq w(t)$.

$$\begin{aligned}
& w(t') \\
= \quad & \{ \text{ property mentioned above } \} \\
& w(t) + (f(x) - f(z)) \cdot (d(z, t) - d(x, t)) \\
\leq \quad & \{ \ f(x) \geq f(z); \quad d(x, t) \geq d(z, t) \ \} \\
& w(t)
\end{aligned}$$

Since t' is obtained from t by swapping x and z only, all elements of C are subtrees of both t and t'. Furthermore, t' contains $\langle y, z \rangle$, and $w(t') \leq w(t)$. Since t is optimal, so is t', which completes our proof.

12.8   Bibliographic Notes

Bresenham's algorithm for drawing a straight line is from [Bre65]. Our discussion of Bresenham's algorithm is similar to [Wir90]. The circle-drawing algorithm is similar to an algorithm presented in [KS63].

Warshall's algorithm was published in [War62]. A similar algorithm for computing the shortest distance for all pairs of points in a graph is from [Flo62].

The oil-spread algorithm is due to [Dij59]. [SP73] shows that this algorithm is optimal under the decision tree model. The name "oil-spread algorithm" was suggested by Peter Hilbers, who didn't like the term "oil-spill algorithm" that I used previously.

The algorithm for recording equivalence classes is due to Martin Rem and can be found in [Dij76]. A thorough discussion of this and related algorithms can be found in [TvL84].

The algorithm for minimization of finite automata is from [vdS85b].

The solution to the "Figure 6" problem is part of the folklore. It is usually attributed to R.W. Floyd. An even simpler and faster algorithm is developed in Exercise 24. It is due to [Bre80]. Its application in Exercise 25 was suggested to me by Robert Harley.

Huffman's algorithm can be found in [Huf52]. The literature contains many proofs of this algorithm. Unfortunately, many of them are wrong. The proof given here was constructed with help from R.J.R. Back.

12.9   Exercises

1. Expand the *mark* operation in the circle-drawing algorithm, to avoid calculation of $y \cdot 64 + x$ **div** 8 and of $2^{x \bmod 8}$ as in the case of the straight line segment.

2. Extend the circle-drawing algorithm to mark all points on the circle, not just one octant. Make sure that every point is marked only once. (This is relevant, for example, if marking inverts the color of a point.)

3. Does the correctness argument of the circle-drawing algorithm apply to the case $r = 0$? If not, where should $r > 0$ have been mentioned? Does the circle-drawing algorithm work if $r = 0$?

4. In the algorithm for drawing a straight line segment, we selected for every x the y value that minimizes the "vertical" distance from the true line. Show that minimizing the Euclidean distance (measured perpendicular to the line) produces the same y value.

5. Write a program for marking all points near the ellipse

   $$(x/a)^2 + (y/b)^2 = 1$$

   where a and b are given positive integers, $0 < a \le b$.

6. Warshall's algorithm has a worst-case running time proportional to $O(N^3)$. What is the running time if we code the algorithm as follows?

```
k := 0;
*[ k ≠ N → i := 0;
    *[ i ≠ N → [   b_ik → j := 0;
                            *[j ≠ N → b_ij := b_ij ∨ b_kj; j := j + 1]
                 ‖ ¬b_ik → skip
                 ];
                 i := i + 1
    ];
    k := k + 1
]
```

On some machines, the inner loop, which ranges over j, can be executed efficiently by so-called bitwise OR instructions, and is partly responsible for the algorithm's reputation of being an efficient one.

If we use variables of a set type instead of an array of booleans, then the coding for the program becomes as follows. Variable s is an array of sets. If we maintain

$$b_{ij} \equiv j \in s_i \quad ,$$

the program reduces to

```
k := 0;
*[ k ≠ N → i := 0;
    *[ i ≠ N → [ k ∈ s_i → s_i := s_i ∪ s_k ‖ k ∉ s_i → skip ];
                 i := i + 1
    ];
    k := k + 1
]   .
```

What is the running time in this case?

7. Warshall's algorithm is based on the numbering of the nodes on paths. One might also base an algorithm on the length of the path, such as the invariant

$$b_{ij} \equiv \text{the original graph has a path from } i \text{ to } j \text{ of length at most } k \quad ,$$

which seems to require only $\log(N)$ steps (doubling k in every step). What is the complexity of each of those steps? Write a program based on this invariant.

8. Consider the case where each edge in the initial graph has a nonnegative length; say b_{ij} is the length of the edge from i to j. If no edge from i to j exists, then $b_{ij} = +\infty$. The length of a path is defined to be the sum of the lengths of the edges forming the path. Write a

program for computing the length of the shortest path between any pair of nodes (again, $+\infty$ if no path exists). Why was the length given to be nonnegative?

9. The transitive reduction of a directed graph is obtained by removing as many edges as possible without changing the transitive closure of the graph. If the graph is acyclic, the transitive reduction is uniquely defined. Write a program for computing the transitive reduction of an acyclic graph.

10. Give a formal correctness proof of the first eq algorithm. In particular, prove that boolean expression $p_1 = q_1$ gives the correct result, based on the invariant and the negation of the two guards.

11. Is it possible that our last version of add increases the path length of any node?

12. In our algorithms, the path that was traversed is shortened in passing. One might change the two algorithms such that paths are first traversed (and left unchanged) to find the unique identifier, and then traversed again to reduce the path lengths to one by assigning the unique identifier as the successor number of every node on the path. Write the two corresponding programs, and compare their efficiency to the two algorithms that we presented.

13. Write a program that, given a nondeterministic, finite-state machine, computes the minimal deterministic, finite-state machine that accepts the same set of strings.

14. Estimate the worst-case complexity of the minimization algorithm.

15. Prove that function r as defined in Section 12.5 has a least solution by proving that the intersection of two sets that each solve equation

$$r(x) \;=\; x \cup r(s(x))$$

is also a solution. It then follows that the intersection of all solutions is the least solution.

16. Prove

$$s(x) \subseteq x \;\Rightarrow\; r(x) = x$$

and

$$r(x) \;=\; r(x \cup s(x)) \qquad .$$

17. Which term in invariant $P1$ implies that the first non-black node on any path from a black node to a white node is grey?

18. Prove the correctness of the algorithm for computing minimal distances.

19. Given an undirected graph in which at least one path exists between any pair of nodes, a spanning tree is defined to be a subset of the edges such that exactly one path exists between any pair of edges. The size of a tree is the sum of the lengths of all edges in it. Write a program for computing the shortest spanning tree.

20. Given an undirected, unrooted tree, write a program for computing the length of a longest path in the graph. Every node is supposed to occur at most once in a path.

21. Given are integers M and N, both positive, and boolean array $b[0..M-1, 0..N-1]$. Furthermore, we have integers x_0, y_0, x_1, and y_1 in the range $0 \le x_0, x_1 < M$ and $0 \le y_0, y_1 < N$. We consider paths between points in a square grid where each square has unit size. A path consists of a number of points that are at the intersection of grid lines. In general, many paths between two given points (x_0, y_0) and (x_1, y_1) achieve the shortest path length. We are now asked to write a program for computing the length of such a shortest path, with the additional restriction that points (x, y) for which $b[x, y]$ is *false* are not on the path, but are "obstacles". If no obstacle-free path exists, the shortest path length is $+\infty$.

22. Show that the number of steps of the first loop in the "Figure 6" program is at most $L + P$, where P is the (minimal) period of the cyclic part of the sequence, and L is the length of the part preceding the cyclic part.

23. Write a program for computing how many numbers occur only once in the entire sequence defined in Section 12.6.

24. Develop an alternative solution to the "Figure 6" problem. Base your solution on the observation that, given L, linear search could be used to determine period P. But since L is unknown, this linear search needs to be restricted to a limited range, say from i to $2i$. If the search fails, i is increased. Writing $g(i)$ for $f^{i-1}(0)$, and

$$p(i, j) = (i < j \le 2i \quad \wedge \quad i \text{ is a power of 2}) \quad ,$$

use invariant Q :

$$p(i, j) \quad \wedge \quad i < 2 \cdot \max(L, P) \quad \wedge$$
$$\forall (m, n : p(m, n) \quad \wedge \quad n < j : g(m) \ne g(n)) \quad .$$

25. The Mandelbrot set (see for example [Man82]), is defined via function $f_c(z) = z^2 + c$ for complex numbers c and z. For fixed c, one considers sequence

$$0, f_c(0), f_c(f_c(0)), \ldots$$

If the modulus of a number in this sequence exceeds 2, then it also does for all subsequent numbers in the sequence. One computes the length of the initial part of the sequence for which all numbers have modulus less than 2, and this length is called $l(c)$. The Mandelbrot set is the set of complex numbers for which $l(c)$ is infinite.

In order to draw a picture of the set, outlining its position in the complex plane, one puts an upper limit on $l(c)$, say some fixed number N. Every point c in the complex plane is given a color based on $l(c)$: the lower $l(c)$, the darker the color. The naive algorithm is

```
function l(c : complex) : integer
|[ var  z : complex;
        j : integer;
    z, j := 0, 0;
    *[j ≠ N  ∧  |z| < 2 → z, j := z² + c, j + 1]
    l := j
]|           .
```

Improve the efficiency of this algorithm by combining it with the cycle-detection algorithm from the previous exercise.

26. Given integer $N > 1$, write a program for computing the period in the decimal expansion of $1/N$.

27. Prove the following property. See Section 12.7 for definitions.

$$w(t(x, z := z, x)) \;=\; w(t) + (f(x) - f(z)) \cdot (d(z, t) - d(x, t))$$

28. Write a program that, given a code tree, encodes a string over A as a bit string. Also write a program that decodes a bit string into an A-string. Feel free to postulate the presence of reasonable, additional information in the representation of the code tree if that simplifies encoding or decoding.

29. Write an efficient program for producing the data structure postulated in the previous exercise, assuming that f is given. (See also Exercise 9.7.)

30. If frequency function f is not given a priori, we might keep a running count of frequencies, and use the running count for constructing the optimal code tree. From one symbol to the next, table f changes little, and the code tree does not change much either. Write a program for increasing by one the frequency count of a given symbol, and update the tree (cf. [Gal78]). See also Exercise 13.17.

13

Concurrent Programs

In the circuitry from which our computers are built more than one thing can be going on at a time. Many signals can be traveling from one component to another, and many components can be computing their outputs concurrently. The environment in which our computers operate is one in which lots of events occur simultaneously. For example, travel agents all over the world are using one computer system for selling airline tickets, and are trying to avoid selling the same ticket to different passengers (with varying degrees of success). The computer that controls your car has a handful of sensors that are communicating their readings to some processor that may thereupon close the throttle, raise the roll bar, and redistribute the pressure on the brakes. All of those components then react concurrently.

The programs that we have discussed so far do not exhibit any form of concurrency. In this chapter, we have a look at concurrent programs. We have at least three reasons for doing so. First, as observed above, concurrency may be part of the problem setting, and, hence, an unavoidable part of the solution. Second, more and more computers are constructed from components that operate concurrently and that have to be programmed individually. Physical arguments show that such multicomputers have the potential of delivering higher performance on many problems than do sequential computers, which execute one program at a time, for the same price. (We will discuss those arguments in a later chapter.) Third, concurrent programs are harder to construct than are sequential ones. We are better prepared for this challenging task when we are aware of the problems, and some of the solution methods. (And most importantly, it is a lot of fun.)

13.1 Mutual Exclusion

Let us start with a simple program. It consists of the concurrent execution of $x := 1$ and $y := 2$, and we write:

$$x := 1 \parallel y := 2 \quad .$$

The statements connected by the vertical bars are called processes. One process is $x := 1$ and the other is $y := 2$. Sometimes we are sloppy and talk about a process as the execution of a statement. What is the result of executing the two processes in parallel? The two processes can be executed independently. One will lead to $x = 1$ and the other to $y = 2$, and when both of them have been completed, we have $x = 1 \ \land \ y = 2$. Problems arise when a dependency exists between the processes. Consider

$$x := 1 \ || \ x := 2 \quad .$$

What is the value of variable x upon completion of this concurrent program? Well, it could be just about everything. If we make no further assumptions about the computer system that executes the program, then we cannot say what the outcome is. In fact, we play our game the other way round by defining what we would like the outcome to be and then seeing whether a reasonably efficient implementation thereof exists. What is a reasonable outcome of the program? I propose that a reasonable outcome is either $x = 1$ or $x = 2$. I don't think it is reasonable to specify that both outcomes are equally likely since that would require an implementation that produces $x = 1$ in 50 percent of the cases and $x = 2$ in the other 50 percent for a large number of runs of the program. This doesn't help you a bit in any individual run of the program. Therefore, all we require is that the outcome satisfy $x = 1 \ \lor \ x = 2$.

Now that we have interference between processes in the form of shared variables, we cannot define the semantics in terms of Hoare triples anymore. Without interference one might hope for a rule like

If $\{ P0 \} \ S0 \ \{ Q0 \}$ and $\{ P1 \} \ S1 \ \{ Q1 \}$ then
$\quad \{ P0 \land P1 \} \ S0||S1 \ \{ Q0 \land Q1 \}$

but in the presence of interference the intermediate states reached during execution of $S0$ and $S1$ play a role and Hoare triples are not adequate. We have a closer look at this below.

What kind of implementations are ruled out by the postulate that the outcome of our program is $x = 1 \ \lor \ x = 2$? Imagine that a variable's value is represented by a certain amount of charge trapped in a capacitor. If one part of the machinery tries to set the capacitor voltage at 1 volt, and another part simultaneously tries to set it at 2 volts, then the result might be a short circuit, or it might be a net voltage level of roughly 1.5 volts, neither of which achieves the required effect. Some mechanism must be installed that guarantees that the two parts of the machine do not operate on the same capacitor at the same time. This is called *mutual exclusion*, and can be achieved by a so-called arbiter. We have hinted at the problems of making arbiters in Chapter 5. Due to the metastable state, it is impossible to build an arbiter that makes a choice within a bounded time. Here we assume that this problem has been solved in a satisfactory manner at the level of the components and then they can be used for ensuring mutually-exclusive access to storage locations. (It requires either that the components operate in synchrony or that the system be robust against possible long arbitration times.) The net effect is that the actions are performed in sequence, but we do not know what the sequence is; it might vary from one execution to the next. In one execution, x might first be set to 1 and then to 2; in another execution, it might be the other way round.

Next, suppose that our variable x is represented by two bits and that the mechanism for mutual exclusion operates at the level of the individual bits. Statement $x := 1$ could be implemented by $x_1 := 0; x_0 := 1$, whereas statement $x := 2$ could be implemented by $x_1 := 1; x_0 := 0$. Since we have made no further assumptions about the mutual exclusion mechanism, it might be that both assignments to x_1 are attempted simultaneously and will result in $x_1 := 0$ first and $x_1 := 1$ second; the assignments to x_0 might occur in opposite order, that is, $x_0 := 0$ first and $x_0 := 1$ second. The result is that x_1 and x_0 are both set to 1 and we have $x = 3$ as the outcome of our concurrent program; similarly $x = 0$ could have resulted. This does not conform with our requirement that the outcome be $x = 1 \ \lor \ x = 2$ and is, therefore, not an acceptable implementation.

The phenomenon observed above is one that we encounter very often: mutual exclusion is provided on some elementary level and is needed on a somewhat larger scale. The example may seem somewhat contrived because variables are not assigned their value bit after bit in most machines. They are, however, assigned their value byte after byte, or word after word, in all machines that I am aware of, so the same problem arises on a slightly larger scale. As soon as you read in the documentation of your machine that, for example, the value of the timer is stored in two words, you have to be alert! If the timer updates the time from $h = 2 \land m = 59$ to $h = 3 \land m = 0$, and another process reads the time simultaneously, you might end up with readings 2:00, 2:59, 3:00, or 3:59. Probably both the first and the last reading are unacceptable, whereas the other two readings are acceptable.

From now on, we assume that mutually-exclusive access is provided to individual scalar variables. No such guarantee is given for larger data structures (only for their individual elements) and a statement like $x := x + 1$ is understood to involve two accesses to x : one for reading and one for writing.

The question that arises is: given mutually-exclusive access to scalar variables, can we construct mutual exclusion between arbitrary actions? If this cannot be done, then we have made a mistake: we have not provided a useful semantics of our programming constructs, namely one that does not lend itself to the construction of larger programs.

Here we go. We focus on the case in which there are two processes that repeatedly perform a so-called critical action, and some noncritical action. The program that we are given is

process 0: $*[true \rightarrow CA_0; \ NCA_0]$ $\|$
process 1: $*[true \rightarrow CA_1; \ NCA_1]$

and we have to add statements to the program to ensure mutual exclusion between CA_0 and CA_1. Our first attempt uses a fresh binary variable that indicates "whose turn it is". (By "fresh" we mean that it is a new variable that does not occur elsewhere in the program.)

> **var** t : *integer*;
> { initially $t = 0 \vee t = 1$ }
> process 0: $*[true \rightarrow *[t \neq 0 \rightarrow skip]; \ CA_0; \ t := 1; \ NCA_0] \ ||$
> process 1: $*[true \rightarrow *[t \neq 1 \rightarrow skip]; \ CA_1; \ t := 0; \ NCA_1]$

This program provides mutual exclusion. We can see this as follows. Action CA_i is executed by process i only when $t = i$ holds (because process i waits until $t = i$ and the other process does not set t to any value other than i). Therefore, condition

$$\text{process 0 executes } CA_0 \ \wedge \ \text{process 1 executes } CA_1$$

implies

$$t = 0 \ \wedge \ t = 1 \quad ,$$

which is *false*, from which the negation of "both in their critical action" follows.

This proof shows the general pattern of proofs of concurrent programs. First, come up with a condition that you think holds in a certain state. Second, verify that it holds when the process in which it occurs reaches the particular state. Third, verify that other processes do not falsify the condition. Fourth, deduce what you want to show from the conditions that you have established. Observe the similarity to invariants (come up with an invariant, show that it is valid, deduce the final condition from the invariant), and also the new aspect: the other processes do not interfere with the validity of the condition. The absence of interference is often the hardest part. For every condition, in every process, you have to check that every action in every other process does not interfere with it. In principle, the amount of work grows tremendously with the number of processes, and you have to be careful in the choice of your conditions and the choice of your program to avoid a job that is undoable.

The solution to the mutual exclusion problem embodied by our program may be correct but it is not very attractive. It has the property that CA_0 and CA_1 are executed in strict alternation. This implies that, if the two CAs or the two NCAs take widely different amounts of time to execute, then the processes will be waiting unnecessarily. In the sequel, we try to develop an algorithm that works properly without making any assumptions about the speed with which processes proceed. This is not a mean trick to make an already hard problem even harder. It is true that some problems admit simple solutions that work only when the speed ratios "are right". However, verifying that this condition is met is often tricky. Furthermore, it would be nice if replacing one part of a program or a computer system with another that has the same functional behavior but runs faster, would allow the whole system to continue operating correctly and, hopefully, faster. If the correctness of some parts relies on specified (and long forgotten) speed ratios, then this fortunate situation may not surface. This principle of replacing one part by another that is at least as good is extremely important; but it is so obvious, and such a vital engineering practice, that it is all too often forgotten. This is the one and only principle on which stepwise refinement is based. You might be surprised by the horror stories that result when this principle is violated. (Ask an older operator in the computer center about the days when a system broke down after a line printer was replaced with a faster one; in many cases, the only fix was to run the faster, more expensive line printer at reduced speed.)

Our next attempt employs two bits of information instead of one. Both processes have a boolean variable whose value is *true* just when the process executes its critical action.

> **var** b : **array** $[0..1]$ **of** *boolean*;
> $\{$ initially $\neg b[0] \ \wedge \ \neg b[1] \ \}$
> process 0: $*[\ true \rightarrow *[b[1] \rightarrow skip];$
> $\qquad\qquad\qquad\qquad b[0] := true; \ \ CA_0; \ \ b[0] := false; \ \ NCA_0$
> $\qquad\quad] \ ||$
> process 1: $*[\ true \rightarrow *[b[0] \rightarrow skip];$
> $\qquad\qquad\qquad\qquad b[1] := true; \ \ CA_1; \ \ b[1] := false; \ \ NCA_1;$
> $\qquad\quad]$

This "solution" is incorrect. Suppose that both processes execute the wait loop that precedes their critical action, and both find the other process' boolean variable to be *false*. Next, both set their own variable to *true*, and execute the critical action: no mutual exclusion. This non-solution is sometimes called the airline industry's solution, since it corresponds to the following algorithm: check whether a ticket is still available; if so, sell it.

Let's shuffle our program a bit and be somewhat more conservative. First, record the process' intention to execute its critical action; then, wait for mutual exclusion.

> **var** b : **array** $[0..1]$ **of** *boolean*;
> $\{$ initially $\neg b[0] \ \wedge \ \neg b[1] \ \}$
> process 0: $*[\ true \rightarrow b[0] := true; \ \ * \ [b[1] \rightarrow skip];$
> $\qquad\qquad\qquad\qquad CA_0; \ \ b[0] := false; \ \ NCA_0$
> $\qquad\quad] \ ||$
> process 1: $*[\ true \rightarrow b[1] := true; \ \ * \ [b[0] \rightarrow skip];$
> $\qquad\qquad\qquad\qquad CA_0; \ \ b[1] := false; \ \ NCA_1$
> $\qquad\quad]$

This solution is as safe as can be with respect to guaranteeing mutual exclusion (it is called "the safe sluice"), but it is a bit too safe: it exhibits a new phenomenon, called *deadlock*. If both processes first set their boolean variable to *true*, and then enter the wait loop, they will never execute the critical action but sit in the loop forever.

In our next attempt, we conclude that it was okay to set the boolean variable before entering the wait loop, but it was not okay to stick to that value while waiting. How about the following version?

```
var b : array [0..1] of boolean;
{ initially ¬b[0]  ∧  ¬b[1]  }
process 0: *[ true → b[0] := true;
                    *[b[1] → b[0] := false;  b[0] := true];
                    CA₀;  b[0] := false;
                    NCA₀
            ] ||
process 1: *[ true → b[1] := true;
                    *[b[0] → b[1] := false;  b[1] := true];
                    CA₁;  b[1] := false;
                    NCA₁
            ]
```

Unfortunately, the same situation that we had before is still possible. For example, if both processes proceed at exactly the same speed, then they may set their own boolean variable to *true*, find the other one to be *true* also, reset their own to *false* and then to *true*, and so on. This form of waiting is called after-you-after-you blocking. It need not be as final as deadlock (it is sometimes called *livelock*), because it might be that the waiting terminates when speed ratios vary a bit. In daily life, this solution is, therefore, an acceptable one. In our cases where the processes might be executed by identical processors, identical speed ratios are not at all uncommon, and so this solution must be rejected. The first real solution to this problem is due to Th.J. Dekker, a Dutch mathematician who came up with it in the mid 1960s. His solution combines the effects of the first and last programs. If there is a tie in the race for entry to the critical action, then the symmetry is broken with the variable that records whose turn it is. In the other situation, that variable plays no role.

```
var b : array [0..1] of boolean;
    t : 0..1;
{ initially ¬b[0]  ∧  ¬b[1]  ∧  (t = 0  ∨  t = 1)  }
```

```
process 0: *[ true → b[0] := true;
                *[ b[1] → [ t = 1 → b[0] := false;
                               *[t = 1 → skip];
                               b[0] := true
                          ‖ t = 0 → skip
                ]          ];
                CA₀;  b[0] := false;  t := 1;
                NCA₀
          ] ‖
process 1: *[ true → b[1] := true;
                *[ b[0] → [ t = 0 → b[1] := false;
                               *[t = 0 → skip];
                               b[1] := true
                          ‖ t = 1 → skip
                ]          ];
                CA₁;  b[1] := false;  t := 0;
                NCA₁
          ]
```

Another solution was published by G.L. Peterson (cf. [Pet81]). The program is surprisingly simple (the correctness argument is not).

```
var b : array [0..1] of boolean;
    t : 0..1;
{ initially ¬b[0] ∧ ¬b[1] }
process 0: *[ true → b[0] := true;  t := 0;
                *[b[1] ∧ t = 0 → skip];
                CA₀;  b[0] := false;
                NCA₀
          ] ‖
process 1: *[ true → b[1] := true;  t := 1;
                *[b[0] ∧ t = 1 → skip];
                CA₁;  b[1] := false;
                NCA₁
          ]
```

The program combines the first algorithm (the "turn" solution, but slightly modified) with the one that might lead to deadlock. In the original paper, it is claimed that the algorithm "is a simple combination of the two". However, if we swap the order of the two assignments that precede the wait loop, then the "simple combination" fails; apparently, there is something not so trivial going on here. Let us, therefore, try to construct a proof of correctness. We have to come up with a condition, P_i, that holds during execution of CA_i, and then we have to show that $P_0 \wedge P_1 = false$ in order to show mutual exclusion. It is clear that $b[i]$ can be one of the conjuncts of P_i. It is also clear that this does not suffice. Upon termination of the wait loop, condition $b[1 - i] \; \wedge \;\; t = i$ is found to be *false*, so we might try to include this as a conjunct in P_i. The two conjuncts would suffice to show mutual exclusion, but, unfortunately, their conjunction is too strong. We cannot show that, for example, there is no interference from process 1 with condition P_0, because condition P_0 does not express enough about process 1; in particular, it does not distinguish between the states that precede execution of $t := 1$ in process 1, and those that follow it. This distinction cannot be expressed with the variables that occur in the program, so we have to introduce something extra to keep track of how far execution of the program has progressed. One method is to label the statements and then refer to the labels. Another method is to introduce auxiliary variables and use them to express the properties we need. Both methods have their attraction; we pursue the latter option. We extend our program with auxiliary variables $a[0]$ and $a[1]$. It would be nice if we could print those variables and the operations on them in a different color, to emphasize that the restriction of one access to a storage location per elementary action does not include references to these auxiliary variables. (Since they are for the proof only, they are not implemented and their operations are not executed.) We emphasize the fact that operations on the auxiliary variables are to be considered as part of the other operations by writing angle brackets. A sequence of actions in angle brackets is understood to be executed as a single action; it is an indivisible action, often referred to as an *atomic action*. (Atomic actions delineate our proof obligations in the sense that interference within atomic actions need not be considered; it does not mean that they have no further substructure.)

$$
\begin{aligned}
&\textbf{var } a, b : \textbf{ array } [0..1] \textbf{ of } boolean; \\
&\quad t : \; 0..1; \\
&\{ \text{ initially } \neg a[0] \;\; \wedge \;\; \neg a[1] \;\; \wedge \;\; \neg b[0] \;\; \wedge \;\; \neg b[1] \;\; \} \\
&\text{process 0: } *[\; true \; \rightarrow \; \langle b[0] := true; \; a[0] := true \rangle; \\
&\qquad\qquad\qquad\qquad \langle t := 0; \; a[0] := false \rangle; \\
&\qquad\qquad\qquad\qquad *[b[1] \;\; \wedge \;\; t = 0 \rightarrow skip]; \\
&\qquad\qquad\qquad\qquad CA_0; \; b[0] := false; \\
&\qquad\qquad\qquad\qquad NCA_0 \\
&\qquad\qquad] \; \| \\
&\text{process 1: } *[\; true \; \rightarrow \; \langle b[1] := true; \; a[1] := true \rangle; \\
&\qquad\qquad\qquad\qquad \langle t := 1; \; a[1] := false \rangle; \\
&\qquad\qquad\qquad\qquad *[b[0] \;\; \wedge \;\; t = 1 \rightarrow skip]; \\
&\qquad\qquad\qquad\qquad CA_1; \; b[1] := false; \\
&\qquad\qquad\qquad\qquad NCA_1 \\
&\qquad\qquad]
\end{aligned}
$$

We claim that P_0 holds during execution of CA_0 where

$$P_0 : \qquad b[0] \;\; \wedge \;\; \neg a[0] \;\; \wedge \;\; (\neg b[1] \;\; \vee \;\; t = 1 \;\; \vee \;\; a[1]) \qquad .$$

First, P_0 holds as a postcondition of the wait loop in process 0, since that loop has invariant $b[0] \land \neg a[0]$, and terminates when $\neg b[1] \lor t = 1$. Second, process 1 does not interfere with condition P_0. Process 1 performs three actions in which variables are updated that occur in P_0, so we have to check those three:

- $b[1] := true;\ a[1] := true$
  This statement falsifies term $\neg b[1]$; because it sets $a[1]$ to $true$, it does not falsify P_0 ;

- $t := 1;\ a[1] := false$
  This statement falsifies term $a[1]$; because it sets t to 1, it does not falsify P_0 ;

- $b[1] := false$
  This statement sets $b[1]$ to $false$ and therefore does not falsify P_0 .

Therefore, P_0 is $true$ and remains $true$ when CA_0 is executed. By symmetry, P_1 is $true$ when CA_1 is executed. We have

$$
\begin{aligned}
& CA_0 \text{ is executed} \quad \land \quad CA_1 \text{ is executed} \\
\Rightarrow \quad & \{ \ P_i \text{ holds during } CA_i \ \} \\
& P_0 \ \land \ P_1 \\
= \quad & \{ \text{ definition of } P_i \ \} \\
& b[0] \ \land \ \neg a[0] \ \land \ (\neg b[1] \ \lor \ t = 1 \ \lor \ a[1]) \ \land \\
& b[1] \ \land \ \neg a[1] \ \land \ (\neg b[0] \ \lor \ t = 0 \ \lor \ a[0]) \\
= \quad & \{ \text{ calculus } \} \\
& b[0] \ \land \ \neg a[0] \ \land \ t = 1 \ \land \ b[1] \ \land \ \neg a[1] \ \land \ t = 0 \\
= \quad & \{ \ (t = 0 \ \land \ t = 1) \ = \ false \ \} \\
& false
\end{aligned}
$$

from which mutual exclusion follows.

We also show absence of deadlock. Deadlock occurs when both processes are in their wait loop. Since no variables change value when both processes are in the wait loop, the two guards are permanently $true$. We have,

$$
\begin{aligned}
& \text{deadlock} \\
\Rightarrow \quad & \{ \text{ the two guards are } true \ \} \\
& b[1] \ \land \ t = 0 \ \land \ b[0] \ \land \ t = 1 \\
= \quad & \\
& false
\end{aligned}
$$

from which absence of deadlock follows.

The two arguments show that mutual exclusion and absence of deadlock are guaranteed. We have not yet established that no process can be locked out: it might be the case that process 0 is the only one that can execute its critical action continuously, and process 1 never succeeds. A property like this one is called a progress property as opposed to the properties that we discussed thus far and that are called safety properties. Safety properties are established by conditions that hold in certain states, but progress properties cannot be dealt with in this way. Therefore, we resort to an informal argument here. Consider process 0. It has one wait loop and if it is locked out it is because it is forced to execute this loop forever. We show, however, that guard $b[1] \wedge t = 0$ is and remains *false*, eventually. We can do so only under the assumption that execution of CA_1 is a terminating activity (and if it isn't, then process 0 can indeed be locked out indefinitely, as can be seen from the mutual-exclusion requirement). After a while, process 1 is doing one of three things: executing NCA_1, executing its wait loop, or repeatedly executing its outer loop. In the first case, $b[1] = false$ and process 0's guard is *false*. In the second case, both processes would be in their wait loops, but we have already shown that this situation does not occur. In the third case, process 1 sets variable t to 1 permanently, and process 0's guard is *false*. Hence, process 0 is not locked out indefinitely.

The mutual-exclusion problem turned out to be a tricky one. The errors that can be made are subtle, and the proofs are subtle. One can come up with indivisible actions that are slightly more complex than just one access to a storage location, but the problems are only marginally less subtle. The problems that we have encountered are, to a large extent, caused by variables that are shared between processes; therefore, operations on them lead to interference. In the sequel, we try an alternate path: we eliminate shared variables altogether. (Serious problems require drastic measures.) Later, we will see that it turns out that computer systems in which the processors have no shared store can be constructed more efficiently than can systems with a shared store.

13.2   A Subtle Mistake

This section is a short intermezzo on a mistake that is sometimes encountered in reasoning about programs, about concurrent programs in particular. The mistake is mixing two notions: being an invariant and being true. Obviously, if a condition is an invariant, then it holds in each and every state reached by executing the program. On the other hand, even if a condition is *true* in every state, then it is not necessarily the case that it is an invariant. Here is an example that demonstrates the difference. Consider programs

$k := 0;$
$*[true \rightarrow \textbf{if } k = 1 \textbf{ then } k := 2]$

and

$k := 0;$
$*[true \rightarrow k := 1]$

and condition $k < 2$. This condition is always true in the first program and it is always true in the second program. If we "merge" the two programs into

$k := 0;$
$*[\ true \rightarrow \textbf{if}\ k = 1\ \textbf{then}\ k := 2$
$\|\ true \rightarrow k := 1$
$]\qquad ,$

then $k < 2$ is no longer always true.

How is the situation with invariants? Condition $k < 2$ is an invariant of the second program, but it is not an invariant of the first and third programs. The reason that it is not an invariant of the first program, even though it is always true, is that we cannot prove

$$\{\ k < 2\ \}\ \textbf{if}\ k = 1\ \textbf{then}\ k := 2\ \{\ k < 2\ \}\qquad .$$

Precondition $k < 2$ does not ensure that postcondition $k < 2$ is established.

In the context of concurrent composition of programs, we have exactly the same phenomenon. In this context, we say that condition P is an invariant if P holds in the initial state and if every atomic statement maintains P, that is, that we have $\{\ P\ \}\ s\ \{P\ \}$ for every statement s in the program. Again, being invariant is a stronger property than being always true. We can use the same example as before if you are willing to consider

$$\textbf{if}\ k = 1\ \textbf{then}\ k := 2$$

as an atomic statement. The exercises give additional examples. The lesson to be drawn from this discussion is that we are really interested in conditions that are invariant and not in conditions that are always true, because the first notion is preserved under parallel composition, whereas the second is not.

13.3   Communication via Channels

When we discussed sequential programs, we did so in terms of an initial and final state, ignoring all input and output, essentially by assuming that the input had already been performed and stored in the relevant variables, and that output still will be performed. We adapted this method to the case of concurrent programs, and ran into the trouble of interference. In this section, we focus on input and output as basic primitives, and see how we can construct concurrent programs out of them.

Input and output are often specified in terms of files, where files are (large) data structures stored in permanent storage. Some files are designated as special files that are not stored anywhere but constitute channels to devices. In fact, these are the true input and output communications, whereas the files in permanent storage form a mechanism for access to some variables whose lifetime is not limited to that of a program. Instead of restricting input and output to devices, we investigate communication between arbitrary processes, provided a communication channel between them exists. We, therefore, introduce channels as part of our program notation, together with input and output statements. A *channel* can be thought of as a communication link between two processes: one sender and one receiver. A communication along a channel takes place when one process executes an output statement on the channel and another process executes an input statement on the same channel. In this case, the value to be output is copied to the second process where it is stored in a variable. A communication, therefore, amounts to a distributed assignment statement: one process provides the variable, the other the expression, and the combined effect is the assignment. There is no automatic buffering: execution of an input or output statement is suspended until the other process is ready to execute the corresponding output or input statement. For channel c, we write $c!e$ for the statement that outputs the value of expression e on channel c, and we write $c?v$ for the statement that stores the received value in variable v. The combined effect of $c!e$ and $c?v$ is equivalent to $v := e$ plus synchronization. Here is an example. Execution of

$$c!29; \quad d?x \quad \|$$
$$c?y; \quad d!41$$

leads to $x = 41 \ \wedge \ y = 29$, no matter what the speed ratio of the two processes is. The input and output actions provide for proper synchronization.

Many of the processes in our programs do not terminate. Here is an example. It is a process that has input channel in and output channel out. It copies the sequence of values received via in to out.

$$copy(in, out) :$$
$$\textbf{var } x : integer;$$
$$*[true \rightarrow in?x; \ out!x]$$

The next example extends the previous one with one local variable, p. It stores the first value received via in in variable p. On channel out, it produces a copy of the sequence of values received via in, with the exception that all multiples of p are removed from the output.

$$filter(in, out) :$$
$$\textbf{var } p, x : integer;$$
$$in?p;$$
$$*[\ true \rightarrow in?x;$$
$$[x \textbf{ mod } p = 0 \rightarrow skip \ \| \ x \textbf{ mod } p > 0 \rightarrow out!x]$$
$$]$$

The third example is a process that generates on channel *out* the sequence of all integer numbers from 2 onwards, in increasing order.

> *generate(out)* :
>   **var** x : *integer*;
> $x := 2$;
> $*[true \rightarrow out!x;\ \ x := x + 1]$

Consider what happens if we run the latter two examples simultaneously, identifying the output of *generator* with the input of *filter*.

> *combine(out)* :
>   **chan** c;
>   *generator(c)* $\|$ *filter(c, out)*

The sequence of numbers produced on channel *out* is the sequence of the odd numbers from 3 on. Consider the program in which we input this sequence into another copy of the *filter* process.

> *combine(out)* :
>   **chan** $c0, c1$;
>   *generator(c0)* $\|$ *filter(c0, c1)* $\|$ *filter(c1, out)*

This yields the sequence of numbers from which multiples of 2 and 3 have been removed. If we construct a sequence of N *filter* processes, then we have the least N primes as variables p in the processes, and the output is a sequence of numbers from which all multiples of those primes have been removed. If we want to use this construction for generating all primes up to some limit L then we have to choose N large enough to make sure that the Nth prime is at least $\sqrt{L}$, and we have to output all the p's. The first problem is solved by recursively creating more processes until the bound is reached. The second problem is solved by adding channels that run in the opposite direction.

> *filter(p, in, out)* :
>   **var** x : *integer*;
> $*[\ true \rightarrow in?x;$
> $[x\ \mathbf{mod}\ p = 0 \rightarrow skip\ \|\ x\ \mathbf{mod}\ p > 0 \rightarrow out!x]$
> $]$
> *sieve(lin, lout)* :
>   **var** p : *integer*; **chan** ri, ro;
>   *lin?p; lout!p*;
> $[\ p^2 \leq L \rightarrow$ *filter(p, lin, ro)* $\|$ *sieve(ro, ri)* $\|$ *copy(ri, lout)*
> $\|\ p^2 > L \rightarrow$ *filter(p, lin, lout)*
> $]$
> **chan** c;
> *generator(c)* $\|$ *sieve(c, out)*

This is a concurrent implementation of Eratosthenes' prime sieve algorithm. This algorithm produces all primes up to L followed by an (infinite) sequence of numbers that may or may not be primes. If we want the program to terminate after producing the primes up to L then some changes are called for. See Exercise 13.

13.4 Buffers

In the programs discussed so far, communicating processes are strictly synchronized by the communication statements: output on a channel and input from the channel are suspended until both processes are ready to proceed. Whichever of the two comes first waits for the second. Although this is a nice symmetric arrangement, it is sometimes a bit inefficient; in many cases it would be just fine to let the sending process proceed and store the value that is being output somewhere until the receiving process is ready for its reception. Progress of the sending process is then not impaired by lack of progress of the receiving process, and this may sometimes lead to smoother operation of the program as a whole. It is almost always important to maintain the order for the messages: they should be received in the order they were sent. A mechanism that provides exactly this is called a buffer. The number of messages that can be stored in the buffer is called the slack, or the buffer capacity. In this section, we have a look at a few buffers. The simplest buffer of all is a one-place buffer. It stores at most one message that has already been sent and has not yet been received. The first program that we wrote was *copy* and it is exactly a one-place buffer.

> $copy(in, out)$:
>   **var** x : $element$;
> $*[true \rightarrow in?x;\ out!x]$

The buffer stores zero messages when execution is just before $in?x$, and it stores one message (in x) when execution is just before $out!x$. We can insert an instance of this process between any send/receive pair and create a channel with slack one instead of slack zero.

How do we go about constructing channels of larger slack? One possibility of creating an N-place buffer is to put N instances of the one-place buffer in series. Doing so has one advantage and one disadvantage: the advantage is that no new constructs are needed; the disadvantage is that a message is copied N times to crawl from the input to the output of the buffer. Since copying does not contribute a lot to progress of the computation proper, we look for another solution. It should be possible to use an array of N locations for storing up to N messages in the buffer. Let $b[0..N-1]$ be the array; let k be the number of messages in the buffer; let the messages be stored from index j on (modulo N); and let $i = j + k$ (modulo N), which implies that the empty array locations are from i on. The actions to be performed are

$$in?b[i]; \quad i,k := (i+1) \bmod N, k+1$$

and

$$out!b[j]; \quad j,k := (j+1) \bmod N, k-1$$

to add an element to the buffer and remove an element from the buffer, respectively. The first action can be chosen only if $k < N$, and the second action only if $k > 0$. Program

```
buffer(in, out, N) :
    var b : array [0..N − 1] of element;
        i, j, k : integer;
    i := 0;  j := 0;  k := 0;
    *[ k < N → in?b[i];  i, k := (i + 1) mod N, k + 1
     ‖ k > 0 → out!b[j];  j, k := (j + 1) mod N, k − 1
     ]
```

is not correct because the choice between the two alternatives is based on the guards only. If both guards are *true*, we do not want an arbitrary choice to be made but we want the choice to be delayed until it becomes clear which communication (via *in* or via *out*) can succeed. The latter is not determined by the buffer process but by the processes with which it communicates. The first alternative is to be chosen if $k < N$ and the other process has reached the point where a communication via *in* can be performed. The second alternative is to be chosen if $k > 0$ and the other process has reached the point where a communication via *out* can be performed. We introduce the *probe* on a channel as boolean function for testing the possibility of completing a communication on a channel: probe $\overline{c}$ on channel c is *true* just when communication via channel c can be performed without first being suspended. It is equivalent to saying that the other process is already suspended on its communication via channel c, and is waiting for the present process to initiate its part of the communication. With this construct, we might be tempted to write the loop in the buffer program as

```
*[ k < N  ∧  in → in?b[i];  i, k := (i + 1) mod N, k + 1
 ‖ k > 0  ∧  out → out!b[j];  j, k := (j + 1) mod N, k − 1
 ]    ,
```

but this is not correct. The loop terminates when both guards are found to be *false*, for example, if neither of the other two processes is ready for input or output. This is not what we want here; what we want is that the buffer process is suspended until at least one of them is ready for a communication. Only then the buffer proceeds to make a choice between the two alternatives. We replace the loop by

$$*[\ true \rightarrow [\ k < N \wedge \overline{in} \rightarrow in?b[i]; \ \ i, k := (i+1) \ \mathbf{mod} \ N, k+1$$
$$\| \ k > 0 \wedge \overline{out} \rightarrow out!b[j]; \ \ j, k := (j+1) \ \mathbf{mod} \ N, k-1$$
$$] \qquad \quad] \qquad ,$$

and we change the semantics of the if-statement. In our sequential programs, we had: an if-statement for which all guards are *false* is equivalent to *abort*, and this is also equivalent to a nonterminating loop. In our concurrent programs, we change this to: an alternative statement is suspended until at least one of the guards is *true*. Only then, an alternative with a *true* guard is selected. For the case of a sequential program, nothing has changed. (Since there are no other processes, a guard that is *false* remains *false* and waiting is indefinite.) But in concurrent programs, a *false* guard may become *true* through the activity of other processes. (Of course, a *true* guard may also become *false*, and this is, in general, something that you want to avoid; we will return to this in the next section.) With this new interpretation of the semantics, the loop achieves exactly the effect we want.

13.5   Merging Two Streams

Consider the program of the prime sieve. It contains a number of *sieve* processes that first send a prime number via channel *lout* and then copy a sequence of primes from *ri* to *lout*. A slight generalization hereof is that we consider the case where we have two sequences of values, and these have to be merged into a single sequence. Here is a solution.

$$merge(inl, inr, out):$$
$$\mathbf{var} \ x : element;$$
$$*[\ true \rightarrow [\ \overline{inl} \rightarrow inl?x; \ \ out!x$$
$$\| \ \overline{inr} \rightarrow inr?x; \ \ out!x$$
$$] \qquad \quad]$$

It copies an element from *inl* to *out*, if one is is available, and similarly for *inr*. What happens if both $\overline{inl}$ and $\overline{inr}$ are found to be *true* ? Well, the semantics of the if-statement does not specify a choice and we have to be content with whatever choice the implementation makes. In such a case, the implementation may always take the first alternative, may make a random choice, or may choose the one that has been *true* for the longest period of time. Suppose it always prefers the first alternative, and suppose furthermore that the process connected to *inl* generates messages at such a high speed that $\overline{inl}$ is always *true* whenever the if-statement is executed. The result is that the second alternative is never chosen and that no communication via channel *inr* takes place. We say that our merge program is an *unfair merge*. A *fair merge* would eventually communicate via both input channels if a message is available on both of them. Can we express a fair merge in our program notation? Yes, but we need a so-called negated probe to do so. One way of writing the program is as follows.

> *fair merge*(*inl*, *inr*, *out*) :
>   **var** x : *element*;
>   *[*true* → [$\overline{inl} \wedge \neg \overline{inr}$ → *inl*?x; *out*!x
>   ‖ $\overline{inr} \wedge \neg \overline{inl}$ → *inr*?x; *out*!x
>   ‖ $\overline{inr} \wedge \overline{inl}$ → *inl*?x; *out*!x; *inr*?x; *out*!x
>   ]   ]

Here is another version.

> *fair merge*(*inl*, *inr*, *out*) :
>   **var** x : *element*;
>   *[*true* → [$\overline{inl}$ → *inl*?x; *out*!x ‖ $\neg\overline{inl}$ → *skip*];
>   [$\overline{inr}$ → *inr*?x; *out*!x ‖ $\neg\overline{inr}$ → *skip*]
>   ]

The disadvantage of the latter program is that it repeatedly checks for the availability of a message on one of the channels, an unattractive phenomenon called busy waiting. The first solution is suspended on the if-statement if no message is available, and this can be implemented without busy waiting.

These fair mergers have guards that may switch from *true* to *false*. For example, condition $\overline{inl} \wedge \neg\overline{inr}$ becomes *false* if the process connected to *inr* reaches its statement that outputs a value on *inr*. The only condition that we use to ensure correctness of the algorithm, however, is $\overline{inl}$, and that part is and remains *true*. The part that switches from *true* to *false* is needed only for ensuring fairness, not for absence of deadlock or any such correctness criterion.

13.6 Data Structures

This is an example where a data structure is stored in one process, and accessed by another process. The data structure in the example is a set of integers, and two operations are provided on the set: one to add an element to the set, the other to scan through the entire set. Both operations are performed via channel communications. Initially, the set is empty. Here is the first version.

```
set(insert, scan) :
    var a : array [0..99] of integer;
        i, n : integer;
    n := 0;
    *[ true → [n < 100 ∧ insert →
                insert?a[n];  i := 0;
                *[a[i] ≠ a[n] → i := i + 1];
                [i = n → n := n + 1 ‖ i < n → skip]
            ‖scan → i := 0;  * [i ≠ n → scan!a[i];  i := i + 1];
                scan! − 1
    ]         ]
```

It is assumed that the set contains at most 100 elements so that they can be stored in an array of size 100. The idea of the *scan* operation is that it is used in the following way.

```
scan?x;
*[x ≠ −1 → operate on x;  scan?x]
```

The assumption that there be at most 100 elements in the set can be relaxed by replacing the fixed-size array with a dynamic data structure. The idea of the *scan* operation is fine as long as −1 is not an element of the set. A better arrangement is to replace terminator −1 with a different convention, for example, by introducing another channel on which the end of the sequence of values is indicated. It would then be used as follows.

```
scan?m;
*[ m → [ next → next?x;  operate on x
       ‖ scan → scan?m
    ]    ]
```

The *set* process first transmits a boolean via *scan*. If it is *false*, the set is empty; if it is *true*, the set is nonempty, and the values are transmitted one after the other via *next*, followed by the value *false* on channel *scan*.

Next, we change the specification of the *scan* operation, and require that the elements of the set be transmitted in increasing order. We might store the elements in increasing order in a linear list, but then insertion is inefficient. Therefore, we store the values in a binary tree with the property that for every node, all elements in its left subtree are smaller than the value stored in the node, and all elements in its right subtree are greater than the value in the node. This representation is inefficient if the elements are inserted in approximately monotonic order; but if they are inserted in random order, it is good, on average.

```
set(insert, scan, next) :
    type ptr = ↑ node;
         node = record v : integer;  l, r : ptr end;
    var t : ptr;  x : integer;
    add(var p : ptr) :
        [ p = nil → new(p);  p↑ := node(x, nil, nil)
        ‖ p ≠ nil ∧ x = p↑.v → skip
        ‖ p ≠ nil ∧ x < p↑.v → add(p↑.l)
        ‖ p ≠ nil ∧ x > p↑.v → add(p↑.r)
        ];
    gen(p : ptr) :
        [ p = nil → skip
        ‖ p ≠ nil → gen(p↑.l);  next!p↑.v;  gen(p↑.r)
        ];
    t := nil;
    *[ true → [ insert → insert?x; add(t)
              ‖ scan ∧ t = nil → scan!false
              ‖ scan ∧ t ≠ nil → scan!true;  gen(t);  scan!false
      ]          ]
```

It is useful to compare this solution to a sequential one in which a set of
procedures is provided that insert an element to a set and scan through the
elements. The insertion procedure should present no particular difficulties.
Our original scan procedure requires that one variable be introduced, corresponding to our variable i, that keeps track of how far we have proceeded
in the scanning operation. It retains its value from one procedure call to the
next, so it is global to the scanning operation, but should not be modified
by any other operations. Our second scan operation would require a much
more complicated global variable than just an integer: the new variable
should store the reference to the present or next node, plus a path from the
root to that node. In our concurrent program, this information is implicit
in the implementation of the recursion, and need not be made explicit. This
is an example in which the concurrent program is not faster but simpler
than a sequential program.

13.7 Matrix Multiplication

In this section, we discuss an algorithm for matrix multiplication. We are
given two square matrices, B and C, of size $n \times n$, and we are interested
in computing their product, $B \times C$, and store it in A; that is, we want
an implementation of $A := B \times C$. We consider a distributed implementation of the simple $O(n^3)$ algorithm and do not try to find a complicated
algorithm of lower complexity, such as an $O(n^{\log_2 7})$ algorithm; we just
focus on an efficient implementation of the simple version. We start with

the assumption that we have a large number of processors. In fact, we assume that we have n^2 processors and we try to come up with an $O(n)$ algorithm. Later we change the algorithm to the case where the number of processors is independent of n, which is a lot more realistic.

First, we look at the distribution of the array elements over the processors. Consider A first. Since the number of processors equals the number of array elements, we might just as well identify the processors in the same way we do the array elements; that is, by using pairs i, j where i and j are in the range 0 through $n - 1$, and storing $A[i, j]$ in processor i, j. Let us assume that processor i, j performs all the computations that are needed for computing the value of its array element. (This is a choice, and a different choice here would give us a different algorithm.) Processor i, j performs

$$A[i, j] := 0; \quad k := 0;$$
$$*[k \neq n \rightarrow A[i, j] := A[i, j] + B[i, k] \cdot C[k, j]; \quad k := k + 1] \qquad ,$$

and if every processor has access to the matrices B and C, then we are done. However, storing a copy of B and a copy of C in each of the n^2 processors requires a total storage capacity proportional to n^4. The storage requirement for a copy of just row i of B and column j of C in processor i, j is proportional to n^3. Let's try to do better; assume that, initially, matrices B and C are distributed in the same way as A. Element i, j is stored in processor i, j. Next, consider step k of the loop, and assume that each processor is executing step k. Each processor i, j needs the value of $B[i, k]$ and of $C[k, j]$, hence n copies of $B[i, k]$ and of $C[k, j]$ are needed at the same time. This is a bit of a problem. Sending $n - 1$ copies of $B[i, k]$ from processor i, k to all other processors with the same row number is a time-consuming operation. What causes all those processors to require the same B-element is the fact that they all use $B[i, 0]$ in the first step, $B[i, 1]$ in the second step, and so on. This is, however, an artifact of our program. All that needs to be computed is $\sum_{k=0}^{n-1} B[i, k] \cdot C[k, j]$, and the order in which those n products are computed and added up is irrelevant. Can we start the different processes with different values of k? If we start them with $k = i$ instead of $k = 0$, then the n processors that need array element $B[i, k]$ need it at different steps. However, they do still need element $C[k, j]$ at the same step. So, the starting point should be a function of both i and j, such as $i + j$. This suggests the program

$$A[i, j] := 0; \quad k := 0;$$
$$*[k \neq n \rightarrow A[i, j] := A[i, j] + B[i, i + j + k] \cdot C[i + j + k, j];$$
$$\qquad k := k + 1$$
$$]\qquad,$$

in which subscript $i + j + k$ is understood to be reduced modulo n. Changing the starting point from 0 to $i + j$ makes sure that only one copy of each array element is needed at a time. (Do not despair if you don't see this right away — it follows in a minute.) In step k, $B[i, i+j+k]$ is needed in processor i, j while in step $k + 1$, it is needed in processor $i, j - 1$. This suggests that elements of B are transmitted along rows, traveling to the next-lower index in every step. Because of the modulo n in the subscripts, these transmissions are "wrapped around" and go from processor $i, 0$ to $i, n-1$. Similarly, elements of C travel along columns from i, j to $i-1, j$ and so on. We, therefore, introduce channels $h[i, j]$ between processors i, j and $i, j + 1$ and channels $v[i, j]$ between i, j and $i + 1, j$. The program requires some "rotations" at initialization. The invariant of the main loop is

$$a = \sum_{l=0}^{k-1} B[i, i+j+l] \cdot C[i+j+l, j] \ \wedge$$
$$b = B[i, i+j+k] \ \wedge \ c = C[i+j+k, j] \ \wedge \ 0 \le k \le n \quad ,$$

and the program for processor i, j is

$$
\begin{aligned}
&b := B[i, j]; \ k := 0; \\
&*[k \ne i \rightarrow b' := b; \ |[h[i,j]?b \ || \ h[i, j-1]!b']|; \ k := k + 1]; \\
&c := C[i, j]; \ k := 0; \\
&*[k \ne j \rightarrow c' := c; \ |[v[i,j]?c \ || \ v[i-1,j]!c']|; \ k := k + 1]; \\
&a := 0; \ k := 0; \\
&*[\ k \ne n \rightarrow a := a + b \cdot c; \ b' := b; \ c' := c; \\
&\qquad |[h[i,j]?b \ || \ h[i,j-1]!b' \ || \ v[i,j]?c \ || \ v[i-1,j]!c']|; \\
&\qquad k := k + 1 \\
&]; \\
&A[i, j] := a \quad .
\end{aligned}
$$

The program multiplies $n \times n$ matrices on an $n \times n$ processor network. Next, we decouple the two sizes and try to find out how a matrix multiplication can be performed efficiently on a collection of p processors, where p is independent of the size n of the matrices. As before, we assume that the elements of A, B, and C are distributed evenly among the p processors. Hence, each processor contains $\frac{n^2}{p}$ elements of each of the three matrices. (To avoid rounding problems, we assume p to be a divisor of n^2.) Again, we assume that each processor performs all the multiplications and additions necessary to compute the part of A that is stored in that processor.

How should the matrices be distributed? If $p = n^2$, we have the old situation, and we could store one element of each matrix in each processor. If $p = n$, then we could store one row or one column of each matrix in a processor, but this is not necessarily the best way to do it; in fact, we will see that it is a poor way. Suppose that element $A[i, j]$ is stored in processor h. In order to compute $A[i, j]$, processor h needs to have row i of B and column j of C (and then performs the dot-product of the two). It would be nice if that row and column could be reused in the computation of a few more elements that reside in processor h so as to reduce the amount of communication. How many rows and columns are needed altogether? Let

$$u = \langle \mathbf{N} i :: \langle \exists j :: A[i,j] \text{ } in \text{ } processor \text{ } h \rangle \rangle \quad , \text{ and}$$
$$v = \langle \mathbf{N} j :: \langle \exists i :: A[i,j] \text{ } in \text{ } processor \text{ } h \rangle \rangle \quad ;$$

then u is the number of rows in B and v is the number of columns in C that are needed for computing all the elements stored in processor h. Since every row and every column contains n elements, $n(u+v)$ elements are to be transmitted from various processors to processor h (minus the few elements that are already in h). Observe that u is also the number of rows in A for which an element resides in h, and that v is the number of columns in A for which an element resides in h. Hence, uv is at least the number of elements of A in h, and since h contains $\frac{n^2}{p}$ elements, we have $uv \geq \frac{n^2}{p}$. Minimizing $n(u+v)$ with respect to the constraint $uv \geq \frac{n^2}{p}$ yields $u = v = \frac{n}{\sqrt{p}}$. This shows that we should try to store the $\frac{n^2}{p}$ elements of A in h in such a way that they are taken from $\frac{n}{\sqrt{p}}$ columns and from $\frac{n}{\sqrt{p}}$ rows. There are many ways of doing this if p is a square (and I don't know how to do it otherwise). If $p = q^2$, then we might number the processors with pairs x, y where x and y range from 0 through $q-1$. One way of distributing the matrix elements is to store element i, j in processor $x, y = iq$ div n, jq div n. This is sometimes called the block-allocation method. Another method is to use $x, y = i$ mod q, j mod q, which is sometimes referred to as grid allocation. Combinations of the two will do, as will permutations of rows and columns obtained from any of them. (In fact, the block-allocation and grid-allocation methods can be obtained from each other by such permutations.) Suppose we use block allocation. What changes in the algorithm? The only change is that the block of matrix elements i, j with $x\frac{n}{q} \leq i < (x+1)\frac{n}{q} \wedge y\frac{n}{q} \leq j < (y+1)\frac{n}{q}$ is considered as one element of a coarser matrix. In our old algorithm, the constant 0 in the assignment to $A[i,j]$ is then understood to be the $\frac{n}{q} \times \frac{n}{q}$ zero matrix; addition $+$ is understood to be matrix addition; and $\cdot$ is matrix multiplication. Variables a, b, c are $\frac{n}{q} \times \frac{n}{q}$ matrices instead of scalars. That's all. (Well, guard $k \neq n$ becomes $k \neq \frac{n}{q}$, and constants i, j are replaced by x, y.)

How much *speedup* do we get from this algorithm? Does it pay off to have q^2 processors working on this matrix multiplication? Let us count the number of communications and the number of arithmetic operations. The number of communications is at most $4(q-1)$ in the initialization, and is exactly $4q$ in the main loop. Each communication involves a block of $\frac{n^2}{q^2}$ elements. Assuming that each communication takes time d per scalar, each process spends at most $\frac{4(2q-1)n^2}{q^2} d$ time in communication. No waiting is involved in the communications in the main loop, since communication is between direct neighbors only, and they are all ready to perform

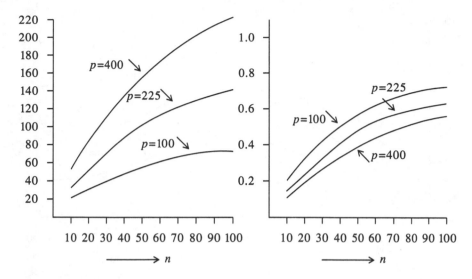

FIGURE 13.1. Speedup and efficiency as functions of n.

all four communications in parallel. The number of arithmetic operations (not counting the arithmetic for incrementing k) is q multiplications and additions of $\frac{n}{q} \times \frac{n}{q}$ matrices, that is, $\frac{2n^3}{q^2}$ arithmetic operations. If each operation takes time f, then the total computation time per processor is $\frac{2n^3}{q^2}f$. Hence, the total execution time is $\frac{4(2q-1)n^2d+2n^3f}{q^2}$.

How do we assess the speedup? We could take the time it takes to run the algorithm on 1 processor and divide it by the time it takes to run it on p processors. This is what is usually done. It seems to be more honest, however, to compare with the time it takes to run the original, sequential algorithm, which was not burdened by any communication overhead. The latter program spends its time exclusively in computation and takes time $2n^3f$. The speedup that our algorithm gives on p processors is (remember $p = q^2$)

$$\frac{2n^3f}{4(2\sqrt{p}-1)n^2d+2n^3f}p \quad ,$$

which is not quite linear in p. Often it is more interesting to look at the efficiency rather than the speedup. The *efficiency* is the speedup divided by the number of processors. It is an indication of how well the processors are being used. The speedup can often be increased a bit by a great increase in the number of processors, but the "law of diminishing returns" makes this unattractive. We have four graphs for the case where $d = f$. The two graphs in Figure 13.1 show speedup and efficiency as functions of n, respectively. The two graphs in Figure 13.2 give speedup and efficiency as

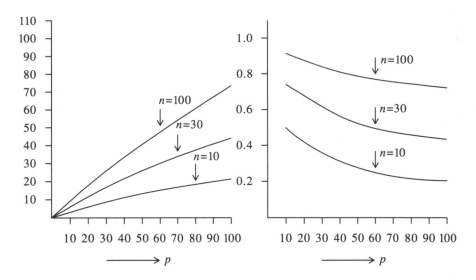

FIGURE 13.2. Speedup and efficiency as functions of p.

functions of p. These graphs exhibit an interesting phenomenon. Consider the last one. It shows that the efficiency goes down as the number of processors increases, and this is known as Amdahl's Law. It is a pessimistic result, and not a very deep one. It is clear that the efficiency goes down when the size of the problem is fixed. It is more useful to take the size into consideration and conclude that "bigger" machines require "bigger" problems in order to use them efficiently. (This is not a very deep result either; it is known as the Law of Conservation of Computing Time.)

One more remark about matrix multiplication. As we have seen, the computing time is $O(n^3)$, and the communication time can be kept down to $O(n^2)$. No matter how poorly the communication is implemented, increasing n eventually causes the computation time to dominate; this in turn, causes the speedup to approach the number of processors. I guess that this is one of the reasons why matrix multiplication is a favorite benchmark algorithm.

13.8   Algorithms that Scale

We are given integer n, $n \geq 0$, and array $a[0..n]$ of $n+1$ real numbers. Let $f(x)$ be the polynomial of order n given by

$$f(x) = \langle \sum i : 0 \leq i \leq n : a[i] \cdot x^{n-i} \rangle \qquad .$$

Of course, we may implement assignment

$$y := f(x)$$

by a loop

$$y := a[0]; \quad k := 0;$$
$$*[\ k \neq n \rightarrow y := y \cdot x + a[k+1]; \quad k := k+1\ ]$$

with invariant

$$y = \langle \sum i : 0 \leq i \leq k : a[i] \cdot x^{k-i} \rangle \ \wedge \ 0 \leq k \leq n \quad .$$

There is not a lot of room for parallelism in this problem as it stands, that is, not if we aim for anything close to linear speedup. The situation changes drastically, however, if we want to apply f not just to one value of x but to a whole sequence of x values. The parallelism does not speed up the computation of any individual $f(x)$ computation, but it may speed up the whole process. In this case, at least two different ways of introducing parallelism are open to us.

One way is to allocate one separate process to each iteration of the loop that computes the polynomial. This leads to a structure of n processes in a *pipeline*, each performing a multiply-and-add step on its input stream. The iterative program used three variables for storing the state: k, y, and x. Variable k is replaced by the identity of the process. Variables y and x need to be communicated between the processes. In the program, channel $c[k]$ is used to communicate both y and x.

```
var c : array [0..n] of chan;
|[ var x : real;
   *[ true → in?x;  c[0]!(a[0], x) ]
]| ||
for all k,  0 ≤ k < n :
   |[ var x, y : real;
      *[ true → c[k]?(y, x);  c[k+1]!(y · x + a[k+1], x) ]
   ]| ||
|[ var x, y : real;
   *[ true → c[n]?(y, x);  out!y ]
]|
```

This solution allows the parallelism to grow with n, the size of the polynomial. It is especially attractive if we can construct inexpensive processors that perform a multiply-and-add step.

The other way of introducing parallelism is to introduce a number of processes that each apply f to a subsequence of the input stream. Here is a possible encoding in which P is the number of processes. Element i of stream *in* is processed by process $i \bmod P$; hence, it is propagated as element $i \textbf{ div } P$ along channel $d[i \bmod P]$, and similarly for output and c. This solution embodies a generally applicable technique that is independent of the structure of f.

```
var d, c : array [0..P − 1] of chan;
|[ var i : int;  x : real;
   i := 0;
   *[ true → in?x;  d[i]!x;  i := (i + 1) mod P ]
]| ||
for all p,  0 ≤ p < P :
   |[ var x, y : real;
      *[ true → d[p]?x;  y := f(x);  c[p]!y ]
   ]| ||
|[ var j : int;  y : real;
   j := 0;
   *[ true → c[j]?y;  out!y;  j := (j + 1) mod P ]
]|
```

An attractive property is that the amount of parallelism is now independent of the degree of the polynomial. This solution has one unattractive property, though. The first and last processes are each connected to P processes; the number of connections increases with the degree of parallelism. It is often easier to construct (fast) channels if the number of connections is fixed, independent of the degree of parallelism. Let us, therefore, try to arrange the processes in a different way. In the program above, the distribution process sends to process p , for every p in the range 0 through $P - 1$. A different arrangement is as follows. The distribution process sends an x value to process 0. Process 0 either applies f to this value x , or it forwards x to process 1. Similarly, process 1 either processes the value it receives or passes it on to the next process, and so on. Each process p is then as follows. (We have added channel $e[p]$ from $p - 1$ to p .)

```
process p :  *[d[p]?x;  c[p]!f(x)] ||
             *[ true → [ e[p + 1] → e[p]?z;  e[p + 1]!z
                       |  d[p]    → e[p]?z;  d[p]!z
             ]          ]
```

The distribution process sends x values via channel $e[0]$. The resulting y values are collected in a similar way. Here we have a choice. Does process p send the result to $p - 1$, which forwards it to $p - 2$, and so on, and we have all y 's output by process 0, or does process p send the result to $p + 1$, and the output is collected from $P - 1$? We list the program for the first choice; the other program is similar. We have added channel $b[p]$ from p to $p - 1$. Outputs are collected from $b[0]$. We make no attempt at receiving the outputs in the same order as the corresponding inputs have been sent: if the input is $x_0 \, x_1 \, x_2$, then the output can be any permutation of $f(x_0) \, f(x_1) \, f(x_2)$. If the order has to be the same, then something needs to be added to this program, such as attaching a sequence number to the messages and a sorter at the output. In some problems, the order is important; in others, it isn't. This scheme of distributing work over processes is known as a processor farm, and is especially attractive if the order of the messages is not important.

$$
\begin{aligned}
\text{process } p: \quad &*[true \rightarrow d[p]?x;\ c[p]!f(x)] \parallel \\
&*[\ true \rightarrow [\ \underline{e[p+1]} \rightarrow e[p]?z;\ e[p+1]!z \\
&\qquad\qquad\quad \| \underline{d[p]} \qquad \rightarrow e[p]?z;\ d[p]!z \\
&\quad\ ] \qquad\qquad] \parallel \\
&*[\ true \rightarrow [\ \underline{b[p+1]} \rightarrow b[p+1]?y;\ b[p]!y \\
&\qquad\qquad\quad \| \underline{c[p]} \qquad \rightarrow c[p]?y;\ b[p]!y \\
&\quad\ ] \qquad\qquad]
\end{aligned}
$$

A process is idle (that is, it is not computing anything) from the time it outputs $f(x)$ until the time it receives its next x value. This idle time can be reduced (or eliminated) by replacing channel $d[p]$ with a buffer, so that the computing process can proceed as soon as it has finished its previous cycle, and having the buffer filled while an f computation is being performed. Usually, a one-place buffer will do, but if communication is slow compared to computation, a larger buffer may be appropriate.

Which solution is to be preferred: the one where the output is taken from the same process as the input is sent to, or the other one? The only difference is in the performance, so let's try to make an estimate of how long each of the two versions takes. Assume that the trick with the buffer works so well that there is no idle time. We count the communication time and computation time. It may be that the arguments and results of f are of a widely different nature, and require widely different amounts of time to transmit. (For example, in a graphics program, x might be the number of a scan line, say $0 \le x < 1024$, whereas $f(x)$ is a sequence of pixels: 1024 numbers of 24 bits each.) Let v be the time it takes to communicate an argument, and w the time it takes to communicate a result; that is, v is the time for communication via e, and w for a communication via b. Let u be the time it takes to compute $f(x)$; that is, we assume that u is independent of x. (This may not be too realistic, but it will do for our purpose here.) Let n_p be the number of x values processed by processor p, and let N be the total number of values processed: $N = \sum_{p=0}^{P-1} n_p$.

Let us first consider the case where input and output to the processor farm are performed at the same end. Processor p spends $u n_p$ time in computation, $(v + w)n_p$ time in receiving and sending its arguments and results, and $2(v + w) \sum_{j=p+1}^{P-1} n_j$ time in passing on arguments to and results from higher-numbered processors. (The factor of 2 is from the fact that each of those messages is both input and output.) We get the best performance if there is no idle time and each processor spends all its time on communication and computation. In this case, we can equate these total times for processors p and $p+1$ and find

$$un_p + (v+w)n_p + 2(v+w)\sum_{j=p+1}^{P-1} n_j =$$
$$un_{p+1} + (v+w)n_{p+1} + 2(v+w)\sum_{j=p+2}^{P-1} n_j$$

$=$ { simplification }

$$un_p - un_{p+1} + (v+w)n_p + 2(v+w)n_{p+1} - (v+w)n_{p+1} = 0$$

$=$

$$(u+v+w)n_p + (v+w-u)n_{p+1} = 0$$

$=$

$$n_{p+1} = \frac{u+v+w}{u-v-w} n_p \quad .$$

Since n_p and n_{p+1} are assumed to be positive, we have $u > v+w$, which means that we can avoid idle time only if the computation time exceeds the communication time per element (which makes sense). Let r stand for $\frac{u+v+w}{u-v-w}$. Observe $r > 1$ and $n_p = r^p n_0$. Hence,

$$\sum_{p=0}^{P-1} n_p = N$$

$=$

$$\sum_{p=0}^{P-1} r^p n_0 = N$$

$=$

$$n_0 = \frac{r-1}{r^P - 1} N \quad .$$

Substituting, we find that each processor spends

$$2(v+w)N + (u-v-w)\frac{r-1}{r^P - 1} N$$

time in communication plus computation. Consider the two limiting cases. If $u \downarrow v+w$, the computing time hardly exceeds the communication time, and the total time tends to $2(v+w)N$, which is the time it takes to send each x value to processor 0 and retrieve $f(x)$ from it. If $u \gg v+w$, the computing time exceeds by far the communication time, and the total time tends to $2(v+w)N + \frac{u}{P}N$, which reflects an almost optimal speedup.

When we consider the case where input is sent to processor 0 and output is taken from $P-1$, we would find

$$n_p = r^p n_0 \quad ,$$

where $r = \frac{u+w+v}{u+w-v}$ and the total time is

$$2vN + (u+w-v)\frac{r-1}{r^P - 1} N \quad ,$$

and we have to assume $u > |v-w|$. We now have three limiting cases. If $w > v$ and $u \downarrow w-v$, the time tends to $2wN$. If $w \leq v$ and $u \downarrow v-w$, the time tends to $2vN$. If $u \gg |v-w|$, then r tends to 1, and the time tends to $2vN + \frac{u+w-v}{P}N$. We find that the case where input and output to the processor farm are performed on different ends has a better performance. Remember, however, that we assumed no idle time. Both farms scale quite well with the number of processors, provided enough work is available, and the communication time is small compared to the computation time.

13.9   Bibliographic Notes

The mutual exclusion problem was first posed in [Dij65]. It contains a description (and proof of correctness) of Dekker's algorithm. Most presentations of mutual exclusion algorithms follow the sequence of algorithms presented in [Dij68]. So does ours.

Peterson's algorithm is from [Pet81]. Our proof is based on [Dij81]. The proof method used here is from [OG76a] and [OG76b]. Exercise 6 is from [Kes82]. More mutual exclusion algorithms can be found in [Ray86].

The difference between "invariant" and "always true" is part of the folklore. See, for example, [vGT90] and [San91]. Exercise 9 is based on an example from [Jon88].

Processes that communicate via channels were introduced in [Hoa78]. The prime sieve is from this paper, where it is attributed to David Gries. Consult [Mar81] for an axiomatic definition of the semantics of the communication primitives. The probe is from [Mar85].

Our discussion of matrix multiplication is based on [Luk91].

13.10   Exercises

1. Construct an algorithm that guarantees that you end up with an acceptable reading of the time, given that the clock process updates first h and then m. It is okay to read the values h and m more than once. If you need some assumptions about the relative speeds of the clock process and the other process, then you may make any reasonable assumption, provided you state it explicitly.

2. What are the possible final values of x and y when executing the following program from an initial state that satisfies $x = y = 0$?

   $$x := y + 1 \;\|\; y := x + 1$$

3. Execution of

   $$\begin{aligned}
   &\textbf{var } i, j, x : integer; \\
   &i := 0; \; j := 0; \; x := 0; \\
   &\|[\; *[i \neq 100 \rightarrow x := x + 1; \; i := i + 1] \; \| \\
   &\quad *[j \neq 100 \rightarrow x := x + 1; \; j := j + 1] \\
   &]\|
   \end{aligned}$$

   leads to 200 executions of $x := x + 1$. Because of the one-access-per-atomic-action rule, this statement is split into two atomic actions, say

   $$\langle x' := x \rangle; \; \langle x := x' + 1 \rangle$$

in the first process, and

$$\langle x'' := x \rangle;\ \ \langle x := x'' + 1 \rangle$$

in the second process. As a result, not all executions of $x := x + 1$ necessarily increase x. What is the range of possible values that x can assume upon completion of this program?

4. Prove that the safe sluice guarantees mutual exclusion. Hint: introduce auxiliary variable y

> **var** b : **array** $[0..1]$ **of** *boolean*;
> $y : 0..1$;
> { initially $\neg b[0]\ \wedge\ \neg b[1]$ }
> process 0:
>   *[*true* $\rightarrow$ $b[0] := true$; * $[b[1] \rightarrow skip]$; $y := 0$;
> CA_0; $b[0] := false$; NCA_0
>   ] ||
> process 1:
>   *[*true* $\rightarrow$ $b[1] := true$; * $[b[0] \rightarrow skip]$; $y := 1$;
> CA_1; $b[1] := false$; NCA_1
>   ]

and show that $y = i\ \wedge\ b[i]$ holds during execution of CA_i.

5. Invert the order of assignments $b[i] := true$ and $t := i$ in process i of Peterson's algorithm, and show that mutual exclusion is no longer guaranteed.

6. Here is variation of Peterson's algorithm (for two processes). It has the property that each variable is modified by only one process, but may be read by both processes. Prove its correctness.

> **var** b : **array** $[0..1]$ **of** *boolean*;
> y : **array** $[0..1]$ **of** *integer*;
> { initially $\neg b[0]\ \wedge\ \neg b[1]\ \wedge\ y[0] = y[1] = 0$ }
> process i : *[*true* $\rightarrow$ $b[i] := true$; $y[i] := y[1 - i] \oplus i$;
>   *$[b[1]\ \wedge\ y[i] = y[1 - i] \oplus i \rightarrow skip]$;
> CA_0; $b[0] := false$;
> NCA_0
>   ]

Symbol $\oplus$ denotes addition modulo 2.

7. Assume that an operation in angle brackets is an indivisible action. Consider a program with one global variable, x, and a local variable, y, for each process. Initially, $x = 1$. Each process is of the form

process i :
$$*[\ true \rightarrow \langle x := x - 1; \ y := x \rangle;$$
$$*[y \neq 0 \rightarrow \langle x := x + 1 \rangle; \ \langle x := x - 1; \ y := x \rangle];$$
$$CA_i;$$
$$\langle x := x + 1 \rangle;$$
$$NCA_i$$
$$]\quad.$$

Show that after-you-after-you blocking is possible. (Note: this solution is sometimes given in terms of indivisible increment and decrement operations where the test $y \neq 0$ is a processor's condition code.)

8. Assume that an operation in angle brackets is an indivisible action. Consider a program with one global variable, x, and a local variable, y, for each process. Initially, $x = 1$ and each $y = 0$. Each process is of the form

process i $:*[\ true \rightarrow *[y = 0 \rightarrow \langle x, y := y, x \rangle];$
$$CA_i;$$
$$\langle x, y := y, x \rangle;$$
$$NCA_i$$
$$]\quad.$$

Show that this solution to the mutual exclusion problem is unfair; that is, in the case of more than two processes, it is possible that two processes alternately execute their critical action while all the other processes are locked out. (Note: this solution is sometimes given in terms of bit-set and bit-test operations where the test $y = 0$ is a processor's condition code.)

9. Consider program

$$p := true; \ q := false;$$
$$\|[\ p := \neg q \ \|\ q := true\ ]\|\quad.$$

Show that p is always true when the first process is executed in isolation. Show that p is always true when the second process is executed in isolation. Show that p is not always true when the first and second processes are executed together as indicated in our program.

Show that $p \wedge \neg q$ is an invariant of the first process but not of the second process.

10. Consider program

$$x := 0;$$
$$\|[\ *[true \rightarrow x := 2x] \ \|\ x := 1\ ]\|\quad.$$

Show that $x = 0 \ \lor \ x = 1$ is always true when the first process is executed in isolation. Show that $x = 0 \ \lor \ x = 1$ is always true when the second process is executed in isolation. Show that $x = 0 \ \lor \ x = 1$ is not always true when the first and second processes are executed together.

11. The *filter* process checks whether x is a multiple of p by comparing to zero the remainder from dividing x by p. The sequence of x values received by the *filter* process is an increasing sequence, so that it is also possible to keep track of the smallest multiple mp of p that is at least x, updating mp whenever a new value for x is received. Adapt the program to eliminate the modulo operation in this way.

12. Can the *sieve* process be simplified to

    $sieve(lin, lout)$:
    　　var $p : integer$; **chan** ro;
    　　$lin?p$; $lout!p$;
    　　[$p^2 < L \rightarrow filter(p, lin, ro) \ || \ sieve(ro, lout)$
    　　$|\!|\ p^2 \geq L \rightarrow filter(p, lin, lout)$
    　　]

    without changing its effect?

13. Change the program so that it produces the primes up to some limit L, and then terminates. Make sure that all processes terminate properly.

14. Construct a program for sorting N numbers using N processes. The processes are connected in a sequence. Each process has one input and one output channel. It inputs N numbers, and outputs the same N numbers, but possibly in a different order. Each process stores in a local variable the maximum of the numbers received so far, and it outputs all values received so far, except the maximum. The maximum is output only after all N values have been input. Formulate this sketch in the form of a program text and explain why this program works correctly, that is, why the collection of processes outputs the N numbers in increasing order.

15. (This problem is similar to the *fringe* problem that we wrote a LISP program for.) Two processes each have a binary tree with labeled leaves. Check whether they have the same fringe. The solution uses a third process: the two processes that each have a tree traverse their trees and send their sequence of labels to the third process, where they are compared.

16. *Conway's problem*: Write a program to read 80-column cards and write them as 125-character lines with the following change: every pair of asterisks ** is to be replaced by an upward arrow ↑ (even if one * is the last character of one card and another * is the first character of the next card). What do you propose to do with more than two consecutive asterisks? The first output line contains slightly more than one and a half card images; exactly how much depends on the asterisks. The problem has an elegant solution consisting of three processes. One process reads the cards and produces a stream of characters from which the card boundaries have disappeared. This stream is input by a second process that outputs a copy thereof in which asterisks have been replaced by arrows. The latter stream of characters is consumed by a process that prints the characters as 125-character lines. Compare your program to a sequential solution.

17. Write a program that consists of two processes. One process reads a sequence of characters from an input channel, and the other process writes the same sequence of characters on an output channel. The only connection between the two processes is a channel along which individual bits are transmitted. Use adaptive Huffman coding to reduce the number of bits transmitted. The idea of the algorithm is presented in Exercise 12.30 and in [Gal78].

18. In our matrix multiplication program we wrote

$$b' := b; \ |[h[i,j]?b \ || \ h[i,j-1]!b']|$$

for the communication of elements of the B matrix. Explain what goes wrong if this is replaced by

$$h[i,j]?b \ || \ h[i,j-1]!b \qquad .$$

19. What is gained or lost by replacing

$$a := a + b \cdot c; \ b' := b; \ c' := c;$$
$$|[h[i,j]?b \ || \ h[i,j-1]!b' \ || \ v[i,j]?c \ || \ v[i-1,j]!c']|$$

    with

$$b' := b; \ c' := c;$$
$$|[\ a := a + b' \cdot c' \ ||$$
$$\quad h[i,j]?b \ || \ h[i,j-1]!b' \ || \ v[i,j]?c \ || \ v[i-1,j]!c'$$
$$]| \qquad ?$$

20. Construct the graphs for speedup and efficiency for the two cases where $d \gg f$ and $d \ll f$.

21. Assume that the matrix-multiplication algorithm is to be executed on a machine with n processors, and that a different distribution scheme of the matrix elements is used: each processor holds one row of B and one column of C. Choose a distribution of matrix A, and compute the number of communications, the speedup, and the efficiency.

22. Construct an algorithm for the LU decomposition of an $n \times n$ matrix on an $n \times n$ processor network.

23. We have discussed processor farms in which all processes are arranged in a linear sequence. Of course, other arrangements can be proposed, such as a balanced binary tree. Carry out performance computations for the case in which input and output to the farm tree are done via the root.

24. In our calculations we have ignored latency: the time that elapses from the moment that an input is given to the moment that the corresponding output appears. Calculate the latency for the two linear processor farms.

14

Implementation Issues: Compilation

In this and subsequent chapters, we look at some implementation issues. We study how the sequential parts of programs can be translated from the program notation that we have been using to the program notation used by a typical machine, such as a sequential machine consisting of one processor and a linear store.

14.1 Translating from One Notation to Another

The translation of programs from one notation, or language, into another is called compilation. Why do we need two different notations for our programs anyway? We have one that we use for writing our programs, and there is supposedly another one used for execution by the machine. (In the context of compilation, the first is called the *source notation* and the second the *object notation*.) The reason is that the requirements for the two notations are quite different:

- the source notation should be suitable for designing programs;

- the object notation should be suitable for mechanical execution.

Of course, the word "suitable" is not very precise. We will go in more details later. Let us give a few examples now.

A major discrepancy between these two notations is the syntactic structure. During execution of a program, the program text is parsed. A piece of program text is parsed each time it is executed. For the sake of efficiency, it is then required that the syntactic structure be simple to parse. The simplest structure is one that can be parsed with a one-state machine, that is, a machine that requires no state information at all. This structure is I^*, where I is a finite set of so-called instructions. Instructions have no further structure; they are not composed of smaller instructions. This structure is used by almost all machines because it allows an extremely simple parsing strategy; in fact, it is so simple that is hardly noticed. The syntactic structure of the statements that we have been using in our source program notation is much "richer" in the sense that it admits statements that are composed from smaller statements and expressions that have other expressions as parts. As we have seen in a previous chapter, parsing such a syntactic structure requires a stack or a set of recursive procedures. Hence, it appears to be profitable to use "structured" statements when designing programs and to have them translated into a sequence of "nonstructured" instructions before execution of the program is undertaken.

The remark applies the same to data as it does to statements. In our source programs, we use booleans, integers, records, arrays, and so on. An array is composed of smaller elements, such as integers or other arrays. When designing programs, the details of the representation of a variable are often postponed until some insight into the relevant operations is gained. Therefore, it is important that operations such as assignments can be written in a way that does not depend on the data type. For example, an integer can be assigned to an integer variable, an array to an array variable; however, although $x := y$ is the same for all data types, it is not the same when it has to be written out in operations on the elementary data types, say integers. A sequence of assignments, or a loop, is then required to implement an array assignment. Hence, some translation from operations on composite data types to sequences of operations on elementary data types has to take place.

Another example of the discrepancy in requirements for the two program notations is the use of names for variables. In the source language, we use identifiers; in the object language, we use natural numbers. In both cases, these names are chosen from a totally ordered collection of potential names, and, at any moment during execution, a subset thereof is in use. A nomenclature is called *closed* if for each pair of names in use, each name in the order between them is also in use; it is called *open,* otherwise. Identifiers in the source program constitute an open nomenclature. (One may use both a and d without being forced to use also identifiers b and c.) During execution, however, a closed nomenclature is preferred, since it admits a simple characterization of the names in use (such as: all names from 0 to 123 are in use), and a simple mapping on a linear store. Furthermore, these names can be encoded with fewer bits, thereby conserving storage space.

There is a slightly different kind of reason for letting the source and object program be different, even if the two notations involved are the same. The reason is that in a "robust" implementation, applying partial functions outside their domain should be avoided. This leads to the addition of statements for checking and, possibly, reporting such erroneous situations. For example, statement $x := sqrt(y)$ might be translated into

$$
\begin{array}{l}
[\ y \geq 0 \rightarrow x := sqrt(y) \\
\|\ y < 0 \rightarrow error('sqrt\ applied\ to\ negative\ argument') \\
]
\end{array}
$$
.

In the next few sections, we consider various issues in more detail.

14.2   Expressions

A sequential computation consists of a sequence of operations, each of which takes a number of arguments and returns a number of results. The results may, in turn, be used as arguments in subsequent operations. If an intermediate result is used more than once, then a variable is needed to hold it and a name is needed to refer to it. In various subcomputations, results may be known to be used only once, and it is then superfluous to introduce a name for them. Expressions in programs serve the purpose of avoiding those names. For example, in $x := (a+b)*(c/d)$, no name is needed to refer to the sum of a and b or to the quotient of c and d. However, memory locations are needed for holding anonymous results until they are needed. In the example, if the sum of a and b is computed before the quotient of c and d is computed, then this sum has to be stored during the division operation until it is needed in the multiplication. In this section, we discuss notations that combine anonymity of intermediate results and suitability for mechanical evaluation.

If results and arguments are anonymous, then the only way of identifying them during execution is by the order in time in which they are created and consumed. The quintessence of a notation for expressions is a relation between the order in which results are created and the order in which arguments are consumed. Two relations suggest themselves: whenever an argument is needed, take either the youngest or the oldest unconsumed result. Under the first regime, expressions can be evaluated with a stack for holding the unconsumed results, and under the second regime, expressions can be evaluated with a queue. The corresponding notations for expressions are called *postfix* and *caudafix*, respectively. We discuss postfix notation first.

A postfix notation is a sequence of literals and operators. A literal is a variable or a constant. An expression is evaluated by evaluating the sequence in order from left to right, where (i) evaluating a literal amounts to pushing its value on top of the stack; and (ii) evaluating an operator amounts to popping the right number of operands from the stack, performing the designated operation, and pushing the result(s) on top of the stack. Operands are taken from the top of the stack because that is where the youngest unconsumed result is located.

The grammar for postfix expressions is

$$pe \longrightarrow lit$$
$$pe \longrightarrow pe\ pe\ op \qquad ,$$

where *lit* stands for a literal (a variable or a constant) and *op* stands for an operator that takes two operands and returns one result. When considering operators $op_{m,n}$ that take m arguments and return n results, $m \geq 0 \land n \geq 1$, we may write

$$pe \quad \longrightarrow \quad exp_1$$
$$exp_0 \quad \longrightarrow \quad \epsilon$$
$$exp_i \quad \longrightarrow \quad exp_{i+m-n} \ op_{m,n} \qquad ,$$

where ϵ is the empty sequence, lit is subsumed in $op_{0,1}$ and we have the latter grammar rule for all $i \geq 1$ and all $m, n, \ i + m \geq n$. Nonterminal exp_i generates all sequences of expressions and operators that produce exactly i results.

The semantics of postfix expressions is formally defined by function $\mathcal{M}$, which when applied to a postfix expression yields the expression in infix notation (cf. Chapter 7). (We might also have $\mathcal{M}$ yield the value of the expression, but then we need to define the value of an infix expression also.) $\mathcal{M}$ adds extra parentheses around any expression that has an operator to avoid ambiguities.

$$\mathcal{M}(e_0 \ e_1 \ op) = (\mathcal{M}(e_0) \ op \ \mathcal{M}(e_1))$$
$$\mathcal{M}(lit) \qquad = lit$$

Next, we want to define function τ so that it maps an expression in infix notation into the corresponding expression in postfix notation; hence, $\mathcal{M}(\tau(e)) = e$ — apart from parentheses. As an example we use the arithmetic expressions, as discussed in Chapter 2, in which $+$ and $-$ have the lowest binding power, $*$ and $/$ have higher, and $\uparrow$ has the highest binding power. Furthermore, $\uparrow$ is right associative and the four other ones are left associative. (This all goes to say that $a - b - c \uparrow d \uparrow e = ((a - b) - (c \uparrow (d \uparrow e)))$.)

$$E \longrightarrow E + T \mid E - T \mid T$$
$$T \longrightarrow T * F \mid T/F \mid F$$
$$F \longrightarrow P \uparrow F \mid P$$
$$P \longrightarrow lit \mid (E)$$

The definition of τ is given by cases.

$$\tau(E + T) = \tau(E) \ \tau(T) \ +$$
$$\tau(E - T) = \tau(E) \ \tau(T) \ -$$
$$\tau(T * F) = \tau(T) \ \tau(F) \ *$$
$$\tau(T/F) \ = \tau(T) \ \tau(F) \ /$$
$$\tau(P \uparrow F) = \tau(P) \ \tau(F) \ \uparrow$$
$$\tau(lit) \qquad = lit$$
$$\tau((E)) \qquad = \tau(E)$$

Property $\mathcal{M}(\tau(e)) = e$, for any infix expression e, follows directly from the definitions of τ, and $\mathcal{M}$.

Note the similarity between the syntax and the definition of τ : the translation of each right-hand side is given in terms of the translation of constituting nonterminal symbols together with some other terminal symbols. Furthermore, the nonterminals occur in the same order in the right-hand side of a rule and in the translation. Therefore, we may weave the translation and the syntax rules into one grammar. In order to be more explicit about the terminal symbols in the infix and the postfix expressions, we denote them slightly differently: terminals from the infix expression (input to the translation) are written in single quotes, whereas terminals from the postfix expression (output of the translation) are written in double quotes.

$$
\begin{aligned}
E &\longrightarrow E\,'{+}'\ T\,''{+}''\mid E\,'{-}'\ T\,''{-}''\mid T\\
T &\longrightarrow T\,'{*}'\ F\,''{*}''\mid T\,'{/}'\ F\,''{/}''\mid F\\
F &\longrightarrow P\,'{\uparrow}'\ F\,''{\uparrow}''\mid P\\
P &\longrightarrow \mathit{lit}\mid '('\,'E\,')'
\end{aligned}
$$

Given a parse tree of a string with respect to this extended grammar, a parse tree of that same string with respect to the original grammar can be obtained by removing all the double-quoted symbols. The corresponding translation is obtained by removing all the single-quoted symbols. Similar to procedure $getsym$ (cf. Chapter 6) for reading the next (single-quoted) symbol from the source program text, we assume the presence of a procedure, $gen(\cdots)$, for appending the next (double-quoted) symbol to the object program text. The parser will now be augmented with calls of gen in order to produce the object program. Applying factorization to F, and the conversion rule to go from $V \longrightarrow Vx|y$ to $V \longrightarrow yx^*$ in the case of E and T, we obtain grammar

$$
\begin{aligned}
E &\longrightarrow T\ ('{+}'\ T\,''{+}''\mid '{-}'\ T\,''{-}'')^*\\
T &\longrightarrow F\ ('{*}'\ F\,''{*}''\mid '{/}'\ F\,''{/}'')^*\\
F &\longrightarrow P\ ('{\uparrow}'\ F\,''{\uparrow}''\mid \epsilon)\\
P &\longrightarrow \mathit{lit}\mid '('\,'E\,')'
\end{aligned}
$$

which leaves us little choice for our augmented parser.

procedure E;
  $|[\ T;$
    $*[\ sym = '{+}' \rightarrow getsym;\ T;\ gen(''{+}'')$
    $\|\ sym = '{-}' \rightarrow getsym;\ T;\ gen(''{-}'')$
    $]$
  $]|$
procedure T;
  $|[\ F;$
    $*[\ sym = '{*}' \rightarrow getsym;\ F;\ gen(''{*}'')$
    $\|\ sym = '{/}' \rightarrow getsym;\ F;\ gen(''{/}'')$
    $]$
  $]|$

procedure F;
$\|[\ P;$
$\quad [\ sym =' \uparrow' \to getsym;\ \ F;\ \ gen('' \uparrow'')$
$\quad \|\ sym \neq' \uparrow' \to skip$
$\quad]$
$]|$
procedure P;
$\|[\ [\ sym \in \{'a'..'z', '0'..'9'\} \qquad \to lit$
$\quad \|\ sym =' ('\qquad\qquad\qquad\qquad \to getsym;\ \ E;$
$\qquad\qquad\qquad\qquad\qquad\qquad\quad [\ sym =')' \to getsym$
$\qquad\qquad\qquad\qquad\qquad\qquad\quad \|\ sym \neq')' \to error$
$\qquad\qquad\qquad\qquad\qquad\qquad\quad]$
$\quad \|\ sym \notin \{'a'..'z', '0'..'9', '('\} \to error$
$\quad]$
$]|$

This concludes our discussion of postfix notation, and we now switch to the discussion of caudafix notation.

A caudafix expression is a sequence of literals and operators. Evaluating a caudafix expression consists of evaluating the sequence in order from left to right. Evaluating a literal amounts to attaching its value to the tail of the queue; and evaluating an operator amounts to detaching operands from the head of the queue, performing the designated operation, and attaching the result(s) to the tail of the queue. We delegate the development of syntax and semantics of caudafix expressions to the exercises. It turns out that an operator need not be textually adjacent to either of its operands, which makes these expressions harder to manipulate (manually).

We give two examples of expressions and their translation in postfix and caudafix notation.

- $a + b * c \uparrow d$
  postfix: $a\ b\ c\ d\ \uparrow\ *\ +$
  caudafix: $c\ d\ b\ \uparrow\ a\ *\ +$

- $(a + b) * (c - d)$
  postfix: $a\ b\ +\ c\ d\ -\ *$
  caudafix: $a\ b\ c\ d\ +\ -\ *$

In the first case, the stack holds up to four values; whereas the queue holds up to three values; and in the second case, we have the reverse situation. In the sequel, we shall assume postfix notation to be used.

An alternative to the use of a stack or a queue for holding intermediate results is to introduce names for these results, and treat those names just like any other variables. For example,

$$x := (a + b) * (c/d)$$

might first be translated to

$$t := a + b; \ u := c/d; \ x := t * u$$

for fresh variables t and u. In many machines, memory consists of a linear store plus a limited set of registers. Registers can be accessed faster than regular storage locations. Often, one tries to allocate frequently used variables to registers. Temporary variables make excellent candidates for being allocated to registers. Allocation of variables is the subject of the next section.

14.3 Nomenclature

We assume that the computer that is going to execute our programs has a linear store, with storage locations numbered from 0. We refer to storage location i as $m[i]$. In this section, we ignore registers. Furthermore, we assume for the moment that the value of a variable fits into one storage location, often referred to as a *word*. We also assume that variables in our source programs are declared, say at the beginning of their block. In order to avoid confusion, we use two different terms for the two different kinds of names: we use the term *identifier* when we refer to the source program, and we use the term *address* when we refer to the object program. We shall discuss the mapping from identifiers to addresses by first looking at blocks and by then including procedures.

14.3.1 BLOCKS

First, we consider the case in which there is only one block and no procedures. A very simple and effective strategy is then to use natural numbers from 0 on for the addresses. A possible assignment of addresses to identifiers is to use the order of declaration. This yields a closed nomenclature for the object names; that is, the addresses in use are a consecutive subsequence of all potential addresses. An example is

$$
\begin{aligned}
&|[\ \textbf{var}\ x, y, z, && \{\ x \to 0, y \to 1, z \to 2\ \} \\
&\qquad\quad i, j, k && \{\ i \to 3, j \to 4, k \to 5\ \} \\
&\quad\ \cdots \\
&]|
\end{aligned}
$$

Next, we take nested blocks into account. We may, however, ignore the block structure and, as before, assign addresses in sequence. As the following example shows, this ignorance is not very attractive.

$B0$: |[**var** a, b, c { $a \rightarrow 0, b \rightarrow 1, c \rightarrow 2$ }

....

$B1$: |[**var** $d, e, f \cdots$]| { $d \rightarrow 3, e \rightarrow 4, f \rightarrow 5$ }

....

$B2$: |[**var** $g, h, i \cdots$]| { $g \rightarrow 6, h \rightarrow 7, i \rightarrow 8$ }

....

]|

During execution of $B2$, addresses 0,1,2,6,7, and 8 are in use; this is not a closed nomenclature, which means that storage is wasted. The identifiers that may occur in the statement part of $B2$ are the identifiers declared in blocks $B0$ and $B2$, and not those declared in $B1$. It would, therefore, be nice if the addresses assigned to identifiers declared in $B2$ were independent of the identifiers declared in $B1$ (and the addresses assigned to them). A possible strategy is to reuse addresses assigned to identifiers declared in blocks other than the textually-enclosing blocks. Our example then leads to

$$a, b, c \rightarrow 0, 1, 2$$
$$d, e, f \rightarrow 3, 4, 5$$
$$g, h, i \rightarrow 3, 4, 5 \quad .$$

As a result, at any moment during execution the address nomenclature is closed. During execution, the set of storage locations used for storing the values of variables grows and shrinks like a *stack*. Although this stack grows at block entry and shrinks at block exit, no actions are required to effect this change of size.

Not only the topmost element of the stack is accessed but each element may be accessed by using its address. In the context of abstract data types one often finds the restriction that only the topmost element can be accessed. In the stack used for expression evaluation, access was to the topmost element only.

14.3.2 PROCEDURES

If we have a program without procedures then for every position in the program text we can say which variables exist when execution reaches that point. In the presence of procedures this is no longer the case. We can still point out which variables can be accessed but many more may exist.

procedure mn;
$\quad |[$ **var** a, b, c
$\qquad$ **procedure** p;
$\qquad |[$**var** $d, e, f \cdots]|$
$\qquad$ **procedure** q;
$\qquad |[$ **var** g, h
$\qquad\quad$ **procedure** r;
$\qquad\qquad |[$ **var** i, j, k
$\qquad\qquad\quad \cdots p \cdots$
$\qquad\qquad]|$
$\qquad\quad \cdots p \cdots r \cdots$
$\qquad]|$
$\qquad \cdots q \cdots p \cdots$
$\quad]|$

During execution of p, variables a, b, c, d, e, and f can be accessed. When p is called from mn, no other variables exist. When called from q, variables g and h exist, even though they are not accessible from p. And if p is recursive, many instances of d, e, and f can exist simultaneously. As a result, the mapping from identifiers to addresses can no longer be a fixed mapping, but it varies during program execution.

The key observation is that variables can be allocated when the procedure to which they are local is called. The memory locations they occupy can be freed when execution of the procedure is completed. If new variables are allocated at the lowest available memory location, just like in the previous section, then the sequence of memory locations holding the variables grows and shrinks like a stack. We had the same effect before we considered procedures. The only difference is that the mapping from identifiers to addresses may now vary during execution. As a result, we have to introduce a variable that indicates the boundary between allocated and free memory locations, sp say. We maintain the invariant

$\quad a$ is an address which is in use $\ \equiv\ 0 \le a < sp$

for all addresses a. Following this scheme, at every procedure entry a sequence of memory locations from sp on is used for all local variables of the procedure, and sp is updated. This sequence of memory locations is called a *procedure frame*, or an *activation record*.

Although the location of a variable may vary from one procedure call to the next, its position within the procedure frame remains the same. In the example, d is always the first variable in the frame of p. As a result, the mapping from identifiers to addresses consists of two parts: a variable part that indicates the memory segment occupied by the procedure frame, and a fixed part that gives the position within the frame. We introduce one variable, say fp, whose value is the beginning address of the memory segment occupied by the procedure that is currently being executed. The

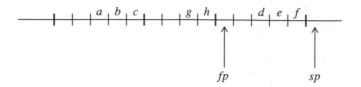

FIGURE 14.1. Three procedure frames.

procedure frame has the following property. Addresses fp and $fp + 1$ contain auxiliary variables; their role is discussed below. Local variables are stored from address $fp + 2$ on. Given fp, the address of a local variable is given by $fp + delta$, where $delta$ is the offset of the local variable from the beginning of the procedure frame. For every variable, $delta$ is fixed. Addressing of variables that are not local to the procedure involves the static link and is discussed below. In Section 14.5, we extend the procedure frame to include parameters.

Figure 14.1 shows the layout of the three procedure frames of mn, q, and p during execution of p when called from mn. More frames may exist at lower addresses, depending on how mn was called. We know how p's local variables are addressed, but we also need to come up with a method for addressing a, b, and c. We cannot use $fp - 7$ to address a because that doesn't work if p is called from mn and the middle one of the three frames is absent. Instead, we use the first anonymous variable in the frame of p to store the frame pointer of procedure mn. Variable a can then be addressed as $m[fp] + 2$. The first anonymous variable in mn's frame contains the frame pointer of the procedure that contains the declaration of mn. The chain of frame pointers that thus arises is called the *static chain*.

Figure 14.2 shows the stack and the static chain during execution of r and then during of execution of p when called from r. Access to a procedure's local variables is immediate. Access to the local variables of the textually enclosing procedure requires one additional memory access to fetch the pointer to that procedure's frame. There is one more memory access for every extra level of nesting, but this number is a static quantity: it does not depend on the number of procedure calls or the level of recursion but on the difference in procedure nesting levels between declaration and use of a variable. In the exercises, we point out methods to make every access immediate.

Next, we look at statements for keeping fp and sp up to date. The only changes occur at entry to or exit from a procedure. At procedure entry, a frame is created. Let k be the frame size, that is, the number of local variables including the auxiliary variables. The actions to be performed are

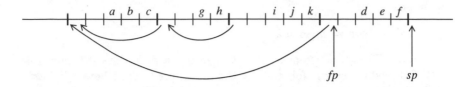

FIGURE 14.2. The static chain.

$$entry: \quad m[sp] :=?; \; fp := sp; \; sp := sp + k$$
$$exit: \quad sp := fp; \; fp := ? \quad .$$

Insufficient information exists to assign a value to $m[sp]$ at procedure entry, and to fp at procedure exit. Procedure entry requires the beginning address of the frame of the textually enclosing procedure. This information depends on the call and the information cannot be part of the compiled procedure body; it has to be supplied at the procedure call. We use a temporary variable called env because it characterizes the environment in which the procedure is executed. This variable is assigned a value in the calling procedure, and is then used at procedure entry.

Procedure exit requires that fp be restored to the value it had upon entry to the procedure. The traditional solution is to store at procedure entry in the procedure frame the value of fp. This value is then assigned to fp upon procedure exit, and it is not used for anything else. The auxiliary variables that thus arise also form a chain, and this is known as the *dynamic chain*. We opt for a different solution, by eliminating fp. With fp gone, there is no need for "its old value". During execution of the procedure, we have invariant

$$fp = sp - k$$

and we can replace all references to fp by $sp - k$. The addressing of variable d within p is changed from $fp + 2$ to $sp - 5 + 2$ (since $k = 5$) which is simplified to $sp - 3$. The address of variable a in mn is changed from $m[fp] + 2$ to $m[sp - 5] + 2$, and so on. We now have

$$entry: \quad m[sp] := env; \; sp := sp + k$$
$$exit: \quad sp := sp - k$$
$$call: \quad env := \text{pointer to frame of the procedure that contains}$$
$$\text{the procedure that is being called}$$

in which k is the size of the frame of the procedure that is being called. If the procedure being called has been declared in the procedure containing the call, then we have

$$call: \quad env := sp - k'$$

where k' is the size of the current frame. If the declaration occurs one level up, we have

$$call: \quad env := m[sp - k']$$

and so on. The sequence of actions to execute a procedure statement is: *call*, followed by *entry*, followed by the procedure body, followed by *exit*. In Section 14.6, we discuss how this sequencing is taken care of. The latter is called *flow of control*. At that point we discuss the role of the second word in the procedure frame.

One improvement is too attractive to omit. The way it stands, addressing a variable in the outermost block leads to following all links of the static chain. However, those variables are found at fixed locations. They are not local to any procedure whose frame can be allocated at different locations during execution. The mapping from these global variables to addresses is fixed and their address can be used instead of the static link. As a result, the last link of the static chain can be eliminated. The chain becomes shorter, and both *call* and *entry* of a procedure that is declared in the outermost block is simplified. All that remains is

$$\begin{aligned} entry: \quad & sp := sp + k \\ exit: \quad & sp := sp - k \end{aligned}$$

where k is the size of the frame without the auxiliary variable for the static link. This improvement helps in two ways: variables declared in the outermost block are addressed without additional memory references, and calls of procedures declared in the outermost block are simplified.

We have glanced over one point. Constant k was the size of the procedure frame. If the stack for storing variables is also the stack for evaluating expressions, then the size of the procedure frame is no longer constant. During evaluation of the expression the frame grows and shrinks. If expression $e + e$ is evaluated, then the occurrences of e are executed with two different frame sizes. Assuming postfix evaluation, the size of the frame is 5 at the time of the first reference and 6 at the second reference. The compiler needs to keep track of the actual frame size during compilation. Constant k is turned into a variable whose value equals the size of the procedure frame. This is a variable in the compiler, not a variable maintained during execution of the program. The result is that expression $e + e$ is compiled into a sequence of three instructions as follows:

load value of variable at address $sp - 2$
load value of variable at address $sp - 3$
add the two values on top of the stack.

This concludes our discussion of nomenclature.

14.4   Assignment Statement

Having discussed variables and expressions, we now turn to their combination in the form of an assignment statement. Inspired by the postfix notation for expressions, we may translate $x := e$ into $x\ e :=$. This is, of course, perfect provided that x leads to pushing the address of x on top of the stack, and not its value. Wherever we need to distinguish between the two, we will write something like $pushvalue(x)$ or $pushaddress(x)$. The instruction corresponding to $:=$ may be thought of as an operator with an address and a value as its two arguments, and with zero results. Its effect is to pop value v from the stack, pop address a from the stack, and perform $m[a] := v$. Another, equally correct translation is $e\ x\ =:$ where $=:$ is an assignment operator with its arguments in reverse order.

Slightly more interesting is the concurrent assignment, such as $x, y := y, x$ which swaps the value of x and y. This example illustrates that, in general,

$$v_0, v_1 := e_0, e_1$$

cannot be translated into

$$v_1\ v_0\ e_0 := e_1 :=\qquad .$$

This translation is incorrect if v_0 occurs in e_1. For the sake of correctness, no $:=$ or $=:$ should precede any of the expressions (including expressions in subscripts in the v_i). Examples of correct translations are

$$v_0\ e_0\ v_1\ e_1 := :=$$

and

$$e_0\ v_0\ e_1\ v_1 =: =:$$

14.5   Parameters

Various parameter-passing mechanisms exist in program notations. In this section, we discuss a possible implementation of some of them. We begin with the simplest and best-understood kind, value parameters. They are exactly like the arguments to the operators in expressions. Therefore, we try to make their implementation identical. In the case of an operator, the arguments are pushed on the stack and then the operator is invoked. Hence, in the case of value parameters, the actual parameters are pushed on the stack and then the procedure is called. Here is an example.

procedure $p(x, y)$;
$\qquad |[\textbf{var}\ a, b;\ \cdots]|$
$p(e, f)$

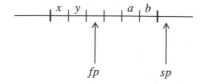

FIGURE 14.3. Stack layout for procedure with parameters.

When the frame for p has been created, the stack is as shown in Figure 14.3. The procedure frame contains two auxiliary variables and local variables a and b. No matter what the location of the procedure frame is, parameters x and y are found at the two locations preceding it. We may, therefore, address x and y as $fp-2$ and $fp-1$, respectively, or as $sp-6$ and $sp-5$. That is all there is to addressing value parameters. Freeing the memory locations they occupy is no big deal either. Upon procedure exit, sp is not decreased by k (see Section 14.3.2) but by k plus the number of parameters.

Result parameters are, in a sense, complementary to value parameters. In this case, variables are listed in the procedure call and expressions are listed at the end of the procedure body. The assignment is to take place after completing the body and before continuing with the statement that follows the call. The obvious implementation is to let the procedure return the values to be assigned on top of the stack, and to postfix the procedure call with the corresponding assignments.

A reference parameter is quite different. It does not stand for a local variable that has an initial value assigned at procedure entry or whose final value is used after procedure exit. It is a local name for a variable identified in the procedure call. A variable is identified by an address. We may allocate a storage location to a reference parameter in the same way we handle value parameters. The difference, however, is that this storage location does not contain a value, but, instead, the address of the variable it stands for. A reference to that variable (via the reference parameter) then consists of two steps: first, the address of the parameter is determined, and the contents of the storage location (which is another address) is fetched; then the latter address is used to access the variable.

In ALGOL or PASCAL, procedures can be passed as parameters. At the call of any procedure, variable env is set to a value that characterizes the scope in which a procedure is executed. All variables global to the procedure being called are in the frame pointed at by env, or can be reached from its static link. If a procedure is called that is not a formal parameter, then this frame can be accessed from the calling procedure. If the procedure is a formal parameter, then this frame does occur in the stack but may not be accessible from the calling procedure. For example, in

```
|[ var a, b, c
   procedure p(procedure q);
     |[var d, e ⋯ q ⋯]|
   procedure r;
     |[ var f, g, h
        procedure s;
          |[var i, j ⋯]|
          ⋯ p(s) ⋯
     ]|
     ⋯ r ⋯
]|
```

the set of variables global to *s* consists of *a*, *b*, *c*, *f*, *g*, *h*, whereas the set of variables accessible at the call contains *a*, *b*, *c*, *d*, *e*. What is needed to address the variables global to a procedure is a pointer to the frame of its textually enclosing procedure — just like *env* that we used before. The only difference is that the value for *env* cannot be computed at the location where the call occurs, it has to be passed as a parameter. In the example, the information needed to pass a procedure as a parameter consists of two parts: the context in which it executes plus the flow-of-control information discussed in the next section. Both are available at the position where the procedure is passed as actual parameter. In some programming languages, procedures that are passed as parameters are restricted to be procedures declared in the outermost block. We have seen that variable *env* need not be assigned a value when such a procedure is called. Hence, such formal procedures can be implemented without representing the scope information, thereby saving one pointer.

14.6   Flow of Control

The object program consists of instructions that are executed in some order. Sometimes the order is not fixed and depends on the outcome of previous instructions. The mechanisms that can be used for causing control to flow from one instruction to the next are discussed in this section. Essentially, two methods exist, which we call the *explicit* and the *implicit sequencing* method. The explicit method is to embed in every instruction the address of the next instruction to be executed. The implicit method is to execute instructions in the order in which they occur in store, with the exception of the so-called jump instructions that transfer control to an explicitly-mentioned storage location. The advantage of explicit control is simplicity; the advantage of implicit control is that it is more efficient in number of bits. Implicit control is also more amenable to pipelined execution, an issue that we will touch upon later. Many processors are constructed out of even simpler processors that are then programmed to interpret our object programs. We will examine an example of such a machine in more detail later, and we will see that the object machine uses the implicit sequencing method, whereas the underlying machine uses the explicit method.

How do the jump instructions encode the address of the next instruction to be executed? Again, various options exist. One is to list the address explicitly as part of the instruction. Another is to specify the distance between the present and the next instruction. The latter, called relative addressing, usually requires fewer bits. It is not unusual to find two relative jump instructions: one for jumps that bridge only a small distance and therefore take only a few bits, and one for jumps that bridge a long distance and therefore require many more bits. In this section, we are not concerned with the actual encoding, and we indicate the address of the next instruction by referring to a label; the label prefixes the target instruction.

As before, we write $\tau(s)$ for the translation of a construct s. We let $\tau(s)$ be a sequence of instructions whose execution starts with the first instruction in the sequence, if any. Upon completion of $\tau(s)$, control flows to the instruction that textually follows $\tau(s)$, whatever instruction that may be. As a result, explicit entry and exit points of an instruction sequence need not be introduced. This protocol allows us to define $\tau(s0;\ s1)$ simply as the catenation of $\tau(s0)$ and $\tau(s1)$. More interesting than sequential composition is the if-statement. We define $\tau(\textbf{if}\ b\ \textbf{then}\ s0\ \textbf{else}\ s1)$ in terms of $\tau(b)$, $\tau(s0)$, and $\tau(s1)$. Remember that $\tau(b)$ is the translation of a boolean expression and, therefore, its execution amounts to producing a boolean value on top of the stack. If it is *true*, $\tau(s0)$ is to be executed, and if it is *false*, $\tau(s1)$ is to be executed. Hence, a so-called conditional jump instruction is required that takes one value from the top of the stack and transfers control to either the next instruction in line or to the address given by the label. We may write $\tau(\textbf{if}\ b\ \textbf{then}\ s0\ \textbf{else}\ s1)$ as

$$\tau(b)$$
conditional jump if *false* to $l0$
$$\tau(s0)$$
jump to $l1$
$l0:\ \tau(s1)$
$l1:$

The symmetry between $s0$ and $s1$ has been distorted, since execution of $s0$ is followed by an unconditional jump to ensure that control flows to the instruction following the whole sequence. Here are a few other translations.

$$\tau(\textbf{if}\ b\ \textbf{then}\ s)\qquad =\qquad \tau(b)$$
conditional jump if *false* to l
$$\tau(s)$$
$l:$

$$\tau(\textbf{repeat } s \textbf{ until } b) \quad = \quad l: \quad \tau(s)$$
$$\tau(b)$$
conditional jump if *false* to l

$$\tau(\textbf{while } b \textbf{ do } s) \quad = \quad l0: \tau(b)$$
conditional jump if *false* to $l1$
$$\tau(s)$$
jump to $l0$
$$l1:$$

All these translations use only the conditional jump if *false* — no conditional jump if *true* is needed. Also, all translations are simple in the sense that the translations of the subparts occur in the same order in the object program text as the subparts occur in the source program. Neither property holds for the following alternative translation of the while statement.

$$\tau(\textbf{while } b \textbf{ do } s) \quad = \quad \text{jump to } l0$$
$$l1: \tau(s)$$
$$l0: \tau(b)$$
conditional jump if *true* to $l1$

The procedure call presents a new aspect. According to the ALGOL 60 report, execution of a procedure call is equivalent to substituting the body at the position of the call, and then executing the expanded text. Textual substitution is not attractive, since it makes the object program much longer than the source program. In the case of recursion, it is not even possible to come up with a finite object text. Obviously, an implementation that avoids textual substitution is called for.

Consider procedure declaration **procedure** p; s and procedure call p. Textual substitution would boil down to the translations

$$\tau(\textbf{procedure } p; s) = \epsilon$$

(no code is generated for the procedure declaration) and $\tau(p) = \tau(s)$ (the translation of the procedure call is the translation of body s). This is the translation that we said is unacceptable and, in fact, it is undoable. A possible solution is to include $\tau(s)$ only once in the object text and to let $\tau(p)$ consist of instructions that cause control to flow from procedure call to procedure body, and vice versa. The first half is easy: to go from call to body, we insert a jump instruction whose argument labels the first instruction of $\tau(s)$. From body to call is less obvious, since a program may contain many different calls of the same procedure. Hence, the instruction executed after the body is completed transfers control to a destination that depends on the call. One "solution" is to let $\tau(s)$ be followed by a jump instruction whose destination label is substituted when calling the procedure. It is a proper solution only if that jump instruction is executed before any other label is substituted in the same instruction. In other words, it is a proper solution only if execution of the procedure body is completed before it is called again. If there is no recursion, then this criterion is met; if there is recursion, then it is violated. For the sake of recursion we need a different implementation. By the way, if the object program text is stored in so-called read only memory (ROM), then it is not possible to substitute for parts of the program text; this is yet another reason for demanding a different implementation.

The procedure that is being completed is the one that was called most recently (and has not yet been completed); this implies that a stack may be used for holding the destinations of jump instructions that terminate procedure bodies. The procedure frame contains a location that has not been used thus far. We use this location for storing this address of the instruction at which execution is to resume, and define τ as

$$\tau(\textbf{procedure } p; s) = \quad lp: \; m[sp] := env; \; m[sp+1] := ra;$$
$$sp := sp + k;$$
$$\tau(s);$$
$$sp := sp - k; \; \text{jump to } m[sp+1]$$

$$\tau(p) \qquad\qquad = \qquad env := \text{pointer to scope}; \; ra := l;$$
$$\text{jump to } lp$$
$$l:$$

in which we recognize *entry*, *exit*, and *call* as discussed in a previous section. For the purpose of efficiently encoding the object text, it is advantageous to introduce one instruction that abbreviates the sequence

$$ra := l;$$
$$\text{jump to } lp$$
$$l:$$

for the procedure call, since label l is then implicit. This label is usually referred to as the *return address*.

14.7   A Word About Big and Small

In the discussion on nomenclature, we have assumed that the value of a variable fits in one storage location, a so-called word. This assumption, however, is not always realistic, as shown in the discrepancy in size between the representation of a boolean, an integer, and an array. We shall first look at methods for dealing with variables whose values are too big to fit in a word. Thereafter, we say a few words about small ones.

A value exceeding the word size is distributed over a number of words. If consecutive words are chosen, they can be characterized by one address together with the number of words. By doing so, the object nomenclature is no longer completely closed since only one of those words is referenced explicitly and the others are referenced implicitly. The larger the values are, the more open the nomenclature becomes and the less efficient the encoding of names becomes. An effective method of making the nomenclature closed again is to introduce *descriptors*. A descriptor is small, that is, it fits in one or two words, and it consists of relevant properties of the large variable to which it corresponds. Instead of storing the large variable in the stack, we may store the large variable anywhere, store its address in the descriptor, and store the descriptor in the stack. A reference to the large variable is then translated into a reference to its descriptor; during execution, this is inspected to derive the address of the large variable. For example, if the address $fp + j$ is used for a variable of n words, then the large variable does not occupy storage locations $fp + j$ through $fp + j + n - 1$ but occupies locations a through $a + n - 1$, where a is the address stored in the descriptor in location $fp+j$. If a descriptor contains nothing more than the address of the variable to which it corresponds, we have $m[fp + j] = a$, and referring to the variable is then called indirect addressing. It is similar to the way in which we handled reference parameters.

A disadvantage of introducing descriptors for large variables is that small and large variables are no longer treated uniformly. (What is the proper size beyond which to use descriptors?) In order to restore uniformity, one might omit descriptors altogether and accept the open nomenclature; or one might use descriptors for all variables, big and small, and accept the overhead of indirect addressing on every reference. In the latter case, one might introduce the trick (or technique) of using two kinds of descriptors, those introduced before and the so-called self-relative descriptors that do not contain the address of the corresponding variable but contain the variable itself. If the distinction between ordinary and self-relative descriptors is part of the descriptor, then the difference may be invisible at the level of the instruction sequence.

Introducing descriptors has repercussions on many of the instructions that we have already discussed, and invites further changes. We mention a few examples.

Within a procedure body, value parameters are treated as local variables. They are initialized by leaving the value of an expression on top of the stack. Since variables have descriptors, values in the stack have to have descriptors. Consequently, instruction *pushvalue(x)* either copies the descriptor of x (if it is self-relative) or copies the value to which the descriptor corresponds and constructs a descriptor for the copy.

In the discussion of translating expressions, we have not dealt with types. They do, however, play a role in the translation, since it is quite reasonable to expect different representations for integer and real numbers, and different operations for integer and real arithmetic. If the type of an arithmetic variable is part of its descriptor, then one add instruction can be used; it is decided during execution whether integer or real addition is to be performed. In passing, it might convert one integer operand to real if the other is a real number. Bits used for conveying type information are often called tag bits.

So far, we have discussed aspects of variables whose representation exceed the word size. Not very much is to be said about the reverse situation in which representations are so small that several of them fit into a single word. It often takes a number of instructions, say three to six, to load or assign a value that is part of a word. If a small variable is distributed over two storage locations, if it crosses a word boundary, it becomes even worse. Therefore, it may, be better to leave holes in store, to not use all bits of a word that contains some small variables. The situation becomes even worse if alignment requirements exist. Alignment is the requirement to make the word boundaries depend on the size of the variable being referenced, such as: if the variable has a size of $8n$ bits, then the word boundary must be at a storage location whose address is a multiple of n. Consequently, if larger variables are referenced, there are fewer word boundaries; this implies that often a variable occupies part of a word only. Since partial words are not identified solely by the address of a storage location, it is usually very hard to implement reference parameters if the argument may be stored as a partial word.

14.8 Arrays

In this section, we concentrate on computing the address of an individual array element, given the beginning address of the array. Consider first the case of an array

   var a : **array** $[l..u]$ **of** *element*

with integers l and u as bounds and elements that each fit in one word. Assume that a occupies storage locations A through $A+u-l$. If the array elements are stored in order of increasing index, the address of element $a[i]$, for $l \le i \le u$, is given by $A+i-l$. Instead of computing $A+(i-l)$, we may compute $(A-l)+i$ and store $A-l$ wherever the address of a needs to be stored (for example, in its descriptor if descriptors are used). This saves one subtraction per index operation. Address $A-l$ is sometimes called the base address or virtual zero address. $A-l$ need not be the address of any of the array elements (namely if $l > 0$ or $u < 0$), and in fact it need not even be an address, for example, if $A < l$.

Next, assume that each element occupies n consecutive storage locations. Array a then occupies locations A through $A+(u-l+1) \cdot n - 1$. Element $a[i]$ is stored in locations $A+(i-l) \cdot n$ through $A+(i-l+1) \cdot n-1$. As before, it may be preferable to rewrite $A+(i-l) \cdot n$ as $(A-l \cdot n)+i \cdot n$ and store $A-l \cdot n$ in the descriptor.

In PASCAL programs, an array element may be an array. For example,

> **var** a : **array** $[l..u]$ **of array** $[m..v]$ **of** *element*

or equivalently

> **var** a : **array** $[l..u, m..v]$ **of** *element*   .

Such a variable is often called a matrix. Assuming that a matrix element occupies one storage location, the previous paragraph applies when choosing n as $n = v - m + 1$. Hence, $a[i]$ occupies locations $A + (i - l) \cdot n$ through $A + (i - l + 1) \cdot n - 1$, and $a[i][j]$, which is equivalent to $a[i, j]$, has offset $j - m$ from the beginning of that stretch. Hence $a[i, j]$ is stored in location $A + (i - l) \cdot n + j - m$. In this case, it may be advantageous to rewrite the expression as $(A - l \cdot n - m) + i \cdot n + j$, and store $A - l \cdot n - m$ in the descriptor.

Another way of implementing the matrix is obtained by trying to make the handling of i (the first index) independent of n (the range of the second index) by transforming all rows into unit size. This can, again, be done by the introduction of descriptors. Each row corresponds to a descriptor, and these descriptors are stored in consecutive storage locations; in turn, one descriptor, which is then the matrix descriptor, corresponds to this sequence. As a consequence, accessing a matrix element avoids a multiplication at the expense of an extra indirection. In this case no relation is assumed between the various rows. They need not be stored consecutively; they need not even have the same size. Hence, this technique is applicable to such rare structures as triangular arrays.

Using either the extra descriptors or the address $A - l \cdot n - m$ may cause problems, however, if the program also refers to $a[i]$ without a second index. In PASCAL programs, one may write something like $a[i] := a[i+1]$ for copying an entire row of the matrix. No such operation on columns exists, which justifies the asymmetry in the implementation. In languages that do not support operations on arrays, such as ALGOL 60 and C, all operations on arrays are on their scalar elements and never on rows or columns. The asymmetry is in this case not justified by the source program notation. We may therefore look for mappings of matrix elements to storage locations that are more symmetric. We mention just one method; it works properly if the matrix is square and the number of rows and columns is a power of 2. Matrix a with n^2 elements is mapped onto storage locations A through $A + n^2 - 1$. The mapping is defined recursively as follows. If $n = 1$, the matrix consists of only one element, which is mapped on location A. If $n = 2k$, the matrix is partitioned into four equally large quadrants, as shown in Figure 14.4. Quadrants are mapped in the same way on the following locations:

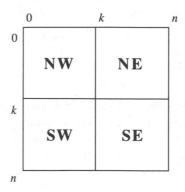

FIGURE 14.4. Partitions of a square matrix.

$$
\begin{aligned}
NW &: A &&\dots A + k^2 - 1 \\
NE &: A + k^2 &&\dots A + 2k^2 - 1 \\
SW &: A + 2k^2 &&\dots A + 3k^2 - 1 \\
SE &: A + 3k^2 &&\dots A + 4k^2 - 1
\end{aligned}
$$

The mapping is applied recursively; each quadrant that consists of more than 1 element is again partitioned into 4 quadrants, and so on. The address of element $a[i, j]$ is then $A + zip(i - l, j - m)$, where

$$
\begin{aligned}
zip(x, y) = [\ & x = 0 \wedge y = 0 \rightarrow 0 \\
\| \ & x > 0 \vee y > 0 \rightarrow zip(x \textbf{ div } 2, y \textbf{ div } 2) \cdot 4 \\
& \qquad\qquad\qquad + (x \textbf{ mod } 2) \cdot 2 + y \textbf{ mod } 2 \\
]&
\end{aligned}
$$

Look at the binary representation of x, y, and $zip(x, y)$ to find out why *zip* is called *zip*. For many pairs i, j the difference in address between $a[i, j]$, $a[i + 1, j]$, and $a[i, j + 1]$ is small, which makes this mapping attractive in a context where "locality" is an important property.

14.9 Side Effects

During execution of a PASCAL program, the type of a variable does not change, and therefore the tag bits mentioned earlier are not needed. It is useful to include in a descriptor those bits whose values do change during execution. Imagine that we have a *resize* operation on arrays that changes the lower and upper bound of a given array to two new values. Array elements that have an index in both the old and new range retain their value; others are undefined. The implementation of this operation is nontrivial and seems to be doable only if the current bounds are stored somewhere, say in the descriptor of the array variable. Consider an assignment of the form $a[i] := e$, where e is an expression that contains a function call and the function has as a side effect that it resizes array a. One way the assignment might have been translated is to determine first the address of the left-hand side $(a[i])$, then determine the value of the right-hand side (e), and finally to perform the assignment. In this case, the assignment might be performed to an array element that is no longer part of the array and might point to an address that, in the meanwhile, has been allocated to a different variable. Such an unfortunate situation can arise in many ways. For example, we may write

$$p\uparrow := e, \qquad a[i] := e, \qquad v.f := e \qquad ,$$

where evaluation of expression e changes pointer p, index i, or the tagfield of variant record v to make field f (in)accessible. Side effects are the result of a function call that changes global variables or parameters.

> **Note:** The side effects mentioned here are a horror. In the design of program notations, attempts have been made to exclude all side effects. Usually, the result is either that the horrible side effects are harder to obtain or that useful side effects are impossible. An example of a useful side effect is a boolean function on an integer argument that checks whether the argument is a prime number. The function might build up a table of prime numbers that it extends from time to time to speed up subsequent calls to the same function. If the table is not used elsewhere, then this side effect is harmless. This technique is known as *memoization*.

Assume that we choose to implement checks for such side effects during program execution. This means that, for example, during evaluation of e in $p\uparrow := e$, checks are to be performed on the absence of assignments to p. To that end, we may include in the descriptor of p a boolean to indicate that p is temporarily unassignable. If an assignment is attempted while the boolean is *true*, then execution of the program is abandoned, and an error message may be produced. Before evaluating e, this boolean in the descriptor of p is set to *true*; and after evaluating e, this boolean is reset to *false*. However, if the function, in turn, contains an assignment $p\uparrow := e'$, then resetting the assignability boolean after completing the latter assignment should leave the boolean *true* because the assignment statement $p\uparrow := e$ has not yet been completed. It turns out that a single boolean is insufficient; what we need is an integer instead of a boolean. If the integer is positive, then the variable is unassignable; if it is zero, then the variable can be assigned a value. Instead of setting the boolean to *true* before evaluating e, and setting it to *false* after evaluating e, the integer is incremented and decremented. This phenomenon, the step from booleans to natural numbers, occurs quite often. Let us call it naturalization.

14.10 Peephole Optimization

The object text that results from translation is a sequence of instructions. In this section, we look at a technique for changing that sequence into another that has the same effect but is shorter, requires less time to execute, or both. Such techniques are generally known under the name optimization, although improvement would be more appropriate. The particular technique we focus on is called peephole optimization. It is based on the observation that any consecutive subsequence of instructions may be replaced by another one that has the same effect.

Why should it be necessary to add peephole optimization as some sort of afterthought? Wouldn't it be much easier to change function τ (the function that defines the translation) in such a way that it produces the improved program text directly? The answer depends a bit on the translation and on the improvements; but in general it is preferable to deal with them separately. In this section, we discuss one simple example. In the next section, we will see more examples. Consider replacing each occurrence of the two-instruction sequence

>   not
>   jump if *false* to *l*

by

>   jump if *true* to *l*

where instruction "not" negates a boolean value on top of the stack.

> **Note**: This replacement is, of course, incorrect if the conditional "jump if *false*" is itself the target of a jump instruction. This provides us with yet another reason for writing explicit labels, because now the absence of a label indicates that control cannot be transferred to an instruction other than by sequential flow of control.

Instruction "not" is generated by the part of the compiler that translates boolean expressions, and the conditional jump is generated by the part that deals with, for example, the repeat statement. We might change τ to produce the shorter form directly.

$$\tau(\textbf{repeat } s \textbf{ until } \neg b) = l : \tau(s)$$
$$\tau(b)$$
$$\text{jump if } \textit{true} \text{ to } l$$
$$\tau(\textbf{repeat } s \textbf{ until } b) \;\; = l : \tau(s)$$
$$\tau(b)$$
$$\text{jump if } \textit{false} \text{ to } l$$

We have to be very careful with such contraptions since it is not clear to which syntactic category b belongs. It is, in the first alternative, definitely not the case that b is an arbitrary boolean expression. For example, to "**repeat** s **until** $\neg p \wedge q$" applies the second alternative of f, not the first. In order to produce an unambiguous definition of f, we are forced to use a lot more case analysis for describing b accurately; most of the syntax for expressions is then found in the repeat statement, and then also in the while statement, in the if statement, and so on. The explosive growth in the definition of τ will be reflected by a similar growth in the size of the compiler. It is much more attractive to stick to a clearly separated translation and optimization, since that allows both of them to be rather simple.

Peephole optimization can be implemented with a window of limited size (the peephole). The window is positioned on the object text, thereby exposing a consecutive subsequence of instructions. This sequence is compared to the patterns for which a replacement has been specified and the substitution is performed if a match exists. Finally, the window is repositioned. Two remarks are in order. First, we show that the result of peephole optimization may depend on the order in which the substitutions are performed. As an example, consider, in addition to the replacement above, replacing each occurrence of

> not
> not

by the empty sequence. Both replacements apply to the three-instruction sequence

> not
> not
> jump if *false* to l

and they lead to

> not   and   jump if *false* to l
> jump if *true* to l

respectively, both of which are irreducible under the two substitutions. In this case, uniqueness is guaranteed by adding the rule to replace

> not   by   jump if *false* to l
> jump if *true* to l

but in other cases it may not always by so easy to find additional rules. Fortunately, uniqueness is not really required. Absence of uniqueness just means that the result is not unique — the improved program will still be equivalent to the original one, but possibly not optimal.

Our second remark concerns the size and repositioning of the window. Usually one restricts movements of the window to be in one direction only, from beginning to end of the text, say. Suppose that the only two replacements are to replace

> not   by   jump if *false* to *l*
> jump if *true* to *l*

and

> not   by   jump if *true* to *l*
> jump if *false* to *l*

A sequence of many instances of "not" followed by a conditional jump is reducible to only a conditional jump, but it requires that the window move backwards a bit after a replacement has been performed. Another solution is to add more substitution patterns: one for every number of "not" occurrences followed by a conditional jump. This, however, requires an unbounded window size. Yet another solution is to add the replacement that two consecutive instances of "not" will be replaced with the empty sequence. Again, these solutions are hard to generalize. A better solution is to let peephole optimization consist of a number of sweeps of the window over the object text. In each sweep, the window moves monotonically over the object text, and sweeps are performed until no further replacements apply. The unbounded window size is thus transformed into an unbounded number of sweeps. A practical compromise between fast translation and optimal object texts is to bound the number of sweeps to one or two, say, since the first sweep usually yields the largest improvement. The restriction to one sweep allows peephole optimization to be straightforwardly incorporated in procedure *gen* ; all that is required is to compare the last few instructions in the sequence generated thus far, plus the new instruction to be appended, to the set of substitution patterns to see whether a replacement applies or not.

14.11   From Stack Machine to Register Machine

In the preceding sections, we have discussed aspects of a program notation that is well suited to automatic execution and suitable as a target for translation. In this section, we discuss what may be done to overcome discrepancies between this notation, which we call the stack machine language, and the notation used by our target computer, which we call the Mosaic machine language. The machine is described in Chapter 16 and has a set of registers instead of a stack. See [Sei92] for a more complete description.

First, and most important of all, a mapping of variables, like *sp*, onto the storage locations of the machine is designed. Our Mosaic machine has some storage locations that require fewer bits and less time to reference than general storage locations: the so-called registers. Therefore, we store sp in one of those registers. We do the same for some of the other "important" variables that play a role in the translation. (When using the addressing scheme that we described in Section 14.3 without fp, then sp is probably the only variable of this kind.)

Next, for each instruction of the stack machine we have to come up with a sequence of Mosaic instructions that has the same effect. Typically, this requires the introduction of a few more local variables. An example of a sequence for adding the two values on top of the stack is as follows. We give the sequence twice, once in a PASCAL-like notation and once in our machine language.

$sp := sp - 1$	DEC	$r11, r11$
$y := m[sp]$	MOVE	$@r11, r1$
$sp := sp - 1$	DEC	$r11, r11$
$x := m[sp]$	MOVE	$@r11, r0$
$x := x + y$	ADD	$r1, r0$
$m[sp] := x$	MOVE	$r0, @r11$
$sp := sp + 1$	INC	$r11, r11$

This translation assumes that sp is stored in register $r11$ and that temporary variables x and y are stored in registers $r0$ and $r1$. This is not the only possible translation. For example,

$sp := sp - 1$	DEC	$r11, r11$
$y := m[sp]$	MOVE	$@r11, r1$
$x := m[sp - 1]$	MOVE	$@r11(-1), r0$
$x := x + y$	ADD	$r1, r0$
$m[sp - 1] := x$	MOVE	$r0, @r11(-1)$

is another possibility. Like many other machines, the Mosaic has addressing modes in which a register is first decreased by one and then used as an address, or first used as an address and then increased by one. In view of these so-called auto-decrement and auto-increment addressing modes (see also Exercise 15), it is more attractive to let the stack expand from higher to lower addresses (and to change the sign of all offsets ...) and consider

$y := m[sp]$	MOVE	$@r11 + +, r1$
$sp := sp + 1$		
$x := m[sp]$	MOVE	$@r11, r0$
$x := x + y$	ADD	$r1, r0$
$m[sp] := x$	MOVE	$r0, @r11$

as a possibility. Because it is shorter than the other ones, this is the one we choose. This single stack-machine instruction leads to four Mosaic instructions. If we simply replace each stack-machine instruction by such a sequence, a technique that is called macro expansion, then the machine code program becomes unacceptably long. Many techniques exist for shortening this text; we mention five. One is to apply peephole optimization on this sequence in exactly the same way as described before. Consider the code for $a := b + c$. The stack-machine code is

> *pushvalue*(*b*)
> *pushvalue*(*c*)
> +
> *pushaddress*(*a*)
> =:

and this leads to

> MOVE $b, @--r11$
>
> MOVE $c, @--r11$
>
> MOVE $@r11++, r1$
> MOVE $@r11, r0$
> ADD $r1, r0$
> MOVE $r0, @r11$
>
> MOVE $\#a, @--r11$
>
> MOVE $@r11++, r1$
> MOVE $@r11++, @r1$

(where we have not concerned ourselves with the addresses for a , b , and c). Straightforward peephole optimization (merely combining two consecutive MOVEs, when the destination of the first is the source of the second) leads to

> MOVE $b, @--r11$
> MOVE $c, r1$
> MOVE $@r11, r0$
> ADD $r1, r0$
> MOVE $r0, @r11$
> MOVE $\#a, r1$
> MOVE $@r11++, @r1$,

which is shorter and faster and, therefore, to be preferred. More extensive peephole optimization can lead to even better code.

The second method is to use the procedure mechanism of the Mosaic machine, which is referred to as a subroutine mechanism. Each sequence of Mosaic instructions representing a stack-machine instruction is turned into a subroutine, and each occurrence of a stack-machine instruction is replaced by a subroutine call. The subroutine call overhead slows down execution, but the length of the machine code is reduced dramatically. In our example, we obtain one instance of

add : MOVE   @$r11 + +, r1$
        MOVE   @$r11, r0$
        ADD $r1, r0$
        MOVE $r0, $@$r11$
        JUMP pi

for the whole program, and an instance of

    CALL add, pi

for every occurrence of the stack-machine instruction for addition. We have introduced register pi (for program index) to handle the flow of control to and from the set of subroutines, which is often called the runtime package.

The third method is based on the observation that the Mosaic program now consists of a set of subroutines plus a long sequence of subroutine calls. Every subroutine call occupies two words, one encoding the call instruction and one encoding the subroutine's label. The first part is the same for all those calls, and we would like to factor out the common part. We do so by just omitting them from the long sequence and by changing the jump instruction that terminates every subroutine in the runtime package.

add : MOVE   @$r11 + +, r1$
        MOVE   @$r11, r0$
        ADD $r1, r0$
        MOVE $r0, $@$r11$
        JUMP   @$pi + +$

This technique halves the length of the long sequence of subroutine calls (by omitting the calls and retaining the arguments only) and is about as fast as the previous method. This technique is often called threaded code, since the runtime package is no longer a set of true subroutines but is a set of instruction sequences, threaded by the rest of the program text, namely, by the long sequence of addresses.

The fourth method is the transition from an open to a closed nomenclature. The long sequence of addresses that results from the previous technique mentions only a few addresses, typically about 50. They form an open nomenclature, and we use 16 bits to encode those 50 or so addresses. A tighter representation is possible by assigning consecutive numbers to the subroutines in the runtime package, replacing the addresses in the long sequence by the corresponding numbers, and including a mapping from these numbers back to the addresses in the Mosaic code. We can now use 6 or 8 bits for every element in the long sequence, thereby shortening it by another significant factor. With this technique, the runtime package is often called an interpreter. The overhead increases again because of the additional storage reference needed to go from a small number to an address.

The fifth technique is the use of a variable mapping of the stack onto the machine's registers and store. We have seen that we used both register $r0$ and $r1$ to hold an element that was the first or second element of the stack. However, they were used only within the short stretch of Mosaic instructions that encodes one stack instruction. We now widen their use a bit by letting the mapping of the stack be one of three possible mappings. We write $m[r11...]$ for the sequence of storage locations from $r11$ on.

(0) The stack is mapped to $m[r11...]$;

(1) The topmost element of the stack is in $r0$ and the remainder is mapped to $m[r11...]$;

(2) The topmost element of the stack is in $r1$, the second element is in $r0$, and the remainder is mapped to $m[r11...]$.

The translation of $a := b + c$ into stack-machine instructions was

> *pushvalue*(b)
> *pushvalue*(c)
> $+$
> *pushaddress*(a)
> $=:$

and we can now generate (assuming that we start in a state where mapping (0) is used)

```
{ mapping (0) }
MOVE      b, r0
{ mapping (1) }
MOVE      c, r1
{ mapping (2) }
ADD       r1, r0
{ mapping (1) }
MOVE      #a, r1
{ mapping (2) }
MOVE      r0, @r1
{ mapping (0) }       ,
```

which is a much better starting point then the translation we had before. Combined with some peephole optimization, this technique gives very good results. In practice, the combination of a variable mapping and a simple peephole optimizer is simpler and more effective than a fixed mapping and an extensive peephole optimizer. Sometimes the mechanism of a variable mapping is also found in hardware. It is then often called associative hardware, or a cache. Such a mechanism requires that the mapping currently being used be maintained during execution of the program. The variable mapping that we have discussed plays a role during compilation only.

14.12   Range Analysis

The idea of having a mapping that differs from instance to instance suggests even more possibilities for generating better code. Not only may the mapping of the stack differ from one place to the next, but also different code sequences can be selected for an operation, depending on the context in which it is used. For example, consider expression i **mod** n. Since the Mosaic does not have a divide instruction, we need, in general, a sequence of instructions for computing the quotient or remainder of integer division. This time-consuming operation requires two orders of magnitude more time than does addition. If, however, it is known that $i \geq 0$ and that n is a power of 2, then the code could select the least-significant $\log(n)$ bits of i. If it is known that $i \geq 0 \ \wedge \ n > 0$ and that i is not much more than n (say $i < 10n$), then the code for $r := i$ **mod** n might be something like

$$r := i; \ \textbf{while } r \geq n \textbf{ do } r := r - n \qquad ,$$

which repeatedly subtracts n to obtain the remainder. Because the quotient was given to be small, this is probably more efficient. If $0 \leq i < 2n$ then the loop might even be replaced with an if-statement. If it is only known that n is not zero, then at least the check to test for division by zero can be omitted. And so on.

A wealth of improvements are possible if certain properties are known about the range of subexpressions. Range analysis is a technique for deriving exactly this kind of information from the source text. It consists of establishing for each expression e values $lo(e)$ and $hi(e)$ that bound e, that is, $lo(e) \leq e \leq hi(e)$. For example, if e is the constant k, then $lo(e) = hi(e) = k$. If e is variable i declared with subrange type 1..10, then $lo(e) = 1$ and $hi(e) = 10$. If e is $e_0 + e_1$, then $lo(e) = lo(e_0) + lo(e_1)$ and $hi(e) = hi(e_0) + hi(e_1)$.

If we have declarations

> **const** $n = \cdots$
> **var** $i : 1..n$
> $a : \textbf{array } [1..n] \textbf{ of } 1..n \qquad ,$

then we may omit bound checks in indexed variables like $a[i]$ or even in $a[(i \textbf{ mod } n) + 1]$. On the other hand, bound checks may be required in assignments to i. However, in the case $i := (i \textbf{ mod } n) + 1$ they can be omitted. Even in constructs like

> **for** $i := 1$ **to** n **do** $a[i] := (i \textbf{ mod } n) + 1 \qquad ,$

no checks are required — neither in assignments to i and $a[i]$ nor for the subscript in $a[i]$.

If a variable is declared without a subrange, then we cannot do better than to take the smallest and largest representable values, respectively.

In this case, range analysis becomes less effective, but usually it is still worthwhile. For an arbitrary integer x, we can still assert that x **mod** 10 is in the range from 0 through 9, and this information can again be used to good advantage. A constant expression is a special case of an expression for which $lo(e) = hi(e)$. The more general and useful technique of range analysis is at least as easy to implement as a technique for distinguishing constant expressions from other expressions.

14.13   Concurrency

In this section, we look at concurrency. One might be tempted to consider an implementation in which one processor per process is available. In many programs, however, at any time many processes are blocked, which would imply that the capacity of many processors goes unutilized. It is therefore more efficient to have a number of processes per processor and to multiplex the processor capacity over the processes that are not blocked. This activity, called process scheduling, is one of the aspects that we discuss here. In this section, we consider the case of multiplexing a single processor. In a later chapter, we briefly look at multiple processors.

The problem of process scheduling first arose in multiprogramming systems: these systems contained only a very small number of processors (one or two) and several "user" programs were run concurrently as independent processes in order to keep the expensive processors busy while a slow input/output operation was performed.

We discuss the implementation of channels and their associated input and output operations also in this section, because these operations cause processes to become blocked or unblocked. These transitions trigger the process scheduling algorithms.

First, we consider the representation of a process. What is the information that is needed to execute an action of any given process? It requires the encoding of the action, plus the variables that it operates on. The action is given by the code plus the program counter, and the variables are given by the contents of the stack plus the registers, if any. Assume that we do the process scheduling in such a way that the contents of the registers are not needed. This simplifies the representation of a process and restricts the moments at which the scheduling comes into action to those moments where the registers contain no useful information.

If the store of the processor is large enough to accommodate the representation of all processes at any time, then disjoint storage segments can be allocated to distinct processes for storing their stacks. Only one instance of the program text, the code, is needed if we restrict ourselves to the case where the code is not modified during execution. If we assume that the program counter is saved on top of the stack, then the stack pointer is the only piece of information needed for representing a process.

The processor capacity is to be multiplexed in a fair way over all processes that are not blocked. To implement this fairness, the processes that
are ready for execution are recorded in a queue. If a processor switches
execution to another process, it selects one from the head of the queue,
and if a suspended process becomes ready for execution it is appended to
the tail of the queue. This leads to the following data structure and operations. Remember that we discuss the case of a single processor. Since the
process multiplexing is done explicitly, we have a lot of control over the
interleaving of actions in different processes. As a result, mutual exclusion
is no problem.

> **type** *process = integer*;
> **var** *readyq* : **record** *hd, tl* : *process* **end**;
>   { initially *readyq.hd = empty* }
> **procedure** *schedule*(*p* : *process*);
> |[{ process *p* is neither executing nor in the ready queue }
>   [*readyq.hd = empty* → *readyq.hd := p*
>   ∥ *readyq.hd ≠ empty* → *m*[*readyq.tl*] := *p*
>   ];
>   *readyq.tl := p*; *m*[*p*] := *empty*
>   ]|
> **procedure** *select*;
> |[{ *readyq.hd ≠ empty* }
>   *sp := readyq.hd*; *readyq.hd := m*[*readyq.hd*]
>   ]|

Some remarks are in order here. A process is identified by its stack pointer.
We assume that it points to the lowest free address of the process's stack.
The first free location will be used for creating a linked list: the list of
processes that are in the ready queue. If the process is not in the ready
queue, this extra word is not used. The extra word is either *empty* for the
last process in the ready queue, or a pointer to the next process in the ready
queue otherwise. The ready queue is empty just when *readyq.hd = empty*.
If it is nonempty, *readyq.tl* identifies the last process in the queue. Constant
empty is chosen to differ from all possible values of the stack pointer.

So much for the ready queue. Operation *schedule*(*p*) adds process *p* to
the ready queue. It does so by using the extra location whose address is
the process's stack pointer (given by *p*) for the link in the ready queue.
Access to this storage location should not interfere with the operation of the
present process — the process that executes *schedule*(*p*) — and therefore
p should not be the executing process. Similarly, it should not be any
process that is already in the ready queue. That is why the precondition
of *schedule* is needed.

Procedure *select* selects a process from the ready queue and continues
its execution. No actions are undertaken to record the state of the present
process; if its state is relevant, it should be recorded before *select* is per-

formed. Statement $readyq.hd := m[readyq.hd]$ removes the first process from the ready queue. Statement $sp := readyq.hd$ sets the processor's stack pointer to the stack pointer of the first process in the ready queue. It assumes that sp is not a variable of the program, but the processor register that contains the stack pointer. Execution of procedure $select$ is then completed with the instruction that continues execution at the location of the procedure call by jumping to the return address found on top of the stack. Due to the assignment to the stack pointer, however, execution continues where the process that has just been removed from the ready queue had been suspended. This is the actual process switching. Because we assumed that no other information than the stack pointer is needed for executing a process, no other actions are required. In particular, no actions to save or restore registers are needed.

Assertion $readyq.hd \neq empty$ has been included as a precondition of procedure $select$. No process can be selected if the ready queue is empty. If all processes would be executed by one processor then we might include a check for this condition, and print a message that a deadlock has occurred if $readyq.hd = empty$. If some process is executed by another processor (including a special-purpose processor such as a peripheral device) then we may not conclude that a deadlock has occurred if the ready queue is empty: it might become nonempty due to the activity of the other processor. The only thing that can be done in this case is to wait until the ready queue becomes nonempty.

$$*[\ readyq.hd = empty \rightarrow skip\ ]$$

The peripheral devices lead to a new phenomenon. Peripherals are often used in conjunction with a so-called interrupt mechanism. If an operation is to be performed by a special-purpose device then the regular processor sends a message with the required information to the device. The device performs the operation and, upon completion, sends a message with completion information to the processor. The receipt of this message triggers execution of a so-called interrupt routine. Upon completion of the interrupt routine, execution of the program that has been interrupted resumes. Here is an example. Suppose that a character is to be read from the keyboard. A command is sent to the device that communicates with the keyboard and the present process is suspended (by storing its stack pointer in some global variable and selecting another process for execution). After a while, when the character has been read, a message is sent to the processor. The interrupt routine then schedules the suspended process. Fine, except that we now have a little problem. Assume that some process executes a $schedule$ operation, finds $readyq.hd = empty$, and is about to assign a new value to $readyq.hd$. Next, the interrupt routine is activated, which also leads to performing a $schedule$ operation, thereby changing $readyq.hd$. Resuming the former program, $readyq.hd$ is now overwritten with the parameter of $schedule$ and, hence, one process is "lost" from the ready queue. The problem is that mutual exclusion is no longer guaranteed, not even on a single-processor system: in the presence of interrupts two programs are interleaved, namely the regular program and the interrupt handler. It is as if two activities are going on concurrently.

The solution to this mutual exclusion problem is one that is a tailor-made solution instead of one of the mutual exclusion algorithms that we discussed in the last chapter. The processor is extended with a new boolean register, the interrupt mask register imr. If a message from a peripheral device arrives, the processor executes the interrupt routine only if imr is $true$ (if interrupts are "enabled"). In case $\neg imr$ (interrupts are "disabled"), execution of the interrupt handler is delayed until imr becomes $true$ again. The operations that call $schedule$ and $select$ are extended with setting imr to $false$ at the beginning and back to $true$ at the end. The interrupt routine saves the value of imr and sets imr to $false$ at its beginning, and restores imr to its previous value upon completion. This ensures that at most one execution of the interrupt routine is active at any time, even if multiple interrupts are received (almost) simultaneously. If the processor is executing the idle loop in which it waits until the ready queue is nonempty, interrupts should not be disabled.

Next, we have a look at the communication actions that trigger execution of the process scheduling operations. Let input and output operations be translated as

$$
\begin{aligned}
c?x &\longrightarrow io(c, x, true) \\
c!x &\longrightarrow io(c, x, false)
\end{aligned}
$$

then it remains to write the code for procedure io. The channels that we have discussed in the previous chapter have the property that at any moment, at most one process is suspended on a communication action on that channel. The action can be either an input or an output action. The process is unblocked by another process that performs the corresponding output or input operation. The second process needs the information of which process is suspended. This information needs therefore be stored in the representation of the channel variable c. Using the fact that at most one process is suspended on c, we choose to implement a channel as a pointer.

$$
\begin{aligned}
c = empty &: \text{no process is suspended on a communication via } c \\
c \neq empty &: \text{one process is suspended on a communication via } c \,; \\
&\quad \text{its stackpointer is given by } c
\end{aligned}
$$

The implementation of a channel and of procedure io is now straightforward.

```
type  channel = process;
procedure io(var c : channel;  var x : msg;  read : boolean);
  [ c = empty → c := sp;  select
  ‖ c ≠ empty → [   read → x := m[m[c − 4]]
                ‖ ¬read → m[m[c − 4]] := x
                ];
                m[c − 5] := m[c − 2];  schedule(c − 4);
                c := empty
  ]
```

Some remarks are in order, mainly notational. In the first alternative, the value of stack pointer register sp is stored in variable c, followed by selecting another process for execution. These two actions correspond to suspending the present process.

In the second alternative, the message is copied from parameter x in the writing process to parameter x in the reading process. The number of words copied depends on the type of x. Since c is the stack pointer of the other process, $m[c − 1]$ is its static link, $m[c − 2]$ is its return address, $m[c − 3]$ is its parameter $read$ and $m[c − 4]$ its parameter x. Since x is a reference parameter, $m[c − 4]$ is the address of the corresponding actual parameter.

In order to schedule the other process for execution, the static link and the three parameters are removed from the top of its stack, and the return address is copied to the top of its stack. The latter is accomplished through $m[c − 5] := m[c − 2]$ and removal of the other four is accomplished by using $c − 4$ as argument to the $schedule$ operation. Upon completion thereof, both the reading and the writing process are ready for execution (one is presently executing, the other is in the ready queue), and no process is suspended on the channel, hence $c := empty$.

So much for the process scheduling algorithms. Is there any reason to believe that the implementation is fair? Does every process get a turn? It may be that a process never performs any input or output operation. With our algorithms, that process never invokes the $select$ operation and, therefore, no other process will ever be executed. One can force a regular invocation of $select$ by equipping the processor with a clock that sends interrupt signals after specified time intervals, called time slices. Upon reception of a time-slice interrupt, the interrupt routine enters the presently executing process at the tail of the ready queue, and selects the process at the head of the queue for execution. See Exercise 19.

Time-slice interrupts effectively introduce concurrency even in one processor. This creates havoc on procedure io since the statements that access the channel variable are no longer mutually exclusive. Time-slice interrupts should be disabled during execution of io.

One aspect that remains is the storage allocation of processes. Without concurrent processes, a stack was used for storing the program's variables.

In the presence of concurrent processes, a single stack no longer suffices. Each process needs its own stack and those stacks grow and shrink independently. When statement

$$S_0 \parallel S_1 \parallel \ldots S_n$$

is executed, a number of stacks are created, and upon completion they are all removed. If we think of these new stacks as linked to the stack of the process that executes the creating statement, then the resulting structure is a tree in which the nodes correspond to the stacks or to the processes. If the size and number of the individual statements can be determined from the program text then a fixed mapping of the stacks on storage locations can be devised. The stack of a process can then be allocated as a fixed-size array in the stack of the creating process. Otherwise, the mapping has to be done during program execution. This is a nontrivial activity that we do not discuss here.

14.14 Assembly

The text generated by a compiler is a sequence of instructions. This sequence is to be encoded in the representation used by the computer that is going to execute the object program. This encoding process is called assembly. Most instructions can be assembled independently of all other instructions. For example, in the Mosaic, the encoding of

MOVE $@r11 + +, r3$

is

0001000010110011   ,

independent of the context in which it occurs. In some cases, a dependency exists. Of course, in jump instructions, the encoding of the address of the next instruction depends on the label, and the address is unknown until (part of) the object program has been assembled. If it is possible to determine the size of each instruction without knowing the addresses corresponding to the labels, then assembly may be done in two phases. In the first phase, the size of each instruction is determined, and thereby the address of each label is also determined. In the second phase, each instruction is assembled. Assembling the jump instructions is then no problem, since the addresses of the labels are known.

Sometimes it is not possible to determine the size of an instruction without knowing the addresses of the labels. For example, in the Mosaic, a jump instruction fits in one word if the destination address is between 0 and 15; otherwise, it requires two words. In many machines, the target address is encoded as a span, which is the difference between the address of the next instruction in sequence and the address of the next instruction to be executed. Since most jump instructions occurring in a program have a small span, it is common practice to provide two different jump instructions; one instruction that fits in one word for small spans and one instruction that requires two words for large spans. The size of the instruction thus becomes span dependent. Making good use of the short encoding of jumps requires a different assembly process — the two-phase assembly will not do. One possibility is first to determine each label's address under the assumption that all jumps are long jumps. In an intermediate phase, for each jump, it is determined whether its destination is within the short span and, if it is, the size of the jump is changed from long to short. All labels that follow the jump have to have their address decreased by one. Finally, the actual assembly is done as before. By converting a long jump into a short jump, the span of no other jump increases. This strategy, therefore, produces a correct result. It may, however, be the case that such a conversion decreases the span of another jump that might thereby become eligible for a short encoding. A second strategy therefore consists of repeating the intermediate phase until no more long jumps can be transformed into short jumps. Even though this is clearly better than the first strategy, it does not necessarily lead to the shortest encoding, as illustrated by the following example.

$l0$: $\cdots$
          JUMP $l1$
          $\cdots$
          JUMP $l0$
          $\cdots$
$l1$: $\cdots$

Let the distance between the two jumps and their destinations be such that if one jump is encoded as a long jump, then the other one has to be encoded as a long jump also; but that if one of them is encoded as a short jump, then the other one may become short also. In the strategy above, jumps are converted from long to short one at a time; therefore, the possibility of short encoding is not discovered. A strategy that produces the optimal result is the following one. First, each label's address is determined as if all jumps are short jumps. Obviously this is not sufficient since for some jumps the destination may be outside the range of the short span. Therefore, in an intermediate phase, each short jump is inspected, and it is determined whether the destination is too far away; if it is, the jump is changed to a long jump. Such a conversion may lead to another jump's destination being out of range; hence, this intermediate phase is repeated until each jump either is long or has a destination that is within its short span. Finally, the actual assembly is done as before.

The two iterative strategies can be contrasted as follows. In the "pessimistic" strategy, the initial coding is correct in the sense that no short jump has a destination outside its span. The encoding is then reconsidered, one jump after the other, and each intermediate encoding is correct. In the "optimistic" strategy, the initial encoding is as short as possible, but it need not be correct. The encoding is then reconsidered, one jump after the other, until correct. Compare these two strategies with strategies for choosing an invariant and a guard of a repetition when the postcondition is of the form $P \wedge Q$.

14.15   Bibliographic Notes

The use of a display (cf. Exercise 6) and a stack for storing and addressing variables is due to [Dij60], [Dij63]. It also uses both a dynamic and a static chain for updating the *display* array. Using these chains without the *display* array was popularized by the portable Pascal compilers. A good discussion of the *display* can be found in [Gri71]. I have been using the version without *display* or dynamic chain for years, but I am not aware of any mention of this scheme in the literature.

Postfix notation is sometimes called *reverse Polish* notation. The Polish logician Łukasiewicz introduced, in 1936, a notation in which the operator precedes the two operands. This is also referred to as prefix notation. Caudafix notation is from [vdS85a]. Prefix, postfix, and caudafix notation share the property that no parentheses and precedence rules are needed. Rumor has it that Łukasiewicz invented his notation because parentheses were hard to produce with his typewriter.

The algorithm for assembling code for span-dependent instructions is from [Szy78].

14.16   Exercises

1. Extend the grammar for arithmetic expressions to include a unary + and −, that is, operators that take one argument and return the argument either unchanged or with the sign changed, respectively. Propose a postfix notation for them also. (You will find that you need different symbols to distinguish the unary operators from their binary relatives.) Give a function that translates the augmented infix grammar to the proposed postfix notation.

2. Give a grammar for caudafix expressions for the case where we have operators $op_{m,n}$ that take m arguments and return n results. Give the semantics by defining $\mathcal{M}$ for caudafix expressions.

3. Give the translation function τ that translates arithmetic expressions from infix to caudafix notation.

4. Suppose that in our postfix notation we do not have separate instruc-

tions for computing the quotient and remainder of integer division, but one instruction that pushes both onto the stack. Adapt τ to handle the new situation, giving the translation for expressions E **div** T and E **mod** T. Do you need to introduce additional operations?

5. Can you invert the procedures that translate infix to postfix expressions, and obtain procedures that translate from postfix to infix?

6. The static chain is used for addressing variables global to a procedure. The number of memory references required for accessing global variables equals the difference in nesting level between declaration and use of the variable. It can be made independent of this difference as follows. Introduce an array, called *display*. Let *display*[0] contain the last pointer of the static chain. Let *display*[1] contain the pointer next to the last, and so on. Hence, *display*[*nl*] contains the frame pointer of the procedure whose local variables have nesting level *nl*. Discuss how variables can be addressed, given array *display*.

7. The previous exercise introduced the *display*. Discuss how this array can be updated at procedure entry and exit. Besides the general case, also consider the special case where procedures are not passed as parameters. It has the following property. The set of variables global to a procedure that is being called is a subset of the set of variables accessible from the procedure containing the call, that is, the set of variables global to the calling procedure plus its local variables. Use this property to show the correctness of the following implementation in which nl is the nesting level of the procedure being called.

$$entry : m[sp] := display[nl];\ display[nl] := sp;\ sp := sp + k$$
$$exit : \quad sp := display[nl];\ display[nl] := m[sp]$$

Constant k is the size of the procedure frame being created.

8. We have given two translations for the while statement. Count the number of loop iterations for which the first is better, for which the second is better, and for which they are equally good.

9. Give a statement s with the property that our translation function τ produces a sequence of labels and instructions $\tau(s)$ in which one of the instructions is labeled with two different labels.

10. Propose a translation for the statement **for** $i := e_0$ **to** e_1 **do** s. Does it make a difference whether i occurs in e_1 or not? Would it be advantageous to know $e_0 \leq e_1$?

11. Prove that the address of element $a[i,j]$ is indeed given by $A + zip(i - l, j - m)$ in the case of the recursive mapping of matrices.

12. If we use the variable mapping of the stack as described in Section 14.11, then we need to come up with three implementations in terms of Mosaic instructions for each stack-machine instruction, one for every mapping encountered at the beginning of the instruction. In the text, we have given the implementation of the add instruction for mappings (0) and (2). Give the implementation if the mapping is (1). What is the mapping at the end of the code sequence that you propose? Give the mappings for the instructions =: and −, which differ from the one for + in the sense that the latter is symmetric in the two arguments that it pops from the stack, whereas the former two are asymmetric.

13. Boolean expressions can be handled in exactly the same way as arithmetic expressions. The method of using a variable mapping has even higher payoff for boolean expressions than it has for arithmetic expressions when the underlying machine has condition codes, as the Mosaic has. Explore this statement of fact by studying two stack-machine instructions. One pops two integer numbers from the stack and pushes 1 onto the stack if the first integer is less than the second, and 0 otherwise. The second instruction is the conditional jump: it pops a value from the stack, and then jumps to the label if the value is 0, and does not jump otherwise. Propose a variable mapping from the stack to the registers and conditions codes, and implement the two stack-machine instructions for the various mappings.

14. Write a subroutine in Mosaic machine code for computing the quotient and remainder of two natural numbers x and y. You may assume $0 \leq x < 2^{15} \wedge 0 < y < 2^{15}$. The numbers x and y are given in $r0$ and $r1$, respectively; hence, mapping (2) applies. Your program may use registers $r0$ through $r5$ only, and no other storage locations (other than for holding the instructions, of course). The values x and y need not be preserved. Indicate which registers hold the results x **div** y and x **mod** y. Prove the correctness of your program. (A program whose running time is proportional to x **div** y is unacceptable; go for a logarithmic solution.)

15. Consider the auto-increment and auto-decrement addressing modes. For example, the Mosaic instructions

$$\text{MOVE} \qquad x, @y + +$$
$$\text{MOVE} \qquad x, @ - -y$$

use postincrement and predecrement. Would it make sense to replace them by preincrement and postdecrement? Indicate how you would implement stack operations (push an element, pop an element, refer to the topmost element without popping it). How would you choose between the two pairs of addressing modes? Does it make sense to have a machine with the pair postincrement/postdecrement?

16. What is the proper definition of the range functions *lo* and *hi* for expressions that contain product, quotient, and remainder?

17. The remark that no checks are required in statements like $i :=$ $(i \textbf{ mod } n) + 1$ depends critically on the assumption that i has a value that has already been checked to be in the proper range. The latter assumption is probably not valid in the case where i has not been initialized. Discuss strategies for checking undefined variables.

18. Complete procedures *schedule*, *select*, and *io* to include the assignments to *imr*.

19. What is wrong with the following implementation of the time-slice interrupt?

   schedule(*sp*); *select*

Give a correct implementation.

20. Assume that statement

$$S_0 \parallel S_1 \parallel \ldots S_n$$

is translated into

$$\begin{aligned} &init(x, n); \; start(l_0, z_0); \; start(l_1, z_1); \; \ldots \; start(l_n, z_n); \\ &\text{jump to } m \,; \\ l_0 : \; &S_0; \; complete(x); \\ l_1 : \; &S_1; \; complete(x); \\ &\vdots \\ l_n : \; &S_n; \; complete(x); \\ m : \; &wait(x) \end{aligned}$$

where x is a fresh variable. Constant z_i is the number of stack locations needed for executing S_i. What data structure would you use for x? Specify and implement operations *init*, *wait*, *start*, and *complete*. State any assumptions you make on the allocation of storage space and addressing of variables.

21. Show that the last strategy for handling span-dependent jumps produces the shortest code.

15

An Example of a Compiler

This chapter contains an example of a small compiler that compiles programs written in a subset of Pascal into instructions for a stack machine, plus a program that acts like the stack machine. The latter is called an interpreter for the stack-machine.

15.1   The Program Notation Pascal-S

In this section, we give a short description of Pascal-S. Pascal-S is small enough to allow a full compiler to be exposed in a handful of pages, and large enough to expose most of the concepts that we have discussed in the previous chapter. We quote from Wirth's paper (cf. [Wir81]), which introduces this particular subset.

> The power of a language and its range of applications largely depend on its *data types* and associated operators. They also determine the amount of effort required to master a language. Pascal-S adheres in this respect largely to the tradition of ALGOL 60. Its primitive data types are the integers, the real numbers, and the boolean truth values. They are augmented in a most important and crucial way by the type *char*, representing the available set of printable characters. Omitted from Pascal are the scalar types and the subrange types.
>
> Pascal-S includes only two kinds of *data structures*: the **array** and the **record** (without variants). Omitted are the set and the file structure. The exceptions are the two standard textfiles input and output which are declared implicitly (but must be listed in the program heading). A very essential omission is the absence of pointer types and thereby of all dynamic structures. Of course, also all packing options (packed records, packed arrays) are also omitted.
>
> The choice of data types and structures essentially determines the complexity of a processing system. Statement and *control structures* contribute very little to it. Hence, Pascal-S includes most of Pascal's statement structures (compound, conditional, selective, and repetitive statements). The only omissions

are the **with** and the **goto** statement. The latter was omitted very deliberately because of the principal use of Pascal-S in teaching the systematic design of well-structured programs. Procedures and functions are included in their full generality. The only exception is that procedures and functions cannot be used as parameters.

In the compiler that we present in this chapter, we have cut down the language even further. We have omitted the real numbers, and the **case** and **for** statements. The pleasure of introducing them is left to the exercises.

Here is an example of a program in Pascal-S. It is an inefficient program for computing Fibonacci numbers. (The inefficiency is not due to Pascal-S; I chose this program because its translation illustrates that recursion does not present any difficulty whatsoever.)

```
program example(input, output);

var i, m: integer;

function f(n: integer): integer;
begin if n<2 then f:= n else f:= f(n-2)+f(n-1) end;

begin write('max = '); read(m);
      i:= 0;
      while i<>m do begin i:= i+1; writeln(i, f(i)) end
end.
```

15.2 The Stack Machine

The compiler generates code for a stack machine. This machine has 43 instructions. It operates on a linear store and two registers, the program counter and the stack pointer. The instruction set is larger than strictly necessary in order to illustrate the operation of a peephole optimizer. For example, an instruction that adds a constant to the value on top of the evaluation stack is superfluous, but often reduces the length of the object code, speeds up execution, and is best generated via a simple peephole optimizer. Various instructions for copying the value of a variable from or to the evaluation stack have been included. Addresses either are constants, or are offsets from the stack pointer, or are generated during execution. Boolean values are represented by integers in the stack machine; boolean value b is represented by $ord(b)$; that is, 1 for *true* and 0 for *false*. Characters are similarly represented by their ordinal values.

We describe the effect of some of the instructions. The description is highly informal. A more rigorous description consists of the procedure *interpret* which appears at the end of the next section.

add   (*add*)
Pop two integers from the stack and then push their sum onto the stack. The stack is found at addresses sp, $sp + 1$, and so on.

eqli   (*equal integers*)
Pop two integers from the stack; then push 1 if they are equal, and 0 if they are different.

ldc   a (*load constant*)
Push constant a onto the stack.

addc   a (*add constant*)
Add constant a to the integer that is on top of the stack.

ldl   a (*load local*)
Push the word at address $sp+$ a onto the stack.

ldla   a (*load local address*)
Push address $sp+$ a onto the stack.

stl   a (*store local*)
Store at address $sp+$ a one word popped from the stack.

jumpz a (*jump if zero*)
Pop one word from the stack. If it is zero, jump to address a.

exit   a (*exit*)
Jump to the address that is on top of the stack. Pop a elements from the stack.

adjs   a (*adjust stack pointer*)
Increase the stack pointer by a.

As an example, we list the object code for the program given before. This listing has been produced by the compiler, but I added comments. Jump and call instructions refer to the address of the target instruction, and do not refer to a label. Execution begins with the instruction at address 0. The offset of a local variable from the stack pointer depends on the number of anonymous results from expression evaluation on the stack.

```
0 :     jump     19      skip code of function f
1 :     ldl      1       begin of f
2 :     ldc      2
3 :     lssi             n<2
4 :     jumpz    8       jump to else part if false
5 :     ldl      1
6 :     stl      3
7 :     jump     18      skip else part
8 :     ldc      0
```

```
 9 :    ldl     2
10 :    addc    -2
11 :    call    1          f(n-2)
12 :    ldc     0
13 :    ldl     3
14 :    addc    -1
15 :    call    1          f(n-1)
16 :    add
17 :    stl     3
18 :    exit    2          end of f
19 :    sets  16382        initialize stack pointer
20 :    ldc   109
21 :    wrc                write('m')
22 :    ldc    97
23 :    wrc                write('a')
24 :    ldc   120
25 :    wrc                write('x')
26 :    ldc    32
27 :    wrc                write(' ')
28 :    ldc    61
29 :    wrc                write('=')
30 :    ldc    32
31 :    wrc                write(' ')
32 :    ldc  16382
33 :    rdi                read(m)
34 :    ldc     0
35 :    stg   16383        i:= 0
36 :    ldg   16383
37 :    ldg   16382
38 :    neqi               i<>m
39 :    jumpz  53          jump to end of loop if false
40 :    ldg   16383
41 :    addc    1
42 :    stg   16383        i:= i+1
43 :    ldg   16383
44 :    ldc     8
45 :    wri                write(i)
46 :    ldc     0
47 :    ldg   16383
48 :    call    1
49 :    ldc     8          write(f(i))
50 :    wri
51 :    wrl                writeln
52 :    jump   36          to beginning of loop
53 :    halt               end.
```

15.3 The Compiler

The compiler has an extremely simple form of peephole optimization in the form of procedure *gen*. It compares the instruction to be generated with the previous instruction and combines the two if possible. This is not done if a label occurs between the two instructions, which is indicated by the boolean *labeled*.

Variables are addressed as discussed in the previous chapter: local variables are addressed relative to the stack pointer, variables in the outermost block are addressed directly, and variables declared in intermediate blocks are addressed via the static chain. Because local variables are addressed with an offset from the stack pointer, the compiler has to keep track of the size of the evaluation stack. Procedure *gen* updates, for every instruction generated, variable *dx*, which represents the value of the stack pointer if $lev = 0$ and the offset from the address of the first variable in the present procedure if $lev > 0$.

We have not tried to make the compiler as efficient as possible. For example, every identifier is compared to all keywords to check whether it is a keyword or not. All identifiers are stored in a linear list, rather than in some tree structure or hash table. All comparisons in the peephole optimizer are done in a linear fashion. We have refrained from using more-efficient algorithms because the present version is probably easier to understand. Any practical compiler, however, would use more-sophisticated algorithms. Also, the error reporting is minimal: not all errors are detected, and errors that are found are presented with a numeric error message; a mnemonic message is more helpful in practice (and requires little extra effort to produce). The compiler stops as soon as one error is detected. No attempts are made to find more errors ("you can stop as soon as you have won") both because it is very hard to do well and because it does not pay off. Experience shows that this would roughly double the size of the compiler, and make it slower; it is just as easy to edit the program and rerun the compiler, given that compilation takes hardly any time.

program *PascalS*(*input*, *output*);

label 99;

const *cxmax* = 2000;   { maximum code array index }
          amax = 16383;   { maximum memory address }

type *opcode* = (*add*, *neg*, *mul*, *divd*, *remd*, *div2*, *rem2*, *eqli*, *neqi*, *lssi*,
                  leqi, *gtri*, *geqi*, *dupl*, *swap*, *andb*, *orb*,
                  load, *stor*, *halt*, *wri*, *wrc*, *wrl*, *rdi*, *rdc*, *rdl*, *eol*,
                  ldc, *ldla*, *ldl*, *ldg*, *stl*, *stg*, *move*, *copy*, *addc*, *mulc*,
                  jump, *jumpz*, *call*, *adjs*, *sets*, *exit*);

```
instr  = record case op : opcode of
                 add, neg, mul, divd, remd, div2, rem2, eqli, neqi, lssi,
                 leqi, gtri, geqi, dupl, swap, andb, orb,
                 load, stor, halt, wri, wrc, wrl, rdi, rdc, rdl, eol :
                     ();
                 ldc, ldla, ldl, ldg, stl, stg, move, copy, addc, mulc,
                 jump, jumpz, call, adjs, sets, exit :
                     (a : integer)
           end;
```

var   code : array[0..cxmax]of instr;
      m   : array[0..amax]of integer;

procedure compile;

const   imax   = 100;   { length of identifier table }
        tmax   = 100;   { length of type table }
        lmax   = 10;   { maximum level }
        al   = 10;   { length of identifiers }
        fabs   = 0;   { standard functions }
        fsqr   = 1;   fodd   = 2;   fchr   = 3;
        ford   = 4;   fwrite = 5;   fwriteln = 6;
        fread = 7;   freadln = 8;   feoln   = 9;
           { standard types }
        intip = 1;   booltip = 2;   chartip = 3;

type   symbol = (ident, number, string, plus, minus, star, lbrack, rbrack,
                  colon, eql, neq, lss, leq, gtr, geq, lparen, rparen, comma,
                  semicolon, period, becomes,
                  beginsym, endsym, ifsym, thensym, elsesym, whilesym,
                  dosym, casesym, repeatsym, untilsym, forsym, tosym,
                  downtosym, notsym, divsym, modsym, andsym, orsym,
                  constsym, varsym, typesym, arraysym, ofsym,
                  recordsym, progsym, funcsym, procsym);
       idkind = (konst, varbl, field, tipe, funkt);
       tpkind = (simple, arrays, records);
       alfa   = packed array[1..al]of char;

var   ch : char;   { last character read }
      cc : integer;   { character count }
      ll : integer;   { line length }
      line : array[1..81]of char;   { present input line }
      sym : symbol;   { last symbol read }
      id : alfa;   { last identifier read }
      num : integer;   { last number read }

```
str : array[1..80]of char;        { last string read }
slen : integer;                   { length of last string }
word : array[beginsym..procsym]of alfa;
cx : integer;                     { code index }
lev : integer;                    { procedure nesting level }
dx : integer;                     { offset in stack }
labeled : boolean;                { next instruction has label }
namelist : array[−1..lmax]of integer;
ix, tx : integer;                 { indices in tables }
itab : array[0..imax]of           { identifier table }
        record name : alfa; link : integer; tip : integer;
          case kind : idkind of
            konst : (val : integer);
            varbl : (vlevel, vadr : integer; refpar : boolean);
            field : (offset : integer);
            tipe  : ();
            funkt : (flevel, fadr, lastpar, resultadr : integer;
                        inside : boolean)
        end;
ttab : array[1..tmax]of           { type table }
        record size : integer;
          case kind : tpkind of
            simple  : ();
            arrays  : (low, high, elemtip : integer);
            records : (fields : integer)
        end;
```

```
procedure error(n : integer);
  var i : integer;
begin for i := 1 to ll do write(line[i]);  writeln;
      for i := 1 to cc − 2 do write(' ');  writeln(' ↑ ');
      writeln( 'error ', n : 1, ' detected' );
      goto 99
end;
```

```
procedure getch;
begin if cc = ll then begin
        if eof(input) then error(100);  ll := 0;  cc := 0;
        while ¬eoln(input) do begin ll := ll + 1;  read(line[ll]) end;
        ll := ll + 1;  read(line[ll])
      end;
      cc := cc + 1;  ch := line[cc]
end;
```

```
procedure getsym;
```

```
    var k : integer; s : symbol; strend : boolean;
begin while ch ∈ [ ' ' , chr(9)] do getch;
    if ch ∈ [ 'a' .. 'z' , 'A' .. 'Z' ] then begin
        k := 0;
        repeat if k ≠ al then begin k := k + 1;  id[k] := ch end;
            getch
        until ch ∉ [ 'a' .. 'z' , 'A' .. 'Z' , '0' .. '9' ];
        while k ≠ al do begin k := k + 1;  id[k] := ' '   end;
        sym := ident;
        for s := beginsym to procsym do
            if word[s] = id then sym := s
    end else if ch ∈ [ '0' .. '9' ] then begin
        num := 0;  sym := number;
        repeat num := num * 10 + (ord(ch) − ord( '0' ));
            getch
        until ch ∉ [ '0' .. '9' ]
    end else if ch = ':' then begin
        getch;
        if ch = '=' then begin getch; sym := becomes end
                    else sym := colon
    end else if ch = '>' then begin
        getch;
        if ch = '=' then begin getch; sym := geq end
                    else sym := gtr
    end else if ch = '<' then begin
        getch;
        if ch = '=' then begin getch; sym := leq end else
        if ch = '>' then begin getch; sym := neq end
                    else sym := lss
    end else if ch = '.' then begin
        getch;
        if ch = '.' then begin getch; sym := colon end
                    else sym := period
    end else if ch = '''' then begin
        slen := 0;  strend := false;  sym := string;
        repeat if cc = ll then error(101);  getch;
            if ch = '''' then begin
                getch;
                if ch = '''' then begin
                    slen := slen + 1;  str[slen] := ch
                end else
                    strend := true
            end else begin
                slen := slen + 1;  str[slen] := ch
            end
```

```
              until strend;
              if slen = 0 then error(102)
        end else if ch = '+' then begin
              getch; sym := plus
        end else if ch = '-' then begin
              getch; sym := minus
        end else if ch = '*' then begin
              getch; sym := star
        end else if ch = '(' then begin
              getch; sym := lparen
        end else if ch = ')' then begin
              getch; sym := rparen
        end else if ch = '[' then begin
              getch; sym := lbrack
        end else if ch = ']' then begin
              getch; sym := rbrack
        end else if ch = '=' then begin
              getch; sym := eql
        end else if ch = ',' then begin
              getch; sym := comma
        end else if ch = ';' then begin
              getch; sym := semicolon
        end else if ch = '{' then begin
              repeat getch until ch = '}';
              getch; getsym
        end else error(103)
end;

procedure check(s : symbol);
begin if sym ≠ s then error(ord(s)) end;

procedure skip(s : symbol);
begin check(s); getsym end;

procedure enter(id : alfa; k : idkind; t : integer);
   var j : integer;
begin if ix = imax then error(104); ix := ix + 1;
      itab[0].name := id; j := namelist[lev];
      while itab[j].name ≠ id do j := itab[j].link;
      if j ≠ 0 then error(105);
      with itab[ix] do begin
          name := id; link := namelist[lev]; tip := t; kind := k
      end;
      namelist[lev] := ix
end;
```

```
function position : integer;
   var i, j : integer;
begin itab[0].name := id;  i := lev;
      repeat j := namelist[i];
            while itab[j].name ≠ id do j := itab[j].link;
            i := i − 1
      until (i < −1) ∨ (j ≠ 0);
      if j = 0 then error(106);  position := j
end;

procedure gen(i : instr);
begin case i.op of
            dupl, eol, ldc, ldla, ldl, ldg :
               dx := dx − 1;
            neg, div2, rem2, swap, load, halt, wrl, rdl,
            addc, mulc, jump, call, sets, exit :
               ;
            add, mul, divd, remd, eqli, neqi, lssi, leqi, gtri,
            geqi, andb, orb, wrc, rdi, rdc, stl, stg, jumpz :
               dx := dx + 1;
            stor, wri, move :
               dx := dx + 2;
            copy :
               dx := dx − i.a + 1;
            adjs :
               dx := dx + i.a
      end;
      if ¬( ((i.op ∈ [addc, adjs])  ∧  (i.a = 0))  ∨
            ((i.op = mulc)  ∧  (i.a = 1))) then
      if labeled then begin
            code[cx] := i;  cx := cx + 1;  labeled := false
      end else if (code[cx − 1].op = ldc)  ∧  (i.op = add) then
            code[cx − 1].op := addc
      else if (code[cx − 1].op = ldc)  ∧  (i.op = mul) then
            code[cx − 1].op := mulc
      else if (code[cx − 1].op = ldc)  ∧  (i.op = neg) then
            code[cx − 1].a := −code[cx − 1].a
      else if (code[cx − 1].op = ldc)  ∧  (code[cx − 1].a = 2)  ∧
            (i.op = divd) then
            code[cx − 1].op := div2
      else if (code[cx − 1].op = ldc)  ∧  (code[cx − 1].a = 2)  ∧
            (i.op = remd) then
            code[cx − 1].op := rem2
      else if (code[cx − 1].op = ldc)  ∧  (i.op = stor) then
```

```
              code[cx − 1].op := stg
        else if (code[cx − 1].op = ldc)  ∧  (i.op = load) then
              code[cx − 1].op := ldg
        else if (code[cx − 1].op = ldla)  ∧  (i.op = stor) then
              code[cx − 1].op := stl
        else if (code[cx − 1].op = ldla)  ∧  (i.op = load) then
              code[cx − 1].op := ldl
        else begin
              code[cx] := i;  cx := cx + 1
end    end;


procedure gen0(op : opcode);
  var i : instr;
begin i.op := op;  gen(i) end;


procedure gen1(op : opcode;  a : integer);
  var i : instr;
begin i.op := op;  i.a := a;  gen(i) end;


function codelabel : integer;
begin codelabel := cx;  labeled := true end;


procedure address(lv, ad : integer);
begin if lv = 0 then
            gen1(ldc, ad)
      else if lv = lev then
            gen1(ldla, ad − dx)
      else begin
            gen1(ldl, −dx);
            while lv + 1 ≠ lev do begin gen0(load);  lv := lv + 1 end;
            gen1(addc, ad)
end    end;


procedure addressvar(ref : integer);
begin with itab[ref] do begin
            address(vlevel, vadr);  if refpar then gen0(load)
end    end ;


procedure mustbe(x, y : integer);
begin if x ≠ y then
      if (ttab[x].kind = arrays) ∧ (ttab[y].kind = arrays)∧
          (ttab[x].low = ttab[y].low) ∧ (ttab[x].high = ttab[y].high)
      then mustbe(ttab[x].elemtip, ttab[y].elemtip)
      else error(107)
end;
```

```
procedure expression(var x : integer);
    forward;

procedure selector(var t : integer; var ref : integer);
    var j, x : integer;
begin t := itab[ref].tip; getsym;
    if sym ∈ [period, lbrack] then begin
        addressvar(ref);  ref := 0;
        while sym ∈ [period, lbrack] do
        case sym of
            period : begin if ttab[t].kind ≠ records then error(108);
                            getsym; check(ident);
                            j := ttab[t].fields; itab[0].name := id;
                            while itab[j].name ≠ id do j := itab[j].link;
                            if j = 0 then error(109);
                            gen1(addc, itab[j].offset);
                            t := itab[j].tip; getsym
                     end;
            lbrack : begin repeat
                                if ttab[t].kind ≠ arrays then error(110);
                                getsym; expression(x); mustbe(intip, x);
                                gen1(addc, −ttab[t].low);
                                t := ttab[t].elemtip;
                                gen1(mulc, ttab[t].size);
                            until sym ≠ comma;
                            skip(rbrack)
end end end        end;

procedure varpar(var t : integer);
    var j : integer;
begin check(ident);  j := position;  selector(t, j);
        if j ≠ 0 then addressvar(j)
end;

procedure standfct(n : integer);
    var x, l : integer;
begin case n of
        fabs :  begin skip(lparen); expression(x); mustbe(intip, x);
                    gen0(dupl);  gen1(ldc, 0);  gen0(lssi);
                    l := codelabel; gen1(jumpz, 0); gen0(neg);
                    code[l].a := codelabel;
                    skip(rparen)
                end;
        fsqr :  begin skip(lparen); expression(x); mustbe(intip, x);
```

```
                gen0(dupl);  gen0(mul);  skip(rparen)
        end;
fodd :  begin skip(lparen);  expression(x);  mustbe(intip, x);
            gen0(rem2);  skip(rparen)
        end;
fchr :  begin skip(lparen);  expression(x);  mustbe(intip, x);
            skip(rparen)
        end;
ford :  begin skip(lparen);  expression(x);  mustbe(chartip, x);
            skip(rparen)
        end;
fwrite, fwriteln :
        begin if n = fwrite then check(lparen);
            if sym = lparen then begin
                repeat getsym;
                    if sym = string then begin
                        for x := 1 to slen do begin
                            gen1(ldc, ord(str[x]));  gen0(wrc)
                        end;
                        getsym
                    end else begin
                        expression(x);
                        if sym = colon then begin
                            mustbe(intip, x);  getsym;
                            expression(x);
                            mustbe(intip, x);  gen0(wri)
                        end else if x = intip then begin
                            gen1(ldc, 8);  gen0(wri)
                        end else if x = chartip then
                            gen0(wrc)
                        else error(111)
                    end
                until sym ≠ comma;
                skip(rparen)
            end;
            if n = fwriteln then gen0(wrl)
        end;
fread, freadln :
        begin if n = fread then check(lparen);
            if sym = lparen then begin
                repeat getsym;  varpar(x);
                    if x = intip then gen0(rdi) else
                    if x = chartip then gen0(rdc)
                            else error(112)
                until sym ≠ comma;
```

$$skip(rparen)$$
end;
        if $n = freadln$ **then** $gen0(rdl)$
end;
   $feoln : gen0(eol)$
end end;

procedure $funcall(i : integer)$;
  var $d, p, x : integer$;
begin $getsym$;
     with $itab[i]$ **do**
     if $flevel < 0$ **then**
       $standfct(fadr)$
     else begin
       if $tip \neq 0$ **then** $gen1(ldc, 0)$; $p := i$; $d := dx$;
       if $sym = lparen$ **then begin**
         repeat $getsym$;
           if $p = lastpar$ **then** $error(113)$; $p := p + 1$;
           if $itab[p].refpar$ **then**
             $varpar(x)$
           else begin
             $expression(x)$;
             if $ttab[x].kind \neq simple$ **then**
               $gen1(copy, ttab[x].size)$
           end;
           $mustbe(itab[p].tip, x)$
         until $sym \neq comma$;
         $skip(rparen)$
       end;
       if $p \neq lastpar$ **then** $error(114)$;
       if $flevel \neq 0$ **then** $address(flevel, 0)$;
       $gen1(call, fadr)$; $dx := d$
end   **end**;

procedure $factor(\textbf{var } t : integer)$;
  var $i : integer$;
begin if $sym = ident$ **then begin**
       $i := position$; $t := itab[i].tip$;
       case $itab[i].kind$ **of**
         $konst$: **begin** $getsym$; $gen1(ldc, itab[i].val)$ **end**;
         $varbl$: **begin** $selector(t, i)$;
                if $i \neq 0$ **then** $addressvar(i)$;
                if $ttab[t].kind = simple$ **then** $gen0(load)$
           end;
         $funkt$: **if** $t = 0$ **then** $error(115)$ **else** $funcall(i)$;

```
                tipe :    error(116)
            end
        end else if sym = number then begin
            gen1(ldc, num);  t := intip;  getsym
        end else if (sym = string) ∧ (slen = 1) then begin
            gen1(ldc, ord(str[1]));  t := chartip;  getsym
        end else if sym = lparen then begin
            getsym;  expression(t);  skip(rparen)
        end else error(117)
end;


procedure term(var x : integer);
    var y : integer;
begin factor(x);
        while sym ∈ [andsym, star, divsym, modsym] do begin
            if sym = andsym then mustbe(booltip, x)
                            else mustbe(intip, x);
            case sym of
                star     : begin getsym;  factor(y);  gen0(mul) end;
                divsym   : begin getsym;  factor(y);  gen0(divd) end;
                modsym : begin getsym;  factor(y);  gen0(remd) end;
                andsym : begin getsym;  factor(y);  gen0(andb) end
            end;
            mustbe(x, y)
    end    end;


procedure simplexpression(var x : integer);
    var y : integer;
begin if sym = plus then begin
            getsym;  term(x);  mustbe(intip, x)
        end else if sym = minus then begin
            getsym;  term(x);  mustbe(intip, x);  gen0(neg)
        end else
            term(x);
        while sym ∈ [orsym, plus, minus] do begin
            if sym = orsym then mustbe(booltip, x) else mustbe(intip, x);
            case sym of
                plus  : begin getsym;  term(y);  gen0(add) end;
                minus : begin getsym;  term(y);  gen0(neg);  gen0(add) end;
                orsym : begin getsym;  term(y);  gen0(orb) end
            end;
            mustbe(x, y)
    end    end;


procedure expression{var x : integer};
```

```
    var op : symbol;  y : integer;
begin simplexpression(x);
      if sym ∈ [eql, neq, lss, leq, gtr, geq] then begin
          if ttab[x].kind ≠ simple then error(118);
          op := sym;  getsym;  simplexpression(y);  mustbe(x, y);
          case op of
              eql  : gen0(eqli);
              neq  : gen0(neqi);
              lss  : gen0(lssi);
              leq  : gen0(leqi);
              gtr  : gen0(gtri);
              geq  : gen0(geqi)
          end;
          x := booltip
end    end;


procedure statement;
   var i, j, t, x : integer;
begin if sym = ident then begin
          i := position;
          with itab[i] do
          case kind of
              varbl : begin selector(t, i);  skip(becomes);
                            expression(x);  mustbe(t, x);
                            if i = 0 then gen0(swap)
                                   else addressvar(i);
                            if ttab[t].kind = simple then
                               gen0(stor)
                            else
                                   gen1(move, ttab[t].size)
                      end;
              funkt : if tip = 0 then
                         funcall(i)
                      else begin
                         if ¬inside then error(119);
                         getsym;  skip(becomes);
                         expression(x);  mustbe(tip, x);
                         address(flevel + 1, resultadr);  gen0(stor)
                      end;
              konst, field, tipe : error(120)
          end
       end else if sym = ifsym then begin
          getsym;  expression(t);  mustbe(booltip, t);  skip(thensym);
          i := codelabel;  gen1(jumpz, 0);  statement;
          if sym = elsesym then begin
```

```
                getsym;  j := codelabel;  gen1(jump, 0);
                code[i].a := codelabel;  i := j;  statement
            end;
            code[i].a := codelabel
        end else if sym = whilesym then begin
            getsym;  i := codelabel;  expression(t);  mustbe(booltip, t);
            skip(dosym);  j := codelabel;  gen1(jumpz, 0);
            statement;  gen1(jump, i);
            code[j].a := codelabel
        end else if sym = repeatsym then begin
            i := codelabel;
            repeat getsym;  statement until sym ≠ semicolon;
            skip(untilsym);  expression(t);  mustbe(booltip, t);
            gen1(jumpz, i)
        end else if sym = beginsym then begin
            repeat getsym;  statement until sym ≠ semicolon;
            skip(endsym)
end    end;


procedure block(l : integer);
    forward;


procedure constant(var c, t : integer);
    var i, s : integer;
begin if (sym = string) ∧ (slen = 1) then begin
            c := ord(str[1]);  t := chartip
        end else begin
            if sym = plus   then begin getsym;  s := +1 end else
            if sym = minus then begin getsym;  s := −1 end
                            else s := 0;
            if sym = ident then begin
                i := position;
                if itab[i].kind ≠ konst then error(121);
                c := itab[i].val;  t := itab[i].tip
            end else if sym = number then begin
                c := num;  t := intip
            end else
                error(122);
            if s ≠ 0 then begin mustbe(t, intip);  c := c * s end
        end;
        getsym
end;


procedure constdeclaration;
    var a : alfa;  t, c : integer;
```

```
begin a := id; getsym; skip(eql); constant(c, t);
      skip(semicolon); enter(a, konst, t); itab[ix].val := c
end;

procedure typ(var t : integer);
  var i, j, sz, ft : integer;
  procedure arraytyp(var t : integer);
    var x : integer;
  begin with ttab[t] do begin
            kind := arrays; getsym; constant(low, x); mustbe(intip, x);
            skip(colon); constant(high, x); mustbe(intip, x);
            if low > high then error(123);
            if sym = comma then
                arraytyp(elemtip)
            else begin
                skip(rbrack); skip(ofsym); typ(elemtip)
            end;
            size := (high − low + 1) ∗ ttab[elemtip].size
  end    end;
begin if sym = ident then begin
            i := position; if itab[i].kind ≠ tipe then error(124);
            t := itab[i].tip; getsym
       end else begin
            if tx = tmax then error(125); tx := tx + 1; t := tx;
            if sym = arraysym then begin
                getsym; check(lbrack); arraytyp(t)
            end else begin
                skip(recordsym);
                if lev = lmax then error(126); lev := lev + 1;
                namelist[lev] := 0; check(ident); sz := 0;
                repeat enter(id, field, 0); i := ix; getsym;
                    while sym = comma do begin
                        getsym; check(ident); enter(id, field, 0);
                        getsym
                    end;
                    j := ix; skip(colon); typ(ft);
                    repeat itab[i].tip := ft; itab[i].offset := sz;
                        sz := sz + ttab[ft].size; i := i + 1
                    until i > j;
                    if sym = semicolon then getsym else check(endsym)
                until sym ≠ ident;
                ttab[t].size := sz; ttab[t].kind := records;
                ttab[t].fields := namelist[lev]; lev := lev − 1;
                skip(endsym)
end    end end;
```

```
procedure typedeclaration;
   var a : alfa;  t : integer;
begin a := id;  getsym;  skip(eql);  typ(t);  skip(semicolon);
       enter(a, tipe, t)
end;


procedure vardeclaration;
   var p, q, t : integer;
begin enter(id, varbl, 0);  p := ix;  getsym;
       while sym = comma do begin
            getsym;  check(ident);  enter(id, varbl, 0);  getsym
       end;
       q := ix;  skip(colon);  typ(t);  skip(semicolon);
       repeat with itab[p] do begin
                    vlevel := lev;  dx := dx - ttab[t].size;  tip := t;
                    vadr := dx;  refpar := false
                 end;
                 p := p + 1
       until p > q
end;


procedure funcdeclaration(isf : boolean);
   var f, p, ps, odx : integer;
   procedure paramlist;
      var r : boolean;  t : integer;
   begin if sym = varsym then begin r := true;  getsym end
                          else r := false;
         check(ident);  p := ix;  enter(id, varbl, 0);  getsym;
         while sym = comma do begin
              getsym;  check(ident);  enter(id, varbl, 0);  getsym
         end;
         skip(colon);  check(ident);  typ(t);
         while p ≠ ix do begin
              p := p + 1;  itab[p].tip := t;  itab[p].refpar := r;
              if r then ps := ps + 1 else ps := ps + ttab[t].size
   end    end;
begin getsym;  check(ident);  enter(id, funkt, 0);  getsym;  f := ix;
    itab[f].flevel := lev;  itab[f].fadr := codelabel;  gen1(jump, 0);
    if lev = lmax then error(127);  lev := lev + 1;  namelist[lev] := 0;
    ps := 1;  odx := dx;
    if sym = lparen then begin
          repeat getsym;  paramlist until sym ≠ semicolon;
          skip(rparen)
    end;
```

```
    if lev > 1 then begin ps := ps + 1;  dx := -1 end
            else dx := 0;
    itab[f].resultadr := ps;  p := f;
    while p < ix do begin
        p := p + 1;
        with itab[p] do begin
            if refpar then ps := ps - 1 else ps := ps - ttab[tip].size;
            vlevel := lev;  vadr := ps
    end end;
    if isf then begin
        skip(colon);  check(ident);  typ(itab[f].tip);
        if ttab[itab[f].tip].kind ≠ simple then error(128)
    end;
    skip(semicolon);
    itab[f].lastpar := ix;  itab[f].inside := true;
    block(itab[f].fadr);  skip(semicolon);  itab[f].inside := false;
    gen1(exit, itab[f].resultadr);  lev := lev - 1;  dx := odx
end;

procedure block{l : integer};
  var d, odx, oix : integer;
begin odx := dx;  oix := ix;
    if sym = constsym then begin
        getsym;  check(ident);
        repeat constdeclaration until sym ≠ ident
    end;
    if sym = typesym then begin
        getsym;  check(ident);
        repeat typedeclaration until sym ≠ ident
    end;
    if sym = varsym then begin
        getsym;  check(ident);
        repeat vardeclaration until sym ≠ ident
    end;
    while sym ∈ [funcsym, procsym] do funcdeclaration(sym = funcsym);
    if l + 1 = codelabel then cx := cx - 1 else code[l].a := codelabel;
    if lev = 0 then
        gen1(sets, dx)
    else begin
        d := dx - odx;  dx := odx;  gen1(adjs, d)
    end;
    statement;
    if lev ≠ 0 then gen1(adjs, odx - dx);  ix := oix
end;
```

```
procedure listcode;
    var i : integer;
begin for i := 0 to cx - 1 do begin
            write(i, ' :      ' );
            case code[i].op of
                add    : writeln( 'add' );
                neg    : writeln( 'neg' );
                mul    : writeln( 'mul' );
                divd   : writeln( 'divd' );
                remd   : writeln( 'remd' );
                div2   : writeln( 'div2' );
                rem2   : writeln( 'rem2' );
                eqli   : writeln( 'eqli' );
                neqi   : writeln( 'neqi' );
                lssi   : writeln( 'lssi' );
                leqi   : writeln( 'leqi' );
                gtri   : writeln( 'gtri' );
                geqi   : writeln( 'geqi' );
                dupl   : writeln( 'dupl' );
                swap   : writeln( 'swap' );
                andb   : writeln( 'andb' );
                orb    : writeln( 'orb' );
                load   : writeln( 'load' );
                stor   : writeln( 'stor' );
                halt   : writeln( 'halt' );
                wri    : writeln( 'wri' );
                wrc    : writeln( 'wrc' );
                wrl    : writeln( 'wrl' );
                rdi    : writeln( 'rdi' );
                rdc    : writeln( 'rdc' );
                rdl    : writeln( 'rdl' );
                eol    : writeln( 'eol' );
                ldc    : writeln( 'ldc   ', code[i].a);
                ldla   : writeln( 'ldla  ', code[i].a);
                ldl    : writeln( 'ldl   ', code[i].a);
                ldg    : writeln( 'ldg   ', code[i].a);
                stl    : writeln( 'stl   ', code[i].a);
                stg    : writeln( 'stg   ', code[i].a);
                move   : writeln( 'move  ', code[i].a);
                copy   : writeln( 'copy  ', code[i].a);
                addc   : writeln( 'addc  ', code[i].a);
                mulc   : writeln( 'mulc  ', code[i].a);
                jump   : writeln( 'jump  ', code[i].a);
                jumpz  : writeln( 'jumpz ', code[i].a);
                call   : writeln( 'call  ', code[i].a);
```

```
                  adjs   : writeln( 'adjs   ', code[i].a);
                  sets   : writeln( 'sets   ', code[i].a);
                  exit   : writeln( 'exit   ', code[i].a)
end     end end;

begin { compile }
    word[beginsym  ] := 'begin     ';
    word[endsym    ] := 'end       ';
    word[ifsym     ] := 'if        ';
    word[thensym   ] := 'then      ';
    word[elsesym   ] := 'else      ';
    word[whilesym  ] := 'while     ';
    word[dosym     ] := 'do        ';
    word[casesym   ] := 'case      ';
    word[repeatsym ] := 'repeat    ';
    word[untilsym  ] := 'until     ';
    word[forsym    ] := 'for       ';
    word[tosym     ] := 'to        ';
    word[downtosym ] := 'downto    ';
    word[notsym    ] := 'not       ';
    word[divsym    ] := 'div       ';
    word[modsym    ] := 'mod       ';
    word[andsym    ] := 'and       ';
    word[orsym     ] := 'or        ';
    word[constsym  ] := 'const     ';
    word[varsym    ] := 'var       ';
    word[typesym   ] := 'type      ';
    word[arraysym  ] := 'array     ';
    word[ofsym     ] := 'of        ';
    word[recordsym ] := 'record    ';
    word[progsym   ] := 'program   ';
    word[funcsym   ] := 'function  ';
    word[procsym   ] := 'procedure ';
    ttab[intip].size := 1;  ttab[intip].kind := simple;
    ttab[chartip].size := 1;  ttab[chartip].kind := simple;
    ttab[booltip].size := 1;  ttab[booltip].kind := simple;
    tx := 3;  namelist[-1] := 0;  lev := -1;  ix := 0;
    enter( 'false     ', konst, booltip);  itab[ix].val := ord(false);
    enter( 'true      ', konst, booltip);  itab[ix].val := ord(true);
    enter( 'maxint    ', konst, intip);  itab[ix].val := 32767;
    enter( 'integer   ', tipe, intip);
    enter( 'char      ', tipe, chartip);
    enter( 'boolean   ', tipe, booltip);
    enter( 'abs       ', funkt, intip);
    itab[ix].flevel := -1;  itab[ix].fadr := fabs;  itab[ix].inside := false;
```

```
enter( 'sqr        ' , funkt, intip);
itab[ix].flevel := −1;  itab[ix].fadr := fsqr;  itab[ix].inside := false;
enter( 'odd        ' , funkt, booltip);
itab[ix].flevel := −1;  itab[ix].fadr := fodd;  itab[ix].inside := false;
enter( 'chr        ' , funkt, chartip);
itab[ix].flevel := −1;  itab[ix].fadr := fchr;  itab[ix].inside := false;
enter( 'ord        ' , funkt, intip);
itab[ix].flevel := −1;  itab[ix].fadr := ford;  itab[ix].inside := false;
enter( 'write      ' , funkt, 0);
itab[ix].flevel := −1;  itab[ix].fadr := fwrite;
enter( 'writeln    ' , funkt, 0);
itab[ix].flevel := −1;  itab[ix].fadr := fwriteln;
enter( 'read       ' , funkt, 0);
itab[ix].flevel := −1;  itab[ix].fadr := fread;
enter( 'readln     ' , funkt, 0);
itab[ix].flevel := −1;  itab[ix].fadr := freadln;
enter( 'eoln       ' , funkt, booltip);
itab[ix].flevel := −1;  itab[ix].fadr := feoln;  itab[ix].inside := false;
namelist[0] := 0;  lev := 0;  cc := 0;  ll := 0;  getch;  getsym;
labeled := true;  cx := 0;  dx := amax + 1;
skip(progsym);  skip(ident);  check(lparen);
repeat getsym;  check(ident);
    if (id ≠ 'input       ' ) ∧ (id ≠ 'output      ' ) then  error(129);
    getsym
until sym ≠ comma;
skip(rparen);  skip(semicolon);  gen1(jump, 0);  block(0);  gen0(halt);
check(period);
listcode
end;


procedure interpret;
    var pc, sp, j, k, n : integer;  i : instr;  c : char;  h : boolean;
begin pc := 0;  h := false;
    repeat i := code[pc];  pc := pc + 1;
        case i.op of
            add  : begin m[sp + 1] := m[sp + 1] + m[sp];  sp := sp + 1 end;
            neg  : m[sp] := −m[sp];
            mul  : begin m[sp + 1] := m[sp + 1] * m[sp];  sp := sp + 1 end;
            divd : begin m[sp + 1] := m[sp + 1] div m[sp];  sp := sp + 1 end;
            remd : begin m[sp + 1] := m[sp + 1] mod m[sp];  sp := sp + 1 end;
            div2 : m[sp] := m[sp] div 2;
            rem2 : m[sp] := m[sp] mod 2;
            eqli : begin m[sp + 1] := ord(m[sp + 1] = m[sp]);  sp := sp + 1 end;
            neqi : begin m[sp + 1] := ord(m[sp + 1] ≠ m[sp]);  sp := sp + 1 end;
            lssi : begin m[sp + 1] := ord(m[sp + 1] < m[sp]);  sp := sp + 1 end;
```

```
  leqi  : begin m[sp + 1] := ord(m[sp + 1] ≤ m[sp]);  sp := sp + 1 end;
  gtri  : begin m[sp + 1] := ord(m[sp + 1] > m[sp]);  sp := sp + 1 end;
  geqi  : begin m[sp + 1] := ord(m[sp + 1] ≥ m[sp]);  sp := sp + 1 end;
  dupl  : begin sp := sp − 1;  m[sp] := m[sp + 1] end;
  swap  : begin k := m[sp];  m[sp] := m[sp + 1];  m[sp + 1] := k end;
  andb  : begin if m[sp] = 0 then m[sp + 1] := 0;  sp := sp + 1 end;
  orb   : begin if m[sp] = 1 then m[sp + 1] := 1;  sp := sp + 1 end;
  load  : m[sp] := m[m[sp]];
  stor  : begin m[m[sp]] := m[sp + 1];  sp := sp + 2 end;
  halt  : h := true;
  wri   : begin write(output, m[sp + 1] : m[sp]);  sp := sp + 2 end;
  wrc   : begin write(output, chr(m[sp]));  sp := sp + 1 end;
  wrl   : writeln(output);
  rdi   : begin read(input, m[m[sp]]);  sp := sp + 1 end;
  rdc   : begin read(input, c);  m[m[sp]] := ord(c);  sp := sp + 1 end;
  rdl   : readln(input);
  eol   : begin sp := sp − 1;  m[sp] := ord(eoln(input)) end;
  ldc   : begin sp := sp − 1;  m[sp] := i.a end;
  ldla  : begin sp := sp − 1;  m[sp] := sp + 1 + i.a end;
  ldl   : begin sp := sp − 1;  m[sp] := m[sp + 1 + i.a] end;
  ldg   : begin sp := sp − 1;  m[sp] := m[i.a] end;
  stl   : begin m[sp + i.a] := m[sp];  sp := sp + 1 end;
  stg   : begin m[i.a] := m[sp];  sp := sp + 1 end;
  move  : begin k := m[sp];  j := m[sp + 1];  sp := sp + 2;  n := i.a;
              repeat n := n − 1;  m[k + n] := m[j + n] until n = 0
          end;
  copy  : begin j := m[sp];  n := i.a;  sp := sp − n + 1;
              repeat n := n − 1;  m[sp + n] := m[j + n] until n = 0
          end;
  addc  : m[sp] := m[sp] + i.a;
  mulc  : m[sp] := m[sp] * i.a;
  jump  : pc := i.a;
  jumpz : begin if m[sp] = 0 then pc := i.a;  sp := sp + 1 end;
  call  : begin sp := sp − 1;  m[sp] := pc;  pc := i.a end;
  adjs  : sp := sp + i.a;
  sets  : sp := i.a;
  exit  : begin pc := m[sp];  sp := sp + i.a end;
        end
      until h
end;

begin compile;
      interpret;
 99 :
end.
```

15.4 Bootstrapping

We have written our compiler and interpreter for some stack machine. If we have a machine available whose instruction set contains exactly the instructions of our hypothetical stack machine, then we might omit the interpreter and have the program executed by that machine. It might also be the case that we want to run our programs on a different machine, for example on a Mosaic. Suppose that we change the compiler to generate Mosaic instructions instead of stack-machine instructions. We may then omit the interpreter and have a Mosaic execute the object program. The compiler, however, is a Pascal program and, for the sake of argument, we assume that no Pascal implementation is available on a Mosaic. (This assumption is certainly valid at the time a new machine is being constructed.) How can we get our compiler to run on a Mosaic? This is a problem that can be solved in essentially two ways, and we discuss both of them. The easiest way is as follows. We can change our compiler and extend the language that it accepts from Pascal-S to Pascal and change the code generation from stack-machine instructions to Mosaic instructions. We go to a friend who has a machine, say an OM, with a Pascal implementation, and we can run our Pascal compiler on the OM. As its input, we can provide it with any Pascal program, for example our Pascal-to-Mosaic compiler. When doing so it compiles this program into an equivalent program written in Mosaic code. This latter version is a Pascal-to-Mosaic compiler that can be run on a Mosaic — and so we are done. This is the easiest and most elegant way. All that it requires is that a Pascal-to-Mosaic compiler be written in Pascal. Well, it also requires the existence of a Pascal compiler on another machine. So, how do we get started on the first machine to have a Pascal compiler? This is done by a process called bootstrapping after the Baron von Münchhausen, who pulled himself out of a swamp by his own bootstraps.

Bootstrapping is the second way of constructing a Pascal compiler that runs on Mosaics. It is much more involved than the method that borrows another machine for a short while. It consists of a number of stages of constructing successively more-evolved compilers. Let us start with our compiler and assume that it generates Mosaic code. Don't worry if the code is inefficient — the only thing that counts right now is that it works. This program is not very big, only about 800 lines, and we might rewrite it by hand into Mosaic code. Because it is not a big program, this is doable. (Of course, we would be done if we could write a Pascal-to-Mosaic compiler in Mosaic code right away, but this is much harder and more error prone than writing it in Pascal and then hand-translating it.) Now we have a Pascal-S-to-Mosaic compiler in Mosaic code (let us call this program x) that can be run on Mosaics. Great! What program shall we give it to compile? Let us rewrite our Pascal-S-to-Mosaic compiler in Pascal-S, giving us program y. It can be compiled by our program x to produce a program

z that behaves exactly like x : it is a Pascal-S-to-Mosaic compiler written in Mosaic code. Next, we write another compiler in Pascal-S, let's say a Pascal-T to Mosaic compiler, written in Pascal-S. Compiling it with z, we get a Pascal-T-to-Mosaic compiler written in Mosaic code, which we can use that for our next step. If Pascal-S is a true subset of Pascal-T, then this new compiler can compile itself. In the next step we, write a Pascal-U-to-Mosaic compiler in Pascal-T, compile it, and obtain a Pascal-U compiler in Mosaic code. We could also rewrite our Pascal-T compiler in Pascal-T by using the language constructs that were added in the step from Pascal-S to Pascal-T, as this might allow for a more concise compiler. We can, in every step, either change the language in which the compiler is written, or change the source language that it compiles, or both. In this way, we go on and on until we have a full Pascal-to-Mosaic compiler, written in Pascal, that compiles itself and other Pascal programs into Mosaic code. It should be evident that this is a laborious process. It is of hardly any practical interest, because we rarely ever find ourselves in the situation where no other compiler is available. And even if no compiler for our own source language is available, we might find a usable compiler for another language on another machine. For example, if we have a C compiler on OM, then we could write a Pascal-to-Mosaic compiler in C and also in Pascal, run the C version on OM with the Pascal version as input, and obtain a Pascal-to-Mosaic compiler in Mosaic code as output. No tiresome bootstrapping is involved.

15.5   Bibliographic Notes

The language Pascal-S is from [Wir81]. This paper also contains a compiler plus interpreter, but it differs substantially from the version we have given here.

15.6   Exercises

1. In a sense, we have been cheating in this compiler. Both in the compiler and in the interpreter, we have been using a record data type in array *code* for representing the instructions. It would be more realistic to assemble the sequence of instructions into a sequence of bit patterns in array m. Also, we have not explained the representation of integers in terms of bits. Discuss both issues and extend the compiler with an assembler. Make sure that array m is the only interface between procedures *compile* and *interpret*.

2. Boolean expressions are implemented in a way similar to arithmetic expressions. Sometimes it may be advantageous to implement them

in a different way. For example, a condition like $b \wedge c$ is currently implemented by first evaluating b and then c, and then computing their conjunction. If, however, the evaluation of b leads to *false*, then the evaluation of c is superfluous; the outcome of $b \wedge c$ is *false*. Describe how this *short-circuit* evaluation of boolean expression might be implemented in the present compiler. Is the effort easier if you are allowed to introduce one or two new instructions? If so, describe their effect.

3. Extend the language to include sets.

4. Extend the language to include the concurrent assignment statement.

5. Extend the language to include the for statement. Make sure that your implementation works in the case where the lower bound equals the smallest possible integer value, in the case where the upper bound is the largest possible integer value, and in the case where the lower bound exceeds the upper bound (and in every other case, of course). Just to remind you: a for-statement is of the form

    > **for** $i := m$ **to** n **do** s

   in which variable i is simply an identifier (not an array element or any such thing). We ignore the case in which do is replaced by **downto**. It may be assumed that execution of statement s does not change variable i or expressions m and n.

6. Extend the language to include functions and procedures as parameters.

7. Remove instructions **divd** and **remd** from the interpreter. Change the compiler to generate instead of these two instructions a call of a subroutine for computing the required result. Use only one extra subroutine for returning both the quotient and remainder of integer division. Make sure that the execution time does not grow linear with the quotient, but with the logarithm of the quotient. For x **div** y and x **mod** y, you may assume $x \geq 0 \ \wedge \ y > 0$. It is okay to include the subroutine in the object code of each program, even if it doesn't need it. Make sure that instructions **div2** and **mod2** are still generated where appropriate.

8. Extend the peephole optimizer to replace every occurrence of

    > load value of i
    > load value of i

   with

```
load value of i
dupl
```

9. Change the compiler in such a way that if $x \neq 1$ then s leads to the following code.

```
        load value of x
        addc    -1
        jumpz   l
        s
l :
```

Do you need to change the peephole optimizer only, or do you have to change more? Do you get the code that you expect if the constant 1 is replaced by 2? What if it is replaced by 0?

10. In the example code given in Section 2, instruction 7 is a **jump** to an **exit** instruction. The **jump** instruction might just as well be replaced by a copy of the **exit** instruction. This change does not make the code any shorter, but reduces its execution time. Discuss how you would implement this improvement.

11. Change the compiler to generate Mosaic code, and change the interpreter to interpret Mosaic code.

12. The storage capacity during execution of *interpret* may be exceeded. One may either check for storage overflow in the interpreter on execution of every instruction that extends the stack, or perform a check less frequently, say once per procedure entry. In the latter case, additional information, to be produced by the compiler, is required. Discuss the nature of the information required. One might even reduce the checks to calls of recursive procedures only. How would you implement this?

16

The Construction of a Processor

In this chapter, we study the construction of a microprocessor, using the circuitry developed in Chapter 5. A microprocessor is a large circuit, and designing a large circuit involves many of the complexities of designing a large program. We try to steer clear of most of those issues and provide only a rough sketch of the circuit.

16.1 Processor Organization

The processor consists of a number of components that are interconnected by a so-called *bus*. A bus is similar to a shared variable in a concurrent program. A major difference, however, is that the kind of circuits we studied in Chapter 5 are driven by a clock that determines when signals, or variables, are accessed. In our concurrent programs, we did not assume any such global synchronization, but made the weaker assumption of fairness: every process proceeds eventually. Because of the synchronization, we describe the bus as a channel rather than as a shared variable.

The processor consists of a number of components. Ignoring the packet interface, which is the component that implements links between processors, we have four parts.

> *processor* : **chan** *bus*
>   *data path* ||
>   *registers* ||
>   *memory interface* ||
>   *controller*

The data path consists of the circuit that implements the arithmetic and logic operations (ALU, for Arithmetic and Logic Unit), together with some internal registers for holding its inputs and outputs.

> *data path* : **var** x, y, w
> $X \parallel Y \parallel ALU \parallel W$

The processor runs on a two-phase non-overlapping clock. The ALU is active during ϕ_1, whereas the bus is active during ϕ_2.

$$X : \quad *[true \rightarrow [\phi_2 \wedge toX \rightarrow bus?x]]$$
$$Y : \quad *[true \rightarrow [\phi_2 \wedge toY \rightarrow bus?y]]$$
$$W : \quad *[true \rightarrow [\phi_2 \wedge fromW \rightarrow bus!w]]$$
$$ALU : \quad *[true \rightarrow [\phi_1 \rightarrow w := function(x, y)]]$$

We still have to figure out conditions like toX, but we postpone doing so until we have collected a few more. In the next section, we see how the ALU computes w as a function of x and y.

Next, we focus on the set of registers. The processor has 16 registers. They are used to hold arguments and results from ALU operations, and to hold addresses that are needed to access storage locations. All accesses to registers are via the bus. The identity of the register that is being accessed is contained as a number in the range 0 through 15 in the instruction that is being executed, which during its execution is stored in variable I. In fact, most instructions specify two registers; most ALU instructions (such as addition) require two operands, and these are contained in two registers. The result is stored in one of those two. Also, the MOVE instruction, which is the one that accesses memory, has two operands; the source and the destination of the copy operation, and each of them may involve a register. The two registers are indicated in two fields of the instruction, referred to as the J and K fields. The remaining 8 bits are referred to as the operation field OP.

var I : **record** OP : 0..255; J, K : 0..15 **end**

Using the instruction register, we may now write the program for the registers.

$$registers : \quad *[\quad true \rightarrow [\quad \phi_2 \wedge fromJ \quad \rightarrow bus!reg[I.J]$$
$$\| \quad \phi_2 \wedge fromK \quad \rightarrow bus!reg[I.K]$$
$$\| \quad \phi_2 \wedge toK \quad \rightarrow bus?reg[I.K]$$
$$] \qquad]$$

By now, we have various processes sending values to channel bus, and also various processes reading from it. In order to ensure correct operation, we must see to it that at any time either no process is sending and no process is receiving, or that one process is sending and one process is receiving. Never shall there be more than one sender or more than one receiver. This synchronization is what we have our clock and the conditions for. The conditions are computed by a process called the controller. The controller derives the conditions from the encoding of the instruction I that is being executed.

The remaining component that interacts with the bus is the memory interface. It is used to transfer words between the processor and the memory. Every memory access requires that an address be specified. One bus cycle is used to transfer the address from the registers, or the ALU output to address latch A. During the next cycle, the data transfer takes place. If

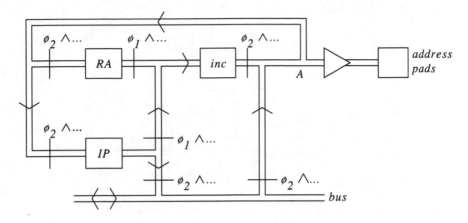

FIGURE 16.1. Memory interface.

the memory access is a write operation, then the value placed on the bus is copied to memory; if the memory access is a read operation then the value stored in memory is copied to the bus. It is the task of the controller to route the proper values to and from the bus. We discuss the controller in a later section. The circuit that implements the memory interface is given in Figure 16.1. We will not study the memory itself.

One value that is often copied to the A register is the instruction pointer (sometimes referred to as the program counter). It is therefore pictured together with the memory interface. It holds the memory location of the next instruction to be executed and is often incremented by one. We might use the ALU for performing the addition with one, but it is more efficient to use a separate circuit for this purpose, since that allows the incrementer and the ALU to operate concurrently. Figure 16.2 shows how an incrementer can be constructed efficiently. Another value that is often copied to address latch A is the so-called refresh address RA. The memory needs to be accessed every so often in order to prevent the contents of the memory cells from slowly leaking away. The processor does not need to access memory in all of its cycles, and the remaining cycles are used to access all storage locations in a round-robin fashion. Variable RA contains the address of the last memory location that has been refreshed. It is also possible to build a memory that needs no refreshing. Essentially, it consists of one flip-flop per memory location. Such a memory, called a static random access memory (SRAM) instead of a dynamic random access memory (DRAM) takes more power and requires more silicon area. Therefore, the DRAM solution is often preferred.

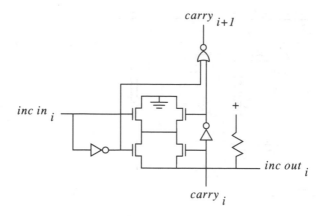

FIGURE 16.2. An incrementer.

16.2   The ALU

In this section we study the ALU, which is a circuit that is given two operands in variables x and y, and computes the result in variable w. The controller computes a number of conditions that indicate which function is to be computed by the circuit. Let us start with studying addition. How do we make an adder? We are given two 16-bit numbers x and y, and we are supposed to compute sum s and carry c. We use subscript i to denote bit i. The least-significant bit is bit 0; the most significant bit is bit 15. Addition can be defined as

$$
\begin{aligned}
s_i &= (x_i + y_i + c_i) \bmod 2 \\
c_{i+1} &= (x_i + y_i + c_i) \operatorname{div} 2 \qquad ,
\end{aligned}
$$

where $c_0 = 0$ and c_{16} is the carry that results from the addition. A direct implementation of this addition is time-consuming if c_{i+1} is determined by c_i because then the carry "ripples through" the adder. Observe, however,

$$
\begin{aligned}
&\text{if } x_i + y_i = 0 \text{ then } c_{i+1} = 0 \qquad \text{"carry kill"} \\
&\text{if } x_i + y_i = 1 \text{ then } c_{i+1} = c_i \qquad \text{"carry propagate"} \\
&\text{if } x_i + y_i = 2 \text{ then } c_{i+1} = 1 \qquad \text{"carry generate"}
\end{aligned}
$$

which suggests to define

$$
\begin{aligned}
g_i &= (x_i + y_i) \operatorname{div} 2 \\
p_i &= (x_i + y_i) \bmod 2
\end{aligned}
$$

and we have

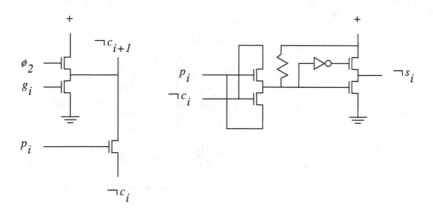

FIGURE 16.3. Computation of c_{i+1} and s_i.

$$c_{i+1} = 0, \quad \text{if } g_i = 0 \wedge p_i = 0$$
$$c_i, \quad \text{if } p_i = 1$$
$$1, \quad \text{if } g_i = 1$$
$$s_i = (p_i + c_i) \bmod 2$$

or equivalently (writing $\neg x$ for $1 - x$)

$$\neg c_{i+1} = 1, \quad \text{if } g_i = 0 \wedge p_i = 0$$
$$\neg c_i, \quad \text{if } p_i = 1$$
$$0, \quad \text{if } g_i = 1$$
$$\neg s_i = (p_i + \neg c_i) \bmod 2 \quad .$$

Remember that we have seen that pull-up circuits are slow, which implies that passing on a high signal takes a long time. In order to speed up passing on a high $\neg c_i$ to $\neg c_{i+1}$, we make the latter signal high before its actual value is computed, and quickly reset it to a low value when necessary. The correct value is needed during ϕ_1, and hence, during the preceding ϕ_2, we can set the signal to a high value. This "trick" is called precharging. The circuits in Figure 16.3 implement the precharging, the computation of c_{i+1}, and the computation of s_i. It remains to design a circuit for computing g_i and p_i, given x_i and y_i.

Figure 16.4 shows a circuit for computing an arbitrary function of two arguments (both result and arguments are binary valued). The function is given by enumeration: for each input combination, the function value is listed. Since only 4 input combinations exist ($x_i, y_i = 0, 0; \ 0, 1; \ 1, 0; \ 1, 1$), a table of 4 entries (labeled G_0, G_1, G_2, G_3) suffices. The circuit implements a form of table lookup. For example, if $x_i = y_i = 0$, g_i is connected to G_0. Similarly for the other three combinations. We use an identical circuit for computing p_i. In the case of addition, the table of values for G and P is as follows.

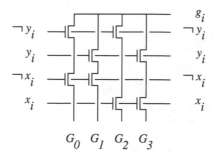

FIGURE 16.4. Circuit for computing an arbitrary function.

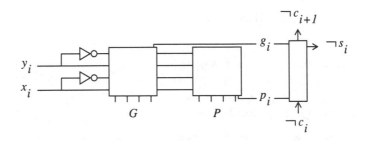

FIGURE 16.5. G, P, and the adder combined.

if x_i, y_i = 0,0	then g_i = 0	and p_i = 0
0,1	0	1
1,0	0	1
1,1	1	0

From the table, we conclude $G_3 G_2 G_1 G_0 = 1000$ and $P_3 P_2 P_1 P_0 = 0110$.
In hexadecimal notation, we find that the controller has to set GP to 86
if the ALU is to perform an addition. Putting it all together, we obtain the
circuit in Figure 16.5.

What happens to c_0 and c_{16} ? In the case of addition, c_0 is set to 0, and
in the case of addition with incoming carry, c_0 is set to the value stored
in the carry-flag. In both cases, c_{16} is the new setting of the carry-flag.

Now that we have a nice circuit for addition, let's find out whether it
can be used for other operations as well. Consider bit-wise conjunction,
which is needed in the AND operation. We have to choose g_i and p_i in
a way that leads to s_i = $x_i \wedge y_i$. The following table gives a possible
implementation. It was obtained by first setting s_i to its proper value, by
choosing $g_i = c_i = c_{i+1} = 0$, and by then figuring out p_i.

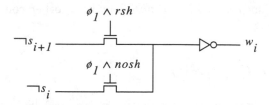

FIGURE 16.6. *ALU* -output shifter.

x_i	y_i	g_i	p_i	c_{i+1}	s_i
0	0	0	0	0	0
0	1	0	0	0	0
1	0	0	0	0	0
1	1	0	1	c_i	1

We find $GP = 08$. In the same way, we construct the table for shifting x over one position to the left. We choose $c_{i+1} = x_i$, $s_i = c_i$.

x_i	y_i	g_i	p_i	c_{i+1}	s_i
0	0	0	0	0	c_i
0	1	0	0	0	c_i
1	0	1	0	1	c_i
1	1	1	0	1	c_i

From s_i follows p_i and from c_{i+1} follows g_i. We find $GP = C0$.

Various operations can be performed by setting GP to the proper value, but not all: operations in which s_i depends on x_{i+1} can not be handled. This dependency occurs in the so-called right-shift operations. Therefore, we add a shifter (see Figure 16.6) at the output of s_i before the final output w_i is computed. It is also possible to combine the ALU and the shifter in parallel because in every cycle at most one of the two is really used. The serial composition has been chosen because it is simpler (only one set of latches and flag computation required) and doesn't require additional time (the slowest path is the computation of the overflow signal V). How are the condition flags computed anyway? We have four of them. Z is set to 1 if the 16-bit result of the ALU operation consists of zeros only, and to 0 otherwise. This requires a big 16-input AND-gate. N is set to the most-significant bit of the result of the ALU operation. C is set to the carry that results from an addition, or to the bit that is shifted out in a shift operation (left or right). V is used to indicate overflow from an arithmetic operation: it is set to one the sum modulo 2 of bits 15 and 16 of the result of the operation when carried out in 17-bit arithmetic. Therefore, V indicates whether the sign-bit of the 16-bit result has the proper value. This completes our discussion of the ALU. We are left with the construction of a controller that issues the proper signals for controlling the operation of the ALU (such as *GP* and *nosh*) and the other components of the processor.

16.3   The Controller

The controller is the component that is, in essence, the implementation of a small program: the interpreter of the machine's instruction set, minus the arithmetic that is performed by the ALU. The program is a simple one. It consists of one loop, and the loop body consists of two actions: first, fetch the next instruction to be executed from memory; second, execute it. Execution boils down to setting all the conditions that we have seen in previous components. How do we execute a program, and compute some signals on the fly? The program could be expressed as a regular expression, which is equivalent to a transition graph (see Chapter 4). The transition graph can be implemented as a circuit consisting of some inputs, outputs, and feedback signals (see Chapter 5). The feedback signals encode the state in which the execution is. The input signals consist of the encoding of the instruction being executed, and a few more that are not of interest right now.

Let us take an example to see what is expected from the controller. Assume that the instruction pointer *IP* points to the instruction

ADD $r0, r1$,

which adds the contents of register $r0$ to that of register $r1$, and stores the result in $r1$. The action by the controller that assigned the proper value to *IP* already caused the 16-bits encoding of the ADD instruction to be transferred to the data input register *IN*. In the first cycle corresponding to the execution of the ADD instruction, the data from memory are copied to instruction register *I*, followed by copying one of the operands of the addition to ALU register *X*.

$\phi_1 \rightarrow I := IN$
$\phi_2 \rightarrow X := reg[I.J]$

In the next cycle, the other operand is copied to ALU register *Y*.

$\phi_1 \rightarrow skip$
$\phi_2 \rightarrow Y := reg[I.K]$

In the third and last cycle, the addition is performed and, simultaneously, the instruction pointer is incremented. Its new value is also stored in address register *A*, causing the next instruction to be copied to data input register *IN*, where it is required for executing the next instruction.

$\phi_1 \rightarrow GP := 86, \; Cin := 0, \; setZNVC, \; nosh, \; inc \; in := IP$
$\phi_2 \rightarrow reg[I.K] := W, \; A := inc \; out, \; IP := A$

The circuitry around IP and A was designed to allow execution of the operations specified in the last two lines without involving the bus. This allows these operations to proceed in parallel with the assignment of the ALU output W to register $reg[I.K]$.

In the sequel, we write the actions to be performed during ϕ_1 and the actions to be performed during ϕ_2 in one line, and we omit the clock signals from the description. It is possible to figure out the clock phase during which an operation is performed by inspecting the circuits. The lines we are writing are just like the lines we were writing at the end of Chapter 5, and they were directly translated into VLSI circuits. Our discussion can therefore be conducted at the level of these lines of program text, and we need not worry about their implementation as a circuit.

So much for the actions that need to be performed. What is the mechanism for performing these actions in this sequence? Well, this is where the input signals and the feedback signals come in. The above sequence goes through three states, and those states are encoded by the feedback signals. Let's call them *decode*, *get*, and *go*, respectively. However, the latter two states are used in the execution sequence of many different instructions, so the instruction itself is also part of the sequencing mechanism. Actually, only the most-significant 8 bits encode the operation; the least-significant 8 bits encode the J and K fields. This leaves us with the following three control lines.

$$st = decode \qquad\qquad \rightarrow I := IN, X := reg[I.J], st := get$$
$$st = get \,\wedge\, I.OP = 01000000 \rightarrow Y := reg[I.K], st := go$$
$$st = go \;\;\wedge\, I.OP = 01000000 \rightarrow GP := 86, Cin := 0, setZNVC,$$
$$nosh, reg[I.K] := W, inc\ in := IP,$$
$$A := inc\ out, IP := A, st := decode$$

This form of sequencing corresponds to what we called *explicit sequencing* in Chapter 14.

We have written $Y := reg[I.K]$ as an abbreviation of *fromK*, *toY*, which copies $reg[I.K]$ to the bus and copies the bus to Y, respectively. Similarly, $reg[I.K] := W$ is short for *fromW*, *toK*. The constructs $inc\ in := IP$, $A := inc\ out$, and $IP := A$ correspond to conditions indicated by dots in Figure 16.1. Consider another instruction, the subtraction of registers. Its set of three lines reads as follows.

$$st = decode \qquad\qquad \rightarrow I := IN, X := reg[I.J], st := get$$
$$st = get \,\wedge\, I.OP = 01000010 \rightarrow Y := reg[I.K], st := go$$
$$st = go \;\;\wedge\, I.OP = 01000010 \rightarrow GP := 29, Cin := 1, setZNVC,$$
$$nosh, reg[I.K] := W, inc\ in := IP,$$
$$A := inc\ out, IP := A, st := decode$$

The first two lines are the same as the first two lines for addition, with the exception of the instruction's encoding. It is much better to combine the two instructions into four lines instead of having six lines. This leads to

$$
\begin{aligned}
st = decode & \rightarrow I := IN, X := reg[I.J], st := get \\
st = get \wedge I.OP = 010000?0 & \rightarrow Y := reg[I.K], st := go \\
st = go \ \wedge I.OP = 01000000 & \rightarrow GP := 86, Cin := 0, setZNVC, \\
& \quad nosh, reg[I.K] := W, inc \ in := IP, \\
& \quad A := inc \ out, IP := A, st := decode \\
st = go \ \wedge I.OP = 01000010 & \rightarrow GP := 29, Cin := 1, setZNVC, \\
& \quad nosh, reg[I.K] := W, inc \ in := IP, \\
& \quad A := inc \ out, IP := A, st := decode
\end{aligned}
$$

in which ? indicates that the corresponding bit of the instruction register I is to be ignored. For every instruction, we concoct a number of control lines, and we exploit the regularities in the instruction encoding so as to combine many lines into fewer lines. Writing a control program is a form of programming that is known as microprogramming. The process of reducing the number of lines is very hard and error prone. Quite often, one can come up with different sets of control lines for implementing an instruction, and which set is chosen is often determined by how well it lends itself to the reduction process.

As mentioned before, the memory needs to be refreshed every now and then. In the above example, it could be done either in state *decode*, in state *get*, or in both. The signals

$$inc \ in := RA, \ A := inc \ out, \ RA := A$$

implement the refresh action.

For the sake of completeness, we mention a few more input signals that did not play a role in the above examples. The conditional jump instructions make a choice between two different actions based on the values of the four flags. It is possible to write all 14 conditional jumps individually, and to write the proper conditions for all 4 flags in each of them, but it makes more sense to devise a special circuit that produces one boolean value (to jump or not to jump) based on the 4 flags and the instruction encoding. This leads to a small special-purpose PLA whose output is an input to the microcode PLA.

The remaining two inputs are signals for indicating that an interrupt has occurred or that a reset has occurred. In state *decode*, a check is carried out to see whether an interrupt has occurred and if so, then some special actions are performed that lead to activating the interrupt handler. If a reset has occurred, then *IP* is set to 0, and in the next cycle, the state is set to *decode*.

It turns out that all together, the Mosaic uses 71 lines to sequence all of its 25 instructions. Five signals are used for the feedback states. Each line contributes one row in the PLA that implements this program. Each input signal contributes one input row of the AND part of the PLA, each output signal contributes one output column of the OR part, and each feedback signal contributes both an input row and an output row.

16.4 Multicomputers

In the previous sections, we have given a bird's-eye view of how a small processor can be constructed. Add a memory chip and a few peripherals and, voilà, we have a complete computer. It is so small that it is aptly known as a microcomputer. What is the essential difference between our humble microcomputer and the supercomputers that make it to the front page of the newspaper? A supercomputer is much more expensive and a lot faster. Two different methods of achieving high speed exist. One method is to come up with a faster implementation of the simple processor; the other method is to use a lot of processors simultaneously. Of course, the two methods can be combined.

Let us have a look at the first method. How can we speed up our simple processor? One of the possibilities is to come up with a more efficient microprogram. For example, if our machine has an instruction for computing the quotient of two numbers, we might have a very inefficient implementation that repeatedly subtracts the denominator from what remains of the numerator, each time incrementing the quotient by one. It is much better to replace this program with a more efficient program, such as shown in Exercise 3.25. While it is rare to find such inefficient microprograms, where they do exist a tremendous improvement may result. Another possibility is to change the circuit. For example, if our machine has an instruction to shift the contents of a register over n positions, and we have the 1-position shifter as shown in Figure 16.6, then it will take n cycles to execute the instructions (plus some for "overhead"); or even $2n$ or $3n$, if we need the same ALU for decrementing n in each step and comparing the resulting against 0. We might replace the simple shifter with a so-called barrel shifter that shifts over n positions in one cycle. The silicon area occupied by the barrel shifter grows with the square of the number of bits in a word, which means that it consumes a lot of silicon. It is not unusual to find that the barrel shifter occupies more area than all the rest of the ALU combined. A third possibility for speeding up the processor is to redesign circuit and microprogram to execute instructions in fewer cycles. One strategy for reducing the number of cycles is *pipelining*. We have seen that the execution of our sample instructions was done in three steps, labeled *decode*, *get*, and *go*. The three steps might be executed by three parallel processes, each dedicated to executing one step. While one of them executes the *go* step of one instruction, another process executes the *get* step of the next instruction, and the third may simultaneously execute the *decode* step of the third instruction. Each instruction still requires three cycles to complete, but since three processes are operating simultaneously, three instructions are executed simultaneously, and the effective rate is one cycle per instruction. Pipelining is found in just about every fast processor. Its major problem is that of dependence of one instruction's execution on the result of a previous instruction that may still be "in the pipeline". For example, if a compare instruction is immediately followed by a conditional jump, the *decode* and *get* processes may have to be suspended for one or two cycles in order for the results of the comparison to become available. This leads to synchronization of the various processes, which in turn causes a dramatic increase in the complexity of each of those processes. Part of the complexity of decoding an instruction may be due to irregularities in the machine's instruction set. Reduction of the number of cycles per instruction may, therefore, require some simplification of the machine's instruction set and is known under the name RISC, for reduced instruction set computer (although the adjective "regular" would be more appropriate). The opposite is also feasible: find out which instructions are often executed in combination, and extend the machine with a new instruction for each such combination. The overhead in the microprogram of loading instructions from memory and decoding them is thereby reduced, and sometimes we may know of a better algorithm for executing the particular combination than for the individual parts. This strategy is known as CISC, or complex instruction set computer. The current trend is away from CISC and towards RISC. One of the reasons is that the frequency of those more complex combinations depends too much on the programming language and on the program. And combinations that are "almost" right are probably even worse than no such combinations at all.

Yet another possibility for making a faster processor is to implement the circuit in a faster technology. We do not have much control over the speed of light, but we may choose a material in which the mobility of the charge carriers is higher, such as gallium arsenide, which would lead to a higher speed of operation. We may also use a technology in which both positively-charged and negatively-charged carriers contribute to the electric current flow. These are known as bipolar technologies. Another method is to shorten the distances traveled by all signals by scaling down the size of the circuit's layout. In those parts of the circuit where delays are dominated by drift of charge carriers in an electric field, such as in a short wire and in the channel of a transistor, scaling down the circuit by a factor α, reduces delay by a factor α. In those parts where delays are dominated by diffusive effects, as in long wires, scaling does not affect the delay. Therefore, scaling can not be expected to be a straightforward job, especially not in the case of circuits that are sensitive to delays. Scaling down is probably the most dramatic factor in the speed of current computers. Every two years, the size of a circuit's layout is approximately halved, in each of the three dimensions. This reduction, which is purely technological progress, has been going on for many years and there is no reason to expect it to stop soon. We are in the extremely fortunate situation where scaling down the size of the circuit in each dimension by a factor α, coupled with decreasing the voltage level at the power supply with a factor α (in order to leave the electric fields in the transistors at the same level), increases the speed of the circuit by a factor α (if we manage to avoid long wires) and simultaneously reduces the power dissipation by a factor α^2, which thereby diminishes the problem of heat dissipation from the chips. It is a remarkable and unusual incentive for advance in VLSI technologies. Actually, one often puts an α^2 times larger circuit on a chip of the same size so that the heat dissipation per chip remains the same.

Another method of building a fast computer is to focus not on using one fast processor, but on using many processors. Again, various ways are open to us for constructing a computer from many processors. One way is to build a so-called shared-memory machine, in which all processors access one, big, shared memory. Access to the memory is destined to be the bottleneck in such a system and one can not expect it to work well with more than a few dozen processors. The more promising way to build a many-processor computer is to equip each processor with its own memory. In such a multicomputer, the processors cannot communicate via shared memory, because there is none. A communication mechanism, which resembles the channels that we used in our concurrent programs (see Chapter 13), is provided instead. Each processor is extended with few links, say four or six, plus some instructions for sending and receiving messages along the links. The processors can be arranged in many different patterns by connecting their links to form a big processor array. If the communication time can be made to grow slowly with the number of processors, then there are hardly any technical limits on the size of a multicomputer. If one manages to write programs that scale with the size of the machine (see Section 13.8), then the multicomputer delivers an almost constant price/performance ratio over an almost unlimited range (from one up). Multicomputers with a few hundred processors are in daily use, and multicomputers with tens of thousands of processors are under construction.

Many problems have to be solved and many choices have to be made in the construction of a multicomputer. The most important one is how to make the communication mechanism fast. For example, one should not choose processors with two links and then arrange them in a linear array. On the average, the delay between sending and receiving a message grows linearly with the number of processors. A better arrangement is a two-dimensional array, requiring four links per processor, and causing the average delay to grow with the square root of the number of processors. Can we do better than the square root? One popular interconnection scheme is called the n-cube. Suppose we identify each of 2^n processors by an n-bit number. Connect two processors if their identifiers differ in exactly one bit. (The case $n = 3$ is the ordinary cube, hence the terminology.) It is easily seen that the maximum distance, measured in links, between any pair of processors is n, and that is a good reason for expecting a short delay in communications. On the other hand, each processor requires n links, so it is a system with a built-in upper limit on its size (given the maximum number of links per processor). Furthermore, one may wonder whether those extra links "are worth it". The n-cube with 2^n processors has a total of $n2^{n-1}$ links. A 2-dimensional mesh with 2^n processors has 2^{n+1} links (minus some $2^{n/2+1}$ at the borders). Apparently, the cube needs more links than does the mesh. Suppose we keep the number of wires in the system constant. (This is a reasonable thing to do, since wires are a significant fraction of the cost.) If the cube uses only 1 wire per link, then the mesh can use

$$\frac{n2^{n-1}}{2^{n+1} - 2^{n/2+1}} \approx \frac{n}{4}$$

wires per link. For $n = 12$, which corresponds to a mere 4096 processors, the mesh can transmit 3 bits in parallel for every bit sent in the cube. On the other hand, the distance (the number of links in a path) is shorter in the cube. But then, the mesh can be laid out with short wires, whereas the cube requires many long wires. And so on. There is no definite formula for putting everything together because many of the parameters depend on the technology, but roughly a 2-dimensional mesh is better for systems up to about a thousand processors, a 3-dimensional mesh is better for systems with about ten-thousand processors, and one would go to 4 or 5 dimensions for a million processors; never would one go to the cube. However, it is not at all necessary to restrict ourselves to one of these regular connection patterns. It appears that a random connection pattern is adequate in almost every aspect (provided it is connected). But it may not be so easy to convince a technician to wire the machine in a random way.

The above discussion of multi-link delays ignores what is going on at the points where links meet, that is, at the processors. One method for sending a message along a multi-link path is to send it to a neighboring processor where it is stored in local memory until the whole message has arrived. Then, it is forwarded to its neighbor on the path, and so on until the message arrives at its destination. This is known as store-and-forward routing. The good thing about it is the fact that it "blocks" only one link per message. The bad thing about it is that it requires buffer storage in every processor en route, the size of those buffers depending on the messages, and it is very slow because at most one link at a time contributes to communicating the particular message. Another method, known as cut-through routing, is to think of the processors as switches, as far as these multi-link messages are concerned. First, all switches are set in the proper position, and then the message goes straight through from the sender to its final destination. This method avoids the buffering, and is a lot faster, but it "blocks" all links of the path for the entire transmission period. A better communication scheme is wormhole routing, which partitions a message into small packets; the packets are sent one after the other using the store-and-forward scheme, but because these small packets are used, the buffer size is the size of the small packet. Also, as soon as a packet has arrived at some processor, it can send it on to the next processor, so that a number of links are transmitting different packets from the same message simultaneously. Since the size of the buffers for storing the small packets is independent of the messages that are communicated, they can be chosen to be small and implemented in some special way outside the memory of the processor and in the part of the circuit that does the actual routing. As a result, the processor and its memory are not interrupted for the forwarding of messages that happen to pass by.

Of course, an interesting problem remains. In Chapter 14, we have seen how variables and statements in a program are mapped to memory locations and instructions. In our concurrent programs, we additionally have processes and channels in between. Therefore, we need to map processes to processors and channels to links. Only in uninteresting cases is there a one-to-one mapping of processes to processors and of channels to links. In general, we have more processes than processors, and channels are mapped to multi-link paths. An algorithm is needed for routing messages to their destination, and it is nontrivial to come up with an efficient algorithm that does not introduce deadlock. Having more than one process per processor is a bonus. Although it introduces some of the problems that we briefly mentioned at the end of Chapter 14, it also solves a problem. In many programs, a message is sent, and then the process waits for another message to come back. If we have only one process per processor, nothing much can be done in the period between the two communication actions. If we have multiple processes per processor, one of the other processes can be executed, until it is waiting for a communication to complete.

We have briefly discussed two ways of improving the performance of our microcomputer to that of a supercomputer: build a fast processor, and use many processors. Of course, both methods can be used in the same system. It appears, however, that speeding up an individual processor is subject to more severe limits than expanding the size of a multicomputer: it is bound more strictly by the law of diminishing returns. We will not go into the many, fascinating aspects of designing efficient computers, but leave the subject right now.

16.5   Bibliographic Notes

The Mosaic circuits that we have discussed are based on [Lut84]. Consult [Sei84], [Sei85], and [Sei90] for discussions of multicomputers. The comparison of cubes and meshes was inspired by [Dal86]. The interaction between technology and computer architecture is discussed in [SM77]. Consult [MC80] for a discussion of scaling of VLSI circuits. These and other computational aspects of VLSI are also found in [Ull84]. Exercise 6 is from [MvdS90].

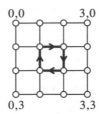

FIGURE 16.7. A deadlocked configuration.

16.6   Exercises

1. Design the circuit for computing the Z, N, and V conditions.

2. Design the circuit for the register array.

3. Propose microcode for an exclusive-or instruction.

4. Propose microcode for the unconditional jump instruction.

5. Assume that wormhole routing in a mesh is used. A message is to be transmitted from $(1,1)$ to $(2,2)$, another message is to be transmitted from $(1,2)$ to $(2,1)$, a third message from $(2,1)$ to $(1,2)$, and a fourth message from $(2,2)$ to $(1,1)$. Assume that the message are long enough to occupy the entire path needed for their transmission. Suppose that the routing algorithm routes all messages in a clockwise fashion. For example, from $(1,1)$ via $(2,1)$ to $(2,2)$. If all messages are sent simultaneously then, after they have all traversed the first link of the path, the configuration is as shown in Figure 16.7. In this configuration we have deadlock. Apparently clockwise routing is not a good algorithm: it suffers from deadlock. Propose an algorithm that routes messages between any pair of processors without introducing deadlock.

6. Consider a complete binary tree of $2^n - 1$ nodes and $2^n - 2$ edges. Each edge except the root has one incoming edge, and each edge except the leaves has two outgoing edges. We can extend the network into a two-in-two-out network by adding two outgoing edges to each leaf and let them go to any unused input of any node. In this way, we add 2^n edges; each node (including every leaf) receives one extra incoming edge, except the root which receives two. There is a lot of freedom in choosing the actual edges, but no matter how you do it, we have the following property. Assume that the above is the communication network of a multicomputer. Assume that the program consists of a complete binary tree of processes in which the

edges correspond to channels. The number of processes may exceed, equal, or be less than the number of processors. Consider the following recursively-defined mapping of the program on the computer. Map the root process to the root processor. If a process has any sub-processes, then it has exactly two subprocesses and it has one channel to each of them. These two channels are mapped on its two outgoing links, one each, and the two subprocesses are mapped on the two processors at the other end of the two links, one each. The result is that every processor has a number of processes. Some processors have more processes than other. Show that, for any complete binary tree, the largest number of processes per processor minus the smallest number of processes per processor is zero or one.

Appendix A

Answers to Some of the Exercises

Answers for Chapter 2

2. Let $f(x)$ be the number of a's minus the number of b's in string x. A string is in the language defined by the grammar just when

   - $f(x) = 1$ and
   - for every proper prefix u of x, $f(u) < 1$.

3. Let the string be given as array $X[0..N-1]$ of length N. We use the notation $X \downarrow i$, (pronounced: X drop i) for $0 \le i \le N$, to denote the tail of length $N-i$ of array X, that is, the sequence from index i on. (Or: X from which the first i elements have been dropped.) We write L for the language denoted by the grammar. L^k is the language consisting of the catenation of k strings from L. We are asked to write a program for computing the boolean value $X \in L$. This may be written as $X \downarrow 0 \in L^1$. The invariant that we choose is obtained by generalizing constants 0 and 1 to variables i and k:

$$P: \quad (X \in L \;=\; X \downarrow i \in L^k) \;\wedge\; 0 \le i \le N \;\wedge\; 0 \le k \quad .$$

We use the following properties:

   (0)   if $X[i] = a$, $i < N$, $k > 0$ then
   $$X \downarrow i \in L^k \;=\; X \downarrow i+1 \in L^{k-1}$$
   (1)   if $X[i] = b$, $i < N$, $k \ge 0$ then
   $$X \downarrow i \in L^k \;=\; X \downarrow i+1 \in L^{k+1}$$
   (2) $X \downarrow N \in L^k \;=\; (k = 0)$
            because $X \downarrow N = \epsilon$ and $\epsilon \in L^k$ for $k = 0$ only
   (3) $X \downarrow i \in L^0 \;=\; (i = N)$
            because $(X \downarrow i = \epsilon) = (i = N)$ and $L^0 = \{\epsilon\}$

The program is

```
{ N ≥ 0 }
k := 1;  i := 0;  { P }
*[ k ≠ 0 ∧ i ≠ N → [ X[i] = a → k := k − 1
```

$$\| X[i] = b \rightarrow k := k+1$$
$$];$$
$$i := i+1 \; \{ \, P \, \}$$

$$];$$
$$\{ \, P \;\; \wedge \;\; (k = 0 \;\; \vee \;\; i = N) \, \}$$
$$[k = 0 \wedge i = N \rightarrow write('\mathbf{yes}') \; \| \; k > 0 \vee i < N \rightarrow write('\mathbf{no}')]$$

The initialization establishes P. The invariance of P follows from properties (0) and (1). Every step increases integer i, and since i is bounded by N, the loop terminates. It does so in a state in which invariant P holds and in which the negation of the guard holds. On account of properties (2) and (3), and in conjunction with P and the negation of the guard, the final statement produces the correct result.

4. We write $\Longrightarrow^k$ for a k-step derivation.

   - induction hypothesis:

     $$(H \Longrightarrow^k x) = (alt(x) \; \wedge \; |x| = k)$$

   - base case, $k = 1$:

     $$H \Longrightarrow^1 x$$
     $$= \qquad \{ \text{ the only production rule that finishes in one}$$
     $$\qquad\qquad \text{step is } H \longrightarrow a \; \}$$
     $$x = a$$
     $$= \qquad \{ \text{ one string } x \text{ of length 1 satisfies } alt(x) \; \}$$
     $$alt(x) \;\; \wedge \;\; |x| = 1$$

   - step, $k > 1$:

     $$H \Longrightarrow^k x$$
     $$= \qquad \{ \text{ the only production rule that does not finish in}$$
     $$\qquad\qquad \text{one step is } H \longrightarrow H \, b \, H \; \}$$
     $$\langle \exists y, z, i, j :: H \Longrightarrow^i y \;\; \wedge \;\; H \Longrightarrow^j z \;\; \wedge \;\; x = ybz \;\; \wedge$$
     $$\qquad i \geq 1 \;\; \wedge \;\; j \geq 1 \;\; \wedge \;\; i + j = k - 1 \rangle$$
     $$= \qquad \{ \text{ induction hypothesis } \}$$
     $$\langle \exists y, z, i, j :: alt(y) \wedge |y| = i \;\; \wedge \;\; alt(z) \wedge |z| = j \;\; \wedge$$
     $$\qquad x = ybz \;\; \wedge \;\; i \geq 1 \;\; \wedge \;\; j \geq 1 \;\; \wedge \;\; i + j = k - 1 \rangle$$
     $$= \qquad \{ \text{ property of } alt \; \}$$
     $$alt(x) \;\; \wedge \;\; |x| = k$$

In our two proofs, each step expresses equality of two conditions, not just implication in one direction. Often, equality of conditions is expressed more easily in formulae than in English. It is a pain in the neck having to say "if and only if" or "just when" all the time.

8. Yes, there is a problem: the grammar is ambiguous. For example, $i/i \times i$ can be parsed as $i/(i \times i)$ or as $(i/i) \times i$.

10. A grammar that generates every string that has twice as many a's as b's is

$$(\{a, b\}, \{S, B\}, \{S \longrightarrow aaSB \mid \epsilon, aB \longrightarrow Ba, B \longrightarrow b\}, S).$$

12. The grammar is

$$(\{a\}, \{B, C, D, R, L, E\}, \textit{rules}, aBRCD)$$

where the (large) set of rules is

$$
\begin{aligned}
BR &\longrightarrow E \\
EC &\longrightarrow E \\
ED &\longrightarrow \epsilon \\
RC &\longrightarrow aaCR \\
Ca &\longrightarrow aC \\
Ba &\longrightarrow aB \\
RD &\longrightarrow LCD \\
CL &\longrightarrow LC \\
BL &\longrightarrow aBR \qquad .
\end{aligned}
$$

First we prove that each string of the form a^{n^2} is in the language, for $n \geq 1$. We do so by proving by mathematical induction that $a^{n^2}BRC^nD$ can be derived, that is, $aBRCD \Longrightarrow^* a^{n^2}BRC^nD$. Basis $n = 1$ follows from the reflexivity of $\Longrightarrow^*$. For all $n \geq 1$, we have

$$
\begin{aligned}
&aBRCD \\
\Longrightarrow^* &\quad \{ \text{ induction hypothesis } \} \\
&a^{n^2}BRC^nD \\
\Longrightarrow^* &\quad \{ \ n \text{ applications of } RC \longrightarrow aaCR \ \} \\
&a^{n^2}B(aaC)^nRD \\
\Longrightarrow^* &\quad \{ \ n(n-1) \text{ applications of } Ca \longrightarrow aC \ \} \\
&a^{n^2}Ba^{2n}C^nRD \\
\Longrightarrow^* &\quad \{ \ 2n \text{ applications of } Ba \longrightarrow aB \ \} \\
&a^{n^2+2n}BC^nRD \\
\Longrightarrow &\quad \{ \ RD \longrightarrow LCD \ \} \\
&a^{n^2+2n}BC^nLCD \\
\Longrightarrow^* &\quad \{ \ n \text{ applications of } CL \longrightarrow LC \ \} \\
&a^{n^2+2n}BLC^{n+1}D \\
\Longrightarrow &\quad \{ \ BL \longrightarrow aBR \ \} \\
&a^{n^2+2n+1}BRC^{n+1}D \qquad .
\end{aligned}
$$

Thus the induction hypothesis holds for $n+1$ also. We conclude that $aBRCD \Longrightarrow^* a^{n^2}BRC^nD$ for all $n \geq 1$. On account of $BR \longrightarrow$

E we then have $aBRCD \Longrightarrow^* a^{n^2} EC^n D$, and n applications of $EC \longrightarrow E$ yields $aBRCD \Longrightarrow^* a^{n^2} ED$, and finally $ED \longrightarrow \epsilon$ yields $aBRCD \Longrightarrow^* a^{n^2}$, for all $n \geq 1$.

Next, we prove that no other strings can be derived from the grammar. For this part of the proof we claim that each derivable string is of one of the four forms:

$$a^{n^2} XRC^{n-i} D, \quad a^{n^2} YLC^{n-i+1} D, \quad a^{n^2} EC^{n-i} D, \quad a^{n^2}$$

where $n \geq 1$, $0 \leq i \leq n$. X is an interleaving of a^{2i} and BC^i, whereas Y is an interleaving of a^{2n} and BC^i. The proof is by mathematical induction on the length of the derivation. For length 0 the claim is true because $aBRCD$ is of the first form (with $n = 1$, $i = 0$). Now, assume the hypothesis holds for some derived string. We show that applying any one of the production rules yields a string of one of the four forms, thus showing that the claim holds for the longer derivation.

$BR \longrightarrow E$ applies to the first form if $i = 0$, that is, $a^{n^2} BRC^n D$, yielding a string of the third form

$EC \longrightarrow E$ applies to the third form if $n > i$, yielding a string of the same form with $i := i + 1$

$ED \longrightarrow \epsilon$ applies to the third form if $n = i$, yielding a string of the fourth form

$RC \longrightarrow aaCR$ applies to the first form if $n > i$, yielding a string of the same form with $i := i + 1$

$Ca \longrightarrow aC$, $Ba \longrightarrow aB$ apply to the first or second form, yielding a string of the same form with X or Y a bit permuted

$RD \longrightarrow LCD$ applies to the first form if $n = i$, yielding a string of the second form

$CL \longrightarrow LC$ applies to the second form if $i > 0$ yielding a string of the same form with $i := i - 1$

$BL \longrightarrow aBR$ applies to the second form if $i = 0$ yielding a string of the first form with $n := n + 1$

We have now established that each string that can be derived from the initial string has some special form, given above. The only strings of this form that are in the language are the strings containing terminal symbols only. Of the four forms above, only the last one qualifies, hence each string in the language is of the form a^{n^2}, for some $n \geq 1$. This completes the second part of the proof.

Here is an alternative solution. First generate $SY^n X^n E$ and observe that the number of $X - Y$ inversions is n^2. Add rule $YX \to XaY$

plus "movers" like $Ya \rightarrow aY$ and $aX \rightarrow Xa$, and "terminators" $SX \rightarrow S$ and $YE \rightarrow E$.

14. The grammar is

$$(\{a, b\},\ \{A, B, M, E\},\ R,\ ME)$$

where R is the set

$$
\begin{aligned}
M &\longrightarrow aMA \mid bMB \mid \epsilon \\
AE &\longrightarrow aE \\
BE &\longrightarrow bE \\
Aa &\longrightarrow aA \\
Ab &\longrightarrow bA \\
Ba &\longrightarrow aB \\
Bb &\longrightarrow bB \\
E &\longrightarrow \epsilon
\end{aligned}
$$

of production rules.

(One may think of this as a program that generates sequences of the form $xMyE$ where x is a sequence of a's and b's, and y is a sequence of a's, b's, A's and B's. The relation between x and y is: the lower-case letters in y form the beginning of x and the capital letters in y form the remainder of x, but in reverse order and written in capitals. Capitals A and B can travel to the right from token M to end E, where they are converted to lower-case.)

First, we prove that each string of the form xx can be derived. This we do by giving a derivation of each such string. We prove by mathematical induction on n that every string of the form $xMxE$ where $x \in \{a, b\}^n$ can be derived from the initial string, that is, $ME \Longrightarrow^* xMxE$. Basis $n = 0$ follows from the reflexivity of $\Longrightarrow^*$. For all $n \geq 0$, we have

$$
\begin{array}{ll}
& ME \\
\Longrightarrow^* & \{ \text{ induction hypothesis } \} \\
& xMxE \\
\Longrightarrow & \{ \text{ application of } M \longrightarrow aMA \ \} \\
& xaMAxE \\
\Longrightarrow^* & \{ \ n \text{ applications of } Aa \longrightarrow aA \text{ and } Ab \longrightarrow bA \ \} \\
& xaMxAE \\
\Longrightarrow & \{ \text{ application of } AE \longrightarrow aE \ \} \\
& xaMxaE
\end{array}
$$

and similarly $ME \Longrightarrow^* xbMxbE$. Thus the induction hypothesis holds for strings of length $n + 1$ also. We conclude that $ME \Longrightarrow^*$

$xMxE$ for all x. On account of $M \longrightarrow \epsilon$ and $E \longrightarrow \epsilon$ we then have $ME \Longrightarrow^* xx$, for all x over $\{a, b\}$.

Next, we prove that no other strings can be derived from the grammar. For this part of the proof we claim that each derivable string is of the form

$$xM^iyE^j$$

where $0 \le i, j \le 1$, and $x = f(y)\, g(y)$. x is a string over $\{a, b\}$ and y is a string over $\{a, b, A, B\}$. Functions f and g map strings over $\{a, b, A, B\}$ to strings over $\{a, b\}$. Informally, f removes all upper-case letters, whereas g removes all lower-case letters, converts upper-case to lower-case, and reverses the order.

$$
\begin{array}{lll}
f(\epsilon) = \epsilon & f(sa) = f(s)\, a & f(sb) = f(s)\, b \\
f(sA) = f(s) & f(sB) = f(s) & \\
g(\epsilon) = \epsilon & g(sa) = g(s) & g(sb) = g(s) \\
g(sA) = a\, g(s) & g(sB) = b\, g(s) &
\end{array}
$$

We will use properties like $f(As) = f(s)$ and $g(As) = g(s)\, a$.

The proof is by mathematical induction on the length of the derivation. For length 0 the claim is true because initial string ME is of the required form with $x = y = \epsilon$. Now, assume that the hypothesis holds for some derived string. We must show that applying any of the 10 production rules to a string of the form above yields again a string of the form above, thus showing that the claim holds for the longer derivation.

$M \longrightarrow aMA$ applies only if $i = 1$ and leads from a string of the form $xMyE^j$ to a string of the form $xaMAyE^j$. Hence we need to show that $xa = f(Ay)\, g(Ay)$, given that $x = f(y)\, g(y)$. Here is the proof.

$$
\begin{aligned}
& f(Ay)\, g(Ay) \\
= \quad & \{ \text{ definition of } f \ \} \\
& f(y)\, g(Ay) \\
= \quad & \{ \text{ definition of } g \ \} \\
& f(y)\, g(y)\, a \\
= \quad & \{ \ x = f(y)\, g(y) \ \} \\
& x\, a
\end{aligned}
$$

$M \longrightarrow bMB$ similar to previous case

$M \longrightarrow \epsilon$ applies only if $i = 1$ and leads from $xMyE^j$ to xyE^j, that is, it is of the same form with $i := 0$.

$AE \longrightarrow aE$ applies only if $j = 1$ and y is of the form zA and leads from xM^izAE to xM^izaE. Hence we have to show that $x = f(za)\, g(za)$, given that $x = f(zA)\, g(zA)$.

$$
\begin{aligned}
& f(za)\ g(za) \\
=\ & \quad \{ \text{ definition of } f \ \} \\
& f(z)\ a\ g(za) \\
=\ & \quad \{ \text{ definition of } g \ \} \\
& f(z)\ a\ g(z) \\
=\ & \quad \{ \text{ definition of } f \ \} \\
& f(zA)\ a\ g(z) \\
=\ & \quad \{ \text{ definition of } g \ \} \\
& f(zA)\ g(zA) \\
=\ & \quad \{ \ x = f(zA)\ g(zA) \ \} \\
& x
\end{aligned}
$$

$BE \longrightarrow bE$ similar to previous case

$Aa \longrightarrow aA$ applies only if y is of the form $uAaw$ and leads from $xM^i uAawE^j$ to $xM^i uaAwE^j$. The argument follows the definitions of f and g in the obvious way.

$Ab \longrightarrow bA$

$Ba \longrightarrow aB$

$Bb \longrightarrow bB$ all three are similar to the previous case

$E \longrightarrow \epsilon$ applies only if $j = 1$ and leads from $xM^i yE$ to $xM^i y$, that is, it is of the same form with $j := 0$.

We have now established that each string that can be derived from the initial string has some special form, given above. The only strings of this form that are in the language are the strings containing terminal symbols only. The only kind that qualifies is the kind with $i = j = 0$ and y free from A's and B's. In the latter case, we have $y = x$ and the general from reduces to xx, which is exactly the set of carré strings. This completes the second part of the proof.

The language is called the carré language because xx can be written as x^2.

Answers for Chapter 3

3. The five derivations are

$$
\begin{aligned}
& ((y = x^2)^x_{x+1})^y_{y+2x+1} \\
=\ & (y = (x+1)^2)^y_{y+2x+1} \\
=\ & y + 2x + 1 = (x+1)^2 \\
=\ & y + 2x + 1 = x^2 + 2x + 1 \\
=\ & y = x^2
\end{aligned}
$$

and

$$
\begin{aligned}
& (((y = x^3 \wedge z = x^2)^x_{x+1})^z_{z+2x+1})^y_{y+3z+3x+1} \\
=\ & ((y = (x+1)^3 \wedge z = (x+1)^2)^z_{z+2x+1})^y_{y+3z+3x+1}
\end{aligned}
$$

$$
\begin{aligned}
&= && (y = (x+1)^3 \wedge z + 2x + 1 = (x+1)^2)^y_{y+3z+3x+1} \\
&= && y + 3z + 3x + 1 = (x+1)^3 \wedge z + 2x + 1 = (x+1)^2 \\
&= && y + 3z + 3x + 1 = (x+1)^3 \wedge z + 2x + 1 = x^2 + 2x + 1 \\
&= && y + 3z + 3x + 1 = (x+1)^3 \wedge z = x^2 \\
&= && y + 3z + 3x + 1 = x^3 + 3x^2 + 3x + 1 \wedge z = x^2 \\
&= && y = x^3 \wedge z = x^2
\end{aligned}
$$

and

$$
\begin{aligned}
&&& ((y^x = z)^x_{x\,\mathbf{div}\,2})^y_{y^2} \\
&= && (y^{x\,\mathbf{div}\,2} = z)^y_{y^2} \\
&= && (y^2)^{x\,\mathbf{div}\,2} = z \\
&= && (y^x = z \wedge even(x)) \vee (y^{x-1} = z \wedge odd(x))
\end{aligned}
$$

and

$$
\begin{aligned}
&&& ((((b \equiv B) \wedge (c \equiv C))^b_{b\equiv c})^c_{b\equiv c})^b_{b\equiv c} \\
&= && (((b \equiv c \equiv B) \wedge (c \equiv C))^c_{b\equiv c})^b_{b\equiv c} \\
&= && ((b \equiv b \equiv c \equiv B) \wedge (b \equiv c \equiv C))^b_{b\equiv c} \\
&= && ((c \equiv B) \wedge (b \equiv c \equiv C))^b_{b\equiv c} \\
&= && (c \equiv B) \wedge (b \equiv c \equiv c \equiv C) \\
&= && (c \equiv B) \wedge (b \equiv C)
\end{aligned}
$$

and

$$
\begin{aligned}
&&& ((((b \equiv B) \wedge (c \equiv C))^b_{b\neq c})^c_{b\neq c})^b_{b\neq c} \\
&= && (((b \neq c \equiv B) \wedge (c \equiv C))^c_{b\neq c})^b_{b\neq c} \\
&= && ((b \neq b \neq c \equiv B) \wedge (b \neq c \equiv C))^b_{b\neq c} \\
&= && ((c \equiv B) \wedge (b \neq c \equiv C))^b_{b\neq c} \\
&= && (c \equiv B) \wedge (b \neq c \neq c \equiv C) \\
&= && (c \equiv B) \wedge (b \equiv C) \qquad .
\end{aligned}
$$

4. The three assignments are

$$
\begin{array}{ll}
z := z \cdot x & (\, y := y - 1 \text{ will not do}) \\
s := s + (n+1)^3 & (\, s := s + n^3 \text{ and } n := n - 1 \text{ will not do}) \\
x := (x - 1)/2 & .
\end{array}
$$

7. From the calculation

$$
\begin{aligned}
& \{P\} \\
& [w \le r \to q, r := q + 1, r - w \parallel w > r \to skip] \\
& \{q \cdot w + r = x \ \wedge \ r \ge 0\} \\
=\ & \quad \{ \text{ definition of if-statement } \} \\
& \{P \wedge w \le r\}\ q, r := q + 1, r - w\ \{q \cdot w + r = x \wedge r \ge 0\}\ \wedge \\
& \{P \wedge w > r\}\ skip\ \{q \cdot w + r = x \wedge r \ge 0\}\ \wedge \\
& P \Rightarrow (w \le r \vee w > r) \\
=\ &
\end{aligned}
$$

$$(P \wedge w \leq r \Rightarrow (q+1) \cdot w + r - w = x \wedge r \geq w) \wedge$$
$$(P \wedge w > r \Rightarrow q \cdot w + r = x \wedge r \geq 0)$$

we conclude that the weakest P is

$$q \cdot w + r = x \ \wedge \ (r \geq w \vee r \geq 0) \qquad .$$

11. The only mistake is that the bound function is not integer valued for negative values of x.

12. The if-statement with n guarded commands

$$\{ \, P \, \} \, [B_0 \rightarrow S_0 \, \| \cdots \| \, B_{n-1} \rightarrow S_{n-1}] \, \{ \, Q \, \}$$

is equivalent to

$$(P \Rightarrow \langle \exists i : 0 \leq i < n : B_i \rangle) \ \wedge$$
$$\langle \forall i : 0 \leq i < n : \{ \, P \wedge B_i \, \} \, S_i \, \{ \, Q \, \} \rangle \qquad .$$

If $n = 0$ this reduces to

$$(P \Rightarrow \textit{false}) \ \wedge \ \textit{true} \qquad ,$$

that is, $P = \textit{false}$ and hence $[\,]$ is equivalent to *abort*.
The do-statement with n guarded commands

$$\{ \, P \, \} \, * [B_0 \rightarrow S_0 \, \| \cdots \| \, B_{n-1} \rightarrow S_{n-1}] \, \{ \, Q \, \}$$

follows from

$$(P \wedge \neg \langle \exists i : 0 \leq i < n : B_i \rangle \ \Rightarrow \ Q) \ \wedge$$
$$\langle \forall i : 0 \leq i < n : P \wedge B_i \Rightarrow bf > 0 \rangle \ \wedge$$
$$\langle \forall i : 0 \leq i < n : \{ \, P \wedge B_i \wedge bf = BF \, \} \, S_i \, \{ \, P \wedge bf < BF \, \} \rangle \qquad .$$

If $n = 0$ this reduces to

$$(P \wedge \neg \textit{false} \ \Rightarrow \ Q) \ \wedge \ \textit{true} \qquad .$$

That is, $P \Rightarrow Q$ and hence $*[\,]$ is equivalent to *skip*.

16. Choose the following invariant relation and bound function.

$P :$ *true*
$bf :$ $y - x$

initialization

obvious, since P is *true*

finalization

$$P \wedge x \geq y \;\Rightarrow\; x \geq y$$

invariance of P

obvious, since P is *true*

decrease of bf

$$
\begin{aligned}
&\quad (bf < BF)^{x,y}_{y,x} \\
&= \qquad \{ \text{ substitution } \} \\
&\quad x - y < BF \\
&\Leftarrow \qquad \{ \; bf = y - x; \;\; \text{add guard } \} \\
&\quad x - y < BF \;\; \wedge \;\; bf = BF \;\; \wedge \;\; x < y
\end{aligned}
$$

bf bounded

$$P \wedge x < y \;\Rightarrow\; bf > 0$$

20. Choose the following invariant relation and bound function.

$$
\begin{aligned}
P: &\quad s = \langle \textstyle\sum i : n \leq i < N : a[i] \cdot x^{i-n} \rangle \;\; \wedge \;\; 0 \leq n \leq N \\
bf: &\quad n
\end{aligned}
$$

initialization

$$N \geq 0 \;\Rightarrow\; (P^n_N)^s_0 \;\text{ since }\; \langle \textstyle\sum i : N \leq i < N : a[i] \cdot x^{i-N} \rangle = 0$$

finalization

$$P \;\; \wedge \;\; n = 0 \;\Rightarrow\; s = \langle \textstyle\sum i : 0 \leq i < N : a[i] \cdot x^{i} \rangle$$

invariance of P

$$
\begin{aligned}
&\quad (P^s_{s \cdot x + a[n]})^n_{n-1} \\
&= \qquad \{ \text{ substitution } \} \\
&\quad (s \cdot x + a[n] = \langle \textstyle\sum i : n \leq i < N : a[i] \cdot x^{i-n} \rangle \wedge 0 \leq n \leq N)^n_{n-1} \\
&= \qquad \{ \text{ substitution } \} \\
&\quad s \cdot x + a[n-1] = \langle \textstyle\sum i : n-1 \leq i < N : a[i] \cdot x^{i-n+1} \rangle \\
&\quad \wedge \; 0 \leq n-1 \leq N \\
&\Leftarrow \qquad \{ \;\; n-1 < N \text{ ensures that the last summation has} \\
&\qquad\qquad \text{at least one term } \} \\
&\quad s \cdot x + a[n-1] = \langle \textstyle\sum i : n \leq i < N : a[i] \cdot x^{i-n} \rangle \cdot x + a[n-1] \\
&\quad \wedge \; 0 \leq n-1 < N \\
&\Leftarrow \qquad \{ \text{ algebra } \} \\
&\quad s = \langle \textstyle\sum i : n \leq i < N : a[i] \cdot x^{i-n} \rangle \;\; \wedge \;\; 0 \leq n-1 < N \\
&= \\
&\quad P \;\; \wedge \;\; n \neq 0
\end{aligned}
$$

decrease of bf

$$n - 1 < n$$

bf bounded

$$P \ \wedge \ n \neq 0 \ \Rightarrow \ n > 0$$

22. Choose the following invariant relation and bound function.

$$P : \quad (a+1)^2 > N \ \wedge \ a \geq 0$$
$$bf : \quad a$$

initialization

$$N \geq 0 \Rightarrow (N+1)^2 > N \ \wedge \ N \geq 0$$

finalization

$$P \ \wedge \ a^2 \leq N \ \Rightarrow a^2 \leq N < (a+1)^2$$

invariance of P

$$
\begin{aligned}
& P^a_{(a+N\,\mathbf{div}\,a)\,\mathbf{div}\,2} \\
= \quad & \{ \text{ substitution } \} \\
& ((a + N \ \mathbf{div} \ a) \ \mathbf{div} \ 2 + 1)^2 > N \wedge (a + N \ \mathbf{div} \ a) \ \mathbf{div} \ 2 \geq 0 \\
\Leftarrow \quad & \{ \ P \Rightarrow (a + N \ \mathbf{div} \ a) \ \mathbf{div} \ 2 \geq 0 \ \} \\
& ((a + N \ \mathbf{div} \ a) \ \mathbf{div} \ 2 + 1)^2 > N \ \wedge \ P \\
\Leftarrow \quad & \{ \ x \ \mathbf{div} \ 2 \geq (x-1)/2 \ \} \\
& ((a + N \ \mathbf{div} \ a - 1)/2 + 1)^2 > N \ \wedge \ P \\
\Leftarrow \quad & \{ \ x \ \mathbf{div} \ a > x/a - 1 \ \} \\
& ((a + N/a - 2)/2 + 1)^2 \geq N \ \wedge \ P \\
= \quad & \{ \text{ arithmetic } \} \\
& (a + N/a)^2 \geq 4 \cdot N \ \wedge \ P \\
= \quad & \{ \text{ arithmetic } \} \\
& (a - N/a)^2 \geq 0 \ \wedge \ P \\
= \quad & \\
& P
\end{aligned}
$$

decrease of bf

$$
\begin{aligned}
& (a)^a_{(a+N\,\mathbf{div}\,a)\,\mathbf{div}\,2} < a \\
= \quad & \{ \text{ substitution } \} \\
& (a + N \ \mathbf{div} \ a) \ \mathbf{div} \ 2 < a \\
\Leftarrow \quad & \\
& a + N \ \mathbf{div} \ a < 2a \\
= \quad &
\end{aligned}
$$

$$N \text{ div } a < a$$
$$\Leftarrow$$
$$a^2 > N$$

bf bounded

$$P \;\Rightarrow\; a \geq 0$$

Remark: we have ignored the problem of division by zero. When we have expression $N \text{ div } a$, we should be able to guarantee $a \neq 0$. The expression is evaluated under condition $a^2 > N$ which implies $a \neq 0$.

23. If $x > 0$ or $y > 0$, $f(x, y)$ is the greatest common divisor of x and y.

Notice $\max(x, x) = x = f(x, 0) = f(x, 0 + 1 \cdot x) = f(x, x)$.

P : $f(X, Y) = f(x, y) \;\wedge\; x \geq 0 \;\wedge\; y \geq 0$
bf : $\lfloor \log(xy + 1) \rfloor$

initialization

  obvious

finalization

$$P \;\wedge\; \neg(x > y > 0) \;\wedge\; \neg(y > x > 0)$$
$$\Rightarrow$$
$$f(X, Y) = f(x, y) \;\wedge\; (x = y \;\vee\; x = 0 \;\vee\; y = 0)$$
$$\Rightarrow \qquad \{ \text{ definition of } f \ \}$$
$$f(X, Y) = \max(x, y)$$

invariance of P; check one alternative, the other is similar

$$P^{x}_{x \bmod y}$$
$$= \qquad \{ \text{ substitution } \}$$
$$f(X, Y) = f(x \bmod y, y) \;\wedge\; x \bmod y \geq 0 \;\wedge\; y \geq 0$$
$$\Leftarrow \qquad \{ \ f \text{ with } x := x \bmod y \text{ and } k := x \text{ div } y \ \}$$
$$f(X, Y) = f(x, y) \;\wedge\; x \bmod y \geq 0 \;\wedge\; y > 0$$
$$\Leftarrow$$
$$P \;\wedge\; x > y > 0$$

decrease of *bf*

We show that $\lfloor \log(xy + 1) \rfloor$ decreases by at least 1 by showing that $\log(xy + 1)$ decreases by at least 1. We check the first alternative, using guard $x > y > 0$; the second alternative is similar.

$$\log((x \bmod y) \cdot y + 1) + 1 \le \log(xy + 1)$$
$$= \qquad \{\ 1 = \log(2)\ \}$$
$$2 \cdot ((x \bmod y) \cdot y + 1) \le xy + 1$$
$$=$$
$$2 \cdot (x \bmod y) \cdot y < xy$$
$$= \qquad \{\ y > 0\ \}$$
$$2 \cdot (x \bmod y) < x$$
$$= \qquad \{\ x = (x \operatorname{\mathbf{div}} y) \cdot y + x \bmod y\ \}$$
$$2 \cdot (x \bmod y) < (x \operatorname{\mathbf{div}} y) \cdot y + x \bmod y$$
$$=$$
$$x \bmod y < (x \operatorname{\mathbf{div}} y) \cdot y$$
$$\Leftarrow \qquad \{\ x \bmod y < y\ \}$$
$$x \operatorname{\mathbf{div}} y \ge 1$$
$$\Leftarrow$$
$$x > y$$

bf bounded: check one alternative, the other one is similar.

$$P \ \wedge\ x > y > 0 \ \Rightarrow\ \log(xy + 1) \ge 0$$

27. $P:$ $y = \langle \sum i : 0 \le i < k : (k - i) \cdot f(i) \rangle\ \wedge$
            $x = \langle \sum i : 0 \le i < k : f(i) \rangle\ \wedge\ 0 \le k \le N$
     $bf:$ $N - k$

initialization

$$P_{0,0,0}^{x,y,k}$$
$$=$$
$$0 = \langle \sum i : 0 \le i < 0 : (0 - i) \cdot f(i) \rangle\ \wedge$$
$$0 = \langle \sum i : 0 \le i < 0 : f(i) \rangle\ \wedge\ 0 \le 0 \le N$$
$$= \qquad \{\ \text{sum over empty range is } 0\ \}$$
$$N \ge 0$$

finalization

$$P \wedge k = N \ \Rightarrow\ y = \langle \sum i : 0 \le i < N : (N - i) \cdot f(i) \rangle$$
is immediate

invariance of P and decrease of bf

$$(((P\ \wedge\ bf < BF)_{k+1}^{k})_{y+x}^{y})_{x+f(k)}^{x}$$
$$= \qquad \{\ \text{substitution}\ \}$$
$$y + x + f(k) = \langle \sum i : 0 \le i < k + 1 : (k + 1 - i) \cdot f(i) \rangle\ \wedge$$
$$x + f(k) = \langle \sum i : 0 \le i < k + 1 : f(i) \rangle\ \wedge$$
$$0 \le k + 1 \le N\ \wedge\ N - k - 1 < BF$$
$$= \qquad \{\ \text{subtract second summation from first}\ \}$$

$$y = \langle \sum i : 0 \le i < k+1 : (k-i) \cdot f(i) \rangle \ \land$$
$$x + f(k) = \langle \sum i : 0 \le i < k+1 : f(i) \rangle \ \land$$
$$0 \le k+1 \le N \ \land \ N-k-1 < BF$$
$$\Leftarrow \qquad \{ \text{ split off the terms with } i = k \,; \ k \ge 0 \ \}$$
$$y = \langle \sum i : 0 \le i < k : (k-i) \cdot f(i) \rangle \ \land$$
$$x + f(k) = \langle \sum i : 0 \le i < k : f(i) \rangle + f(k) \ \land$$
$$0 \le k < N \ \land \ N-k-1 < BF$$
$$\Leftarrow$$
$$P \ \land \ k \ne N \ \land \ bf = BF$$

bf bounded

$$P \ \land \ k \ne N \ \Rightarrow \ k < N \ = \ bf > 0$$

40. Let $c(x, m, n)$ be the number of combinations in which x can be produced from at most m stamps in the range 1 through n ($m, n \ge 0$).

$$c(0, m, n) = 1$$
$$c(x, 0, n) = 0 \qquad \text{for } x > 0, n \ge 0$$
$$c(x, m, 0) = 0 \qquad \text{for } x > 0, m \ge 0$$
$$c(x, m, n) = \langle \sum i : 0 \le i \cdot v[n] \le x \ \land \ i \le m :$$
$$c(x - i \cdot v[n], m - i, n - 1) \rangle$$
$$\text{for } x > 0, m > 0, n > 0$$

The procedure is as follows.

procedure $p(x, m, n : integer;$ **var** $y : integer);$
$\{ \ 0 \le x = x' \land 0 \le m = m' \land 0 \le n = n' \le N \land y = y' \ \}$
$|[$ **var** $k : integer;$
$[\ x = 0 \qquad\qquad\qquad\qquad \to y := y + 1$
$\| \ x > 0 \land (m = 0 \lor n = 0) \ \to skip$
$\| \ x > 0 \land m > 0 \ \land \ n > 0 \to$
$\qquad k := 0;$
$\qquad *[\ k \le m \land k \cdot v[n] \le x \to$
$\qquad\qquad p(x - k \cdot v[n], m - k, n - 1, y); \ k := k + 1$
$\qquad] \qquad]$
$]|$
$\{ \ y = y' + c(x', m', n') \ \}$

The problem to compute $c(x, M, N)$ is now solved by the following statements.

$$y := 0; \ p(x, M, N, y) \ \{ \ y = c(x, M, N) \ \}$$

43. We prove $f(i + j - 1) = f(i)f(j) + f(i - 1)f(j - 1)$ for all i, j by induction on j.

- base: for all $i \geq 1, j = 1$:
$$f(i + 1 - 1) = f(i) \cdot 1 + f(i - 1) \cdot 0$$
- step: for all $i \geq 1, j > 1$:

$$f(i + j - 1)$$

$=$

$$f((i + 1) + (j - 1) - 1)$$
$$\{ \text{ induction hypothesis: } i, j := i + 1, j - 1 \ \}$$
$$f(i + 1)f(j - 1) + f(i)f(j - 2)$$

$=$

$$\{ \ f(i + 1) = f(i) + f(i - 1) \ \}$$
$$f(i)f(j - 1) + f(i - 1)f(j - 1) + f(i)f(j - 2)$$

$=$

$$\{ \ f(j) = f(j - 1) + f(j - 2) \ \}$$
$$f(i)f(j) + f(i - 1)f(j - 1)$$

The correctness of the program follows from the following calculations for the case where $n \geq 2$.

- if $odd(n)$ then $n = 2k + 1$ and the postcondition of statement $fib(n \ \mathbf{div} \ 2, x, y)$ is $n' = 2k + 1 \wedge x = f(k) \wedge y = f(k + 1)$.

$$f(n')$$

$=$

$$\{ \ i, j := k + 1, k + 1 \ \}$$
$$f(k + 1)f(k + 1) + f(k)f(k)$$

and

$$f(n' + 1)$$

$=$

$$\{ \ i, j := k + 2, k + 1 \ \}$$
$$f(k + 2)f(k + 1) + f(k + 1)f(k)$$

$=$

$$f(k + 1)f(k + 1) + f(k)f(k + 1) + f(k + 1)f(k)$$

- if $even(n)$ then $n = 2k$ and the postcondition of statement $fib(n \ \mathbf{div} \ 2, x, y)$ is $n' = 2k \wedge x = f(k) \wedge y = f(k + 1)$.

$$f(n')$$

$=$

$$\{ \ i, j := k + 1, k \ \}$$
$$f(k + 1)f(k) + f(k)f(k - 1)$$

$=$

$$f(k + 1)f(k) + f(k)f(k + 1) - f(k)f(k)$$

and

$$f(n' + 1)$$

$=$

$$\{ \ i, j := k + 1, k + 1 \ \}$$
$$f(k + 1)f(k + 1) + f(k)f(k)$$

Answers for Chapter 4

2. We construct a transition graph and derive a right-linear grammar from it. The graph in Figure A.1 has 3 nodes, one for every possible

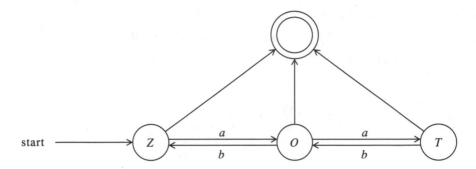

FIGURE A.1. Transition graph.

value of the number of a's minus the number of b's, namely, 0, 1, and 2. The corresponding nodes are labeled Z, O, and T. Z is the initial node and we would like every node to act as a final node, although we have allowed only one final node so far. We can realize this by adding one node and let it be the final node, and by adding transitions labeled with ϵ from each of the three existing nodes to the new node. The corresponding grammar is

$$(\ \{a, b\},$$
$$\{Z, O, T\},$$
$$\{Z \longrightarrow aO \mid \epsilon, \ O \longrightarrow aT \mid bZ \mid \epsilon, \ T \longrightarrow bO \mid \epsilon\},$$
$$Z) \qquad .$$

5. First we prove $\epsilon + \epsilon = \epsilon$.

$$\epsilon + \epsilon$$
$$= \qquad \{ \ e = ee \text{ with } e := \epsilon \ \}$$
$$\epsilon + \epsilon\epsilon$$
$$= \qquad \{ \ \epsilon^* = \epsilon, \text{ proved in the text } \}$$
$$\epsilon + \epsilon\epsilon^*$$
$$= \qquad \{ \ \epsilon + ee^* = e^*, \text{ proved in the text, with } e := \epsilon \ \}$$
$$\epsilon^*$$
$$= \qquad \{ \ \epsilon^* = \epsilon, \text{ proved in the text } \}$$
$$\epsilon$$

Here is the proof of $e + e = e$.

$$e + e$$
$$= \qquad \{ \ e = ee \text{ twice } \}$$
$$ee + ee$$
$$= \qquad \{ \ e(f + g) = ef + eg \text{ with } f, g := \epsilon, \epsilon \ \}$$
$$e(\epsilon + \epsilon)$$

$$= \qquad \{\ \epsilon + \epsilon = \epsilon\ \}$$
$$\qquad e\epsilon$$
$$= \qquad \{\ e\epsilon = e\ \}$$
$$\qquad e$$

6. First we prove $\epsilon + e^* = e^*$.

$$\epsilon + e^*$$
$$= \qquad \{\ e^* = \epsilon + ee^*,\ \text{proved in the text}\ \}$$
$$\epsilon + \epsilon + ee^*$$
$$= \qquad \{\ \epsilon + \epsilon = \epsilon,\ \text{proved in the previous exercise}\ \}$$
$$\epsilon + ee^*$$
$$= \qquad \{\ \epsilon + ee^* = e^*,\ \text{proved in the text}\ \}$$
$$e^*$$

Here is the proof of $e^* e^* = e^*$.

$$e^* e^* = e^*$$
$$= \qquad \{\ e^* = \epsilon + e^*\ \}$$
$$e^*(\epsilon + e^*) = e^*$$
$$= \qquad \{\ e(f + g) = ef + eg\ \text{with}\ f, g := \epsilon, \epsilon\ \}$$
$$e^* \epsilon + e^* e^* = e^*$$
$$= \qquad \{\ f\epsilon = f\ \text{with}\ f := e^*\ \}$$
$$e^* + e^* e^* = e^*$$
$$= \qquad \{\ e^* = \epsilon + e^*\ \}$$
$$\epsilon + e^* + e^* e^* = e^*$$
$$= \qquad \{\ \text{distribution};\ \epsilon\ \text{is unit element}\ \}$$
$$\epsilon + (\epsilon + e^*)e^* = e^*$$
$$= \qquad \{\ e^* = \epsilon + e^*\ \}$$
$$\epsilon + e^* e^* = e^*$$
$$= \qquad \{\ e^* = e^{**}\ \text{twice}\ \}$$
$$\epsilon + e^* e^{**} = e^{**}$$
$$= \qquad \{\ f^* = \epsilon + f f^*\ \text{with}\ f := e^*\ \}$$
$$true$$

9. Either change is fine, but the combination is not. The graph that would then be produced by the expression $a + b^*$ defines the language denoted by expression $a + b^* + b^* a$, which is quite a different language.

13. Each rule in a left-linear grammar is of the form $A \longrightarrow Bx$ or $A \longrightarrow x$ for $A, B \in N$, $x \in T^*$. The set of nonterminals is the set of nodes. The set of terminals is the set of symbols used in labeling the edges. Each edge from A to B with label x yields a rule $B \longrightarrow Ax$. For initial node A add rule $A \longrightarrow \epsilon$. The final node Z is the initial nonterminal, that is, the initial string of the grammar.

15. First solving for C, then B, next A and finally E, all the time strictly following the given procedure, yields

$$((a + b(aa)^* ab)(bb + ba(aa)^* ab)^* (ba(aa)^* b + a) + b(aa)^* b)^*$$

or, equivalently,

$$(aa + bb + (ab + ba)(aa + bb)^*(ab + ba))^* \qquad .$$

19. Let k be greater than the number of non-ϵ-edges of a transition graph that corresponds to L. For a string whose length is at least k, any path from initial to final node contains a cycle with at least one non-ϵ-edge. The cycle can be traversed n times, for all $n \geq 0$.

20. We assume that $\{a^i b^i \mid i \geq 0\}$ is regular and obtain a contradiction. According to the Pumping Lemma, for sufficiently large i, $a^i b^i$ can be written as xyz where y is nonempty and $xy^n z$ is in the language, for all $n \geq 0$. If y consists of a's only or of b's only then the number of a's differs from the number of b's in $xy^n z$ for all $n \neq 1$. If y consists of both a's and b's then we do not have all a's to the left of all b's in $xyyz$.

Answers for Chapter 5

1. The first circuit computes $\neg(a \wedge ((b \wedge c) \vee d))$ and the other circuit computes $a \equiv b$, which in the jargon is sometimes called exclusive-nor instead of equivalence.

3. Possible disjunctive normal forms are

$$(a \wedge b) \vee (c \wedge d) \vee (b \wedge c)$$
$$(a \wedge b) \vee (\neg a \wedge \neg b)$$
$$(a \wedge b \wedge c) \vee (\neg a \wedge \neg b \wedge c) \vee (\neg a \wedge b \wedge \neg c) \vee (a \wedge \neg b \wedge \neg c)$$
$$(a \wedge b \wedge c) \vee (\neg a \wedge \neg b \wedge \neg c)$$
$$(\neg a \wedge \neg b \wedge \neg e) \vee (\neg b \wedge \neg c) \vee (\neg b \wedge \neg d \wedge \neg e) \qquad .$$

5. First we construct boolean expressions for the outputs in terms of the inputs. We use the names l, e, and g for the three outputs $x < y$, $x = y$, and $x > y$ respectively. The 2-bit number x is denoted by booleans $x0$ and $x1$: $x1 \equiv \text{'}(x \text{ div } 2 = 1)$ and $x0 \equiv (x \bmod 2 = 1)$; similar for y. We have

$$
\begin{aligned}
&l \\
= \quad &x < y \\
= \quad &x \text{ div } 2 < y \text{ div } 2 \ \vee \\
&(x \text{ div } 2 = y \text{ div } 2 \ \wedge \ x \bmod 2 < y \bmod 2) \\
= \quad &(\neg x1 \wedge y1) \ \vee \\
&(((\neg x1 \wedge \neg y1) \vee (x1 \wedge y1)) \ \wedge \ (\neg x0 \wedge y0))
\end{aligned}
$$

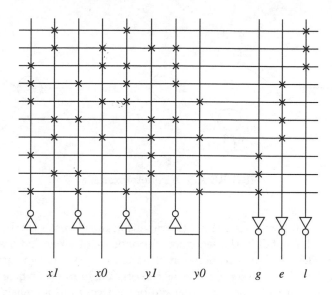

$$x1 \quad\quad x0 \quad\quad y1 \quad\quad y0 \quad\quad\quad g \quad\quad e \quad\quad l$$

FIGURE A.2. PLA for $>$, $=$, and $<$.

$$= (\neg x1 \wedge y1) \vee$$
$$(\neg x1 \wedge \neg y1 \wedge \neg x0 \wedge y0) \quad \vee \quad (x1 \wedge y1 \wedge \neg x0 \wedge y0)$$

and similarly

$$g$$
$$= (\neg y1 \wedge x1) \vee$$
$$(\neg y1 \wedge \neg x1 \wedge \neg y0 \wedge x0) \quad \vee \quad (y1 \wedge x1 \wedge \neg y0 \wedge x0) \quad\quad ,$$

and finally

$$e$$
$$= x = y$$
$$= x \ \mathbf{div}\ 2 = y \ \mathbf{div}\ 2 \quad \wedge \quad x \ \mathbf{mod}\ 2 = y \ \mathbf{mod}\ 2$$
$$= ((\neg x1 \wedge \neg y1) \quad \vee \quad (x1 \wedge y1)) \wedge$$
$$((\neg x0 \wedge \neg y0) \quad \vee \quad (x0 \wedge y0))$$
$$= (\neg x1 \wedge \neg y1 \wedge \neg x0 \wedge \neg y0) \quad \vee \quad (\neg x1 \wedge \neg y1 \wedge x0 \wedge y0) \quad \vee$$
$$(x1 \wedge y1 \wedge \neg x0 \wedge \neg y0) \quad \vee \quad (x1 \wedge y1 \wedge x0 \wedge y0) \quad\quad .$$

This yields the PLA in Figure A.2.

6. Assume that we have a transition graph. We show that we can obtain
an equivalent graph in which each transition is labeled with exactly
one symbol (not ϵ). First, we observe that labels of two or more
symbols are not needed since a transition labeled with a sequence of
n symbols ($n > 1$) can be changed into a path of n transitions

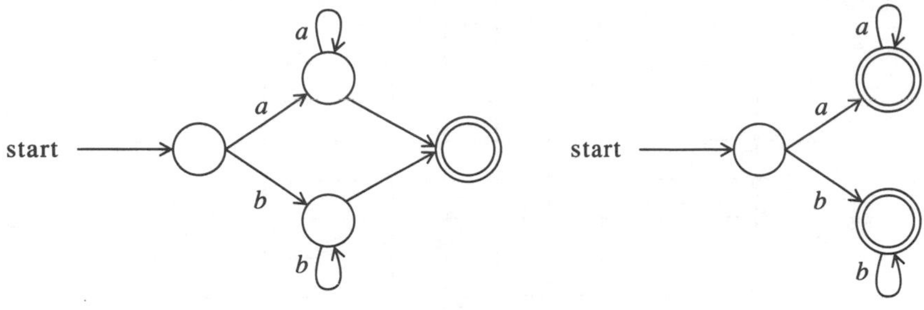

FIGURE A.3. A counterexample.

via $n-1$ new states; the i th transition in this path is labeled with the i th symbol in the sequence. Second, we observe that transitions labeled with ϵ can be eliminated as follows. We make a new graph that has the same set of nodes as the original graph (in which no label is a sequence of more than one symbol). It contains a transition from node x to node y labeled with symbol a, just when the original graph has a path from x to y whose labeling is a. (Such a path consists of zero or more transitions labeled with ϵ, followed by one transition labeled with a, followed by zero or more transitions labeled with ϵ.) The initial node of the original graph is also the initial node of the new graph. The new graph has a set of final nodes and we have to define what it is. A node in the new graph is a final node just when there is a path in the original graph from this node to the final node in which all transitions are labeled ϵ. (This includes the original final node itself, since there is an empty path from it to the final node.)

Figure A.3 shows an example of a transition graph that requires either ϵ-transitions or more than one final node.

Multiple final nodes present no serious problem in the implementation. A string is in the language if a properly labeled path exists, leading from the initial node to some final node. The circuits as described give a boolean value per node: a path from initial to the node exists just when the boolean value is *true*. A path to some final node exists just when at least one of the boolean values corresponding to the various final nodes is *true*. Therefore, the existential quantification in the new graphs translates into one OR gate that computes the disjunction of the boolean values involved. If there are no final nodes at all, this disjunction is *false*; in this case, the language is the empty set and the whole circuit might be "optimized" to produce only the constant value *false*.

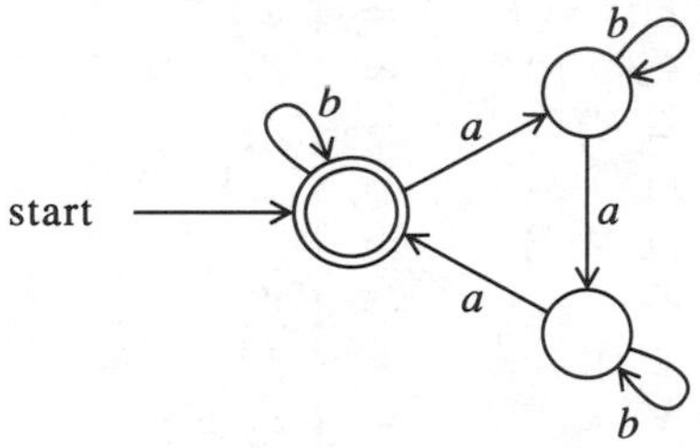

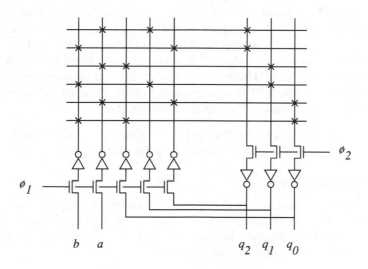

FIGURE A.4. Transition graph for Exercise 5.9.

FIGURE A.5. Circuit for Exercise 5.9.

9. The transition graph without ϵ transitions is given in Figure A.4, and the corresponding circuit is given in Figure A.5. Signal q_0 is the output.

Answers for Chapter 6

1. The transformed grammar is as follows. We have included the terminal symbol $\perp$ to mark the end of the input. We have also listed the lookahead set for each rule.

$$
\begin{aligned}
S &\longrightarrow a[i] := E \perp \mid i\ R\ \perp \\
R &\longrightarrow := E \mid \epsilon \mid (E\ M) \\
M &\longrightarrow \epsilon \mid ,E\ M \\
E &\longrightarrow V \\
V &\longrightarrow i \mid a[i]
\end{aligned}
$$

$$
\begin{aligned}
L(S &\longrightarrow a[i] := E \perp) = \{'a'\} \\
L(S &\longrightarrow i\ R\ \perp) \quad = \{'i'\} \\
L(R &\longrightarrow := E) \qquad = \{':'\} \\
L(R &\longrightarrow \epsilon) \qquad\quad = \{'\perp'\} \\
L(R &\longrightarrow (E\ M)) \quad = \{'('\} \\
L(M &\longrightarrow \epsilon) \qquad\quad = \{')'\} \\
L(M &\longrightarrow, E\ M) \qquad = \{','\} \\
L(E &\longrightarrow V) \qquad\quad = \{'i', 'a'\} \\
L(V &\longrightarrow i) \qquad\qquad = \{'i'\} \\
L(V &\longrightarrow a[i]) \qquad\quad = \{'a'\}
\end{aligned}
$$

4. A possible solution is to introduce an extra nonterminal symbol, such as T. The set of strings that can be derived from S is the same as in the original grammar. The set of strings that can be derived from T is a subset thereof, namely all those in which the number of occurrences of **then** equals the number of occurrences of **else**. These are exactly the strings that can be included between **then** and **else** without introducing an ambiguity.

$$
\begin{aligned}
S &\longrightarrow \textbf{if } b \textbf{ then } T \textbf{ else } S \mid \textbf{if } b \textbf{ then } S \mid \textbf{while } b \textbf{ do } S \mid a \\
T &\longrightarrow \textbf{if } b \textbf{ then } T \textbf{ else } T \mid \textbf{while } b \textbf{ do } T \mid a
\end{aligned}
$$

Answers for Chapter 7

1. When the program is executed it produces an output text that is equivalent to the program text. This is similar to the idea of self-reference which is at the heart of the Liar's paradox, of the halting problem, and of Gödel's theorem.

2. The proof of $\mathcal{M}(H) = \neg\mathcal{M}(H)$ is:

$$
\begin{aligned}
&\mathcal{M}(H) \\
= \quad& \{ \text{ definition of } H \ \} \\
&\mathcal{M}(\text{'} \neg \texttt{M(H)}\text{'}) \\
= \quad& \{ \text{ definition of } \mathcal{M}(\text{'} \neg \text{'} x) \ \} \\
&\neg\mathcal{M}(\text{'M(H)'}) \\
= \quad& \{ \text{ definition of } \mathcal{M}(\text{'M(} \text{'} x \text{'}\text{)'}) \ \} \\
&\neg\mathcal{M}(\text{'H'}) \\
= \quad& \{ \text{ definition of } \mathcal{M}(\text{'H'}) \ \} \\
&\neg\mathcal{M}(H) \quad .
\end{aligned}
$$

5. We have

$$
\begin{aligned}
&(p \wedge q) \vee r \equiv p \wedge (q \vee r) \\
= \quad& \{ \text{ golden rule } p \vee q \equiv p \equiv q \equiv p \wedge q \ \} \\
&(p \vee q \equiv p \equiv q) \vee r \equiv p \wedge (q \vee r) \\
= \quad& \{ \text{ disjunction distributes through equivalence } \}
\end{aligned}
$$

$$p \vee q \vee r \equiv p \vee r \equiv q \vee r \equiv p \wedge (q \vee r)$$
$=$ { golden rule $p \vee (q \vee r) \equiv p \equiv q \vee r \equiv p \wedge (q \vee r)$ }
$$p \vee r \equiv p$$
$=$ { definition of implication }
$$r \Rightarrow p \qquad .$$

6. We have

$$(p \wedge q) \vee (q \wedge r) \vee (r \wedge p)$$
$=$ { distribution }
$$(q \wedge (p \vee r)) \vee (r \wedge p)$$
$=$ { distribution }
$$((q \wedge (p \vee r)) \vee r) \wedge ((q \wedge (p \vee r)) \vee p)$$
$=$ { distribution }
$$(q \vee r) \wedge (p \vee r \vee r) \wedge (q \vee p) \wedge (p \vee p \vee r)$$
$=$ { idempotence }
$$(p \vee q) \wedge (q \vee r) \wedge (r \vee p)$$

and

$$p \Rightarrow q$$
$=$ { definition implication }
$$\neg p \vee q$$
$=$ { definition explication }
$$\neg p \Leftarrow \neg q$$

and

$$p \wedge (p \Rightarrow q)$$
$=$ { definition implication }
$$p \wedge (\neg p \vee q)$$
$=$ { complement rule }
$$p \wedge q$$

and

$$q \vee (p \Rightarrow q)$$
$=$ { definition implication }
$$q \vee (\neg p \vee q)$$
$=$ { idempotence }
$$\neg p \vee q$$
$=$ { definition implication }
$$p \Rightarrow q$$

and

$$p \equiv q$$
$=$ { mutual implication }

$$(p \Rightarrow q) \wedge (q \Rightarrow p)$$
$$=\qquad \{ \text{ definition of implication } \}$$
$$(\neg p \vee q) \wedge (\neg q \vee p)$$
$$=\qquad \{ \text{ distribution } \}$$
$$(\neg p \wedge \neg q) \vee (\neg p \wedge p) \vee (q \wedge \neg q) \vee (q \wedge p)$$
$$=$$
$$(p \wedge q) \vee (\neg p \wedge \neg q) \qquad .$$

7. For couple c, let $c.h$ be the age of the husband and $c.w$ the age of the wife. The two given properties are

(0) $\langle \mathbf{MAX}c :: c.h \rangle = \langle \mathbf{MAX}c :: c.w \rangle$
(1) $\langle \forall c, d :: c.h \ \mathbf{min} \ d.w = c.w \ \mathbf{min} \ d.h \rangle$

For every couple c we have

$$c.h$$
$$=\qquad \{ \ c.h \leq \langle \mathbf{MAX}d :: d.h \rangle \ \}$$
$$c.h \ \mathbf{min} \ \langle \mathbf{MAX}d :: d.h \rangle$$
$$=\qquad \{ \ (0) \ \}$$
$$c.h \ \mathbf{min} \ \langle \mathbf{MAX}d :: d.w \rangle$$
$$=\qquad \{ \ \mathbf{min} \ \text{distributes over} \ \mathbf{max} \ \}$$
$$\langle \mathbf{MAX}d :: c.h \ \mathbf{min} \ d.w \rangle$$
$$=\qquad \{ \ (1) \ \}$$
$$\langle \mathbf{MAX}d :: c.w \ \mathbf{min} \ d.h \rangle$$
$$=\qquad \{ \ \mathbf{min} \ \text{distributes over} \ \mathbf{max} \ \}$$
$$c.w \ \mathbf{min} \ \langle \mathbf{MAX}d :: d.h \rangle$$
$$=\qquad \{ \ (0) \ \}$$
$$c.w \ \mathbf{min} \ \langle \mathbf{MAX}d :: d.w \rangle$$
$$=\qquad \{ \ c.w \leq \langle \mathbf{MAX}d :: d.w \rangle \ \}$$
$$c.w \qquad .$$

8. Number the light bulbs 0 through $n - 1$. Let boolean $b(i, k)$ be: light bulb i is on after pushing the button k times. Therefore, the initial state of bulb i is $b(i, 0)$. We have to prove $b(i, n)$, for all i. Pushing the button once amounts to

(0) $b(i, k + 1) \equiv b(i, k) \equiv b(i + 1, k)$

for all $i, k \geq 0$. The first argument of b is understood to be reduced modulo n. We show

(1) $b(i, k + j) \equiv b(i, k) \equiv b(i + j, k)$

for all $i, k \geq 0$, j a power of 2.
The proof is by induction on j.

- $j = 1$: from (0)
- $j \geq 1$: We have

$$
\begin{aligned}
& b(i, k + 2j) \\
= \quad & \{\ (1) \text{ with } k := k + j\ \} \\
& b(i, k + j) \equiv b(i + j, k + j) \\
= \quad & \{\ (1) \text{ twice; second time with } i := i + j\ \} \\
& b(i, k) \equiv b(i + j, k) \equiv b(i + j, k) \equiv b(i + j + j, k) \\
= \quad & \{\ \text{calculus}\ \} \\
& b(i, k) \equiv b(i + 2j, k) \quad .
\end{aligned}
$$

We conclude our result from

$$
\begin{aligned}
& b(i, n) \\
= \quad & \{\ (1) \text{ with } j, k := n, 0\ ;\ n \text{ is a power of 2}\ \} \\
& b(i, 0) \equiv b(i + n, 0) \\
= \quad & \{\ \text{first argument of } b \text{ is reduced modulo } n\ \} \\
& true \quad .
\end{aligned}
$$

By the way, the property that all n light bulbs are on after pushing the button n times, independently of the initial configuration, is not only implied by but equivalent to the property that n is a power of 2. We omit the proof thereof.

Answers for Chapter 8

4. First we write a program for computing the number of distinct values in a. Due to the monotonicity of a, it is 1 more than the number of direct neighbors that differ in value, hence

$$
R: \quad x = 1 + \langle \mathbf{N}i : 0 < i < N : a[i - 1] < a[i] \rangle
$$

which suggests

$$
\begin{aligned}
& P: \quad x = 1 + \langle \mathbf{N}i : 0 < i < k : a[i - 1] < a[i] \rangle \ \wedge\ 1 \leq k \leq N \\
& bf: \quad N - k
\end{aligned}
$$

The program is

```
x, k := 1, 1;  { P }
*[ k ≠ N → [ a[k − 1] < a[k] → x := x + 1
           ▯ a[k − 1] = a[k] → skip
           ];
           k := k + 1  { P }
 ]
```

initialization:

$$P_{1,1}^{x,k}$$
$$= \quad \{ \text{ substitution } \}$$
$$1 = 1 + \langle \mathbf{N}i : 0 < i < 1 : a[i-1] < a[i] \rangle \;\wedge\; 1 \le 1 \le N$$
$$= \quad \{ \text{ definition of } \langle \mathbf{N}... \rangle, \text{ given } \}$$
$$true$$

finalization:

$$P \;\wedge\; k = N$$
$$\Rightarrow \quad \{ \text{ substitution } \}$$
$$R$$

invariance of P:

$$P_{k+1}^{k}$$
$$= \quad \{ \text{ substitution } \}$$
$$x = 1 + \langle \mathbf{N}i : 0 < i < k+1 : a[i-1] < a[i] \rangle \;\wedge$$
$$1 \le k+1 \le N$$
$$\Leftarrow \quad \{ \text{ domain split; strengthen } 1 \le k+1 \text{ to allow it } \}$$
$$x = 1 + \langle \mathbf{N}i : 0 < i < k : a[i-1] < a[i] \rangle$$
$$\qquad + \langle \mathbf{N}i : 0 < i = k : a[i-1] < a[i] \rangle \;\wedge$$
$$1 \le k \;\wedge\; k+1 \le N$$

This corresponds to the state between the if-statement and the increase of k. The correctness of the if-statement then follows from

$$(P_{k+1}^{k})_{x+1}^{x}$$
$$\Leftarrow \quad \{ \text{ see above; substitution } \}$$
$$x + 1 = 1 + \langle \mathbf{N}i : 0 < i < k : a[i-1] < a[i] \rangle$$
$$\qquad\qquad + \langle \mathbf{N}i : 0 < i = k : a[i-1] < a[i] \rangle \;\wedge$$
$$1 \le k \;\wedge\; k+1 \le N$$
$$\Leftarrow \quad \{ \text{ second count is 1 if } a[k-1] < a[k] \}$$
$$P \;\wedge\; k \ne N \;\wedge\; a[k-1] < a[k]$$

and

$$P_{k+1}^{k}$$
$$\Leftarrow \quad \{ \text{ see above } \}$$
$$x = 1 + \langle \mathbf{N}i : 0 < i < k : a[i-1] < a[i] \rangle$$
$$\qquad + \langle \mathbf{N}i : 0 < i = k : a[i-1] < a[i] \rangle \;\wedge$$
$$1 \le k \;\wedge\; k+1 \le N$$
$$\Leftarrow \quad \{ \text{ second count is 0 if } a[k-1] = a[k] \}$$
$$P \;\wedge\; k \ne N \;\wedge\; a[k-1] = a[k]$$

bf bounded:

$$P \;\wedge\; k \ne N \;\Rightarrow\; bf > 0$$

termination:

bf is decreased by 1 in every step of the iteration.

The next program computes the maximum length of any plateau. If a plateau of a certain positive length exists then also a plateau of length one less exists. Hence, the maximum plateau length can be described as the value x for which a plateau of length x exists, but no plateau of length $x+1$ exists. Due to the monotonicity of a, this can be formulated as follows.

$$R: \quad \langle \exists i : x-1 \leq i < N : a[i-x+1] = a[i] \rangle \ \wedge$$
$$\langle \forall i : x \leq i < N : a[i-x] < a[i] \rangle$$

This suggests an invariant and a bound function.

$$P: \quad \langle \exists i : x-1 \leq i < k : a[i-x+1] = a[i] \rangle \ \wedge$$
$$\langle \forall i : x \leq i < k : a[i-x] < a[i] \rangle \ \wedge \ 1 \leq k \leq N$$
$$bf: \quad N-k$$

The program is

```
x, k := 1, 1;  { P }
*[ k ≠ N → [ a[k − x] < a[k] → skip
           [] a[k − x] = a[k] → x := x + 1
           ];
           k := k + 1  { P }
 ]        .
```

initialization:

$$P_{1,1}^{x,k}$$
$$= \quad \{ \text{ substitution } \}$$
$$\langle \exists i : 0 \leq i < 1 : a[i] = a[i] \rangle \ \wedge$$
$$\langle \forall i : 1 \leq i < 1 : a[i-1] < a[i] \rangle \ \wedge \ 1 \leq 1 \leq N$$
$$= \quad \{ \text{ definition of } \langle \exists ... \rangle, \ \langle \forall ... \rangle, \text{ given } \}$$
$$\textit{true}$$

finalization:

$$P \ \wedge \ k = N$$
$$\Rightarrow \quad \{ \text{ substitution } \}$$
$$R$$

invariance of P:

$$P_{k+1}^{k}$$
$$= \quad \{ \text{ substitution } \}$$
$$\langle \exists i : x-1 \leq i < k+1 : a[i-x+1] = a[i] \rangle \ \wedge$$
$$\langle \forall i : x \leq i < k+1 : a[i-x] < a[i] \rangle \ \wedge$$
$$1 \leq k+1 \leq N$$

$\Leftarrow \quad$ { domain split; strengthen $1 \le k+1$ to allow it }
$$(\langle \exists i : x-1 \le i < k : a[i-x+1] = a[i]\rangle \ \vee$$
$$a[k-x+1] = a[k]) \ \wedge$$
$$\langle \forall i : x \le i < k : a[i-x] < a[i]\rangle \ \wedge \ a[k-x] < a[k] \ \wedge$$
$$2 \le k+1 \le N$$

This corresponds to the state between the if-statement and the increase of k. The correctness of the if-statement then follows from

$$P^k_{k+1}$$
$\Leftarrow \quad$ { see above; definition of P }
$$P \ \wedge \ k \ne N \ \wedge \ a[k-x] < a[k]$$

and

$$(P^k_{k+1})^x_{x+1}$$
$\Leftarrow \quad$ { see above; substitution }
$$(\langle \exists i : x \le i < k : a[i-x] = a[i]\rangle \ \vee \ a[k-x] = a[k]) \ \wedge$$
$$\langle \forall i : x \le i < k : a[i-x-1] < a[i]\rangle \ \wedge$$
$$a[k-x-1] < a[k] \ \wedge \ 2 \le k+1 \le N$$
$\Leftarrow \quad$ { $a[i-x-1] \le a[i-x], \ a[k-1] \le a[k]$ }
$$P \ \wedge \ k \ne N \ \wedge \ a[k-x] = a[k]$$

bf bounded:

$$P \ \wedge \ k \ne N \ \Rightarrow \ bf > 0$$

termination:

bf is decreased by 1 in every step of the iteration.

7. Our program stores the least N elements in array $h[0..N-1]$. The program consists of a loop with invariant P.

$P: \quad \langle \forall i : 0 \le i < k : h[i]$ is the least-but-i element of $H\rangle \ \wedge$
$\quad\quad 1 \le k \le N$
$bf: \quad N-k$

```
h[0] := 1;  k := 1;
*[ k ≠ N → x := 0;  *[2 · h[x] ≤ h[k−1] → x := x + 1];
              y := 0;  *[3 · h[y] ≤ h[k−1] → y := y + 1];
              z := 0;  *[5 · h[z] ≤ h[k−1] → z := z + 1];
              [ 3 · h[y] ≥ 2 · h[x] ≤ 5 · h[z] → h[k] := 2 · h[x]
              | 5 · h[z] ≥ 3 · h[y] ≤ 2 · h[x] → h[k] := 3 · h[y]
              | 2 · h[x] ≥ 5 · h[z] ≤ 3 · h[y] → h[k] := 5 · h[z]
              ];
              k := k + 1
]
```

The loop contains three linear searches, assigning to x the least value for which $2 \cdot h[x] > h[k-1]$, and similarly for y and z. The smallest of the three "candidates" $2 \cdot h[x]$, $3 \cdot h[y]$, and $5 \cdot h[z]$, is then added to the array. (Expression $a \geq b \leq c$ is read as $a \geq b \wedge b \leq c$.) We can make the program more efficient by adding the invariants of those three inner loops to the invariant of the outer loop. This allows each linear search to start from the point where it terminated the previous time, instead of starting from 0. The extension of P is

$$\langle \forall j : 0 \leq j < x : 2 \cdot h[j] \leq h[k-1] \rangle \quad \wedge$$
$$\langle \forall j : 0 \leq j < y : 3 \cdot h[j] \leq h[k-1] \rangle \quad \wedge$$
$$\langle \forall j : 0 \leq j < z : 5 \cdot h[j] \leq h[k-1] \rangle$$

and the program becomes

```
h[0] := 1;  k := 1;  x, y, z := 0, 0, 0;
*[ k ≠ N → *[2 · h[x] ≤ h[k − 1] → x := x + 1];
           *[3 · h[y] ≤ h[k − 1] → y := y + 1];
           *[5 · h[z] ≤ h[k − 1] → z := z + 1];
           [ 3 · h[y] ≥ 2 · h[x] ≤ 5 · h[z] → h[k] := 2 · h[x]
           | 5 · h[z] ≥ 3 · h[y] ≤ 2 · h[x] → h[k] := 3 · h[y]
           | 2 · h[x] ≥ 5 · h[z] ≤ 3 · h[y] → h[k] := 5 · h[z]
           ];
           k := k + 1
 ]      ,
```

or even

```
h[0] := 1;  k := 1;  x, y, z := 0, 0, 0;
*[ k ≠ N → *[2 · h[x] ≤ h[k − 1] → x := x + 1];
           *[3 · h[y] ≤ h[k − 1] → y := y + 1];
           *[5 · h[z] ≤ h[k − 1] → z := z + 1];
           [ 3 · h[y] ≥ 2 · h[x] ≤ 5 · h[z] → h[k] := 2 · h[x];
                                              k, x := k + 1, x + 1
           | 5 · h[z] ≥ 3 · h[y] ≤ 2 · h[x] → h[k] := 3 · h[y];
                                              k, y := k + 1, y + 1
           | 2 · h[x] ≥ 5 · h[z] ≤ 3 · h[y] → h[k] := 5 · h[z];
                                              k, z := k + 1, z + 1
 ]      ]      .
```

By the way, the three inner loops are iterated at most once per step of the outer loop and may, therefore, be replaced with if-statements.

9. Define C as $C = \langle \mathbf{N} i, j : 0 \leq i < j < N : w[i] + w[j] = A \rangle$. Postcondition R, invariant P and bound function bf are as follows.

$$R : \quad C = c$$

$$P: \quad C = c + \langle \mathbf{N}i,j : m \le i < j < n : w[i] + w[j] = A \rangle \ \wedge$$
$$\qquad 0 \le m \ \wedge \ n \le N$$
$$bf: \quad n - m$$

program:

$$c, m, n := 0, 0, N; \quad \{ P \}$$
$$*[\ m < n - 1 \rightarrow [\ w[m] + w[n-1] < A \rightarrow m := m + 1$$
$$\qquad\qquad\qquad \| \ w[m] + w[n-1] > A \rightarrow n := n - 1$$
$$\qquad\qquad\qquad \| \ w[m] + w[n-1] = A \rightarrow c, m, n :=$$
$$\qquad\qquad\qquad\qquad\qquad\qquad\qquad\qquad c + 1, m + 1, n - 1$$
$$\quad] \qquad\qquad\qquad]$$

initialization:

$$P_{0,0,N}^{c,m,n}$$
$$=$$
$$C = 0 + \langle \mathbf{N}i,j : 0 \le i < j < N : w[i] + w[j] = A \rangle \ \wedge$$
$$0 \le 0 \ \wedge \ N \le N$$
$$= \qquad \{ \text{ definition of } C \ \}$$
$$\textit{true}$$

finalization:

$$P \ \wedge \ m \ge n - 1$$
$$\Rightarrow \qquad \{ \text{ substitution } \}$$
$$C = c + \langle \mathbf{N}i,j : n - 1 \le m \le i < j < n : w[i] + w[j] = A \rangle$$
$$\Rightarrow \qquad \{ \text{ numeric quantification over an empty range is 0 } \}$$
$$R$$

invariance of P :

$$P_{m+1}^{m}$$
$$= \qquad \{ \text{ substitution } \}$$
$$C = c + \langle \mathbf{N}i,j : m + 1 \le i < j < n : w[i] + w[j] = A \rangle \ \wedge$$
$$0 \le m + 1 \ \wedge \ n \le N$$
$$\Leftarrow \qquad \{ \text{ domain split; strengthen } 0 \le m + 1 \text{ to allow it } \}$$
$$C = c + \langle \mathbf{N}i,j : m \le i < j < n : w[i] + w[j] = A \rangle$$
$$\qquad - \langle \mathbf{N}i,j : m = i < j < n : w[i] + w[j] = A \rangle \ \wedge$$
$$0 \le m < n - 1 < N$$
$$\Leftarrow \qquad \{ \ w[m] + w[j] \le w[m] + w[n-1] \text{ for } j < n \ \}$$
$$P \ \wedge \ w[m] + w[n-1] < A \ \wedge \ m < n - 1$$

$$P_{n-1}^{n}$$
$$= \qquad \{ \text{ substitution } \}$$
$$C = c + \langle \mathbf{N}i,j : m \le i < j < n - 1 : w[i] + w[j] = A \rangle \ \wedge$$
$$0 \le m \ \wedge \ n - 1 \le N$$
$$\Leftarrow \qquad \{ \text{ domain split; strengthen } n - 1 \le N \text{ to allow it } \}$$

$$C = c + \langle \mathbf{N}i, j : m \le i < j < n : w[i] + w[j] = A \rangle$$
$$\quad - \langle \mathbf{N}i, j : m \le i < j = n - 1 : w[i] + w[j] = A \rangle \ \wedge$$
$$0 \le m < n - 1 < N$$
$$\Leftarrow \quad \{ \ w[i] + w[n - 1] \ge w[m] + w[n - 1] \ \text{for} \ i \ge m \ \}$$
$$P \ \wedge \ w[m] + w[n - 1] > A \ \wedge \ m < n - 1$$

$$P^{c,m,n}_{c+1,m+1,n-1}$$
$$= \quad \{ \ \text{substitution} \ \}$$
$$C = c + 1 +$$
$$\quad \langle \mathbf{N}i, j : m + 1 \le i < j < n - 1 : w[i] + w[j] = A \rangle \ \wedge$$
$$0 \le m + 1 \ \wedge \ n - 1 \le N$$
$$\Leftarrow \quad \{ \ \text{domain split; strengthen range of} \ m \ \text{and} \ n \ \}$$
$$C = c + 1 + \langle \mathbf{N}i, j : m \le i < j < n : w[i] + w[j] = A \rangle$$
$$\quad - \langle \mathbf{N}i, j : m = i < j < n - 1 : w[i] + w[j] = A \rangle$$
$$\quad - \langle \mathbf{N}i, j : m < i < j = n - 1 : w[i] + w[j] = A \rangle$$
$$\quad - \langle \mathbf{N}i, j : m = i < j = n - 1 : w[i] + w[j] = A \rangle$$
$$\wedge \ 0 \le m < n - 1 < N$$
$$\Leftarrow \quad \{ \ \text{monotonicity of} \ w \ \}$$
$$P \ \wedge \ w[m] + w[n - 1] = A \ \wedge \ m < n - 1$$

bf bounded:

$$P \ \wedge \ m < n - 1 \ \Rightarrow \ bf > 0$$

termination:

bf is decreased by 1 or 2 in every step of the iteration.

11. We define function *lcp* as the function that returns the number given by the longest common prefix of the representation of two given numbers.

$$lcp(a, b) = \langle \mathbf{MAX}k, l : a \ \mathbf{div} \ 10^k = b \ \mathbf{div} \ 10^l : b \ \mathbf{div} \ 10^l \rangle$$

(We have omitted the range $k \ge 0 \wedge l \ge 0$.) We have the following properties.

$$lcp(a, a) = a$$
$$lcp(a \ \mathbf{div} \ 10, b) = lcp(a, b) \qquad \text{if} \ a > b$$
$$lcp(a, b) = lcp(b, a)$$

We give a proof of the second property, since this one may not be obvious.

$$lcp(a \ \mathbf{div} \ 10, b)$$
$$=$$
$$\langle \mathbf{MAX}k, l : k \ge 0 \wedge a \ \mathbf{div} \ 10^{k+1} = b \ \mathbf{div} \ 10^l : b \ \mathbf{div} \ 10^l \rangle$$

$$= \qquad \{ \ a > b \ \Rightarrow \ a \neq b \ \textbf{div} \ 10^l \ \text{for all} \ l \geq 0 \ \}$$
$$\langle \textbf{MAX}k, l : k \geq -1 \wedge a \ \textbf{div} \ 10^{k+1} = b \ \textbf{div} \ 10^l : b \ \textbf{div} \ 10^l \rangle$$
$$= \qquad \{ \ \text{replace} \ k+1 \ \text{by} \ k \ \}$$
$$\langle \textbf{MAX}k, l : k \geq 0 \wedge a \ \textbf{div} \ 10^k = b \ \textbf{div} \ 10^l : b \ \textbf{div} \ 10^l \rangle$$
$$=$$
$$lcp(a, b)$$

Given two numbers a and b, we are to write a program for computing $lcp(a, b)$. As an invariant we propose something similar to the invariant of Euclid's gcd algorithm, namely introduce variables x and y with the property that their lcp equals the lcp that was asked for.

$$P: \qquad lcp(a, b) = lcp(x, y) \ \wedge \ x \geq 0 \ \wedge \ y \geq 0$$

Since $lcp(x, x) = x$ the program will reduce x and y from their initial values a and b to equality under invariance of P. The bound function is, therefore, $x + y$. Since $x := x \ \textbf{div} \ 10$ maintains P if $x > y$ (cf. the second property) we obtain the following program.

$$x, y := a, b;$$
$$*[\ x > y \rightarrow x := x \ \textbf{div} \ 10 \ \| \ y > x \rightarrow y := y \ \textbf{div} \ 10 \ ]$$

12. Postcondition R, invariant P and bound function bf are as follows.

$$R: \quad X^Y = z$$
$$P: \quad X^Y = z \cdot x^y \ \wedge \ x > 0 \ \wedge \ y \geq 0$$
$$bf: \quad \lfloor \log(y) \rfloor$$

program:

$$x, y, z := X, Y, 1; \quad \{ \ P \ \}$$
$$*[\ y > 0 \ \wedge \ even(y) \rightarrow x, y := x^2, y/2$$
$$\| \ y > 0 \ \wedge \ odd(y) \rightarrow x, y, z := x^2, (y-1)/2, z \cdot x$$
$$]$$

initialization:

$$P_{X,Y,1}^{x,y,z}$$
$$=$$
$$X^Y = 1 \cdot X^Y \ \wedge \ X > 0 \ \wedge \ Y \geq 0$$
$$= \qquad \{ \ \text{given} \ \}$$
$$true$$

finalization:

$$P \ \wedge \ y = 0$$
$$\Rightarrow \qquad \{ \ \text{arithmetic} \ \}$$
$$R$$

invariance of P :

$$P_{x^2,y/2}^{x,y}$$
$=$ { substitution }
$X^Y = z \cdot (x^2)^{(y/2)}$ $\wedge$ $x^2 > 0$ $\wedge$ $y/2 \geq 0$
$\Leftarrow$ { arithmetic }
P $\wedge$ $y > 0$ $\wedge$ $even(y)$

$$P_{x^2,(y-1)/2,z\cdot x}^{x,y,z}$$
$=$ { substitution }
$X^Y = z \cdot x \cdot (x^2)^{((y-1)/2)}$ $\wedge$ $x^2 > 0$ $\wedge$ $(y-1)/2 \geq 0$
$\Leftarrow$ { arithmetic }
P $\wedge$ $y > 0$ $\wedge$ $odd(y)$

bf bounded:

$P \wedge y > 0 \Rightarrow bf \geq 0$

termination:

bf is decreased by at least 1 in every step of the iteration since
y is at least halved.

Slight variations of the algorithm are

$x, y, z := X, Y, 1;$ $\{ P \}$
$*[\ y > 0$ $\wedge$ $even(y) \rightarrow x, y := x^2, y/2$
$\ \|\ y > 0$ $\wedge$ $odd(y)\ \rightarrow y, z := y - 1, z \cdot x$
$\ ]$

and

$x, y, z := X, Y, 1;$ $\{ P \}$
$*[\ y \neq 0 \rightarrow *[even(y) \rightarrow x, y := x^2, y/2];$
$\qquad y, z := y - 1, z \cdot x$
$\ ]$.

They also take logarithmic time, but this is a slightly harder to see.

16. Define C as

$$C = \langle \mathbf{N}x, y : 0 \leq x \leq y : x^2 + y^2 = N \rangle \quad .$$

Postcondition R, invariant P and bound function *bf* are as follows.

$R:$ $C = c$
$P:$ $C = c + \langle \mathbf{N}x, y : a \leq x \leq y \leq b : x^2 + y^2 = N \rangle$ $\wedge$
$\qquad 0 \leq a$
$bf:$ $b - a$

program:

$$a, b, c := 0, round(\sqrt{N}), 0; \quad \{ P \}$$
$$*[\ a \leq b \rightarrow [\ a^2 + b^2 < N \rightarrow a := a + 1$$
$$\| \ a^2 + b^2 > N \rightarrow b := b - 1$$
$$\| \ a^2 + b^2 = N \rightarrow a, b, c := a + 1, b - 1, c + 1$$
$$] \qquad\qquad]$$

(It doesn't matter whether *round* rounds up or down.)

initialization:

$$P^{a,b,c}_{0,round(\sqrt{N}),0}$$

$=$

$$C = 0 + \langle \mathbf{N}x, y : 0 \leq x \leq y \leq round(\sqrt{N}) : x^2 + y^2 = N \rangle \ \wedge$$
$$0 \leq 0$$

$=$ \qquad { definition of C }

true

finalization:

$$P \ \wedge \ a > b$$

$\Rightarrow$ \qquad { numeric quantification over an empty range is 0 }

$$R$$

invariance of P :

$$P^a_{a+1}$$

$=$ \qquad { substitution }
$$C = c + \langle \mathbf{N}x, y : a + 1 \leq x \leq y \leq b : x^2 + y^2 = N \rangle \ \wedge$$
$$0 \leq a + 1$$

$\Leftarrow$ \qquad { domain split }
$$C = c + \langle \mathbf{N}x, y : a \leq x \leq y \leq b : x^2 + y^2 = N \rangle$$
$$\quad - \langle \mathbf{N}x, y : a = x \leq y \leq b : x^2 + y^2 = N \rangle \ \wedge$$
$$0 \leq a \leq b$$

$\Leftarrow$ \qquad { monotonicity: $a^2 + y^2 \leq a^2 + b^2$ for $y \leq b$ }
$$P \ \wedge \ a^2 + b^2 < N \ \wedge \ a \leq b$$

$$P^b_{b-1}$$

$=$ \qquad { substitution }
$$C = c + \langle \mathbf{N}x, y : a \leq x \leq y \leq b - 1 : x^2 + y^2 = N \rangle \ \wedge$$
$$0 \leq a$$

$\Leftarrow$ \qquad { domain split }
$$C = c + \langle \mathbf{N}x, y : a \leq x \leq y \leq b : x^2 + y^2 = N \rangle$$
$$\quad - \langle \mathbf{N}x, y : a \leq x \leq y = b : x^2 + y^2 = N \rangle \ \wedge$$
$$0 \leq a \leq b$$

$\Leftarrow$ \qquad { monotonicity: $x^2 + b^2 \geq a^2 + b^2$ for $x \geq a$ }
$$P \ \wedge \ a^2 + b^2 > N \ \wedge \ a \leq b$$

$$P^{a,b,c}_{a+1,b-1,c+1}$$

$$=\qquad \{\text{ substitution }\}$$
$$C = c + 1 + \langle Nx, y : a + 1 \le x \le y \le b - 1 : x^2 + y^2 = N\rangle$$
$$\wedge\ \ 0 \le a + 1$$

$$\Leftarrow\qquad \{\text{ domain split }\}$$
$$C = c + 1 + \langle Nx, y : a \le x \le y \le b : x^2 + y^2 = N\rangle$$
$$- \langle Nx, y : a < x \le y = b : x^2 + y^2 = N\rangle$$
$$- \langle Nx, y : a = x \le y < b : x^2 + y^2 = N\rangle$$
$$- \langle Nx, y : a = x \le y = b : x^2 + y^2 = N\rangle\ \wedge$$
$$0 \le a \le b$$

$$\Leftarrow\qquad \{\text{ monotonicity of } x^2 + y^2 \ \}$$
$$P\ \wedge\ a^2 + b^2 = N\ \wedge\ a \le b$$

bf bounded:

$$P\ \wedge\ a \le b\ \Rightarrow\ bf \ge 0$$

termination:

bf is decreased by 1 or 2 in every step of the iteration.

We might speed up execution of the program by eliminating the expression $a^2 + b^2$ from the program. We do so by our standard method of introducing a fresh variable whose value equals the expression that we want to eliminate, that is, we extend the invariant with the conjunct

$$v = a^2 + b^2$$

and update the value of v whenever a or b changes. This can be done efficiently since, for example,

$$(a + 1)^2 + b^2\ =\ a^2 + 2a + 1 + b^2\qquad .$$

We can replace the initialization $b := round(\sqrt{N})$ by a linear search

$$b := 0;\ \ *[b^2 < N \to b := b + 1]$$

and obtain our final program. (We have made another minuscule change by switching to $v = a^2 + b^2 - N$.)

$$a, b, c, v := 0, 0, 0, -N;\ \ *[v < 0 \to b, v := b + 1, v + 2b + 1];$$
$$\{\ P\ \}$$
$$*[\ a \le b \to$$
$$[\ v < 0 \to a, v := a + 1, v + 2a + 1$$
$$\|\ v > 0 \to b, v := b - 1, v - 2b + 1$$
$$\|\ v = 0 \to a, b, c, v := a + 1, b - 1, c + 1, v + 2a - 2b + 2$$
$$]\ \ ]$$

25. Let

$$s(p, q) \;=\; \langle \sum i : p \le i < q : f(i) \rangle$$

and observe that $s(p, q)$ is a decreasing function of p and an increasing function of q. Furthermore, $p < q \;\equiv\; s(p, q) > 0$. Let

$$n(i, j) \;=\; \langle \mathbf{N} p, q : i \le p \;\wedge\; j \le q \;\wedge\; p < q : s(p, q) = A \rangle$$

for all $i < j$. In order to establish

$$R: \qquad n(1, 2) = c$$

the saddleback search suggests invariant

$$P: \qquad n(1, 2) = c + n(i, j) \;\wedge\; 1 \le i < j$$

and bound function

$$2L - i - j$$

in which $f(L) > A$. The invariant is established if the state satisfies $c = 0 \;\wedge\; i = 1 \;\wedge\; j = 2$ and postcondition R is established if the state satisfies $P \;\wedge\; f(i) > A$. We are interested in increasing i, or j, or both, and we calculate the preconditions of those three actions. At least one of those actions should also increase c and, for reasons of symmetry, we try to do it in the action that increases both i and j. First, the increase of i:

$$P^i_{i+1}$$

$=$ $\quad$ { substitution }

$\quad n(1, 2) = c + n(i + 1, j) \;\wedge\; 1 \le i + 1 < j$

$=$ $\quad$ { substitution }

$\quad n(1, 2) = c + n(i, j) - \langle \mathbf{N} q : j \le q \wedge i < q : s(i, q) = A \rangle$

$\quad \wedge\; 1 \le i + 1 < j$

$\Leftarrow$ $\quad$ { monotonicity of s }

$\quad P \;\wedge\; s(i, j) > A \;\wedge\; i + 1 < j$

$=$ $\quad$ { property of s }

$\quad P \;\wedge\; s(i, j) > A \;\wedge\; s(i + 1, j) > 0$

$\Leftarrow$

$\quad P \;\wedge\; s(i, j) > A \;\wedge\; f(i) \le A$

and second, the increase of j:

$$P_{j+1}^j$$

$=$ { substitution }
$n(1,2) = c + n(i, j+1) \quad \wedge \quad 1 \le i < j+1$
$=$ { substitution }
$n(1,2) = c + n(i,j) - \langle \mathbf{N}p : i \le p \wedge p < j : s(p,j) = A \rangle$
$\wedge\; 1 \le i < j+1$
$\Leftarrow$ { monotonicity of s }
$P \;\wedge\; s(i,j) < A$

and third, the increase of both i and j :

$$P_{c+1,i+1,j+1}^{c,i,j}$$

$=$ { substitution }
$n(1,2) = c + 1 + n(i+1, j+1) \quad \wedge \quad 1 \le i+1 < j+1$
$=$ { substitution }
$n(1,2) = c + 1 + n(i,j)$
$\qquad\qquad - \langle \mathbf{N}q : j < q \;\wedge\; i < q : s(i,q) = A \rangle$
$\qquad\qquad - \langle \mathbf{N}p : i < p \;\wedge\; p < j : s(p,j) = A \rangle$
$\qquad\qquad - \langle \mathbf{N}p,q : i = p \;\wedge\; j = q : s(p,q) = A \rangle$
$\wedge\; 1 \le i+1 < j+1$
$\Leftarrow$ { monotonicity of s }
$P \;\wedge\; s(i,j) = A$.

These guards are a strong incentive to add

$$x \;=\; s(i,j)$$

to the invariant. The program can then be coded as follows.

```
c, i, j, x := 0, 1, 2, f(1);
*[ x > A  ∧  f(i) ≤ A → i, x := i + 1, x − f(i)
 ‖ x < A              → j, x := j + 1, x + f(j + 1)
 ‖ x = A              → c, i, j, x := c + 1, i + 1, j + 1,
                                  x − f(i) + f(j + 1)
 ]
```

26. Of course it is possible to use the solution to the previous problem and substitute i for $f(i)$ but then the running time is proportional to A rather than $\sqrt{A}$. The sum of the sequence of $q - p$ consecutive integers from p on is $\langle \sum i : p \le i < q : i \rangle$. Let us consider the sequences in order of their length. What is the simplest sequence of length k ? It is

1, 2, $\cdots$, k which has sum $\frac{1}{2}k(k+1)$.

The second simplest sequence of length k is

2, 3, $\cdots$, $k+1$ which has sum $\frac{1}{2}k(k+1)+k$

(because each of its k elements is increased by 1). The n th simplest sequence of length k is

n, $n+1$, $\cdots$, $k+n-1$ which has sum $\frac{1}{2}k(k+1)+(n-1)k$.

It follows that the number of sequences of length k with sum A equals the number of occurrences of A in

$$\frac{1}{2}k(k+1), \ \frac{1}{2}k(k+1)+k, \ \cdots, \ \frac{1}{2}k(k+1)+(n-1)k, \ \cdots$$

which is 1 when

$$\frac{1}{2}k(k+1) \leq A \ \wedge \ (A - \frac{1}{2}k(k+1)) \bmod k = 0$$

and 0 otherwise. This leads directly to the following invariant

c = the number of sequences with sum A and length
less than k $\wedge$ $1 \leq k$

and program.

```
c, k := 0, 1;
*[ k(k+1)/2 ≤ A →
     [ (A − k(k+1)/2) mod k = 0 → c := c + 1
     ‖ (A − k(k+1)/2) mod k ≠ 0 → skip
     ];
     k := k + 1
   ]
```

Strengthening the invariant with $e = A - \frac{1}{2}k(k+1)$ leads to the final solution.

```
c, k, e := 0, 1, A − 1;
*[ e ≥ 0 → [ e mod k = 0 → c := c + 1
           ‖ e mod k ≠ 0 → skip
           ];
           k := k + 1;  e := e − k
   ]
```

Answers for Chapter 9

1. One second corresponds to $n \approx 9$ for the first and $n \approx 4$ for the second program. If we assume that the time elapsed since the "Big Bang" is $1.5.10^{10}$ years or $4.7 * 10^{17}$ seconds, we find $n \approx 27$ for the first and $n \approx 419$ for the second program.

4. Sorting can be viewed as performing a judiciously-chosen permutation on the given array to transform it into a sorted array. Therefore, sorting takes at least as much time as finding the right permutation. If all n numbers are different then there are $n!$ different permutations. If we construct a comparison tree, as in the case of searching, then each leaf corresponds to a possible choice, and the number of leaves is, therefore, at least $n!$. The height of a binary tree with at least $n!$ leaves is at least $\log_2(n!)$. The result follows from

$$
\begin{aligned}
&\log_2(n!) \\
\approx\quad & \{ \text{ Stirling's approximation } \} \\
&\log_2((\tfrac{n}{e})^n \sqrt{2\pi n}) \\
=\quad & \\
&n\log_2(n) - n\log_2(e) + \log_2(\sqrt{2\pi n}) \\
\approx\quad & \{ \text{ consider large } n \} \\
&n\log_2(n) \quad .
\end{aligned}
$$

7. The new elements that are added to the bag are generated in ascending order. Therefore, one may introduce a second array that is also in ascending order, just like the given array, and add new elements always to the tail of the second array. The minimum element that is to be removed from the bag is the smaller of the two elements that are at the heads of the two arrays when both are nonempty, and it is the head element of the nonempty array if one of the arrays is empty.

8. If we count only comparisons, the value is 2, since the first condition is *false* in all steps except the last, and therefore the second boolean is also evaluated in all steps except the last. This program is even less efficient than the one with the first and second alternative in reverse order.

Answers for Chapter 10

3. The function is well-defined because in every recursive call the arguments are lexicographically less than (m, n) and there is a lower bound (both numbers 0).

Of course, we may try to compute $A(3, 6)$ by applying the definition a number of times and reduce $A(3, 6)$ to

$A(2, A(3, 5))$ to

$A(2, A(2, A(3, 4)))$ to

$A(2, A(2, A(2, A(3, 3))))$ to

$A(2, A(2, A(2, A(2, A(3, 2)))))$ to

$A(2, A(2, A(2, A(2, A(2, A(3, 1))))))$ to

$A(2, A(2, A(2, A(2, A(2, A(2, A(3, 0)))))))$ to

$A(2, A(2, A(2, A(2, A(2, A(2, A(2, 1))))))) $ and so on.

However, this is going to take us 172233 steps and it is usually faster to be smarter. One way to avoid the calculational problem is to observe

$$A(0, n) = n + 1$$
$$A(1, n) = n + 2$$
$$A(2, n) = 2n + 3$$
$$A(3, n) = 2^{n+3} - 3$$

from which we infer $A(3, 6) = 509$.

6. $(define\ (replace\ (lambda\ (x\ y\ z)$
                    $(cond\ ((atom\ z)\ (cond\ ((eq\ x\ z)\ y)$
                                            $(t\ z)))$
                            $(t\ (cons\ (replace\ x\ y\ (car\ z))$
                                      $(replace\ x\ y\ (cdr\ z)))))))))$

8. $(define$
              $(intersect\ (lambda\ (x\ y)$
                    $(cond\ ((null\ x)\ nil)$
                            $((member\ (car\ x)\ y)$
                                $(cons\ (car\ x)\ (intersect\ (cdr\ x)\ y)))$
                            $(t\ (intersect\ (cdr\ x)\ y)))))$
              $(setdif\ (lambda\ (x\ y)$
                    $(cond\ ((null\ x)\ nil)$
                            $((member\ (car\ x)\ y)\ (setdif\ (cdr\ x)\ y))$
                            $(t\ (cons\ (car\ x)\ (setdif\ (cdr\ x)\ y))))))$
              $(eqset\ (lambda\ (x\ y)$
                    $(cond\ ((null\ (setdif\ x\ y))\ (null\ (setdif\ y\ x)))$
                            $(t\ nil)))))$

11. The solution involves function *collect* that computes the union of set *s* and all non- *nil* atoms in *x*.

        $(define\ (allatoms\ (lambda\ (x)$
                    $(collect\ x\ nil)))$
              $(collect\ (lambda\ (x\ s)$
                    $(cond\ ((atom\ x)\ (cond\ ((eq\ x\ nil)\ s)$
                                            $((member\ x\ s)\ s)$
                                            $(t\ (cons\ x\ s))))$
                            $(t\ (collect\ (car\ x)\ (collect\ (cdr\ x)\ s)))))))$

13. Since *reduce* is defined for nonempty lists only, the base case is the list of one element. The program is as follows.

$$(define\ (reduce\ (lambda\ (op\ x)$$
$$(cond\ ((null\ (cdr\ x))\ (car\ x))$$
$$(t\ (op\ (car\ x)\ (reduce\ op\ (cdr\ x))))))))$$

The result of

$$(reduce\ (lambda\ (a\ b)\ b)\ x)$$

for nonempty list x is the last element of list x.

15. The function definition follows the recursive definition of the derivative of an expression:

$$\frac{d}{dx}x = 1$$
$$\frac{d}{dx}y = 0\ \text{for all constants and variables}\ y\ \text{different from}\ x$$
$$\frac{d}{dx}(e+f) = \frac{d\ e}{dx} + \frac{d\ f}{dx}$$
$$\frac{d}{dx}(e \times f) = \frac{d\ e}{dx}f + e\frac{d\ f}{dx}$$

$$(define$$
$$(deriv\ (lambda\ (e\ x)$$
$$(cond\ ((atom\ e)\ (cond\ ((eq\ e\ x)\ (quote\ 1))$$
$$(t\ (quote\ 0))))$$
$$((eq\ (car\ e)\ (quote\ plus))$$
$$(list\ (quote\ plus)$$
$$(deriv\ (cadr\ e)\ x)$$
$$(deriv\ (caddr\ e)\ x)))$$
$$((eq\ (car\ e)\ (quote\ times))$$
$$(list\ (quote\ plus)$$
$$(list\ (quote\ times)$$
$$(deriv\ (cadr\ e)\ x)$$
$$(caddr\ c))$$
$$(list\ (quote\ times)$$
$$(cadr\ e)$$
$$(deriv\ (caddr\ e)\ x)))))))$$
$$(list\ (lambda\ (a\ b\ c)$$
$$(cons\ a\ (cons\ b\ (cons\ c\ nil))))))$$

19. The definition of subtraction follows that of addition, except that the carry is computed differently. Since we have no representation for negative numbers, the result is valid only if y is at most x. We obtain our definition of the subtraction function as follows.

$$\mathcal{M}(xa) - \mathcal{M}(yb) - c$$
$$= \quad \{\ \mathcal{M}(xa) = \mathcal{M}(x) \cdot 2 + a\ \}$$
$$\mathcal{M}(x) \cdot 2 - \mathcal{M}(y) \cdot 2 - c \cdot 2 - b \cdot 2 + a + b + c$$
$$=$$

$$(\mathcal{M}(x) - \mathcal{M}(y) - c - b + (a + b + c) \textbf{ div } 2) \cdot 2$$
$$+(a + b + c) \textbf{ mod } 2$$
$=$ { induction hypothesis }
$$\mathcal{M}(subt(x, y, c + b - (a + b + c) \textbf{ div } 2) \cdot 2$$
$$+(a + b + c) \textbf{ mod } 2$$
$=$ { this is going to be our definition of $subt$ }
$$\mathcal{M}(subt(xa, yb, c))$$

This suggest that $subt$ is a copy of sum except that the carry is computed differently: $c + b - (a + b + c) \textbf{ div } 2$ instead of $(a + b + c) \textbf{ div } 2$. If so desired, one might simplify the first alternative in $subt$ since it is applied only to arguments that lead to a nonnegative result. For multiplication we have:

$$\mathcal{M}(x) \cdot \mathcal{M}(ya)$$
$=$
$$\mathcal{M}(x) \cdot (a + 2 \cdot \mathcal{M}(y))$$
$=$
$$\mathcal{M}(x) \cdot \mathcal{M}(y) \cdot 2 + a \cdot \mathcal{M}(x)$$
$=$ { induction hypothesis }
$$\mathcal{M}(mult(x, y)) \cdot 2 + a \cdot \mathcal{M}(x)$$
$=$ { this is going to be our definition of $mult$ }
$$\mathcal{M}(mult(x, ya))$$

```
(define
   (mult (lambda (x y)
      (cond ((null y) (quote (0)))
            ((eq (car y) (quote 0))
               (cons (quote 0) (mult x (cdr y))))
            (t (add x (cons (quote 0) (mult x (cdr y))))))))
   (sub (lambda (x y) (subt x y (quote 0))))
   (subt (lambda (x y c)
      (cond ((null x) (cond ((eq c (quote 0)) y)
                           (t (subt (quote (1)) y (quote 0)))))
            ((null y) (cond ((eq c (quote 0)) x)
                           (t (subt x (quote (1)) (quote 0)))))
            (t (cons (mod2 (car x) (car y) c)
                     (subt (cdr x) (cdr y)
                           (sub2 (car x) (car y) c)))))))
   (sub2 (lambda (a b c)
      (cond ((eq a b) c)
            (t b)))))
```

21. Function *hanoi* has four parameters; the first parameter is the name of the first stack; the second parameter is the name of the second

stack; the third parameter is the name of the third stack; the fourth parameter is the list of disks as initially found on the first stack, in the order from bottom to top. The result is a list of moves. Each move is a list of three elements, the first of which is the name of the disk being moved, the second is the name of the stack from which the disk is moved, and the third is the name of the stack to which the disk is moved. The number of moves is as small as possible. The moves are in the order in which performing the moves leads to moving all disks from the first to the third stack. Initially, the second and third stacks are empty. Never is a larger disk on top of a smaller disk. One disk is moved at a time.

```
(define
    (hanoi (lambda (from via to disks)
        (do from via to disks ()))))
    (do (lambda (from via to disks rest)
        (cond ((null disks) rest)
            (t (do from
                    to
                    via
                    (cdr disks)
                    (cons (move (car disks) from to)
                        (do via
                            from
                            to
                            (cdr disks)
                            rest)))))))
    (move (lambda (disk from to)
        (cons disk (cons from (cons to nil)))))
    (null (lambda (x)
        (cond ((atom x) (eq x nil))
            (t nil))))
)
```

An example of a call is

```
(hanoi gold silver brass (huge big medium small tiny))
```

and this leads to a sequence of 31 moves.

23. The results of running the programs are

```
t
t
nil
nil
```

t
does not terminate
does not terminate

and the proper meanings are

true,
true,
false,
false,
true,

undefined since both *true* and *false* lead to a contradiction,
undefined since both *true* and *false* are logically consistent.

27. The following changes will implement a version of the Schorr–Waite
graph marking algorithm. Consult [Gri79] for a proof of the algorithm.

```
program lisp(input, output);
...
var ...
    inuse : array[1..n]of 0..3;
...
procedure mark(p : object);
    var q, t : object;
begin  q := nil;
        while p ≠ nil do begin
            inuse[p] := inuse[p] + 1;
            t := a[p];  a[p] := d[p]; d[p] := q;  q := t;
            if (inuse[p] = 3) ∨ ((q > 0) ∧ (inuse[q] = 0)) then begin
                t := q;  q := p;  p := t
    end    end end;
procedure collectgarbage;
    var i : 1..n;
begin for i := 1 to n do inuse[i] := 0;
        mark(olp);  mark(alp);
        for i := 1 to n do
            if inuse[i] = 0 then begin d[i] := Free;  Free := i end;
        if Free = nil then erm(4)
    end;
```

29. Extend function *eval* as follows.

```
(eval (lambda (e a)
    (cond ((atom e) (cond ((eq e nil) nil)
                          ((eq e t) t)
                          (t (assoc e a)))))
```

$$(((atom\ car\ e))$$
$$(cond\ ((eq\ (car\ e)\ (quote\ quote))\ (cadr\ e))$$
$$((eq\ (car\ e)\ (quote\ cond))\ (evcon\ (cdr\ e)\ a))$$
$$((eq\ (car\ e)\ (quote\ if))\ (evif\ (cdr\ e)\ a))$$
$$(t\ (apply\ (car\ e)\ (evlis\ (cdr\ e)\ a)\ a))))$$
$$(t\ (apply\ (car\ e)\ (evlis\ (cdr\ e)\ a)\ a)))))$$
$$(evif\ (lambda\ (e\ a)$$
$$(cond\ ((eval\ (car\ e)\ a)\ (eval\ (cadr\ e)\ a))$$
$$(t\ (eval\ (caddr\ e)\ a)))))$$

32. The single-statement version is wrong. Consider the case where

$$cons(a[x],\ a[y])$$

takes the last cell from the free list. Let the result it constructs be
called r. The next call of *cons* will then invoke the garbage collector,
and since object r has not been added to object list *olp* or association list *alp*, it is not reachable from the roots of the graph and will
be appended to the free list by the garbage collector. Consequently,
the call of *cons* in $alp := cons(r,\ alp)$ adds to the association list
an object that is also in the free list, and havoc will result.

Answers for Chapter 11

3. $x, y := y, x - y$

7. An invariant that shows that the product is computed is $X \cdot Y = z + x \cdot y \ \land \ 0 \le y < 2^k$. (We do not verify this.) The extra term that we need in the invariant is $0 \le z < x$. It is maintained by both alternatives of the if-statement:

$$(0 \le z < x)^{x,y,z,k}_{2x,(y-1)/2,z+x,k+1} \qquad\qquad (0 \le z < x)^{x,y,k}_{2x,y/2,k+1}$$
$$= \qquad\qquad\qquad\qquad\qquad =$$
$$0 \le z + x < 2x \qquad\qquad\qquad 0 \le z < 2x$$
$$\Leftarrow \qquad\qquad\qquad\qquad\qquad \Leftarrow$$
$$0 \le z < x \qquad\qquad\qquad\qquad 0 \le z < x$$

We postulate that the conditions $z \ge x/2$ and $z < x/2$ are postconditions of the first and second alternative respectively. This is verified
by

$$(z \ge x/2)^{x,y,z,k}_{2x,(y-1)/2,z+x,k-1} \qquad\qquad (z < x/2)^{x,y,k}_{2x,y/2,k-1}$$
$$= \qquad\qquad\qquad\qquad\qquad =$$
$$z + x \ge 2x/2 \qquad\qquad\qquad z < 2x/2$$
$$= \qquad\qquad\qquad\qquad\qquad =$$
$$z \ge 0 \qquad\qquad\qquad\qquad\qquad z < x$$

both of which follow from the term added to the invariant. The inverse of our annotated program

$$x, y, z, k := X, Y, 0, N;$$
$$*[\ k \neq 0 \rightarrow$$
$$\quad [\ odd(y) \rightarrow x, y, z, k := 2x, (y - 1)/2, z + x, k - 1 \ \{z \geq x/2\}$$
$$\quad \|\ even(y) \rightarrow x, y, k := 2x, y/2, k - 1 \qquad\qquad \{z < x/2\}$$
$$\quad]\ ]$$
$$\{X \cdot Y = z \ \wedge \ y = 0\}$$

is therefore

$$*[\ k \neq N \rightarrow [\ z \geq x/2 \rightarrow x, y, z, k := x/2, 2y + 1, z - x/2, k + 1$$
$$\qquad\qquad\qquad \|\ z < x/2 \rightarrow x, y, k := x/2, 2y, k + 1$$
$$\quad] \qquad\qquad] \qquad .$$

The latter program computes the quotient (in y) and remainder (in z) when dividing the initial value of z by the initial value of $x/2^N$. (If x is not a multiple of 2^N initially, then the program will evaluate $x/2$ for an odd value of x, and this operation is undefined.) The claim can be verified by checking that

$$Z = z + x \cdot y \ \wedge \ 0 \leq z < x = X \cdot 2^{N-k}$$

is an invariant of the inverse program, where Z is the initial value of z and where $X \cdot 2^N$ is the initial value of x. An annotated version of the program is

$$\{\ z = Z \ \wedge \ x = X \cdot 2^N \ \wedge \ X \neq 0\ \}$$
$$y, k := 0, 0;$$
$$\{\ inv : Z = z + x \cdot y \ \wedge \ 0 \leq z < x = X \cdot 2^{N-k} \ \wedge$$
$$\qquad 0 \leq k \leq N\ \}$$
$$*[\ k \neq N \rightarrow [\ z \geq x/2 \rightarrow x, y, z, k := x/2, 2y + 1, z - x/2, k + 1$$
$$\qquad\qquad\qquad \|\ z < x/2 \rightarrow x, y, k := x/2, 2y, k + 1$$
$$\quad] \qquad\qquad]$$
$$\{\ Z = z + x \cdot y \ \wedge \ 0 \leq z < x = X, \text{ hence}$$
$$\quad z = Z \ \textbf{mod} \ X \ \wedge \ y = Z \ \textbf{div} \ X\ \} \qquad .$$

8. An invariant that shows the correctness of the original program is

$$\gcd(X, Y) = \gcd(x, y) \ \wedge \ 2XY = xu + yv \ \wedge$$
$$x > 0 \ \wedge \ y > 0 \qquad .$$

This is verified for the first alternative by

$$\quad (inv)^{x,v}_{x-y,v+u}$$
$$=$$

$$\gcd(X, Y) = \gcd(x - y, y) \quad \wedge \quad 2XY = (x - y)u + y(v + u)$$
$$\wedge \ x - y > 0 \ \wedge \ y > 0$$

$$=$$

$$inv \ \wedge \ x > y$$

which follows from the invariant and the guard. The other alternative follows by symmetry. From the negation of the guards we have $x = y$ upon termination, which implies

$$\gcd(X, Y) = x = y \ \wedge \ X \cdot Y = \gcd(X, Y) \cdot (u + v)/2 \quad .$$

Combined with the fact that

$$X \cdot Y = \gcd(X, Y) \cdot \text{lcm}(X, Y)$$

for all X, Y, the postcondition follows. (Termination follows from decrease of the variant function $x + y$.)

If we add the term $u > 0 \ \wedge \ v > 0$ to the invariant then we are led to conclude that $v > u$ holds as a postcondition of the first alternative, whereas $u > v$ holds as a postcondition of the second alternative. Hence, the inverse program executes $x, v := x + y, v - u$ if $v > u$ and symmetrically for the second case. The original program is initialized in a state where $x + y = u + v$ and this condition is falsified by each step of the loop, as can be verified by adding $x + y \leq u + v$ to the invariant. As a result, the inverse program reads

$$*[\ x + y \neq u + v \to [\ v > u \to x, v := x + y, v - u$$
$$\| \ u > v \to y, u := y + x, u - v$$
$$]\qquad\qquad\qquad]\qquad .$$

10. The initial entropy is $-\sum_i p_i \cdot \log(p_i)$, where $p_i = 1/8$ for each of the eight states. Hence, the initial entropy is $3\log(2)$ bits. Consider the following table of initial and final states.

| | before | | | after | |
a	b	c	a	b	c
false	false	false	false	false	false
false	false	true	true	true	false
false	true	false	false	false	false
false	true	true	true	true	false
true	false	false	false	false	false
true	false	true	true	true	false
true	true	false	false	false	true
true	true	true	true	true	true

Only four distinct final states exist and they occur either once or three times in the table, hence their probabilities are $1/8$ and $3/8$. Consequently, the final entropy is

$$-(1/8\log(1/8) + 1/8\log(1/8) + 3/8\log(3/8) + 3/8\log(3/8))$$

which is 1.18 bits less than the initial entropy.

11. The initial state has entropy $-100 \cdot (\frac{1}{100}\log(\frac{1}{100})) = 6.644$ bits.

- Execution of $i,j := i+j, i+j$ leads to one of 19 possible states. The probability of $i = j = k$ is $\frac{k+1}{100}$ for $0 \leq k \leq 9$ and $\frac{19-k}{100}$ for $9 \leq k \leq 18$. The entropy is therefore

$$-\sum_{k=0}^{8} 2 \cdot \frac{k+1}{100}\log(\frac{k+1}{100}) - \frac{10}{100}\log(\frac{10}{100}) = 4.031$$

  bits. The entropy reduction is 2.613 bits.

- Execution of $i,j := i + j, i - j$ leads to one of 100 possible states, all with equal probability. There is no entropy reduction.

- Execution of $i,j := i + j, |i - j|$ is almost the same as the previous one, except that those 45 final states with $j < 0$ are mapped to those with $j > 0$. The entropy is therefore $-45 \cdot \frac{2}{100}\log(\frac{2}{100}) - 10 \cdot \frac{1}{100}\log(\frac{1}{100}) = 5.744$ bits. The entropy reduction is 0.900 bits.

- Execution of $i,j := j, i$ leads to one of 100 possible states, all with equal probability. There is no entropy reduction.

- Execution of $i,j := i$ **div** $2, j$ **div** 2 leads to one of 25 possible states, all with equal probability: each final state results from four initial states. The entropy reduction is 2 bits.

- Execution of $i,j := i$ **mod** $2, j$ **mod** 2 leads to one of 4 possible states, all with equal probability. The final entropy is therefore 2 bits. The entropy reduction is 4.644 bits.

- Execution of $i,j := \max(i,j), \min(i,j)$ leads to one of 55 possible states. In 45 states the condition $i > j$ holds and they may arise from 2 initial states each; in 10 states we have $i = j$ and they arise from 1 initial state each. The entropy is therefore $-45 \cdot \frac{2}{100}\log(\frac{2}{100}) - 10 \cdot \frac{1}{100}\log(\frac{1}{100}) = 5.744$ bits. The entropy reduction is 0.900 bits.

- Execution of $[\, i \leq j \rightarrow i := 0 \,\|\, i > j \rightarrow j := 0 \,]$ leads to one of 19 possible states. The probability of $i = 0, j = k$ is $\frac{k+1}{100}$ for $0 \leq k \leq 9$ and the probability of $i = k, j = 0$ is $\frac{k}{100}$ for $0 \leq k \leq 9$. The entropy is therefore $-\sum_{k=0}^{9} \frac{k+1}{100}\log(\frac{k+1}{100}) - \sum_{k=0}^{9} \frac{k}{100}\log(\frac{k}{100}) = 4.031$ bits. The entropy reduction is 2.613 bits.

- Execution of $*[i > j \rightarrow i := i-1]$ is equivalent to $i := \min(i, j)$ and leads to one of 55 possible states. The final states with $i < j$ have one initial state each; there are 45 of these and they have probability $\frac{1}{100}$ each. The probability of $i = j = k$ is $\frac{10-k}{100}$ for $0 \le k \le 9$. The entropy is therefore $-\sum_{k=0}^{9} \frac{10-k}{100} \log(\frac{10-k}{100}) - 45 \cdot \frac{1}{100} \log(\frac{1}{100}) = 5.171$ bits. The entropy reduction is 1.473 bits.

13. The gate with outputs

   - a and $a \equiv b$ is not universal: the only functions that can be computed are continued equivalences, like $a \equiv a \equiv b \equiv b$ and they can all be simplified to $a \equiv b$, or a, b, *true*, or *false*; so, for example, neither an OR- nor an AND-function can be constructed; the gate is reversible: a can be reconstructed from the a output and b can be reconstructed as the outcome of $a \equiv (a \equiv b)$, which shows that the gate is its own inverse;

     if $a = false$ and $b = false$ then no ball goes in and one must come out, which cannot be done with the rules that we have used since those imply the "law of conservation of billiard balls".

   - $a \lor b$ and $a \land b$ is not universal since its two outputs are monotonic functions and, hence, a negation cannot be computed; the gate is not reversible since the two outputs are symmetric in a and b;

     no: irreversible gates cannot be built from reversible (billiard ball) gates without adding constant inputs and without generating "garbage" outputs.

   - $\neg(a \lor b)$ and $\neg(a \land b)$ is universal; the gate is not reversible since the two outputs are symmetric in a and b;

     no.

   - $\neg(a \lor b)$ and a is universal; the gate is not reversible since the two outputs do not depend on b if a is *true*;

     no.

   - $a \Rightarrow b$ and $b \Rightarrow a$ is universal; the gate is not reversible since $a = b = true$ and $a = b = false$ produce the same output;

     no.

Answers for Chapter 12

8. Replace assignment $b_{ij} := b_{ij} \lor (b_{ik} \land b_{kj})$ in Warshall's algorithm by assignment $b_{ij} := \min(b_{ij}, b_{ik} + b_{kj})$.

Negative lengths lead to problems if there is a cycle in which the path lengths add up to a negative number: going around the loop repeatedly then keeps decreasing the length, making the minimum $-\infty$.

17. The term $s(x) \subseteq x \cup y$.

24. With postcondition R,

$$R: \qquad g(i) = g(j) \ \wedge \ \forall(n : i < n < j : g(i) \neq g(n))$$

we have, $Q \ \wedge \ g(i) = g(j) \ \Rightarrow \ R$. The program is

$$
\begin{aligned}
&i, j := 1, 2; \\
&*[\ g(i) \neq g(j) \to [j = 2i \to i := j \ \| \ j < 2i \to skip]; \\
&\qquad\qquad\qquad j := j + 1 \\
&\ ] \qquad .
\end{aligned}
$$

We verify the invariance of Q.

Initialization:

$$Q_{1,2}^{i,j}$$

$=$

$$
\begin{aligned}
&p(1,2) \ \wedge \ 1 < 2 \cdot \max(L, P) \ \wedge \\
&\forall(m, n : p(m, n) \ \wedge \ n < 2 : g(m) \neq g(n))
\end{aligned}
$$

$=$ $\{\ P \geq 1 \ \}$

$true$.

Invariance in first alternative:

$$(Q_{j+1}^{j})_{j}^{i}$$

$=$

$$
\begin{aligned}
&p(j, j + 1) \ \wedge \ j < 2 \cdot \max(L, P) \ \wedge \\
&\forall(m, n : p(m, n) \ \wedge \ n < j + 1 : g(m) \neq g(n))
\end{aligned}
$$

$=$

$$
\begin{aligned}
&j \text{ is a power of 2} \ \wedge \ j < 2 \cdot \max(L, P) \ \wedge \\
&\forall(m : p(m, j) : g(m) \neq g(j)) \ \wedge \\
&\forall(m, n : p(m, n) \ \wedge \ n < j : g(m) \neq g(n))
\end{aligned}
$$

$\Leftarrow$ $\{\ p(i, j) \wedge p(m, j) \ \Rightarrow \ i = m \ \}$

$\qquad Q \ \wedge \ g(i) \neq g(j) \ \wedge \ j = 2i \ \wedge \ i < \max(L, P)$

$\Leftarrow$ $\{\ \text{see note below} \ \}$

$\qquad Q \ \wedge \ g(i) \neq g(j) \ \wedge \ j = 2i \qquad .$

Note: We distinguish between two cases.

- If $L \leq i$ then $Q \wedge g(i) \neq g(j) \ \Rightarrow \ j < i + P$ on account of $\forall(i : L \leq i : g(i) = g(i + P))$ and the fact that P is as small as possible. Hence $Q \wedge g.i \neq g.j \wedge j = 2i \ \Rightarrow \ i < P \leq \max(L, P)$.

- If $i < L$ then $i < \max(L, P)$.

Invariance in second alternative (we ignore $i < 2 \cdot \max(L, P)$):

$$Q^j_{j+1}$$

$=$

$$p(i, j+1) \;\wedge$$
$$\forall(m, n : p(m, n) \;\wedge\; n < j+1 : g(m) \neq g(n))$$

$=$

$$p(i, j+1) \;\wedge\; \forall(m : p(m, j) : g(m) \neq g(j)) \;\wedge$$
$$\forall(m, n : p(m, n) \;\wedge\; n < j : g(m) \neq g(n))$$

$\Leftarrow \qquad \{\; p(i,j) \wedge p(m,j) \;\Rightarrow\; i = m \;\}$

$\qquad Q \;\wedge\; g(i) \neq g(j) \;\wedge\; j < 2i \quad .$

Since j increases by 1 in every iteration of the loop, and since the invariant implies that j is bounded from above, the loop terminates.

We conclude with the program text in terms of f instead of g. Variables x and y satisfying $x = g(i) \;\wedge\; y = g(j)$ have been introduced.

$$i, j, x, y := 1, 2, 0, f(0);$$
$$*[\; x \neq y \rightarrow [j = 2i \rightarrow i, x := j, y \;\|\; j < 2i \rightarrow skip];$$
$$\qquad j, y := j+1, f(y)$$
$$]$$

27. For x a subtree of code tree t, let $cw(x, t)$ be the weight that x contributes to the weight of t. Formally,

$$cw(x, t) \;=\; \langle \sum a : a \in L(x) : f(a) \cdot d(a, t) \rangle \quad .$$

We have

$$cw(x, t)$$

$=$ $\quad \{$ definition $\}$

$$\langle \sum a : a \in L(x) : f(a) \cdot d(a, t) \rangle$$

$=$ $\quad \{$ property of path length $\}$

$$\langle \sum a : a \in L(x) : f(a) \cdot (d(a, x) + d(x, t)) \rangle$$

$=$ $\quad \{$ arithmetic $\}$

$$\langle \sum a : a \in L(x) : f(a) \cdot d(a, x) \rangle$$
$$+ d(x, t) \cdot \langle \sum a : a \in L(x) : f(a) \rangle$$

$=$ $\quad \{$ definitions $\}$

$$w(x) + d(x, t) \cdot f(x) \quad .$$

If x and z are disjoint subtrees of t, and if $t' = t(x, z := z, x)$, then

$$w(t) \;=\; cw(x, t) + cw(z, t) + rest$$
$$w(t') \;=\; cw(x, t') + cw(z, t') + rest$$

in which the two *rest* 's are equal. Consequently,

$$w(t')$$
$$= \quad \{ \text{ eliminate } rest \ \}$$
$$cw(x, t') + cw(z, t') + w(t) - cw(x, t) - cw(z, t)$$
$$= \quad \{ \text{ arithmetic; previous property } \}$$
$$w(t) + w(x) + d(x, t') \cdot f(x) + w(z) + d(z, t') \cdot f(z)$$
$$- w(x) - d(x, t) \cdot f(x) - w(z) - d(z, t) \cdot f(z))$$
$$= \quad \{ \text{ arithmetic; } d(x, t) = d(z, t'); \quad d(z, t) = d(x, t') \ \}$$
$$w(t) + (f(x) - f(z)) \cdot (d(z, t) - d(x, t)) \quad ,$$

which proves the property.

Answers for Chapter 13

3. All values in the range $2 \leq x \leq 200$ are possible outcomes.

6. The proof is identical to the proof of Peterson's algorithm in which every occurrence of t is replaced by $y[0] \oplus y[1]$.

14. The program for each process is

```
sort(in, out) :
    var i, x : integer;
    in?x;  i := 1;
    *[ i ≠ N → in?y;  i := i + 1;
            [ x ≥ y → out!y
            ‖ x ≤ y → out!x;  x := y
    ]           ];
    out!x
```

Number the process from 0 on (input is to 0, output is from $N-1$). The input to process k is a sequence of N integers. The largest k elements thereof are in the last k positions of the sequence and they occur in ascending order. The invariant of the loop is: i values have been input so far. The maximum thereof is x and the remaining $i-1$ values have been output. If $i + k > N$ then the last $k + i - N - 1$ elements of the output sequence so far are the largest $k + i - N - 1$ elements so far, and they are in ascending order.

15. The two processes that store a tree execute

```
procedure fringe(root : tree, chan frc, eqc)
    var eq : boolean
    procedure traverse(t : tree)
    [  leaf(t) → traverse(t.l);
                        [eq → traverse(t.r)‖¬eq → skip]
    ‖ ¬leaf(t) → frc!t.label;  eqc?eq
    ]
‖[ eq := true;  traverse(root);
    [eq → frc! ⊥ ;  eqc?eq‖¬eq → skip]
]‖
```

and the third process executes

```
procedure cmp(chan frc0, frc1, eqc0, eqc1)
    var lab0, lab1 : label
‖[ ‖[frc0?lab0 ‖ frc1?lab1]‖;
    *[ lab0 = lab1 ≠⊥→ ‖[eqc0!true ‖ eqc1!true]‖;
                             ‖[frc0?lab0 ‖ frc1?lab1]‖
    ];
    ‖[eqc0!lab0 = lab1 ‖ eqc1!lab0 = lab1]‖
]‖
```

and the result is stored in the boolean eq in the two processes containing the tree. The constant $\perp$ indicates a value that differs from any label occurring in either of the two trees. It is used to indicate the end of the fringe transmitted to the process performing the comparison. Communication between the tree-storing processes and the comparison process consists of pairs: both tree-storing processes send a label, the other process returns a boolean to both of them. Communication ceases as soon as the boolean is *false* (indicating that the two fringes are different) or when the boolean follows two $\perp$'s (indicating that the two fringes are equal).

17. Before we can construct programs for converting a stream of characters to a stream of bits, and vice versa, we have to decide upon a representation of a code tree. One method is to enumerate the nodes in the tree starting with 1 for the root, and assigning $2i$ and $2i + 1$ to the two children of node i, unless i is a leaf. This numbering is not attractive since it leads to gaps in the numbering if the tree is not balanced. A consequence of gaps is that the arrays used are larger than necessary. If the frequency of each character is at least twice the frequency of the next most frequent character, the coding tree degenerates to a list, and the numbers grow exponentially in the number of characters. A better enumeration is suggested by the following theorem, due to [Gal78]. We introduce some terminology first. Each of the leaves of a code tree has a frequency assigned to it, viz.

the frequency of the corresponding character. We also assign a frequency to the other nodes in the tree, defined recursively as the sum of the frequencies of its children. Two distinct nodes are called siblings if they have the same parent. A binary code tree is said to have the sibling property if each node, except the root, has a sibling and if the nodes can be enumerated in order of nonincreasing frequency with each node adjacent to its sibling.

> Theorem: a binary code tree is a Huffman tree just when
> it has the sibling property.

For a proof we refer to [Gal78]. The enumeration that the theorem suggests is to simply enumerate the nodes in order of nonincreasing frequency. The children of nonleaf nodes are given by array *succ* : the two children of node i are $succ[i]$ and $succ[i] + 1$. Array *succ* makes it possible to traverse the tree from root to leaves, as required for the decoding process. In order to permit efficient traversal from leaves to root, as required for the encoding process, we introduce array *pred*, where

$$pred[succ[i]] \ = \ pred[succ[i] + 1] \ = \ i$$

for each nonleaf node i. The correspondence between characters and leaves needs to be represented also. We use arrays *ch* and *leaf* : character c corresponds to leaf $leaf[c]$, and we have $c = ch[leaf[c]]$. Finally, we need to decide on how to indicate which nodes are leaves. We use constant *null* for this purpose, that is, $succ[i] = null$ just when i is a leave. This completes our choice for the representation of a Huffman tree. Given such a tree, we can construct the processes for transforming a stream of characters into a stream of bits (encoding), and vice versa (decoding). We consider decoding first. Decoding requires that a number of bits be consumed from the input and that a character be produced at the output. The number of input bits depends on the coding tree, and is not fixed a priori. We do know, however, that they encode a path from the root to a leaf and, therefore, the best way of decoding the character is to consume the input bits while tracking the path in the coding tree. Every input bit corresponds to one step from an internal node in the tree to one of its two children. The traversal is terminated when a leaf is reached, and then we know what the corresponding character is.

```
decoder :
    *[ true → i := root;
            *[succ[i] ≠ null → bits?b;  i := succ[i] + b];
            out!ch[i]
    ]
```

Encoding requires the construction of a sequence of bits, again corresponding to the path from the root to a leaf. Given the representation,
however, the path is more easily constructed in the opposite direction, starting at the proper leaf and proceeding towards the root. We
use an additional array for storing the encoded path leading from the
present node, node i, to the leaf, $leaf[c]$. When the path is traversed
all the way to the root, the encoding is transmitted in the opposite
order of its construction. One may, alternatively, use a recursive procedure for traversing the path from leaf to root and transmit the
sequence of bits in reverse order. The length of the bits sequence,
and hence the required size of the auxiliary array or the depth of the
recursion, equals the number of edges in the path from leaf to root. If
a tree with N leaves is perfectly balanced then this length is $\log(N)$.
If, however, the tree degenerates to a list, all lengths from 1 through
$N - 1$ exist.

$encoder$:

$$*[\ true \rightarrow\ in?c;\ \ i := leaf[c];\ \ p := 0;$$
$$*[\ i \neq root \rightarrow\ a[p] := i - succ[pred[i]];$$
$$p := p + 1;\ \ i := pred[i]$$
$$];$$
$$*[p \neq 0 \rightarrow p := p - 1;\ \ bits!a[p]]$$
$$]$$

Next, we look at updating the tree. Array $freq$ is used to maintain a
running count of the frequencies. Whenever a character is processed,
the frequency of its corresponding leaf is incremented. In order to
make sure that the frequencies of other nodes are consistent, the
frequencies of all nodes on the path from the leaf to the root are
incremented. However, whenever the frequency of a node other than
the root is incremented, the enumeration may have to be reviewed:
incrementing an element of array $freq$ may cause $freq$ to be no longer
nonincreasing. This is the one and only reason for reorganizing the
tree. In the sequel we shall find it advantageous if the frequencies of a
node and its parent differ. This is always the case, except if the sibling
has frequency 0. We, therefore, assume that each of the frequencies
is at least 1 instead of 0. This may be implemented by letting $freq$
be 1 more than the actual number of occurrences.

We noticed that, for nodes i on the path from leaf to root, $freq[i]$ is
to be incremented, while renumbering the nodes to keep $freq$ nonincreasing. Renumbering is, therefore, called for when $freq[i]$ is to be
incremented and $freq[i-1] = f[i]$, and i is not the root. The latter
implies that $i - 1$ is also a node in the tree; it may or may not be a
sibling of i; it may or may not have the same distance from the root.
However, since all frequencies are positive we know that $i - 1$ is not

a parent of i, nor vice versa. To maintain the monotonicity of *freq* it is possible to swap the subtrees rooted at $i-1$ and i, that is, swap nodes i and $i-1$ in the numbering, and then increment $freq[i-1]$. However, many nodes with equal frequency may exist and, hence, we either have to do the swapping repeatedly, or find the least index j for which $freq[j] = f[i]$, swap the two subtrees rooted at j and i and then increment $f[j]$. Observe, again, that j is well-defined because all frequencies are positive. In the program, parameter i is the index of the leaf whose frequency is to be incremented.

$$
\begin{aligned}
&increment\ frequency(i): \\
&\quad *[\ i \neq root \rightarrow \\
&\qquad j := i;\ *[freq[j-1] = freq[i] \rightarrow j := j-1]; \\
&\qquad [\ j = i \rightarrow skip \\
&\qquad \|\ j < i \rightarrow succ[i], succ[j] := succ[j], succ[i]; \\
&\qquad\qquad\qquad ch[i], ch[j] := ch[j], ch[i]; \\
&\qquad\qquad [\ succ[i] = null \rightarrow leaf[ch[i]] := i \\
&\qquad\qquad \|\ succ[i] \neq null \rightarrow pred[succ[i]] := i; \\
&\qquad\qquad\qquad\qquad\qquad\qquad pred[succ[i]+1] := i \\
&\qquad\qquad]; \\
&\qquad\qquad [\ succ[j] = null \rightarrow leaf[ch[j]] := j \\
&\qquad\qquad \|\ succ[j] \neq null \rightarrow pred[succ[j]] := j; \\
&\qquad\qquad\qquad\qquad\qquad\qquad pred[succ[j]+1] := j \\
&\qquad\ ]\qquad\quad]; \\
&\qquad freq[j] := freq[j] + 1;\ i := pred[j] \\
&\quad]; \\
&freq[root] := freq[root] + 1
\end{aligned}
$$

The only aspect that we have not dealt with is initialization. A simple and effective initialization is a balanced binary code tree in which all characters have their frequency count set to 1. Here is the text of the complete program.

```
program Huffman;

const  n     = 128;
       null  = -1;

type tree = record leaf : array [char] of integer;
                   succ, pred, freq : array [0..2(n - 1)] of integer;
                   ch : array [0..2(n - 1)] of char;
                   root : integer
             end;
        bit = 0..1;

var bits : chan of bit;
```

```
procedure init tree(var t : tree);
    var i : integer;
begin for i := 1 to 2(n − 1) do
            t.pred[i] := (i + 1) div 2 − 1;
        for i := 2(n − 1) downto n − 1 do begin
            t.succ[i] := null; t.freq[i] := 1;
            t.ch[i] := chr(i − n + 1); t.leaf[chr(i − n + 1)] := i
        end;
        for i := n − 2 downto 0 do begin
            t.succ[i] := 2i + 1;
            t.freq[i] := t.freq[t.succ[i]] + t.freq[t.succ[i] + 1]
        end;
        t.root := 0
end;


procedure increment freq(var t : tree; i : integer);
    var j, x : integer;  y : char;
begin while i ≠ t.root do begin
        j := i;  while t.freq[j − 1] = t.freq[i] do j := j − 1;
        if j < i then begin
            x := t.succ[i];  t.succ[i] := t.succ[j];  t.succ[j] := x;
            y := t.ch[i];  t.ch[i] := t.ch[j];  t.ch[j] := y;
            if t.succ[i] = null then
                t.leaf[t.ch[i]] := i
            else begin
                t.pred[t.succ[i]] := i;  t.pred[t.succ[i] + 1] := i
            end;
            if t.succ[j] = null then
                t.leaf[t.ch[j]] := j
            else begin
                t.pred[t.succ[j]] := j;  t.pred[t.succ[j] + 1] := j
            end
        end;
        t.freq[j] := t.freq[j] + 1;  i := t.pred[j]
    end;
    t.freq[t.root] := t.freq[t.root] + 1
end;


procedure decoder;
    var t : tree; i : integer; c : char; b : bit;
begin init tree(t);
    repeat i := t.root;
        while t.succ[i] ≠ null do begin
            bits?b;  i := t.succ[i] + b
```

```
            end;
            c := t.ch[i];
            cobegin
                increment freq(t, i);
                write(c)
            coend
        until c = '.';
        writeln
    end;

    procedure encoder;
        var  t : tree;  c : char;  i, p : integer;
             a : array [0..n − 2] of bit;
    begin init tree(t);
        repeat read(c);  i := t.leaf[c];  p := 0;
            while i ≠ t.root do begin
                a[p] := i − t.succ[t.pred[i]];  p := p + 1;
                i := t.pred[i]
            end;
            cobegin
                increment freq(t, t.leaf[c]);
                while p ≠ 0 do begin
                    p := p − 1;  bits!a[p]
                end
            coend
        until c = '.'
    end;
    begin writeln('adaptive Huffman coding');
        writeln('type input followed by a period');
        cobegin encoder; decoder coend
    end.
```

Answers for Chapter 14

2. The grammar is

$$
\begin{array}{ll}
ce & \longrightarrow exp_1 \\
exp_0 & \longrightarrow \epsilon \\
exp_i & \longrightarrow exp_{i-1} \; lit \mid exp_{i+1} \, op
\end{array}
$$

for binary operators, and

$$
\begin{array}{ll}
ce & \longrightarrow exp_1 \\
exp_0 & \longrightarrow \epsilon \\
exp_i & \longrightarrow exp_{i+m-n} \, op_{m,n}
\end{array}
$$

for operators $op_{m,n}$ that take m arguments and return n results. The semantics are formally defined by function $\mathcal{M}$ that when applied to a sequence of category exp_i yields a sequence of i expressions in infix notation.

$$\mathcal{M}(\epsilon) \qquad\qquad = \epsilon$$
$$\mathcal{M}(seq\ lit) \quad\ = \mathcal{M}(seq)\ lit$$
$$\mathcal{M}(seq\ op) \quad = s\ (v0\ op\ v1)$$
$$\text{where}\ v0\ v1\ s = \mathcal{M}(seq)$$

3. We want function τ to map an infix expression into the corresponding caudafix expression. It is, however, simpler to extend the domain of τ to sequences of infix expressions, and the range to sequences of caudafix expressions. For the sake of brevity, we restrict ourselves here to fully parenthesized infix expressions. We shall see to it that

$$\mathcal{M}(\tau(\epsilon)) \qquad\ = \epsilon$$
$$\mathcal{M}(\tau(seq\ e)) = \mathcal{M}(\tau(seq))\ value(e) \qquad .$$

The definition of τ is by cases.

$$\tau(\epsilon) \qquad\qquad\qquad = \epsilon$$
$$\tau(seq\ lit) \qquad\qquad = \tau(seq)\ lit$$
$$\tau(seq\ (e_0\ op\ e_1)) \qquad = \tau(e_0\ e_1\ seq)\ op$$

The order of seq, e_0, and e_1 is different in the left- and right-hand sides of the last line; this implies that a slightly more complicated translation scheme is asked for.

4. Assume that instruction $\div$ has the following effect: it pops an element y from the stack, it pops an element x from the stack, it pushes x **div** y on the stack, and it pushes x **mod** y on the stack. The translation of x **div** y is then to perform $\div$ on x and y, and to delete the remainder, leaving the quotient on the stack. The translation of x **mod** y is to perform $\div$ on x and y, and to delete the quotient, leaving the remainder on the stack. Deleting an element from the top of the stack can be performed by the sequence $0 * +$ but deleting the next element from the stack seems not to be so easy. We therefore propose to add an instruction $swap$ that exchanges the two topmost stack elements. The definition of τ is now as follows.

- $\tau(x\ \textbf{div}\ y) = \tau(x)\ \tau(y) \div 0 * +$
- $\tau(x\ \textbf{mod}\ y) = \tau(x)\ \tau(y) \div swap\ 0 * +$

6. A variable with nesting level nl and offset $delta$ in its procedure frame is addressed as $display[nl] + delta$, independent of the nesting level of the currently executing procedure. Array $display$ is typically a short array, its size rarely exceeding four elements. It is attractive to store the array in registers, making access to variables without intermediate memory references.

7. Given *fp*, array *display* can be assigned the proper value through
the sequence of assignments

$display[nl] := fp;$
for $i := nl - 1$ **downto** 0 **do** $display[i] := m[display[i + 1]]$

in which *nl* is the nesting level at which the statements are executed.
The update is done at every procedure entry (and *nl* corresponds to
the body of the procedure being called) and upon completion of every
procedure call (and *nl* corresponds to the body of the procedure in
which the call occurs). Updating array *display* at every procedure
exit can be avoided by creating a new array *display* in every procedure frame.

The procedure entry statements set *display[nl]* to the correct value.
From the property given in the exercise, it follows that *display[i]* already has the correct value for each $0 \le i < nl$. The procedure exit
statements seem to set only *display[nl]* to the value it had before
procedure entry. We have to show that also those elements with index $i > nl$ (but at most the nesting level of the procedure in which
the call occurs) have their old value. This follows from the following
observation, which can be proved by induction.

> After procedure exit, all elements of array *display*, includ-
> ing those with an index exceeding the present nesting level,
> have the same value as before the corresponding procedure
> entry.

8. Let *n* be the number of times that the body *s* of the loop is executed,
for one execution of the whole while-statement. We count the number
of instructions executed to complete execution of the while-statement,
ignoring the instructions in *b* and *s* since they are the same in
both cases. In the case of the first translation, we find that $2n + 1$
jump instructions are being executed, and in the case of the second
translation this number is $n + 2$. Hence, the first translation is better
if $n = 0$, the two are equal if $n = 1$, and the second translation is
better if $n \ge 2$.

12. If we start out with mapping (1) then addition can be implemented
with

MOVE $r11 + +, r1$
ADD $r1, r0$

which leads to a state in which mapping (1) is valid.

An implementation of $=:$ starting from mapping (0) is

MOVE $r11 + +, r0$
MOVE $r11 + +, @r0$

An implementation of =: starting from mapping (1) is

    MOVE $r11++, @r0$

An implementation of =: starting from mapping (2) is

    MOVE $r0, @r1$

All three lead to a state in which mapping (0) applies.

An implementation of $-$ starting from mapping (0) is

    MOVE $r11++, r1$
    MOVE $r11++, r0$
    SUB $r1, r0$

An implementation of $-$ starting from mapping (1) is

    MOVE $r11++, r1$
    SUB $r0, r1$
    MOVE $r1, r0$

An implementation of $-$ starting from mapping (2) is

    SUB $r1, r0$

All three lead to a state in which mapping (1) applies.

Answers for Chapter 15

5. Code for

    for $i := m$ to n do s

of the form

    $i := m$;
    while $i \leq n$ do begin s; $i := i + 1$ end

is incorrect if $n = maxint$. Similarly,

    $i := m - 1$;
    while $i < n$ do begin $i := i + 1$; s end

fails if $m = minint$. The following code will always do.

    $i := m$;
    if $i \leq n$ then
        loop
            s
        exit if $i = n$
            $i := i + 1$
        end

This can be compiled as follows.

```
                load value of m
                dupl
                store value in i
                load value of n
                leqi
                jumpz   l1
    l0 :        s
                load value of i
                load value of n
                neqi
                jumpz   l1
                load value of i
                addc    1
                store value in i
                jump    l0
    l1 :
```

The code for computing n occurs twice; it might be attractive to compute the value once, and keep a copy on top of the stack for later references. This value is deleted from the stack upon completion of the loop.

```
                load value of m
                store value in i
                load value of n
                dupl
                load value of i
                geqi
                jumpz   l1
    l0 :        s
                dupl
                load value of i
                neqi
                jumpz   l1
                load value of i
                addc    1
                store value in i
                jump    l0
    l1 :        adjs    1
```

The procedure that compiles a statement is extended with the following code, which also takes care of the case of a downto where the variable needs to be decremented. It requires adding an integer variable d to procedure *statement* ; it is the increment of the loop variable.

```
    else if sym = forsym then begin
        getsym; check(ident);  i := position;  t := itab[i].tip;
        if itab[i].kind ≠ varbl then error(130);
        if ttab[t].kind ≠ simple then error(131);
        getsym; skip(becomes); expression(x); mustbe(t, x);
        addressvar(i); gen0(stor);
        if sym = downtosym then
            d := -1
        else begin
            check(tosym);  d := 1
        end;
        getsym; expression(x); mustbe(t, x); gen0(dupl);
        addressvar(i); gen0(load);
        if d = 1 then gen0(geqi) else gen0(leqi);
        j := codelabel; gen1(jumpz, 0);
        skip(dosym); statement;
        gen0(dupl); addressvar(i); gen0(load);
        gen0(neqi); x := codelabel; gen1(jumpz, 0);
        addressvar(i); gen0(load); gen1(addc, d);
        addressvar(i); gen0(stor); gen1(jump, j + 1);
        code[j].a := codelabel; code[x].a := codelabel;
        gen1(adjs, 1)
end
```

7. The two occurrences of

$$code[cx] := i; cx := cx + 1$$

in procedure *gen* are replaced by

```
if i.op ∈ [divd, remd] then begin
    code[cx].op := call;  code[cx].a := divmod;  cx := cx + 1;
    if i.op = divd then begin
        code[cx].op := swap;  cx := cx + 1
    end;
    code[cx].op := adjs;  code[cx].a := 1;  cx := cx + 1;
end else begin
    code[cx] := i;  cx := cx + 1
end
```

and an integer *divmod* is declared in procedure *compile*. Procedure *gendivmod* is declared (in *compile*, following the declaration of *codelabel*) and it is called just prior to the call of *block*(0) at the end of *compile*.

```
    procedure gendivmod;
```

```
        var l0, l1, l2, l3 : integer;
     begin divmod := codelabel;
           gen1(ldc, 0);  gen1(ldl, 3);  gen1(ldl, 3);
           l0 := codelabel;
           gen1(ldl, 1);  gen1(ldl, 1);  gen0(geqi);
           l1 := codelabel;  gen1(jumpz, 0);
           gen1(mulc, 2);
           gen1(jump, l0);
           l2 := codelabel;  code[l1].a := l2;
           gen1(ldl, 0);  gen1(ldl, 5);  gen0(neqi);
           l3 := codelabel;  gen1(jumpz, 0);
           gen0(div2);
           gen1(ldl, 2);  gen1(mulc, 2);  gen1(stl, 3);
           gen1(ldl, 1);  gen1(ldl, 1);  gen0(geqi);
           gen1(jumpz, l2);
           gen1(ldl, 1);  gen1(ldl, 1);  gen0(neg);  gen0(add);
           gen1(stl, 2);
           gen1(ldl, 2);  gen1(addc, 1);  gen1(stl, 3);
           gen1(jump, l2);
           code[l3].a := codelabel;
           gen1(adjs, 1);  gen1(stl, 4);  gen1(stl, 2);  gen1(exit, 1)
     end;
```

This procedure generates code as if the following function had been declared.

```
     function  divmod(x, y : integer)
        var q, r, w : integer;
     begin q := 0;  r := x;  w := y;
           while r ≥ w do w := w * 2;
           while w ≠ y do begin
                w := w div 2;  q := q * 2;
                if r ≥ w then begin r := r − w;  q := q + 1 end
           end ;
           return(r, q)
     end;
```

This function works fine (see Chapter 3) as long as we may ignore integer overflow. Overflow occurs in the first loop if $x > maxint/2$. The two lines

```
divd : begin m[sp + 1] := m[sp + 1] div m[sp];  sp := sp + 1 end;
remd : begin m[sp + 1] := m[sp + 1] mod m[sp];  sp := sp + 1 end;
```

are removed from the interpreter.

Answers for Chapter 16

3. The microcode for these instructions is identical to that for the ADD instruction, except that $GP := 86$ is replaced by $GP := 08$ in the case of AND, and by $GP := 06$ in the case of XOR.

6. Height h of a node is defined as its distance in the original tree from the root. Hence, $0 \leq h < n$. A node at height h has two incoming edges, one from a node with height $h - 1$ and one from a node with height $n - 1$. (The number $h - 1$ is to be read modulo n, that is $h - 1 = n - 1$ if $h = 0$.) We introduce $k_{h,i}$ and $s_{h,i}$. A node at height h contains $k_{h,i}$ processes whose distances is i from the root process, and $s_{h,i}$ processes whose distances is at most i from the root process.

$$
\begin{aligned}
k_{0,0} &= 1 \\
k_{h,0} &= 0 && \text{for } 0 < h < n \\
k_{h,i} &= k_{h-1,i-1} + k_{n-1,i-1} && \text{for } 0 \leq h < n, i > 0 \\
s_{h,i} &= \textstyle\sum_{j=0}^{i} k_{h,j} && \text{for } 0 \leq h < n, i \geq 0
\end{aligned}
$$

The homogeneity of the mapping is expressed by the property that for each i numbers l_i and c_i exist with

$$
\begin{aligned}
k_{h,i} &= c_i && \text{if } h \neq l_i \\
k_{h,i} &= c_i + 1 && \text{if } h = l_i \\
s_{h,i} &= 2c_i + 1 && \text{if } h \leq l_i \\
s_{h,i} &= 2c_i && \text{if } h > l_i \quad .
\end{aligned}
$$

The property follows by mathematical induction on i using the following induction hypothesis.

$$
\begin{aligned}
l_i &= i \bmod n \\
c_0 &= 0 \\
c_{i+1} &= 2c_i && \text{if } i \bmod n \neq n - 1 \\
c_{i+1} &= 2c_i + 1 && \text{if } i \bmod n = n - 1
\end{aligned}
$$

Appendix B

Bibliography

[Apt81]   K.R. Apt.   Ten years of Hoare's logic, a survey, part 1. *ACM Transactions on Programming Languages and Systems*, 3(4):431–483, 1981.

[AU72]   A.V. Aho and J.D. Ullman. *The Theory of Parsing, Translation and Compiling*. Prentice-Hall, 1972.

[Bac94]   P. Bachmann. *Die Analytische Zahlentheorie*. Teubner, 1894.

[Bac79]   R.C. Backhouse. *Syntax of programming Languages, Theory and Practice*. Series in Computer Science (C.A.R. Hoare, ed.). Prentice-Hall International, 1979.

[Bac86]   R.C. Backhouse. *Program Construction and Verification*. Series in Computer Science (C.A.R. Hoare, ed.). Prentice-Hall International, 1986.

[Ben73]   C.H. Bennett. Logical reversibility of computation. *IBM Journal of Research and Development*, 6:525–532, 1973.

[Ben82]   C.H. Bennett. The thermodynamics of computation - a review. *International Journal of Theoretical Physics*, 21:905–940, 1982.

[BL85]   C.H. Bennett and R. Landauer. The fundamental physical limits of computation. *Scientific American*, pages 38–46, July 1985.

[BM]   R.S. Boyer and J S. Moore. MJRTY, a fast majority-voting algorithm. Unpublished manuscript.

[Bre65]   J.E. Bresenham. Algorithm for computer control of a digital plotter. *IBM Systems Journal*, 4(1):25–30, 1965.

[Bre80]   R.P. Brent. An improved Monte Carlo factorization algorithm. *BIT*, 20:176–184, 1980.

[Bro89]   M. Broy, editor. *Constructive Methods in Computing Science*, NATO ASI Series. Springer Verlag, 1989.

[BW88]   R.S. Bird and P. Wadler. *Introduction to Functional Programming*. Series in Computer Science (C.A.R. Hoare, ed.). Prentice-Hall International, 1988.

[Cho59]   N. Chomsky. On certain formal properties of grammars. *Information and Control*, 2:137–167, 1959.

[Chu41]   A. Church. *The Calculi of Lambda-Conversion*, volume 6 of *Annals of Mathematical Studies*. Princeton University Press, 1941.

[CM73]   T.J. Chaney and C.E. Molnar. Anomalous behavior of synchronizer and arbiter circuits. *IEEE Transactions on Computers*, C-22:421–422, 1973.

[CU90]   W. Chen and J.T. Udding. Program inversion: more than fun! *Science of Computer Programming*, 15:1–13, 1990.

[Dal86]   W.J. Dally. *A VLSI Architecture for Concurrent Data Structures*. PhD thesis, California Institute of Technology, 1986. Caltech technical report TR 5209.

[dB82]   J. de Bakker. *Mathematical Theory of Program Correctness*. Series in Computer Science (C.A.R. Hoare, ed.). Prentice-Hall International, 1982.

[DeR71]   F.L. DeRemer. Simple LR(k) grammars. *Communications of the ACM*, 14(7):453–460, 1971.

[DeR74]   F. DeRemer. Review of formalisms and notations. In *Compiler Construction*, volume 21 of *Lecture Notes in Computer Science*, chapter 2.A, pages 37–56. Springer-Verlag, 1974.

[DF88]   E.W. Dijkstra and W.H.J. Feijen. *A method of programming*. Addison-Wesley, 1988.

[Dij59]   E.W. Dijkstra. A note on two problems in connexion with graphs. *Numerische Mathematik*, 1:269–271, 1959.

[Dij60]   E.W. Dijkstra. Recursive programming. *Numerische Mathematik*, 2:312–318, 1960.

[Dij63]   E.W. Dijkstra. An ALGOL60 Translator for the X1. *Annual review in Automatic Programming*, 3:329–345, 1963.

[Dij65]   E.W. Dijkstra. Solution of a problem in concurrent programming control. *Communications of the ACM*, 8(9), 1965.

[Dij68]   E.W. Dijkstra. Cooperating sequential processes. In F. Genuys, editor, *Programming Languages*. Academic Press, 1968.

[Dij75]   E.W. Dijkstra. Guarded commands, nondeterminacy and formal derivation of programs. *Communications of the ACM*, 18:453–457, 1975.

[Dij76]   E.W. Dijkstra. *A Discipline of Programming*. Prentice-Hall, 1976.

[Dij78]   E.W. Dijkstra. Program inversion. EWD 671. Technological University Eindhoven, 1978.

[Dij81]   E.W. Dijkstra. An assertional proof of a program by G.L. Peterson. EWD 779. Technological University Eindhoven, 1981.

[DS90]   E.W. Dijkstra and C.S. Scholten. *Predicate calculus and program semantics*. Springer-Verlag, 1990.

[Fey84]   R.P. Feynman. Quantum mechanical computers. *Optics News*, pages 11–20, 1984.

[Flo62]   R.W. Floyd. Algorithm 97: shortest path. *Communications of the ACM*, 5(6):345, 1962.

[Flo67]   R.W. Floyd. Assigning meaning to programs. In *Mathematical Aspects of Computer Science*, pages 19–32. XIX American Mathematical Society, 1967.

[FT82]   E. Fredkin and T. Toffoli. Conservative logic. *International Journal of Theoretical Physics*, 21:219–253, 1982.

[Gal78]   R.G. Gallager. Variations on a Theme by Huffman. *IEEE Transactions on Information Theory*, 24:668–674, 1978.

[Gri71]   D. Gries. *Compiler Construction for Digital Computers*. John Wiley and Sons, 1971.

[Gri79]   D. Gries. The Schorr-Waite graph marking algorithm. *Acta Informatica*, 11:223–232, 1979.

[Gri81]   D. Gries. *The Science of Programming*. Springer-Verlag, 1981.

[Gri82]   D. Gries. A note on the standard strategy for developing loop invariants and loops. *Science of Computer Programming*, 12:207–214, 1982.

[GvdS90]   D. Gries and J.L.A. van de Snepscheut. Inorder traversal of a binary tree and its inversion. In E.W. Dijkstra, editor, *Formal Development of Programs and Proofs*, University of Texas at Austin Year of Programming Series, pages 37–42. Addison-Wesley, 1990.

[HA72]   C.A.R. Hoare and D.C.S. Allison. Incomputability. *Computing Surveys*, 4(3):169–178, 1972.

[Heh84]   E.C.R. Hehner. *The Logic of Programming*. Series in Computer Science (C.A.R. Hoare, ed.). Prentice-Hall International, 1984.

[Heh89]   E.C.R. Hehner. Termination is timing. In J.L.A. van de Snepscheut, editor, *Mathematics of Program Construction*, volume 375 of *Lecture Notes in Computer Science*, pages 36–47. Springer Verlag, 1989.

[Heh90]   E.C.R. Hehner. Beautifying Gödel. In W.H.J. Feijen, A.J.M. van Gasteren, D. Gries, and J. Misra, editors, *Beauty is our business - a birthday salute to Edsger W. Dijkstra*, pages 163–172. Springer-Verlag, 1990.

[Heh92]   E.C.R. Hehner, 1992. Private communication.

[Hem80]   C. Hemerik. Formal derivation of a list processing program. *Information Processing Letters*, 10(3):124–126, 1980.

[Hoa62]   C.A.R. Hoare. Quicksort. *Computer Journal*, 5:10–15, 1962.

[Hoa69]   C.A.R. Hoare. An axiomatic approach to computer programming. *Communications of the ACM*, 12:576–580,583, 1969.

[Hoa71]   C.A.R. Hoare. Proof of a program FIND. *Communications of the ACM*, 14:39–45, 1971.

[Hoa78]   C.A.R. Hoare. Communicating sequential processes. *Communications of the ACM*, 21(8):666–677, 1978.

[HU69]   J.E. Hopcroft and J.D. Ullman. *Formal languages and their relation to automata*. Addison-Wesley, 1969.

[Huf52]   D.A. Huffman. A method for the construction of minimum redundancy codes. *Proceedings IRE*, 40:1098–1101, 1952.

[Jon88]   J.E. Jonker, 1988. Private communication.

[Jon92]   C.B. Jones. The search for tractable ways of reasoning about programs. Technical Report UMCS-92-4-4, University of Manchester, 1992.

[Kal90]   A. Kaldewaij. *Programming: The Derivation of Algorithms*. Series in Computer Science (C.A.R. Hoare, ed.). Prentice-Hall International, 1990.

[Kes82]   J.L.W. Kessels. Arbitration without common modifiable variables. *Acta Informatica*, 17:135–141, 1982.

[Kle56]   S.C. Kleene. *Representation of Events in Nerve Nets and Finite Automata*. Automata Studies, Princeton University Press, 1956.

[Knu71]   D.E. Knuth. Top-down syntax analysis. *Acta Informatica*, 1:79–110, 1971.

[Knu73]   D.E. Knuth. *The Art of Computer Programming, Vol. 3: Sorting and Searching*. Addison-Wesley, 1973.

[Knu76]   D.E. Knuth. Big omicron and big omega and big theta. *SIGACT News*, April-June:18–24, 1976.

[Koh70]   Z. Kohavi. *Switching and Finite Automata Theory*. McGraw-Hill, 1970.

[Kru75]   F.E.J. Kruseman Aretz. A LISP interpreter written in ALGOL 60. Eindhoven University of Technology, 1975. class handouts.

[KS63]   H.B. Keller and J.R. Swenson. Experiments on the lattice problem of Gauss. *Mathematics of Computation*, XVII(83):223–230, 1963.

[KS90]   A. Kaldewaij and B. Schoenmakers. Searching by elimination. *Science of Computer Programming*, 14(2-3):229–242, 1990.

[Lan65]   P. Landin. A correspondence between ALGOL 60 and Church's Lambda Notation. *Communications of the ACM*, 8:89–101, 158–165, 1965.

[LS68]   P.M. Lewis II and R.E. Stearns. Syntax-directed transduction. *Journal of the ACM*, 15:464–488, 1968.

[Luc61]   P. Lucas. Die strukturanalyse von formelübersetzern. *Elektron. rechenanl.*, 3:159–167, 1961.

[Luk91]   J.J. Lukkien. *Parallel Program Design and Generalized Weakest Preconditions*. PhD thesis, Groningen University, 1991. also, Caltech technical report TR 90-16.

[Lut84]   C. Lutz. Design of the Mosaic processor. Master's thesis, California Institute of Technology, 1984. Caltech technical report TR 5129.

[Man82]   B.B. Mandelbrot. *The Fractal Geometry of Nature*. Freeman, 1982.

[Man89]   U. Manber. *Introduction to Algorithms*. Addison-Wesley, 1989.

[Mar81]   A.J. Martin. An axiomatic definition of synchronization primitives. *Acta Informatica*, 16:219–235, 1981.

[Mar83]   A.J. Martin. A general proof rule for procedures in predicate transformer semantics. *Acta Informatica*, 20:301–313, 1983.

[Mar85]   A.J. Martin. The probe: an addition to communication primitives. *Information Processing Letters*, 20:125–130, 1985. and (21)107.

[MC80]   C.A. Mead and L.A. Conway. *Introduction to VLSI Systems*. Addison Wesley, 1980.

[McC60]   J. McCarthy. Recursive functions of symbolic expressions and their computation by machine, Part I. *Communications of the ACM*, 3(4):184–195, 1960.

[MG82]   J. Misra and D. Gries. Finding repeated elements. *Science of Computer Programming*, 2:143–152, 1982.

[Mor79]   J.M. Morris. Traversing binary trees simply and cheaply. *Information Processing Letters*, 9(5):197–200, 1979.

[Mor90]   C. Morgan. *Programming from Specifications*. Series in Computer Science (C.A.R. Hoare, ed.). Prentice-Hall International, 1990.

[MvdS90]   A.J. Martin and J.L.A. van de Snepscheut. An interconnection network for distributed recursive computations. *IEEE Transactions on Computers*, 39(11):1393–1395, 1990.

[Nau63]   P. Naur. Revised report on the Algorithmic Language ALGOL 60. *Communications of the ACM*, 6(1):1–17, 1963.

[OG76a]   S.S. Owicki and D. Gries. An axiomatic proof technique for parallel programs. *Acta Informatica*, 6:319–340, 1976.

[OG76b]   S.S. Owicki and D. Gries. Verifying properties of parallel programs. *Communications of the ACM*, 19(5):279–285, 1976.

[Pet81]   G.L. Peterson. Myths about the mutual exclusion problem. *Information Processing Letters*, 12(3):115–116, 1981.

[Ray86]   M. Raynal. *Algorithms for mutual exclusion*. The MIT Press, 1986.

[San91]   B.A. Sanders. Eliminating the substitution axiom from UNITY logic. *Formal Aspects of Computing*, 3:189–205, 1991.

[Sci73]   Science and the citizen. *Scientific American*, 228:43–44, 1973.

[Sei80]   C.L. Seitz. System timing. In C.A. Mead and L.A. Conway, editors, *Introduction to VLSI Systems*, chapter 7. Addison Wesley, 1980.

[Sei84]   C.L. Seitz. Concurrent VLSI architectures. *IEEE Transactions on Computers*, C-33(12):1247–1265, 1984.

[Sei85]   C.L. Seitz. The Cosmic Cube. *Communications of the ACM*, 28(1):22–33, 1985.

[Sei90]   C.L. Seitz. Multicomputers. In C.A.R. Hoare, editor, *Developments in Concurrency and Communication*, pages 131–200. Addison Wesley, 1990.

[Sei92]   C.L. Seitz. Submicron systems architecture, semiannual technical report. Technical Report CS 92-17, California Institute of Technology, 1992.

[SFM $^+$ 85] C.L. Seitz, A.H. Frey, S. Mattisson, S.D. Rabin, D.A. Speck, and J.L.A. van de Snepscheut. Hot-Clock nMOS. In H. Fuchs, editor, *1985 Chapel Hill Conference on VLSI*, pages 1–17. Computer Science Press, 1985.

[SM77]   I.E. Sutherland and C.A. Mead. Microelectronics and computer science. *Scientific American*, 237:210–228, 1977.

[SP73]   P.M. Spira and A. Pan. On finding and updating shortest paths and spanning trees. *Conference record, IEEE 14th Annual Symposium on Switching and Automata Theory*, pages 82–84, 1973.

[SW67]   H. Schorr and W.M. Waite. An efficient machine-independent procedure for garbage collection in various list structures. *Communications of the ACM*, 10:501–506, 1967.

[Szy78]   T.G. Szymanski. Assembling code for machines with span-dependent instructions. *Communications of the ACM*, 21:300–308, 1978.

[Tar85]   R.E. Tarjan. Amortized computational complexity. *SIAM Journal on Algebraic and Discrete Methods*, 6:306–318, 1985.

[Tur36]   A.M. Turing. On computable numbers with an application to the Entscheidungsproblem. *Proc. London Math. Soc.*, pages 230–265, 1936. A correction, 544-546.

[Tur49]   A.M. Turing. On checking a large routine. *Report of a Conference on High-Speed Automatic Calculating Machines*, pages 67–69, 1949.

[TvL84]   R.E. Tarjan and J. van Leeuwen. Worst-case analysis of set union algorithms. *Journal of the ACM*, 31(2):245–281, 1984.

[Ull84]   J.D. Ullman. *Computational Aspects of VLSI.* Computer Science Press, 1984.

[vdS85a]   J.L.A. van de Snepscheut.   Evaluating expressions with a queue. *Information Processing Letters,* 20:65–66, 1985.

[vdS85b]   J.L.A. van de Snepscheut. *Trace Theory and VLSI Design,* volume 200 of *Lecture Notes in Computer Science.* Springer-Verlag, 1985.

[vdS91]   J.L.A. van de Snepscheut. Inversion of a recursive tree traversal. *Information Processing Letters,* 39(5):265–267, 1991.

[vdS92]   J.L.A. van de Snepscheut. A LISP programming exercise. *Information Processing Letters,* 42:103–108, 1992.

[vG90]   A.J.M. van Gasteren. *On the shape of mathematical arguments,* volume 445 of *Lecture Notes in Computer Science.* Springer-Verlag, 1990.

[vGT90]   A.J.M. van Gasteren and G. Tel. Comments on "On the proof of a distributed algorithm": always-true is not invariant. *Information Processing Letters,* 35:277–279, 1990.

[vN66]   J. von Neumann. Fourth University of Illinois lecture. In A.W. Burks, editor, *Theory of Self-Reproducing Automata.* University of Illinois Press, 1966.

[War62]   S. Warshall. A theorem on Boolean matrices. *Journal of the ACM,* 9(1):11–12, 1962.

[Wir81]   N. Wirth. Pascal-S: A subset and its implementation. In D.W. Barron, editor, *Pascal: the language and its implementation,* pages 199–259. John Wiley and Sons, 1981.

[Wir90]   N. Wirth. Drawing lines, circles, and ellipses in a raster. In W.H.J. Feijen, A.J.M. van Gasteren, D. Gries, and J. Misra, editors, *Beauty is our business, a birthday salute to Edsger W. Dijkstra,* pages 427–434. Springer-Verlag, 1990.

Index

Texts and Monographs in Computer Science

(continued from page ii)

Texts and Monographs in Computer Science

(continued)

Dexter C. Kozen
The Design and Analysis of Algorithms
1992. X, 320 pages, 72 illus.

E.V. Krishnamurthy
Error-Free Polynomial Matrix Computations
1985. XV, 154 pages

David Luckham
Programming with Specifications: An Introduction to ANNA, A Language for Specifying Ada Programs
1990. XVI, 418 pages, 20 illus

Ernest G. Manes and Michael A. Arbib
Algebraic Approaches to Program Semantics
1986. XIII, 351 pages

Robert N. Moll, Michael A. Arbib, and A.J. Kfoury
An Introduction to Formal Language Theory
1988. X, 203 pages, 61 illus.

Helmut A. Partsch
Specification and Transformation of Programs
1990. XIII, 493 pages, 44 illus.

Franco P. Preparata and Michael Ian Shamos
Computational Geometry: An Introduction
1988. XII, 390 pages, 231 illus.

Brian Randell, Ed.
The Origins of Digital Computers: Selected Papers, 3rd Edition
1982. XVI, 580 pages, 126 illus.

Thomas W. Reps and Tim Teitelbaum
The Synthesizer Generator: A System for Constructing Language-Based Editors
1989. XIII, 317 pages, 75 illus.

Thomas W. Reps and Tim Teitelbaum
The Synthesizer Generator Reference Manual, 3rd Edition
1989. XI, 171 pages, 79 illus.

Arto Salomaa and Matti Soittola
Automata-Theoretic Aspects of Formal Power Series
1978. X, 171 pages

Texts and Monographs in Computer Science